THE VICTORIA HISTORY
OF THE
COUNTIES OF ENGLAND

A HISTORY OF
WILTSHIRE

VOLUME XIV

Oxford University Press, Walton Street, Oxford OX2 6DP
Oxford   New York   Toronto
Delhi   Bombay   Calcutta   Madras   Karachi
Petaling Jaya   Singapore   Hong Kong   Tokyo
Nairobi   Dar es Salaam   Cape Town
Melbourne   Auckland

and associated companies in
Berlin   Ibadan

Oxford is a trademark of Oxford University Press

Published in the United States by
Oxford University Press, New York

British Library Cataloguing in Publication Data
A History of Wiltshire.——(The Victoria
history of the counties of England)
Vol. 14: Malmesbury Hundred
1. Wiltshire——History
I. Crowley, D. A.
II. University of London
Institute of Historical Research
III. Series
942.3

ISBN 0 19 722779 1

Distributed by Oxford University Press until 1 January 1994
thereafter by Dawsons of Pall Mall

Printed in Great Britain
by The Bath Press, Avon

942.31

942.31

THE VICTORIA HISTORY
OF THE
COUNTIES OF ENGLAND

EDITED BY C. R. ELRINGTON

THE UNIVERSITY OF LONDON
INSTITUTE OF
HISTORICAL RESEARCH

INSCRIBED TO THE
MEMORY OF HER LATE MAJESTY
QUEEN VICTORIA
WHO GRACIOUSLY GAVE THE TITLE TO
AND ACCEPTED THE DEDICATION
OF THIS HISTORY

A HISTORY OF

WILTSHIRE

EDITED BY D. A. CROWLEY

VOLUME XIV

MALMESBURY HUNDRED

PUBLISHED FOR

THE INSTITUTE OF HISTORICAL RESEARCH

BY

OXFORD UNIVERSITY PRESS

1991

CONTENTS OF VOLUME FOURTEEN

LIST OF ILLUSTRATIONS

Thanks are rendered to the following for permission to reproduce material: AT & T Telecommunications UK Ltd., Mr. and Mrs. G. H. Baker, the British Library, Cambridge University Committee for Aerial Photography, the Courtauld Institute of Art (photographs of the Buckler paintings in Devizes Museum), Mrs. J. Giles, Mr. J. Lardy, Malmesbury Civic Trust, Lt.-Col. S. A. Pitman (photograph of overmantel at Eastcourt House), the Royal Commission on the Historical Monuments of England, Mr. Brian Thatcher, Maj. A. R. Turnor, Wiltshire Archaeological and Natural History Society, and Wiltshire Library and Museum Service.

LIST OF ILLUSTRATIONS

LIST OF MAPS AND PLANS

The maps listed below were drawn by K. J. Wass from drafts prepared by D. A. Crowley, Jane Freeman, and Janet H. Stevenson. The plan of Crudwell church was drawn by A. P. Baggs. The parish and other boundaries are taken from inclosure award, tithe award, and other maps of the earlier 19th century, from Ordnance Survey maps of the later 19th, and, on the maps of Brokenborough and of Malmesbury boundaries, from later Ordnance Survey maps.

EDITORIAL NOTE

LIKE the fourteen earlier volumes of the *Victoria History of Wiltshire*, the present volume has been prepared under the supervision of the Wiltshire Victoria County History Committee. The origin and early constitution of that Committee are described in the Editorial Note to Volume VII, the first to be published, and the new arrangements introduced in 1975 are outlined in the Editorial Note to Volume XI. The arrangements for financing the research and writing of the Wiltshire History were modified in 1990, after the District Councils of Kennet, Salisbury, North Wiltshire, and West Wiltshire had agreed to increase their contributions to the Committee's funds so that Thamesdown Borough Council, the successor to Swindon Borough Council which in 1947 had jointly set up the Wiltshire V.C.H., should not continue to meet a disproportionate share of the cost. To those five District Councils and to the Wiltshire County Council, the major financial contributor, the University of London again offers its profound thanks for their support of the Wiltshire V.C.H. Committee, whose collaboration in the enterprise is also acknowledged once more with warm gratitude.

Thanks are also offered to the large number of people who have helped in the compilation of the volume by granting access to documents and buildings in their ownership or care, by providing information, or by giving advice. Most of them are named in the footnotes to the articles with which they helped and a few in the preamble to the List of Illustrations. Special mention must be made of the assistance given by the County Archivist (Mr. K. H. Rogers until September 1990) and his staff, and of the information and access to documents given by the Clerk to the Burgesses and Freemen of Malmesbury (Mr. L. Grey).

The *General Introduction* to the *Victoria County History*, published in 1970, and its *Supplement* published in 1990 give an outline of the structure and aims of the series as a whole, with an account of its origins and progress.

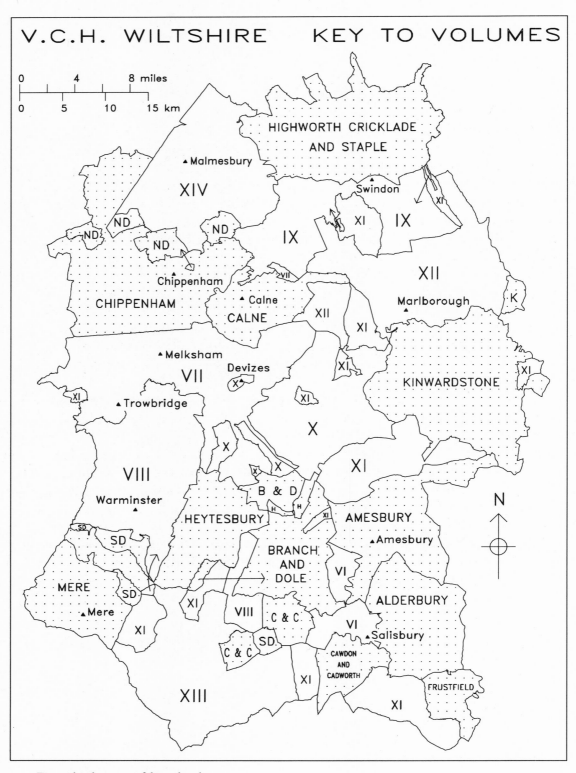

V.C.H. WILTSHIRE   KEY TO VOLUMES

HIGHWORTH CRICKLADE AND STAPLE

XIV

ND ND ND ND

Chippenham

CHIPPENHAM

Malmesbury

IX

XI IX

Swindon

XII

Marlborough

K

Calne

CALNE

XII

XI

Melksham

VII

Devizes

X

XI

XI

Trowbridge

XI

XI

KINWARDSTONE

XI

X

VIII

Warminster

SD

SD

MERE

SD

Mere

XI

XIII

X

X

B & D

HEYTESBURY

H

H

XI

AMESBURY

Amesbury

XI

VI

BRANCH AND DOLE

VIII

C & C

SD

C & C

VI

ALDERBURY

Salisbury

CAWDON AND CADWORTH

XI

XI

FRUSTFIELD

XI

N

Detached parts of hundreds:
B & D Branch and Dole   **ND** North Damerham   **H** Heytesbury
C & C Cawdon and Cadworth **SD** South Damerham   **K** Kinwardstone

Contents of Volumes:
I–V General chapters
VI Wilton, Salisbury; Underditch hundred; part of Branch and Dole hundred
VII Bradford, Melksham, and Potterne and Cannings hundreds
VIII Warminster, Westbury, and Whorwellsdown hundreds
IX Kingsbridge hundred
X Swanborough hundred; Devizes
XI Downton hundred and Elstub and Everleigh hundred
XII Ramsbury and Selkley hundreds; Marlborough
XIII Chalke and Dunworth hundreds
XIV Malmesbury hundred

WILTSHIRE
VICTORIA COUNTY HISTORY COMMITTEE

As at 20 September 1990

COUNCILLOR MRS. V. C. S. LANDELL MILLS,
  Chairman
COUNCILLOR A. J. MASTERS   *Representing the Wiltshire County Council*
COUNCILLOR COL. H. D. ROGERS, O.B.E.
COUNCILLOR MRS. P. RUGG

COUNCILLOR MISS P. E. G. COURTMAN
COUNCILLOR DR. J. M. G. KIRKALDY   *Representing the Kennet District Council*

COUNCILLOR THE HON. MRS. J. I. MORRISON
COUNCILLOR J. RHIND-TUTT   *Representing the Salisbury District Council*

COUNCILLOR M. H. FANNING
COUNCILLOR A. E. MAYER   *Representing the Thamesdown Borough Council*

MISS D. J. MATTHEWS   *Representing the North Wiltshire District Council*

COUNCILLOR A. J. C. PEARCE   *Representing the West Wiltshire District Council*

MR. C. R. ELRINGTON   *Representing the Central Committee of the Victoria County History*

MR. H. F. SEYMOUR   *Representing the Wiltshire Archaeological and Natural History Society*

Co-opted Members

THE REVD. CANON B. G. CARNE   MISS SUSAN REYNOLDS
DR. R. F. HUNNISETT   MR. BONAR SYKES
MR. M. J. LANSDOWN

MR. D. M. KENT, *Hon. Secretary*
MR. E. J. P. THORNTON, *Hon. Treasurer*

LIST OF CLASSES OF DOCUMENTS
IN THE PUBLIC RECORD OFFICE
USED IN THIS VOLUME
WITH THEIR CLASS NUMBERS

Clerks of Assize
ASSI 24	Western Circuit, Miscellaneous Books

Chancery
		Proceedings
C 1		Early
C 2		Series I
C 3		Series II
C 5		Six Clerks Series, Bridges
C 10		Whittington
C 33		Judicial Proceedings (Equity Side), Entry Books of Decrees and Orders
C 54		Close Rolls
C 66		Patent Rolls
C 78		Decree Rolls
		Masters' Exhibits
C 104		Tinney
C 108		Farrar
C 112		Rose
C 116		Court Rolls
		Inquisitions post mortem
C 135		Series I, Edw. III
C 138		Hen. V
C 139		Hen. VI
C 140		Edw. IV and V
C 142		Series II
C 260		Files (Tower and Rolls Chapel), Recorda

Court of Common Pleas
		Feet of Fines
CP 25(1)		Series I
CP 25(2)		Series II
CP 40		Plea Rolls
CP 43		Recovery Rolls

Duchy of Lancaster
DL 1	Equity Proceedings, Pleadings Depositions and Examinations
DL 3	Series I
DL 4	Series II
DL 29	Ministers' Accounts
DL 30	Court Rolls
DL 42	Miscellaneous Books
DL 43	Rentals and Surveys
DL 44	Special Commissions and Returns

Exchequer, King's Remembrancer
		Entry Books of Decrees and Orders
E 123		Series I
E 126		Series IV
E 134		Depositions taken by Commission
E 150		Inquisitions post mortem, Series II

E 159	Memoranda Rolls
E 178	Special Commissions of Inquiry
E 179	Subsidy Rolls, etc.

Exchequer, Augmentation Office
E 301	Certificates of Colleges and Chantries
E 305	Deeds of Purchase and Exchange
E 309	Enrolments of Leases
E 310	Particulars for Leases
E 315	Miscellaneous Books
E 317	Parliamentary Surveys
E 318	Particulars for Grants of Crown Lands

Exchequer, Lord Treasurer's Remembrancer's and Pipe Offices
E 370	Miscellaneous Rolls
E 372	Pipe Rolls

Ministry of Education
ED 2	Parish Files
ED 7	Public Elementary Schools, Preliminary Statements
ED 21	Public Elementary School Files
ED 49	Endowment Files, Elementary Education

Registry of Friendly Societies
		Rules and Amendments
FS 1		Series I
FS 3		Series II
FS 4		Indexes, Series II

Home Office
HO 52	Correspondence and Papers, Municipal and Provincial
HO 67	Acreage Returns
HO 107	Census Returns, 1841
HO 129	Ecclesiastical Returns

Indexes
IND	Indexes, Various

Board of Inland Revenue
IR 18	Tithe Files
IR 29	Tithe Apportionments
IR 30	Tithe Maps

Justices Itinerant
JUST 1	Eyre Rolls, Assize Rolls, etc.
JUST 3	Gaol Delivery Rolls

Exchequer, Office of the Auditors of Land Revenue
LR 2	Miscellaneous Books

Ministry of Agriculture, Fisheries, and Food
MAF 68	Agricultural Returns, Parish Summaries

Privy Council Office
PC 1	Papers, mainly unbound

LIST OF CLASSES OF DOCUMENTS

Prerogative Court of Canterbury
PROB 6   Act Books, Administrations
PROB 11   Registered Copies of Wills

Court of Requests
REQ 2   Proceedings

General Register Office
RG 4   Non-parochial registers
          Census Returns
RG 9   1861
RG 11   1881

Special Collections
SC 2   Court Rolls
SC 6   Ministers' Accounts

Court of Star Chamber
          Proceedings
STAC 1   Hen. VII
STAC 2   Hen. VIII
STAC 8   Jas. I

Court of Wards and Liveries
WARD 7   Inquisitions post mortem

NOTE ON ABBREVIATIONS

Among the abbreviations and short titles used are the following:

Abbrev. Plac.	*Placitorum Abbreviatio*, ed. W. Illingworth (Record Commission, 1811)
Acct. of Wilts. Schs	*An Account of Schools for the Children of the Labouring Classes in the County of Wiltshire*, H.C. 27 (1859 Sess. 1), xxi (2)
Acts of P.C.	*Acts of the Privy Council of England* (H.M.S.O. 1890–1964)
Alum. Cantab.	*Alumni Cantabrigienses*, ed. J. and J. A. Venn
Alum. Oxon.	*Alumni Oxonienses*, ed. J. Foster
Arch. Jnl.	*Archaeological Journal*
Aubrey, *Nat. Hist. Wilts.* ed. Britton	John Aubrey, *Natural History of Wiltshire*, ed. John Britton (London, 1847)
Aubrey, *Topog. Coll.* ed. Jackson	*The Topographical Collections of John Aubrey*, ed. J. E. Jackson (Devizes, 1862)
B.L.	British Library Add. MS. Additional Manuscript Eg. Ch. Egerton Charter Harl. Ch. Harleian Charter Lansd. Ch. Lansdowne Charter
Bodl. Libr.	Bodleian Library
Bk. of Fees	*The Book of Fees* (H.M.S.O. 1920–31)
Bracton's Note Bk.	H. de Bracton, *Note Book*, ed. F. W. Maitland (London, 1887)
Burke, *Commoners*	J. Burke and others, *A History of the Commoners* (London, 1833–8)
Burke, *Ext. & Dorm. Baronetcies*	J. Burke and others, *Extinct and Dormant Baronetcies*
Burke, *Ext. & Dorm. Peerages*	J. Burke and others, *Extinct and Dormant Peerages*
Burke, *Land. Gent.*	J. Burke and others, *Landed Gentry*
Burke, *Peerage*	J. Burke and others, *A Dictionary of the Peerage*
Cal. Chart. R.	*Calendar of the Charter Rolls preserved in the Public Record Office* (H.M.S.O. 1903–27)
Cal. Close	*Calendar of the Close Rolls preserved in the Public Record Office* (H.M.S.O. 1892–1963)
Cal. Cttee. for Compounding	*Calendar of the Proceedings of the Committee for Compounding, etc. 1643–60* (H.M.S.O. 1889–92)
Cal. Cttee. for Money	*Calendar of the Proceedings of the Committee for the Advance of Money, 1642–6* (H.M.S.O. 1888)
Cal. Fine R.	*Calendar of the Fine Rolls preserved in the Public Record Office* (H.M.S.O. 1911–62)
Cal. Inq. Misc.	*Calendar of Inquisitions Miscellaneous (Chancery) preserved in the Public Record Office* (H.M.S.O. 1916–68)
Cal. Inq. p.m.	*Calendar of Inquisitions post mortem preserved in the Public Record Office* (H.M.S.O. 1904–88)
Cal. Inq. p.m. Hen. VII	*Calendar of Inquisitions post mortem, Henry VII* (H.M.S.O. 1898–1955)
Cal. Papal Reg.	*Calendar of Papal Registers: Papal Letters* (H.M.S.O. and Irish Manuscripts Commission, 1893–1986)
Cal. Pat.	*Calendar of the Patent Rolls preserved in the Public Record Office* (H.M.S.O. 1891–1986)
Cal. S.P. Dom.	*Calendar of State Papers, Domestic Series* (H.M.S.O. 1856–1972)
Calamy Revised, ed. Matthews	*Calamy Revised: being a Revision of Edmund Calamy's Account of the Ministers and others Ejected and Silenced, 1660–2*, by A. G. Matthews (1934)

Camden, *Brit.* (1806)	W. Camden, *Britannia*, with additions by R. Gough (1806)
Cat. Anct. D.	*Descriptive Catalogue of Ancient Deeds in the Public Record Office* (H.M.S.O. 1890–1915)
Ch. Com.	Church Commissioners
Char. Com.	Charity Commission
Close R.	*Close Rolls of the Reign of Henry III preserved in the Public Record Office* (H.M.S.O. 1902–75)
Coll. Topog. et Gen.	*Collectanea Topographica et Genealogica*, (London, 1834–43)
Colvin, *Brit. Architects*	H. Colvin, *A Biographical Dictionary of British Architects, 1600–1840* (1978)
Complete Peerage	G. E. C[ockayne] and others, *The Complete Peerage* (2nd edn. 1910–59)
Compton Census	*The Compton Census of 1676: a critical edition*, ed. A. Whiteman (British Academy Records of Social and Economic History, N.S. x)
T. Cox, *Magna Brit.*	T. Cox, *Magna Britannia Antiqua et Nova* (London, 1738)
Crockford	*Crockford's Clerical Directory*
Cur. Reg. R.	*Curia Regis Rolls preserved in the Public Record Office* (H.M.S.O. 1922–79)
D. & C. Sar	dean and chapter of Salisbury
D.N.B.	*Dictionary of National Biography*
Dugdale, *Baronage*	W. Dugdale, *The Baronage of England* (London, 1675–6)
Dugdale, *Mon.*	W. Dugdale, *Monasticon Anglicanum*, ed. J. Caley and others (London, 1817–30)
E.H.R.	*English Historical Review*
Educ. Enq. Abstract	*Abstract of Returns relative to the State of Education in England*, H.C. 62 (1835), xliii
Educ. of Poor Digest	*Digest of Returns to the Select Committee on the Education of the Poor*, H.C. 224 (1819), ix (2)
Ekwall, *Eng. Place-Names*	E. Ekwall, *The Concise Oxford Dictionary of English Place-Names* (4th edn. 1960)
Endowed Char. Wilts.	*Endowed Charities of Wiltshire*, H.C. 273 (1908), lxxx (northern division); H.C. 273–i (1908), lxxxi (southern division)
Eton Coll. Mun.	Muniments of Eton College, Bucks.
Eulogium Hist.	*Eulogium (Historiarum sive Temporis): Chronicon ab Orbe Condito usque ad Annum Domini MCCCLXVI; a Monacho quodam Malmesburiensi Exaratum*, ed. F. S. Haydon (Rolls Series, 1858)
Feud. Aids	*Inquisitions and Assessments relating to Feudal Aids preserved in the Public Record Office* (H.M.S.O. 1899–1920)
Finberg, *Early Wessex Chart.*	H. P. R. Finberg, *Early Charters of Wessex* (Leicester, 1964)
G.E.C. Baronetage	G. E. C[ockayne], *Complete Baronetage* (1900–9)
G.R.O.	General Register Office
Geneal.	*The Genealogist* (1877–1919)
Gent. Mag.	*Gentleman's Magazine* (1731–1867)
Geol. Surv.	Geological Survey
H.C.	House of Commons
H.M.S.O.	Her (His) Majesty's Stationery Office
Harl. Soc.	Harleian Society
Hist. MSS. Com.	Royal Commission on Historical Manuscripts
Hist. Parl.	*The History of Parliament*
Hoare, *Mod. Wilts.*	Sir Richard Colt Hoare and others, *The History of Modern Wiltshire* (London, 1822–43)
Inq. Non.	*Nonarum Inquisitiones in Curia Scaccarii*, ed. G. Vandersee (Record Commission, 1807)
Jnl. Brit. Arch. Soc.	*Journal of the British Archaeological Association*

NOTE ON ABBREVIATIONS

Kelly's Dir.	*Kelly's Directory*
Kelly's Handbk.	*Kelly's Handbook to the Titled, Landed and Official Classes*
L.J.	*Journals of the House of Lords*
L. & P. Hen. VIII	*Letters and Papers, Foreign and Domestic, of the Reign of Henry VIII* (H.M.S.O. 1864–1932)
Lamb. Palace Libr.	Lambeth Palace Library
Land. Util. Surv.	Land Utilisation Survey
Leland, *Itin.* ed. Toulmin Smith	*Itinerary of John Leland*, ed. L. Toulmin Smith (1907–10)
Lewis, *Topog. Dict. Eng.*	S. Lewis, *Topographical Dictionary of England*
Lond. Gaz.	*London Gazette*
Longleat Mun.	Longleat House Muniments
Medieval Arch.	*Medieval Archaeology*
N.S.	New Series
Nat. Bldgs. Rec.	National Buildings Record (*formerly* National Monuments Record) of the Royal Commission on Historical Monuments of England
Nat. Soc. *Inquiry, 1846–7*	*Result of the Returns made to the General Inquiry made by the National Society, 1846–7* (1849)
Nightingale, *Wilts. Plate*	J. E. Nightingale, *Church Plate of Wiltshire* (Salisbury, 1891)
O.S.	Ordnance Survey
O.S.D.	Ordnance Survey Drawings
J. Ogilby, *Brit.*	J. Ogilby, *Britannia* (1675)
Orig. Rec. ed. G. L. Turner	*Original Records of Early Nonconformity under Persecution and Indulgence*, ed. G. L. Turner (1911–14)
P.N. Wilts. (E.P.N.S.)	J. E. B. Gover, Allen Mawer, and F. M. Stenton, *Place-Names of Wiltshire* (English Place-Name Society, xvi)
P.R.O.	Public Record Office (see above, p. xiv)
P.R.S., Pipe R. Soc.	Pipe Roll Society
Pat. R.	*Patent Rolls of the Reign of Henry III preserved in the Public Record Office* (H.M.S.O. 1901–3)
Pevsner, *Wilts.* (2nd edn.)	Nikolaus Pevsner, *Buildings of England: Wiltshire*, revised by Bridget Cherry (1975)
Phillipps, *Mon. Inscriptions N. Wilts.*	Sir Thomas Phillipps, *Monumental Inscriptions in Wiltshire* (North Wiltshire) (priv. print. 1821)
Phillipps, *Wilts. Inst.*	*Institutiones Clericorum in Comitatu Wiltoniae*, ed. Sir Thomas Phillipps (priv. print. 1825)
Pigot, *Nat. Com. Dir.*	Pigot, *National Commercial Directory*
Plac. de Quo Warr.	*Placita de Quo Warranto*, ed. W. Illingworth and J. Caley (Record Commission, 1818)
Poor Law Abstract, 1804	*Abstract of Returns relative to the Expense and Maintenance of the Poor* (printed by order of the House of Commons, 1804)
Poor Law Abstract, 1818	*Abstract of Returns relative to the Expense and Maintenance of the Poor*, H.C. 82 (1818), xix
Poor Law Com. 2nd Rep.	*Second Annual Report of the Poor Law Commissioners for England and Wales*, H.C. 595 (1836), xxix (1)
Poor Rate Returns, 1816–21	*Poor Rate Returns, 1816–21*, H.C. 556, Supplementary App. (1822), v
Poor Rate Returns, 1822–4	*Poor Rate Returns, 1822–4*, H.C. 334, Supplementary App. (1825), iv
Poor Rate Returns, 1825–9	*Poor Rate Returns, 1825–9*, H.C. 83 (1830–1), xi
Poor Rate Returns, 1830–4	*Poor Rate Returns, 1830–4*, H.C. 444 (1835), xlvii
Princ. Regy. Fam. Div.	Principal Registry of the Family Division, Somerset House
R.O.	Record Office
Red Bk. Exch.	*The Red Book of the Exchequer*, ed. H. Hall (Rolls Series, 1896)
Reg.	Register

Reg. Chichele	*The Register of Henry Chichele, Archbishop of Canterbury*, ed. E. F. Jacob (Canterbury and York Society, 1934–47)
Reg. Ghent	*Registrum Simonis de Gandavo, Diocesis Saresbiriensis*, ed. C. T. Flower and M. C. B. Dawes (Canterbury and York Society, 1934)
Reg. Hallum	*The Register of Robert Hallum, Bishop of Salisbury*, ed. J. Horn (Canterbury and York Society, 1982)
Reg. Langton	*The Register of Thomas Langton, Bishop of Salisbury*, ed. D. P. Wright (Canterbury and York Society, 1985)
Reg. Malm.	*Registrum Malmesburiense*, ed. J. S. Brewer and C. T. Martin (Rolls Series, 1879–80)
Reg. Martival	*The Registers of Roger Martival, Bishop of Salisbury*, ed. K. Edwards and others (Canterbury and York Society, 1959–75)
Reg. Regum Anglo-Norm.	*Regesta Regum Anglo-Normannorum, 1066–1154*, ed. H. W. C. Davis and others (1913–69)
Reg. St. Osmund	*Vetus Registrum Sarisberiense alias Dictum Registrum Sancti Osmund Episcopi*, ed. W. H. R. Jones (Rolls Series, 1883–4)
Rep. Com. Eccl. Revenues	*Report of the Commissioners appointed to Inquire into the Ecclesiastical Revenues of England and Wales* [67], H.C. (1835), xxii
Return of Non-Provided Schs.	*Return of Schools Recognised as Voluntary Public Elementary Schools*, H.C. 178–xxxi (1906), lxxxviii
Returns relating to Elem. Educ.	*Returns relating to Elementary Education*, H.C. 201 (1871), lv
Rot. Chart.	*Rotuli Chartarum, 1199–1216*, ed. T. D. Hardy (Record Commission, 1837)
Rot. Cur. Reg.	*Rotuli Curiae Regis, 6 Richard I to 1 John*, ed. F. Palgrave (Record Commission, 1835)
Rot. Hund.	*Rotuli Hundredorum temp. Hen. III & Edw. I*, ed. W. Illingworth and J. Caley (Record Commission, 1812–18)
Rot. Litt. Claus.	*Rotuli Litterarum Clausarum, 1204–1227*, ed. T. D. Hardy (Record Commission, 1833–44)
Rot. Litt. Pat.	*Rotuli Litterarum Patentium, 1201–16*, ed. T. D. Hardy (Record Commission, 1835)
Rot. Parl.	*Rotuli Parliamentorum* [1783]
Sar. Chart. and Doc.	*Charters and Documents illustrating the History of the Cathedral, City, and Diocese of Salisbury, in the Twelfth and Thirteenth Centuries, etc.* ed. W. Dunn Macray (Rolls Series, 1891)
Soc. Antiq.	Society of Antiquaries of London
Tax. Eccl.	*Taxatio Ecclesiastica Angliae et Walliae auctoritate P. Nicholai IV circa A.D. 1291*, ed. S. Ayscough and J. Caley (Record Commission, 1802)
Topog. and Gen.	*The Topographer and Genealogist*, ed. J. G. Nichols (London, 1846)
Univ. Brit. Dir.	*Universal British Directory of Trade, Commerce, and Manufacture*, ed. P. Barfoot and J. Wilkes (1791–8)
V. & A. Mus.	Victoria and Albert Museum
V.C.H.	*Victoria County History*
Valor Eccl.	*Valor Ecclesiasticus temp. Hen. VIII*, ed. J. Caley and J. Hunter (Record Commission, 1810–34)
W.A.M.	*Wiltshire Archaeological and Natural History Magazine*
W.A.S. (Libr.)	Wiltshire Archaeological and Natural History Society (Library in the Museum, Long Street, Devizes)
W.N. & Q.	*Wiltshire Notes and Queries* (Devizes, 1896–1917)

W.R.O.	Wiltshire Record Office
	Principal classes used:
	    A Quarter Sessions records
	    D Salisbury Diocesan records
	    EA Enclosure Awards
	    F County Council records
	    G Rural District and Borough Council records

NOTE ON ABBREVIATIONS

W.R.S.	Wiltshire Record Society (*formerly* Records Branch of W.A.S.)
Walker Revised, ed. Matthews	*Walker Revised; being a Revision of John Walker's Sufferings of the Clergy during the Grand Rebellion, 1642–60*, ed. A. G. Matthews
Walters, *Wilts. Bells*	H. B. Walters, *Church Bells of Wiltshire* (Devizes, 1927–9)
Wm. of Malmesbury, *Gesta Regum Angl.*	*Willelmi Malmesbiriensis Monachi de Gestis Regum Anglorum Libri Quinque; Historiae Novellae Libri Tres*, ed. W. Stubbs (Rolls Series, 1887–9)
Williams, *Cath. Recusancy*	J. A. Williams, *Catholic Recusancy in Wiltshire, 1660–1791* (Catholic Record Society, 1968)
Dr. Williams's Libr.	Dr. Williams's Library, 14 Gordon Square, London W.C. 1
Wilts. Cuttings	Volumes of newspaper and other cuttings in W.A.S. Libr.
Wilts. Inq. p.m. 1242–1326	*Abstracts of Wiltshire Inquisitiones post mortem in the reigns of Henry III, Edward I, and Edward II, 1242–1326*, ed. E. A. Fry (Index Library, xxxvii)
Wilts. Inq. p.m. 1327–77	*Abstracts of Wiltshire Inquisitiones post mortem in the reign of Edward III, 1327–77*, ed. Ethel Stokes (Index Library, xlviii)
Wilts. Inq. p.m. 1625–49	*Abstracts of Wiltshire Inquisitiones post mortem in the reign of Charles I, 1625–49*, ed. G. S. and E. A. Fry (Index Library, xxiii)
Wilts. Q. Sess. Rec. ed. Cunnington	*Records of the County of Wiltshire from the Quarter Sessions Rolls of the 17th Century*, ed. B. H. Cunnington (Devizes, 1932)
Wilts. Tracts	Collections of tracts in W.A.S. Libr.

INTRODUCTION

MALMESBURY hundred in north-west Wiltshire is flat, well drained land, not an area of hill forts and henge monuments, but one of dense and apparently prosperous settlement in the Saxon period. Malmesbury was the site of an early and wealthy abbey around which a town grew up, and the place names, including Norton, Sutton, Somerford, Stanton, Crudwell, and the evocative Charlton, are typically Saxon. At the Conquest Malmesbury was as developed as any town in Wiltshire, and the two hundreds which later merged as Malmesbury hundred probably contained as many villages to the square mile as any other in the county. Malmesbury stands on a promontory above the Sherston and Tetbury branches of the Bristol Avon; Oaksey and Brinkworth are sited on ridges, but nearly all the other villages are beside streams. Many are mentioned in Malmesbury abbey charters but the boundaries ascribed to them may be much later than the purported dates of the charters: nevertheless some boundaries, notably the Foss Way and other roads, and the Avon, its Sherston branch, and its tributaries Gauze, Brinkworth, and Woodbridge brooks, are clearly ancient and suggest an early end to intercommoning by villages. A straight line dividing several pairs of parishes in the south part of the hundred suggests a later end to it there, and isolated examples of intercommoning persisted throughout the Middle Ages.

Most of the hundred is in Wiltshire's Cotswold country where Cornbrash and limestone and clay of the Forest Marble outcrop: to the south-east, where the clay soils are heavier, part is in the Cheese country. The Cotswold country was noted for sheep-and-corn husbandry, and nearly every principal village in the hundred is known to have had open fields and common pastures in the Middle Ages. There was apparently little dispersed settlement before the 16th century and the villages remained small. Malmesbury, a focus for many of them, never had a market to rival Tetbury, Cirencester, or Chippenham, and the success of its cloth industry was spasmodic. Although the town expanded westwards in the 19th and 20th centuries the two branches of the Avon prevented expansion in the other three directions, and, poorly served by railways and modern roads, it has remained commercially undeveloped. In the 20th century a few of the villages, Hullavington, Brinkworth, and Sutton Benger, have grown substantially; there has been new building in most of the others, perhaps encouraged by the proximity of the M4 motorway and fast rail services, but a few, including Norton, Foxley, Draycot Cerne, and Garsdon, have remained very small. At various times some hamlets have dwindled to single farmsteads, but the hundred is not an area of lost villages.

The land was inclosed mainly in the 16th and 17th centuries, especially, it seems, in the early and mid 17th century. For some small groups of open fields, like those of Foxley, Dauntsey, and Brinkworth, there is little evidence of inclosure. Where there is evidence of a large group, as for Brokenborough, Charlton, and Hullavington, the fields can be seen to have been inclosed at first piecemeal, afterwards in stages by agreed inclosures over a long period, in some places preceded, in others followed, by inclosure of common pasture. Only at Crudwell and Stanton St. Quintin was inclosure of open arable by Act. After inclosure much land was laid to grass, and in the later 19th century and early 20th there was dairy farming throughout the hundred. Since 1939 much of the land has again been ploughed. Common meadow land at Seagry was not inclosed until 1883, and in many places vestiges of common pasture in wide lanes and on small greens remain visible.

There was in the hundred a lack of woodland consistent with early settlement and early division of the land, but most villages preserved small areas of ancient woodland: in the south-west, for example, Corston, Rodbourne, Hullavington, Surrendell, Bradfield, Norton, Foxley, and Bremilham all had 10–20 a. Villages further north or east may have taken wood from the purlieus of Braydon forest. The forest itself was reduced to an area east of the hundred in 1300, but until the 1630s both the forest and its purlieus, parts of which were called Minety or Charlton quarter and Brinkworth quarter, remained open for feeding in common by cattle from villages with land adjoining them. Soon after 1630, when the forest was inclosed, each village with a valid claim to such pasture rights was allotted a specified part of the purlieus: in Malmesbury hundred Oaksey, Crudwell, Hankerton, Cloatley, Brokenborough, Charlton, Milbourne, Garsdon, Lea, Cleverton, Little Somerford, and Brinkworth received allotments, those for Brinkworth, Charlton, and Hankerton being the largest. Over most of the allotments the land was inclosed and improved and new farmsteads were built, but some parts were assigned as common pasture and remained such until the early 19th century. Some allotments adjoined the land of the villages for which they were made and were parts of the relevant parishes; others, detached, were either absorbed by surrounding parishes or transferred to them statutorily in the 19th century.

In several parishes Malmesbury abbey had large demesne buildings, some of which were erected or repaired in a building boom of the later 13th century, but only two large medieval barns, at Brokenborough and Crudwell, survive. In Malmesbury and generally throughout the hundred the few medieval domestic buildings which survive are largely hidden by later alterations: Abbey House in Malmesbury is over a 13th-century undercroft, a farmhouse at Sutton Benger contains the remains of a 13th-century chapel, Dauntsey House has an early 14th-century hall range, and Garsdon Manor includes a 14th-century cruck roof. Many farmhouses were rebuilt in the 17th century, and in many villages gabled houses of stone with stone-slated roofs and mullioned windows are a prominent feature: to the south-east, where there was less stone and more woodland, there are timber-framed houses of that date. In the 17th and 18th centuries, after inclosure, more farmsteads were built outside the villages. Rebuilding continued in the 19th century, but there are fewer 19th-century planned farmsteads on new sites than elsewhere in the county, presumably because around Malmesbury the farms, mostly devoted to dairying, remained small. In the later 20th century Malmesbury was limited as a commercial centre, and the villages around it, in many of which farming activities had ceased, offered little employment. Where the land was worked from outside the village, farm buildings were either converted for residence or replaced by new housing.

Malmesbury abbey owned c. 23,000 a. of the hundred, besides more outside it, but few of its records survive and no detailed account of the estate can be given. There was nothing to rival it after the Dissolution, but the Howards, earls of Suffolk and of Berkshire, held four of the abbey's manors, c. 10,000 a. after the increases of the 1630s, and later more, and theirs was the grandest mansion in the hundred. Their house, built for Sir Henry Knyvett, an energetic Elizabethan squire keen to promote local military organization, was embraced in the early 17th century by Charlton Park which has stylistic similarity to Audley End. The Longs and their descendants the earls of Mornington and the Earls Cowley owned Draycot Cerne for over 450 years and built up an estate around it with large houses at Draycot and Seagry. The estate of the Dauntsey and Danvers families, which may have originated soon after the Conquest and included Malmesbury borough after the Dissolution, disintegrated after *c.* 1650. In the 18th and 19th centuries large estates were held by the Foxes, Lords Holland, and the Bouveries, earls of Radnor, but most estates were small and the manor houses not much more than farmhouses. Malmesbury, among the most rotten of boroughs, was usually represented in parliament by local men, and only in the later 18th century were the seats disputed by the Howards and Foxes.

The division of the hundred into parishes and the arrangements for churches to be served, as complex as elsewhere in Wiltshire, were presumably much influenced by Malmesbury abbey which took the great tithes from most of its estates. Even in an area of many villages some parishes on its estates were large, taking in several villages and hamlets; the churches on two, Brokenborough and Charlton, were dependent on St. Mary's church in Malmesbury's suburb Westport, and those on two more, Hankerton and Lea, were for long dependent chapels. Away from the abbey's estates, however, the parishes, such as Bremilham, Foxley, and Seagry, were small. The abbey church became the parish church of Malmesbury after the Dissolution, elsewhere much medieval work survives in the churches, and there is a Saxon church in Westport. Local incumbents included two enthusiastic providers of garden allotments for the poor, and at Stanton St. Quintin, Bertrand Pleydell-Bouverie, a son of the earl of Radnor, carved a fine stone pulpit for the church. Quakerism was strong, various dissenting groups, including Moravians, established themselves in Malmesbury and Westport, and in the earlier 19th century Brinkworth was the centre from which southern England was evangelized by Primitive Methodists.

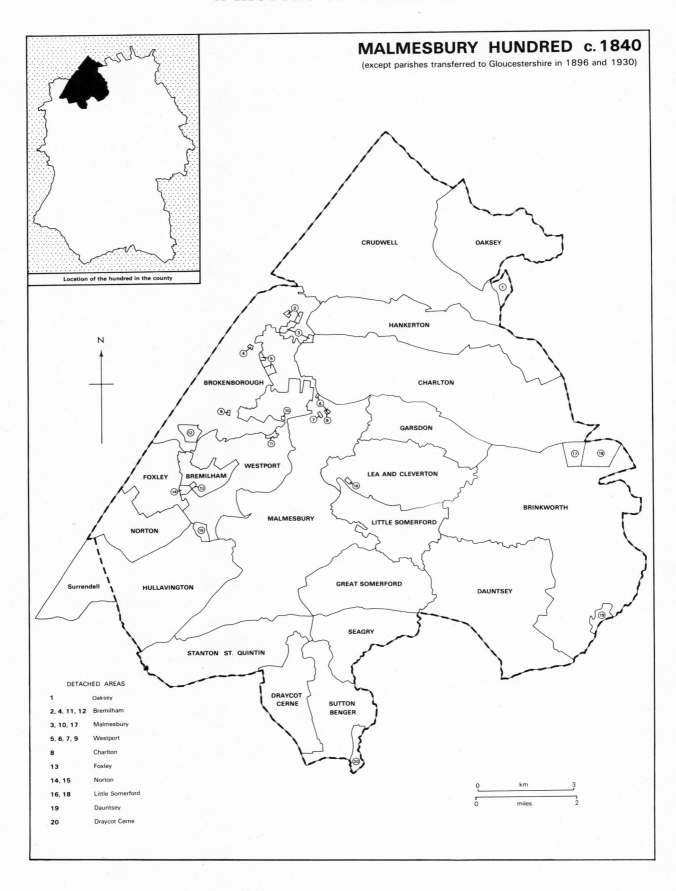

MALMESBURY HUNDRED c.1840

(except parishes transferred to Gloucestershire in 1896 and 1930)

Location of the hundred in the county

N

CRUDWELL

OAKSEY

HANKERTON

CHARLTON

BROKENBOROUGH

GARSDON

LEA AND CLEVERTON

FOXLEY

BREMILHAM

WESTPORT

MALMESBURY

LITTLE SOMERFORD

BRINKWORTH

NORTON

Surrendell

HULLAVINGTON

GREAT SOMERFORD

DAUNTSEY

SEAGRY

STANTON ST. QUINTIN

DRAYCOT CERNE

SUTTON BENGER

DETACHED AREAS

1	Oaksey
2, 4, 11, 12	Bremilham
3, 10, 17	Malmesbury
5, 6, 7, 9	Westport
8	Charlton
13	Foxley
14, 15	Norton
16, 18	Little Somerford
19	Dauntsey
20	Draycot Cerne

km 0 3

miles 0 2

MALMESBURY HUNDRED

IN north-west Wiltshire in 1066 a hundred was called Cicemethorn and another Sutelesberg, both presumably after their meeting places. In 1084 Cicemethorn, later called Chedglow, contained estates mainly north of Malmesbury, and Sutelesberg, then called Startley, estates mainly south of Malmesbury. Chedglow included Brokenborough, Charlton, Crudwell, Garsdon, Kemble, and Long Newnton, all belonging to Malmesbury abbey; Ashley, Oaksey, and possibly Poole Keynes; and small estates called Chedglow and Malmesbury.[1] The Brokenborough and Crudwell estates included lands which later became separate estates,[2] and in 1084 the composition of Chedglow hundred may have been roughly as in the early 14th century when it was Ashley, Brokenborough, Charlton, Crudwell (including Chedglow, Chelworth, and Eastcourt), Garsdon, Hankerton, Kemble (including Ewen), Lea and Cleverton, nearly all Malmesbury parish (including Burton Hill, Corston, Milbourne, and Rodbourne, but excluding the borough), Long Newnton, Oaksey, Poole Keynes, and Sutton Benger.[3] In 1084 Startley hundred contained estates called Bradfield, Brinkworth, Draycot, Foxley, Hullavington, Christian Malford, Norton, and Stanton, and a small one called Chedglow; and it may have contained more.[4] In the early 14th century it contained Bremilham, Brinkworth (including Grittenham), Christian Malford, Dauntsey (including Smithcot), Draycot Cerne, Easton Piercy in Kington St. Michael parish, Foxley, Hullavington (including Bradfield but not Surrendell), Norton, Seagry, Great Somerford, Little Somerford, and Stanton St. Quintin.[5] Easton Piercy was in Thorngrove hundred in 1084; Surrendell was in Dunlow hundred in 1084,[6] in Chippenham hundred in the 14th century and later.[7] The part of Westport parish outside Malmesbury borough is likely to have been in Chedglow hundred.

In 1086 Malmesbury borough may already have been privileged and was not part of either Chedglow or Startley hundred. The borough and both hundreds belonged to the Crown,[8] in the 1130s were held by Roger, bishop of Salisbury,[9] and in 1215 were granted at fee farm to Malmesbury abbey.[10] Because the grant was of Malmesbury and three hundreds, and in the period 1226–8 the third hundred was called Malmesbury,[11] it has been suggested that there was an earlier urban Malmesbury hundred, but that is unlikely.[12] It is more likely that what were granted in 1215 and called Malmesbury hundred were regalian rights within the borough.[13] While in Malmesbury abbey's hands, however, Chedglow and Startley hundreds and the borough coalesced. That some places were assigned to both hundreds, or to the wrong one, in the period 1268–89 suggests that the distinction had already been blurred by then.[14] It was largely abandoned after 1334, and in 1377 Malmesbury hundred

[1] V.C.H. Wilts. ii, pp. 115, 196.
[2] Below, Brokenborough, manor; Crudwell, manors.
[3] V.C.H. Wilts. iv. 298.   [4] Ibid. ii, p. 212.
[5] Ibid. iv. 301.   [6] Ibid. ii, pp. 204–5.
[7] Ibid. iv. 298; Taxation Lists (W.R.S. x), 27, 61; Q. Sess. 1736 (W.R.S. xi), p. 136.
[8] V.C.H. Wilts. ii, pp. 113, 115; below, Malmesbury, introduction.
[9] Reg. Regum Anglo-Norm. iii, no. 784.
[10] Rot. Chart. (Rec. Com.), 213.
[11] Bk. of Fees, i. 379.
[12] J. Tait, Medieval Eng. Boro. 53; cf. V.C.H. Wilts. v. 44, 46–7.
[13] Cf. below, Malmesbury, local govt. (manorial govt.).
[14] P.R.O., JUST 1/998A, rot. 30 and d.; JUST 1/1006, rot. 44 and d.

included Malmesbury borough and, with the possible exception of Christian Malford, all the places in Chedglow and Startley hundreds in 1334. Westport was clearly in the hundred in 1377;[15] Christian Malford was later in North Damerham hundred.[16]

Malmesbury hundred had in it c. 37 tithings. Those which were never parishes included, at various times, Grittenham in Brinkworth parish, Eastcourt in Crudwell, Smithcot in Dauntsey, Cloatley in Hankerton, Cleverton in Lea and Cleverton, and Burton Hill, Corston, Milbourne, and Rodbourne in Malmesbury.[17] Kemble and Poole Keynes, transferred to Gloucestershire in 1896, Ashley and Long Newnton, transferred to Gloucestershire in 1930,[18] and Easton Piercy are outside the scope of this volume, but Surrendell is included.

Malmesbury abbey held the hundred at fee farm until the Dissolution.[19] In 1566, 1583, and 1586 the Crown leased it to the burgesses of Malmesbury,[20] in 1588 to Sir John Danvers and his sons Charles and Henry, in 1595 to Sir Henry Knyvett, and in 1607 to Thomas Howard, earl of Suffolk, and his wife Catherine.[21] In 1611 it sold the hundred to Sir Richard Grobham (d. 1629).[22] Malmesbury hundred passed to Sir Richard's eventual heir, his sister Joan, wife of John Howe. Joan was succeeded by her son Sir John Howe, Bt., and the hundred passed in the direct male line to Sir Richard Howe, Bt. (d. 1703), and Sir Richard Howe, Bt. (d. s.p. 1730).[23] That Sir Richard was succeeded by his cousin John Howe (cr. Baron Chedworth 1741, d. 1742), and the hundred descended with the Chedworth title to John Howe (d. 1762), Henry Howe (d. 1781), and John Howe (d. 1804). That last Lord Chedworth devised the hundred for sale[24] and it was bought by Sir John St. Aubyn, Bt., who sold it in 1813 to Joseph Pitt. In 1840 Pitt sold it to Joseph Neeld,[25] the owner in 1845.[26]

In 1255 the sheriff was taking a total of £3 6s. 8d. for cert money and tithing penny and £1 6s. 8d. for sheriff's aid at his twice-yearly tourns,[27] and in 1535 the hundred was worth £4 12s. to Malmesbury abbey.[28] In the later 16th century the hundred was worth £6 11s. 8d.[29]

Chedglow hundred presumably met at Chedglow and the name Cicemethorn has been thought to suggest that it met at a thorn tree there.[30] According to tradition Startley hundred met at Startley ash on Startley common in Great Somerford.[31] Before 1215 the constable of Malmesbury castle held fortnightly courts for Startley hundred, and possibly for Chedglow, at Malmesbury,[32] and after 1215 three-weekly courts of the two hundreds may have been held together at Malmesbury.[33] With Malmesbury abbey's consent Glastonbury abbey withdrew its men of Christian Malford from the hundred courts in 1244,[34] but an attempt in the period 1242–54 to withdraw Ashley was unsuccessful.[35] Malmesbury abbey held the courts until the Dissolution.[36] In 1561–2 they were held by the Crown about every three weeks, often on a Saturday, and dealt with infringements of the assize of bread and of ale,

[15] V.C.H. Wilts. iv. 309–10.
[16] Ibid. 328.
[17] Below, local govt. sections of par. hists.
[18] V.C.H. Wilts. iv. 340, 351, 354–5.
[19] Valor Eccl. (Rec. Com.), ii. 122.
[20] P.R.O., C 66/1312, mm. 36–7; ibid. E 310/26/153, f. 40; E 310/26/154, f. 6.
[21] Ibid. C 66/1312, mm. 36–7; C 66/1436, m. 32; Cal. S.P. Dom. 1603–10, 359.
[22] P.R.O., C 66/1870, no. 3; Wilts. Inq. p.m. 1625–49 (Index Libr.), 103–7.
[23] V.C.H. Wilts. xi. 170; for the Howe fam., Complete Peerage, iii. 156–7; P.R.O., CP 25(2)/987/3 Anne Trin.
[24] P.R.O., CP 25(2)/1476/22 Geo. III East.; W.R.O. 530.
[25] Aubrey, Topog. Coll. ed. Jackson, 206.
[26] W.R.O. 1305/203, petition, 1845.
[27] Rot. Hund. (Rec. Com.), ii (1), 230, 235.
[28] Valor Eccl. (Rec. Com.), ii. 119.
[29] P.R.O., E 310/26/153, f. 40.
[30] P.N. Wilts. (E.P.N.S.), 53.
[31] W.A.M. xxxi. 322; W.R.O., EA/98.
[32] Bodl. MS. Wood Empt. 5, f. 4.
[33] V.C.H. Wilts. v. 63–4; Reg. Malm. ii. 178–9; Cur. Reg. R. xi, p. 281.
[34] P.R.O., CP 25(1)/250/4, no. 24.
[35] Reg. Malm. ii. 178–9.
[36] Valor Eccl. (Rec. Com.), ii. 119, 122.

suitors who failed to attend or pursue complaints, and pleas of debt. A toll called the Tolsey was paid on St. Aldhelm's day (25 May) and St. James's day (25 July).[37] Later the courts were held by the lords of the hundred, and in the early 19th century they were for the recovery of small debts. Between 1840 and 1845 they were held every three weeks and presided over as registrar or judge by an attorney who issued an average of 19 original summonses at each court. The registrar's judgements were neither reversed nor impugned, debts were paid, and in 1845 the lord and inhabitants of the hundred petitioned to enlarge the jurisdiction of the court for the recovery of debts not exceeding £20.[38]

Before 1215 the constable of Malmesbury castle held twice-yearly courts called great hundreds at Startley.[39] Tourns for both Chedglow and Startley hundreds were held by the sheriff at Cowfold in Malmesbury parish in 1255 or earlier[40] and in 1439 when they were jointly called Malmesbury hundred.[41] In the 16th century tourns were held at Malmesbury: in the period 1502–11 they were for Malmesbury hundred,[42] but in 1561–2 law days for Chedglow hundred were held the day after those for Startley hundred.[43] In Chedglow hundred the men on Malmesbury abbey's estates and on Oaksey manor, virtually the whole hundred apart from Ashley, were free from the sheriff's jurisdiction in the mid 13th century.[44] In 1275 the jurors of Startley hundred complained that after 1215, with Malmesbury abbey's consent, they were compelled to make payments at law days nominally for Chedglow hundred, to which the sheriff could presumably enforce little attendance, and that the sheriff and the abbey shared the income.[45] Malmesbury abbey's men of Brinkworth, Grittenham, and Norton had presumably been withdrawn from the Startley tourn by 1255;[46] Stanton St. Quintin was withdrawn c. 1258 but later attended;[47] Hullavington was withdrawn c. 1264, afterwards attended, was withdrawn again c. 1443,[48] but attended in the early 16th century;[49] and Draycot Cerne, Foxley, and Great Somerford were temporarily withdrawn in the 1260s.[50] There is no record of attendance by Bremilham or Dauntsey, which were apparently withdrawn by a member of the Dauntsey family before 1275.[51] Extensive liberties granted in 1340 to John Moleyns in estates at Brinkworth and Lea included view of frankpledge which was exercised at Lea.[52] In 1439 and 1511 tithingmen of Ashley, Draycot Cerne, Easton Piercy, Foxley, Hullavington, Seagry, Somerford, and Stanton St. Quintin attended the tourn for Malmesbury hundred,[53] and in 1562 only Ashley, Draycot Cerne, Easton Piercy, Foxley, Seagry, and Somerford paid cert to the sheriff.[54]

One man acted as the sheriff's serjeant in Chedglow and Startley hundreds in the period 1189–94,[55] and in 1255 one man served as bailiff for the two hundreds.[56] The bailiff or steward was paid £4 yearly in the 16th century, and in 1545 William Stumpe, a leading inhabitant of Malmesbury and purchaser of some of the abbey's estates, was appointed.[57] In 1613 the right of the constable of Malmesbury hundred

[37] P.R.O., SC 2/209/16, rot. 2 and d.
[38] W.R.O. 1305/203, petition, 1845.
[39] Bodl. MS. Wood Empt. 5, f. 4.
[40] Rot. Hund. (Rec. Com.), ii (1), 230.
[41] W.A.M. xiii. 116–17.
[42] P.R.O., SC 2/208/29, ff. 9v.–10; W.R.O. 192/26, ff. 4v.–5, 23, 24v.
[43] P.R.O., SC 2/209/16, rot. 2 and d.
[44] Rot. Hund. (Rec. Com.), ii (1), 230.
[45] Ibid. 272.
[46] Ibid. 230. For the abbey's tenure of those places, below, Brinkworth, manors; Norton, manor.
[47] W.A.M. xiii. 117; below, Stanton St. Quintin, local govt.
[48] Below, Hullavington, local govt.

[49] P.R.O., SC 2/208/29, f. 20v.; W.R.O. 192/26, ff. 4v.–5, 23, 24v.
[50] P.R.O., JUST 1/998A, rot. 30 and d.
[51] Rot. Hund. (Rec. Com.), ii (1), 273. For the Dauntseys' tenure of those places, below, Bremilham, manor; Dauntsey, manors.
[52] Cal. Chart. R. 1327–41, 468; below, Brinkworth, local govt.; Lea and Cleverton, local govt.
[53] W.A.M. xiii. 116–17; W.R.O. 192/26, ff. 4v.–5, 23, 24v.
[54] P.R.O., E 370/12/17; E 370/16/19.
[55] V.C.H. Wilts. v. 9; Abbrev. Plac. (Rec. Com.), 13–14.
[56] Rot. Hund. (Rec. Com.), ii (1), 239.
[57] Valor Eccl. (Rec. Com.), ii. 122; L. & P. Hen. VIII, xx (1), p. 676; P.R.O., E 310/26/153, f. 40.

to arrest the ringleaders of an anti-inclosure riot was challenged by the keeper of the king's race in Cole park (in Malmesbury parish).[58] Besides the high constable there were two petty constables in 1639,[59] and there were two constables in the 18th century.[60]

[58] *Acts of P.C.* 1613–14, 92–3.
[59] *Cal. S.P. Dom.* 1639, 206, 246, 284, 536.

[60] *Q. Sess. 1736* (W.R.S. xi), p. 43.

BREMILHAM

BREMILHAM,[1] which in 1731 consisted of a main part 3 km. WSW. of Malmesbury and of five detached portions, was one of the smallest of Wiltshire parishes. In 1731 it measured, excluding roads, water, and waste, c. 440 a. Three of the detached portions, Brokenborough field and two fields called Hankerton Corner, a total of 97 a., were virtually encompassed by Brokenborough; the other two, New leaze, 5 a. SSE. of Brokenborough field, and 8 a. called the Light in the 19th century were encompassed by Westport parish, and the Light was very near Malmesbury. About 1840 New leaze was considered part of Westport, but a field of 2 a. north of Brokenborough village and encompassed by Brokenborough parish was considered part of Bremilham.[2] In 1871 Bremilham parish was c. 458 a.[3]

The main part of the parish was separated from Brokenborough to the north by the Sherston branch of the Bristol Avon. That river was a boundary c. 1100 marking the southern edge of Malmesbury abbey's estate called Brokenborough,[4] which Bremilham was thus apparently outside. A tributary of the Avon was part of Bremilham's boundary with Foxley to the west.[5] To the south Bremilham parish adjoined Malmesbury common: the boundary between them had possibly been made by the early 13th century when the lord of Bremilham manor had hedges apparently marking his boundaries to the south.[6] A grant of Bremilham's tithes in 1179[7] either reflected or led to its status as a parish. The detached portions presumably joined the parish because they and their tithes belonged to the lord of Bremilham manor.[8] In the early 13th century the lord of that manor had land and pasture rights apparently north of the Avon,[9] which may have led to a later lord's ownership of the detached portions; the lord of the manor owned them in the 17th century.[10] The parish was dissolved in 1884. Four detached portions were added to Brokenborough, the fifth to Westport; the main part was added to Foxley parish[11] and, as part of that, was added to Norton parish in 1934.[12] From the 16th century the principal farm in Bremilham parish was called Cowage.[13] That name became an altern-

ative name for the parish,[14] and after the parish was dissolved the name Bremilham was little used.

The main part of the parish made an arc mostly south of a southwards bend of the Avon. Two tributaries cross it from west to east, the southern being the stream which separated Foxley and Bremilham. It is nearly flat, below 76 m. beside the Avon. Kellaways Clay outcrops in the slightly higher southern part, Cornbrash nearer the Avon. In a small area in the north-west corner more Kellaways Clay outcrops, there partly covered by sand and gravel. The Avon and both the tributaries have exposed narrow bands of clay of the Forest Marble and deposited alluvium.[15] Bremilham had much meadow for so small a parish. Its other land is suitable for arable and pasture. In the 17th and 18th centuries the Cornbrash was favoured for arable, the Kellaways Clay for pasture. Cowage Grove, 11 a. in the south-west corner, is apparently ancient woodland.[16]

The east–west Malmesbury–Sherston road through Foxley crosses the former parish: it was part of the main Oxford–Bristol road in the late 17th century[17] but was superseded in importance by a road north of the parish turnpiked in 1756.[18] So small a parish had few inhabitants, although in 1377 the number of poll-tax payers, 31, was higher than that for either Foxley or Norton.[19] From the 16th century or earlier there was apparently no more than a single farm in the parish,[20] and in 1811 there were only 14 inhabitants.[21] By 1841 the number had risen to 47, of whom 14 lived at the Light.[22] The population had fallen to 25 by 1881, but in 1891 the main part of the former parish had 27 inhabitants, the Light 17.[23]

Earliest settlement in the parish may have been in the timber buildings, short distances east and south of the present Cowage Farm, revealed by air photography in 1975 and afterwards partly excavated. Among the eastern buildings one, apparently apsidal, was possibly a church.[24] Bremilham church had apparently been built on its present site on the Cornbrash between the Avon and the southern tributary by the late 12th or the late 13th century.[25] Its proximity to the house and buildings of Cowage, formerly Bremilham, Farm,

[1] A map of the par. is below, s.v. Norton. This article was written in 1987. Maps used include O.S. Maps 6", Wilts. VIII, XIII (1888–9 edns.); 1/25,000, ST 88, ST 98 (1958–9 edns.); 1/50,000, sheet 173 (1974 edn.).
[2] W.R.O. 1198/1; ibid. Bremilham and Brokenborough tithe awards; P.R.O., HO 107/1181.
[3] Census, 1871.
[4] Arch. Jnl. lxxvii. 46–7.
[5] W.R.O., tithe award.
[6] Reg. Malm. ii. 185–7.
[7] Cal. Chart. R. 1257–1300, 157–9.
[8] For Brokenborough's tithes, below, Brokenborough, manor; for Westport's, ibid. Westport, manors.
[9] Reg. Malm. ii. 185–7.
[10] W.R.O., A 1/310, roll 1, Wm. Estcourt; ibid. 130/25, lease, Estcourt to Webb, 1699; 212B/27/11/1, deed, Smith to Smith, 1647.
[11] V.C.H. Wilts. iv. 348 n., 360 n.; for the transfer to Brokenborough, O.S. Map 6", Wilts. VIII (1889 edn.).
[12] V.C.H. Wilts. iv. 355 n.

[13] W.R.O. 212B/5141; P.R.O., SC 6/Hen. VIII/3986, rot. 99d.
[14] e.g. Phillipps, Wilts. Inst. ii. 28.
[15] Geol. Surv. Map 1", solid and drift, sheet 251 (1970 edn.).
[16] W.R.O. 212A/27/11/1, deed, Smith to Smith, 1647; 1198/1.
[17] J. Ogilby, Brit. (1675), pl. 79.
[18] V.C.H. Wilts. iv. 257, 269; L.J. xxviii. 581.
[19] V.C.H. Wilts. iv. 309.
[20] Taxation Lists (W.R.S. x), 80; P.R.O., C 3/62/35.
[21] V.C.H. Wilts. iv. 342.
[22] P.R.O., HO 107/1181.
[23] V.C.H. Wilts. iv. 342, 348 n., 360 n.
[24] Arch. Jnl. cxliii. 240–50. The ideas, expressed ibid. 253, that Bremilham was the site of Mailduib's monastery and that there is evidence 'of a major sixth/seventh-century settlement' at Bremilham are fanciful, and the discussion, ibid. 253–7, of 'Hercology of the Par. of Bremilham' is unsound.
[25] Below, church.

suggests that it was built when there was already a farmstead on the site, and the sites of earlier settlement had presumably been deserted by the time that church was built. In 1731 the church and those of Cowage Farm were the only buildings in the main part of the parish. Cowage Farm is an 18th-century L-shaped farmhouse which was altered and extended in the 19th century. It apparently replaced a larger house which was standing in 1731.[26] The extensive farm buildings include a large barn, which may also be 18th-century, and an enclosed stockyard. North of them the Avon is crossed by an 18th-century three-arched stone bridge. A pair of cottages was built at the east corner of Cowage Grove between 1773 and 1828:[27] it was demolished between 1921 and 1956.[28] Another pair was built beside the Malmesbury–Sherston road near Cowage Farm between 1885 and 1897,[29] and another pair beside them c. 1945.[30]

On the detached parts of the parish there were buildings only at the Light on the edge of Malmesbury. Most of the Light was bounded to the north by the Malmesbury–Sherston turnpike road. It was crossed by the lane called Dark Lane in 1987.[31] A messuage may have stood there in 1699.[32] A dwelling house there in 1731 stood on the south side of the Malmesbury–Sherston road.[33] Buildings south of Dark Lane were used for tanning in the 18th and 19th centuries and incorporated a dwelling house.[34] By 1884 a few other buildings had been erected on the land, including, north of the Malmesbury–Sherston road, a school for Westport and Malmesbury parishes;[35] after 1884, as part of the built-up area of Malmesbury, more of the land was used for housing and commerce and some for quarrying stone.[36] The dwelling house standing in 1731, later called the Light, was replaced by or incorporated in a much larger house in the later 19th century. In 1987 that house was used as a nursing home. Few of the tannery buildings survive.

MANOR. Malmesbury abbey claimed to have held *BREMILHAM* before the Conquest as part of its estate called Brokenborough, and very likely did so. Bremilham was apparently the 2 hides of its land, granted to one of its knights after 1066, which were held by William in 1086.[37] The abbey

was overlord until the Dissolution.[38]

Bremilham may have belonged to Miles of Dauntsey in the mid 12th century. It passed from Miles's son Miles to the younger Miles's son Richard, to Richard's son Matthew of Bremilham (fl. 1199–1208), and to Matthew's son Richard of Bremilham (d. s.p. before 1249).[39] In 1249 Agnes, daughter of another Richard of Bremilham, conveyed the estate to Roger Dauntsey,[40] the grandson of the younger Miles Dauntsey;[41] Agnes was presumably Matthew's sister and Roger's cousin. In 1257 Bremilham was conveyed to Roger's brother Gilbert (d. by 1282) for life and, if another brother Richard (d. by 1275) survived Gilbert, to Richard in tail.[42] Until 1656 Bremilham belonged to the owners of Dauntsey.[43] It was held by Richard's son Richard (fl. 1292), Sir Richard Dauntsey (fl. 1349), Sir John Dauntsey[44] (d. 1391), Sir John Dauntsey (d. 1405), and Sir Walter Dauntsey[45] (d. 1420), passed to Walter's sister Joan (d. 1457),[46] her son Edmund Stradling (d. 1461), John Stradling[47] (d. 1471), and, presumably, Edward Stradling (d. 1487) and Anne Stradling (d. 1539), wife of Sir John Danvers, and was held by Silvester Danvers (d. 1551),[48] Sir John Danvers (d. 1594), and Sir John's relict Elizabeth (d. 1630), wife of Sir Edward Carey.[49] By 1625 Bremilham had passed to Sir John's son Henry,[50] from 1626 earl of Danby (d. 1644),[51] and in 1628 was settled on the marriage of Henry's brother Sir John Danvers[52] (d. 1655), a regicide.[53] In 1656 Sir John's trustees sold it to Thomas Estcourt,[54] knighted in 1661,[55] of Sherston Pinkney.[56]

Estcourt (d. 1683)[57] in 1669 settled Bremilham on his marriage with Anne Kirkham.[58] It passed to their son William[59] (d. 1727) and to William's son Charles, who in 1731 sold it to Robert Holford, a master in Chancery.[60] Holford (d. 1753)[61] was succeeded in turn by his son Peter (d. 1803) and Peter's son Robert (d. 1838), each also a master in Chancery: Robert's heir was his brother George (d. 1839), who was succeeded in turn by his son R. S. Holford (d. 1892) and R. S. Holford's son Sir George Holford.[62] In 1897 the manor was called the Cowage estate and consisted of 459 a., nearly all the old Bremilham parish and 49 a. of adjoining land in Brokenborough and Westport parishes.[63] Sir George Holford sold the estate in

[26] W.R.O. 1198/1.
[27] *Andrews and Dury, Map* (W.R.S. viii), pl. 13; O.S. Map 1", sheet 34 (1828 edn.).
[28] O.S. Maps 6", Wilts. XIII. NW. (1925 edn.); 1/25,000, ST 98 (1959 edn.).
[29] Ibid. 6", Wilts. XIII (1888 edn.); W.A.S. Libr., sale cat. ii, no. 19.
[30] W.R.O., G 7/760/169. [31] Ibid. tithe award.
[32] Ibid. 212A/27/11/1, deed, Estcourt to Carpenter, 1699.
[33] Ibid. 1198/1.
[34] Ibid. tithe award; below, econ. hist.
[35] O.S. Map 6", Wilts. VIII (1889 edn.); below, educ.
[36] O.S. Map 6", Wilts. VIII. SW. (1900 edn.).
[37] *V.C.H. Wilts.* ii, pp. 88, 125–6.
[38] P.R.O., C 142/247, no. 100.
[39] B.L. Add. MS. 15667, f. 38v.; for Matthew, *Rot. Cur. Reg.* (Rec. Com.), i. 225; *Cur. Reg. R.* v. 232; for Ric. of Bremilham (fl. early 13th cent.), *Bradenstoke Cart.* (W.R.S. xxxv), p. 75; *Reg. Malm.* ii. 185–7; *Civil Pleas, 1249* (W.R.S. xxvi), p. 144.
[40] P.R.O., CP 25(1)/251/15, no. 30.
[41] B.L. Add. MS. 15667, f. 38v.
[42] Ibid.; P.R.O., CP 25(1)/251/19, no. 4; *Cat. Anct. D.* iii, A 4636; *Sel. Cases in K.B.* iv (Selden Soc. lxxiv), pp.

37–43; *Rot. Hund.* (Rec. Com.), ii (1), 272–3.
[43] Below, Dauntsey, manors.
[44] *Feet of F. 1327–77* (W.R.S. xxix), p. 73; *Abbrev. Plac.* (Rec. Com.), 228.
[45] *Cal. Inq. p.m.* xviii, p. 363.
[46] *Feet of F. 1377–1509* (W.R.S. xli), pp. 88, 121.
[47] P.R.O., C 140/1, no. 12.
[48] Ibid. C 142/94, no. 88.
[49] Ibid. C 142/247, no. 100.
[50] W.R.O. 212A/27/11/1, deed, Smith to Smith, 1647.
[51] *Complete Peerage*, iv. 48–9.
[52] W.R.O. 212A/27/11/1, deed, Danvers to Coppin, 1652.
[53] *D.N.B.*
[54] W.R.O. 212A/27/11/1, deed, Coppin to Estcourt, 1656.
[55] *Alum. Oxon. 1500–1714*, ii. 466.
[56] For the Estcourts, Burke, *Land. Gent.* (1937), 710–11.
[57] P.R.O., PROB 11/373, ff. 248v.–249.
[58] W.R.O. 212A/27/11/1, deed, Estcourt and Kirkham, 1669.
[59] Ibid. 212A/27/11/1, deed, Estcourt to Carpenter, 1699.
[60] Ibid. 212A/27/11/2, deeds, Estcourt and Holford.
[61] *V.C.H. Glos.* xi. 286.
[62] Burke, *Land. Gent.* (1898), i. 741; *Alum. Cantab. 1752–1900*, iii. 413.
[63] W.A.S. Libr., sale cat. ii, no. 19.

1915 to Tom Rich, who in 1928 sold 137 a. north of the Avon and in 1942 sold Cowage farm to Mrs. D. Hartman. In 1950 Mrs. Hartman sold the farm to H. I. Coriat, and in 1955 Coriat sold it to Mr. W. L. Collins who owned it in partnership with Mr. K. L. Collins in 1987.[64]

ECONOMIC HISTORY. In the early 13th century villeins may have cultivated some Bremilham land, but most was apparently demesne. Richard of Bremilham, then lord of Bremilham manor, and Malmesbury abbey agreed to change, or to confirm new, agrarian practices on the open fields of Brokenborough and of Burton Hill in Malmesbury parish. Men of Corston and Rodbourne were given a right of way over Bremilham land, but it seems that none but Richard and his villeins might cultivate it or keep animals on it. They, on the other hand, retained pasture rights on temporarily inclosed arable apparently north of the Avon and on land tilled by the men of Corston and Rodbourne, and Richard was granted wood each year from Hyam wood and elsewhere.[65]

There is no later evidence of villeins or customary tenants at Bremilham, and Bremilham farm, later called Cowage farm, was apparently the only farm in the 16th century.[66] In the early 17th century it was leased for years on lives and sublet. In 1647 it consisted of nearly all the main part of the parish, the farmhouse and farm buildings, 68 a. of arable, c. 52 a. of meadow, and 138 a. of pasture, and of 84 a., arable and pasture, of the detached lands.[67] The farm was possibly in hand while William Estcourt lived in Bremilham in the early 18th century, but from 1716 to 1915 was held by tenant farmers.[68] In 1731 Cowage farm measured 402 a., 144 a. of arable, 43 a. of meadow, and 215 a. of pasture: it included the detached parts of the parish called Brokenborough field and New leaze, a total of 84 a., all pasture, and 318 a. in the main part of the parish. Cowage Grove, 11 a., and the detached lands called Hankerton Corner, 10 a. of arable and 8 a. of pasture, were not part of the farm.[69] In 1739 c. 7 a. in Westport parish were added to the farm,[70] which they adjoined,[71] and later c. 64 a. in Brokenborough north and south of Brokenborough field were added to extend the farm north to the Malmesbury–Sherston road.[72]

About 1839 Bremilham parish included c. 141 a. of arable, c. 269 a. of grassland, and 20 a. of woodland, of which a total of 389 a. was in Cowage farm.[73] In 1867 there were less than 100 a. of arable in the parish: cows, pigs, and particularly sheep were kept.[74] Cowage farm was 459 a. in 1897 when it included a total of 80 a. in Brokenborough and Westport parishes: it included only 71 a. of arable.[75] It was worked with land in Foxley in the earlier 20th century[76] when sheep and cows were kept on it. From 1928 it was a farm of 323 a. south of the Avon, nearly all the main part of the old Bremilham parish. Between 1942 and 1955 the farm was used first for dairying, later for tillage. From 1955 to 1984 it was a pig, beef, and arable farm, from 1984 beef and arable.[77] A brick kiln stood in the east part of the old parish in the late 19th century.[78]

The Light, the detached land near Malmesbury, was held by members of the Lyne family, tanners, from 1730 or earlier.[79] A tannery stood on it in 1731.[80] In 1815 the tannery incorporated a bark mill, a tanyard, drying sheds, a leather house, and a counting house.[81] Matthew Thompson tanned there from 1848 or earlier to the 1880s when it was apparently closed.[82]

LOCAL GOVERNMENT. There is no record of a court of Bremilham manor, and, because it was so small, there was little government of the parish by itself in the 18th century. In 1724 the tenant of Cowage farm was expected to do in Bremilham what churchwardens, overseers of the poor, surveyors of highways, and tithingmen would do elsewhere.[83] Between 1775–6 and 1835–6 expenditure on the poor varied from £10 in 1775–6 to £65 in 1823–4. Occasionally the figures seem high for so small a parish: several times they exceeded those of Bremilham's larger neighbour Foxley. In 1802–3 and 1814–15 three adults were relieved permanently. The parish joined Malmesbury poor-law union in 1835,[84] and became part of North Wiltshire district in 1974.[85]

CHURCH. An early apsidal church may have stood at Bremilham.[86] It is likely that a church stood there in 1179 when Amesbury priory was granted the tithes of Bremilham,[87] and from then the priory possibly had the duty to provide chaplains to serve it. Although re-issues of the charter confirmed the grant to Amesbury priory,[88] in 1298 the lord of Bremilham manor held the advowson, there was a rector,[89] and, as he was later, the rector was almost certainly entitled to the tithes of the parish. In 1298 and the 14th century the use of the word chapel to describe Bremilham church[90]

[64] Inf. from Mrs. B. Collins, Cowage Farm.
[65] Reg. Malm. ii. 185–7.
[66] Taxation Lists (W.R.S. x), 80; P.R.O., C 3/62/35.
[67] W.R.O. 212A/27/11/1, deed, Smith to Smith, 1647.
[68] Ibid. A 1/310, roll 1, Estcourt; A 1/345/57; ibid. 212A/27/11/4, leases; ibid. Inland Revenue, val. reg. 9; W.A.S. Libr., sale cat. ii, no. 19. [69] W.R.O. 1198/1.
[70] Ibid. 212A/27/11/3, deed, Garlick to Holford, 1739.
[71] Ibid. 1198/2.
[72] W.A.S. Libr., sale cat. ii, no. 19.
[73] W.R.O., tithe award, where the totals of land use for the par. seem to be miscalculated.
[74] P.R.O., MAF 68/151, sheet 3.
[75] W.A.S. Libr., sale cat. ii, no. 19.
[76] W.R.O., G 7/515/5; inf. from Maj. A. R. Turnor, Foxley Manor, Norton.
[77] Inf. from Mrs. Collins.

[78] O.S. Maps 6″, Wilts. VIII (1889 edn.), VIII. SW. (1900 edn.).
[79] W.R.O. 212A/27/11/4, lease, Estcourt to Lyne, 1730.
[80] Ibid. 1198/1. [81] Ibid. 149/101/7.
[82] Kelly's Dir. Wilts. (1848 and later edns.); O.S. Map 6″, Wilts. VIII (1889 edn.).
[83] W.R.O. 212A/27/11/4, lease, Estcourt to Richens, 1724.
[84] Poor Law Abstract, 1804, 566–7; 1818, 498–9; Poor Rate Returns, 1816–21, 188; 1822–4, 228; 1825–9, 219; 1830–4, 212; Poor Law Com. 2nd Rep. App. D, 559; App. E, 406–7.
[85] O.S. Map 1/100,000, admin. areas, Wilts. (1974 edn.).
[86] Above, introduction.
[87] Cal. Chart. R. 1257–1300, 157–9.
[88] Dugdale, Mon. ii. 336.
[89] Reg. Ghent (Cant. & York Soc.), ii. 576. For refs. in this section to lords of the manor, above, manor.
[90] Phillipps, Wilts. Inst. i. 1, 27, 42, 46, 75.

perhaps looks back to the earlier arrangements to serve it. The living remained a rectory. Under agreements of 1873 between the ordinary and the owner of Cowage farm and between the owner of Cowage farm, the patron of Foxley, and the patron of Bremilham, and by an Order in Council of 1874, Bremilham church became a mortuary chapel and in 1893, when the rector of Foxley was appointed rector of Bremilham, Foxley and Bremilham rectories were united.[91] Bremilham churchyard was last used for a burial in 1904.[92] The united benefice was united with the benefice of Sherston Magna with Easton Grey and Luckington with Alderton in 1986. Bremilham was to remain a separate parish under the Order in Council of 1874, but in 1986 Foxley with Bremilham was considered one parish.[93]

The advowson of Bremilham belonged to the lords of the manor from 1298 or earlier to 1629.[94] In 1406 the king presented because Walter Dauntsey was his ward, but his candidate was denied admittance because there was an incumbent rector. The king presented, successfully, for the same reason in 1411.[95] In 1417 and 1420 feoffees presented, in 1430 and 1433 Joan Dauntsey's husband Sir John Stradling presented, in 1439, 1444, and 1445 her husband John Dewale presented, and in 1465 Edmund Stradling's relict Elizabeth and her husband William Lygon presented.[96] The Crown presented in 1559, possibly by lapse,[97] and in 1594,[98] again possibly by lapse. From Henry, earl of Danby (d. 1644), the advowson passed to his nephew Henry, son of Sir John Danvers (d. 1655). It was among estates settled by Henry (d. 1654) to pay his father's debts and the Crown took it from, and returned it to, Henry Danvers's trustees in 1661 when Sir John Danvers was attainted.[99] The trustees presented in 1666 and 1675, and in 1681 Sir Thomas Estcourt, lord of Bremilham manor, presented, presumably by grant of a turn.[1] The advowson passed to Henry Danvers's niece Anne[2] (d. s.p. 1685), wife of Thomas Wharton (d. 1715) who, as Baron Wharton, presented in 1703 and, as earl of Wharton, in 1713.[3] In 1729 it was presumably among the estates forfeited for treason by Thomas's son Philip, duke of Wharton.[4] It was acquired, presumably by purchase with other of Wharton's possessions in 1743, by Sir John Rushout, Bt., who presented in 1760. Rushout was succeeded as owner by his son Sir John Rushout, Bt. (cr. Baron Northwick 1797, d. 1800), whose relict Rebecca

presented in 1804 and son the Revd. George Rushout-Bowles presented in 1838, 1839, and 1840.[5] The advowson apparently passed with the Northwick title to Northwick's son John, Baron Northwick (d. 1859), and to George's son George, Baron Northwick (d. s.p.s. 1887). That last Northwick's relict Elizabeth, Baroness Northwick (d. 1912), presented in 1893 and afterwards had the right to present at the second, and thereafter at every third, vacancy of the united benefice.[6] No later presentation by that right is known, and at those turns, in 1946 and 1963, the university of Oxford and the Crown presented respectively.[7] No representative of Lady Northwick was apparently on the board of patronage set up in 1986 for the benefice of Sherston Magna, Easton Grey, Luckington, Alderton and Foxley with Bremilham.[8]

Valuations at £4 2s. in 1535,[9] c. £3 c. 1561,[10] and c. £16 in 1649[11] show the living to have been no richer than might be expected from the smallness of the parish. In 1766 it was augmented by lot with £200 from Queen Anne's Bounty.[12] Further augmentations by lot in 1807 and 1812 were set aside in, respectively, 1808 and 1813.[13] The income of £121 c. 1830 was low, but the parish was very small and the curate's stipend no more than £25.[14] In 1704 the rector was entitled to all tithes from the whole parish. The augmentation of 1766 was apparently used to buy tithes arising from land in Brokenborough parish: the rector owned such tithes in 1786 when all his tithes were worth c. £23.[15] The tithes from Brokenborough, valued at £34, were commuted in 1840, those from Bremilham, at £106, in 1841.[16] The rector claimed c. 1561 that he was being deprived of the glebe by the tenant of Bremilham farm who had held it by lease for 24 years, in 16 of which there had been no incumbent.[17] There was no glebe in 1704 or later.[18]

No rector is known to have lived in the parish, and few held the living for life. Richard le Dean, presented in 1298, was licensed to study for three years.[19] Between 1411 and 1445 incumbencies averaged three years.[20] William Clarke, rector 1465–1514,[21] was in 1478 licensed to hold another benefice.[22] From c. 1543 to 1559 none would accept the rectory because it was so poor.[23] From 1595 most rectors were pluralists: Richard Jeane, rector 1595–1627, was rector of Foxley;[24] Edward Bridges, rector 1627–66, was rector of North Wraxall and vicar of Seagry[25] and preached at Bremilham four times a year;[26] John Stumpe, rector

[91] *Lond. Gaz.* 15 May 1874, pp. 2575–6; Bristol R.O., EP/A/1/6, pp. 33, 47; W.R.O. 11/175; 592/10; Ch. Com. file, NB 5/137C, pt. 1.   [92] W.R.O. 592/8.
[93] *Lond. Gaz.* 15 May 1874, p. 2576; Ch. Com. file, NB 5/137C, pt. 1.
[94] Phillipps, *Wilts. Inst.* (index in *W.A.M.* xxviii. 214).
[95] *Cal. Pat.* 1405–8, 173; P.R.O., CP 40/584, rot. 276; Phillipps, *Wilts. Inst.* i. 77, 100.
[96] Phillipps, *Wilts. Inst.* (index in *W.A.M.* xxviii. 214); Aubrey, *Topog. Coll.* ed. Jackson, pedigree at p. 217, where Edmund is called Edw.
[97] *Cal. Pat.* 1558–60, 123; P.R.O., C 3/62/35.
[98] Phillipps, *Wilts. Inst.* i. 234.
[99] Aubrey, *Topog. Coll.* ed. Jackson, 226–7, pedigree at p. 217; W.R.O. 529/243.   [1] Phillipps, *Wilts. Inst.* ii. 28, 33, 37.
[2] P.R.O., CP 25(2)/806/1 Jas. II East.
[3] *Complete Peerage*, xii (2), 608; Phillipps, *Wilts. Inst.* ii. 47, 52.   [4] *Complete Peerage*, xii (2), 612.
[5] Below, Malmesbury, manors; Phillipps, *Wilts. Inst.* ii. 79, 97, 104; Bristol R.O., EP/A/1/4, where the 1838 presen-

tation was said, apparently erroneously, to be by the Revd. Chas. Rushout-Bowles. For the Rushouts, L. G. Pine, *New Ext. Peerage*, 208.
[6] *Lond. Gaz.* 15 May 1874, pp. 2575–6; Bristol R.O., EP/A/3/29; above.   [7] Below, Foxley, church.
[8] Ch. Com. file, NB 5/137C, pt. 1.
[9] *Valor Eccl.* (Rec. Com.), ii. 139.
[10] P.R.O., C 3/62/35.   [11] *W.A.M.* xli. 6.
[12] C. Hodgson, *Queen Anne's Bounty* (1864), p. cccxxxv.
[13] Ch. Com. file, F 603.
[14] *Rep. Com. Eccl. Revenues*, 826–7.
[15] W.R.O., D 1/24/26/1–2.   [16] Ibid. tithe awards.
[17] P.R.O., C 3/62/35.
[18] W.R.O., D 1/24/26/1–2; ibid. tithe award.
[19] *Reg. Ghent* (Cant. & York Soc.), ii. 576, 836.
[20] Phillipps, *Wilts. Inst.* i. 100, 102–3, 106, 111, 121, 123, 127, 129–30, 135–6.   [21] Ibid. 155, 191.
[22] *Cal. Papal Reg.* xiii (2), 667.   [23] P.R.O., C 3/62/35.
[24] Phillipps, *Wilts. Inst.* i. 234; ii. 14.
[25] *W.N. & Q.* vii. 547.   [26] *W.A.M.* xli. 6.

1675–81, was rector of Foxley and vicar of Norton;[27] Edmund Wayte, rector 1681–1703,[28] was vicar of Norton and rector of Great Somerford where he lived;[29] John Harris, rector 1703–13,[30] was vicar of Norton and rector of Easton Grey;[31] Simon Crook, rector 1729–60, was rector of Foxley.[32] Daniel Freer, rector 1760–93,[33] was described to the bishop as a madman:[34] in 1783 he held no other cure and held a weekly service in the church. There was then no surplice, no plate, and no register, and communion had been celebrated only once since 1760. Freer was in conflict with his principal parishioner, John Bennett, the tenant of Cowage farm, whose farm buildings were very near the church. Bennett would not attend services and Freer complained that he 'made a pigsty' of the rectory house:[35] since no rector is known to have been resident and Freer lived in Westport the claim perhaps justifies the description of Freer. John Britton commented that the tenant of Cowage farm was inconvenienced because his landlord did not own the advowson and c. 1801 recorded monthly services.[36] John Nicholas, rector 1804–36, was vicar of Westport and rector of Fisherton Anger[37] and during his incumbency curates usually took monthly services at Bremilham.[38] A congregation of 35 attended the service held on Census Sunday in 1851.[39] From 1899 to 1946 the united benefice of Foxley with Bremilham was held with Norton vicarage, from 1951 to 1983 with the vicarage of Corston with Rodbourne.[40]

Bremilham church was undedicated. In 1731 and 1809 it consisted of a nave 25 ft. by 13 ft. and a chancel 13 ft. by 11 ft.: the side walls were 10 ft. high.[41] In 1809 it had a western timber bellcot, the chancel had two 13th-century lancet windows in the south wall, and the nave had a round-headed south doorway and 16th-century windows in the south and west walls.[42] Between 1839 and 1886,[43] presumably c. 1874, the church was demolished and a small chapel with a western bellcot was built on the site of the chancel. Under the agreements of 1873 which led to its closure Cowage farm was charged with the maintenance of the chapel.[44]

At the single communion service held between 1760 and 1783 Foxley's plate was used.[45] Bremilham had a chalice and two patens in the earlier 20th century.[46] The single bell, cast by Roger Purdue at Bristol in 1677, was hung in Foxley church after 1874, possibly in 1923, and Foxley's bell, which was cracked, was placed in Bremilham mortuary chapel.[47] The oldest register to survive begins in 1814.[48] Transcripts of the 17th and 18th centuries show that in many years there was no burial, marriage, or christening in the church.[49]

NONCONFORMITY. William Estcourt, lord of Bremilham manor 1683–1727, lived at Cowage Farm until 1723–4[50] and was a Roman Catholic.[51] The tenant of Cowage farm would not attend church in the late 18th century,[52] but there is no evidence of formal protestant nonconformity in the parish.

EDUCATION. In 1858 a school for 16 children of Bremilham and Foxley was being held in a cottage beside Cowage Grove by a woman who lived in Norton.[53] It may have been closed in the 1880s, when a school was held in Foxley, or in 1894 when a new Foxley school was built.[54] The Malmesbury and Westport school at the Light was built c. 1850.[55]

CHARITY FOR THE POOR. None known.

BRINKWORTH

BRINKWORTH village is 8.5 km. ESE. of Malmesbury.[56] The parish, shaped like Africa, is one of the largest in north Wiltshire: it contains the village with several small outlying settlements nearby, Grittenham hamlet, and many scattered farmsteads. The north part of the parish was Brinkworth tithing, the south Grittenham tithing.[57] About 1320 c. 300 a. east of the village

[27] Phillipps, *Wilts. Inst.* ii. 33, 37; W.R.O., D 1/48/1, f. 23.   [28] Phillipps, *Wilts. Inst.* ii. 37, 47.
[29] W.R.O., D 1/48/2, f. 24; D 1/51/1, ff. 46, 48v.; D 1/54/12/1.
[30] Phillipps, *Wilts. Inst.* ii. 47, 52.
[31] W.R.O., D 1/51/1, ff. 65–6; below, Norton, church.
[32] Phillipps, *Wilts. Inst.* ii. 62, 79.
[33] Ibid. 79, 97.
[34] W.R.O., D 1/48/4, p. 57.
[35] *Vis. Queries, 1783* (W.R.S. xxvii), pp. 43–4.
[36] J. Britton, *Beauties of Wilts.* iii. 132.
[37] *Rep. Com. Eccl. Revenues*, 826–7; below, Charlton, church.
[38] W.R.O. 592/7; Ch. Com. files, F 603; NB 5/137c, pt. 1.   [39] P.R.O., HO 129/252/2/14/19.
[40] Below, Foxley, church.
[41] W.R.O. 1198/1; B.L. Add. MS. 36409, f. 30.
[42] Watercolour by J. Buckler in W.A.S. Libr., vol. vi. 21. The date is from B.L. Add. MS. 36409. See below, plate facing p. 237.
[43] O.S. Map 6″, Wilts. VIII (1889 edn.); W.R.O., tithe award.
[44] W.R.O. 592/10.
[45] *Vis. Queries, 1783* (W.R.S. xxvii), p. 43.
[46] W.R.O. 592/4E.
[47] Ibid.; Walters, *Wilts. Bells*, 91, 293; below, Foxley, church.   [48] W.R.O. 592/7.
[49] Ibid. bishop's transcripts, bdles. 1–3.
[50] Ibid. 212A/27/11/4, lease, Estcourt to Richens, 1724.
[51] Williams, *Cath. Recusancy* (Cath. Rec. Soc.), 61, 239.
[52] *Vis. Queries, 1783* (W.R.S. xxvii), p. 43.
[53] *Acct. of Wilts. Schs.* 10.   [54] Below, Foxley, educ.
[55] Ibid. Malmesbury, educ.
[56] This article was written in 1989.
[57] Maps used include O.S. Maps 1″, sheets 34 (1828 edn.), 157 (1968 edn.); 1/50,000, sheet 173 (1974 edn.); 1/25,000, ST 98, SU 08 (1959 edns.); 6″, Wilts. IX, XIV (1887–8 and later edns.).

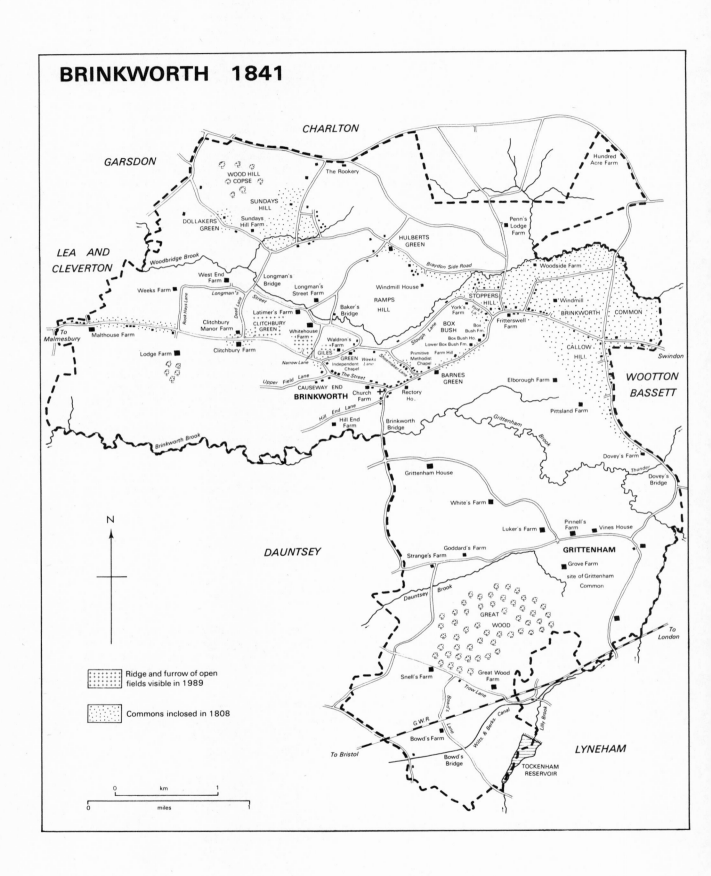

BRINKWORTH 1841

GARSDON

CHARLTON

Hundred Acre Farm

WOOD HILL COPSE

The Rookery

SUNDAYS HILL

DOLLAKERS GREEN

Sundays Hill Farm

Penn's Lodge Farm

LEA AND CLEVERTON

HULBERTS GREEN

Woodbridge Brook

Braydon Side Road

Woodside Farm

West End Farm

Longman's Bridge

Weeks Farm

Longman's Street Farm

Windmill House

Longman's Street

STOPPERS HILL

Windmill

BRINKWORTH COMMON

Latimer's Farm

Baker's Bridge

RAMPS HILL

York's Farm

Fritterswell Farm

Dean Lane

Rook Hays Lane

To Malmesbury

Malthouse Farm

Clitchbury Manor Farm

CLITCHBURY GREEN

Whitehouse Farm

Waldron's Farm

Slough Lane

Box Bush Fm.

BOX BUSH

Box Bush Ho.

Lower Box Bush Fm.

CALLOW HILL

Swindon

Lodge Farm

Clitchbury Farm

GILES GREEN

Narrow Lane

Independent Chapel

Weeks Lane

Shoemaker Lane

Farm Hill

Primitive Methodist Chapel

WOOTTON BASSETT

Upper Field Lane

The Street

BARNES GREEN

Elborough Farm

CAUSEWAY END

BRINKWORTH

Church Farm

Rectory Ho.

Pittsland Farm

Hill End Lane

Brinkworth Bridge

Grittenham Brook

Hill End Farm

Dovey's Farm

Brinkworth Brook

Grittenham House

Thunder

Dovey's Bridge

N

DAUNTSEY

White's Farm

Luker's Farm

Pinnell's Farm

Vines House

Goddard's Farm

GRITTENHAM

Strange's Farm

Grove Farm

site of Grittenham Common

Dauntsey Brook

GREAT WOOD

To London

Snell's Farm

Great Wood Farm

Bowd's Lane

Trow Lane

Wilts & Berks. Canal

Lilly Brook

LYNEHAM

| | Ridge and furrow of open fields visible in 1989 |
| | Commons inclosed in 1808 |

G.W.R.

Bowd's Farm

To Bristol

Bowd's Bridge

TOCKENHAM RESERVOIR

0   km   1

0   miles   1

were apparently lost to the parish when the lord of Brinkworth manor allowed them to be inclosed in Vasterne park, and they became part of Wootton Bassett parish.[58] Brinkworth village was never in Braydon forest, but it was near its 13th-century boundaries, and from 1300, when the area of the forest was greatly reduced, to 1630, when it was inclosed,[59] part of the purlieus of the forest was called Brinkworth quarter: the parts of the purlieus claimed as Brinkworth's and Grittenham's were presumably defined, as other parts were.[60] When the purlieus were inclosed in the early 1630s much of Brinkworth quarter, possibly as much as 1,250 a., became part of Brinkworth parish.[61] Other parts of the quarter allotted to Milbourne in Malmesbury and to Little Somerford, a total of 309 a., were transferred to Brinkworth in 1884.[62] To the south-east 42 a., a detached part of Dauntsey, were transferred to Brinkworth in 1884 and, to the south, a total of 16 a. were transferred from Dauntsey and Lyneham between 1891 and 1901: Brinkworth parish thereafter measured 2,459 ha. (6,075 a.).[63]

Streams and roads mark much of the parish boundary. That with Dauntsey, the east–west part of which was marked by Brinkworth brook, had been fixed by the early 13th century;[64] that with Wootton Bassett, marked by a road and Lilly brook, is presumably of c. 1320.[65] In the 13th century the southern boundary of Braydon forest followed Grittenham brook on the east:[66] from the Brinkworth village, passed east of the village on a roughly north-west and south-east line, and followed Brinkworth brook on the east:[66] from the early 1630s the parish's northern boundary was marked by a road at its east and west ends, from 1884 for its whole length. Woodbridge brook also marked a small part of the parish's eastern boundary, and Lilly brook the south-east boundary with Tockenham and Lyneham.

Oxford Clay outcrops over the entire parish except in a small area of the south-east, where sand, silt, and clay of the Lower Corallian outcrop. Brinkworth, Woodbridge, and Lilly brooks have all deposited alluvium.[67] The whole parish drains westwards to the Bristol Avon and is crossed by east–west ridges and valleys. Brinkworth brook flows across the centre, and near Grittenham hamlet, where it divides Brinkworth and Grittenham tithings, it is called Grittenham brook. The south is drained by its feeders Thunder brook and Lilly brook and by Dauntsey brook, which rises near Grittenham hamlet. Woodbridge brook and its feeders drain the north. The highest land, over 130 m., is in the south-east and, over 120 m., in the north-east and north-west. Sundays Hill, Ramps Hill, and Callow Hill, all in the north, are

over 110 m. The part of the parish which was in Braydon forest was well wooded, the south part contains ancient woodland, and the centre contained open arable, but most of the parish has long been grassland.

The main Swindon–Malmesbury road through Brinkworth village crosses the north part of the parish from east to west on high ground: it was turnpiked in 1809 and disturnpiked in 1876.[68] Parallel to it in the south the London and south Wales motorway was built on lower-lying land and opened in 1971.[69] Elsewhere the parish was served by lanes, the courses of some of which were altered at inclosure in the early 19th century and when the motorway was built. Baker's bridge and Longman's bridge over Woodbridge brook, and Brinkworth bridge and Dovey's bridge over Brinkworth brook, were so called in 1773.[70] The Wilts. & Berks. canal was constructed across the southern tip of the parish, where seven locks carried it over rising ground, and opened c. 1801. To feed it, a reservoir was made on the Brinkworth–Lyneham boundary. The canal was closed in 1914.[71] In 1989 the towpath and the remains of a lock were visible at Bowd's bridge and the reservoir was used for leisure. The G.W.R. London–Bristol line was built north of the canal and opened in 1841.[72] A line which branched from it at Wootton Bassett to provide a more direct link to south Wales was built south of Brinkworth village, where there was a station, and opened in 1903.[73] The station was closed in 1961.[74]

The sum at which Brinkworth and Grittenham together were assessed for taxation in 1334 was among the higher for Startley hundred. There were 123 poll-tax payers in Brinkworth and 69 in Grittenham in 1377.[75] Assessments for taxation in the 16th and 17th centuries were consistently among the highest in Malmesbury hundred.[76] The population rose from 923 to 1,042 between 1801 and 1811 when 910 lived in Brinkworth and 132 in Grittenham. In 1841 the increase of Brinkworth's population to 1,307 and of Grittenham's to 387 was attributed to the presence of 235 G.W.R. labourers in the parish. After falling to 1,273 between 1841 and 1861 the population of the parish increased to 1,436 between 1861 and 1871 because newly built cottages attracted labourers. Thereafter, despite the transfer of 9 people to the parish in 1884, it declined, and had reached 850 by 1931. With the building of new houses in Brinkworth village from 1934 the population grew steadily, and was 1,173 in 1981.[77]

BRINKWORTH. Its site, on the ridge between Brinkworth brook and Woodbridge brook used by the Swindon–Malmesbury road, suggests that the

[58] Cal. Pat. 1317–21, 431–2.
[59] V.C.H. Wilts. iv. 402–6, 445.
[60] W.R.O. 88/1/52; below, Charlton, introduction.
[61] For the boundaries, below.
[62] Census, 1891; below, Malmesbury, introduction; Little Somerford, introduction.
[63] Census, 1891; 1901; cf. P.R.O., IR 29/38/95; IR 30/38/95.
[64] Arch. Jnl. lxxvi. 168–9.
[65] Above.
[66] V.C.H. Wilts. iv. 444–5.
[67] Geol. Surv. Maps 1", solid and drift, sheet 252 (1974 edn.); 1/50,000, drift, sheet 266 (1974 edn.).
[68] V.C.H. Wilts. iv. 257, 271.

[69] Rep. Co. Surveyor, 1971–2 (Wilts. co. council), 3.
[70] Andrews and Dury, Map (W.R.S. viii), pl. 14.
[71] V.C.H. Wilts. iv. 273, 277; O.S. Map 6", Wilts. XIV (1887 edn.).
[72] V.C.H. Wilts. iv. 282.
[73] Ibid. 289.
[74] C. R. Clinker, Clinker's Reg. Closed Passenger Sta. 1830–1980, p. 19.
[75] V.C.H. Wilts. iv. 301, 309.
[76] Taxation Lists (W.R.S. x), 30, 48–9; P.R.O., E 179/197/153; E 179/198/261; E 179/198/287; E 179/199/356; E 179/199/399; E 179/259/20.
[77] V.C.H. Wilts. iv. 319, 323, 342; Census, 1961; 1971; 1981.

village is ancient. In Brinkworth tithing in 1773 small outlying settlements west of the village were at Clitchbury Green, Giles Green, and Causeway End, north of it at Dollakers Green and Woodbridge Green, later Hulberts Green, and east of it at Barnes Green and Box Bush, and there were many outlying farmsteads.[78] Since then Brinkworth village has spread west and east along the main road to take in Causeway End, Barnes Green, Box Bush, and more recent settlement east of Box Bush as part of the village, and a new settlement called Callow Hill has grown, but there is still much scattered settlement. The older houses in the tithing are built of a variety of materials.

Brinkworth, for which the Swindon–Malmesbury road made a street, may for long have been a small village grouped around its church with, also on the south side of the street, the demesne farmstead west of it and the rectory house east of it. The farmstead, Church Farm, includes a house of the 17th century which was extended south and east in the 19th. There was an inn in the village in 1654,[79] and the White Lion was open in 1719 and 1755.[80] The Waggon and Horses east of Church Farm had been opened by 1903 and was closed between 1956 and 1966.[81] The Three Crowns, between the church and the rectory house, was open in 1801[82] and 1989. Street Farm, on the north side of the Street, was built in 1763 and extended in 1985.[83] Cottages for paupers and a workhouse stood near the church in the earlier 19th century.[84] A friendly society begun in 1834 did not prosper, but one based at Brinkworth Primitive Methodist chapel flourished 1866–87 and another, the Brinkworth Mutual Club and Institute, at the school 1899–1912.[85] A cemetery was opened c. 1886 north of the Street.[86] New cottages were built in the later 19th century and, north of Church Farm, two pairs of council houses in 1934 and two more pairs in 1938.[87] The south part of the village in 1773 consisted of buildings in Hill End Lane, so called c. 1808,[88] and in the mid 19th century a school was built south of the church in the lane afterwards called School Hill. Hill End Lane became the approach to Brinkworth station in 1903 when a stationmaster's house and three cottages, all red-brick, were built on it and a new lane was made south of the railway line. Also south of the line Brooklands, an estate of 35 council houses, was built c. 1953.[89]

The buildings at Causeway End in 1773 included a nonconformist chapel and possibly Causeway End House, which was built in the later 18th century. None of those at Barnes Green survives: Barnes Green Farm was rebuilt and a nonconformist chapel and cottages built in the earlier

19th century. Four farmhouses at Box Bush survive from 1773.[90] Farm Hill, possibly 17th-century, has two storeys and attics, Box Bush Farm was built in the early 18th century, and Lower Box Bush Farm retains some stone-rubble walling. Box Bush House was built of red brick in the early 18th century: in the early 19th a large two-storeyed range with a mansard roof and a three-bayed south entrance front, also of red brick, was built against the south side. Further east Fritterswell Farm was also built in the 18th century and extended in the 19th, and settlement extended along the main road after the common land was inclosed in 1808.[91] The Suffolk Arms on the north side was open from the earlier 20th century.[92] In 1989 there was a continuous line of settlement from Causeway End to the Suffolk Arms. Mostly since c. 1970 new private houses have been built at Causeway End, in the main part of Brinkworth village, and in small estates at Barnes Green, in York's Lane, west of Fritterswell Farm, and north of Fritterswell Farm in an area called Stoppers Hill.[93]

Callow Hill grew as a settlement in the earlier 19th century around the junction of the Swindon–Malmesbury road and a new lane made when Brinkworth common was inclosed. Several cottages had been built there by 1841.[94] The Royal George inn on the south side of the main road was open from 1884 or earlier to c. 1970 and East End Farm was built north of the junction in the early 20th century. In the later 19th century more houses were built in the lane south of the junction, and in the later 20th small groups of private houses in the south-west angle of the lane and the road.[95]

Of the buildings in 1773 around the green formed by the wide verges of the Swindon–Malmesbury road, together called Clitchbury Green, only Clitchbury Manor Farm, standing in 1763, survives.[96] All beside the main road, Clitchbury Farm was built to the south between c. 1808 and c. 1840, Brinkworth House to the east in stone between c. 1840 and 1884,[97] and Clitchbury Manor, a double-fronted red-brick house, to the west in the early 20th century.

The open fields of Brinkworth may have been worked from farmsteads in the village in the Middle Ages, the dispersal of farmsteads beginning only after the fields had been inclosed at some date before 1587.[98] In 1773 lanes parallel to the Swindon–Malmesbury road may have marked the north and south extent of the former open-field arable.[99] Upper Field Lane, so called c. 1808, ran from Causeway End south-west and north to a junction on the main road with Rook Hays Lane, which ran north to Longman's Street.[1] Coins and a tile kiln found nearby suggest that Longman's

[78] *Andrews and Dury, Map* (W.R.S. viii), pl. 14.
[79] P.R.O., C 5/381/65.
[80] W.R.O. 88/4/5.
[81] Ibid. G 7/516/2–3; *Kelly's Dir. Wilts.* (1903).
[82] Soc. Antiq. MS. 817, iii, p. 27.
[83] Dates on ho.
[84] Glos. R.O., D 2242/IV/3/1, deed, earl of Suff. to Luce, 1839; below, local govt.
[85] P.R.O., FS 4/Wilts./55, nos. 295, 360, 511.
[86] W.R.O. 953/16.
[87] Dates on hos.
[88] *Andrews and Dury, Map* (W.R.S. viii), pl. 14; W.R.O., EA/131.
[89] O.S. Maps 1/25,000, 41/08 (1948 edn.), SU 08 (1959 edn.).
[90] *Andrews and Dury, Map* (W.R.S. viii), pl. 14; below, nonconf.

[91] Below, econ. hist.
[92] *Kelly's Dir. Wilts.* (1903, 1907).
[93] Cf. O.S. Map 1/50,000, sheet 173 (1974 edn.).
[94] Ibid. 1″, sheet 34 (1828 edn.); C. Greenwood, *Map of Wilts.* (1820); P.R.O., IR 30/38/42.
[95] O.S. Maps 1/50,000, sheet 173 (1974 edn.); 6″, Wilts. XIV (1887 edn.); W.R.O., G 7/516/3.
[96] *Andrews and Dury, Map* (W.R.S. viii), pl. 14; B.L. Maps, M.T. 6b., 3 (10).
[97] W.R.O., EA/131; P.R.O., IR 29/38/42; IR 30/38/42; O.S. Map 6″, Wilts. XIV (1887 edn.).
[98] Below, econ. hist.
[99] *Andrews and Dury, Map* (W.R.S. viii), pl. 14.
[1] W.R.O., EA/131.

Street is of Romano-British origin.[2] Following Woodbridge brook, it was near the 13th-century boundary of Braydon forest. From c. 1808 or earlier its eastern end was called Slough Lane, and in 1989 it was a wide green road. Five lanes, Dead (so called in 1736), Narrow, Weeks, Almshouse (later Shoemaker), and York's, linked Longman's Street and Slough Lane with the Swindon–Malmesbury road.[3] About nine farmsteads have been built in those lanes and four are of the late 16th or early 17th century. Weeks Farm, mostly rebuilt in the 19th century, retains a plan of c. 1600 and a timber-framed wall; Whitehouse Farm, built c. 1700, was apparently preceded by a house called Gaggs Place c. 1581;[4] Giles Green Farm, much altered, was built in the early 17th century as a timber-framed house. Waldron's Farm is a cruciform stone house built c. 1600: it was presumably built for a Walrond and, because of its plan, possibly for a recusant.[5] The rooms were arranged round a central staircase, two service rooms and a hall respectively in the shorter north and south wings, and a kitchen and parlour in the longer west and east ones. There is a moat on the north side of the house. Of the other farmhouses Lodge Farm was built in the 18th century and enlarged c. 1909, Longman's Street Farm is a red-brick house of the mid 18th century, York's was rebuilt in 1873 for John Collingborn,[6] West End Farm was rebuilt in the 20th century, and Latimer's was demolished c. 1955.[7] Of other scattered settlement in Slough Lane in 1773 none survived in 1884.[8]

Four other farmsteads in the south part of Brinkworth tithing in 1773 were also on old inclosures.[9] Three stood, like Fritterswell Farm, beside the edge of Brinkworth common, formerly part of the purlieus of Braydon: both Elborough Farm and Pittsland Farm are red-brick and stone-slated houses of the 18th century extended in the 19th, and Dovey's Farm was rebuilt in the later 19th century. South-west of the village, Hill End Farm is a 17th-century house.

On the former purlieus of Braydon forest north of Woodbridge brook, inclosed land since c. 1631,[10] c. 15 scattered farmsteads have been built, 3 beside the road along the northern parish boundary, and c. 8 beside a lane, roughly parallel to that road and Woodbridge brook, across the middle of the purlieus. Part of the lane was called Braydon Side in 1787 or earlier.[11] No more than two 17th-century farmhouses survive: Sundays Hill Farm is a tall house with a one-room plan built of coursed rubble with a stone-slated roof in the later 17th century; Park, formerly Hundred Acre, Farm, possibly also built in the 17th century, was extended and altered in the 19th and 20th centuries. Most of the other farmsteads have been rebuilt on sites occupied in 1773.[12] Penn's Lodge

is a substantial farmhouse of the later 19th century; Somerford, formerly Rookery, Farm was rebuilt in the earlier and enlarged in the later 19th century. The buildings at Dollakers Green have been demolished, and Hulberts Green Farm at Woodbridge Green was rebuilt in the 20th century.

Farmsteads were also built on new sites in the 19th century. To the east several were built on Brinkworth common, presumably after it was inclosed, and to the west Malthouse Farm was built beside the Swindon–Malmesbury road between c. 1808 and c. 1840.[13]

GRITTENHAM may have been a small village in the early Middle Ages. If so, its site is unknown and it presumably became depopulated in the 16th century, when the lord of the manor apparently ejected copyholders at inclosure, or in the 17th, when the lord was said to have demolished cottages and to have forced the inhabitants to move to Brinkworth village.[14] Apparently in the later 16th century a manor house, Grittenham House, was built.[15] A new farmhouse was built near it in 1865[16] and Grittenham House was ruinous c. 1895.[17] Nothing of Grittenham House survived in 1989 but a large pond near its site is possibly to be associated with it.

In 1773 and 1989 settlement in Grittenham tithing was in scattered farmsteads,[18] although a school,[19] a few cottages, and a chapel,[20] all built in the 19th century, form a group with Pinnell's Farm and Luker's Farm along an east–west lane in the north-east quarter of the tithing. The c. 12 farmsteads make a ring around woodland and former common pasture[21] in the centre of the tithing. Some were built in the later 16th or earlier 17th century, possibly to replace those in Grittenham village. Grove Farm, on the former common, was built as a timber-framed house of four bays, of which the westernmost was of one storey, and has a north lobby entrance. A red-brick extension was built on the east in the 19th century. On the north side of the common Vines House was built as a timber-framed east–west range in the earlier 17th century, possibly with a weatherboarded east wing of one storey and attics.[22] The central portion of the house was rebuilt in coursed rubble in the earlier 18th century, and early 17th-century panelling with a carved frieze depicting fabulous beasts was reset in a first-floor room. The east wing was rebuilt in brick in the later 19th century, and c. 1970 a two-storeyed red-brick north wing was built. Also on the north side Goddard's Farm is a timber-framed house built in three stages with a north entrance front c. 1600. The east end of the south front and the east gable are weatherboarded, and the roof was formerly thatched. West of it Strange's Farm was built in the 17th century

[2] V.C.H. Wilts. i (1), 46; inf. from Mr. C. K. Currie, 15 Claudeen Close, Swaythling, Southampton.
[3] W.R.O., EA/131; ibid. 88/2/12.
[4] P.R.O., C 142/193, no. 43.
[5] Ibid. C 142/372, no. 165; Wilts. Inq. p.m. 1625–49 (Index Libr.), 297–300; below, manors.
[6] Date on ho.; W.R.O. 1409/42.
[7] Inf. from Mr. R. Sheppard, Longman's Street Farm.
[8] Andrews and Dury, Map (W.R.S. viii), pl. 14; O.S. Map 6", Wilts. XIV (1887 edn.).
[9] Andrews and Dury, Map (W.R.S. viii), pl. 14.
[10] Below, econ. hist.

[11] Coroners' Bills, 1752–96 (W.R.S. xxxvi), p. 98.
[12] Andrews and Dury, Map (W.R.S. viii), pl. 14.
[13] W.R.O., EA/131; P.R.O., IR 30/38/42.
[14] P.R.O., C 104/137/1.
[15] Cf. below, manors.
[16] Date on ho.
[17] F. N. Macnamara, Memorials of Danvers Fam. 544.
[18] Andrews and Dury, Map (W.R.S. viii), pl. 14.
[19] Below, educ.
[20] Ibid. nonconf.
[21] Ibid. econ. hist.
[22] Photo. in possession of Mrs. P. S. Mitchell, Vines Ho.

of one storey and attics with a three-room plan and a thatched roof. On the south side of the wood Great Wood Farm in Trow Lane was built in the 16th century as a small timber-framed house of one storey and attics, in the early 17th century its south-east end was rebuilt as a cross wing, and in the 19th century a brick and slate house was added south-east of that. Bowd's Farm in Bowd's Lane, rebuilt in red brick in the 18th century, retains a 17th-century plan. The other farmhouses standing in 1773[23] were rebuilt in the 19th or 20th century. Snell's Farm in Trow Lane was built in the earlier 19th century[24] and the farmhouse was rebuilt in Tudor style in the earlier 20th. Six estate cottages were built in 1862–3,[25] possibly those which attracted labourers to the parish between 1861 and 1871,[26] and in the earlier 20th century three pairs of red-brick gabled estate cottages were built in Tudor style. Little has been built in the tithing in the mid and later 20th century and the farmhouse of White's Farm, standing south-east of Grittenham House in 1773,[27] has been demolished.

MANORS AND OTHER ESTATES.

A 5-hide estate that became *BRINKWORTH* manor was held in 1066 by Malmesbury abbey which claimed to have been given it by Leofsige, a nobleman.[28] The abbey held the manor until the Dissolution.[29]

The Crown granted Brinkworth manor in 1544 to William Stumpe[30] (d. 1552). Stumpe was succeeded by his son Sir James Stumpe[31] (d. 1563), from whom the manor passed to his wife Isabel (d. 1573), later wife of Thomas Stafford, and to his daughter Elizabeth.[32] Elizabeth (d. 1585) and her husband Sir Henry Knyvett in 1584 conveyed the manor to Thomas Howard[33] (cr. earl of Suffolk 1603, d. 1626), the husband of their daughter Catherine (d. 1638).[34] Before 1630 the manor passed from Catherine to her son Thomas Howard, earl of Berkshire[35] (d. 1669), and it descended like Charlton manor with the earldom of Berkshire and from 1745 with the earldom of Suffolk.[36] In 1840 Thomas Howard, earl of Suffolk and of Berkshire, owned 1,793 a. in the parish.[37] Thomas's son Charles (d. 1876) sold 1,117 a. in c. 1858:[38] the remainder, in the north-west part of the parish, passed like Charlton to Michael Howard, earl of Suffolk and of Berkshire, who

sold it in 1960 to Southery Farms Ltd., controlled by A. H. Jarrard. Between 1963 and 1967 Southery Farms sold the land as three farms.[39] Each of the farms sold in 1858 and the 1960s has apparently descended separately.

In 1572 Henry and Elizabeth Knyvett sold White's place, later *WEEKS* farm, and other land to Thomas Davis or Taylor[40] (d. 1586). The farm passed to Thomas's son James[41] (d. by 1597), and to James's nephew Anthony Davis or Taylor.[42] Anthony sold the farm in 1632 to John Browning,[43] who sold it in 1657 to John Lyeford.[44] Lyeford sold it in 1665 to John Weeks[45] (d. 1678), who devised it, subject to rent charges for the poor of Brinkworth, to his grandson John Weeks,[46] perhaps the John Weeks holding land in Brinkworth in 1736.[47] Thomas, earl of Suffolk and of Berkshire, owned the 105-a. farm in 1834 or earlier.[48] Charles, earl of Suffolk and of Berkshire, sold it in 1858 to Nathaniel Young,[49] the owner in 1876.[50] Weeks farm was owned in 1905 by W. G. Faussett,[51] in 1910 by John Selwood,[52] 1927–65 by H. J. Selwood,[53] and in 1989 by Mr. M. A. Maslin.[54]

In 1066 Tochi held 5 hides in Brinkworth. Miles Crispin held them in 1086, and Humphrey held them of him.[55] Parts of the estate were possibly later held by Roger Charlton, Robert of Lea, Adam of Purton, John Mautravers, and John Mauduit, who each held land freely in Brinkworth in the later 13th century.[56] Only Mauduit's holding, which may have grown after the later 13th century, has been traced further.

Mauduit was presumably the Sir John Mauduit (d. 1302) who was succeeded by his nephew Sir John Mauduit (d. 1347). In 1340 Sir John conveyed his estate to his son-in-law John Moleyns,[57] who in that year was granted liberties there, including free warren in his demesne land of what was then called the manor of *BRINKWORTH*.[58] From John Moleyns (d. 1360) the manor descended in the direct male line to Sir William (d. 1381), Sir Richard (d. 1384), Sir William (d. 1425), and Sir William (d. 1439). The last William's heir was his daughter Eleanor (d. 1476), who married Sir Robert Hungerford, Lord Hungerford and Moleyns (attainted 1461, d. 1464), and secondly Sir Oliver Manningham (d. 1499).[59] Sir Oliver apparently held the manor until his death,[60] when it reverted to Eleanor's granddaughter Mary Hungerford, *suo jure* Baroness

[23] *Andrews and Dury, Map* (W.R.S. viii), pl. 14.
[24] O.S. Map 1″, sheet 34 (1828 edn.); P.R.O., IR 30/38/42.
[25] Dates on hos.
[26] *V.C.H. Wilts.* iv. 323.
[27] *Andrews and Dury, Map* (W.R.S. viii), pl. 14.
[28] Finberg, *Early Wessex Chart.* pp. 105–6; *V.C.H. Wilts.* ii, p. 125.
[29] *Valor Eccl.* (Rec. Com.), ii. 121.
[30] *L. & P. Hen. VIII*, xix (2), p. 414.
[31] P.R.O., C 142/97, no. 121.
[32] Ibid. C 142/135, no. 1; ibid. REQ 2/37/75; *V.C.H. Wilts.* xi. 8.
[33] *Hist. Parl., Commons*, 1558–1603, ii. 420–3; W.R.O. 88/1/89–90.
[34] For the earls of Suff. and of Berks., *Complete Peerage*, ii. 150–1; xii (1), 462–81.
[35] P.R.O., C 5/405/40.   [36] Below, Charlton, manors.
[37] P.R.O., IR 29/38/42; IR 30/38/42.
[38] W.R.O. 88/10/22.
[39] Inf. from Mr. H. P. Terry, the Old Forge, Great Rissington, Cheltenham, Glos.
[40] W.R.O. 88/2/42; 88/4/3/3.   [41] Ibid. 88/4/3/4.

[42] Ibid. 88/4/3/5.   [43] Ibid. 88/2/46; 88/4/3/8–9.
[44] Ibid. 88/4/3/16.
[45] Ibid. 88/4/3/21.
[46] P.R.O., PROB 11/358, ff. 105–107v.; below, educ., charities.
[47] *Q. Sess. 1736* (W.R.S. xi), p. 142.
[48] *Endowed Char. Wilts.* (N. Div.), 140; P.R.O., IR 29/38/42; IR 30/38/42.
[49] W.R.O. 88/10/22.   [50] Ibid. 374/130/15.
[51] *Endowed Char. Wilts.* (N. Div.), 141.
[52] W.R.O., Inland Revenue, val. reg. 15.
[53] Ibid. G 7/515/2; G 7/516/1–3.
[54] Local inf.
[55] *V.C.H. Wilts.* ii, p. 146.
[56] *Reg. Malm.* i. 246–8, 278; ii. 389, 392.
[57] *Feet of F. 1327–77* (W.R.S. xxix), pp. 62–4; below, Little Somerford, manor.
[58] *Cal. Chart. R. 1327–41*, 468.
[59] For the Hastings, Hungerford, and Moleyns fams., *Complete Peerage*, vi. 618–24, 654–7; ix. 39–43; P.R.O., C 139/99, no. 31, f. 4.
[60] P.R.O., CP 40/925, rot. 333; ibid. SC 2/209/57.

Botreaux, Hungerford, and Moleyns (d. *c.* 1533), who married first Edward Hastings, Lord Hastings (d. 1506), and secondly Sir Richard Sacheverell (d. 1534). Mary's heir was her son George Hastings, Lord Hastings (cr. earl of Huntingdon 1529, d. 1544),[61] from whom the estate passed to his son Francis, earl of Huntingdon (d. 1560), and grandson Henry Hastings, earl of Huntingdon.[62] Lord Huntingdon sold the manor, apparently in portions.[63]

An estate at *CLITCHBURY*, consisting of land which had almost certainly belonged to Lord Huntingdon, was accumulated by John Stratton (d. 1624) who bought 84 a. from Anthony Geering and his wife Martha, land from Robert Cripps, and in 1618 land from Edmund Estcourt and his wife Margaret. The estate passed to Stratton's son Edward.[64] In 1647 Edward conveyed it to Edward Ernle and his son Walter, who in 1648 together sold it to Edward Goddard.[65] Either that Edward Goddard or another sold it in 1700 to John Waldron (fl. 1726).[66] The estate, later Clitchbury Manor farm, passed to Waldron's son John, whose assigns sold it in 1763 to Henry Fox, Baron Holland.[67] It passed like Grittenham manor to Mary, Lady Holland,[68] and was owned in 1989 by Mr. W. Scott.[69]

Other land once Lord Huntingdon's was held in 1575 by Thomas Walrond and his wife Eleanor.[70] *WALDRON'S* farm passed to Edward Walrond (d. 1605), to his relict Dorothy (d. 1612), and to their sons Francis (d. 1613) and Richard (d. 1640). Richard was succeeded by his son Edward.[71] The farm was owned 1786–1831 by Maurice Bennett, in 1833 by a Mr. Green,[72] and *c.* 1840 by J. S. Buckland, who owned 51 a. in the parish.[73] In the 20th century Waldron's was a farm of less than 20 a.

Gaggs place, later *WHITEHOUSE* farm, was held by Henry Richman (d. 1581) and passed to his son John.[74] Members of the Baskett family owned the farm, 58 a. *c.* 1840, from 1781 to 1866;[75] V. Sheppard owned it in 1927,[76] Mr. J. Sheppard in 1989.[77]

Malmesbury abbey's claim to have held *GRITTENHAM* before the Conquest as part of its estate called Brokenborough is likely to have been justified. Between 1066 and 1086 the abbey may have granted it to one of its knights, and the hide held in 1086 by an Englishwoman was almost certainly Grittenham.[78] The abbey recovered the estate,[79] perhaps soon after 1086, and held it until the Dissolution.[80]

In 1541 the Crown granted the manor to John Ayliffe (knighted 1549, d. 1556) and his wife Elizabeth (fl. 1560). From the Ayliffes it passed in the direct male line to John[81] (d. 1579), John[82] (d. 1631), Sir George[83] (d. 1643), John (d. 1645), and George[84] (d. 1713). The manor passed with Foxley manor from George to his relict Judith (d. 1716),[85] to their son John (d. 1722), and to their daughter Judith (d. 1737), to Susanna Horner (d. 1758), and to Henry Fox.[86] From Henry Fox (cr. Baron Holland 1763, d. 1774) the manor passed from father to son with the Holland title to Stephen Fox (d. 1774), Henry Fox (d. 1840), who took the surname Vassall in 1800, and Henry Fox (d. 1859). The manor, *c.* 1,761 a. *c.* 1840,[87] passed with Foxley to Mary, Lady Holland (d. 1889), Leopold Fox-Powys (d. 1893), and Thomas Powys, Baron Lilford,[88] who sold it in 1895 to George Llewellen Palmer.[89] In the earlier 20th century Palmer sold the *c.* 11 farms of the manor separately, and each has descended separately.[90]

ECONOMIC HISTORY. Of the two 5-hide estates at Brinkworth in 1086 one had 1 hide in demesne, the other 4: on Malmesbury abbey's demesne hide were 3 *servi* and 2 ploughteams, on Miles Crispin's 4, which may have been mostly woodland, was 1 team. A total of 9 *villani*, 8 bordars, 21 coscets, and 18 cottars had 7 teams on 4 hides. Grittenham was the tenth hide.[91]

BRINKWORTH. In the Middle Ages there was open arable at Brinkworth, presumably north and south of the Swindon–Malmesbury road, and a south field was mentioned in the later 13th century. In the 16th century fields were called East, West, Lye, and Windmill.[92] Sheep-and-corn husbandry was presumably practised, and until 1320 the manor had 300 a. of waste east of the village.[93] John Moleyns's estate included 51 a. of cultivated demesne arable *c.* 1340,[94] and in 1340 he was licensed to inclose a wood and impark 160 a.:[95] the estate contained *c.* 100 a. of inclosures in 1493.[96] In the earlier 16th century the demesne of Brinkworth manor, including four several pastures, was held in portions by lessees: of 40

---

[61] *Hist. MSS. Com.* 78, *Hastings*, i, p. 313.
[62] P.R.O., CP 40/1198, Carte rott. 24d.–27.
[63] Below.
[64] *Wilts. Inq. p.m.* 1625–49 (Index Libr.), 205–6; P.R.O., CP 25(2)/371/16 Jas. I East.
[65] W.R.O. 11/103–4.   [66] Ibid. 11/111–14.
[67] Ibid. 11/122; B.L. Maps, M.T. 6b., 3 (10).
[68] W.R.O. 11/128; below.
[69] Inf. from Mrs. F. Scott, West End Farm, Brinkworth.
[70] P.R.O., CP 25(2)/239/17 Eliz. I East.
[71] Ibid. C 142/372, no. 165; *Wilts. Inq. p.m.* 1625–49 (Index Libr.), 297–300.
[72] W.R.O., A 1/345/58A.
[73] P.R.O., IR 29/38/42; IR 30/38/42.
[74] Ibid. C 142/193, no. 43.
[75] Ibid. IR 29/38/42; IR 30/38/42; W.R.O. 1363/4; ibid. A 1/345/58A.   [76] W.R.O., G 7/515/2.
[77] Inf. from Mr. J. Sheppard, Whitehouse Farm.
[78] Finberg, *Early Wessex Chart.* pp. 105–6; *V.C.H. Wilts.* ii, pp. 88, 125–6.
[79] *Tax. Eccl.* (Rec. Com.), 193.
[80] *Valor Eccl.* (Rec. Com), ii. 121.

[81] *L. & P. Hen. VIII*, xvi, p. 426; *Wilts. Pedigrees* (Harl. Soc. cv/cvi), 1; Phillipps, *Wilts. Inst.* i. 220, 223; P.R.O., C 142/108, no. 123.   [82] P.R.O., C 142/191, no. 112.
[83] *Wilts. Inq. p.m.* 1625–49 (Index Libr.), 175–6. This descent of the Ayliffe fam. corrects that at *V.C.H. Wilts.* xii. 188.
[84] P.R.O., CP 25(2)/744/16 Chas. II East.; ibid. PROB 11/199, ff. 73 and v., 425v.–426; W.R.O., bishop's transcripts, Lydiard Tregoze, bdle. 1B.
[85] P.R.O., PROB 6/89, f. (orig. foliation) 251; PROB 6/92, f. (orig. foliation) 144.   [86] Below, Foxley, manor.
[87] *Complete Peerage*, vi. 541–5; P.R.O., IR 29/38/42.
[88] Below, Foxley, manor.
[89] W.A.S. Libr., sale cat. xxxii, no. 26.
[90] W.R.O., Inland Revenue, val. reg. 15; ibid. G 7/515/2; inf. from the owners.   [91] *V.C.H. Wilts.* ii, pp. 125, 146.
[92] *Reg. Malm.* ii. 183–4; W.R.O. 88/2/46.
[93] *Cal. Pat.* 1317–21, 431–2; *V.C.H. Wilts.* ix. 190.
[94] N. Fryde, 'Medieval Robber Baron', *Medieval Legal Rec.* ed. R. F. Hunnisett and J. B. Post, 210.
[95] *Cal. Chart. R.* 1327–41, 468.
[96] P.R.O., CP 40/925, rot. 336 and d.

customary holdings only 11 were measured in yardlands and most were apparently small inclosed pasture farms.[97] There was a grazier in the parish c. 1509.[98]

The open fields had been inclosed by 1587 when no corn was grown on Brinkworth manor. Some meadow may still have been used in common, Brinkworth marsh was a common pasture of 200 a. for sheep, and the men of Brinkworth were entitled to feed cattle in Braydon forest and its purlieus. The demesne farm was further broken up, possibly as inclosure of the arable progressed, and in 1587 the 333 a. of demesne were leased in 23 portions. There were then 33 copyholders, some of whom were apparently still required to make hay in the custom meadow, and 25 cottagers. Large numbers of sheep may have been grazed, and on the numerous small pasture farms butter and cheese were produced for the markets at Cirencester (Glos.) and Marlborough.[99] Further inclosure may have been carried out by the lord of the manor c. 1614,[1] and inhabitants of Brinkworth were accused in 1612 of grubbing up woodland to make pastures.[2] In the earlier 17th century c. 220 a. of Brinkworth manor were in 24 leaseholds. The largest farms were the remnant of the demesne with 55 a., Pittslands, so called, with 40 a., and one with 37 a. On three of the smaller holdings new houses had been built. The manor had 28 copyholds: the largest was 81 a., 3 had c. 45 a. each, 5 had 30–35 a., 5 had 20–30 a., and the rest fewer than 20 a. each. The fields were of 1–15 a., and one of 12 a. in Windmill field was described as a recent inclosure.[3]

Braydon forest was inclosed in 1630[4] and the purlieus were inclosed soon afterwards. Of Brinkworth's part of the purlieus, the larger area, to the north and west and possibly as much as 1,000 a., much of which was probably wooded, was reserved by the lord of the manor and then or later converted to farmland. By agreement with the lord in 1631 the smaller area, to the east and south-east and apparently c. 250 a., was divided into Brinkworth common, for the tenants of Brinkworth manor, and a common of 50 a. for the cottagers of Brinkworth. Smaller common pastures also remained at Barnes Green, Clitchbury Green, Giles Green, Dollakers Green, Hulberts Green, Sundays Hill, and, still visible in 1989, beside roads in the north part of the parish.[5] New farms to the north included Hundred Acre, later Park, farm, and Penn's Lodge farm which contained 54 a. of former purlieus in the later 18th century.[6] To the south-east Dovey's farm, 80 a. in 1671, contained 14 a. of the former purlieus.[7] Except for woodland, the whole parish was still grassland c. 1680 when dairy farming was prevalent.[8]

That Brinkworth manor had 46 leaseholders and 43 copyholders in 1704 suggests that farms then were still very small,[9] but in 1800, when c. 1,000 a. of the manor were in 14 farms, they were apparently larger. An unlocated farm, Hammonds, was then 320 a., Penn's Lodge farm 177 a., and the former demesne, Church farm, 131 a.: none of the other 11 was over 60 a.[10] In 1808 the common pastures of Brinkworth were divided and allotted by Act.[11] About 1840 the average size of the 18 farms of Brinkworth manor was 100 a., the glebe farm was c. 150 a., and another c. 1,100 a. of Brinkworth tithing were in many farms of which only Lodge, 216 a., and Clitchbury, 110 a., were over 100 a.[12]

GRITTENHAM. In 1540 Grittenham manor consisted of demesne land leased in five portions and some copyholds.[13] The open field in the tithing may have been inclosed in the later 16th century when the demesne was in hand and the lords of the manor apparently ejected copyholders, added copyhold land to the demesne, and converted arable to meadow and pasture.[14] The men of Grittenham claimed the right to feed animals in Braydon forest and its purlieus and, after dispute c. 1631, c. 100 a. of the purlieus were allotted to the lord of the manor. The allotment, however, was in Minety and presumably of no benefit to the tenants of Grittenham.[15] About 1680 the demesne, 414 a. of grassland, remained in hand: 230 a. were meadow, 182 a. were pasture, and 44 cows, 36 other cattle, and 200 ewes were kept on it. The tenanted land was in 13 small farms and the tenants had a large common east of Great Wood.[16] The common had been inclosed by c. 1840 when there were 14 farms in the tithing. The former demesne was in Grittenham House farm, 174 a., White's, 104 a., and Snell's, 188 a.; six other farms were of 100–150 a.; and Grove or Common farm, 90 a., was on the former common.[17]

There was little arable in the parish c. 1840.[18] In 1867 grain was grown on a little over half the 530 a. of arable. Only 3 a. were arable in 1936, but during the Second World War c. 650 a. were ploughed. Only 222 a. were arable in 1966, but between 1976 and 1986 a further c. 180 a. were ploughed. Most of the parish was permanent grassland in 1867: nearly half was for hay 1876–1936. More temporary grass was grown after 1946, c. 293 a. in 1966, and 517 ha. in 1976. Between 1867 and 1985 c. 1,000 cows were usually in the parish and large herds of pigs were also kept. Sheep averaged 465 between 1867 and 1926, and 1,171 were kept in 1936. Few were kept after the Second World War.[19]

There were still c. 40 farms in the parish in

[97] P.R.O., SC 6/Hen. VIII/3986, rott. 124–6.
[98] L. & P. Hen. VIII, i (1), p. 224.
[99] W.R.O. 88/2/44; P.R.O., C 3/106/11.
[1] W.R.O. 88/1/117; 88/1/119.
[2] Early-Stuart Tradesmen (W.R.S. xv), pp. 66–7.
[3] W.R.O. 88/2/46.   [4] V.C.H. Wilts. iv. 403–6.
[5] Andrews and Dury, Map (W.R.S. viii), pl. 14; W.R.O. 88/9/1G; 88/9/11.
[6] W.R.O. 88/2/53; 88/2/56.   [7] Ibid. D 1/24/27/1.
[8] P.R.O., E 134/32 Chas. II East./7.   [9] W.R.O. 88/2/53.
[10] Ibid. 88/2/56.   [11] Ibid. EA/131.
[12] P.R.O., IR 29/38/42; IR 30/38/42.

[13] Ibid. SC 6/Hen. VIII/3986, rott. 126d.–127.
[14] Ibid. C 1/1110, no. 41; C 1/1156, nos. 35–6; C 104/137/1.
[15] Ibid. E 134/26 Chas. II East./9; W.R.O. 88/10/52.
[16] P.R.O., E 126/13, ff. 292–294v.; E 134/32 Chas. II East./7.
[17] Ibid. IR 29/38/42; IR 30/38/42.   [18] Ibid.
[19] Ibid. MAF 68/151, sheet 2; MAF 68/493, sheet 5; MAF 68/1063, sheet 4; MAF 68/1633, sheet 6; MAF 68/2203, sheet 14; MAF 68/2773, sheet 9; MAF 68/3319, sheet 10; MAF 68/3814, no. 137; MAF 68/4182, no. 137; MAF 68/4552, no. 137; MAF 68/5004, no. 137; MAF 68/5505, no. 137; MAF 68/6032, no. 137.

1989, but some of the smaller ones were not worked. Clitchbury Manor farm and West End farm were worked together as a 312-a. farm, Manor farm at Grittenham was 298 a., and *c.* 14 farms were of 100–250 a. Most were dairy farms, some, including Manor, were mixed, and on a few cattle were reared for beef.[20]

Brinkworth had woodland 1 furlong by 4 furlongs and 4 furlongs square in 1086.[21] Malmesbury abbey's Brinkworth manor was subject to forest law *c.* 1190, and the woodland was presumably north of the village and within the 13th-century boundaries of Braydon forest. Although Brinkworth's woods were apparently disafforested in 1300,[22] they remained part of the purlieus. After the Dissolution a dispute over them between the Crown and Sir James Stumpe and his wife Isabel, who claimed them as part of Brinkworth manor, was ended in 1587 when the Crown conveyed them to Sir Henry Knyvett for £50 yearly.[23] The woods, *c.* 800 a. in 1587, were in New park, Ox Thick, Wickhurst, Woodhill, and Blackmore.[24] As part of the purlieus they remained under some forest laws, and in the period 1595–1623 were tended by an underforester and by woodwards who attended Braydon swanimote courts.[25] After the purlieus were inclosed *c.* 1631 most of the woodland was apparently grubbed up. Outside the purlieus the only woodland in Brinkworth manor in 1544 was in hedges surrounding inclosures.[26] Wood Hill copse, planted before 1773, was 44 a. *c.* 1840:[27] it was grubbed up before *c.* 1875,[28] presumably to form Woodhill farm. In 1541 Grittenham manor contained Great Wood, 180 a., of which part may have been open to the tenants' animals.[29] There were service trees (*pyrus sorbus*) in it in the 17th century,[30] and in the 17th and 19th it was in coppices.[31] In 1989 it was still a wood of *c.* 180 a.

A watermill, possibly on Brinkworth brook, was part of Grittenham manor in the 16th century.[32] In the Middle Ages a windmill may have stood east of Ramps Hill where a field was later called Windmill piece.[33] Although most surrounding land was pasture a windmill for grinding corn was built between 1808 and 1828 on Brinkworth common,[34] apparently for Abraham Young, who owned it *c.* 1840. It had a stone tower hung with stone slates, a domed cap, six sails, and a fantail. It had additional steam power *c.* 1871, and from *c.* 1880 was powered entirely by a gas engine installed by Westport Ironworks, Malmesbury. The mill was still working *c.* 1939. Milling afterwards ceased, the mill became ruinous, and in 1980 only the foundations remained.[35]

There is evidence of clothmaking in Brinkworth: John Clarke had 24 yd. of fine woollen cloth and 7½ yd. of coarse cloth at Brinkworth in the earlier 16th century,[36] Robert Lewen (d. 1580), a Devizes woollen draper, bought land in Brinkworth,[37] William Trebett of Brinkworth was admitted a freeman of the Weavers' Company of London in 1653,[38] George Matthews was a weaver in 1688,[39] Thomas Mapson was a drugget maker and woolcomber 1722–5,[40] and in 1757 the stock of Joseph Stratton, a woolstapler, was destroyed in a fire at his house in Brinkworth.[41] Although in 1831 most men in the parish were employed in agriculture, 47 in Brinkworth and 3 in Grittenham were engaged in retail trades.[42] A stonemason was based in the parish *c.* 1903, and a basket maker 1923–39. Bricks were made in the parish 1927–31 by the Brinkworth Brick Co.[43] In 1957 Mr. A. Watson established a depot and offices in Brinkworth for oil and petrol distribution. In 1989 the firm had 250 employees of whom 14 worked in offices built at Causeway End *c.* 1980.[44] Two haulage contractors were based in the parish in 1989.

LOCAL GOVERNMENT. In 1289 the abbot of Malmesbury claimed as an ancient right gallows and view of frankpledge in Brinkworth.[45] Manor courts were held in 1473 or earlier.[46] Records of views and manorial courts survive for the period 1544–1778. The views and courts were held twice a year: their business was recorded separately, although they were held on the same day. From 1736 views were held yearly in autumn, manorial courts only when business required it. At later 16th-century views, pleas of debt were heard, common assault was punished, and infringements of the assize of bread and of ale were presented: at the courts, manorial officials were elected, heriots were paid, encroachments on the waste were presented, use of the common pastures was regulated, and licences to sublet were granted. In 1572 offences included brawling, breaking and entering, and the keeping of greyhounds; in 1575 a scold was sent to the stocks and a man of suspect character was reported for setting his neighbours a bad example. In 1576 15 men were presented for playing bowls. In 1660 an unlicensed and disorderly alehouse was reported and tenants were enjoined to make hedges and bridges between fields.[47]

In 1340 John Moleyns was granted extensive liberties over his manor of Brinkworth.[48] A tithingman and tenants attended views and courts held at Lea in 1487 and 1510–14. The Brinkworth homage presented flooded roads and ditches, the

---

[20] Inf. from the owners or occupiers of farms in the par.
[21] *V.C.H. Wilts.* ii, pp. 125, 146.
[22] Ibid. iv. 402.
[23] B.L. Lansd. MS. vi, no. 21; P.R.O., E 123/12, f. 232.
[24] W.R.O. 88/2/44.
[25] *V.C.H. Wilts.* iv. 403–6.
[26] P.R.O., E 318/Box 20/1074, rot. 5.
[27] Ibid. IR 29/38/42; IR 30/38/42; *Andrews and Dury, Map* (W.R.S. viii), pl. 17.
[28] O.S. Map 6", Wilts. IX (1888 edn.).
[29] P.R.O., E 318/Box 1/14, rot. 2.
[30] Aubrey, *Nat. Hist. Wilts.* ed. Britton, 56.
[31] P.R.O., E 134/32 Chas. II East./7; ibid. IR 29/38/42; IR 30/38/42.
[32] Ibid. C 142/108, no. 123; ibid. SC 6/Hen. VIII/3986, rott. 126d.–127.

[33] Ibid. IR 29/38/42; IR 30/38/42; W.R.O. 88/2/46.
[34] W.R.O., EA/131; O.S. Map 1", sheet 34 (1828 edn.).
[35] M. Watts, *Wilts. Windmills*, 12, 26–9; *Kelly's Dir. Wilts.* (1939); P.R.O., IR 29/38/42; IR 30/38/42.
[36] P.R.O., STAC 2/26/431.
[37] Ibid. PROB 11/62, ff. 282v.–283v.
[38] *W.A.M.* xxxviii. 574.
[39] W.R.O. 88/2/53.
[40] *Wilts. Apprentices* (W.R.S. xvii), pp. 16, 31, 84.
[41] B.L., Church Briefs, A. iv. 6.
[42] *Census*, 1831.
[43] *Kelly's Dir. Wilts.* (1903 and later edns.).
[44] Inf. from Mr. A. Watson, Watsons Petroleum.
[45] P.R.O., JUST 1/1006, rot. 44.
[46] Ibid. STAC 1/2/99.
[47] W.R.O. 88/2/6–12; 88/2/21; 88/2/23–9.
[48] *Cal. Chart. R. 1327–41*, 468.

illegal felling of trees, and ruinous tenements.[49] Courts for Grittenham manor were held 1517–22[50] and in 1550.[51]

At vestry meetings, recorded from 1746, separate officers were appointed for Brinkworth and for Grittenham, which were rated together.[52] In the later 18th century and earlier 19th Grittenham had four or five highway surveyors whose yearly expenditure 1761–1833 averaged £30.[53]

A house near Brinkworth church given to the parishioners by Malmesbury abbey in 1478 was used as a workhouse after the Reformation. The poor law was vigorously administered in the parish in the later 18th century. The workhouse, for which a master was appointed each spring, had 20 inmates in the summer of 1779, 30 in the winter of 1779–80, and in 1781–2 an average £30 was spent monthly on indoor relief.[54] In 1802–3 nearly half the inhabitants of the parish were paupers: £1,222 was spent on relieving 194 adults and 216 children continuously and another 20 people occasionally.[55] About a quarter of the inhabitants were paupers 1812–15: in 1812–13 £2,723 was spent on continuous relief for 153 adults, of whom 38 were in the workhouse, and occasional relief for another 50; and in 1814–15 £1,276 was spent on relieving 133 adults continuously and 81 occasionally.[56] Spending remained very high 1816–34 and was frequently the highest of any parish in the hundred, including Malmesbury.[57] The workhouse remained open until the parish joined Malmesbury poor-law union in 1835.[58] The vestry assisted a total of 110 people to emigrate to Quebec in 1842–3, 1847, and 1852.[59] The parish was included in North Wiltshire district in 1974.[60]

CHURCH. A church stood at Brinkworth in 1151.[61] It was served by a rector in the earlier 13th century and, despite papal and royal licences of 1248 and 1340 respectively for Malmesbury abbey to appropriate it,[62] the living remained a rectory and in 1961 was united with that of Dauntsey.[63]

Until the Dissolution Malmesbury abbey had the right to present the rector and usually did so.[64] The rectory was disputed between a nominee of the pope, who provided a rector in 1330,[65] and a nominee of the king: on the grounds that the king presented when the abbey was vacant his nominee was instituted in 1331.[66] In 1342 the abbey granted the advowson for three years to William de Bohun, earl of Northampton, who presented in 1344. The earl and the king disputed the advowson in 1346, when the king again claimed to present because the abbey was vacant, and the king's nominee was instituted.[67] Papal provisees continued to claim the benefice 1346–52, but none was apparently instituted and the king presented again in 1361.[68] Cecily, duchess of York, the mother of Edward IV, presented in 1462, presumably by grant of a turn, and in 1521 John and Thomas Huntbache did so by grant of a turn.[69] The advowson was granted in 1541 to John Ayliffe, and descended with Grittenham manor.[70] By grants of a turn Richard Tanner presented in 1567 and Rowland Wilson and Nicholas Crispe presented jointly in 1629.[71] Henry, Lord Holland, sold the advowson in 1830 to Pembroke College, Oxford.[72] The college transferred it in 1927 to the bishop of Bristol, who became patron of the united benefice in 1961.[73]

The benefice, the richest in Malmesbury deanery, was valued at £10 in 1291,[74] £200 in 1650,[75] and £873 c. 1830.[76] The rector took all tithes from the parish except the great tithes from the demesne of Malmesbury abbey. The excepted tithes were leased by the abbey to the rector 1222 × 1246 for a pension of 4s. The lease was for life but the payment of a pension to the abbey by the rector in 1265 and 1291 suggests that later rectors also held those tithes.[77] Later, however, the demesne was tithe free. In 1840 the rector's tithes were valued at £780 and commuted.[78]

After 1279 Malmesbury abbey gave land to the rector.[79] The glebe was 80 a. in 1671 and included a farmhouse called Dovey's. More land was afterwards acquired: in 1705 and 1783 the rector had 114 a.,[80] and c. 1840 150 a. which included land allotted at inclosure in 1808.[81] The rector sold 7 a. in 1897, 124 a. including Dovey's farm in 1919,[82] the rectory house and 7 a. in 1955, and 2 a. in 1965:[83] 3 a. of glebe remained in 1989.[84]

The rectory house standing in 1671[85] was replaced in the mid 18th century. The house is of stone and brick and, **H**-shaped with a long central east–west range between projecting north–south wings, possibly on the plan of the old house. There was originally a north entrance front, the west end contained two parlours, the east end contains service rooms, and the central range is a long hall

[49] P.R.O., SC 2/208/28; SC 2/209/57, rot 2 and d.
[50] Ibid. C 1/1156, nos. 35–6.
[51] Ibid. REQ 2/118/8.
[52] W.R.O. 1607/27.
[53] Ibid. 1607/69.
[54] Ibid. 1607/47; 1607/70.
[55] V.C.H. Wilts. iv. 342; Poor Law Abstract, 1804, 566–7.
[56] Poor Law Abstract, 1818, 498–9.
[57] Poor Rate Returns, 1816–21, 188; 1822–4, 228; 1825–9, 219; 1830–4, 212.
[58] Poor Law Com. 2nd Rep. App. D, 559.
[59] W.R.O. 1607/71.
[60] O.S. Map 1/100,000, admin. areas, Wilts. (1974 edn.).
[61] Reg. Malm. i. 349.
[62] Cal. Papal Reg. i. 249; Cal. Pat. 1338–40, 431.
[63] Ch. Com. file, NB 5/21.
[64] Phillipps, Wilts. Inst. (index in W.A.M. xxviii. 214).
[65] Cal. Papal Reg. ii. 325, 349.
[66] Cal. Pat. 1330–4, 38, 152, 175; Phillipps, Wilts. Inst. i. 27; P.R.O., CP 40/285, rot. 27.
[67] Phillipps, Wilts. Inst. i. 39, 41, 55; Cal. Pat. 1345–8, 166, 238, 311; P.R.O., C 260/65, no. 11; ibid. CP 40/348, rot. 547.
[68] Cal. Papal Reg. iii. 184; Cal. Pat. 1348–50, 71, 204, 253, 315, 565; 1350–4, 2, 395; 1361–4, 110.
[69] Phillipps, Wilts. Inst. i. 152, 195.
[70] P.R.O., E 318/Box 1/14; above, manors.
[71] Phillipps, Wilts. Inst. i. 223; ii. 14.
[72] Pembroke Coll., Oxf., Mun. 31/1/3–4.
[73] Ch. Com. files, NB 5/21; 88092.
[74] Tax. Eccl. (Rec. Com.), 189.
[75] W.A.M. xli. 8.
[76] Rep. Com. Eccl. Revenues, 826–7.
[77] Reg. Malm. i. 417; ii. 73–4; Tax. Eccl. (Rec. Com.), 189.
[78] P.R.O., IR 29/38/42; IR 30/38/42.
[79] W.R.O. 88/2/6.
[80] Ibid. D 1/24/27/1–3.
[81] Ibid. EA/131; P.R.O., IR 29/38/42; IR 30/38/42.
[82] Pembroke Coll., Oxf., Mun. 31/1/6–7.
[83] Ch. Com. deeds 462737, 491332.
[84] Inf. from Deputy Dioc. Sec., Dioc. Bd. of Finance, Church Ho., 23 Gt. Geo. Street, Bristol.
[85] W.R.O., D 1/24/27/1.

passage[86] with a room south of it. The south parlour was extended south to create a large drawing room c. 1830,[87] the inside of the house was altered in the earlier 20th century, and in the later 20th north service rooms were built between the wings and the north parlour became an entrance hall with a west door. A new rectory house was built in 1955.[88]

The wealth of the living attracted able men. Guiscard de Pardies, a Frenchman instituted in 1312, had no English and was ordered to appoint a chaplain to serve Brinkworth. He was apparently a canon lawyer employed by Malmesbury abbey.[89] In 1335 a royal clerk, John of Badminton, rector 1331–44, was licensed to study for three years,[90] and in 1408 William Lombard, rector 1403–17, was licensed to take a year's leave.[91] Andrew Sparrow or Herbard, rector 1419–21, was also a canon of St. David's,[92] Richard Machon (d. c. 1492) was also rector of Crudwell and, from 1486, precentor of St. David's, and John Lichfield, rector 1493–1511, was also rector of St. Augustine's, Watling Street, London, and, from 1496, of Childrey (Berks.).[93] Thomas Head, rector 1511–21, was also rector of Milton (Kent),[94] and Edward Hutchins (d. 1629) was a canon of Salisbury.[95] Tobias Crispe, rector 1629–42, was a proponent of antinomianism.[96] William Dowdeswell, instituted in 1643, was deprived before 1650 and restored in 1660.[97] The intruded minister, John Harding, in 1650 paid a fifth of the benefice's income to Dowdeswell.[98] The laxity displayed towards the cure by Francis Cary, rector 1671–1711, prompted the bishop to dispatch to Brinkworth a curate, whom, on pain of sequestration, Cary was to employ at £30 yearly.[99] Curates often served the cure or assisted the rector in the 17th century and early 18th. One, Richard Copson, was instituted as rector in 1711.[1] In 1783 the rector held two Sunday services, and preached each Sunday morning, for a congregation which averaged 150–200 people. Communion was celebrated at Easter, Whitsun, Michaelmas, and Christmas for 12–20. The rector was also rector of Wellow (Hants), where he lived for part of the year, and employed a curate at Brinkworth.[2] Matthew Marsh, rector 1802–40, was a pluralist among whose preferments were the chancellorship and the subdeanery of Salisbury.[3] From 1804 his curate was Henry Wightwick, rector of Little Somerford. Wightwick lived in the rectory house at

Brinkworth, held two Sunday services, and preached on Sunday mornings, Christmas day, and Good Friday.[4] Henry's brother Charles, at whose suggestion Pembroke College bought the advowson,[5] was presented by the college as rector in 1841, and until 1935 all the rectors were fellows of the college.[6] On Census Sunday in 1851 a congregation of 250 attended morning service, fewer afternoon service.[7] A curate assisted the rector 1884–92[8] and in 1922 when services were sometimes held in Grittenham school. From 1936 to 1949 the living was held by R. E. Ramsay, the suffragan bishop of Malmesbury.[9]

Brinkworth shared with Brokenborough, Charlton, and Hankerton in Lady Frances Winchcombe's Bible charity established by deed of 1706. In 1834 Brinkworth's share, £1, was spent on Bibles and prayer books for children at Weeks's charity school. There was £10 of Brinkworth's share in hand in 1902, and in 1903 £2 was spent on books for nonconformists and £2 on books for churchgoers.[10]

The church of ST. MICHAEL, so called in 1763[11] but St. Peter's in 1248[12] and 1512,[13] is built of stone rubble with ashlar dressings and has a chancel, an aisled nave with south porch, and a west tower.[14] The church which stood in 1151 may have been rebuilt in the late 12th century or early 13th. The east wall of the south aisle, which contains part of a blocked lancet window, and that of the north aisle are of that period and suggest that the church was cruciform. The chancel and chancel arch were rebuilt in the 14th century, and in the 15th the tower was built, possibly to replace a central tower. The south aisle, standing in the 15th century, and the nave were rebuilt, and the north aisle and the porch built, in the early 16th century. In the early 18th a west gallery was built[15] and, possibly then, the nave was fitted with box pews.[16] In 1879 the chancel was rebuilt in 14th-century style.[17] The entire church was restored, and the area below the gallery enclosed to form a baptistery, under the direction of C. E. Ponting in 1902–3. The pulpit, altar table, and font cover were placed in the church in the 1630s.[18]

Brinkworth was rich in plate in the 16th century. In 1553 the king's commissioners took 32 oz. and left 9½ oz. In 1989 the parish owned a chalice hallmarked for 1631, a flagon hallmarked for 1637, and a paten hallmarked for 1718.[19] There were four bells in 1553. In 1925 a new treble cast by

[86] Ibid. D 1/24/27/2–3.   [87] W.A.M. xliii. 173.
[88] Ch. Com. deed 491332.
[89] Reg. Ghent (Cant. & York Soc.), ii. 800; Reg. Martival (Cant. & York Soc.), i. 423, 426–7; iii, p. 142.
[90] A. B. Emden, Biog. Reg. Univ. Oxf. to 1500, i. 90; Phillipps, Wilts. Inst. i. 27, 39.
[91] Reg. Hallum (Cant. & York Soc.), p. 97; Phillipps, Wilts. Inst. i. 89, 106.
[92] Emden, op. cit. iii. 1739–40; Cal. Papal Reg. vii. 176.
[93] Cal. Papal Reg. xvi, p. 71; Reg. Langton (Cant. & York Soc.), p. 43; Emden, op. cit. ii. 1144, 1201.
[94] Phillipps, Wilts. Inst. i. 190, 195; Emden, op. cit. ii. 900.
[95] Phillipps, Wilts. Inst. ii. 14; Alum. Oxon. 1500–1714, ii. 778.
[96] W.N. & Q. vii. 385–7.
[97] Walker Revised, ed. Matthews, 384.
[98] Calamy Revised, ed. Matthews, 247; W.A.M. xli. 8.
[99] Phillipps, Wilts. Inst. ii. 31, 51; P.R.O., C 104/131/1.
[1] Subscription Bk. 1620–40 (W.R.S. xxxii), p. 67; Phillipps, Wilts. Inst. ii. 51; W.R.O., bishop's transcripts, bdles. 1–2.

[2] Vis. Queries, 1783 (W.R.S. xxvii), pp. 45–6.
[3] Phillipps, Wilts. Inst. ii. 103; Alum. Oxon. 1715–1886, iii. 916.
[4] W.R.O., bishop's transcripts, bdle. 3; Ch. Com. file, NB 5/21; below, Little Somerford, church.
[5] Pembroke Coll., Oxf., Mun. 31/1/1.
[6] W.A.M. xlvii. 296; Bristol R.O., EP/A/3/31.
[7] P.R.O., HO 129/252/1/8/11.   [8] W.A.M. xlvi. 114.
[9] Who Was Who, 1951–60, 903–4; Ch. Com. files, NB 5/21; K 10643.
[10] Endowed Char. Wilts. (N. Div.), 140, 142; below, Charlton, church.
[11] J. Ecton, Thesaurus (1763), 402.
[12] Cal. Papal Reg. i. 249.
[13] L. & P. Hen. VIII, i (2), p. 1525.
[14] Cf. J. Buckler, watercolour in W.A.S. Libr., vol. vi. 2 (1809).   [15] A carved date of 1707 has been reset.
[16] Panelling from pews of that date has been re-used in the tower.
[17] W.R.O. 1607/37.   [18] W.A.M. xl. 107–9.
[19] Nightingale, Wilts. Plate, 193–4; inf. from the rector.

Mears & Stainbank was added to the ring of five cast by William and Roger Purdue in 1663.[20] Registers of marriages, baptisms, and burials begin in 1653 and are complete.[21]

NONCONFORMITY. Two parishioners declined to receive Easter communion in 1584.[22] There were 35 nonconformists in the parish in 1676.[23] Several who refused to attend church, have their children baptized, or pay church rates in the period 1662–83[24] were Quakers. Their society, consisting chiefly of members of the Edwards, Reynolds, Scull, and Young families 1662–1752,[25] was at first associated with that of Lea.[26] In 1674 it met in Anthony Edwards's barn.[27] Two Quakers emigrated to Philadelphia c. 1683.[28] The group certified a meeting house in 1690[29] and may have had a burial ground at Brinkworth until 1734 or later.[30] Its numbers declined in the mid 18th century and in 1752 it ceased to attend the Chippenham monthly meeting.[31]

Presbyterians or Independents met in a house at Brinkworth in 1689.[32] Independency was promoted in the parish c. 1740 by John Cennick,[33] and a chapel at Causeway End was built in 1741.[34] Another group, possibly also of Independents, met in Brinkworth in 1742, and in 1743 Presbyterians also held services there.[35] Some Independents joined the Moravian church after 1745[36] and met in the later 18th century and early 19th in Vines House at Grittenham.[37] In 1783 Causeway End chapel and a Moravian meeting house, presumably Vines House, were both served by ministers but apparently little used.[38] Independents met at Bowd's Farm, Grittenham, in 1798.[39] An average congregation of 150 attended each of the two Sunday services held in Causeway End chapel in 1850–1.[40] That chapel was closed between 1939 and 1954.[41]

Primitive Methodism was brought to Brinkworth in 1824 by Samuel Heath. Brinkworth became the centre of a circuit in 1826–7,[42] from which much of southern England was evangelized.

Meetings were held in houses until a chapel was built at Barnes Green in 1828.[43] A new chapel, medium sized and of stone, was built in 1860,[44] in 1907 was attended by 42 adults,[45] and was still used for services in 1989. Registrations of births and baptisms survive for 1829–37.[46]

Primitive Methodists met in a house at Grittenham from 1835.[47] A congregation of 48 attended each of two services held on Census Sunday in 1851.[48] A small iron chapel was opened in 1894, attended in 1907 by 22 adults,[49] and closed c. 1975.[50] A chapel for Primitive Methodists[51] was built at Callow Hill in 1889. The Salvation Army held weekday services in it in 1896.[52] It was closed between 1955 and 1971.[53]

EDUCATION. John Weeks (d. 1678) bequeathed a rent charge of £5 for teaching 10 poor children of Brinkworth tithing to read.[54] Children were taught in 1778 and 1859 in a cottage on the north side of the Swindon–Malmesbury road.[55] In 1783 the rector and the parishioners were each giving £5 5s. for more children to be taught,[56] and in 1808 the lords of Brinkworth and Grittenham manors also contributed.[57] The school had c. 40 pupils in 1818,[58] 60–70 in 1833.[59] A new school was built in 1868 and enlarged c. 1870, and c. 1887 a school board for Brinkworth tithing was formed.[60] Average attendance was 130 in 1906–11, 95 in 1926–7, and 107 in 1937–8.[61] The rent charge was extinguished in 1957. Weeks's educational charity and the Winchcombe Bible charity were merged to become an educational trust for the school and parish.[62] In 1989 the school had 82 children and 4 teachers.[63]

A school at Grittenham was opened in 1864.[64] It had 39 pupils on return day in 1871[65] and an average of 39 in 1906.[66] Numbers had declined to 20 by 1927 when the school was closed.[67]

Other schools were held in the parish in the 19th century. Girls were taught in a charity school c. 1808,[68] in 1818 a school for 15–20 children was supported by subscription,[69] and in 1833 schools

[20] Walters, *Wilts. Bells*, 38–9, 248; inf. from the rector.
[21] W.R.O. 1607/1–12. Bishop's transcripts for 1572–3, 1582–3, 1605–10, 1619–23, and 1632 are ibid. Marriages are printed in *Wilts. Par. Reg. (Mar.)*, ed. W. P. W. Phillimore and J. Sadler, x. 19–43.
[22] W.R.O., D 1/43/5, f. 21.
[23] *Compton Census*, ed. Whiteman, 128.
[24] W.R.O., D 1/54/1/1, no. 54; D 1/54/6/1, no. 52; D 1/54/10/1, no. 30.
[25] *W.N. & Q.* ii–vii, *passim*.
[26] *V.C.H. Wilts.* iii. 118.
[27] W.R.O., D 1/54/6/1, no. 52.   [28] *W.N. & Q.* iv. 139.
[29] *Meeting Ho. Certs.* (W.R.S. xl), p. 3.
[30] *W.N. & Q.* vii. 180, 515.   [31] *V.C.H. Wilts.* iii. 127.
[32] *Meeting Ho. Certs.* (W.R.S. xl), p. 1.
[33] *V.C.H. Wilts.* iii. 130.
[34] *Meeting Ho. Certs.* (W.R.S. xl), p. 24; J. L. Osborn, *Villages of N. Wilts.* 35.
[35] *Meeting Ho. Certs.* (W.R.S. xl), p. 25.
[36] *V.C.H. Wilts.* iii. 131.
[37] Evidence of Vines fam. supplied by Mrs. P. S. Mitchell, Vines Ho.
[38] *Vis. Queries, 1783* (W.R.S. xxvii), pp. 45–6.
[39] *Meeting Ho. Certs.* (W.R.S. xl), p. 51.
[40] P.R.O., HO 129/252/1/8/12.
[41] *Kelly's Dir. Wilts.* (1939); G.R.O. Worship Reg., cancellations, no. 31934.
[42] *V.C.H. Wilts.* iii. 143; W. C. Tonks, *Victory in the Villages*, 86, 99, 122–3.
[43] *Meeting Ho. Certs.* (W.R.S. xl), pp. 108, 110, 113, 120;

Tonks, op. cit. 36–7; P.R.O., IR 29/38/42; IR 30/38/42.
[44] Date on chapel; see plate facing p. 173.
[45] Tonks, op. cit. 23–4.   [46] P.R.O., RG 4/3326.
[47] *Meeting Ho. Certs.* (W.R.S. xl), p. 138.
[48] P.R.O., HO 129/252/1/9/14.
[49] Tonks, op. cit. 23–4, 137.
[50] Inf. from Mrs. K. J. Ody, Pinnell's Farm.
[51] See plate facing p. 173.
[52] W.R.O. 1571/27.
[53] Ibid. 1571/28; G.R.O. Worship Reg., cancellations, no. 41214.
[54] P.R.O., PROB 11/358, ff. 105–107v.
[55] *Acct. of Wilts. Schs.* 10; P.R.O., IR 29/38/42; IR 30/38/42; W.R.O. 1607/70.
[56] *Vis. Queries, 1783* (W.R.S. xxvii), pp. 45–6.
[57] Lamb. Palace Libr., MS. 1732.
[58] *Educ. of Poor Digest*, 1020.
[59] *Educ. Enq. Abstract*, 1030.
[60] *Endowed Char. Wilts.* (N. Div.), 143–4; P.R.O., ED 7/130, no. 39; W.R.O. 782/15/1.
[61] *Bd. of Educ., List 21, 1908–9* (H.M.S.O.), 500; *1912*, 548; *1927*, 358; *1938*, 421.
[62] Inf. from the rector; above, church.
[63] Inf. from the head teacher.
[64] P.R.O., ED 7/130, no. 40.
[65] *Returns relating to Elem. Educ.* 420–1.
[66] *Return of Non-Provided Schs.* 39.
[67] *Bd. of Educ., List 21, 1927* (H.M.S.O.), 358; *1932*, 406.
[68] Lamb. Palace Libr., MS. 1732.
[69] *Educ. of Poor Digest*, 1020.

were attended by *c.* 45 and by 20–30.[70] In 1859 Primitive Methodists supported a school attached to their chapel.[71] It was perhaps the school attended by 102 children on return day in 1871.[72]

CHARITIES FOR THE POOR. John Weeks (d. 1678) bequeathed £10 a year to the poor of Brinkworth and stipulated that no family was to receive more than 2*s*. 6*d*. or less than 6*d*.[73] In 1834, 1904 (when 116 people received a gift),[74] and 1952 (when 82 did so) the £10 was distributed as the donor intended.[75]

By will proved 1815 Hannah Nichols gave £200 for blankets for old people at Christmas. The capital was afterwards augmented, and in the 1830s, when the income was £10, blankets were given to each poor family every four years. Blankets were given in alternate years to all paupers in the parish *c.* 1905,[76] and in 1952 £8 was spent on blankets for 10 people.[77]

Weeks's eleemosynary charity and Nichols's charity were amalgamated in 1957 and most of the income was afterwards distributed at Christmas. Payments were made to 24 people in 1988.[78] From 1967 Brinkworth parishioners were entitled to be admitted to an almshouse in Dauntsey.[79]

BROKENBOROUGH

BROKENBOROUGH village is 2.5 km. north-west of Malmesbury abbey.[80] In 1086 Malmesbury abbey's large estate called Brokenborough included Corston and other land near Malmesbury, and in title deeds the abbey gave an even larger estate the name Brokenborough.[81] In the 11th century and earlier Brokenborough was almost certainly a village with its own lands; later a manor and a tithing were called Brokenborough, but the church was not a parish church and until 1984 was dependent on, successively, Westport and Charlton churches.[82] Brokenborough relieved its own poor[83] and in the 19th and 20th centuries was a civil parish.[84]

The Romano-British settlement now called White Walls stood where the Roman Foss Way crossed the Sherston branch of the Bristol Avon on the edge of Brokenborough parish,[85] but no earlier remains have been discovered in the parish. A monk of Malmesbury wrote in the later 14th century that a royal residence and its manor of both heathens and Christians was at 'Kairdureburgh which is now called Brukeburgh or Brokenbern',[86] and words were later intruded to imply that a castle had stood at Brokenborough.[87] The statement perpetuated a tradition that King Athelstan (d. 939) had a palace at Brokenborough. The monk's apparent claim that earlier kings of Wessex lived at Brokenborough is implausible, and the notion that demolished buildings, which may have been some of Malmesbury abbey's demesne farm, had been a royal palace[88] has not been substantiated. The Celtic name Kairdureburgh, not recorded until the 14th century, possibly refers to a fortified camp, of which there is no evidence, and may be spurious. Although it appears in a charter reputed to be of 956 the name Brokenborough is not known to have been used before the 11th century. It may refer to a broken barrow, but no nearby barrow is known; it is more likely to refer to a broken hill,[89] perhaps to the steep sided valley beside which the village stands. Although the evidence that early Saxon kings had a fortified palace on the site of a Celtic stronghold which was renamed Brokenborough may be discounted, the village, on an elevated site near a stream, may nevertheless have been an early Saxon settlement. In the early Middle Ages it seems to have been well populated, economically prosperous, and prominent among Malmesbury abbey's estates,[90] and that may be why the abbey called a very large estate Brokenborough and associated Brokenborough with its supposed patrons.[91]

Boundaries of what the abbey claimed had been its Brokenborough estate in 956 were drawn up in the 11th or 12th century and took in, among others, lands later in the parishes of Ashley and Long Newnton (both now Glos.), Crudwell, Malmesbury, and Westport. The only parts to have been later boundaries of Brokenborough parish were the Sherston Avon and, between that and the Tetbury (Glos.) branch of the Avon, the Foss Way.[92] The rest of the parish boundaries are irregular and marked by prominent features only in short stretches. Until the 19th century they were ill defined and uncertain, presumably because in the Middle Ages the tithes from Brokenborough and nearly all its neighbours were due to Malmesbury abbey, and after the Dissolution many were in lay hands and merged.[93] The parish lies north-

[70] *Educ. Enq. Abstract*, 1030.   [71] *Acct. of Wilts. Schs.* 10.
[72] *Returns relating to Elem. Educ.* 420–1.
[73] P.R.O., PROB 11/358, ff. 105–107v.
[74] *Endowed Char. Wilts.* (N. Div.), 140–1.
[75] W.R.O., Char. Com., Brinkworth.
[76] *Endowed Char. Wilts.* (N. Div.), 140, 142; P.R.O., PROB 11/1572, f. 102.
[77] W.R.O., Char. Com., Brinkworth.
[78] Inf. from the rector.
[79] Char. Com. file; below, Dauntsey, charities.
[80] This article was written in 1987. Maps used include O.S. Maps 1/50,000, sheet 173 (1974 edn.); 1/25,000, ST 88, ST 98 (1958–9 edns.); 6″, Wilts. VIII (1889 and later edns.).

[81] Below, manor.   [82] Ibid. church.
[83] Ibid. local govt.   [84] *V.C.H. Wilts.* iv. 342.
[85] Ibid. i (1), 68.
[86] *Eulogium Hist.* (Rolls Ser.), i. 225.
[87] Dugdale, *Mon.* i. 257.
[88] Aubrey, *Topog. Coll.* ed. Jackson, 210–11.
[89] *P.N. Wilts.* (E.P.N.S.), 53–4.
[90] Below, econ. hist.
[91] *V.C.H. Wilts.* iii. 213.
[92] *Arch. Jnl.* lxxvii. 42–54. T. R. Thomson attempted to plot the whole boundary on maps in W.A.S. Libr.
[93] Below, manor; ibid. Charlton, manors; Crudwell, manors; Hankerton, manors; Westport, manors.

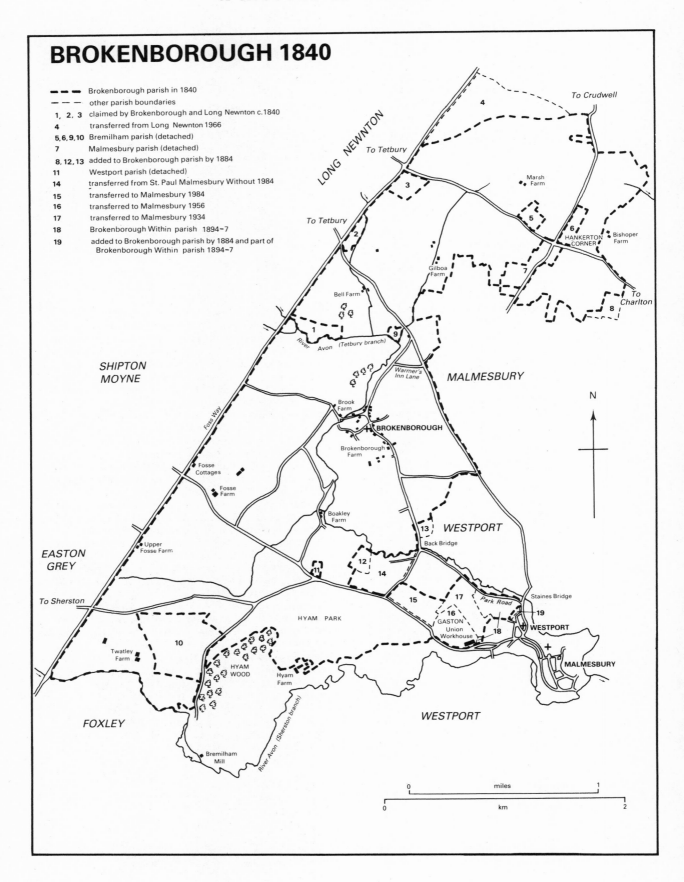

BROKENBOROUGH 1840

- - - Brokenborough parish in 1840
- - - other parish boundaries

1, 2, 3	claimed by Brokenborough and Long Newnton c.1840
4	transferred from Long Newnton 1966
5,6,9,10	Bremilham parish (detached)
7	Malmesbury parish (detached)
8, 12,13	added to Brokenborough parish by 1884
11	Westport parish (detached)
14	transferred from St. Paul Malmesbury Without 1984
15	transferred to Malmesbury 1984
16	transferred to Malmesbury 1956
17	transferred to Malmesbury 1934
18	Brokenborough Within parish 1894–7
19	added to Brokenborough parish by 1884 and part of Brokenborough Within parish 1894–7

east and south-west and is separated from Malmesbury by Westport parish.[94] It encompassed several islands of neighbouring parishes,[95] presumably because those lands and their tithes had been acquired by the lords of neighbouring manors. The lord of Bremilham manor held land in the open field of Brokenborough in the earlier 13th century:[96] in 1731 his successor owned 97 a. of Bremilham parish in three pieces surrounded or almost surrounded by Brokenborough,[97] and c. 99 a. in four pieces in 1840.[98] The lords of Whitchurch and Milbourne manor in Malmesbury and of Thornhill manor in Westport held land or tithes in Brokenborough in the 16th century,[99] and detached portions of both parishes, c. 30 a. in all, were encompassed by Brokenborough in 1840.[1] In 1371 and 1534 a field called Worthy, sometimes said to be in Brokenborough, Westport, and Malmesbury,[2] in 1478 land on the north side of the Tetbury Avon near Malmesbury,[3] and in 1577 Bremilham Mill on the Sherston Avon[4] were ascribed to Brokenborough: none was later. In the later 16th century land called Wakely Hill was disputed between Brokenborough and Milbourne;[5] mounds marked off Brokenborough from Long Newnton in 1584,[6] suggesting that part of the boundary was not then the Foss Way; and in 1649 and 1785 Hyam park was said to be partly in Brokenborough and partly in Westport.[7] The boundary between the two parishes was drawn across Hyam park in 1838: Hyam Farm and Hyam wood were assigned to Westport, a field called the Gaston, c. 25 a. near Malmesbury on which the union workhouse was built in 1838, was assigned to Brokenborough.[8]

In 1840 the parish was bounded on the south by the Sherston Avon and the new boundary of 1838, already slightly amended, and on the north-west by the Foss Way: watercourses and roads also marked some of the northern and eastern boundaries. At its south-east corner the parish adjoined the built-up area of Malmesbury and Westport.[9] Between 1840 and 1884 several fields on Brokenborough's irregular eastern boundary, of which one was the site of Malmesbury fever (isolation) hospital between the 1890s and 1933 and others took Brokenborough's boundary eastwards along Burnham Road and to the north-west side of Shipton Hill in Westport, a total of c. 13 a., were transferred to Brokenborough from Westport, and a detached ½ a. of Brokenborough beside

Park Road surrounded by Westport was transferred to Westport; and in 1884 the islands of Malmesbury, Westport, and Bremilham, a total of c. 130 a., were transferred to Brokenborough.[10] Three fields adjoining the east side of the Foss Way but not each other, a total of 32 a. belonging to the lord of Long Newnton manor, were claimed by both Brokenborough and Long Newnton c. 1840.[11] They were ascribed to Long Newnton in 1881, and in 1889 Brokenborough measured 2,634 a.[12] From 1872 two parts of the south-east corner of the parish, c. 19 a., were in Malmesbury urban sanitary district, from 1886 Malmesbury municipal borough.[13] In 1894 they and the lands between Foundry Road and Burnham Road and on the north-west side of Shipton Hill became a separate parish called Brokenborough Within, and from then the remainder of Brokenborough parish was called Brokenborough Without. In 1897 Brokenborough Within was merged with Westport St. Mary Within, and Brokenborough Without was again called Brokenborough.[14] A further 25 a. at the south-east corner were transferred to Malmesbury municipal borough in 1934,[15] and a further 25 a., the Gaston, on which the workhouse stood, in 1956.[16] The three fields ascribed to Long Newnton in 1881, a further 76 a. of Long Newnton adjoining the Foss Way to the west and Brokenborough to the south, and the width of the Foss Way itself were transferred to Brokenborough in 1966.[17] After that Brokenborough measured 1,085 ha. (2,681 a.).[18] In 1984 a further 9 ha. at the south-east corner were transferred to Malmesbury and 12 ha. of St. Paul Malmesbury Without parish were transferred to Brokenborough.[19]

The land is undulating, highest at over 110 m. in the north, lowest at below 76 m. in the south-east. It drains mainly to the Tetbury Avon which flows from north-west to south-east across it. There is flat land in the north and west crossed by the Foss Way, and the site of an airfield on the watershed of the Thames and the Bristol Avon is in the north. To the south and east the Tetbury Avon, called the Ingelbourne in the 11th or 12th century,[20] has cut the steep sided valley to which the parish name may refer. To the north and west the outcrops are mainly limestone and clay of the Forest Marble, to the south mainly Kellaways Clay and Cornbrash. Sand and gravel lie in various parts and the streams have deposited alluvium. There are several geological faults.[21] Nearly all the land

[94] Below, Westport, map.
[95] W.R.O., tithe award.
[96] *Reg. Malm.* ii. 185–7.
[97] W.R.O. 1198/1.
[98] Ibid. tithe awards.
[99] *Cal. Pat.* 1547–8, 194; P.R.O., E 315/102, ff. 28–9.
[1] W.R.O., tithe award.
[2] Ibid. 88/1/114; P.R.O., E 315/104, f. 198 and v.; ibid. JUST 3/156, rot. 15d.
[3] W.R.O. 88/1/16.
[4] Ibid. 88/2/21, view 29 Mar. 1577.
[5] Ibid. 88/2/21, view 23 Sept. 16 Eliz. I; 88/2/22, view 28 Mar. 28 Eliz. I; 88/2/34.
[6] Ibid. 88/2/22, view 24 Sept. 1584.
[7] Ibid. 88/5/46/4, Mitford's opinion; *Cal. Cttee. for Compounding*, iii. 1969.
[8] *W.A.M.* xlvii. 565; W.R.O. 1589/68.
[9] W.R.O., tithe award.
[10] Ibid.; *Census*, 1891; O.S. Map 6″, Wilts. VIII (1889 and

later edns.). For the survey dates of the 1889 map see the later edns. For the hosp., below, Malmesbury, public services. Malmesbury and Westport street names are those of 1989: the streets are mapped below, p. 133.
[11] W.R.O., tithe award.
[12] O.S. Map 6″, Wilts. VIII (1889 edn.).
[13] *V.C.H. Wilts.* iv. 352 n. For Malmesbury U.S.D., below, Malmesbury, introduction.
[14] *Census*, 1901.
[15] *V.C.H. Wilts.* iv. 342 n.; O.S. Map 1″, sheet 157 (1940 edn.).
[16] *Census*, 1961; O.S. Map 1″, sheet 157 (1968 edn.).
[17] W.R.O., Wilts. co. council, clerk's office papers, 247.
[18] *Census*, 1981.
[19] Statutory Instruments, 1984, no. 387, N. Wilts. (Parishes) order.
[20] *Arch. Jnl.* lxxvii. 46; below, Malmesbury, introduction.
[21] Geol. Surv. Map 1″, solid and drift, sheet 251 (1970 edn.).

is suitable for either tillage or pasture with, especially in the south, meadow land beside the streams.[22]

The principal roads through the parish, converging on Malmesbury from Sherston and Tetbury, were turnpiked in 1756.[23] Until c. 1778 the Tetbury road was part of the route between Cirencester (Glos.) and Malmesbury.[24] The Sherston road and a road which branched from it to Shipton Moyne (Glos.) were possibly made on their present routes at inclosure c. 1640.[25] Across the north end of the parish the Charlton–Tetbury road, called New Leaze Lane in 1639,[26] was turnpiked in 1798;[27] where it enters Brokenborough from the east the land was called Hankerton Corner from c. 1613[28] or earlier. The Malmesbury–Tetbury road was disturnpiked in 1874, the other roads in 1876.[29] Brokenborough village is served by a road which links it to the Tetbury road and to Malmesbury: to the south the road crosses the Tetbury Avon and the parish boundary at Back bridge, and where it marked the parish boundary nearer Malmesbury is called Park Road. Of other roads in 1773 two, that linking the north part of Brokenborough village with the Shipton Moyne road, and Warmer's Inn Lane north of Brokenborough village, remain tracks; a road across the north end of the parish from the west end of Crudwell parish to Malmesbury, and a road from the Back bridge road to the Tetbury road went out of use between 1840 and the early 1880s.[30]

Brokenborough's assessment for taxation is likely to have been low in 1334 when it was returned with Burton Hill in Malmesbury,[31] but at 120 the number of poll-tax payers in 1377 was high.[32] The parish was of average wealth in the 16th century[33] and was later not densely populated: 75 adults lived in it in 1676.[34] In 1801 the population was 211: it had risen to 283 by 1831. Of 429 inhabitants 131 lived in the union workhouse in 1841, 160 of 443 in 1851. A decrease in the population from 503 in 1861 to 444 in 1871 was attributed to emigration. The population was 381 in 1891. In the three years of its existence Brokenborough Within had c. 60 inhabitants. Brokenborough's population was 317 in 1901 and 1951: a sharp rise to 388 between 1901 and 1911 was possibly caused by increased use of the workhouse or the isolation hospital. The land transferred to Malmesbury in 1934 had a population of 5 in 1931.[35] New building west of Malmesbury after the Second World War was partly in Brokenborough, and the land transferred to Malmesbury in 1956 had a population of 80 in 1951. Further building for Malmesbury in Brokenborough's south-east corner caused Brokenborough's population to reach 413 in 1961 and 556 in 1971. In 1981 it was 532:[36] away from Malmesbury the parish was sparsely populated.

Brokenborough village is on high ground near the Tetbury Avon roughly in the middle of the parish. To the south the farmsteads called Twatley in 1640[37] and Boakley in 1678,[38] each beside a branch of the Avon, may be on old sites, but in the Middle Ages there seems to have been little settlement outside the village. Following inclosure five new farmsteads were built in the west and north in the 18th century or early 19th and it is very likely that house sites in the village were given up then.[39] In 1989 the village remained small.

In the village, centred on the church, most of the older buildings are of local stone. In the Middle Ages extensive demesne farm buildings belonging to Malmesbury abbey stood to the south slightly away from the village. A late-medieval barn of 10 bays with 2 east transeptal entrances, 9 raised cruck trusses, and walls with plain buttresses survives. A larger and possibly earlier barn and a farmhouse stood on a moated site south of it until demolished in the mid 17th century.[40] The demesne land was later worked from Brokenborough Farm at the south end of the village street.[41] The farmhouse has an apparently 17th-century north range of two storeys and attics to which a south wing was added in the 18th century. Respectively north-west and west of the church, Brook Farm and another house are 18th-century farmhouses extended in the 19th century. In the street are a house apparently of the 17th or 18th century and two small farmhouses and a cottage apparently of the 18th. North of the church a small farmhouse was much enlarged and altered in the later 20th century. South of the church the Rose and Crown is a small 18th-century house extended in the 19th century: it was called the Crown in 1731,[42] the Rose and Crown in 1740.[43] In the street 11 houses are 20th-century: they include 4 council houses built in 1954,[44] a large house of the 1960s, and 2 stone houses built as a pair c. 1980.[45] Along the street sites from which buildings have been removed are evident.

Outside the village Boakley is the oldest farmhouse.[46] It was built in the later 17th century with a staircase in a semicircular rear projection, and a rear wing was added in the 19th century. From 1773 or earlier some of the farm buildings have been on a higher site further south[47] where an apparently 18th-century barn survives, and a new house was built further south in 1961.[48] Upper Fosse Farm is a small early 18th-century house,

[22] Below, econ. hist.
[23] V.C.H. Wilts. iv. 257, 269; L.J. xxviii. 581.
[24] Below, Malmesbury, introduction.
[25] W.R.O. 88/2/24, views 14 Sept. 16 Chas. I, 28 Sept. 17 Chas. I; below, econ. hist.
[26] W.R.O. 88/2/24, view 1 Oct. 15 Chas. I.
[27] Ibid. 88/5/46/3; L.J. xli. 655.
[28] W.R.O. 88/2/46, f. 64v.
[29] V.C.H. Wilts. iv. 269; 14 & 15 Vic. c. 76 (Local and Personal).
[30] Andrews and Dury, Map (W.R.S. viii), pl. 16; W.R.O., tithe award; O.S. Map 6", Wilts. VIII (1889 edn.).
[31] V.C.H. Wilts. iv. 298.   [32] Ibid. 309.
[33] Taxation Lists (W.R.S. x), 30, 51; P.R.O., E 179/197/155.
[34] Compton Census, ed. Whiteman, 129 n.

[35] V.C.H. Wilts. iv. 323, 342, 352.
[36] Census, 1961; 1971; 1981; below; ibid. Malmesbury, introduction.
[37] W.R.O. 88/2/24, view 14 Sept. 16 Chas. I.
[38] Ibid. 88/2/26, view 2 Oct. 1678.
[39] Below; ibid. econ. hist.
[40] Aubrey, Topog. Coll. ed. Jackson, 211.
[41] Below, econ. hist.
[42] W.R.O. 1198/1.
[43] Ibid. 88/3/3, ct. rec., 1740.
[44] W.R.O., G 7/360/9.
[45] Local inf.
[46] For Twatley, below, manor.
[47] Andrews and Dury, Map (W.R.S. viii), pl. 16.
[48] Inf. from Mr. E. J. Baldwin, Bob Hills, Brokenborough.

extended in the early 19th century westwards and by the addition of a rear north wing. Fosse Farm is an **L**-shaped house of the early or mid 18th century extended to form a square in the 20th: its symmetrical south front has a stone doorcase and rusticated quoins. Gilboa Farm is also 18th-century, Bell Farm is of *c.* 1800, Marsh Farm is of the early 19th century, and Boakley Cliff Farm is mid 19th-century. Beside the Foss Way an apparently 18th-century house, possibly that called Red Lion House in 1773,[49] later Fosse Cottages,[50] was rebuilt in 1938.[51] At the junction of the road through the village and the Tetbury road, an area called Sunset Hill in 1919,[52] are a 19th-century house and a pair of cottages of the early 20th. Beside the Sherston road a row of 10 estate cottages was built in vernacular style with gabled stone roofs mainly in the period 1919–40,[53] and beside each of the Tetbury road, the Charlton–Tetbury road, and the Sherston road a pair of estate cottages was built *c.* 1900. A public house beside the Sherston road was called the Bull in the early 1880s, the Red Bull in 1899[54] and 1987.

The workhouse was the only building in the south-east corner of the parish in 1840,[55] but others may have been erected by 1872 when Malmesbury urban sanitary district took in two pieces of land. In 1884 those lands had on them a bacon curing factory beside Park Road and buildings in Burnham Road, at the north-west end of Foundry Road, and at the south end of Bremilham Road. The land on the north-west side of Shipton Hill and between Foundry Road and Burnham Road transferred to Brokenborough by 1884 then had on it houses, cottages, and industrial buildings in Foundry Road and Shipton Hill and the police station in Burnham Road. A large house, Burnham House, was built in Burnham Road between 1884 and 1899.[56] Other houses to be built on what was Brokenborough Within include cottages in Burnham Road, council houses at the east end of Athelstan Road, at the east end of Pool Gastons Road, and in Hobbes Close, an estate of private houses on the site of the bacon factory near Staines bridge, and private houses in St. Aldhelm's Road and at the east end of Old Alexander Road.

On the 25 a. transferred to Malmesbury in 1934 eight council houses were built in Pool Gastons Road in 1932.[57] Other council houses were later built in the same road, at the west end of Athelstan Road, in Avon Road, Alexander Road, Newnton Grove, and near the swimming pool built in 1961.[58] To the north, part of the housing estate called White Lion Park was built.[59] On the 25 a. transferred to Malmesbury in 1956 the workhouse,

closed in 1933,[60] was converted in 1937 and 1938 to 20 houses called Bremilham Terrace,[61] a total of 58 council houses was built in Corn Gastons in 1954 and 1956,[62] Malmesbury secondary modern school was built in 1954,[63] and council houses in Bremilham Rise later replaced Bremilham Terrace.[64] On the 9 ha. transferred to Malmesbury in 1984 the Parklands estate of 34 council houses and 21 old people's bungalows was built in 1958,[65] *c.* 30 sheltered homes for old people were built in 1965,[66] and 26 council houses and 28 old people's bungalows were built in 1968.[67]

Long Newnton airfield, half in Brokenborough, was laid out as a decoy for Kemble airfield in 1940, and almost immediately began to be used to train for night flying. In 1941 it had two runways, a perimeter track, and four hangars, and more hangars were built in 1942. The airfield was used only for storage after 1945: most later reverted to agriculture but a few buildings, including the control tower, survived in 1987.[68]

MANOR AND OTHER ESTATES. In 1086 Malmesbury abbey held a 50-hide estate called Brokenborough. The abbey later claimed that an estate of 100 *mansae* called Brokenborough was granted to it by King Edwy in 956 and that in 1065 King Edward confirmed to it a 50-hide estate called Brokenborough. The estate in 1086 included Corston in Malmesbury, is likely to have included Bremilham, Cowfold in Malmesbury, and Grittenham in Brinkworth, and possibly included Rodbourne in Malmesbury, Sutton Benger, and lands later in Westport parish: of all those only Corston was mentioned in Domesday Book. The abbey claimed that the estate in 1065 included Bremilham, Corston, Cowfold, Grittenham, Rodbourne, and Sutton Benger; the boundaries appended to what it claimed was a copy of Edwy's grant of 956 took in much more of its 13th-century Wiltshire estate, but omitted part of it alienated in the late 11th century. It is doubtful that Edwy and Edward made grants in the terms cited by the abbey,[69] and very likely that the abbey held Brokenborough village, its land, and other nearby land from or soon after the abbey's foundation. In 1086 the places included in the large estate called Brokenborough may have been separate entities, as they all were later. The manor of *BROKENBOROUGH* was held by the abbey until the Dissolution.[70] In 1552 the king gave the manor, except a meadow and some woodland, to John Dudley, duke of Northumberland, in an exchange,[71] and in 1553 Northumberland sold it

[49] *Andrews and Dury, Map* (W.R.S. viii), pl. 16.
[50] O.S. Map 6″, Wilts. VIII (1889 edn.).
[51] W.R.O., G 7/760/105.
[52] O.S. Map 6″, Wilts. VIII. NW. (1924 edn.).
[53] Ibid. Wilts. VIII. SW. (1924 edn.); W.R.O., G 7/505/1.
[54] O.S. Maps 6″, Wilts. VIII (1889 edn.), VIII. SW. (1900 edn.).
[55] W.R.O., tithe award.
[56] O.S. Map 6″, Wilts. VIII (1889 and later edns.); above; for the factory, below, Malmesbury, trade and ind.
[57] W.R.O., G 21/350/1; date on bldg.
[58] For the swimming pool, below, Malmesbury, public services.
[59] Below, Westport, introduction.
[60] *W.A.M.* xlvii. 151.

[61] W.R.O., G 21/132/21.
[62] Ibid. G 7/505/1; G 21/132/3.
[63] Below, Malmesbury, educ.
[64] Ibid. introduction.
[65] W.R.O., G 7/360/10.
[66] Ibid. 2248/1.
[67] Inf. from Housing and Property Services Dept., N. Wilts. district council, Chippenham.
[68] C. Ashworth, *Action Stations*, v. 118–19.
[69] *V.C.H. Wilts.* ii, pp. 88, 125–6; Finberg, *Early Wessex Chart.* pp. 91, 105–6; *Reg. Malm.* i. 311–13, 321–5; above, Bremilham, introduction, manor. The boundaries are recited in *Arch. Jnl.* lxxvii. 42–54; cf. maps in W.A.S. Libr.
[70] *Valor Eccl.* (Rec. Com.), ii. 118–19, 122.
[71] *Cal. Pat.* 1550–3, 369–70.

to Sir James Stumpe,[72] the owner of Charlton manor and other of Malmesbury abbey's estates. The Crown granted the excepted lands to Stumpe through an agent in 1559. Stumpe (d. 1563) settled Brokenborough on his wife Isabel[73] (d. 1573), later wife of Thomas Stafford:[74] the conveyance was found to be imperfect and in 1565 his trustees leased the manor to the Staffords. Stumpe had a daughter Elizabeth (d. 1585), wife of Henry Knyvett (knighted 1574, d. 1598), and in 1566 the trustees conveyed the manor to the Knyvetts.[75] From 1598 to 1987 Brokenborough descended with Charlton manor in the Howard family and with the earldoms of Suffolk and Berkshire.[76] The manor included c. 2,200 a. c. 1840;[77] 155 a. of Twatley farm were sold in 1857,[78] c. 220 a. of Hyam farm were sold between 1912 and 1927,[79] and Marsh farm, c. 260 a., was sold c. 1985. In 1987 the Charlton Park estate owned 1,548 a. in Brokenborough parish.[80]

In the late 12th or early 13th century Malmesbury abbey granted 1 yardland in Brokenborough to be held freely by Wibert son of William.[81] In 1242–3 William le Theyn held an estate there assessed as $\frac{1}{10}$ knight's fee.[82] William apparently had a son Miles whose son Geoffrey le Theyn claimed land in Brokenborough against relatives in 1249.[83] Other members of the Theyn family held land in Brokenborough in the 1260s but apparently not after 1268 when William Theyn conveyed an estate there and in Charlton to Roger Charlton.[84] The land in Brokenborough descended with that in Charlton in the Charlton family, of which Wibert son of William may have been a member.[85] It belonged to Robert Charlton (fl. 1387),[86] Walter Charlton (d. by 1444),[87] Wibert Charlton (fl. 1454),[88] and John Charlton. In 1478 John sold it to Sir Roger Tocotes[89] (d. 1492).[90] Tocotes may have settled it on his wife's son Sir Richard Beauchamp, Lord St. Amand, whose son Anthony St. Amand[91] may have held it in 1526.[92] About 24 a. of it apparently passed with the Charlton land to the Long family of Draycot Cerne and was merged with Brokenborough manor in the early 17th century.[93] The rest of the estate was apparently bought in 1535 by William Stumpe from another Roger Tocotes.[94] Stumpe (d. 1552) was succeeded by his son Sir James Stumpe[95] (d. 1563), and his part of the estate, 88 a. in 1558,[96] passed with Brokenborough manor to Henry and Elizabeth Knyvett,[97] who conveyed it to Sir James's brother John in 1564.[98] John Stumpe (d. 1600) held other lands in Brokenborough.[99] What had been Sir Roger Tocotes's was apparently what became FOSSE,[1] later Upper Fosse, farm. It passed to Stumpe's son James (d. 1602) and to James's son William, a minor in 1602,[2] who was presumably the William Stumpe who held the land in 1644.[3] Thomas Stumpe held it in 1671[4] and 1680.[5] Fosse farm belonged to William Robins in 1737. In 1760 Anne Robins, a widow, sold it to Mary Pitt[6] (d. by 1829), a widow, later wife of Stiles Rich. It passed to Mary Pitt's grandson Alfred Pitt who sold the farm, 60 a., to Thomas, earl of Suffolk and of Berkshire, in 1837.[7] It was absorbed by Brokenborough manor.

In 1242–3 John Mautravers held land in Brokenborough assessed as $\frac{1}{4}$ knight's fee.[8] An estate, assessed as $\frac{1}{4}$ knight's fee in 1428[9] and possibly the same, was conveyed in 1340 by Sir John Mauduit to his son-in-law John Moleyns (d. 1360),[10] who in the same year was granted free warren in the demesne lands.[11] The estate descended in the Moleyns, Hungerford, and Hastings families with Lea manor to Henry Hastings, earl of Huntingdon,[12] who sold it to Anthony Webb in 1571.[13] Webb apparently sold the estate, c. 42 a., to William Bailey in 1593.[14] Bailey (d. 1621) had a son Giles[15] (d. 1645 or 1646) who devised land in Brokenborough to his grandsons Giles Bailey and Anthony Bailey.[16] In 1655 Anthony Bailey held the land later called BOAKLEY farm, c. 88 a.[17] Later owners of the farm were said to be Giles Bailey, Daniel Bennett (fl. c. 1758), Daniel's son Giles (fl. 1780), Giles Bailey Bennett (fl. 1810), and Daniel's grandson Daniel Bennett of Faringdon House (Berks., now Oxon.).[18] The farm, 90 a., was for sale in 1816.[19] Sarah Godwin owned it in 1839,[20] H. F. Gibson in 1910,[21] and the Misses Geneste in 1928.[22] In 1934 it was bought from

[72] Cal. Pat. 1550–3, 258; P.R.O., CP 25(2)/65/533, no. 23.
[73] P.R.O., C 142/135, no. 1; W.R.O. 88/1/43.
[74] V.C.H. Wilts. xi. 8.
[75] P.R.O., C 3/108/18; C 142/257, no. 82; W.R.O. 88/1/58; 88/1/61.
[76] Below, Charlton, manors.
[77] W.R.O., tithe award.
[78] Ibid. 137/125/58.
[79] Below, Westport, manors.
[80] Inf. from Mr. A. Witchell, Messrs. Humberts, 10 St. Mary Street, Chippenham.
[81] Reg. Malm. ii. 396.
[82] Bk. of Fees, ii. 733, where Theyn is called Vain. Cf. Reg. Malm. ii. 389–90.
[83] Civil Pleas, 1249 (W.R.S. xxvi), pp. 90, 148.
[84] P.R.O., CP 25(1)/251/21, nos. 29, 33; ibid. JUST 1/998A, rot. 16.
[85] Below, Charlton, manors.
[86] Cal. Close, 1385–9, 454, 462.
[87] Feet of F. 1377–1509 (W.R.S. xli), pp. 68–9.
[88] W.R.O. 88/1/17B; P.R.O., C 1/17, no. 174.
[89] Feet of F. 1377–1509 (W.R.S. xli), p. 157.
[90] Cal. Inq. p.m. Hen. VII, i, p. 369.
[91] Complete Peerage, xi. 302–3; W.R.O. 88/1/17.
[92] P.R.O., CP 25(2)/46/319, no. 26.
[93] W.R.O. 88/2/46, f. 60; below, Charlton, manors; ibid. Draycot Cerne, manor.
[94] W.R.O. 88/1/22.

[95] W.N. & Q. viii. 394–5.
[96] W.R.O. 88/2/41.
[97] Above.
[98] W.R.O. 88/1/46.
[99] Below.
[1] W.R.O. 88/2/45.
[2] W.N. & Q. viii. 533–4.
[3] W.R.O. 1589/61, lease, Westport to Bailey, 1644.
[4] Ibid. 88/2/18.
[5] Ibid. 88/2/26, view 28 Apr. 1680.
[6] Ibid. 88/10/12.
[7] Ibid. 88/5/30.
[8] Bk. of Fees, ii. 733.
[9] Feud. Aids, v. 236.
[10] Feet of F. 1327–77 (W.R.S. xxix), pp. 62–4; Complete Peerage, ix. 39.
[11] Cal. Chart. R. 1327–41, 468.
[12] Below, Lea and Cleverton, manors.
[13] W.R.O. 88/1/72.
[14] Ibid. 79B/13, deed, Webb to Bailey, 1593; lease, Bailey to Woodroffe, 1593; 88/2/45; 130/25, deed, Webb to Pinkney, 1587.
[15] P.R.O., C 142/415, no. 89.
[16] W.R.O. 79B/13, will of Giles Bailey.
[17] Ibid. 79B/13, marriage articles, 1655.
[18] Ibid. 88/3/10; 88/5/24; ibid. A 1/345/61.
[19] Ibid. 315/28/4.
[20] Ibid. tithe award.
[21] Ibid. Inland Revenue, val. reg. 9.
[22] Ibid. G 7/501/1.

the Genestes by J. E. Baldwin (d. 1982), members of whose family, including his son Mr. E. J. Baldwin, owned the farm, c. 130 a., in 1987.[23]

In the early 15th century John West, a prominent local official, may have held land freely in Brokenborough,[24] as another John West did in the early 16th century. The later John's son Henry held c. 180 a. which he sold to William Stumpe (d. 1552) in 1551–2. Stumpe's son Sir James[25] (d. 1563), the owner of Brokenborough manor from 1553, leased WEST'S to West (d. c. 1557) and his wife Anne (fl. 1570) for life. In 1564 Anne and her husband Thomas Feltham disputed the freehold with Sir James's daughter Elizabeth and her husband Henry Knyvett.[26] The Knyvetts apparently held it in 1581,[27] and in 1622 John Morley, Henry West's grandson, quitclaimed to their grandson Thomas, Lord Howard.[28] The estate, which may have included the site of Twatley Farm, was absorbed by Brokenborough manor.[29]

Several small estates in Brokenborough held freely in the Middle Ages included one conveyed by Thomas of Purton to Adam Sturmy[30] who apparently held it in 1236.[31] Purton gave a rent of 2s. from it to Bradenstoke priory.[32] Robert Sturmy of Seagry, who had a son Adam, conveyed 1 yardland in Brokenborough, possibly the same land, to Thomas Goter in 1311.[33] Possibly in the early 13th century, certainly from the late 13th, land in Brokenborough was part of an estate centred on Purton:[34] in 1421 some was part of a manor called Gascrick,[35] and in 1476 some, with land in Purton, was given to endow the Wootton and York chantry in Ramsbury church. The chantry was apparently dissolved c. 1539.[36] Another estate was held by John Malliard (d. 1534) whose son Thomas[37] in 1546 sold it to Matthew King[38] (fl. 1570).[39] Land belonged to St. Mary's chantry in Westport church in 1478:[40] what was said to be that land was acquired by King from Henry and Elizabeth Knyvett in 1564.[41] King's land was acquired by his son-in-law John Stumpe in 1571[42] and passed with Stumpe's other land.[43]

From 1249 or earlier to 1928 land in Brokenborough was part of Bremilham manor, as were the detached parts of Bremilham parish encompassed by Brokenborough until 1884. In 1249 the lord of Bremilham held 36 a. in the open fields,[44] a total of 51 a. c. 1600[45] and of 64 a. in 1897.[46] In

the 16th century and early 17th other freeholds in Brokenborough parish included a total of c. 85 a.[47] Some of that descended with Foxley manor,[48] some with Whitchurch and Milbourne manor in Malmesbury.[49]

TWATLEY farm was bought in 1857 by T. G. Smith[50] (d. 1908), from 1871 the lord of Easton Grey manor. Smith's heir was his sister Honora (d. 1916), wife of the Revd. George Wilder, and members of the Wilder family owned the farm in 1910. It was bought c. 1925, possibly from Honora's son and heir Graham Wilder, by H. C. Cox (d. c. 1945).[51] Cox, a Canadian, deputy master of the Beaufort hunt, until 1939 lived at Twatley mainly in the winter: he used the estate as a base from which to hunt and added more land to it.[52] The farmhouse, later called Whatley Manor, was apparently rebuilt in the 18th century. Presumably between 1857 and 1871 it was enlarged by incorporating or replacing a range of outbuildings to the north-west.[53] R. R. Neeld lived in the house in the period 1899–1924 or longer.[54] Cox altered the inside and added a west wing. He greatly extended the stable court, built other stables and coach houses, and laid out ornamental gardens and a small park. On the Sherston road Smith built the east lodge, Cox the west lodge.[55] Cox's executors sold the estate to H. I. Coriat and his wife Priscilla, who owned it until c. 1957.[56] It later belonged to R. J. Rennie who c. 1961 divided it. In 1987 Whatley Manor was a hotel and Twatley Manor farm, with buildings converted from some of Cox's stables and coach houses, belonged to Mr. J. E. Willis.[57]

Malmesbury abbey owned the tithes from Brokenborough,[58] and after the Dissolution they were part of Brokenborough manor.[59] When the tithes were commuted in 1840 Thomas, earl of Suffolk and of Berkshire, owned nearly all the land and great tithes of the parish. Great tithes on their own land, a total of 23 a., were owned by John Hill and George Woodruffe. Great tithes owned by the rector of Bremilham from 117 a. and by Thomas and Mary Anne Gaby from 12 a. were commuted.[60]

ECONOMIC HISTORY. Malmesbury abbey's large estate called Brokenborough was assessed at

[23] Inf. from Mr. E. J. Baldwin, Bob Hills, Brokenborough.
[24] Cal. Fine R. 1430–7, 69, 195; P.R.O., C 1/14, no. 1.
[25] W.N. & Q. viii. 393–5; W.R.O. 88/1/34; 88/2/41.
[26] W.R.O. 88/2/17; 130/1A, lease, Stumpe to West, 1552; P.R.O., C 3/107/14; above.
[27] W.R.O. 88/1/85.
[28] Ibid. 88/1/131.   [29] Ibid. 88/2/34.
[30] Cat. Anct. D. ii, C 2029, 2240.
[31] Close R. 1234–7, 341.
[32] Bradenstoke Cart. (W.R.S. xxxv), p. 75.
[33] Cat. Anct. D. ii, C 3448, 5410.
[34] Ibid. vi, C 6036; P.R.O., SC 12/1/1, rot. 14; above.
[35] Cat. Anct. D. iii, C 2969.
[36] Ibid. vi, C 6194; V.C.H. Wilts. xii. 44.
[37] P.R.O., C 142/56, no. 98.
[38] Ibid. CP 25(2)/46/324, no. 25.
[39] W.R.O. 88/2/17, view 28 Sept. 12 Eliz. I.
[40] Ibid. 88/1/16.
[41] Ibid. 88/1/52.
[42] Cal. Pat. 1575–8, p. 502; P.R.O., C 3/107/49.
[43] W.R.O. 88/2/46, f. 60v.; above.
[44] P.R.O., CP 25(1)/251/15, no. 30; inf. from Mrs. B. Collins, Cowage Farm, Norton; above, Bremilham, introduction, manor.
[45] W.R.O. 88/2/45.
[46] W.A.S. Libr., sale cat. ii, no. 19.
[47] W.R.O. 88/2/45; 88/2/46, ff. 60–61v.
[48] e.g. Cal. Pat. 1549–51, 301; below, Foxley, manor.
[49] e.g. L. & P. Hen. VIII, xx (2), p. 539; below, Malmesbury, manors.
[50] W.R.O., A 1/345/61; ibid. 88/10/22, sale cat., 1857.
[51] P. Saunders, Almost a Fairy Story: Hist. of Easton Grey, hist. notes by R. E. Sandell; W.R.O., Inland Revenue, val. reg. 9; ibid. A 1/355/239; local inf.
[52] V.C.H. Wilts. iv. 371; local inf.
[53] W.R.O., tithe award; O.S. Map 6″, Wilts. VIII (1889 edn.); above.
[54] Kelly's Dir. Wilts. (1899 and later edns.); W.R.O., A 1/355/234.
[55] W.R.O., tithe award; O.S. Map 6″, Wilts. VIII (1889 and later edns.); local inf.
[56] W.R.O., A 1/355/379; ibid. G 7/505/1; local inf.
[57] Local inf.
[58] P.R.O., SC 6/Hen. VIII/3986, rott. 101d.–102.
[59] Ibid. E 305/20/Box H/8.
[60] W.R.O., tithe award.

50 hides in 1086; what became Brokenborough parish may have been 14. With 64 ploughteams on land for 60 the estate was fully exploited, mostly by *villani*, and there was a small proportion of demesne. There were 8 mills, 50 a. of meadow, 30 a. of pasture, and woodland 3 leagues by 2, but Brokenborough village is likely to have had a small proportion of them.[61] In 1210 its Brokenborough estate was the abbey's most valuable, and, with 64 oxen, was stocked for arable farming: the very high value suggests that land elsewhere was accounted for with Brokenborough's.[62]

In the early 13th century Brokenborough's arable and pastures were clearly open, and between then and the earlier 18th century they were inclosed by stages. Between 1222 and 1246 inhooks were proposed and probably made, with corn sown on temporarily inclosed fallow which would otherwise have been common pasture for sheep. The lord and tenants of Bremilham then had land and pasture rights in the open field.[63] In the late 14th century the land of Brokenborough remained open.[64] Although there was a Little field in 1369,[65] most arable was in two apparently roughly equal fields, called West and North in 1249.[66] There were common pastures, and both meadow land and woodland were apparently commonable. Malmesbury abbey's demesne was the largest holding[67] but between them the customary tenants, *c.* 27 in 1284, may have held much more land. The customary works by tenants may have been enough to cultivate the demesne[68] which in 1396 included 180 a. of arable and 15 a. of meadow and had on it 4 avers, 24 oxen, 2 cows, and 200 sheep.[69] Later evidence shows that the customary tenants of Brokenborough had to provide 21 mowers and 21 haymakers for each of two demesne meadows, a total of 28 a., and 4 of each for a third, 3 a. Customary tenants from Sutton Benger helped to mow the two meadows.[70] A large barn was built on the demesne in the late 13th century,[71] another in the late Middle Ages,[72] and a farmhouse called the place house was referred to *c.* 1600.[73] In 1478 the arable strips of the demesne, customary tenants, and freeholders were apparently intermingled, and by then the demesne had apparently been leased.[74] In the early 16th century most of it was leased as a single farm; some meadow lands and the woodland and warren of Hyam which may have been in Westport parish, were leased separately. In 1539–40 the *c.* 20 customary holdings, some

of 2 or more yardlands, totalled *c.* 20 yardlands[75] and the *c.* 6 freeholds possibly totalled *c.* 10 yardlands.[76]

The common pastures of Brokenborough were possibly in the extreme north and extreme southeast. They had been inclosed by the mid 16th century.[77] That in the south-east, Gaston, may have been *c.* 75 a.;[78] evidence of *c.* 1613 shows that in the north, called New leaze after inclosure, to have been 150–200 a.[79] At inclosure New leaze was divided, and allotments, mainly of between 5 a. and 15 a., were added to most holdings.[80] Other land, especially parts of the demesne and freeholds, was in closes in the 16th century;[81] in the 1570s Hyam park, partly in Brokenborough, was enlarged,[82] and *c.* 1600 formerly common meadows were apparently several.[83] Most arable, however, remained open and in West and North fields. There was still a small third field, called South in 1558 and later, but few held land in it. Cultivation in West and North fields was apparently in small strips,[84] and in the 16th century small parts of both fields were used as meadow.[85] Other parts, in which the demesne lay, may have been inclosed in the later 16th century.[86] Feeding in the fields was supervised by the manor court, and in 1580 the homage met to consider a proposal to inclose West field. Sheep were usually stinted at two for each acre held.[87] About 1613 West field and North field were each *c.* 425 a.; a further 116 a. of West and 25 a. of North were said to have been inclosed.[88] Nearly all of both fields was inclosed between then and *c.* 1700. Newly inclosed lands and the inclosure process were frequently mentioned in the mid 17th century,[89] but there is no evidence of formal agreement. In the 1660s John Aubrey referred to much recent, and continuing, inclosure at Brokenborough, a new preference for wheat to barley, and conversion of arable to pasture.[90] There was 200 a. or more of open field in 1672,[91] but after *c.* 1700 apparently only a small and fragmented residue survived.[92] From then until the later 20th century nearly all the parish was a patchwork of closes averaging *c.* 10 a.[93]

Although Brokenborough was outside Braydon forest at every perambulation,[94] rights to wood and pasture in the forest or its purlieus were claimed in 1570 or earlier by the tenants of Brokenborough manor:[95] the claims possibly originated in some by Malmesbury abbey for its whole estate. Cattle were driven from Brokenborough to be turned into

[61] *V.C.H. Wilts.* ii, pp. 125–6; above, manor.
[62] *Interdict Doc.* (Pipe R. Soc. N.S. xxxiv), 16, 23.
[63] *Reg. Malm.* ii. 185–7; P. Vinogradoff, *Villainage in Eng.* 226.
[64] B.L. Add. MS. 6165, p. 110.
[65] P.R.O., JUST 3/156, rot. 11.
[66] Ibid. CP 25(1)/251/15, no. 30.
[67] B.L. Add. MS. 6165, p. 110.
[68] *Reg. Malm.* i. 182–5, 203.
[69] B.L. Add. MS. 6165, p. 110.
[70] W.R.O. 88/2/34; 88/2/43; 88/2/45.
[71] *Reg. Malm.* ii. 367.
[72] Above, introduction.   [73] W.R.O. 88/2/45.
[74] Ibid. 88/1/16.
[75] P.R.O., SC 6/Hen. VIII/3986, rott. 101–2.
[76] W.R.O. 88/2/45.
[77] Ibid. 88/1/38; 88/2/41; P.R.O., C 1/1319, no. 64.
[78] W.R.O. 88/2/17, ct. baron 28 Sept. 12 Eliz. I; 88/2/41; 88/2/45. The name Gaston survives.
[79] W.R.O. 88/2/46, ff. 60v.–69. New Leaze Lane was so called in 1639: above, introduction.

[80] W.R.O. 88/2/45.
[81] Ibid. 88/1/38; 88/2/41.
[82] Ibid. 88/1/75; 88/1/82.
[83] Ibid. 88/2/45.
[84] Ibid.; 88/2/43.
[85] Ibid. 88/2/17, ct. baron 4 Sept. 15 Eliz. I; 88/2/21, view 22 Sept. 1575; 88/2/45.
[86] Cf. ibid. 88/1/38; 88/2/45.
[87] Ibid. 88/2/17; 88/2/21, especially view 24 Sept. 22 Eliz. I; 88/2/23–4; 88/2/29.
[88] Ibid. 88/2/46, ff. 60–69v.
[89] e.g. ibid. 79B/13, marriage articles, 1656; 88/2/24; 1589/61, lease, Westport to Bailey, 1644.
[90] Aubrey, *Topog. Coll.* ed. Jackson, 211.
[91] W.R.O. 88/2/52.
[92] Ibid. 88/2/19; 88/2/37B, pp. 19–25.
[93] W.R.O., tithe award map; O.S. Maps 6", Wilts. VIII. NE., NW., SW. (1924 edn.); below.
[94] *V.C.H. Wilts.* iv. 444–5.
[95] B.L. Stowe MS. 1046, f. 45. Comment about the forest is below, Charlton, introduction, econ. hist.

the purlieus at Stonehill in Charlton. They were not restricted to any part of the forest or purlieus and were not stinted.[96] In 1576 the manor court ordered the tenants to appoint a herdsman to keep their cattle in the forest for a fortnight in September.[97] In Charlton quarter Brokenborough manor was said to have woodland within a 2-mile perimeter, in 1590 said to be 100 a., and 4 a. of heath, presumably a clearing.[98] Braydon was disafforested in 1630, and in 1631 Thomas, earl of Berkshire, lord of Brokenborough manor and other manors nearer the forest, inclosed parts of the purlieus in respect of all those manors,[99] but apparently none was added to any farm in Brokenborough.

Until the 18th century it seems that nearly all the farms in the parish were based in Brokenborough village: Twatley and Boakley were the exceptions.[1] The demesne, which in 1556 included a total of 280 a. in West and North fields, had been leased in portions by 1590. The largest portion, Brokenborough farm, was c. 290 a. c. 1600 when it included only 33 a. of open field. Hyam park, c. 201 a. in Brokenborough and Westport in 1649, was still leased separately, and by 1590 farms of 80 a. and 50 a., mainly in the open fields, had apparently been made from the demesne. In 1590 most of the c. 23 copyholds and c. 6 freeholds included land in each main open field and an allotment of New leaze.[2] A total of c. 990 a. was copyhold c. 1613, of c. 310 a. freehold. Apart from Brokenborough farm there were some 25 farms in the parish averaging c. 50 a. with only one exceeding 100 a.,[3] and that was the pattern of tenure throughout the 17th century and in the early 18th.[4]

In the 18th century new farmsteads were built on inclosures outside the village. Those called Fosse, Upper Fosse, and Gilboa were built between 1700 and 1773, and those called Marsh and Bell between 1773 and 1820.[5] In the later 18th century the farms were reorganized and made fewer.[6] As part of an attempt to improve the Charlton Park estate John, earl of Suffolk and of Berkshire, in 1809 advertised, apparently in vain, for tenants from Northumberland and Scotland for seven farms in Brokenborough: it was intended to increase arable and introduce mechanical threshing.[7] About 1840 there were 817 a. of arable and 1,772 a. of grassland in the parish in 10 main farms. Based in the village Brokenborough farm, 530 a., was half arable and half pasture, and Brook farm, 52 a., was mostly pasture. Twatley farm, 302 a., was also half arable and half pasture, but Boakley, c. 100 a., Bell, 140 a., Gilboa, 269 a., and Marsh, 263 a., were predominantly pasture.

Upper Fosse farm, then called Butts, and Fosse farm, a total of c. 220 a., were worked together. In the north-east 162 a., more arable than pasture, were in Bishoper farm based in Hankerton; in the south 240 a., mostly pasture, were in Hyam farm based in Westport.[8]

More of the parish was converted to grassland between the mid 19th century and the early 20th. The farms based in the parish included c. 650 a. of arable in 1887, only c. 350 a. in 1937. In 1887 they had on them 147 cows, 257 other cattle, 581 sheep, and 143 pigs; 315 cows, 168 other cattle, 432 sheep, and 74 pigs in 1937.[9] By 1910 land had been taken from Brokenborough farm, then 254 a., to enlarge Brook, then 281 a. Fosse farm was then 238 a., Upper Fosse 163 a., Bell 121 a., Marsh 263 a., Gilboa 236 a., and Boakley c. 100 a. Between 1857, when it was 153 a., and the mid 1920s Twatley farm may have been used as much for sport as agriculture. In 1910 Bishoper farm and Hyam farm still included a total of c. 400 a. in the parish, and Cowage (Bremilham) farm 64 a.[10] In 1920 Boakley Cliff was a small dairy farm.[11]

The pattern changed again in the 1960s and 1970s. Much land was taken in hand as part of the Charlton Park estate, much pasture was ploughed, and the average size of the fields was greatly increased. In 1987 c. 1,350 a. of Brokenborough parish were worked with land in Charlton by that estate from Brokenborough Farm and buildings near Charlton Park: a large new grain store stood at the junction of the road through the village and the Tetbury road. There was pasture in the east and a dairy at Brokenborough Farm, but in most of the west and north cereals were grown. Bishoper farm included c. 200 a., mostly arable, in the parish,[12] and Marsh farm, c. 260 a., was also mainly arable. Boakley was a mainly dairy farm of c. 130 a.,[13] and Hyam still included c. 200 a., mainly pasture, in the parish.[14] The Twatley estate was used mainly to feed horses from c. 1925 to c. 1945. In the later 20th century Twatley Manor farm was worked from converted stables and coach houses of Whatley Manor and included land in Easton Grey.[15]

Brokenborough parish never seems to have contained much woodland. Hyam and Twatley were woods in the early 13th century[16] and the 16th.[17] Later the woods of Hyam park were assigned to Westport parish[18] and Twatley farm contained no woodland.[19] In 1840 there were 4 a. of woodland in the parish,[20] and in the later 20th century several small plantations were made.[21]

In the later 13th century three mills may have been part of Brokenborough manor.[22] One, still

[96] W.R.O. 88/10/52.
[97] Ibid. 88/2/21, view 21 Sept. 1576.
[98] Ibid. 88/2/34; 88/2/43.
[99] Ibid. 88/9/11; *W.N. & Q.* vii. 452–4.
[1] Above, introduction.
[2] *Cal. Cttee. for Compounding*, iii. 1969; W.R.O. 88/1/38; 88/2/43; 88/2/45; 88/9/2.
[3] W.R.O. 88/2/46, ff. 60–9.
[4] Ibid. 88/2/19.
[5] *Andrews and Dury, Map* (W.R.S. viii), pl. 16; C. Greenwood, *Map of Wilts.* (1820); above, introduction.
[6] W.R.O. 88/2/56–7.
[7] Ibid. 88/10/9; *V.C.H. Wilts.* iv. 88.
[8] W.R.O., tithe award.

[9] P.R.O., MAF 68/1120, sheet 10; MAF 68/3850, no. 120.
[10] W.R.O., Inland Revenue, val. reg. 9; ibid. 137/125/58; above, manor.
[11] W.A.S. Libr., sale cat. xvii, no. 61.
[12] Inf. from Mr. A. Witchell, Messrs. Humberts, 10 St. Mary Street, Chippenham.
[13] Inf. from Mr. E. J. Baldwin, Bob Hills, Brokenborough.
[14] Inf. from Mrs. U. Cox Cox, Hyam Farm, Malmesbury.
[15] Local inf.   [16] *Reg. Malm.* i. 187.
[17] P.R.O., E 315/104, f. 198.
[18] W.R.O. 1589/68.
[19] Ibid. 137/125/58.   [20] Ibid. tithe award.
[21] Inf. from Mr. Witchell.
[22] *Reg. Malm.* i. 186–7.

held freely as part of the manor in the 16th and 17th centuries, was Bremilham Mill in Westport.[23] A water mill was held by copy in the 16th century,[24] by lease in the 17th:[25] it may have been near Back bridge,[26] either in Brokenborough parish or Westport. No certain site of a mill in Brokenborough parish is known.

It is unlikely that Brokenborough shared much in the Malmesbury cloth industry, but a weaver and a wool spinner were mentioned in 1349,[27] a broad weaver in the 1660s,[28] and a clothier in 1680.[29] A bacon factory, a slaughterhouse, and the Westport ironworks were on the land which was for three years Brokenborough Within parish.[30] In the late 1920s and the 1930s, and in the 1980s when it was an hotel, Whatley Manor provided employment in the parish.[31]

LOCAL GOVERNMENT. Malmesbury abbey had regalian rights in Brokenborough and in the later 14th century or earlier held view of frankpledge there.[32] In 1340 John Moleyns was granted liberties which included view of frankpledge,[33] but neither he nor his descendants seems to have exercised them in respect of their Brokenborough estate. In the early 16th century the abbey held view of frankpledge with a manor court twice a year at Brokenborough:[34] in 1549 it was claimed that before the Dissolution it was attended by the men of Lea and Cleverton because no court was held at Lea.[35] No Lea business was done at Brokenborough after the Dissolution.

Court records from the mid 16th century to the early 19th survive for Brokenborough manor.[36] For most of that period courts called view of frankpledge with the court of the manor were held twice yearly, in spring and autumn. In the early part of the period the distinction between the two types of court was observed: a jury affirmed the tithingman's presentments and the homage presented manorial business. Later a single panel acted as jurors and homage. In the later 16th century and earlier 17th the taking of strays and of excess tolls by millers were frequently presented under leet jurisdiction. Less frequently unsworn males over 12 were ordered to take an oath of allegiance, participants in affrays and unlawful games were punished, and tapsters were amerced. Failures to practice archery and to keep bows and arrows were presented in the earlier 17th century,[37] as was misuse of greyhounds.[38] The homage presented deaths of tenants and surrenders of copyholds, misuse of common pastures, and buildings out of repair:

the court made rules for common pasturage and fixed penalties for infringements, ordered repairs to boundaries, gates, and watercourses, dealt with other copyhold and agrarian business, and elected officers. In 1579 a court punished a suitor for refusing to doff his cap and for other contumacy,[39] in 1625 an overseer of highways for neglect,[40] and in 1631 an inhabitant for idleness.[41] Open-field husbandry still gave rise to business in the courts in the later 17th century, as did the condition of hedges, ditches, and roads; but the business was becoming stereotyped and in the 18th century most business concerned copyhold tenure and the appointment of officers. Throughout the period courts baron in addition to the biannual court were occasionally held for copyhold business.

Brokenborough relieved its own poor.[42] The cost was £61 in 1775–6. It rose from £55 in the early 1780s to £282 in 1802–3, a rate of increase above average. Continuous relief was given to 26 adults, and occasional relief to 59, in 1802–3, to 21 and 12 respectively in 1812–13. The cost of poor relief was usually between £200 and £300 a year in the early 19th century but above £300 from 1816–17 to 1821–2 and in 1829–30 and 1830–1. Although the annual changes were smaller than in some parishes the cost of poor relief in Brokenborough was usually about average for a parish of its size.[43] The parish became part of Malmesbury poor-law union in 1835[44] and of North Wiltshire district in 1974.[45]

CHURCH. Brokenborough church had apparently been built by the 12th century.[46] In 1248 it may have been served by Malmesbury abbey[47] which took the tithes of Brokenborough.[48] From 1341 or earlier to 1879 it was a chapel of Westport church, and from 1879 to 1984 a chapel of Charlton church.[49] In the early 16th century, because Brokenborough village was sometimes separated by flood water from Westport church, the bishop consecrated Brokenborough church for christenings and marriages and authorized burials.[50] Corpses were buried at Brokenborough in the 17th century and later. Marriages were apparently solemnized at Brokenborough in the 17th century and early 18th, but from c. 1744 only at Westport or Charlton.[51] Brokenborough church was licensed for marriages in 1933.[52] In 1984 a benefice, in the gift of the Church Trust Fund, and a parish of Brokenborough were created and united with those of Malmesbury with Westport: Malmesbury became the parish church.[53]

[23] W.R.O. 88/2/43; below, Westport, econ. hist.
[24] P.R.O., SC 6/Hen. VIII/3986, rot. 101; W.R.O. 88/2/43. [25] W.R.O. 88/2/49.
[26] Ibid. 88/2/24, view 19 Apr. 18 Chas. I.
[27] W.A.M. xxxiii. 400. [28] W.R.O., D 1/42/62.
[29] Williams, Cath. Recusancy (Cath. Rec. Soc.), 334.
[30] Below, Malmesbury, trade and ind.
[31] Local inf. [32] P.R.O., JUST 3/156, rot. 11.
[33] Cal. Chart. R. 1327–41, 468.
[34] P.R.O., E 315/104, f. 198 and v.
[35] Ibid. REQ 2/14/97.
[36] Para. based on W.R.O. 88/2/17–27; 88/2/29; 88/2/33; 88/3/3.
[37] e.g. ibid. 88/2/24, views 16 Apr. 5 Chas. I, 14 Apr. 7 Chas. I.
[38] Ibid. 88/2/24, view 26 Sept. [2] Chas. I.
[39] Ibid. 88/2/21, view 3 Apr. 1579.

[40] Ibid. 88/2/24, view 22 Sept. 1 Chas. I.
[41] Ibid. view 14 Apr. 7 Chas. I.
[42] Ibid. tithe award.
[43] Poor Law Abstract, 1804, 566–7; 1818, 498–9; Poor Rate Returns, 1816–21, 188; 1822–4, 228; 1825–9, 219; 1830–4, 212.
[44] Poor Law Com. 2nd Rep. App. D, 559.
[45] O.S. Map 1/100,000, admin. areas, Wilts. (1974 edn.).
[46] Below.
[47] Reg. Malm. i. 411. [48] Above, manor.
[49] Inq. Non. (Rec. Com.), 167; Lond. Gaz. 7 Mar. 1879, pp. 1957–60; below.
[50] W.R.O., D 1/42/21, ff. 18v.–21v.
[51] Ibid. 1795/1; 1813/6–7; ibid. bishop's transcripts, bdle. 1; Lond. Gaz. 7 Mar. 1879, pp. 1957–8.
[52] W.R.O. 1795/5.
[53] Ch. Com. file, NB 5/116B; inf. from Ch. Com.

The vicar of Westport received moduses in respect of demesne land and of the part of Hyam park in Brokenborough. In 1784–5 he successfully claimed the full value of the small tithes from all the rest of the parish. The tithes were commuted in 1840.[54] There was no glebe in Brokenborough parish.

Until the Reformation the church contained a wheel of 18 small bells rung at the Elevation of the Host.[55] In 1380 the rector of Kellaways may have served Brokenborough,[56] and from the 16th century a curate served apparently more often than the vicar of Westport.[57] In the early 16th century the inhabitants of Brokenborough provided a lodging for a curate and agreed to add 33s. 4d. a year to the curate's stipend when one lived in Brokenborough, but there is evidence that none did for long.[58] The church lacked the *Paraphrases* of Erasmus in 1553[59] and the parishioners implied in 1556 that their expectation of two Sunday services was not being met.[60] The early 17th-century curate Thomas Hobbes, father of the philosopher Thomas Hobbes, was not resident and the parishioners complained that too few sermons were preached.[61] In 1650 they again protested that the church was not well served,[62] and it was claimed in 1665 that no service was held on 12 consecutive Sundays.[63] In 1783 the vicar held a service on alternate Sundays, celebrated communion four times with c. 12 communicants, and catechized.[64] On Census Sunday in 1851 the afternoon service was attended by 61.[65] In the earlier 20th century a service was held every Sunday: communion was celebrated 16 times in 1910 and in 1953, 30 times in 1939.[66] From 1706 Brokenborough received £1 a year from the Lady Frances Winchcombe charity to buy Bibles and prayer books; in 1904 some of the income was spent on books for the Sunday school.[67]

The church of *ST. JOHN THE BAPTIST*, so called in 1763,[68] is of coursed rubble with limestone ashlar dressings and consists of a chancel with north vestry and a nave with north aisle and porch and east belfry. The nave, small and with thick walls, and the chancel, almost square, were apparently built in the 12th century or earlier. The aisle, with a four-bay arcade, was built c. 1200, and, possibly about then, the chancel arch was rebuilt. In the 14th century new windows were made in the east and south walls of the chancel and the

south doorway of the nave was renewed. Apparently in the early 16th century, the date of its doorway and windows, the aisle was rebuilt, probably to a greater width. In the late 16th century or early 17th the only window in the south wall of the nave was heightened and given a dormer roof. The south doorway had been blocked and its porch demolished by the early 19th century. About 1800 the tall window was removed and a wooden belfry replaced or encased a stone bellcot.[69] The church was restored in 1883[70] when much of the exterior stonework was renewed, the north porch was rebuilt, the vestry was added, and the roofs were renewed. An early 17th-century pulpit survives.

The church had 3½ oz. of plate in 1553. In 1987 it had a chalice hallmarked for 1651, a silver paten, and a silver-plated paten.[71] There were two bells and a sanctus bell in 1553. The single bell, cast by John Rudhall in 1801, was rehung in 1977 when the belfry was repaired.[72] The registers of baptisms and burials are complete from 1697:[73] marriages are recorded for the period 1709–44.[74]

NONCONFORMITY. In 1674 two men were presented for not attending church,[75] and a papist and a protestant dissenter lived in the parish in 1676.[76] Meeting houses for Independents were certified in 1815 and 1816.[77] A small chapel for Primitive Methodists was built in 1873[78] and used until c. 1963.[79]

EDUCATION. A day school was started in 1825 and was attended by 17 boys and 5 girls in 1833. Each year the Elizabeth Hodges educational charity gave £2 for three boys to be taught.[80] The school, attended by 20–30, was held in a cottage in 1858,[81] and in 1871 was attended by 12 boys and 21 girls.[82] Two buildings were used by schools in 1881,[83] and later a dame school for small children, to which the charity still paid £2, was held until the 1920s in a room adjoining the post office.[84] In the mid 19th century a school was held in the union workhouse in the south-east corner of the parish.[85]

CHARITY FOR THE POOR. None known.

[54] W.R.O. 88/5/46/4, copy bill, Mitford's opinion, observations regarding Westport vicarage; ibid. tithe award; below, Charlton, church.
[55] Aubrey, *Topog. Coll.* ed. Jackson, 211.
[56] W.R.O., D 1/2/4, f. 47v.
[57] Ibid. D 1/43/1, ff. 24v., 133v.; ibid. bishop's transcripts, bdles. 1–3.
[58] Ibid. D 1/42/21, ff. 18v.–21v.
[59] Ibid. D 1/43/1, f. 133v.
[60] Ibid. D 1/43/2, f. 19v.
[61] Ibid. D 1/42/21, ff. 18v.–21v.; A. Rogow, *Thomas Hobbes*, 25–35.
[62] *W.A.M.* xli. 6.   [63] W.R.O., D 1/42/62.
[64] *Vis. Queries, 1783* (W.R.S. xxvii), pp. 228–9.
[65] P.R.O., HO 129/252/2/11/12.
[66] W.R.O. 1795/4.
[67] *Endowed Char. Wilts.* (N. Div.), 145–6; below, Charlton, church.
[68] J. Ecton, *Thesaurus*, 403. In 1851 the church was called St. Bartholomew's presumably by mistake: P.R.O., HO 129/252/2/11/12.
[69] Pencil drawing by Thomas Hearne in church; B.L. Add.

MS. 36409, f. 28v.; J. Buckler, watercolour in W.A.S. Libr., vol. vi. 19.
[70] J. L. Osborn, *Villages of N. Wilts.* 43; date on rainwater heads.
[71] Nightingale, *Wilts. Plate*, 195; inf. from Mr. P. Redford, 8 Sherston Road.
[72] Walters, *Wilts. Bells*, 42; inf. from Mr. Redford.
[73] W.R.O. 1795/1. Bishop's transcripts for other years in the 17th cent. are ibid.
[74] Ibid. 1795/1; ibid. bishop's transcripts, bdle. 2.
[75] Ibid. D 1/54/6/1, no. 44.
[76] *Compton Census*, ed. Whiteman, 129 n.
[77] *Meeting Ho. Certs.* (W.R.S. xl), pp. 76, 79.
[78] *Kelly's Dir. Wilts.* (1895).
[79] W.R.O. 2244/18.
[80] *Educ. Enq. Abstract*, 1031; for the char. below, Malmesbury, educ.   [81] *Acct. of Wilts. Schs.* 48.
[82] *Returns relating to Elem. Educ.* 420–1.
[83] O.S. Map 6", Wilts. VIII (1889 edn.).
[84] *Endowed Char. Wilts.* (N. Div.), 146; W.R.O., F 8/210/3; inf. from Mr. E. J. Baldwin, Bob Hills, Brokenborough.
[85] *Acct. of Wilts. Schs.* 32.

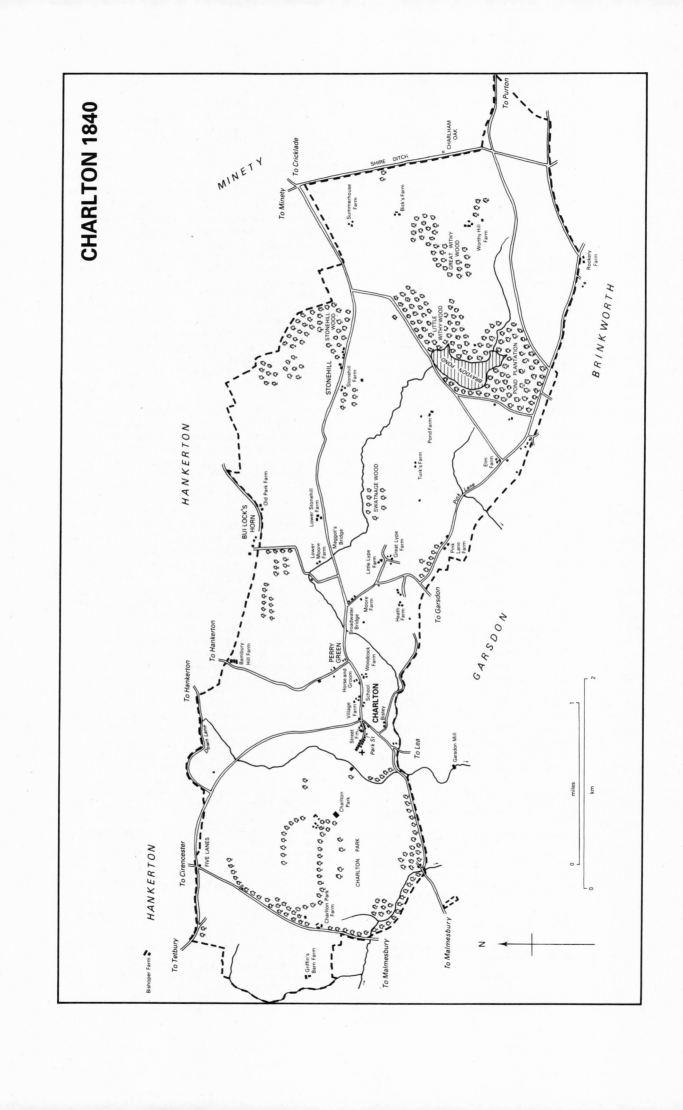

CHARLTON 1840

CHARLTON

CHARLTON, 3 km. ENE. of Malmesbury, is a small village in a large parish.[86] The parish is rectangular, on an east and west axis, and measures 9.6 km. by 2.5 km., 1,929 ha. (4,766 a.). Its name, which may indicate that early in its history the village was dependent on a larger settlement nearby,[87] and its proximity to Malmesbury, where an abbey stood from the 7th century,[88] suggest that Charlton originated as a settlement for tenants of the abbey. Characteristically of the Wiltshire places so called[89] Charlton was a street village, belonged to the abbey, had in it a prosperous tenantry and little demesne,[90] and was not an early parish. Its church may have been served first by Malmesbury abbey but was a chapel of Westport from the later 13th century until it became a parish church in 1879.[91] Charlton, however, relieved its own poor[92] and in the 19th century was a civil parish.[93]

Charlton's boundaries were recited in the late 11th century or later. Marked by a stream and a road on the south, a stream on the west, and Hankerton on the north they approximated to the later boundaries of the west half of the parish.[94] Down Lane was the boundary with Hankerton in the 16th century[95] and later. The east half of the parish was outside the boundaries c. 1100.[96] The western boundary of Braydon forest in 1225 may then have been the eastern boundary of Charlton: it touched Pink Lane and Swatnage wood. The forest was extended westwards to include Charlton village in 1228, reduced in 1279 to its boundaries of 1225, and reduced further in 1300 when the western boundary was redrawn c. 4 km. to the east.[97] The area between the eastern boundary of Charlton, as defined in 1225, and the western boundary of the forest, as defined in 1300, was among the forest purlieus of which each village near the forest later claimed a particular part.[98] The part claimed and perambulated by Charlton approximated to what the later parish included: the east boundary was Shire ditch dividing it from Minety (then Glos.) and, north and south of Charlham oak, from the forest. Its other boundaries, recited in 1585,[99] 1595,[1] and c. 1600,[2] have not been plotted precisely. From c. 1580 the lord of Charlton manor and the lord of Cloatley manor

in Hankerton disputed part of the purlieus and, almost certainly after the dispute was heard in the Exchequer in 1595, a triangle formed by the Cricklade–Malmesbury road, Shire ditch, and a line from Charlham oak to Stonehill wood, formerly claimed for Cloatley,[3] became Charlton land. In 1630 the Crown inclosed Braydon forest mainly on its boundaries of 1300,[4] and by 1631 the lords of many manors near the forest, including Charlton, had inclosed those parts of the purlieus claimed for their respective manors. Much dispute, two public meetings in the great lodge of the forest, and some compromise followed.[5] The lord of Charlton manor conceded to Garsdon possibly c. 200 a. to the south,[6] and to Oaksey a triangle of c. 100 a., much of the triangle earlier claimed by Cloatley;[7] and if, as seems likely, Brokenborough's woodland was the 84 a. adjoining Brinkworth east of Shire ditch,[8] he added it to Charlton manor. The boundary of the manor became the parish boundary. The triangle of c. 100 a. was apparently regained by the lord of Charlton manor by purchase in the later 17th century,[9] and by the parish. Minor changes were made to the boundaries in the 19th century: that with Hankerton along the Cricklade–Malmesbury road was redefined in 1809,[10] and c. 1882 a detached 2 a. of Charlton WSW. of the village was transferred to Malmesbury and further adjustments were made to Charlton's boundaries with Garsdon, Hankerton, and Malmesbury.[11] Since then the boundaries have been unchanged.

The west part of Charlton parish, containing the older settlement, embraces outcrops of Cornbrash and of clay and limestone of the Forest Marble; Kellaways Clay outcrops near the southern boundary, where there are several small areas of gravel deposits, and around Charlton village.[12] The land is mainly flat, at over 107 m. highest in the north and at below 76 m. lowest in the south where tributaries of the Bristol Avon meet. It favours both arable and pasture and was the site of Charlton's open fields.[13] Kellaways Sand has been exposed in the centre of the parish and in the 17th century was dug.[14] Oxford Clay outcrops in all the east part of the parish, overlain in a few places by glacial deposits. In the centre and east

---

[86] This article was written in 1988. Maps used include O.S. Maps 1", sheet 157 (1968 edn.); 1/50,000, sheet 173 (1974 edn.); 1/25,000, ST 98–9, SU 08 (1959 edns.); 6", Wilts. VIII–IX (1888–9 edns.).
[87] H. P. R. Finberg, 'Charltons and Carltons', *Lucerna*, 144–60.
[88] *V.C.H. Wilts.* iii. 211.
[89] Ibid. x. 33–40; xi. 23, 55–9; xiii. 142, 147–8. Charlton in Hungerford is touched on in *V.C.H. Berks.* iv. 184, 193–4.
[90] Below, econ. hist.
[91] Ibid. church.   [92] Ibid. local govt.
[93] *V.C.H. Wilts.* iv. 343.
[94] *Arch. Jnl.* lxxvii. 8–12.
[95] W.R.O. 88/2/22, view 7 Apr. 27 Eliz. I.
[96] *Arch. Jnl.* lxxvii. 11.
[97] *V.C.H. Wilts.* iv. 444–5, where the citation of the 1228 boundaries omits their ref. to Charlton. Cf. *Close R.* 1227–31, 103.
[98] P.R.O., E 178/2408; W.R.O. 88/10/52.

[99] W.R.O. 88/2/22, view 7 Apr. 27 Eliz. I. For Charlham (Charlton) oak, *W.A.M.* xlv, map at p. 564.
[1] P.R.O., E 134/37 Eliz. I East./13.
[2] W.R.O. 88/2/34.
[3] P.R.O., E 134/37 Eliz. I East./13; below, Hankerton, introduction.
[4] *V.C.H. Wilts.* iv. 406.   [5] W.R.O. 88/10/52.
[6] *W.N. & Q.* vii. 453–4.
[7] W.R.O. 88/1/141; 663/8.
[8] P.R.O., E 134/37 Eliz. I East./13; above, Brokenborough, econ. hist.
[9] Below, manors.
[10] W.R.O., EA/132.
[11] Ibid. tithe award; O.S. Maps 6", Wilts. VIII–IX (1888–9 edns.); *Census*, 1891.
[12] Para. based on Geol. Surv. Maps 1", solid and drift, sheets 251 (1970 edn.), 252 (1974 edn.).
[13] Below, econ. hist.
[14] W.R.O. 88/2/25, view 26 Oct. 23 Chas. I; 88/2/27.

the land, declining westwards from 134 m. on the east boundary to below 91 m., undulates more than in the west. An east–west stream was dammed to form Broad water, later Braydon pond, 6 a. c. 1600:[15] the pond, 40 a., had its present shape in 1773.[16] The clay, unfavourable to arable, can support woodland and has been much used as pasture: it was open to Braydon forest and its purlieus until the 17th century. From the later 16th century to the earlier 18th the contrast between the two halves of the parish was softened: the open fields in the west were inclosed and, after 1631, much clay land to the east was inclosed and improved. From the mid 18th century to the mid 20th most of the parish was a patchwork of fields divided by hedges and averaging c. 10 a., and from the later 19th to the mid 20th most fields were pasture. In the 15th and 16th centuries there was a park called Stonehill north of the Cricklade–Malmesbury road.[17] From the later 16th century land around Charlton Park was imparked:[18] the park wall, recorded in the early 17th century,[19] reached in 1773 to the village, where it divided the park and the churchyard, and ran for 1.5 km. on the east side of what became the Cirencester (Glos.) to Malmesbury road and for 1.5 km. on the north side of the Cricklade–Malmesbury road.[20] Much of the wall, including a later northern part along the road from Hankerton to Tetbury (Glos.), survived in 1988.

The Cirencester–Malmesbury road runs north and south across the west part of the parish, and the Cricklade–Malmesbury road east and west marking parts of the boundary at the north-east and south-west corners; the old Oxford–Bristol road crosses the south-east corner of the parish[21] also marking part of the boundary. The Cricklade–Malmesbury road ran through the purlieus of Braydon forest.[22] In the centre of the parish it crosses a tributary of the Avon at Maggot's bridge and Broadwater bridge, and in the west it forms the east part of Charlton village street. Before Charlton Park was built and land around it imparked[23] the road almost certainly formed the whole street, being diverted southwards when the park was walled.[24] The Oxford–Bristol road, linking Purton and Malmesbury, may also have been diverted after the purlieus were inclosed in 1631, and it declined in importance in the 18th century.[25] The Cricklade–Malmesbury road was turnpiked in 1756, disturnpiked in 1876; the Cirencester–Malmesbury road was completed across Hankerton parish and turnpiked in 1778, disturnpiked

in 1874.[26] Tetbury Way was turnpiked in 1798:[27] it ran from Charlton church to meet the Cirencester–Malmesbury road and the Hankerton–Tetbury road, Down Lane, at a junction called Five Lanes. In 1808 it was replaced by a road, further from Charlton Park, which made a crossroads with the Cricklade–Malmesbury road and the west part of Charlton street and met Down Lane east of Five Lanes.[28] The turnpike house at the crossroads was apparently built c. 1808. The road was disturnpiked in 1876.[29] In 1773 and 1988 other roads linked Charlton to Hankerton, Garsdon, and Lea.[30] To the east the courses of the lanes may have been made or altered when the purlieus were inclosed, and were so when Charlton's common pastures were inclosed c. 1808. Pink Lane remains on the course it followed in 1773, but a westwards extension to link the farmhouses called Heath and Bisley became a footpath in the 19th century, and to the north a roughly parallel road linking Great Lype Farm, Turk's Farm, and Braydon pond also became a footpath.[31] A new turnpike road proposed in 1819 would have linked Garsdon Mill in Garsdon and the Cricklade–Malmesbury road east of Perry Green, enabled the road along the south side of the park to be closed, and taken traffic away from Charlton village, but was not built.[32] About 1626, in the later 17th century, and in the later 18th proposals for a Thames–Avon canal through Charlton came to nought.[33]

Charlton is a street village which was surrounded by its open fields:[34] taken with its name, that arrangement suggests that Charlton was planned as a settlement, possibly soon after Malmesbury abbey's foundation in the late 7th century. No other settlement in the parish has grown to be more than a hamlet. There were several farmsteads and possibly a hamlet called Kingershay east of the village in the Middle Ages.[35] Cottages were built on the waste there in the 16th century,[36] more farmsteads were built after the purlieus were inclosed,[37] and Stonehill, where there was a nonconformist chapel in the 19th century,[38] may have ranked as a hamlet. In the west farmsteads were built away from the village in the 16th century and later[39] and Perry Green at the east end of the street became a hamlet in the 19th century. Charlton had 152 poll-tax payers in 1377, apart from Malmesbury the highest number for a parish in the hundred.[40] In the 16th century the parish was perhaps of average prosperity,[41] but from the 1560s the presence of a large manor house[42] increased the population and overall

---

[15] W.R.O. 88/2/24, view 28 Sept. 2 Chas. I; 88/2/34.
[16] *Andrews and Dury, Map* (W.R.S. viii), pl. 17.
[17] Below, econ. hist.; C. Saxton, *Map of Wilts.* (1576).
[18] Below, manors, econ. hist.
[19] *W.A.M.* xxviii. 169; W.R.O. 88/2/45.
[20] *Andrews and Dury, Map* (W.R.S. viii), pls. 16–17.
[21] J. Ogilby, *Brit.* (1675), pl. 79.
[22] *V.C.H. Wilts.* iv. 445.
[23] Below, manors.
[24] Cf. O.S. Map 6″, Wilts. VIII (1889 edn.).
[25] Below, Malmesbury, introduction.
[26] *V.C.H. Wilts.* iv. 257, 269; *L.J.* xxviii. 581; xxxv. 436; 14 & 15 Vic. c. 76 (Local and Personal); below, Hankerton, introduction.
[27] *L.J.* xli. 655; W.R.O. 88/5/46/3; for the name ibid. 88/2/49.
[28] *W.A.M.* xlii. 619; W.R.O. 88/5/46/3.

[29] *V.C.H. Wilts.* iv. 269; 14 & 15 Vic. c. 76 (Local and Personal).
[30] *Andrews and Dury, Map* (W.R.S. viii), pl. 17.
[31] Ibid.; C. Greenwood, *Map of Wilts.* (1820); O.S. Maps 1″, sheet 34 (1828 edn.); 6″, Wilts. VIII (1889 edn.); W.R.O., tithe award, which shows the junction of Pink Lane and the Garsdon road incorrectly; below, econ. hist.
[32] W.R.O., A 1/370/22HC.
[33] Aubrey, *Nat. Hist. Wilts.* ed. Britton, 30–2; *W.A.M.* xlii. 399.
[34] For the fields, below, econ. hist.
[35] Below.
[36] W.R.O. 88/2/43.
[37] Below.
[38] Ibid. nonconf.
[39] Below.
[40] *V.C.H. Wilts.* iv. 309.
[41] *Taxation Lists* (W.R.S. x), 30.
[42] Below, manors.

wealth of the parish. The tithingman listed 125 adult males living in the parish in 1775.[43] The population increased from 1801, when it was 428, to 1851, when it was 690. A decline from 621 in 1861 to 565 in 1871 was attributed to emigration. From 612 in 1881 the population had fallen to 367 by 1931. After the Second World War temporary housing in Charlton park brought about an increase, to 654 in 1951,[44] but in 1961 there were only 376 inhabitants. In 1981 the population was 427.[45]

To judge from the number of landholders Charlton village was already populous in 1086 but grew little between then and the later 13th century.[46] The site of its church, at the extreme west end of the street, suggests that the church was built when the village was already mature and that the building of Charlton Park west of the village in the 1560s and the imparking of land between the house and the church[47] prevented it from growing westwards. It is possible that buildings west of the church were removed when the park wall was brought up to the village, probably in the earlier 17th century, but air photography does not reveal them.[48] The west part of the street, ending at the park gates,[49] has been called Park Street since the later 19th century.[50] Demesne farm buildings erected in the late 13th century[51] may have been on the south side of the street near the church, a site later used by the Howards, lords of Charlton manor, for a dower house. Most of the dower house was burned down in 1877:[52] parts of it survive in the large house, called Charlton Cottage, which replaced it. On the north side of the street near the church is a run of c. 7 stone cottages: one, gabled, may be 17th-century or older; most of the others are apparently 18th-century. Also on the north side is an early 18th-century farmhouse, and Street Farm, near the crossroads, is late 18th-century. A pair of 19th-century cottages stands on each side of the street, and on the south side other buildings apparently range in date from the late 18th century to the late 19th. From the later 16th century the number of farmsteads in the street may have declined as more were built away from the village.[53] In the later 20th century 18 private houses were built on vacant sites in Park Street and several farm buildings were converted to dwellings. The church house, mentioned in the later 16th and earlier 17th centuries,[54] may have been near the church. Another house in Park Street was a police station in the mid 20th century.[55] East of the crossroads the buildings

straggled more. On the north side Village Farm was built c. 1700 in an **L** shape. The symmetrical main front, of two storeys with attics and of five bays, has three tall gables and ovolo-moulded mullion and transom windows. The back range was made taller, possibly in the later 18th century, and the angle of the **L** was partly filled in the later 19th. The original newel stair and two bolection-moulded stone fireplaces survive. At the east end of the street the Horse and Groom, an inn from 1822 or earlier,[56] was apparently built in the later 18th century and extended in the early 19th: a friendly society formed in 1833 met there.[57] Opposite the Horse and Groom, Woodcock Farm seems likely to be the house in the street largely rebuilt in the earlier 18th century.[58] On each side of the street is another small 18th-century farmhouse, the village school is on the south side, and the village hall, rebuilt in 1981–2,[59] is on the north side. In the later 20th century nine private houses were built and farm buildings of Village Farm and Woodcock Farm were converted for residence. In the south-east angle of the crossroads four old people's bungalows and 12 other council houses were built in 1953.[60] Beside the Cricklade–Malmesbury road a little south of the village a children's hospital with 11 beds, endowed by Lady Victoria Howard, was built in 1870.[61] In the 20th century, when patients were selected by the Invalid Children's Aid Society, the endowment was supplemented by fees and subscription. The hospital was closed in 1953.[62] The village was designated a conservation area in 1973.[63]

West of the village the manor house, called Charlton Park from the 18th century,[64] was visited by James I,[65] and parliamentary cavalry were garrisoned there in the Civil War. In 1667 John Dryden wrote *Annus Mirabilis* there,[66] and in the 18th and 19th centuries the owners, members of the Howard family, presumably had a large household. In the First World War part of the house was a Red Cross hospital[67] and in and after the Second a boarding school was in it. From the early 1950s to 1981, when it was divided into 18 apartments, it was not lived in.[68] In the south part of the park 71 dwellings were made from huts in the period 1950–3:[69] they went out of use c. 1967[70] and were removed.

In the 13th century the estate called Kingershay may have included small farmsteads in a hamlet of that name:[71] its site may have been at or near that of Pond Farm,[72] in Braydon forest until 1300 and thereafter in the purlieus.[73] That site was

[43] W.R.O. 88/3/4.
[44] Ibid. G 7/505/1; *V.C.H. Wilts.* iv. 323, 343.
[45] *Census*, 1961; 1981.
[46] *V.C.H. Wilts.* iv. 9 and n.
[47] Below, manors.
[48] Wilts. co. council, air photos., 1971, 1981.
[49] See plate facing p. 61.
[50] O.S. Map 6″, Wilts. VIII. SE. (1901 edn.).
[51] *Reg. Malm.* i. 367.
[52] Soc. Antiq. MS. 817, iv, p. 2.
[53] Below.
[54] W.R.O. 88/2/1, view 27 Sept. 13 Eliz. I; 88/2/24, view 30 Mar. 14 Chas. I.
[55] Ibid. G 7/505/1.
[56] Ibid. A 1/326/3.
[57] P.R.O., FS 1/776A, no. 236.
[58] W.R.O. 88/10/3.
[59] Char. Com. file.

[60] W.R.O., G 7/505/1.
[61] *V.C.H. Wilts.* v. 344.
[62] W.R.O., L 2, Charlton (N.W.); ibid. G 7/505/1.
[63] Inf. from Co. Planning Officer, Co. Hall, Trowbridge.
[64] *Andrews and Dury, Map* (W.R.S. viii), pl. 17.
[65] *Cal. S.P. Dom.* 1619–23, 171.
[66] Aubrey, *Topog. Coll.* ed. Jackson, 212, 263.
[67] Wilts. Cuttings, xv. 74.
[68] Ibid. xxix. 147; *Daily Telegraph*, 1 Apr. 1981; below, educ.
[69] W.R.O., G 7/505/1.
[70] Inf. from Housing and Property Services Dept., N. Wilts. district council, Chippenham.
[71] *Reg. Malm.* i. 184–5. In this and the following 4 paras. inf. dated 1773 is from *Andrews and Dury, Map* (W.R.S. viii), pls. 16–17.
[72] Cf. W.R.O. 130/1B, lease, earl of Berks. to Waters, 1674.
[73] Above.

called Braydon End in 1773. The use of the names North, South, and East Kingershay from the 15th century to the 17th[74] suggests that settlement was not then nucleated. Pond Farm, which has extensive farm buildings, was rebuilt in the later 20th century, and Pond Hill Farm incorporates a small 19th-century house. Nearby, Turk's Farm, an L-shaped house of one storey and attics on a cross-passage plan with a contemporary farm building, was built c. 1630 when the purlieus were inclosed.

Stonehill, later Cockroost, Farm is an apparently 18th-century house which with a group of cottages east of it on the north side of the Cricklade–Malmesbury road made up Stonehill hamlet in 1773 and 1988: the four cottages to survive are apparently 18th- or 19th-century. Two houses were built beside Cockroost Farm in the later 20th century.

Perry Green hamlet consists of buildings beside the road to Hankerton. After the vicarage house was built there in the later 19th century,[75] the road was called Vicarage Lane. Cottages may have been built there in the 16th century and the 17th.[76] Two buildings stood at the south end of the lane in 1773: one, a small farmhouse apparently of the 18th century, survives, as do three other small apparently late 18th-century houses and a pair of 19th-century cottages. A pair of council houses was built at the junction of Vicarage Lane and the main road in 1945[77] and several houses have been built in the lane since then.

The pattern of scattered settlement in the parish has changed little from when it was set, apparently between the late 16th century and the early 18th. Unusually for so large a Wiltshire parish only one new farmstead was built in the 19th century.[78] In the west part of the parish Bambury Hill Farm was built c. 1575:[79] a 17th-century farmhouse and farm buildings of various dates were on the site in 1988. South of Charlton village was a farmstead called Bisley in 1773 and later: a 17th- or 18th-century farmhouse, a cottage or outbuilding much altered in the later 20th century to form a house, and a house of c. 1930 survive there. In the west part of the park Charlton Park Farm, later Home Farm, consisting of a farmhouse and a regular farmyard with a barn and cattle sheds was built in the late 18th century:[80] the house was later extended. Griffin's Barn Farm west of it consists of an early 18th-century barn, a late 18th-century house, and later farm buildings. In the north-west corner of the parish a pair of cottages was built c. 1932,[81] and near Charlton Park Farm are two pairs, one of stone and red brick of the later 19th century and one of the early 20th in vernacular style.

In the centre of the parish Old Park Farm was built c. 1800, Bullock's Horn Farm in the later 20th century; Lower Moore Farm incorporates a mid 18th-century farmhouse;[82] and Moore Farm incorporates a small 18th-century farmhouse, near which are several small dwellings of the 19th and 20th centuries. Heath, now Langley's, Farm consists of a long two-storeyed east–west range of the 17th century with a lobby entrance to the south and a stair turret projecting to the north: in the early 18th century a short wing was built at the east end and the old east end was refronted. Lower Stonehill Farm incorporates an early 18th-century house and a possibly contemporary barn: in 1773 a farmstead further east, demolished before 1828,[83] bore the name. Lype and Pink Lane were place names from the 13th century or earlier[84] and may have been hamlets. Great Lype and Little Lype were separate farmsteads in the later 18th century[85] and 1988. Great Lype incorporates a house probably built in the 17th century as a single storey with attics and raised to two storeys and extended in the early 19th; Little Lype incorporates a house possibly of the 17th century and another of the later 20th. The present Pink Lane Farm is a farmhouse of 17th-century or earlier origin, extended and altered, with extensive buildings. On the north side of Pink Lane buildings standing in 1773 were removed in the mid 19th century.[86] Both Elm Farm and Newhouse Farm occupy sites in use in 1773. Elm Farm incorporates a farmhouse possibly of the early 19th century; a small house was built for Newhouse farm in the early 20th. Nearby is a small 18th-century farmhouse and several houses of the 19th and 20th centuries.

At the east end of the parish Summerhouse, formerly Hundred Acre, Farm, Worthy Hill Farm, and Bick's Farm may have originated in the early 18th century. Hundred Acre House was apparently a large house built in 1740 for John Carey: in 1773 it had a summer house to the south. The main house was replaced in the late 19th century by a house apparently built for C. A. Kemble.[87] Worthy Hill farmhouse is a double-pile red-brick house of the period 1730–50 with a contemporary barn and stable of red brick and a late 18th-century open cattle shed of stone. Bick's farmhouse and most of the farm buildings were rebuilt in the later 20th century. Beside the Purton road east of Worthy Hill Farm, Eighty Acre Farm, built c. 1857,[88] was called Bourne Valley Farm in 1988: Grove Farm was built west of it in the later 20th century. A late 19th-century stone cottage with red-brick dressings and a substantial late 20th-century house are nearby.

An electricity sub-station partly in Hankerton was built near Stonehill wood in 1970.[89] A water tower was built on the watershed of the Thames and Avon north-east of Braydon pond in 1981.[90]

MANORS AND OTHER ESTATES. To judge

---

[74] W.R.O. 88/1/16; 88/2/46.
[75] Below, church.
[76] W.R.O. 88/2/34; B.L. Add. Ch. 59236.
[77] W.R.O., G 7/505/1.
[78] Below.
[79] W.R.O. 88/2/34; 88/2/43.
[80] No bldg. on the site is on *Andrews and Dury, Map* (W.R.S. viii), pl. 16 (1773).
[81] W.R.O., G 7/501/1.
[82] Not marked on *Andrews and Dury, Map* (W.R.S. viii), pl. 17 (1773).

[83] O.S. Map 1″, sheet 34 (1828 edn.).
[84] *P.N. Wilts.* (E.P.N.S.), 55.
[85] W.R.O. 88/2/57.
[86] Ibid. tithe award; O.S. Map 6″, Wilts. IX (1888 edn.).
[87] Plaque and initials on ho.; below, manors.
[88] Below, econ. hist.
[89] Inf. from Property Services Manager, C.E.G.B., Bedminster Down, Bridgwater Road, Bristol.
[90] Inf. from Supply Controller, Wessex Water, Quay Ho., the Ambury, Bath.

from its name[91] Charlton belonged to Malmesbury abbey from or soon after the abbey's foundation in the 7th century,[92] but the charter of 681 recording the grant to the abbey of 15 *cassati* near Tetbury, to which the recital of Charlton's boundaries was appended, is likely to have referred to Charlton in Tetbury. By interpolation the abbey also claimed, almost certainly falsely, to have been granted Charlton near Malmesbury in 844 by a charter of King Ethelwulf.[93] Aelfheah, ealdorman of Hampshire, devised Charlton to the abbey *c.* 970:[94] his had possibly been a temporary tenure under the abbey. Malmesbury abbey held Charlton in 1086[95] and *CHARLTON* manor until the Dissolution.[96] The abbey considered Kingershay a small estate separate from Charlton in the late 13th century[97] but not later.

In an exchange in 1545 the Crown granted the manor to Thomas Wriothesley, Baron Wriothesley,[98] who in the same year returned it to the Crown in another exchange.[99] In 1547 the Crown granted the manor to Edward Seymour, duke of Somerset[1] (d. 1552). In 1552 the Crown resumed it on Somerset's attainder and granted it to John Dudley, duke of Northumberland,[2] and in 1553 Northumberland sold it to Sir James Stumpe[3] (d. 1563). Stumpe's heir was his daughter Elizabeth (d. 1585), wife of Henry Knyvett (knighted 1574, d. 1598).[4] Charlton manor passed in 1598 to the Knyvetts' daughter Catherine (d. 1638) and her husband Thomas Howard, Lord Howard (cr. earl of Suffolk 1603, d. 1626).[5] From 1631 it included all but perhaps *c.* 500 a. of the parish.[6] It was settled on the Howards' younger son Thomas[7] (from 1622 Baron Howard and Viscount Andover, cr. earl of Berkshire 1626, d. 1669), a royalist, who was allowed to compound for his sequestered estates in 1653.[8] The manor and the earldom of Berkshire passed in succession to Thomas's sons Charles (d. 1679) and Thomas (d. 1706), and to his great-grandson Henry Howard (d. 1757) who inherited the earldom of Suffolk in 1745. Charlton manor and the earldoms of Suffolk and Berkshire have since descended together. Henry was succeeded by his grandson Henry Howard (d. 1779) and Henry's posthumous son Henry (d. 1779), whose heir was his granduncle Thomas Howard (d. 1783). Thomas was succeeded by his third cousin John Howard (d. 1820) and he by his son Thomas (d. 1851). In 1839 Lord Suffolk owned all but *c.* 180 a. of the parish.[9] The manor and earldoms descended in the direct male line to

Charles Howard (d. 1876), Henry (d. 1898), Henry (d. 1917), Charles (d. 1941), and Michael Howard, earl of Suffolk and of Berkshire. In 1959 Lord Suffolk sold *c.* 2,500 a., the east half of the parish apart from Braydon pond and the woodland around it.[10] The pond and woodland were sold later,[11] and in 1978 Lord Suffolk sold 260 a. mainly south-east of Charlton village.[12] In 1988 he owned 1,471 a. of Charlton parish.[13] The land sold in 1959, *c.* 20 farms, was bought by Southery Farms Ltd., then controlled by A. H. Jarrard.[14] In the few years after 1959 Southery Farms sold the farms, mostly to the tenants. In 1988 the land of Charlton not owned by Lord Suffolk, *c.* 3,000 a., was in *c.* 20 separately owned holdings of which the largest was *c.* 250 a.[15]

A house at Charlton, on open land away from the village, was built for Henry Knyvett:[16] it was presumably begun after 1563, when his wife inherited the manor, and was apparently first occupied by the Knyvetts in 1568 or 1569.[17] The house had a main north–south range as the east side, and ranges extending westwards from each end of it as the north and south sides, of an enclosed and roughly square courtyard.[18] Knyvett did not build as large a house as he intended[19] but was not justified in calling it a poor cottage as he did in 1596.[20] His daughter Catherine extended and altered the house after his death in 1598. The principal addition was a west range including a loggia, with a long gallery above it, two-storeyed west wings, and stair turrets with domes and parapets in the re-entrant angles. The second floor was probably added then to the old part of the house and the whole building was given uniformity by large mullioned and transomed windows and an elaborate roofline.[21] There are stylistic similarities to the much larger house at Audley End in Saffron Walden (Essex) which Catherine's husband built between *c.* 1603 and 1616.[22] Changes were made to the inside of the house, later called Charlton Park, in the late 17th or early 18th century when some rooms were subdivided to make closets; and the courtyard elevations may then have been given sash windows.[23] In the 1770s great changes were put in hand by the elder Henry, earl of Suffolk and of Berkshire (d. 1779), with Matthew Brettingham as architect.[24] He rebuilt most of the south range: the new south front, with sash windows to light taller rooms, was built on the line of an earlier central projection. In the east range Knyvett's hall, which was at the north end, was

[91] Above, introduction.
[92] For the abbey, *V.C.H. Wilts.* iii. 210–11.
[93] Finberg, *Early Wessex Chart.* pp. 69, 73, 199–200, 206–9. *V.C.H. Wilts.* iii. 211 seems wrong to say that any grant purported to be of the 680s referred to Charlton near Malmesbury.
[94] D. Whitelock, *A.-S. Wills*, pp. 22, 121.
[95] *V.C.H. Wilts.* ii, p. 126.
[96] *Valor Eccl.* (Rec. Com.), ii. 120.
[97] *Reg. Malm.* i. 184–5.
[98] *L. & P. Hen. VIII*, xx (1), pp. 524–5.
[99] Ibid. xx (2), p. 220.
[1] *Cal. Pat.* 1547–8, 125, 131–2.
[2] Ibid. 1550–3, 369–70; *Complete Peerage*, xii (1), 62–4.
[3] *Cal. Pat.* 1550–3, 258; P.R.O., CP 25(2)/65/533, no. 23.
[4] *W.N. & Q.* viii. 445–9.
[5] W.R.O. 88/1/87; P.R.O., C 142/257, no. 82; inf. about the Howards' geneal. and titles is from *Complete Peerage*, ii. 150–1; xii (1), 462–82; *Who's Who, 1987*, 1695.
[6] W.R.O. 88/2/46–7; 88/2/49.   [7] Ibid. 88/1/118.

[8] *Cal. Cttee. for Compounding*, iii. 1968–9.
[9] W.R.O., tithe award.
[10] *Wilts. Gaz. and Herald*, 27 Aug. 1959.   [11] Local inf.
[12] Wilts. Cuttings, xxviii. 242, 254.
[13] Inf. from Mr. A. Witchell, Messrs. Humberts, 10 St. Mary Street, Chippenham.
[14] *Wilts. Gaz. and Herald*, 27 Aug. 1959.   [15] Local inf.
[16] W.R.O. 88/2/21, ct. 18 June 17 Eliz. I, view 20 Sept. 1576.
[17] Ibid. 88/1/64–5; 88/1/68.
[18] J. Harris, *Cat. of Brit. Drawings*, pl. 24.
[19] W.R.O. 88/2/34.
[20] H. Knyvett, *Defence of the Realm* (Tudor and Stuart Libr.).
[21] See plates facing pp. 44, 45.
[22] Colvin, *Brit. Architects*, 455.
[23] Harris, *Cat. of Brit. Drawings*, pl. 24; a view of the ho. *c.* 1750 is in 'Andover Scrapbk.', Kenwood Ho., Lond.
[24] Colvin, *Brit. Architects*, 158.

demolished, and a large central dining room was built behind a sash-windowed façade: to the north and south east wings and stair turrets similar to those on the west front were built. The central courtyard was roofed over as a large two-storeyed hall, lit by a central dome, with staircases and galleries on its north and south sides.[25] On the west front the domes and parapets of the stair turrets were altered and cresting above the central porch was replaced by a pierced parapet. The inside of the house had not been completely refitted by 1779, when Lord Suffolk died, and apparently remained unfinished throughout the 19th century.[26] The long gallery was panelled and decorated between 1900 and 1911,[27] and work on the central hall may have been finished only about then.[28] Between 1978 and 1981 the house was converted into flats[29] and many of the rooms, but not the dining room or central hall, were divided. Immediately north of the house a kitchen block was built in the 19th century and joined to the north-east corner by a tunnel. North of that is a square stable court, three sides of which were probably built in the mid 19th century.[30] The south-east side, with wings at each end to form a court open to the south-east, is probably of the 1770s: it was converted into a house c. 1950. Farm buildings west of the stables are mostly of the 18th and 19th centuries.

By c. 1600 the gardens and yards of Charlton Park, c. 20 a., had been enclosed by a high wall, and there was a park.[31] In the later 18th century a walled garden survived north-west of the house, beyond it was an enclosure with a regular plantation which may have been an orchard, and a short avenue was across the south-west of the house. By 1773, possibly by c. 1610, the park had been extended eastwards to the village; winding paths through a wood indicate that it had reached its full extent to the south-west by the early 18th century;[32] and in 1808 it was further enlarged to the north-east.[33] Capability Brown, who was at Charlton in 1768, proposed alterations to the house which were not accepted, and drew sketches for water near the house and for a kitchen garden and offices.[34] The walled kitchen gardens at the west edge of the park in 1773 were probably by Brown, and after 1773 a small lake was made south-east of the house and the last of the formal gardens

removed.[35] The kitchen garden was a flower garden in the earlier 20th century.[36] In 1773 the principal approach to the house was apparently along the old course of the Cricklade–Malmesbury road, from the south and from the village westwards.[37] A new drive with an entrance lodge was made from the Cirencester–Malmesbury road in the late 18th century, possibly c. 1778 when the road was turnpiked,[38] and lodges were built at the old south entrance to the park in the mid 19th century.

In 1086 Ranulph Flambard held at Charlton lands assessed at a total of 3 hides, but precisely where they lay is obscure.[39]

In the late 12th century or early 13th Malmesbury abbey granted to Wibert son of William a small manor and a corrody for service in the abbey and as the abbey's forester.[40] Wibert's estate later passed in the Charlton family of which he may have been the progenitor. It was possibly held by Thomas Charlton in 1242–3[41] and by Wibert Charlton in 1283–4.[42] Roger Charlton bought a freehold in Charlton from William Theyn in 1268[43] and it apparently passed to his son Roger: a licence to build an oratory in his house at Charlton was granted to either the father or the son.[44] Later the Charltons' two estates seem to have been united.[45] Wibert Charlton (fl. 1347,[46] d. by 1362)[47] may have held the united estate. Robert Charlton's estate in 1387 included what had been Wibert son of William's:[48] it was later reputed a manor, called *CHARLTON TANTUM* in 1608[49] when it included c. 200 a. and pasture rights.[50] Robert's estate passed to his son Walter (d. by 1428) and to Walter's son Wibert (fl. 1454).[51] John Charlton, who was escheator of Wiltshire and of Hampshire,[52] held it in 1473[53] and sold it in 1478 to Sir Roger Tocotes[54] (d. 1492). On Tocotes's attainder in 1484 the estate was granted for life to his wife's son Sir Richard Beauchamp, from 1491 Lord St. Amand (d. 1508).[55] Tocotes recovered his lands and in 1492 conveyed the estate to St. Amand[56] who devised it for life to his illegitimate son Anthony St. Amand, with reversion to Henry Long[57] (later knighted, d. 1556).[58] The estate passed to Long between 1530[59] and 1541[60] and descended with Draycot Cerne manor to Sir Robert Long (d. 1581) and Sir Walter Long,[61] who in 1608 sold it to Thomas, earl of Suffolk.[62] It was thereupon merged with Charlton manor.

[25] See plate facing p. 44.
[26] *Gent. Mag.* lxxvi (1), 211; J. Britton, *Beauties of Wilts.* iii. 63; Wilts. Cuttings, ix. 192.
[27] *W.A.M.* xxxvii. 338; see below, plate facing p. 44.
[28] Cf. J. A. Gotch, *Archit. of Renaissance in Eng.* ii. 5; see below, plate facing p. 44.
[29] Wilts. Cuttings, xxix. 147.
[30] O.S. Map 6″, Wilts. VIII (1889 edn.); W.R.O., tithe award.
[31] W.R.O. 88/2/34.
[32] Ibid. 88/2/45; *Andrews and Dury, Map* (W.R.S. viii), pls. 16–17; painting by H. F. de Cort, Suff. coll., Rangers Ho., Blackheath, Lond.
[33] W.R.O. 88/5/46/3.
[34] D. Stroud, *Capability Brown*, 102.
[35] *Andrews and Dury, Map* (W.R.S. viii), pl. 17; painting by de Cort; J. Buckler, watercolour in W.A.S. Libr., vol. x. 28.
[36] *Country Life*, 14 Oct. 1933.
[37] *Andrews and Dury, Map* (W.R.S. viii), pl. 17.
[38] Above, introduction.
[39] *V.C.H. Wilts.* ii, p. 126.
[40] *Reg. Malm.* ii. 396.

[41] *Bk. of Fees*, ii. 733. A further possible ref. to Thomas is ambiguous: ibid. 716.
[42] *Reg. Malm.* i. 154.
[43] P.R.O., CP 25(1)/251/21, no. 33.
[44] *Reg. Malm.* ii. 343–5.   [45] Ibid. i. 276.
[46] *Wilts. Inq. p.m.* 1327–77 (Index Libr.), p. 184.
[47] *Cal. Close*, 1360–4, 341.   [48] W.R.O. 88/1/3A.
[49] P.R.O., CP 25(2)/369/6 Jas. I Mich.
[50] W.R.O. 88/1/118.
[51] *Cal. Close*, 1454–61, 38; *Feud. Aids*, v. 236; vi. 538; P.R.O., C 1/17, no. 174.
[52] *Cal. Pat.* 1476–85, 128.
[53] W.R.O. 88/1/4.
[54] Ibid. 88/1/16; *Feet of F. 1377–1509* (W.R.S. xli), pp. 157–8.
[55] *Cal. Pat.* 1476–85, 416; *Complete Peerage*, xi. 302–3.
[56] W.R.O. 88/1/17.
[57] *Cal. Close*, 1500–9, pp. 346–7.
[58] P.R.O., C 142/110, no. 167.
[59] *Extents for Debts* (W.R.S. xxviii), p. 52.
[60] P.R.O., SC 6/Hen. VIII/3986, rot. 110d.
[61] Below, Draycot Cerne, manor.
[62] P.R.O., CP 25(2)/369/6 Jas. I Mich.

Between 1208 and 1222 Malmesbury abbey granted to Henry Lype 1 yardland almost certainly at Lype.[63] Henry's successors apparently included Edith Lype, a freeholder in 1283–4,[64] and Roger Lype, a freeholder in the later 13th century.[65] An estate bought in 1489 by Hugh Martin from Richard, son and heir of William Short, and his wife Joan included land at Lype,[66] seems likely to have been what was later *GREAT LYPE* farm,[67] and may have been what the Lypes held. It was owned in 1541 by Anthony Martin[68] (d. 1570) who was succeeded in turn by his sons Robert[69] (d. 1577) and Roger[70] (d. 1595). Roger, a clothier of Steeple Ashton, was succeeded by his son Roger[71] who in 1606 held Lype House and 91 a. with pasture rights.[72] Henry Martin owned the estate in 1637.[73] It passed to his son Henry (d. 1689), to Henry's son Michael, who held it until 1723 or later, to Michael's nephew Roger, who held it 1731–9 or longer, and to Roger's nephew Michael Martin who in 1752 sold it[74] to Humphrey Woodcock (d. 1754). Woodcock devised it to his nephew Charles Williamson[75] (d. 1760) whose executors sold the estate in 1763 to Henry, earl of Suffolk and of Berkshire.[76] Great Lype farm, c. 150 a., was among the lands sold by Michael, earl of Suffolk and of Berkshire, in 1959. In 1961 it was bought by J. B. Walker (d. 1971) and in 1988 belonged to his son Mr. J. A. Walker and daughter Miss J. J. Walker.[77]

Besides those of the Charltons and Lypes there were several other freeholds in Charlton in the Middle Ages. Until its dissolution a chantry at Cirencester in honour of Jesus held a small one.[78] In the later 13th century Richard of Lea and his son Richard held 1½ hide in Charlton and land in Lea:[79] some of that estate was possibly among lands entered on in 1340 by John Moleyns, lord of Lea manor, and formerly Ralph of Combe's.[80] Land in Charlton descended with Lea manor in the Moleyns, Hungerford, and Hastings families.[81] In 1571 Henry Hastings, earl of Huntingdon, sold his small estate in Charlton, called *EDWARDS*, to Anthony Webb.[82] Edwards, 30 a., may have descended to Webb's grandson Anthony Webb but from 1595[83] its descent is obscure. Thomas Burrows owned it c. 1672,[84] Adam Burrows in 1702, and it remained in the Burrows family until 1737[85] or later. It is likely to have been bought by Humphrey Woodcock and to have passed to Charles Williamson who settled land on the marriage of his

niece Sarah Kyffin and Matthew Sloper.[86] Before 1780 Sloper's trustees sold Edwards to John Paul (d. 1789). Paul devised it to his nephew Josiah Paul Paul (formerly Josiah Paul Tippetts) who in 1795 sold it to John, earl of Suffolk and of Berkshire.[87] It was merged with Charlton manor.

In 1540–1 Roger Young was a freeholder in Charlton.[88] His was possibly the freehold there which William Roberts (d. c. 1547) settled on himself for life and on his grandson Giles Roberts.[89] Apparently between 1590[90] and 1594 Giles Roberts sold his estate to Justinian Smith[91] (d. c. 1602)[92] whose son Richard owned 95 a. and pasture rights in 1606[93] and sold them in 1609 to Thomas, earl of Suffolk.[94] The lands were merged with Charlton manor.

In 1606 freeholds of 33 a. and 32 a. with pasture rights belonged, respectively, to John Palmer and Robert Ring, and there were other small freeholds.[95] Palmer's belonged to William Palmer, rector of Little Somerford, in 1625[96] and 1646,[97] but their descents are otherwise obscure. Some of the lands may have been in John Turk's freehold which in 1724 was settled on the marriage of his granddaughter Hester Phelps and Thomas Jones (d. 1768). The Joneses' estate passed to their son John, who owned 107 a. c. 1780, and to John's son Thomas: in 1804 Thomas Jones sold the estate to John, earl of Suffolk and of Berkshire,[98] and it was absorbed by Charlton manor.

SUMMERHOUSE farm, 105 a. c. 1780,[99] originated as an inclosure of 100 a. of the purlieus of Braydon forest: it was apparently the triangle conceded to Sir Nevill Poole, the lord of Oaksey manor, by Thomas, earl of Berkshire, in 1633. It was bought, apparently in the later 17th century, by an earl of Berkshire from Giles Poole, Sir Ralph Dutton, and John Waters, possibly trustees, but did not descend with Charlton manor. It was bought in 1740 by John Carey (d. 1752) who devised it to his nephew John Carey. The nephew was succeeded by his sisters Jane (d. 1786), wife of the Revd. Richard Brooke (d. before 1809), and Mary (d. s.p. 1806), wife of Richard Fowler, tenants in common. The farm passed to the Brookes' son Samuel (d. 1837), to Samuel's son S. B. Brooke (d. 1869), and to S. B. Brooke's nephew the Revd. Charles Kemble (d. 1874) and his wife Charlotte.[1] In 1882 Charlotte Kemble assigned it to her son C. A. Kemble,[2] and it belonged to a Kemble in 1910.[3] Later owners

---

[63] *Reg. Malm.* i. 435–6. [64] Ibid. 154.
[65] Ibid. ii. 280.
[66] *Feet of F. 1377–1509* (W.R.S. xli), p. 163.
[67] Evidence supplied by Miss J. J. Walker, Great Lype Farm.
[68] P.R.O., SC 6/Hen. VIII/3986, rot. 110d.
[69] W.R.O. 88/2/1, ct. baron 29 Sept. 12 Eliz. I.
[70] Ibid. 88/2/21, view 27 Sept. 1577.
[71] Ibid. 88/2/22, view 23 Sept. 1584; P.R.O., C 142/242, no. 39 (2).
[72] W.R.O. 88/2/49.
[73] Ibid. 88/2/35.
[74] Ibid. 88/3/4–6; 88/5/4; ibid. wills, archd. Wilts., 1718, will of Hen. Martin; for the death in 1689, ibid. 1813/1.
[75] Ibid. 280/18, copy will of Humphrey Woodcock; 280/25, copy decree, 1757.
[76] Ibid. 88/5/4; 280/39.
[77] Above; inf. from Miss Walker.
[78] *Valor Eccl.* (Rec. Com.), ii. 448; *Cal. Pat.* 1560–3, 566–7; P.R.O., E 309/2/25, no. 1.
[79] *Reg. Malm.* i. 247–8; ii. 277–8.
[80] *Feet of F. 1327–77* (W.R.S. xxix), pp. 62–4; *Cal. Close, 1339–41,* 458–9.
[81] Below, Lea and Cleverton, manors.
[82] W.R.O. 88/1/72.
[83] Ibid. 130/25, deed, Webb to Pinkney, 1587; P.R.O., C 2/Eliz. I/E 4/68.
[84] W.R.O. 88/2/50. [85] Ibid. 88/3/4.
[86] Ibid. 280/18, copy will of Chas. Williamson.
[87] Ibid. 88/5/9; ibid. A 1/345/91; A. T. Lee, *Hist. Tetbury,* 221–2.
[88] P.R.O., SC 6/Hen. VIII/3986, rot. 110d.
[89] Ibid. C 1/1465, no. 48; C 3/376/7.
[90] W.R.O. 88/2/43. [91] Ibid. 88/1/96; 88/1/109.
[92] *W.N. & Q.* viii. 467. [93] W.R.O. 88/2/49.
[94] Ibid. 88/1/109. [95] Ibid. 88/2/49.
[96] Ibid. 88/2/23; below, Little Somerford, church.
[97] W.R.O. 88/2/25, view 8 Oct. 22 Chas. I.
[98] Ibid. 88/2/57; 88/5/10. [99] Ibid. 88/2/57.
[1] Ibid. 88/1/141; 663/8. For the inclosures, above, introduction; below, econ. hist.
[2] W.R.O. 856/3. [3] Ibid. Inland Revenue, val. reg. 11.

included Frederick Hays, 1924–39 or longer,[4] and Mrs. D. J. Woolford who in 1984 sold the farm to Mr. M. H. Wood, the owner in 1988.[5]

All the great tithes from Charlton belonged to Malmesbury abbey.[6] After the Dissolution all tithes of corn and hay were granted with Charlton manor[7] and descended with it. In 1840 those arising from 2,238 a. were merged with the land, those from 6 a. were commuted: the remainder of the parish was free from great tithes.[8]

ECONOMIC HISTORY. Charlton had land for 13 ploughteams in 1086 but only 9½ teams were there. On its demesne Malmesbury abbey had 2 teams and 7 serfs; 23 *villani*, 13 cottars, and 2 coscets had a total of 5 teams; and Ranulph Flambard had 2½ teams. About half Flambard's land was formerly held by the abbey's *villani*. The three types of land, the demesne, 12 hides worth £8, and the customary and thegnland, a total of 8 hides worth £2, were not valued in proportion to the number of teams on them:[9] a possible explanation is that extensive uncultivated land east of the village was deemed demesne.

In the Middle Ages there seems to have been little inclosed land outside Charlton village. The arable was in open fields, possibly two in 1333,[10] three in 1396 and later: in 1409 they were called East, West, and Grandon. Meadow land was commonable,[11] there was feeding in common in the purlieus of Braydon forest, and between the arable and the purlieus lay common pastures in the 16th century[12] and almost certainly in the Middle Ages. As might be expected from the name of the village,[13] demesne land was not extensive despite its high valuation in 1086. It was stocked with 16 oxen *c.* 1210.[14] Later in the 13th century it was in hand[15] and enlarged. The pasture called Stonehill was inclosed from the waste by the sacrist of Malmesbury abbey and given to the abbot in an exchange, the pasture called Middle Hurst was added to the demesne after the abbot acquired by exchange the freeholders' pasture rights in it, and six customary holdings were taken in hand. Dairy farming on the demesne is implied by the description of Stonehill as a cow pasture.[16] New farm buildings were erected in the later 13th century[17] and buildings stood on Stonehill pasture in 1292.[18] In 1396 there were 90 a. of demesne in the open fields and 12 a. in the common meadows. Customary works were almost certainly sufficient to cultivate it.[19] By the mid 15th century Stonehill had apparently been imparked and stocked with deer,[20]

but in the early 16th it was one of *c.* 10 leased demesne pastures, most lying apparently between the arable and the purlieus. A lease in 1519 of the arable and rights to common pasture[21] was presumably not the first. Charlton manor comprised three types of customary holding in the later 13th century, yardlands, ½-yardlands, and Monday lands, and five types of tenant: there were 3 freeholders, 12 yardlanders, 14 ½-yardlanders, 9 acremen, and 8 gavelmen. In addition Malmesbury abbey's land at Kingershay was then a separate small manor with 4–5 customary tenants,[22] and in the early 15th century Walter Charlton's estate, also partly at Kingershay, had on it four tenants each holding between 10 a. and 20 a.[23] In 1541 Charlton manor had 6 freeholders, 31 customary tenants, and 2 tenants at will. Some held what had earlier been more than one customary holding but it is unlikely that, excluding pasture rights, any holding in the parish, including the demesne of Charlton manor, exceeded 100 a.[24]

Between *c.* 1541 and *c.* 1631 only about half Charlton parish was farmland: east of a line roughly from Bullock's Horn in Hankerton to Pink Lane Farm was largely woodland and rough pasture open to similar land north and south and to Braydon forest to the east.[25] In the west half of the parish there were still three main open fields, but references to Middle, North, and Hay fields suggest subdivision.[26] In the later 16th century there was piecemeal inclosure, and Hay field was inclosed by agreement in 1572. Much of Grandon field and part of West field were inclosed. In addition, exchanges of strips in the fields were often agreed on[27] and in 1583 a meeting was arranged for all the tenants of Charlton manor, including freeholders, to decide on bringing together into larger tracts all the strips in the fields.[28] That meeting failed whether it was intended to promote inclosure or only to rearrange the strips.[29] By the early 17th century, however, apparently by exchange, amalgamation, and inclosure,[30] demesne land had been removed from the open fields. In 1616 the open fields contained 678 a. shared among 45 occupants and divided into 1,000 strips: most of West field, 216 a., was presumably west of what was later the Cirencester–Malmesbury road, Grandon field, 22 a., was apparently south or south-east of Charlton village, and Home, formerly East, field, 440 a., was north of and adjoined the village.[31] The custom had apparently long been for a hay crop to be taken in small parts of the fields:[32] in 1578, for example, the practice was apparently to make

---

[4] W.R.O., G 7/510/1; *Kelly's Dir. Wilts.* (1939).
[5] Inf. from Mr. M. H. Wood, Summerhouse Farm.
[6] *Reg. Malm.* i. 206; *Valor Eccl.* (Rec. Com.), ii. 118; P.R.O., SC 6/Hen. VIII/3986, rot. 112.
[7] P.R.O., C 66/768, m. 33.
[8] W.R.O., tithe award.
[9] *V.C.H. Wilts.* ii, p. 126.
[10] W.R.O. 88/1/1.
[11] Ibid. 88/1/6; B.L. Add. MS. 6165, pp. 109–10.
[12] Below.   [13] Above, introduction.
[14] *Interdict Doc.* (Pipe R. Soc. N.S. xxxiv), p. 23.
[15] *Reg. Malm.* i. 203, 205–6.
[16] Ibid. ii. 232–9, 277–81, 322–3.
[17] Ibid. i. 367.
[18] Ibid. ii. 375–9.
[19] Ibid. i. 203; B.L. Add. MS. 6165, pp. 109–10.
[20] P.R.O., C 1/18, no. 172.

[21] Ibid. SC 6/Hen. VIII/3986, rot. 111d.
[22] *Reg. Malm.* i. 154–7, 184–5.
[23] *Feet of F. 1377–1509* (W.R.S. xli), pp. 68–9; W.R.O. 88/1/16.
[24] P.R.O., SC 6/Hen. VIII/3986, rott. 110d.–112d.
[25] W.R.O. 88/2/34; below.
[26] W.R.O. 88/2/1, view 15 Sept. 5 Eliz. I, ct. baron 23 Jan. 14 Eliz. I; 88/2/21, ct. baron 18 June 17 Eliz. I; 88/2/34.
[27] Ibid. 88/2/1, especially ct. baron 23 Jan. 14 Eliz. I; 88/2/21–2. For W. field, below.
[28] *Album H. M. Cam* (Univ. Louvain), 30–1; W.R.O. 88/2/22, view 29 Aug. 1583.
[29] W.R.O. 88/2/47.   [30] Below.
[31] W.R.O. 88/2/47. Statute measure is given: by estimation the area was 897 a. For the location of Grandon field, ibid. 88/2/22, ct. 21 Dec. 28 Eliz. I.
[32] e.g. ibid. 88/2/1, view 15 Sept. 5 Eliz. I.

The central hall

The long gallery

CHARLTON: CHARLTON PARK

CHARLTON
Charlton Park from the west in 1809

MALMESBURY
Abbey House from the north-west in 1809

hay on inclosures in the fallow field,[33] and 12 a. of meadow were in the open fields in 1616.[34] Other meadow land also remained commonable and some was held in rotation.[35] The Moor, 20 a., and the Heath, 30 a., were common pastures east of the village mostly south of the Cricklade–Malmesbury road. North of them Inner down, 10 a., was used in common from 1 August to 2 February.[36] In 1606 there were, apparently, 30–40 farms in the parish, all but a few based in the village, and still none exceeding 100 a.[37]

West of the village Sir Henry Knyvett built Charlton Park[38] on part of West field, and in 1572 he bought out a copyholder and thereafter gave parts of that copyhold and demesne elsewhere in the open fields in exchange for 45 a. or more of Rudge furlong in West field.[39] About 1610 the park around the house was said to measure 350 a. and to have in it woodland, deer, and 15 a. of meadow.[40] In addition, mainly around the village, perhaps c. 300 a. of the open fields had been inclosed as parts of farms by 1606. East of the village Stonehill was again imparked. It was for a time called the new park and was paled: a keeper was appointed in 1576.[41] It was called the old park c. 1610 when it was said to measure c. 400 a. and to include woodland and 35 a. of meadow.[42] Inclosed demesne pastures and meadows west or south of Stonehill park continued to be held on leases[43] and in the later 16th century three farms, Bambury Hill, with buildings first erected c. 1575 on land inclosed from Hay field, and two called Lype, were based there.[44] Cultivation was extended further eastwards between 1610 and 1620 when Stonehill park was apparently leased in portions for agriculture; a new farm, with buildings and 60 a., had been created from the park by 1618.[45]

Although its boundaries were defined several times in the 13th and 14th centuries and unchanged after 1300[46] Braydon forest was not inclosed, and on all sides woods and pastures also lay open outside the boundaries of 1300. In the 16th century those woods and pastures were called the purlieus and were in four quarters, of which Charlton or Minety quarter was one. Inhabitants of, and tenants of manors in, parishes near the forest were allowed to keep cattle freely throughout the year in the purlieus and the forest, and the forest officers freely entered the purlieus to hunt or protect deer: that was the custom in the 16th century and almost certainly long before. Except for those accustomed to feed cattle in the forest but without land adjoining the purlieus, to drive

cattle was forbidden, but Charlton cattle could be turned into the purlieus from the Heath or the Moor and left to wander. Although the purlieus were open, boundaries across them to divide the land of separate manors were recognized.[47] Braydon was disafforested in 1630 and inclosed, and the Crown, as owner of the forest, gave up its rights over the purlieus.[48] Thomas, earl of Berkshire, lord of Charlton manor, inclosed Charlton's part of the purlieus in 1631.[49] The land inclosed was described as bushy and woody and overgrown with bracken and bramble.[50] By agreement with the freeholders and other tenants of Charlton manor Lord Berkshire took most of it to be improved for his own use.[51] Part was left as woodland and possibly c. 1,000 a. became several farmland.[52] In place of their feeding for cattle in the forest and the purlieus the farmers of Charlton accepted 400 a. in Charlton's part of the purlieus as a common pasture, called Charlton common, and the cottagers of Charlton were allotted a common of 50 a. In 1631 gates and gaps were left for both commons to be open to parts of the purlieus outside Charlton while Lord Berkshire disputed with the lords of other manors the extent of his inclosures, but from 1633 the two commons were exclusive to Charlton.[53]

In the west half of the parish open fields were still cultivated in the 18th century, and a third field, Middle, was apparently taken from Home field; but consolidation of strips into larger tracts and inclosure continued,[54] and it is unlikely that there were more than vestiges of the open fields c. 1760. Most inclosure was apparently in the period 1709–48 when Humphrey Woodcock was steward of Charlton manor. Woodcock owned an estate in Charlton, was a copyholder and leaseholder, and favoured inclosure: he was dismissed by Henry, earl of Suffolk and of Berkshire, who accused him of breaches of trust and false accounting throughout his period of office.[55] Little land was granted by copy after c. 1731,[56] the number of farms was reduced, and the consolidation of strips and inclosure presumably accelerated. Most of the land was apparently worked from farmsteads in the village: based outside it Bambury Hill farm was 195 a. c. 1780, and Griffin's Barn farm was 205 a. worked from buildings west of the Cirencester–Malmesbury road.[57] Also in the west half deer were kept in Charlton park in 1674.[58] In 1760 the park measured c. 245 a.[59] When in hand it was partly used for stock rearing but sometimes it was leased and within its walls West field, c. 60 a., remained arable.[60] The park was enlarged

[33] Ibid. 88/2/21, view 20 Mar. 1577.
[34] Ibid. 88/2/47.
[35] Ibid. 88/2/34; 88/2/49.
[36] Ibid. 88/2/34. For the locations, ibid. 88/2/43; *Andrews and Dury, Map* (W.R.S. viii), pl. 17.
[37] W.R.O. 88/2/49.   [38] Above, manors.
[39] W.R.O. 88/2/1, ct. baron 23 Jan. 14 Eliz. I; 88/2/21, ct. baron 18 June 17 Eliz. I, view 20 Sept. 1576.
[40] Ibid. 88/2/45.
[41] Ibid. 88/2/49; Saxton, *Map of Wilts.*
[42] W.R.O. 88/2/45.
[43] Ibid. 88/2/49.
[44] Ibid. 88/2/34; 88/2/43.
[45] Ibid. 88/2/34; B.L. Add. Ch. 59193.
[46] *V.C.H. Wilts.* iv. 402–3.
[47] P.R.O., E 178/2408; W.R.O. 88/10/52. For Charlton's boundaries, above, introduction.

[48] P.R.O., E 178/2470.
[49] *W.N. & Q.* vii. 453–4.
[50] W.R.O. 88/10/52.
[51] Ibid. 88/9/1F.
[52] Below.
[53] W.R.O. 88/9/1F. For the disputes, ibid. 88/1/141; 88/9/11; *W.N. & Q.* vii. 453–4.
[54] W.R.O. 88/2/37B, lease, earl of Berks. to Woodcock, 1738; 88/5/3; ibid. D 1/24/216/1.
[55] Ibid. 88/2/37B, leases, 1716, 1724, 1738; 88/10/3; above, manors.
[56] W.R.O. 88/2/37A.
[57] Ibid. 88/2/56–7; *Andrews and Dury, Map* (W.R.S. viii), pls. 16–17.
[58] *W.A.M.* iii. 377–8.
[59] W.R.O. 88/5/46/4, partic. of park, 1760.
[60] Ibid. 88/2/56; 88/9/26, acct. bk. 1757; ibid. tithe award.

c. 1770 for more deer to be kept[61] and in 1773 its walls enclosed *c*. 675 a.[62] In the east half of the parish the land was improved after 1631 and there was hedging, ditching, and tree felling in the late 1630s.[63] In the 18th century the average size of the closes there was under 10 a. Acreages of farms which existed in 1631 were increased and new farms created. The largest, Worthy Hill farm, measured 457 a. *c*. 1780. Others then included Stonehill, 410 a., Kynaston, later Pond, 142 a., Hundred Acre, later Summerhouse, 105 a., Pink Lane, 291 a., Great Lype, 250 a., and Little Lype, 107 a. Between the former open fields to the west and the former purlieus to the east the Heath and the Moor, respectively 45 a. and 54 a. *c*. 1780, remained for use in common[64] and there were other smaller areas of common pasture called Pink Lane, Perry Green, and Broad Green.[65] The 50-a. pasture allotted to the cottagers in 1631 was apparently not marked out until 1660 or later.[66] That and the 400-a. common pasture were respectively south and north of Braydon pond.[67] Despite encroachments on them all those pastures were still used in common *c*. 1780.[68] In 1660 stinting on the commons was related to contributions to church rates, 6 sheep to 1*d*., 1 beast or 1 horse to 2*d*.[69] In 1698 it was based on the value of holdings, 20 sheep for every £10, 1 horse for every 8 sheep, and cattle at the rate of 1 for every 4 sheep.[70]

The common pastures were inclosed, presumably mostly by agreement, *c*. 1808.[71] No new farm was created and most of the new inclosures went to enlarge farms:[72] trees were planted around Braydon pond.[73] North of Braydon pond Thomas, earl of Suffolk and of Berkshire, held 55 a. as field gardens in 1839:[74] they were replaced, possibly before 1898, by 71 a. of garden allotments near the south-east corner of the parish,[75] and the 71 a. became farmland in the mid 20th century.[76] In 1809 John, earl of Suffolk and of Berkshire, tried to improve his estate by converting pasture to arable, erecting new buildings and installing threshing machines, and fertilizing and draining land: new tenants, especially from Scotland and Northumberland, were invited, but few tenancies changed.[77] In 1839 the average size of the fields remained *c*. 10 a. and the parish still had about six times as much grassland as arable: more arable was in the west than the east but no farm had more arable than grass. In 1839 Park farm, 205 a. worked from buildings beside the Cirencester–Malmesbury road, was wholly within the walls of Charlton park, which had again been enlarged in 1808, and 408 a. of the park were in hand.[78] Deer

were kept *c*. 1867 but not *c*. 1892.[79] The other farms in the west in 1839 were Street, 260 a. including land imparked in 1808, Village, 106 a., others of 81 a. and 27 a. based in the street, Woodcock, 143 a., Bambury Hill, 255 a. including 67 a. in Hankerton, and Griffin's Barn, 230 a. including 50 a. in Malmesbury. Bishoper farm based in Hankerton included 75 a. of Charlton west of the Cirencester–Malmesbury road. In the centre and east the farms were Heath, 116 a., Great Lype, 221 a., Little Lype, 126 a., Lower Moore, 23 a., Old Park, 316 a. including 82 a. in Hankerton, Lower Stonehill, 198 a., Stonehill, 138 a., Pond, 177 a., Pink Lane, 111 a., Elm, 199 a., Worthy Hill, 321 a., Bick's, 160 a., and Summerhouse, 173 a. including 59 a. in Hankerton. Of the south-east corner of the parish Moonsleaze farm, based in Purton, included 85 a., and Rookery farm and another farm, both based in Brinkworth, included respectively 135 a. and 97 a.[80] The 85 a. of Moonsleaze farm was later, possibly from 1857, Eighty Acre farm.[81] In 1887 the parish contained 596 a. of arable, 160 a. of grass under rotation, and 3,764 a. of permanent grassland: 1,006 sheep, 525 pigs, 465 cows, and 534 other cattle were kept.[82] There may have been some market gardening in the south-east.[83]

The 19th-century pattern of farming in Charlton continued until the Second World War. In 1910 much more of the park than in 1839 was in Park farm, 541 a. worked from the buildings beside the Cirencester–Malmesbury road and from others near Charlton Park, but most of the other farms were smaller than in 1840 and there were several new small farms: by then Elm farm had been halved and Turk's taken from Old Park.[84] In 1939 only 5 of 30 farms based in Charlton parish exceeded 150 a.[85] There were then only *c*. 200 a. of arable. Sheep and pigs were still kept but most farming was dairying: 820 cows and 248 other cattle were kept in 1937.[86]

After 1939 more land was ploughed, but dairy and cattle farming also increased: 1,000 a. were arable and *c*. 2,700 cattle were kept in the parish in 1977.[87] The fields were made much larger. Most of the arable was in the west where much land of the Charlton Park estate was taken in hand. In 1988 over half the 1,000 a. in hand were arable, with woodland and pasture for beef cattle in the park: the farmland was worked from the buildings near Charlton Park and from Brokenborough. The tenanted farms, Griffin's Barn, 194 a., and Bambury Hill, 206 a., were both arable and dairy farms. The *c*. 70 a. of Bishoper farm in Charlton remained arable.[88] In 1988 the centre and east of

[61] *W.A.M.* xlii. 619; Wilts. Cuttings, xiv. 216.
[62] *Andrews and Dury, Map* (W.R.S. viii), pls. 16–17; W.R.O., tithe award.
[63] W.R.O. 88/2/35.   [64] Ibid. 88/2/56–7.
[65] Ibid. 88/2/5, view 23 Oct. 1778.   [66] Ibid. 88/2/2.
[67] Ibid. tithe award; *Andrews and Dury, Map* (W.R.S. viii), pl. 17.
[68] W.R.O. 88/2/5, view 23 Oct. 1778; 88/2/57.
[69] Ibid. 88/2/2.   [70] Ibid. 88/2/27, view 20 Oct. 1698.
[71] Ibid. 88/5/13; Britton, *Beauties of Wilts.* iii. 62–3.
[72] Cf. *Andrews and Dury, Map* (W.R.S. viii), pl. 17; W.R.O., tithe award; above, introduction.
[73] Britton, *Beauties of Wilts.* iii. 62–3.
[74] W.R.O., tithe award.
[75] O.S. Map 6″, Wilts. IX (1888 and later edns.).
[76] Cf. ibid. Wilts. IX. SW. (1925 edn.).

[77] *V.C.H. Wilts.* iv. 88; W.R.O. 88/10/9.
[78] W.R.O., tithe award; ibid. 88/5/46/3.
[79] *W.N. & Q.* ii. 251.
[80] W.R.O., tithe awards; ibid. 88/10/22, summary of estates, 1855.
[81] Ibid. 88/10/22, sale cat., 1857; O.S. Map 6″, Wilts. IX (1888 edn.).
[82] P.R.O., MAF 68/1120, sheet 10.
[83] O.S. Map 6″, Wilts. IX (1888 edn.).
[84] W.R.O., Inland Revenue, val. reg. 11.
[85] *Kelly's Dir. Wilts.* (1939).
[86] P.R.O., MAF 68/3850, no. 138; [1st] Land Util. Surv. Map, sheets 103–4.
[87] P.R.O., MAF 68/5556, no. 138.
[88] Inf. from Mr. A. Witchell, Messrs. Humberts, 10 St. Mary Street, Chippenham.

the parish was mainly pasture and worked in 15–20 farms. Little Lype, Old Park, Elm, Lower Stonehill, and Bick's remained dairy farms, cereals were grown on Pink Lane farm, and there were large buildings for cattle on Pond, Worthy Hill, and Heath farms, for pigs on Bullock's Horn farm, and for chickens near Pink Lane Farm. Turk's farm was used for rearing cattle and horses, Summerhouse farm for a riding school, and the Braydon pond estate for shooting and fishing. Land near Charlton's boundary with Brinkworth was worked from Brinkworth.[89]

In 1086 Charlton had little woodland, 2 furlongs by 1 furlong,[90] and with access to the woody grounds to the east and to Braydon forest may have needed no more. Charlton Thorns, 16 a., and Swatnage coppice, 6 a., were woods in the 16th century[91] when many trees also grew in Charlton's part of the purlieus: woods of c. 40 a. and 20 a. referred to c. 1600 are likely to have been in the purlieus.[92] Charlton Thorns was possibly what was later called Dellas wood and Stonehill wood.[93] Woodland was in both parks in the early 17th century[94] but after 1631 some was almost certainly cleared from the east part of the parish.[95] There were c. 220 a. of woodland c. 1780. The woods included Stonehill, 64 a., Swatnage, 14 a., Great Withy, 29 a., and Little Withy, 12 a.: most of the remainder was in Charlton park.[96] More trees were planted in the 19th century, including Pond plantation, c. 194 a., c. 1808. There were c. 480 a. of woodland in 1839,[97] 500 a. in 1910 when 450 a. were in the east.[98] Most of that woodland remained in 1988.

A mill with 12 a. of meadow and 15 a. of pasture was at Charlton in 1086,[99] and a mill was part of Charlton manor in the mid 13th century.[1] In the 16th century a copyhold water mill was near the parish boundary SSW. of the church.[2] It was a grist mill,[3] called Smith's in 1773 when it was within the park.[4] It may have gone out of use about then.[5] A windmill was part of the manor c. 1600, when it was in hand,[6] and in the earlier 17th century.[7] It was in the north-west part of the parish near the Charlton–Tetbury road.[8]

Non-agricultural trades developed little at Charlton. A weaver was mentioned in 1577,[9] shoemakers and a parchment maker in the early 18th century;[10] and there was a slaughterhouse at Perry Green in the early 19th century[11] and a saw mill near Elm Farm in the 20th.[12] A haulage business was run from Pink Lane Farm in the later 20th century.

LOCAL GOVERNMENT. Malmesbury abbey held view of frankpledge for Charlton, at Hocktide and Martinmas, in the later 13th century[13] and at the Dissolution,[14] and spring and autumn views continued to be held with manor courts until the 18th century.[15] From 1563 to 1598 the lord of Charlton manor was Sir Henry Knyvett,[16] whose treatise of 1596 on the defence of the realm shows him to have favoured local organization for defence and suggests that he was aware of his powers to enforce the law locally,[17] and in that period Charlton's courts were very active. That and the thread of efficiency and good organization which runs through local government in Charlton to the 19th century may be partly due to Knyvett's impact on a community whose origin[18] implied social and economic co-operation.

In the later 16th century the view of frankpledge was distinguished from the manor court, but later the two were held together; from the 16th century to the 18th additional courts baron were sometimes held. Leet business was done in the later 16th century and the 17th. In the later 16th the tithingman presented infractions of the assize of bread and of ale, millers for taking excess toll, and strays: his presentments were affirmed by jurors who corporately made additional presentments. Assaults were sometimes presented by the tithingman, sometimes by the jurors. Later the jurors made all presentments.[19] Other matters dealt with in the later 16th century under leet jurisdiction included the administering of the oath of allegiance to young men,[20] the tithing's failure to have the statutory rook net,[21] the playing of unlawful games,[22] and the harbouring of suspect women.[23] In 1564 the court ordered that the statutes should be complied with and that vagabonds, beggars, and the suspected should be taken to the constable for punishment. Thefts were punished by three hours in the stocks in 1564,[24] a day in the stocks in 1584;[25] and the making of a pillory was required in 1565. To sell ale between Easter and Whitsun was in 1565 forbidden to all but the parish clerk.[26] Archery practice was enjoined in 1579.[27] In the earlier 17th century a single body of jurors made presentments

[89] Inf. from Miss J. J. Walker, Great Lype Farm; local inf.
[90] V.C.H. Wilts. ii, p. 126.
[91] W.R.O. 88/2/43.
[92] Ibid. 88/2/34; 88/10/52.
[93] Andrews and Dury, Map (W.R.S. viii), pl. 17; O.S. Map 6″, Wilts. IX (1888 edn.).
[94] W.R.O. 88/2/45.
[95] Above.
[96] W.R.O. 88/2/57.
[97] Ibid. tithe award; above.
[98] W.R.O., Inland Revenue, val. reg. 11.
[99] V.C.H. Wilts. ii, p. 126.
[1] Reg. Malm. ii. 143–4.
[2] P.R.O., SC 6/Hen. VIII/3986, rot. 111; W.R.O. 88/2/22, view 7 Apr. 27 Eliz. I; 88/2/43.
[3] W.R.O. 88/2/34.
[4] Andrews and Dury, Map (W.R.S. viii), pl. 17.
[5] Cf. W.R.O. 88/2/57; ibid. tithe award.
[6] Ibid. 88/2/34.
[7] Ibid. 88/2/24, view 30 Mar. 14 Chas. I.
[8] Ibid. D 1/24/216/1.
[9] Sess. Mins. (W.R.S. iv), 28.

[10] Wilts. Apprentices (W.R.S. xvii), pp. 28, 121, 135.
[11] W.R.O., tithe award.
[12] Kelly's Dir. Wilts. (1939).
[13] Reg. Malm. i. 156–7.
[14] P.R.O., SC 6/Hen. VIII/3986, rot. 111d.
[15] W.R.O. 88/2/1–5; 88/2/21–5; 88/2/27; 88/2/29; 88/2/33. The 2 following paras. are based on those rec.
[16] Above, manors.
[17] Knyvett, Defence of the Realm.
[18] Above, introduction.
[19] For the later 16th cent. W.R.O. 88/2/1; 88/2/21–2; 88/2/29; 88/2/33.
[20] e.g. ibid. 88/2/22, view 29 Aug. 1583.
[21] Ibid. 88/2/1, view 3 Sept. 15 Eliz. I; 24 Hen. VIII, c. 10; 8 Eliz. I, c. 15.
[22] W.R.O. 88/2/21, view 18 Sept. 1578.
[23] Ibid. view 23 May 24 Eliz. I.
[24] Ibid. 88/2/1, view 27 Mar. 6 Eliz. I, ct. baron 18 Sept. 6 Eliz. I.
[25] Ibid. 88/2/22, view 23 Sept. 1584.
[26] Ibid. 88/2/1, ct. baron 26 Mar. 7 Eliz. I.
[27] Ibid. 88/2/21, view 2 Apr. 1579.

under leet jurisdiction and acted as the homage, and similar business was done.[28] In addition to bakers, tapsters, and millers a butcher was presented.[29] The prohibition against harbouring the suspected was extended to oblige those subletting to indemnify the parish and later to deny right of settlement to those thought likely to become a charge on the parish: in 1635 an inhabitant was penalized for failing to eject his own mother from his house.[30] From the later 17th century the courts continued to appoint the tithingman but dealt with little leet business.[31] The office of tithingman, like that of reeve, passed in the order in which the bread was received at holy communion.[32]

From the mid 16th century to the early 18th the most important business of the manor courts, apart from the normal recording of surrenders of and admittances to copyholds, was to confirm agreed changes in the way that the open fields and common pastures were used, and, by listing and amercing transgressors, to inhibit bad agrarian practice and establish precedent. Matters ranged from the recital of the boundaries of the manor in 1585[33] and the agreement with the lord following the inclosure of Braydon forest[34] to orders to scour ditches, ring pigs, brand cattle, tie up bitches in season, and share in paying a mole catcher.[35] The court appointed a hayward, a reeve, and overseers of the fields,[36] and in 1636 levied a rate to pay the hayward 2s. a week for overseeing the new common pastures.[37] Of particular and persistent concern was the maintenance of boundaries, both to restrict animals and demarcate, the limiting of common of pasture to certain times and numbers and kinds of animals, and the achievement of piecemeal inclosures of arable and pasture. The homage's adjudication in minor agrarian disputes was also recorded,[38] and in the later 16th century pleas between tenants were heard. In one a tenant demanded the return of the lower half of his wife's petticoat which, without his consent, she had pledged to buy firewood: the court allowed the gagee to keep the garment but ordered its full value to be rendered.[39] In 1580 tenants were forbidden to implead each other at any but the lord's court unless 40s. or more was claimed.[40] In the 18th century the courts continued to witness transfers of copyholds, new rules for husbandry were sometimes recorded and some new inclosures referred to, and officers were appointed, but most of their business was by then stereotyped and they had declined as an agent of local government.[41]

Charlton relieved its own poor and was apparently doing so in the 1570s.[42] Overseers' accounts

are complete from 1707 to 1835[43] when the parish joined Malmesbury poor-law union.[44] In each year one overseer served from Easter to Michaelmas, another from Michaelmas to Easter. Expenditure was divided between monthly doles and *ad hoc* payments for such things as shoes, clothes, fuel, funerals, rents, and, occasionally, repairs to buildings. Usually more was spent on doles than other payments: from April to September 1737, for example, £29 of the £39 spent was given as doles to c. 17 recipients. In 1751–2 £132 was spent. In the late 1760s and early 1770s the parish may have had a workhouse[45] but otherwise the method of poor relief was not changed. Expenditure rose in the late 18th century: it was £131 in 1775–6, £187 in 1791–2, £375 in 1798–9, and £809 in 1800–1. In 1802–3 monthly doles were paid to 30. Between then and 1835 with some fluctuation expenditure decreased, but it was often above average for a parish of Charlton's size and in several years exceeded £500.[46] The parish owned six cottages in Charlton in 1839.[47] In its first year Malmesbury union kept three Charlton paupers in the workhouse and relieved a further 44.[48] In 1974 the parish became part of North Wiltshire district.[49]

Overseers of highways were sometimes appointed in the manor court in the later 16th century,[50] presumably *ad hoc*, and in 1634 accounts were demanded from the overseers.[51] In the late 18th century two surveyors of highways were appointed each year.[52]

CHURCH. Charlton church was standing in the late 12th century.[53] It was called a chapel in 1248 and may then have been served by Malmesbury abbey, which took the tithes of Charlton,[54] but in the later 13th century was a daughter of Westport church.[55] The vicar of Westport took small tithes from Charlton and had a house and land there,[56] presumably all given by Malmesbury abbey, and in 1346 the abbey ordered the vicar to repair the chancel of Charlton church because the church was a chapel of Westport.[57] The church's status may have been in question in 1437–8 when, apparently to oblige the vicar or the abbey to repair the chancel, the parishioners denied that there was right of burial at Charlton and by implication that Charlton was a parish church. Bodies, which the parishioners said were taken to Malmesbury, were presumably buried at Westport.[58] From the 17th century or earlier baptisms, marriages, and burials were all at Charlton,[59] and, presumably because the glebe was at

[28] W.R.O. 88/2/23–5.   [29] e.g. ibid. 88/2/23.
[30] Ibid. 88/2/21, view 2 Apr. 1579; 88/2/24, views 25 Sept. 10 Chas. I, 4 Apr. 11 Chas. I, 30 Mar. 14 Chas. I.
[31] Ibid. 88/2/2–5; 88/2/27.
[32] B.L. Stowe MS. 1046, f. 47.
[33] W.R.O. 88/2/24, view 7 Apr. 27 Eliz. I.
[34] Ibid. 88/2/24, view 28 Sept. 13 Chas. I; above, econ. hist.
[35] e.g. W.R.O. 88/2/21, views 23 Sept. 1575, 2 Apr. 1579, 26 Mar. 22 Eliz. I; 88/2/24, view 23 Apr. 12 Chas. I.
[36] e.g. ibid. 88/2/1, view 15 Sept. 5 Eliz. I, ct. baron 3 Sept. 15 Eliz. I.
[37] Ibid. 88/2/24, view 23 Apr. 12 Chas. I.
[38] e.g. ibid. 88/2/22, view 1 Apr. 26 Eliz. I.
[39] Ibid. view 29 Mar. 28 Eliz. I.
[40] Ibid. 88/2/21, view 26 Mar. 22 Eliz. I.
[41] Ibid. 88/2/3–5.

[42] Ibid. 88/2/21, view 2 Apr. 1579.
[43] Para. based on ibid. 88/5/46/10; 1813/19–26.
[44] *Poor Law Com. 2nd Rep.* App. D, 559.
[45] W.R.O. 1813/20; 1813/29.
[46] Ibid. 1813/21–3; *Poor Law Abstract, 1804,* 566–7; *1818,* 498–9; *Poor Rate Returns, 1816–21,* 188; *1822–4,* 228; *1825–9,* 219; *1830–4,* 212.
[47] W.R.O., tithe award.   [48] Ibid. 1813/32.
[49] O.S. Map 1/100,000, admin. areas, Wilts. (1974 edn.).
[50] W.R.O. 88/2/1, ct. baron 26 Mar. 7 Eliz. I; 88/2/22, view 7 Apr. 27 Eliz. I.
[51] Ibid. 88/2/24, view 9 Apr. 10 Chas. I.
[52] Ibid. 1813/17–18.   [53] Below.
[54] *Reg. Malm.* i. 411–12.   [55] Ibid. ii. 343–5.
[56] Below.   [57] *Reg. Malm.* ii. 419–21.
[58] W.R.O., D 1/2/9, ff. (2nd foliation) 52v.–54.
[59] Ibid. bishop's transcripts, bdle. 1.

Charlton where several vicars lived,[60] Charlton was often mistaken for the mother church.[61] Its dependence on Westport was apparently marked by no more than the incumbent's title of vicar of Westport, but it remained dependent until 1879. Charlton with Brokenborough then became a separate parish served by a perpetual curate with Charlton as the parish church: Brokenborough church, also a daughter of Westport until 1879, became a chapel of ease in the new parish with no right of marriage until 1933. The Crown, patron of Westport, became patron of the new living.[62] The benefice was united with the vicarage of Hankerton in 1954 and the bishop of Bristol became joint patron: in 1961 the archbishop of Canterbury presented by lapse.[63] Brokenborough was detached from the benefice in 1984. In 1987 Charlton, without Hankerton, was joined to Lea and Cleverton and to Garsdon to form a new benefice: the bishop of Bristol and the Church Society Trust became joint patrons.[64]

In the late 13th century and later the vicar of Westport took small tithes from Charlton apart from Malmesbury abbey's demesne.[65] They were worth £25 in 1705.[66] In 1784–5 the vicar successfully refused compositions agreed with his predecessors.[67] Thereafter moduses were paid for the Charlton demesne land and Charlton park, and the full value of the small tithes was paid in respect of 2,250 a.[68] In 1794 John, earl of Suffolk and of Berkshire, paid the vicar a total of £260 for the moduses, the small tithes from Charlton and Brokenborough, and a lease of the glebe,[69] from 1800 £280, and from c. 1812 £430.[70] The tithes were commuted in 1840.[71] From 1879 the vicar of Charlton with Brokenborough was entitled to the rent charges from Charlton and Brokenborough and to the glebe.[72]

The vicar of Westport held land in Charlton c. 1286.[73] It was possibly 1 yardland and in 1409 and later included land in the open fields.[74] A house on it in 1438[75] was not one in which later vicars lived. By 1671, when the glebe was estimated as 56 a., it had long been used as a barn and there was no glebe house.[76] The glebe, all in Charlton, was 46 a. in 1839.[77] A large glebe house built in Vicarage Lane c. 1876[78] became the vicarage house of the new benefice in 1879.[79] It was sold in 1974. The new vicarage house built in its garden in 1973 was sold in 1981.[80] The diocesan board of finance

sold 35 a. of the glebe in 1982 and retained 5 a. in 1988.[81]

In the Middle Ages a house, called Our Lady's house, and 4 a. were given for masses in Charlton church.[82] Prescribed ornaments were not in the church in 1556.[83] The vicar of Westport apparently lived at Charlton in 1438,[84] and in the 17th century vicars lived and held services at Charlton. A house, apparently newly built, was leased to the vicar in 1609.[85] Matthew Whitley, vicar from 1650 or earlier to 1670, lived at Charlton, sometimes employed a curate, and was accused of persistent drunkenness, solemnizing a clandestine marriage, and claiming skill in palmistry.[86] Except in the mid 18th century most later vicars themselves held services at Charlton.[87] John Hollinworth, curate from 1768, vicar 1782–1800, lived at Charlton and solemnized there many marriages which might have been expected to take place at Westport.[88] In 1783 he held at Charlton a Sunday service every week and communion four times a year.[89] John Nicholas, vicar 1800–36,[90] lived at Charlton until c. 1810. John, earl of Suffolk and of Berkshire, added £150 a year to Nicholas's income c. 1812 to provide for additional services at Charlton, but the two quarrelled and Nicholas left Charlton: he was rector of Fisherton Anger, where he lived c. 1818 to 1825, and of Bremilham, and employed a curate to serve Charlton.[91] Thomas, earl of Suffolk and of Berkshire, favoured evangelicalism and appointed a scripture reader. In 1850 the reader was accused by the vicar, G. H. H. Hutchinson, of convoking congregations and convicted of allowing his cottage to be used as an uncertified place of worship: he was replaced by a second curate.[92] Only 90 attended the service at Charlton on Census Sunday in 1851, a congregation said to be smaller than usual.[93] Soon afterwards Alfred Church, later professor of Latin at University College, London, was curate.[94] Services in the earlier 20th century were more frequent and in 1933, for example, communion was celebrated 75 times at Charlton.[95]

In 1706 Frances Winchcombe, daughter of Thomas, earl of Berkshire (d. 1706), gave a rent charge of £4 for prayer books and Bibles for poor children in Charlton and other parishes: Charlton's share was £1. In the 19th century and early 20th the income was spent on such books to be given to children or sold cheaply to adults.[96]

The church of ST. JOHN THE BAPTIST, so

[60] Below. [61] e.g. W.A.M. xli. 7.
[62] Lond. Gaz. 7 Mar. 1879, pp. 1957–8; above, Brokenborough, church.
[63] Ch. Com. file, NB 5/3B. [64] Inf. from Ch. Com.
[65] Reg. Malm. ii. 322–3; W.A.M. xli. 7.
[66] W.R.O. 413/450.
[67] Ibid. 88/5/46/4, copy bill, Mitford's opinion, Ryder's opinion, observations on Westport vicarage.
[68] Ibid. tithe award.
[69] Ibid. 88/5/46/4, tithe acct.
[70] Soc. Antiq. MS. 817, iii, p. 135.
[71] W.R.O., tithe award.
[72] Lond. Gaz. 7 Mar. 1879, p. 1958.
[73] Reg. Malm. ii. 322–3. [74] W.R.O. 88/1/6.
[75] Ibid. D 1/2/9, f. (2nd foliation) 54.
[76] Ibid. D 1/24/216/1; D 1/54/6/1, no. 33.
[77] Ibid. tithe award.
[78] A new vicar was instituted in 1876: ibid. 1795/6.
[79] Lond. Gaz. 7 Mar. 1879, p. 1958.
[80] Inf. from Ch. Com.
[81] Inf. from Deputy Dioc. Sec., Dioc. Bd. of Finance, Church Ho., 23 Gt. Geo. Street, Bristol.
[82] P.R.O., C 66/1046, m. 1; W.R.O. 88/2/1, ct. baron 28 Mar. 15 Eliz. I.
[83] W.R.O., D 1/43/2, f. 20.
[84] Ibid. D 1/2/9, f. (2nd foliation) 54.
[85] Ibid. bishop's transcripts, bdle. 1; ibid. D 1/42/62; ibid. 88/2/46.
[86] Ibid. D 1/42/62; W.N. & Q. vii. 549–50; W.A.M. xli. 7.
[87] W.R.O., D 1/51/1, passim; ibid. bishop's transcripts, bdles. 2–3.
[88] Ibid. D 1/48/4; ibid. bishop's transcripts, bdle. 3; ibid. 1813/6–7.
[89] Vis. Queries, 1783 (W.R.S. xxvii), pp. 228–9.
[90] Alum. Oxon. 1715–1886, iii. 1020; W.R.O., D 1/48/4.
[91] Rep. Com. Eccl. Revenues, 852–3; Soc. Antiq. MS. 817, iii, p. 135.
[92] Devizes Gaz. 5 Apr. 1900; Hansard, 3rd ser. cxxxviii, p. 1843.
[93] P.R.O., HO 129/252/1/6/8.
[94] Devizes Gaz. 5 Apr. 1900; Alum. Oxon. 1715–1886, 251.
[95] W.R.O. 1813/12.
[96] Endowed Char. Wilts. (N. Div.), 217–18; W.R.O. 1795/6.

called in 1763,[97] consists of a chancel with north chapel and south vestry, a nave with north aisle and north and south porches, and a west tower against which is an extension of the aisle, and is of coursed rubble with ashlar dressings. The chancel and the nave and its four-bay arcade and its aisle were built in the late 12th century. In the early 14th the aisle may have been rebuilt and was extended westwards, the chapel and tower were built, and windows in the chancel and nave were renewed. Other windows in the chancel[98] and in the nave and nave aisle were renewed in the 15th century when the south porch was added. A large south window was inserted in the nave in the late 16th century or early 17th, and the upper stage of the tower was apparently rebuilt in the 17th century. A canopied monument to Sir Henry Knyvett (d. 1598) and his wife Elizabeth (d. 1585)[99] stood under an arch between the chancel and chapel until 1864 or later:[1] afterwards it was moved to the north wall of the chapel and the arch was replaced by a two-bayed arcade. The church was restored in 1874–5: the vestry was built, the original triple-lancet east window of the chancel was replaced by a window with geometrical tracery and a similar window was placed in the west wall of the tower, a gallery incorporating carved wood from Sherborne House (Glos.) was removed from the west end of the nave aisle, and the church was reseated.[2] A wooden rood screen and a pew, which was used by the earls of Suffolk and of Berkshire, incorporated elaborate 16th-century carving, and extended across nearly the whole width of the nave and nave aisle at their east end, were removed, and the pulpit, dated 1630, was moved from half way along the north wall to the south-east corner of the nave.[3] The north porch was built in the 19th century. A 17th-century altar table remains in use, 17th-century woodwork survives in the pulpit, and wood from the screen and the Suffolk pew has been re-used as an organ case in the chapel. The church, which was reroofed in 1926,[4] contains a late 12th-century font reset on a 17th-century base.

In 1553 the king took 3 oz. of plate and left a chalice of 11 oz. In 1988 the parish owned a chalice, a paten, and a flagon, all hallmarked for 1706 and given by Lady Frances Winchcombe and her father, and an almsdish given in 1851.[5]

There were three bells and a sanctus bell in 1553. A new peal was cast by Abraham Rudhall in 1712: a bell cast by John Rudhall in 1805 hangs in the ring of five as a replacement. The bells were in poor condition in 1924 and 1988.[6]

The registers are complete from 1661.[7]

NONCONFORMITY. Thomas, earl of Berkshire (d. 1669), and Charles, earl of Berkshire (d. 1679), were papists, and seven papists lived at Charlton in 1676. There was no papist there in 1680.[8]

Quakers lived at Charlton from the later 17th to the mid 18th century,[9] and in 1669 there may have been Presbyterians there,[10] but in 1676 only three protestant nonconformists were in the parish.[11] A meeting house for dissenters was certified in 1717. An Independent meeting house was certified in 1800, a Baptist one in 1819, another one, at Stonehill, in 1827, and possibly others in 1818 and 1833.[12] A small Primitive Methodist chapel was built at Stonehill in 1836: afternoon and evening services on Census Sunday in 1851 were attended by 38 and 35 respectively.[13] It had apparently been closed by 1882.[14]

EDUCATION. A day school, largely paid for by Thomas, earl of Suffolk and of Berkshire, was attended by 21 boys and 11 girls in 1833.[15] Charlton Park National school and a schoolhouse were built in the east part of the village in 1838.[16] Two dame schools were also held in 1846–7.[17] In 1858 c. 75 attended Charlton Park school, where land was provided for industrial instruction.[18] There were 76 pupils in 1871[19] and 73 in 1902.[20] Average attendance remained above 70 until the early 1930s: 49 children attended in 1935–6.[21] The school was closed in 1975.[22] A boarding school for c. 50 girls, Wings school, was in Charlton Park during the Second World War and until the early 1950s.[23]

CHARITY FOR THE POOR. Mary Howard, daughter of Thomas, earl of Berkshire (d. 1706), gave 8 a. in Brokenborough, the Poor's land, to the second poor of Charlton. In 1834 the rent from the land was £8 10s. and sums of between 2s. 6d. and 7s. were given at Christmas.[24] The charity, which was regulated by Scheme in 1925, gave small sums at Christmas until 1979: £5 17s. was distributed among 30 in 1950. The land was sold in 1960, and in the 1980s the charity made occasional gifts.[25]

[97] J. Ecton, *Thesaurus*, 403.
[98] J. Buckler, watercolour in W.A.S. Libr., vol. vi. 10.
[99] *Topog. and Gen.* i. 469–70.   [1] *W.A.M.* xlii. 184.
[2] *Kelly's Dir. Wilts.* (1939); W.R.O. 88/5/49; Soc. Antiq. MS. 817, iii, p. 139.
[3] *W.A.M.* xlii. 183; *Devizes Gaz.* 5 Apr. 1900. The date 1630 is on surviving woodwork.
[4] J. L. Osborne, *Villages of N. Wilts.* 47.
[5] Nightingale, *Wilts. Plate*, 194–5; inf. from the incumbent, Lea Rectory.
[6] Walters, *Wilts. Bells*, 49; W.R.O. 1813/14; inf. from the incumbent.
[7] W.R.O. 1813/1–11. Early 17th-cent. bishop's transcripts are ibid.
[8] Williams, *Cath. Recusancy* (Cath. Rec. Soc.), 239, 316.
[9] *W.N. & Q.* ii. 427, 463, 569; iii. 122; iv. 307; vi. 134.
[10] *Orig. Rec.* ed. G. L. Turner, i. 108; ii. 1056.
[11] *Compton Census*, ed. Whiteman, 129 n.

[12] *Meeting Ho. Certs.* (W.R.S. xl), pp. 19, 56, 84, 90, 114, 132.
[13] P.R.O., HO 129/252/1/6/9; W.R.O., tithe award.
[14] *Return of Churches*, H.C. 401, p. 228 (1882), 1; O.S. Map 6", Wilts. IX (1888 edn.).
[15] *Educ. Enq. Abstract*, 1032.
[16] P.R.O., ED 7/130, no. 62.
[17] Nat. Soc. *Inquiry, 1846–7*, Wilts. 12–13.
[18] *Acct. of Wilts. Schs.* 48.
[19] *Returns relating to Elem. Educ.* 420–1.
[20] W.R.O., F 8/220/1.
[21] *Bd. of Educ., List 21, 1908–38* (H.M.S.O.).
[22] W.R.O., list of primary schs. closed since 1946.
[23] Wilts. Cuttings, xxix. 147; inf. from Mrs. E. Seymour, Luccombe Mill, Bratton; local inf.
[24] *Endowed Char. Wilts.* (N. Div.), 217–18.
[25] W.R.O., L 2, Charlton; Char. Com. file; inf. from Mrs. M. E. Jones, 16 Pikefield.

CRUDWELL

CRUDWELL village[26] is 6 km. north-east of Malmesbury.[27] It took its name either from the stream flowing through it or from the mineral spring south-east of the church.[28] Besides Crudwell village the large triangular parish, 1,983 ha. (4,899 a.), contains Eastcourt village and Chelworth, Murcott, Chedglow, and West Crudwell hamlets.

The boundaries of Malmesbury abbey's large estate called Brokenborough, which included Crudwell village and other parts of the parish, were described in the later 11th century or early 12th, but none has been convincingly identified with the later boundaries of Crudwell parish.[29] The boundaries of Chelworth, Murcott, and Eastcourt were described separately about the same time. Those of Murcott and Eastcourt included watercourses which may have been those later dividing Crudwell parish from Hankerton. Eastcourt's south-eastern boundary, Braydon or Swill brook,[30] was a boundary of Braydon forest in the 13th century and of its purlieus from 1300 until the forest was inclosed in 1630. In the early 1630s the purlieus were divided among the lords of manors adjoining them: c. 300 a. south-east of Braydon brook were allotted to the lords of Crudwell and Eastcourt manors and became part of the parish.[31] The parish's western boundary followed the Foss Way under an agreement of 1208 × 1222.[32] The eastern boundary with Oaksey, on its present course in 1591, follows a stream in the south and Quallstocks Lane in the north.[33] The southern boundary on Windmill Hill, earlier common to men of Crudwell and Hankerton, was defined only at the parliamentary inclosure of Hankerton in 1809.[34] In 1896 the north-eastern boundary with Kemble, and in 1930 the western one with Long Newnton and Ashley, became county boundaries when those parishes were transferred to Gloucestershire.[35]

Crudwell lies in the valley of the Upper Thames.[36] A feeder of Braydon brook flows south-eastwards across the parish and two more rise south-west of Crudwell village. The highest land, at 135 m., is in the north, the lowest, below 90 m., in the south-east. Clay and limestone of the Forest Marble outcrop in most parts, Cornbrash around Eastcourt; nearly all the parish is suitable for both arable and pasture. Kellaways Clay and Oxford Clay outcrop in the south-east corner, where there is woodland, and there was formerly woodland further north-west around Chelworth.

Across the north part of the parish oolite outcrops in a dry east–west valley and its three northern tributaries: it has been quarried in several places.[37] Alluvium has been deposited by Braydon brook and its feeders, extensively along the south-east boundary. The relief is gentle, and high ground in the north and south-west has been used for airfields.

The Foss Way along the western boundary remained the main Bath–Cirencester road until a more westerly road through Tetbury (Glos.) was turnpiked in 1743.[38] The Crudwell section of the Foss Way may have continued to take traffic from Cirencester to Malmesbury and Chippenham until 1778 when a new road was built to link Crudwell village and Five Lanes junction in Charlton as part of a Cirencester–Malmesbury turnpike road. That road was disturnpiked in 1874.[39] Only a very small part of the Crudwell section of the Foss Way has been made up. The Crudwell–Minety road was called London Way at Eastcourt in the mid 17th century,[40] and in 1773 as in 1989 crossed Braydon brook at Pill bridge.[41] It was turnpiked in 1810 and disturnpiked in 1864.[42] Until 1778 Malmesbury was reached from Crudwell village by Crudwell or Tetbury Lane leading west to the Foss Way or by a road leading through Murcott and Hankerton: both survive, but from c. 1825 the Murcott road has led from the Malmesbury road south of the village and not from the village itself.[43] A lane also links Crudwell to Ashley, and Tetbury Lane and Crudwell Lane lead on to Long Newnton and Tetbury. North of Crudwell village an east–west road in the dry valley crosses the parish from Oaksey to Culkerton in Ashley: Tuners Lane links it to the west part of Crudwell village. In the east Quallstocks Lane, on its present course in 1591[44] and only a path in 1989, and other lanes and footpaths have linked Eastcourt, Oaksey, Chelworth, and Kemble. The road between Crudwell and Kemble was improved c. 1937 when the Cirencester–Malmesbury road was diverted through Kemble to avoid a runway.

Neolithic artifacts have been found in the parish, and a Bronze-Age bowl barrow may have been at Chedglow. Romano-British remains, including skeletons and coins at Murcott, have also been found.[45] No township in the parish was highly assessed for taxation in 1334. In 1377 the parish was apparently one of the most populous in the

[26] This article was written in 1988–9.
[27] Maps used include O.S. Maps 1", sheets 34 (1828 edn.), 157 (1968 edn.); 1/50,000, sheets 163, 173 (1974 edns.); 1/25,000, 31/99 (1951 edn.); 6", Wilts. III–IV, VIII–IX (1886–9 and later edns.).
[28] P.N. Wilts. (E.P.N.S.), 56; Aubrey, Nat. Hist. Wilts. ed. Britton, 23.
[29] Arch. Jnl. lxxvii. 42–53, 120; T. R. Thomson attempted to plot them on maps in W.A.S. Libr.
[30] Arch. Jnl. lxxvii. 111–24.
[31] V.C.H. Wilts. iv. 406–7, 444; P.R.O., C 3/452/68; W.R.O. 374/8.
[32] Reg. Malm. ii. 220–1; V.C.H. Wilts. iii. 230.
[33] W.A.M. vi. 198; below, Oaksey, introduction.
[34] Beds. R.O., L 26/1149, rot. 6d.; L 33/41; W.R.O., EA/132.

[35] V.C.H. Wilts. iv. 315.
[36] Para. based on Geol. Surv. Maps 1", solid and drift, sheets 251 (1970 edn.), 252 (1974 edn.).
[37] Below, econ. hist.
[38] V.C.H. Wilts. iv. 254–7, 268; L.J. xxvi. 241; J. Ogilby, Brit. (1675), pl. 55.
[39] V.C.H. Wilts. iv. 257, 269; L.J. xxxv. 436; Andrews and Dury, Map (W.R.S. viii), pls. 16–17; 14 & 15 Vic. c. 76 (Local and Personal).
[40] W.R.O. 374/8.
[41] Andrews and Dury, Map (W.R.S. viii), pl. 17.
[42] V.C.H. Wilts. iv. 257, 271; L.J. xlvii. 761.
[43] C. Greenwood, Map of Wilts. (1820); O.S. Map 1", sheet 34 (1828 edn.).
[44] W.A.M. vi. 198.
[45] V.C.H. Wilts. i (1), 62, 169.

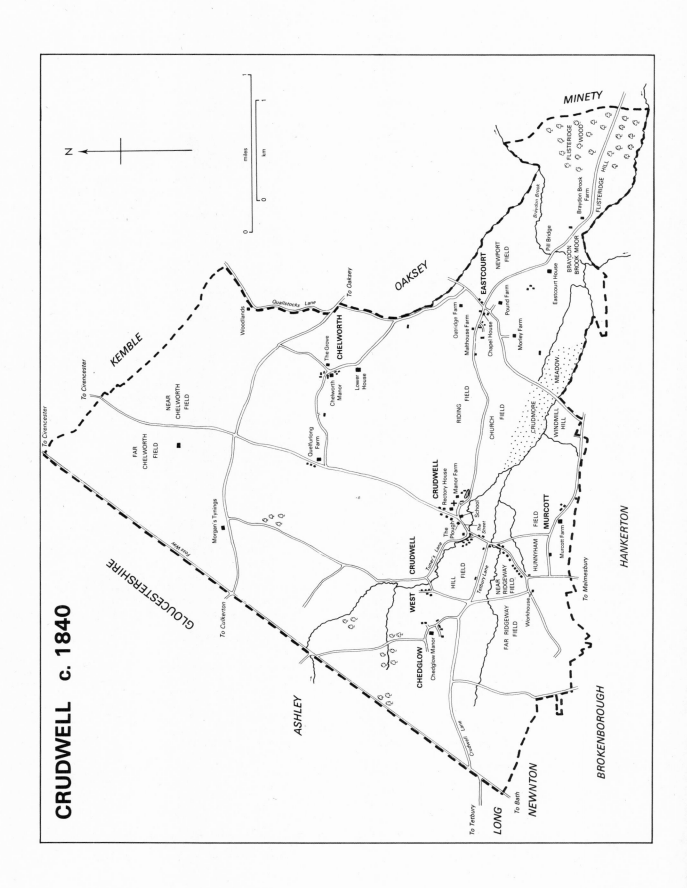

CRUDWELL c. 1840

MINETY

FLISTERIDGE
WOOD
FLISTERIDGE HILL
Braydon Brook Farm
BRAYDON BROOK MOOR
Pill Bridge
Braydon Brook

OAKSEY

EASTCOURT
NEWPORT FIELD
Eastcourt House

Oatridge Farm
Pound Farm
Malthouse Farm
Chapel House
Morley Farm

Qualstocks Lane
To Oaksey

Woodlands

KEMBLE

CHELWORTH
The Grove

To Cirencester

NEAR CHELWORTH FIELD

Chelworth Manor
Lower House

RIDING FIELD

CHURCH FIELD

MEADOW.

CRUDMORE

WINDMILL HILL

FAR CHELWORTH FIELD

Quelfurlong Farm

To Cirencester

Morgan's Tynings

CRUDWELL
Rectory House
Manor Farm
School
The Plough
The Street

MURCOTT
Murcott Farm

HUNNYHAM FIELD

HANKERTON

Foss Way

To Culkerton

WEST CRUDWELL
Turner's Lane

HILL FIELD

Tetbury Lane

NEAR RIDGEWAY FIELD

Workhouse

To Malmesbury

GLOUCESTERSHIRE

ASHLEY

CHEDGLOW
Chedglow Manor

FAR RIDGEWAY FIELD

Crudwell Lane

To Tetbury
To Bath

LONG NEWNTON

BROKENBOROUGH

N

miles
km

52

hundred: of 151 taxpayers 60 lived at Crudwell, 57 at Eastcourt, 20 at Chedglow, and 14 at Chelworth.[46] In the 16th century and earlier 17th Crudwell's assessments for taxation were among the highest in Malmesbury hundred.[47] The population fell from 512 in 1801 to 467 in 1811, but rose thereafter. Of the 681 inhabitants in 1841, 358 lived at Crudwell, 156 at Eastcourt, 58 at Chelworth, 55 at Chedglow, and 54 at Murcott. The population had risen to 799 by 1861, fluctuated in the period 1871–91, and fell to 574 in 1931. With the building of new houses after c. 1936 it rose again and was 924 in 1981.[48]

CRUDWELL church stands on a knoll, with the demesne farmstead east of it around the mineral spring and the rectory house west of it: Crudwell was an early endowment of Malmesbury abbey[49] and those sites were presumably used from the early Middle Ages. In 1230 the demesne farmstead included a hall, a large fishpond, and a chapel dedicated to St. Laurence. In the period 1260–96 the chancel of the chapel was reconstructed, the hall and fishpond were repaired, and new buildings, including a large stone-slated barn, two thatched barns, and two houses, were constructed. The farmstead was surrounded by a wall, the main gate of which still stood c. 1670.[50] It was apparently replaced in the 18th century or earlier by Manor Farm, in 1773 and 1820 called Paradise Farm,[51] a small farmhouse of stone rubble. A staircase was afterwards constructed in Manor Farm at the north end of its west side, and in the early 19th century the house was extended to the south-west by an L-shaped range with a symmetrical south front. The fishpond survived in 1989 when a large medieval barn was being made into a house. A church house may have stood near the church in 1597 and c. 1670,[52] and a school was built west of the church in the 17th century.[53]

Later settlement in the village was all west of the church,[54] where the older buildings are of stone, some with stone-slated roofs. In 1773 there were buildings in the Street and Tuners Lane but no more than one of those standing then survives. From 1778 the Street was part of the Cirencester–Malmesbury road, more houses were built beside it, including a toll house at the junction with Tetbury Lane,[55] and the village was extended southwards. On the east side a terrace of cottages was built in the later 18th century and a terrace of neo-Gothic cottages in 1847.[56] On the west side the Plough inn, open in 1841, was built in the

later 18th century and extended in the 19th; north of it Crudwell House, built in the earlier 19th century,[57] is of three storeys with an ashlared south front of three bays with a central Doric porch. Where a feeder of Braydon brook is forded at the junction of the Street and Tuners Lane is a small green, the cottages on the north and west sides of which in 1773[58] were rebuilt in the 19th century. To the south Town Farmhouse was built in the early 19th century,[59] and the Wheatsheaf inn, open in 1859,[60] a nonconformist chapel,[61] and estate and other cottages were also built in the 19th century. The straightening of the road between c. 1960 and c. 1980 created a small green at the junction with the lane to Chedglow,[62] and more houses have been built there.

On the east side of Tuners Lane 4 pairs of council houses were built in 1936, 4 pairs in 1938,[63] and 12 houses c. 1950. Private houses built in the village from c. 1980 include a total of c. 75 in estates on the east side of Tuners Lane called Day's Court and Brookside, and north and south of Tetbury Lane called the Dawnays and the Butts. The village became a conservation area in 1975.[64]

WEST CRUDWELL was a hamlet in 1268.[65] There was settlement in 1696 and 1773 east and west of a lane which connected Tetbury Lane and Tuners Lane.[66] On the east side of the lane were three farmhouses in 1805,[67] two c. 1840.[68] Only West Crudwell Farm stood in 1879, and the lane was its drive.[69] West Crudwell Farm was rebuilt in the earlier, and extended in the later, 19th century.

CHEDGLOW, so called by the 12th century,[70] gave its name to the hundred which presumably met there in the early Middle Ages,[71] and was a small village in 1377.[72] It was called Church Leaze in 1773 and 1820,[73] possibly by mistake. Settlement c. 1840 was on either side of a lane linking Tetbury Lane and the Foss Way, with Chedglow Manor and Oliver House on the west side and Manor Farmhouse and cottages on the east.[74] Oliver House was built as a long east–west range, possibly in the 18th century, and a south wing at the west end was added in the early 19th century: other additions are of the later 19th century and the 20th. Manor Farmhouse is a small 17th-century house and the cottages north of it are also 17th century.

CHELWORTH, less populous than Chedglow in 1377, remained a small settlement c. 1840.[75] It

[46] V.C.H. Wilts. iv. 298, 309.
[47] Taxation Lists (W.R.S. x), 29–30, 49; P.R.O., E 179/197/153; E 179/198/261; E 179/198/287; E 179/199/356; E 179/199/399; E 179/259/20.
[48] V.C.H. Wilts. iv. 346; Census, 1961; 1971; 1981.
[49] Below, manors.
[50] Reg. Malm. ii. 60–5, 366–7; Aubrey, Topog. Coll. ed. Jackson, 215–16.
[51] Andrews and Dury, Map (W.R.S. viii), pl. 17; Greenwood, Map of Wilts.
[52] W.N. & Q. vii. 336; Beds. R.O., L 26/1156.
[53] Below, educ.   [54] See plate facing p. 61.
[55] Andrews and Dury, Map (W.R.S. viii), pl. 17; Beds. R.O., L 25/168; L 26/1177, f. 104.
[56] Date and initials WM on ho.
[57] P.R.O., IR 29/38/93; IR 30/38/93.
[58] Andrews and Dury, Map (W.R.S. viii), pl. 17.
[59] Beds. R.O., L 25/168.

[60] Kelly's Dir. Wilts. (1859).   [61] Below, nonconf.
[62] O.S. Maps 6″, Wilts. ST 99 SW. (1960 edn.); 1/10,000, ST 99 SW. (1982 edn.).
[63] Dates on hos.
[64] Inf. from Co. Planning Officer, Co. Hall, Trowbridge.
[65] P.R.O., JUST 1/998A, rot. 4.
[66] Andrews and Dury, Map (W.R.S. viii), pl. 17; Beds. R.O., L 33/41.
[67] Beds. R.O., L 25/168; L 26/1177, ff. 38–42.
[68] P.R.O., IR 29/38/93; IR 30/38/93.
[69] O.S. Map 6″, Wilts. III (1886 edn.).
[70] P.N. Wilts. (E.P.N.S.), 57.
[71] Above, Malmesbury hund.
[72] V.C.H. Wilts. iv. 309.
[73] Andrews and Dury, Map (W.R.S. viii), pl. 17; Greenwood, Map of Wilts.
[74] P.R.O., IR 29/38/93; IR 30/38/93.
[75] Ibid.; V.C.H. Wilts. iv. 309.

lies along three lanes with its centre at their junction.[76] South-west of the junction Chelworth Manor was built to an **L**-shaped plan in the 18th century. Its short south wing was extended southwards to make a new entrance front in the mid 19th century, and c. 1920 the house was extended westwards and altered in Cotswold vernacular style. The Grove, in 1989 called Chelworth Farmhouse, is a small, gabled, 17th-century house enlarged in the 19th century. A circular well house on a small green was built at the junction in the early 19th century, and a range of 17th-century cottages, a three-storeyed house of the early 19th century, and a pair of estate cottages of 1881 are nearby.[77] Lower House was built south of Chelworth Manor in the 18th century. To the west, beside land called Church Green in 1879,[78] cottages were built c. 1800. The easternmost was greatly enlarged and called Chelworth House c. 1936 when many pieces of mainly 19th-century carved stonework were built into its walls.[79] About 1980 an estate of 29 houses was built north-east of the Grove.[80] West of the hamlet Quelfurlong Farm, called Aubrey's House in 1696,[81] Quelverland in 1773,[82] Quelverlong c. 1840,[83] was rebuilt, and cottages were erected north of it, in the later 19th century.

EASTCOURT was almost as populous as Crudwell in 1377,[84] and in the Middle Ages had a chapel of ease.[85] In 1696 and 1773 settlement was around the junction of the Crudwell–Minety and Oaksey–Hankerton roads.[86] To remove a stagger from the crossroads, where a toll house was built, the Minety road was remade on a more easterly course between the junction and Pill bridge when it was turnpiked in 1810.[87] Near the junction in the Crudwell road, called Eastcourt Lane, a large farmhouse of the 17th century or earlier 18th was called Malthouse Farm;[88] opposite, on the south side, are a former malthouse, possibly 18th-century, and a kiln. A school was built in Eastcourt Lane in the mid 19th century.[89] South-east of the junction a line of houses marks the old course of the Minety road. The northernmost is Pound Farm, an **L**-shaped 17th-century house with an asymmetrical north-east entrance front. Eastcourt House is the southernmost.[90] Other farmsteads were built away from the village in all four directions. To the north Oatridge Farm was built in the mid 17th century. It comprised three rooms and had a south-west entrance front, mullioned and transomed windows, and a newel staircase near the north-west chimney stack. Later in the 17th century a staircase with turned balusters was built

in a short wing which projected from the east end of the north-east side of the house. The easternmost room, which retains a transverse beam decorated with mid 17th-century plasterwork, was fitted with two bolection-moulded doors c. 1700. In the 18th century the staircase was incorporated in a larger wing. To the south Morley Farm was built on a three-room plan with a cross passage in the 16th century, and rebuilt in the earlier 17th. Additions were built on the west in the 19th and 20th centuries. A dry moat south of the house may mark the site of a medieval house. To the south-east Braydon Brook Farm was among several houses standing in the mid 17th century and presumably built after Braydon was disafforested c. 1630:[91] the south entrance front of Braydon Brook Farm was rebuilt in the 18th century, much of the interior was refitted in the 19th, and the south front was again rebuilt c. 1930. To the west Eastcourt, formerly Eastcourt Field, Farm was built north of Eastcourt Lane in the period 1840–79.[92] Of cottages built on the waste c. 1597 at Eastcourt, and near Braydon brook and Flisteridge wood, none survives.[93]

MURCOTT consisted of a farmstead and a few other buildings on the south side of the Hankerton road in 1696 and 1773.[94] Murcott Farm was rebuilt c. 1710[95] as a long north–south range, and has a seven-bayed east entrance front with mullioned and transomed windows and a central doorway. The interior was refitted and a long west wing was built at the south end in the 19th century. In the early 20th, a short west wing and a corridor connecting it to the long wing were built. On the north side of the lane cottages were built c. 1800, on the south side a house called Murcott Park was built in the earlier 19th century,[96] and Murcott remained a hamlet in 1989. A parish revel was held in the 17th century, possibly, as c. 1862, in August at Murcott.[97]

Outside the village and hamlets there was little settlement before the 19th century, although a house at Woodlands, rebuilt in the 19th century, stood in 1696.[98] On the north side of the Oaksey–Culkerton road two farmsteads were built in the 19th century, Gipsy's Lodge near the boundary with Oaksey between 1840 and 1879, and Morgan's Tynings, including a farmhouse, a pair of cottages, and later a bungalow, before c. 1840:[99] a third farmstead and a factory, the Pinnegar works, were built in the 20th century. Further north two other farmsteads originated in the 19th century and a pair of estate cottages was built

[76] Andrews and Dury, Map (W.R.S. viii), pl. 17; Beds. R.O., L 33/41.
[77] Date on bldg.
[78] O.S. Map 6″, Wilts. III (1886 edn.).
[79] W.R.O., G 7/760/41.
[80] O.S. Maps 1/50,000, sheet 173 (1974 edn.); 1/10,000, ST 99 SE. (1982 edn.).
[81] Beds. R.O., L 33/41.
[82] Andrews and Dury, Map (W.R.S. viii), pl. 17.
[83] P.R.O., IR 30/38/93.
[84] V.C.H. Wilts. iv. 309.
[85] Below, church.
[86] Andrews and Dury, Map (W.R.S. viii), pl. 17; Beds. R.O., L 33/41.

[87] Beds. R.O., L 25/168; L 26/1177, f. 104; O.S. Map 1″, sheet 34 (1828 edn.); above.
[88] O.S. Map 1/10,000, ST 99 SE. (1982 edn.).
[89] Below, educ.
[90] Ibid. manors.
[91] W.R.O. 374/8.
[92] O.S. Map 6″, Wilts. III (1886 edn.); P.R.O., IR 30/38/93.
[93] Beds. R.O., L 26/1156.
[94] Ibid. L 33/41; Andrews and Dury, Map (W.R.S. viii), pl. 17.
[95] W.R.O. 212A/27/23/2.
[96] Beds. R.O., L 25/168; P.R.O., IR 30/38/93.
[97] Aubrey, Topog. Coll. ed. Jackson, 215–16.
[98] Beds. R.O., L 33/41.
[99] P.R.O., IR 30/38/93; O.S. Map 6″, Wilts. III (1886 edn.).

beside the Cirencester–Malmesbury road in 1878.[1] In the west corner of the parish Chedglow barn was being made into a house in 1989.

R.A.F. Kemble was established from 1937 in the north corner of the parish and opened in 1938. The station was part of Maintenance Command and chiefly used for aircraft storage; several large hangars were built. In the period 1969–83 the Red Arrows, a permanent team which performed flying displays, was based there. In 1983 the station became part of Logistics Command, and servicing and repair work was undertaken, mainly for the United States Air Force.[2] The airfield buildings include a headquarters and a housing estate called the Firs. A small part of Long Newnton airfield is in the west corner of the parish.[3]

MANORS AND OTHER ESTATES. Although Malmesbury abbey's claim to have received 10 hides at Crudwell in 854 from King Ethelwulf may have been without foundation, long before the Conquest it is likely to have held a large estate there to which other land was added. In the period 871–99 King Alfred gave 4 hides at Chelworth, then part of an estate in Kemble, to a thegn, Dudig, for lives, with reversion to the abbey. Dudig sold his interest to Ordlaf, who in 901 exchanged the lands with Malmesbury abbey. At Eastcourt 10 *manentes* were held by the abbey, alienated, and restored by King Edgar in 974. The abbey claimed that in 1065 its Crudwell estate, 40 hides, also included land at Murcott and Hankerton and, since both were later part of that estate, the claim may be true.[4] A tenant held the Chelworth land in 1066 and William held it in 1086:[5] it was possibly the estate of 5 hides later held by Simon St. Owen. The assertion by Simon's son Ernulf that his grandfather had received it by royal grant suggests that it had been resumed, possibly by William II. Ernulf gave Chelworth to the abbey in the period 1141–59.[6] Andrew of Murcott (d. *c.* 1202) held freely of the abbey 1 hide at Murcott but no later freeholder is recorded.[7] The abbey retained its Crudwell estate until the Dissolution,[8] after which Hankerton and Cloatley in Hankerton became separate estates.[9]

In 1544 the Crown granted CRUDWELL manor, including land at Chelworth, Eastcourt, and Murcott, and later called the manor of Crudwell with Eastcourt, to John de Vere, earl of Oxford, and his wife Dorothy.[10] The earl sold it

in 1552 to John Lucas[11] (d. 1556) from whom it passed to his son Thomas[12] (knighted 1571,[13] d. 1611). Sir Thomas was succeeded by his relict Mary (d. 1613) and son Thomas[14] (d. 1625). From Thomas the manor passed to his son John[15] (knighted 1638,[16] cr. Baron Lucas of Shenfield 1645, d. 1671). Lord Lucas was succeeded by his daughter Mary (cr. Baroness Lucas of Crudwell 1663, d. 1702), wife of Anthony Grey, earl of Kent. Thereafter the manor passed with the barony[17] to Mary's son Henry Grey (cr. marquess of Kent 1706, duke of Kent 1710, and Marquess Grey 1740; d. 1740), and to Henry's grand-daughter Jemima Campbell, *suo jure* Marchioness Grey (d. 1797), wife of Philip Yorke, earl of Hardwicke. Jemima's heir, her daughter Amabel Yorke,[18] Baroness Lucas (cr. Countess de Grey 1816, d. *s.p.* 1833), relict of Alexander Hume-Campbell, styled Lord Polwarth, in 1810 sold 892 a. at Eastcourt, including Braydon Brook, Malthouse, Oatridge, and Pound farms, to Joseph Pitt:[19] that land afterwards descended with Eastcourt manor.[20] From Amabel, the manor, earldom, and barony passed to her nephew Thomas Weddell, formerly Robinson, Baron Grantham (d. 1859), who in 1833 took the name de Grey instead of Weddell. Earl de Grey owned *c.* 3,257 a. in Crudwell *c.* 1841[21] and was succeeded in the manor and barony of Lucas by his daughter Anne (d. 1880), relict of George Cowper, Earl Cowper.[22] The manor and barony descended to Anne's son Francis Cowper, Earl Cowper (d. *s.p.* 1905), and successively to Francis's nephew Auberon Herbert (d. *s.p.* 1916)[23] and niece Nan (d. 1958), from 1917 the wife of H. L. Cooper.[24] Between 1919 and 1923 Nan, Lady Lucas, sold the manor in portions. In 1919 T. W. Ferris (d. 1925) bought Manor farm, *c.* 350 a., in 1927 his trustees sold it to W. W. Saunders, and in 1935 Saunders sold it to Gonville and Caius College, Cambridge. In 1967 the college sold it to Mr. J. J. Blanch, the owner in 1989.[25] Lady Lucas sold *c.* 668 a. at Chelworth, possibly to T. H. Sampson, the owner in 1927. In 1943 that estate was bought for Mr. A. B. Blanch, the owner in 1989.[26] Murcott farm, *c.* 190 a., belonged to W. Payne in 1927:[27] in 1989, when it was 210 a., it belonged to Mr. N. G. Hughes.[28] Other farms, including Quelfurlong, 617 a. in 1919, West Crudwell, 231 a., Field Barn, 232 a., Odd, 200 a., Morgan's Tynings, 183 a.,[29] and Woodlands, have also descended separately.

In 1066 Ulwi held 1 hide and 1½ yardland at CHEDGLOW. Ernulf of Hesdin held the estate

[1] Date on bldg.

[2] C. Ashworth, *Action Stations*, v. 115–17; inf. from the Officer Commanding, R.A.F. Kemble; Defence Land Agent, Durrington.

[3] Above, Brokenborough, introduction.

[4] Finberg, *Early Wessex Chart.* pp. 74, 76, 78, 99, 105–6; V.C.H. Wilts. ii, p. 89.

[5] *V.C.H. Wilts.* ii, p. 126.

[6] Ibid. iii. 216–17; *Reg. Malm.* ii. 323–6.

[7] P.R.O., CP 25(1)/250/2, no. 33.

[8] *Valor Eccl.* (Rec. Com.), ii. 120.

[9] Below, Hankerton, manors.

[10] L. & P. Hen. VIII, xix (1), p. 286.

[11] P.R.O., CP 40/1151, Carte rot. 3.

[12] Ibid. C 142/107, no. 40.

[13] W. A. Shaw, *Kts. of Eng.* ii. 75.

[14] P.R.O., C 142/322, no. 156; mon. in St. Giles's church, Colchester (Essex).

[15] P.R.O., WARD 7/74, no. 73.

[16] Shaw, *Kts. of Eng.* ii. 205.

[17] P.R.O., DL 30/127/1905; for the Lucas fam., *Complete Peerage*, viii. 241–6.

[18] Beds. R.O., L 26/1177.

[19] Ibid. L 19/26.

[20] Below.

[21] P.R.O., IR 29/38/93.

[22] W.R.O., A 1/345/131.

[23] Ibid. Inland Revenue, val. reg. 4.

[24] *Who Was Who, 1951–60*, 680.

[25] *W.A.M.* xliii. 224; inf. from the Archivist, Gonville and Caius Coll., Camb.; Mrs. H. Blanch, Manor Farm.

[26] W.R.O., Inland Revenue, val. reg. 4; ibid. G 7/515/7; inf. from Mr. A. B. Blanch, Chelworth Manor.

[27] W.R.O., G 7/515/7.

[28] Inf. from Mr. N. G. Hughes, Murcott Farm.

[29] Beds. R.O., L 23/1036–7; L 23/1039–40.

in 1086[30] and it passed to his daughter Maud, wife of Patrick of Chaworth.[31] The overlordship of the estate, ½ knight's fee in 1242–3, was later held by another Patrick of Chaworth (d. 1257) and by his sons Pain of Chaworth (d. 1278) and Sir Patrick of Chaworth (d. 1315). Sir Patrick's heir, his daughter Maud,[32] married Henry, earl of Lancaster (d. 1345), and was succeeded by her son Henry (cr. duke of Lancaster 1351, d. 1361). The heirs of Henry, duke of Lancaster, were his daughters Maud (d. s.p. 1362), wife of William, duke of Bavaria, and Blanche (d. 1369), wife of John of Gaunt (cr. duke of Lancaster 1362, d. 1399). The overlordship was assigned to Maud and from her passed to Blanche. From Blanche it descended to her son Henry of Lancaster, whose estates were annexed to the Crown on his accession as Henry IV in 1399.[33] The overlordship of the duchy of Lancaster was last mentioned in 1626.[34]

Before 1202 the ½ knight's fee was held successively by Adam of Standen and his son Godfrey of Standen or St. Martin. In 1203 it was held by Godfrey's relict Alice and her husband Walter de la Hay,[35] and in 1242–3 by Hugh of Standen.[36] The mesne lordship was not mentioned again.

What was later called Chedglow manor was held of Standen by Walter Pendock in 1242–3.[37] Hugh Pendock held it c. 1258,[38] and in 1281 Hugh's daughters and coheirs, Beatrice, Maud, Josiana, and Agnes, held it.[39] Henry of Rodbourne, who held the estate in 1361, may have been a descendant of Walter Pendock.[40] The same estate was held by Thomas Packer (d. 1554), from whom it descended in the direct line to John Packer[41] (d. 1607), Thomas Packer[42] (d. 1623), and John Packer.[43] From that John (d. 1664) Chedglow manor passed to his relict Anne and, after her death c. 1670, to her executors. John Packer, grandnephew of John Packer (d. 1664), apparently held the manor in 1712[44] and was possibly the John Packer who sold it in 1722 to Richard Gastrell[45] (d. 1739). Gastrell was succeeded by his son John, who in 1754 sold the manor to James Clutterbuck.[46] In 1759 Clutterbuck sold it to William Earle[47] (d. 1774), whose son Giles sold it to John Freeman in 1785.[48] From 1795 to 1803 the manor was held in moieties by Elizabeth Freeman and Thomas Baldwin. William Peacey (d. 1815) bought it c. 1803 and was succeeded by his son Robert, who held c. 547 a. in the parish c. 1840.[49]

William Peacey, the owner in 1865,[50] sold the estate in 1900 to Hugh Baker (d. 1960), who was succeeded by his niece, Mrs. B. Capper (d. 1973). Her son, Mr. C. Capper, was the owner in 1989.[51]

Chedglow Manor was built to an L-shaped plan in the 18th century and incorporated re-used 16th-century beams. In 1761 there was a long avenue west of the house.[52] The south front of the east–west range was rebuilt and the north end of the north–south range was extended in the earlier 19th century, and in the later 19th the south front was heightened. A new north-west entrance front was built in the angle of the ranges in the 20th century.

In 1086 Alfred of Marlborough held 1 hide and 1 yardland in Chedglow with half a house in Malmesbury. The overlordship of the estate, ⅕ knight's fee, passed like the honor of Ewyas and manor of Teffont Evias to Robert Tregoze (d. 1265). It was last mentioned in 1242–3. Edward held the land of Alfred in 1086. In 1242–3 Henry of Chelworth held it of Robert Tregoze, and William Foliot and Ralph of Startley held it of Henry.[53] Ralph's daughter Maud settled land in Chedglow on Simon of Ford, his wife Ellen, and his daughters Alice and Margery in 1317.[54] The land was possibly that held in 1464–5 by John Moody.[55] Moody's Chedglow land passed like Foxley manor to his son Edmund (d. 1509), and in turn to Edmund's relict Elizabeth and son John[56] (d. 1549). That John's son John[57] owned it in 1586: he possibly sold it about then to John Packer,[58] the owner of Chedglow manor, and it was later part of the manor.

Two thegns holding 1 hide and 1½ yardland at Chedglow in 1066 could choose their overlord. Miles Crispin was overlord in 1086, and the overlordship descended with the honor of Wallingford (Berks., late Oxon.) to 1300 or later. A thegn, Siward, held the land of Miles in 1086.[59] In 1242–3 Adam of Purton and Hugh Peverell held 5½ yardlands in Chedglow.[60] Adam later held the entire estate but before 1293 conveyed it for a mass for his soul in Ashton Keynes church.[61] In 1549 the Crown, through agents, sold it to Thomas Walton,[62] the owner in 1586.[63] The estate was possibly that owned in 1647 by Edmund Estcourt[64] which Giles Estcourt sold to Richard Alexander in 1699. Richard Alexander, perhaps the same, and William Alexander sold it in 1729 to Richard Gastrell,[65] and it was added to Chedglow manor.

[30] V.C.H. Wilts. ii, p. 140.
[31] Ibid. p. 110.
[32] Bk. of Fees, ii. 728; Cal. Inq. p.m. i, pp. 113–15; V.C.H. Devon, i. 567–8.
[33] Complete Peerage, vii. 396–419; Cal. Inq. p.m. i, pp. 93, 110; Cal. Close, 1360–4, 208.
[34] P.R.O., C 142/406, no. 54.
[35] Ibid. CP 25(1)/250/3, no. 4; Cur. Reg. R. ii. 119, 205, 288.
[36] Bk. of Fees, ii. 728.
[37] Ibid.
[38] Cal. Inq. p.m. i, pp. 113–15.
[39] Feet of F. 1272–1327 (W.R.S. i), p. 19.
[40] Cal. Inq. p.m. xi, pp. 93, 110; Cal. Close, 1360–4, 208.
[41] P.R.O., C 142/106, no. 84.
[42] Ibid. C 142/296, no. 116.
[43] Ibid. C 142/406, no. 54.
[44] Ibid. C 5/260/2; ibid. PROB 11/332, ff. 56v.–57v.
[45] W.R.O. 149/76/10, deed, Packer to Gastrell, 1722.
[46] Ibid. 1636/1, deed, Gastrell to Clutterbuck, 1754.
[47] Ibid. 1636/1, deed, Clutterbuck to Earle, 1759.
[48] Ibid. 1636/1, deed, Earle to Freeman, 1785. For the Earles, below.

[49] W.R.O., A 1/345/131; ibid. 149/77/4; P.R.O., IR 29/38/93; IR 30/38/93.
[50] Harrod's Dir. Wilts. (1865).
[51] Inf. from Mr. C. Capper, Chedglow Manor; mon. in churchyard.
[52] Map of 1761 at Chedglow Manor.
[53] V.C.H. Wilts. ii, pp. 110, 142; xiii. 187; Bk. of Fees, ii. 725.
[54] Feet of F. 1272–1327 (W.R.S. i), p. 97.
[55] Feet of F. 1377–1509 (W.R.S. xli), pp. 143–5.
[56] Below, Foxley, manor; P.R.O., C 142/24, no. 26.
[57] P.R.O., C 142/92, no. 112.
[58] Ibid. CP 43/14, rot. 20.
[59] V.C.H. Wilts. ii, pp. 111, 146; V.C.H. Berks. iii. 523–6; Cal. Inq. p.m. iii, p. 466.
[60] Bk. of Fees, ii. 742.
[61] Cal. Inq. Misc. i, pp. 449–50.
[62] Cal. Pat. 1548–9, 185–7; P.R.O., REQ 2/16/101.
[63] P.R.O., CP 25(2)/241/28 Eliz. I East.
[64] Glos. R.O., D 1571/F 24.
[65] Ibid. D 474/T 14, deed, Gastrell to Sandford, 1744, endorsement.

In 1066 Edward and Siward each held ½ yardland in Chedglow. Almeric de Drewes dispossessed them and Durand of Gloucester held the estates in 1086.[66] Neither estate has been traced further.

In 1086 Tovi held 2 hides and 1 yardland in Chelworth of Malmesbury abbey.[67] That was possibly the estate held in 1314 by John, later Sir John, Bradenstoke and his wife Elizabeth.[68] They conveyed their estate, later called *CHELWORTH* manor or Bradenstoke's, in 1358 to Gilbert of Berwick[69] (d. 1361) and it descended to Gilbert's daughter Agnes, the wife of John Roches.[70] From John's and Agnes's son Sir John Roches[71] (d. 1400)[72] the manor passed to his relict William (d. 1410), and in 1411 was apparently allotted to John's and William's daughter Elizabeth, the wife of Sir Walter Beauchamp (d. 1430). It passed to Elizabeth's son Sir William Beauchamp (from 1449 Lord St. Amand, d. 1457)[73] and to his relict Elizabeth, who married Sir Roger Tocotes. In 1477 Elizabeth and Sir Roger assigned Chelworth manor to Elizabeth's son Sir Richard Beauchamp (from 1491 Lord St. Amand, d. 1508). Lord St. Amand was succeeded by John Baynton (d. 1516), the great-grandson of Elizabeth, wife of Sir Walter Beauchamp, and John by his son Sir Edward Baynton (d. 1544) and grandson Andrew Baynton.[74] Andrew Baynton sold the manor in 1547 to Nicholas Snell, who sold it in 1553 to William Earle[75] (d. 1586). Earle devised it to his son Thomas[76] (d. 1618), and it passed to Thomas's son Thomas[77] (will proved 1638) and daughter Margaret, the wife of John Partridge. John and his and Margaret's son Thomas owned it c. 1649.[78] Margaret Glanvill's estate, which she owned in 1684–5,[79] was apparently Chelworth manor and was later called the Grove. Thomas Snell owned it in 1696.[80] William Mill (will proved 1765) devised the estate, 105 a. in 1785, to his daughter Elizabeth (d. 1825). It was held by her husband, Toby Walker Sturge (d. 1841), and passed to their sons William, Samuel, Daniel, and Toby Walker as tenants in common. William sold his share to his brothers c. 1841 and the estate may have been sold c. 1843.[81] Thomas Buckland owned it 1865–80.[82] Grove farm, 82 a., was bought, possibly c. 1883,[83] by John Sampson, who owned it 1885–9. Jane Sampson, who may have sold some

of the land, owned it 1895–1915,[84] A. J. Telling 1927–31,[85] a Mrs. Jackson-Freeman in 1946,[86] and S. Kekewich (d. 1980) in 1956.[87] In 1978 Kekewich sold the 20-a. estate to J. C. Brownlow, who owned only 10 a. in 1989.[88]

Malmesbury abbey granted 3 yardlands in Eastcourt to Miles Kecy, to whose son Miles the land was confirmed in the early 12th or early 13th century.[89] That estate was possibly the origin of *EASTCOURT* manor, which belonged in 1533 to Sir Edward Baynton (d. 1544). His son Andrew sold it in 1555 to Henry Sharington, who sold it in 1556 to Thomas Walton (will proved 1593) and Thomas's wife Margaret.[90] The manor was later owned by Sir Henry Poole (d. 1632), whose son Sir Nevill[91] sold it before 1658 to Giles Earle (will proved 1677). Earle devised it to his nephew Thomas Earle[92] (knighted 1681, d. 1696): it passed in turn to Thomas's son Giles[93] (d. 1758), Giles's son William (d. 1774), William's wife Susanna (d. 1796 or 1797), and William's son Giles.[94] About 1807 Giles sold it to Joseph Pitt[95] (d. 1842), M.P. for Cricklade, who in 1810 added to it the Eastcourt land of Crudwell manor.[96] In 1844 Pitt's Eastcourt estate was sold to J. R. Mullings[97] (d. 1859). From Mullings it passed in turn to his sons Joseph Mullings (d. 1860) and A. R. Mullings (d. 1885). A. R. Mullings took the name Randolph in place of Mullings in 1877 and was succeeded by his son J. R. Randolph[98] (d. 1936),[99] who in the period 1910–27 sold Eastcourt Field, Malthouse, Oatridge, and Pound farms, a total of c. 670 a.[1] Randolph's executors sold the rest of the estate c. 1937 to C. E. D. Cooper, who in 1945 sold Eastcourt House and 480 a. to Maj., later Lt.-Col., S. A. Pitman, the owner in 1989.[2]

Eastcourt House was built in the years 1658–62 for Giles Earle. He, his nephew Thomas Earle, Thomas's family, and the south front of the house are depicted on a carved wooden overmantel in the drawing room. The carving shows a six-bayed house with an asymmetrically placed porch and, on the north side of the house at the east end, a turret surmounted by a cupola with a weathervane.[3] The house may have been L-shaped, with a service wing at the east end on the north side. The dining room retains a contemporary fireplace, panelling, and doorcases, and on the two floors above it a 17th-century staircase has been reset.

[66] *V.C.H. Wilts.* ii, pp. 46, 142, 146.   [67] Ibid. p. 126.
[68] *Feet of F.* 1272–1327 (W.R.S. i), p. 89.
[69] *Feet of F.* 1327–77 (W.R.S. xxix), p. 112.
[70] *V.C.H. Wilts.* xi. 243; *Cal. Inq. p.m.* xi, pp. 32–3.
[71] *Cal. Close, 1396–9,* 500.
[72] *Cal. Inq. p.m.* xviii, pp. 128–9.
[73] *Complete Peerage,* xi. 301–2; P.R.O., C 139/164, no. 18, rot. 10.
[74] *Cal. Inq. p.m. Hen. VII,* i, pp. 304, 306, 313; *Complete Peerage,* xi. 302–3; *V.C.H. Wilts.* vii. 180–1; P.R.O., E 150/982, no. 6.
[75] P.R.O., E 159/378, rot. 229.
[76] Ibid. PROB 11/69, ff. 161v.–163.
[77] Ibid. PROB 11/132, ff. 101–2.
[78] Ibid. C 3/456/47; ibid. PROB 11/178, ff. 210 and v., 263.
[79] Beds. R.O., L 26/1157.   [80] Ibid. L 33/41.
[81] Ibid. L 19/11–13; P.R.O., IR 29/38/93; IR 30/38/93; ibid. PROB 11/1856, ff. 396v.–399.
[82] *Harrod's Dir. Wilts.* (1865); *Kelly's Dir. Wilts.* (1880); W.R.O., A 1/345/131; ibid. 971/2.
[83] W.R.O. 374/130/34.
[84] Ibid. Inland Revenue, val. reg. 4; *Kelly's Dir. Wilts.* (1885 and later edns.).

[85] *Kelly's Dir. Wilts.* (1923 and later edns.); W.R.O., G 7/515/7.   [86] W.R.O., G 7/516/1.
[87] Ibid. G 7/516/2; mon. in churchyard.
[88] Inf. from Mr. J. C. Brownlow, Chelworth Farmhouse.
[89] *Reg. Malm.* ii. 67–8; *V.C.H. Wilts.* iii. 230.
[90] P.R.O., E 150/982, no. 6; ibid. E 159/378, rot. 229; ibid. PROB 11/82, ff. 321v.–322v.
[91] *Wilts. Inq. p.m. 1625–49* (Index Libr.), 148–50.
[92] M. F. Keeler, *Long Parl.* 309–10; P.R.O., PROB 11/353, ff. 123v.–124.
[93] *Hist. Parl., Commons, 1660–90,* ii. 251; P.R.O., PROB 11/435, ff. 165–6.
[94] *Hist. Parl., Commons, 1715–54,* ii. 1–2; P.R.O., PROB 11/1000, ff. 166–9; PROB 11/1292, ff. 214–20.
[95] W.R.O., A 1/345/132.
[96] *Hist. Parl., Commons, 1790–1820,* iv. 806–7; above.
[97] W.R.O. 374/130/35.
[98] Burke, *Land. Gent.* (1871), ii. 959; (1937), 1889–90.
[99] *Who Was Who, 1929–40,* 1121.
[1] W.R.O., Inland Revenue, val. reg. 4; ibid. G 7/515/7.
[2] Inf. from Mrs. S. A. Pitman, Eastcourt Ho.
[3] See plate facing p. 60. The weathervane, inscribed GE 1662, stood beside the N. doorway in 1989.

A room west of the dining room was fitted with bolection-moulded panelling in the early 18th century. A large block incorporating a staircase hall to the north was built on the west side of the house in the mid 18th century: it too retains contemporary fittings. In 1773 the house stood in a small park with a lake to the south.[4] In the 19th century the centre of the south front was extended and the south porch, dated 1658, was reset in the north front at the centre of a two-storeyed corridor built between the staircase hall and the service wing. Mahogany doors in the house may have been brought from Norfolk House, London.[5]

In the earlier 13th century Malmesbury abbey held land called Morley as part of its Kemble estate, and was overlord of the Morley land in 1361 or later.[6] Miles held MORLEY in the earlier 12th century, and his estate descended to his daughter Millicent and was claimed in 1200 by his grandson Miles of Morley.[7] In 1221 Miles of Morley established his right to ¼ knight's fee in Kemble and Morley.[8] Miles of Morley and Ralph of Hurley held that estate in 1242–3.[9] Geoffrey of Morley held it in 1283–4,[10] and in 1325 Geoffrey of Morley (fl. 1333) and his wife Felice settled the estate on themselves and Roger Norman,[11] who was granted free warren in his demesne lands in 1337.[12] Roger (d. 1349) was succeeded by his grandson Giles Norman[13] (d. 1361), who held a house and c. 108 a. From Giles, Morley passed to his cousin Margaret, the wife of John Chamberlain.[14] In 1363 Richard Cavendish and his wife Gillian, John Glemsford and his wife Beatrice, and William Chamberlain and his wife Christine, possibly Margaret's daughters and their husbands, conveyed the estate to Sir Gilbert Despenser and James de Lacy.[15] Despenser (d. 1382) sold his interest to Lacy,[16] and in 1384 Lacy's feoffees sold Morley to Robert Charlton and Robert's wife Catherine.[17] Robert, then Sir Robert, Charlton held it in 1391,[18] Sir Robert's son Walter in 1412,[19] and Walter's relict Joan Charlton in 1428.[20] In 1696 Morley farm was owned by Giles Earle.[21] It passed like Eastcourt manor to J. R. Randolph.[22] In 1927 G. H. Godwin owned Morley farm, 204 a.,[23] A. D. Godwin owned it in 1946,[24] E. F. Crocker in 1956,[25] and Mr. A. H. Brassey in 1988.[26]

In 1066 Guerlin held by lease 3 hides in Crudwell of Malmesbury abbey. Ebrard held the estate of the abbey in 1086.[27] It was possibly the estate, then 4 hides, which the abbey granted to Andrew of Stanton c. 1181.[28] Andrew's estate, which was possibly at West Crudwell, was held in the 13th

century for ¼ knight's fee by four or five tenants, one of whom in 1283–4 was the sacrist of Malmesbury abbey.[29]

In 1304–5 Reynold of Bradfield conveyed 6¾ a., which may formerly have been part of Stanton's estate, to his sister Margery and her husband Richard of Crudwell. The land descended to Richard's grandson John Chedglow, who in 1368 granted it and the reversion of 1 yardland in West Crudwell to Malmesbury abbey.[30]

In 1222 Malmesbury abbey appropriated all the great tithes of Crudwell except those from Chedglow manor.[31] They were granted in 1544 to John, earl of Oxford,[32] and descended with Crudwell manor. In 1842, by which time those from 2,197 a. had been merged, tithes owned by Thomas, Lord de Grey, from 1,306 a., were valued at £316 and commuted, and tithes owned by Joseph Pitt, from 30 a., were valued at £7 13s. and commuted.[33]

ECONOMIC HISTORY. In 1086 Malmesbury abbey's 40-hide Crudwell estate, almost certainly including land at Eastcourt, Murcott, and Hankerton, could support 25 ploughteams and did so. On the 18 demesne hides were 5 *servi* with 4 teams, and 48 *villani*, 24 bordars, 10 cottars, and 7 coliberts had a total of 18 teams. There were 24 a. of meadow. Three of the 40 hides were held by Ebrard and included demesne on which were 5 *servi* and 3 ploughteams, and 7 *villani* and 1 bordar had only 1 team between them. There were 9 a. of meadow. The land at Chelworth added to Crudwell manor in the mid 12th century had 2 teams, 6 *servi*, 6 bordars, and 8 a. of meadow in 1086.[34]

Crudwell manor had on it 40 oxen and 2 draught animals in 1210.[35] A large pasture astride the Foss Way, presumably west of Crudwell village, was common to the men of Crudwell, Chedglow, Ashley, and Long Newnton until 1208 × 1222 when that part east of the Foss Way was allotted to Crudwell.[36] In the later 14th century Crudmore was a common meadow in the south part of the parish.[37] In 1283–4 Crudwell manor had 17 tenants at Crudwell, 12 at Chelworth, 30 at Eastcourt, 6 at West Crudwell, and 10 at Murcott.[38] The demesne was presumably in hand when extensive new buildings were erected between 1260 and 1296.[39] In 1396 the manor had land in open fields around Chelworth, west and south of Crudwell village, and at Eastcourt. The demesne, on which were 5 bondmen, included 200 a. of that land,

[4] *Andrews and Dury, Map* (W.R.S. viii), pl. 17.
[5] Inf. from Mrs. Pitman.
[6] *Bk. of Fees*, ii. 733; *Cal. Inq. p.m.* xi, pp. 206–7; P.R.O., CP 25(1)/250/4, no. 9.
[7] *Rot. Cur. Reg.* (Rec. Com.), ii. 274.
[8] P.R.O., CP 25(1)/250/4, no. 9.
[9] *Bk. of Fees*, ii. 733.
[10] *Reg. Malm.* i. 152–3, 248.
[11] *Feet of F.* 1272–1327 (W.R.S. i), p. 119; 1327–77 (W.R.S. xxix), pp. 39–40.
[12] *Cal. Chart. R.* 1327–41, 389.
[13] *Wilts. Inq. p.m.* 1327–77 (Index Libr.), 206–7.
[14] *Cal. Inq. p.m.* xi, pp. 206–7.
[15] *Feet of F.* 1327–77 (W.R.S. xxix), p. 125; *Cal. Close, 1360–4*, 549.
[16] *Cal. Inq. p.m.* xv, pp. 235–6.
[17] *Cal. Close, 1381–5*, 420.
[18] Ibid. 1389–92, 362.
[19] Ibid. 1409–13, 312.
[20] *Feud. Aids*, v. 236.
[21] Beds. R.O., L 33/41.
[22] Above.
[23] W.R.O., G 7/515/7.
[24] Ibid. G 7/516/1.
[25] Ibid. G 7/516/2.
[26] Inf. from Mr. A. H. Brassey, Morley Farm.
[27] *V.C.H. Wilts.* ii, p. 126.
[28] *Pipe R. 1181* (P.R.S. xxx), 96.
[29] *Bk. of Fees*, ii. 733; *Reg. Malm.* i. 144–5, 152–3, 246.
[30] B.L. Cott. MS. Faust. B. viii, ff. 174v.–177.
[31] *Reg. Malm.* i. 264–7; W.R.O., D 1/24/65/4.
[32] *L. & P. Hen. VIII*, xix (1), p. 286.
[33] P.R.O., IR 29/38/93.
[34] *V.C.H. Wilts.* ii, p. 126; above, manors.
[35] *Interdict Doc.* (Pipe R. Soc. n.s. xxxiv), 22.
[36] *Reg. Malm.* ii. 220–1.
[37] B.L. Cott. MS. Faust. B. viii, ff. 176v.–177.
[38] *Reg. Malm.* i. 144–9.
[39] Ibid. ii. 366–7.

20 a. in common in Crudmore, and common of pasture for 200 sheep and 38 other animals, mainly oxen.[40] Some Eastcourt tenants apparently worked each Monday for the lord.[41] There is no evidence that men of Hankerton, tenants of Crudwell manor, had much land in Crudwell parish in the Middle Ages, but in the 16th century they claimed right of common on Windmill Hill, apparently successfully.[42] In 1532 the demesne, including pasture called Woodlands, was leased to members of the Poole family. Other pasture called Woodlands was leased in 1511. In 1540–1 c. 55 yardlands were in only 24 copyholds of which half were at Eastcourt. The largest copyhold, 8 yardlands, included land at Murcott, and there were others of 5 yardlands and 4 yardlands at Crudwell or Chelworth: those at Eastcourt, where 6 were of 1 yardland, were on average smaller.[43] In 1597 former copyholds were held on lease, 7 in Crudwell village, 3 at Chelworth, 2 at West Crudwell, 4 at Murcott, and 21 at Eastcourt: the largest were at Murcott, most of the smaller ones still at Eastcourt.[44]

The owners of land in Crudwell parish had rights to feed animals in Braydon forest and its purlieus until c. 1630. Of the c. 250 a. of the purlieus south-east of Braydon brook then allotted to the lord of Crudwell manor c. 27 a., Braydon Brook moor, remained common pasture. The rest, divided, inclosed, and improved, was added to farms in the parish and some was ploughed. The c. 50 a. allotted to the lord of Eastcourt manor was added to the adjoining Oaksey park which he also owned. In 1649 the arrangements made c. 1630 were disputed by the lord of Chelworth manor, apparently unsuccessfully.[45]

Throughout the 18th century c. 1,000 a. of open field and common pasture lay around Crudwell, Chelworth, Murcott, and Eastcourt, but most of Crudwell manor was inclosed land. Morgan's Tynings farm, c. 175 a., was formed between 1724 and 1755, on new inclosures to judge from its name. Quelfurlong farm, 454 a. c. 1755, was mainly a dairy farm; Oatridge farm, held 1734–9 by Daniel Oatridge, a Tetbury cheese factor, may also have been a dairy farm. Six other farms were of more than 200 a. c. 1755, two based in Crudwell village, two at Chelworth, one of 383 a. at Eastcourt, and Woodlands farm, 265 a. Other farms included Murcott, 180 a., one of 119 a. at West Crudwell, one of 142 a. at Eastcourt, and 11 of less than 100 a.[46]

In 1805 the open arable around Chelworth was in Far and Near Chelworth fields, west and south of Crudwell village in Hill, Hunnyham, and Far and Near Ridgeway fields, and around Eastcourt in Newport, Church, and Riding fields. There were small common pastures including one of 13

a. on Windmill Hill and others totalling 4 a. at Chelworth Lane and Chelworth Green. Braydon Brook moor was then several.[47] In 1815 it was agreed to inclose the open arable and common pastures and to re-allot old inclosures, and an Act was passed in 1816: the land was presumably inclosed soon afterwards but an award was not made until 1841.[48]

The four small estates at Chedglow in 1086, a total of c. 4 hides and ½ yardland, could support 2 ploughteams and 6 oxen and included small amounts of demesne and of meadow land; one had an exceptionally large pasture of 1½ yardland.[49] Later in the Middle Ages Chedglow possibly had its own open fields, North and West. The lord of Chedglow manor held land in the open fields of Crudwell and in Crudmore meadow,[50] for which 18 a. were allotted at inclosure,[51] but the land of Chedglow had all been inclosed by 1761.[52]

There was c. 1840 marginally more arable, 2,280 a. in the north, west, and south-east parts of the parish, than pasture, 2,251 a. Both arable and pasture fields were large, 20–30 a., but tended to be smaller near the settlements. In the north only Quelfurlong farm, 260 a., and a 206-a. farm at Chelworth were entirely pasture. Farms of 375 a., 221 a., and 94 a. at Chelworth, and Morgan's Tynings, 185 a., were all arable: at Chelworth only Grove farm, 128 a., had both arable and pasture. Three farms based in Crudwell village, Manor, 268 a., and others of 35 a. and 16 a., were entirely pasture. South of the village Murcott farm, 134 a., included only one field of arable, 26 a.; west of the village West Crudwell farm, 45 a., was entirely pasture, and a 113-a. farm at West Crudwell and Chedglow Manor farm, 547 a., contained both arable and pasture. All the farms in the south-east were in the Eastcourt estate: a 309-a. farm with farmsteads at Malthouse and Pound Farms, Oatridge, 230 a., Morley, 200 a., and farms of 87 a. and 59 a. all contained arable and pasture; only Eastcourt Manor farm, 115 a., contained no arable. In 1863 c. 45 a. were still in Oaksey park. A new farm, Eastcourt Field, later Eastcourt, 165 a., was formed between c. 1840 and 1879 with a new farmstead between Eastcourt and Crudwell villages.[53]

Later in the 19th century less land was ploughed, and in 1936 only about a sixth of the parish was arable.[54] In the period 1936–66 arable increased to half the parish. Wheat was the chief cereal crop 1867–1936, and turnips and swedes were grown on nearly half the c. 500 a. under root crops 1867–1916. Barley replaced wheat as the main cereal 1946–76. Until c. 1956 about three quarters of the grassland was permanent pasture, more thereafter. In 1937 the c. 260 a. of R.A.F.

[40] B.L. Add. MS. 6165, p. 109; ibid. Cott. MS. Faust. B. viii, ff. 176v.–177; Beds. R.O., L 25/168; L 26/1177.
[41] P.R.O., SC 6/Hen. VIII/3986, rot. 104d.
[42] Beds. R.O., L 26/1149, rot. 6d.; W.R.O., EA/132.
[43] P.R.O., SC 6/Hen. VIII/3986, rott. 103d.–105.
[44] Beds. R.O., L 26/1156.
[45] Ibid. L 25/168; L 26/1177, f. 106; W.R.O. 374/8; P.R.O., C 3/452/68; above, introduction; below, Oaksey, manor.
[46] Beds. R.O., L 19/71; L 19/75; L 19/164; L 26/1159; L 30/8/2/3; W.R.O. 212A/27/23/2, deed, 1710.
[47] Beds. R.O., L 25/168; L 26/1177; Glos. R.O., D 674B/P 74.
[48] L.J. l. 649, 743; Beds. R.O., L 30/11/301/313; W.R.O.,

EA/160; P.R.O., IR 29/38/93; IR 30/38/93.
[49] V.C.H. Wilts. ii, pp. 140, 142, 146.
[50] W.R.O. 149/76/10, deed, 1722.
[51] Ibid. EA/160.
[52] Map of 1761 in Chedglow Manor.
[53] P.R.O., IR 29/38/93; IR 30/38/93; O.S. Map 6″, Wilts. III (1886 edn.); W.R.O. 374/129/41.
[54] Para. based on P.R.O., MAF 68/151, sheet 1; MAF 68/493, sheet 6; MAF 68/1063, sheet 15; MAF 68/1633, sheet 3; MAF 68/2203, sheet 5; MAF 68/2773, sheet 9; MAF 68/3319, sheet 10; MAF 68/3814, no. 139; MAF 68/4182, no. 139; MAF 68/4552, no. 139; MAF 68/5004, no. 139; MAF 68/5505, no. 139.

Kemble ceased to be used for agriculture.[55] Most of the new grassland in the parish in the later 19th century and earlier 20th was used for cattle rearing and dairy farming: there were usually over 1,000 cattle in the parish in the period 1867–1926, more after the Second World War. Sheep farming, however, declined only after c. 1930: there were usually over 2,500 sheep in the parish 1867–1926, and the land was sometimes used for large flocks later. Pigs were also numerous 1867–1976. There were c. 25 farms in the parish 1906–16, of which the largest were Chelworth, 668 a., Quelfurlong, 594 a., Chedglow, 577 a., and Crudwell Manor, 547 a. including Morgan's Tynings.[56] Odd and Lower Odd farms at Chelworth were formed in the early 20th century.[57] In 1966 four of the 25 farms were 1,000 a. or more.

In 1985 the farmland was again half pasture and half arable. Wheat was again the chief cereal crop, and 1,150 cows and 3,150 sheep were kept.[58] The north and west parts of the parish were mainly arable, the east mainly grassland, in 1989. Of c. 20 farms Chelworth Manor, 650 a., Chedglow Manor, 610 a., Crudwell Manor, 350 a., Lower Odd, 238 a. including Odd, and Quelfurlong, 210 a., were all mainly arable. Cattle for beef were also reared on Lower Odd farm, and Morgan's Tynings, c. 200 a., was a mixed farm. Eastcourt House farm, 480 a., Murcott farm, 210 a., and Oatridge farm, 200 a., were all grassland, Murcott for sheep, Oatridge for beef cattle. Eastcourt, 350 a., was an arable and dairy farm with a pedigree herd of Holstein Friesian cattle. Smaller farms included Crudwell Court, 107 a. on which wheat and potatoes were grown and cattle reared for beef, and West Crudwell, 100 a., a sheep farm.[59] Horses were trained at Oliver House Stud in 1984[60] and 1989.

There was woodland 2 leagues square in Malmesbury abbey's Crudwell estate in 1086, when three estates at Chedglow each had 1 a. of wood.[61] In the early Middle Ages there was also woodland near Chelworth hamlet: some, possibly to the north-east where Woodlands was a large pasture in 1540–1, was assarted before c. 1150.[62] A wood called Flisteridge, which Malmesbury abbey claimed c. 1257 had been included in Braydon forest between 1199 and 1216, was used for pasture by the tenants of Crudwell and other manors as part of the purlieus of the forest, but in 1278 the abbey successfully excluded from the wood between 29 September and 11 November tenants

of Oaksey manor who claimed pannage in it for the whole year.[63] Very little of the c. 300 a. of the purlieus allotted for Crudwell and Eastcourt manors c. 1630 was woodland in the later 18th century. Flisteridge wood was planted on 112 a. of that land between 1773 and c. 1840 and remained a wood of that size in 1989. About 1840 there were also 12 a. of plantation and coppices at Chedglow.[64]

An inhabitant of Crudwell bought wool at Cirencester c. 1615 to sell speculatively,[65] and a weaver lived in the parish in 1736.[66] Limestone has been quarried in the north part of the parish from the 18th century or earlier. There was a quarry at Chedglow in 1774, and quarries, one with a lime kiln, were worked on the north side of the Oaksey–Culkerton road in the 19th and 20th centuries.[67] A public stone pit on Windmill Hill was allotted to the inhabitants of Crudwell parish in 1841.[68] Masons were based in the parish from the 18th century to the 1930s.[69] There was a chandler's shop at Crudwell in 1773.[70] From c. 1867 to 1964 manufacturers of veterinary chemicals and medicines, Thomas Pettifer & Son, from 1883 Stephen Pettifer & Sons Ltd., were based in Crudwell, from c. 1889 at Mayfield House, and held 1911–15 a royal warrant for Santovin, a worm drench for sheep.[71]

A factory for the manufacture of agricultural machinery was opened on c. 4 a. south of Kemble airfield by Mr. A. B. Blanch c. 1943 and called the Pinnegar works. About 1947 A. B. Blanch & Co. Ltd., from 1952 the Alvan Blanch Development Co. Ltd., moved to Chelworth Manor, and in 1989 still made agricultural machinery, chiefly for export. Agricultural machinery continued to be made at the Pinnegar works under the management of Blanch-Lely until 1969, when the factory was bought by Rigid Containers Ltd., manufacturers of corrugated paper and fibreboard cases. The factory was on a 7-a. site in 1989 and 100 people were employed in it.[72] J. T. Carpenter & Sons, a firm of haulage contractors, had a depot in Crudwell village in 1989.

Mayfield House was a hotel from c. 1965,[73] and Crudwell Court, formerly the Rectory, was one from 1986.[74]

The only mill on Malmesbury abbey's Crudwell estates in 1086 was at Chelworth.[75] Men of Crudwell may also have ground corn at the abbey's mill at Charlton 1246–60.[76] A mill at Crudwell in the later 13th century and earlier 14th may have

[55] Inf. from Defence Land Agent, Durrington; above, introduction.
[56] Kelly's Dir. Wilts. (1907); W.R.O., Inland Revenue, val. reg. 4.
[57] Inf. from Mr. R. J. Wilson, Lower Odd Farm.
[58] P.R.O., MAF 68/5980, no. 139.
[59] Inf. from Mrs. H. Blanch, Manor Farm; Mr. A. R. Thornton, Crudwell Ct. Farm; Mrs. C. Browning, W. Crudwell Farm; Mrs. S. A. Pitman, Eastcourt Ho.; Mr. C. Hart, Eastcourt Farm; Mr. N. G. Hughes, Murcott Farm; Mrs. D. E. Hislop, Oatridge Farm; Mr. A. B. Blanch, Chelworth Manor; Mr. Wilson; Mr. P. G. Dyke, Quelfurlong Farm; T. H. Clark & Sons, Morgan's Tynings Farm; Mr. C. Capper, Chedglow Manor.
[60] Daily Telegraph, 8 Feb. 1984.
[61] V.C.H. Wilts. ii, pp. 126, 140, 142, 146.
[62] Reg. Malm. i. 455; ii. 323–6; P.R.O., SC 6/Hen. VIII/3986, rot. 103d.
[63] V.C.H. Wilts. iv. 402, 405; below, Oaksey, econ. hist.

[64] Andrews and Dury, Map (W.R.S. viii), pl. 17; P.R.O., IR 29/38/93; IR 30/38/93.
[65] Early-Stuart Tradesmen (W.R.S. xv), p. 89.
[66] Q. Sess. 1736 (W.R.S. xi), p. 142.
[67] Coroners' Bills, 1752–96 (W.R.S. xxxvi), p. 57; P.R.O., IR 29/38/93; IR 30/38/93; Beds. R.O., L 19/13; W.R.O. 374/130/34; ibid. Inland Revenue, val. reg. 4; O.S. Map 1/25,000, 31/99 (1951 edn.).
[68] W.R.O., EA/160.
[69] Wilts. Apprentices (W.R.S. xvii), p. 72; Kelly's Dir. Wilts. (1890 and later edns.); Beds. R.O., L 19/264.
[70] Meeting Ho. Certs. (W.R.S. xl), p. 29.
[71] Kelly's Dir. Wilts. (1867 and later edns.); inf. from Mr. J. Pettifer, 9A Roland Gardens, Lond. SW. 7.
[72] Inf. from Mr. A. B. Blanch, Chelworth Manor; Mr. E. C. J. Bussey, Rigid Containers Ltd., Crudwell.
[73] W.R.O., G 7/516/3.
[74] Inf. from Mrs. S. Howe, Crudwell Ct.
[75] V.C.H. Wilts. ii, p. 126.   [76] Reg. Malm. ii. 143–4.

NORTON
Norton Manor, built *c.* 1623, from the south-west

CRUDWELL
Overmantel depicting Eastcourt House, built 1658–62, and the Earle family

CRUDWELL: THE VILLAGE CENTRE IN THE EARLY 20TH CENTURY

DAUNTSEY: THE SCHOOL AND ALMSHOUSE, BUILT 1864–6

CHARLTON: PARK STREET IN THE MID 20TH CENTURY

been the windmill which was ruinous in 1396 or earlier[77] and presumably stood on Windmill Hill. There may have been a watermill on Braydon brook south-east of Eastcourt village before 1696.[78]

LOCAL GOVERNMENT

Records of courts called view of frankpledge with court of the manor for Crudwell manor are extant for 1562–1602, 1617–26, 1671–84, and 1710.[79] By 1815 no court had been held for many years.[80] A court leet and court baron was revived in 1830, held only when business required it, and discontinued in 1917. Courts were held twice yearly in the 16th and 17th centuries. The business of the view was recorded in Latin, that of the manor court separately in English. At the views a tithingman each for Crudwell and Eastcourt was elected, cert money was paid, and bakers and brewers were presented for giving short measure. The manor court appointed a reeve and a hayward each autumn and sheeptellers from 1673, regulated common husbandry, was told of stray animals which had been impounded, and ordered roads, ditches, ponds, and boundary stones to be maintained. Members of the Wygold family, bondmen of the manor, were licensed to live outside it in 1562 and 1570 but in 1576 and 1617 were said to do so without permission. In 1623 fines of 10s. were imposed for playing skittles. In the 15th and 16th centuries a tithingman from Chedglow attended courts held for the honor of Wallingford, paid cert money, and invariably had nothing to present.[81]

About a quarter of the parishioners received poor relief in 1803: 10 were in the workhouse south-west of the village and about a third of the £577 raised by the poor rate was spent on them. Work was also provided for those relieved outside the workhouse.[82] In the years 1813–15 about a quarter were still relieved, but then at an average cost of £735: 11 were in the workhouse, and outside it 35 were relieved continuously, 56 occasionally.[83] In 1816 only £392 was spent on the poor, but in the years 1817–34 the average £632 spent yearly was surpassed among the parishes of the area only by Brinkworth and Malmesbury.[84] Crudwell became part of Malmesbury poor-law union in 1835.[85] Vestries, which were meeting by 1775,[86] were, like the courts, held in the workhouse in the earlier 19th century.[87] Crudwell became part of North Wiltshire district in 1974.[88]

CHURCH

Crudwell church, apparently standing in the 10th or 11th century,[89] belonged to Malmesbury abbey in 1151 when Hankerton church was dependent on it. The abbey later presented a rector, apparently between 1151 and 1191.[90] Hankerton became a separate parish in 1445.[91] Crudwell rectory was united with Ashley rectory in 1955, and in 1987 Crudwell and Ashley became part of a new benefice with Oaksey, Hankerton, and Long Newnton.[92]

The abbot of Malmesbury presented rectors until the Dissolution, except in 1361 and 1510 when the king presented because the abbey was vacant, and in 1392 when, presumably with the abbot's consent, the king presented one of his clerks.[93] The Crown granted the advowson to John, earl of Oxford, in 1544[94] and it descended with Crudwell manor. In 1552 John Lucas leased it for 60 years to Thomas Walton, whose assigns John White and Robert Earle presented in 1554 and 1580 respectively. The lords thereafter presented, except in 1763 when Reginald Lygon did so, presumably by grant of a turn.[95] In 1834 Thomas, Earl de Grey, sold the advowson to William Maskelyne[96] (d. 1840), who presented his son William Maskelyne (d. 1866) as rector.[97] That rector inherited the advowson and devised it to his wife Sarah, who in 1867 presented Oswald Smith. Afterwards Smith bought the advowson and in 1888 his trustee Jason Smith presented W. A. Sole (d. 1898), who himself afterwards bought the advowson. Sole's trustees remained patrons[98] and in 1955 became entitled to present alternately and in 1987 jointly at three of four turns.[99]

In 1291 the rectory was valued at £6 13s. 4d.[1] It was worth £18 in 1535,[2] £96 in 1650.[3] Its average income of £487 in the years 1829–31 made the benefice one of the richer in Malmesbury deanery.[4]

Until 1222 rectors were apparently entitled to the whole income of the church, paying a pension of £2 to Malmesbury abbey. In 1222, under arrangements to become effective on the death of the incumbent rector, the abbey appropriated most of the great tithes, extinguished the pension, and allotted to the rector the great tithes from Chedglow manor, the hay tithes from the abbey's demesne in the parish, and all the small tithes.[5] The new rector challenged those arrangements c. 1230 but in 1231 they were confirmed by the pope.[6] The rector's tithes were valued at £589 in 1842 and commuted.[7]

[77] Ibid. 273; *Inq. Non.* (Rec. Com.), 166; B.L. Add. MS. 6165, p. 109.
[78] Beds. R.O., L 33/41.
[79] Para. based on ibid. L 26/1149–52; L 26/1154–5; P.R.O., DL 30/127/1905; W.R.O. 1165/8.
[80] Beds. R.O., L 30/11/301/313.
[81] For the honor cts., P.R.O., SC 2/212/2, rot. 4; SC 2/212/9, rot. 2d.; SC 2/212/14; SC 2/212/18, rot. 4; SC 2/212/19, rot. 15; SC 2/212/20, rot. 1; SC 2/212/24, rot. 3d.
[82] Ibid. IR 29/38/93; IR 30/38/93; *Poor Law Abstract, 1804,* 566–7.
[83] *Poor Law Abstract, 1818,* 498–9.
[84] *Poor Rate Returns, 1816–21,* 188; *1822–4,* 228; *1825–9,* 219; *1830–4,* 212.
[85] *Poor Law Com. 2nd Rep.* App. D, 559.
[86] *Endowed Char. Wilts.* (N. Div.), 372; W.R.O. 1609/19.
[87] W.R.O. 1165/8, pp. 1, 4.
[88] O.S. Map 1/100,000, admin. areas, Wilts. (1974 edn.).
[89] Below.
[90] *Reg. Malm.* i. 264–7, 348–52, 359–63.

[91] For the hist. of its church, below, Hankerton.
[92] Ch. Com. file, NB 5/3B.
[93] Phillipps, *Wilts. Inst.* (index in *W.A.M.* xxviii. 218); *V.C.H. Wilts.* iii. 223, 225; *Cal. Pat.* 1391–6, 188.
[94] *L. & P. Hen. VIII,* xix (i), p. 286.
[95] Phillipps, *Wilts. Inst.* (index in *W.A.M.* xxviii. 218); *Cal. Pat.* 1578–80, pp. 281, 292; Beds. R.O., L 26/1176.
[96] Beds. R.O., L 19/36.
[97] *Alum. Oxon. 1715–1886,* iii. 923; mon. in church.
[98] Bristol R.O., EP/A/3/133; P.R.O., PROB 11/1928, ff. 31v.–40; mon. in churchyard.
[99] Ch. Com. file, NB 5/3B.
[1] *Tax. Eccl.* (Rec. Com.), 189.
[2] *Valor Eccl.* (Rec. Com.), ii. 137.
[3] *W.A.M.* xli. 7.
[4] *Rep. Com. Eccl. Revenues,* 830–1.
[5] *Reg. Malm.* i. 264–7; W.R.O., D 1/24/65/4; P.R.O., IR 29/38/93; IR 30/38/93.
[6] *Reg. Malm.* ii. 60–5.
[7] P.R.O., IR 29/38/93.

In 1222 the rector retained all the glebe, which included land in Hankerton.[8] He had a house, 1 carucate, and 5 a. of meadow in 1341.[9] The glebe, including 1 yardland in Hankerton, was c. 113 a. in the 17th century and early 18th. The Hankerton land was transferred after 1704 to the vicar of Hankerton, and in the 19th century the rector had 72 a.[10] The glebe house and c. 33 a. were sold in 1929, 17 a. in the years 1949–51, and in 1989 there were c. 13 a. In 1932–3 a new house was built of stone with a stone-slated roof.[11] That was sold in 1976[12] and replaced by the Butts, which was sold in 1985. The house sold in 1929, Crudwell Court, is an early 18th-century L-shaped house with a long north–south range. At the west end of the south wing, beyond which it projected to the south, a second north–south range with a west entrance front was built parallel to the first before c. 1805. It was heightened and extended west by a shorter range in the later 19th century. Northwest of the house a circular stone pigeon house, possibly also 18th-century, formerly had a conical roof of stone slates.[13]

St. John's chapel at Eastcourt, dependent on Crudwell church in the 12th century,[14] stood on Eastcourt Lane near the junction with the Oaksey–Hankerton road.[15] It was not used after the Reformation and nothing of it survived in 1989. Few medieval rectors are likely to have been resident. John of Abingdon, rector in 1230, was cardinal priest of the church of St. Praxedes, Rome.[16] Henry Mauley, also rector of Tyringham (Bucks.), was in 1253 licensed to hold a third benefice.[17] William Lawton, apparently in minor orders when he was instituted c. 1299, was licensed in 1300 to study abroad for two years, and was ordained priest on his return. A chaplain served Crudwell during his absence.[18] Richard Machon, rector from 1479 to c. 1492, was a pluralist whose other preferments included the rectory of Brinkworth and, from 1486, the precentorship of St. David's.[19] Furnishings stolen from the church before 1550[20] had not been replaced by 1556.[21] The *Paraphrases* of Erasmus was lacking in 1550, and in 1553 communion was celebrated infrequently because few parishioners attended.[22] Samuel Alsop, instituted in 1645, was ejected before 1650.[23] The ministers who served the cure during the Interregnum may have been negligent, for in 1662 the church lacked a surplice, an altar cloth, a dish for the communion bread, and the Book of Homilies.[24] In the 17th century most rectors, including Daniel Harford,

rector 1670–9 and a fellow of Magdalen College, Oxford, 1664–77, seem to have resided.[25] The rectors were patrons of Hankerton, although their patronage was sometimes challenged, and in the years 1699–1782, 1785–1855, and 1903–9 were also vicars of Hankerton.[26] George Ingram, from 1761 Viscount Irvine, rector 1719–63, was a canon of Westminster Abbey and chaplain to the House of Commons from 1724;[27] he employed a curate at Crudwell.[28] James Wiggett, rector from 1782 to 1839,[29] served Hankerton as curate before presenting himself as vicar in 1785. He held a Sunday service at Crudwell and another at Hankerton, alternately in the morning and afternoon, and other services at Crudwell on great festivals and fast days. The sacrament, administered four or more times a year c. 1783, was sometimes received by many communicants.[30] At Crudwell in 1850–1 average congregations of 300 attended morning services, of 400 afternoon services.[31] A priest-in-charge served Crudwell 1982–7,[32] and in 1989 the rector lived in Oaksey.

The church of *ALL SAINTS* was so called in 1763.[33] It is of rubble and ashlar and comprises a chancel with north chapel, an aisled and clerestoried nave with south porch, and an aisled west tower.[34] The proportions of the narrow, thin-walled nave suggest that the church may have been built in the 11th century. The tower was probably built after the nave but before the two-bayed north nave aisle which was built c. 1200. In the early 13th century a south transept was built. The chancel was rebuilt in the later 13th century, and soon afterwards the north aisle was extended east to form the chapel. The south aisle, divided from the nave by a two-bayed arcade and incorporating the transept, of which the east wall survives, was built in the 14th century. At the same time the tower was altered and the clerestory built. In the 15th century the south aisle was extended westwards and partly rebuilt, the porch, two-storeyed and embattled, was built, a wooden screen was erected in the north aisle, and the nave, tower, and tower aisles were refenestrated. The centre and west arch of the south aisle were apparently renewed in the early 20th century. Glass depicting the seven sacraments and given by John Dow and his wife Joan in the mid 15th century is in a window in the north aisle. Carved bench ends incorporate the royal arms of 1509–47: they may be of that date but were possibly given later by Thomas Walton (will proved 1593).[35] The 15th-century wood-

[8] *Reg. Malm.* i. 264–7.
[9] *Inq. Non.* (Rec. Com.), 166.
[10] W.R.O., D 1/24/65/3–4; P.R.O., IR 29/38/93; IR 30/38/93; below, Hankerton, church.
[11] Ch. Com. files 11352, E 6109, H 8742, PG 766; inf. from Deputy Dioc. Sec., Dioc. Bd. of Finance, Church Ho., 23 Gt. Geo. Street, Bristol.
[12] Inf. from the rector, Oaksey.
[13] Inf. from Mrs. S. Howe, Crudwell Ct.; Beds. R.O., L 25/168.
[14] *Reg. Malm.* i. 264–7, 348–52.
[15] Beds. R.O., L 25/168; L 26/1177, f. 70.
[16] *Reg. Malm.* i. 60–2.
[17] *Cal. Papal Reg.* i. 284.
[18] Phillipps, *Wilts. Inst.* i. 3; *Reg. Ghent* (Cant. & York Soc.), ii. 842, 859.
[19] A. B. Emden, *Biog. Reg. Univ. Oxf. to 1500*, ii. 1201.
[20] W.R.O., D 1/43/1, f. 21v.
[21] Ibid. D 1/43/2, f. 20v.
[22] Ibid. D 1/43/1, ff. 21v., 129.

[23] Phillipps, *Wilts. Inst.* ii. 22; *W.A.M.* xli. 7.
[24] W.R.O., D 1/54/1/1, no. 60.
[25] Ibid. bishop's transcripts, bdle. 1; *Alum. Oxon. 1500–1714*, ii. 650; mon. in church.
[26] Phillipps, *Wilts. Inst.* (indexes in *W.A.M.* xxviii. 218, 221); *Crockford* (1907, 1926); below, Hankerton, church.
[27] *Complete Peerage*, vii. 75.
[28] W.R.O., bishop's transcripts, bdles. 2–3.
[29] Phillipps, *Wilts. Inst.* ii. 91; *Clergy List* (1859); mon. in church.
[30] *Vis. Queries, 1783* (W.R.S. xxvii), pp. 81, 114; Ch. Com. file, NB 5/3B.
[31] P.R.O., HO 129/252/1/3/5.
[32] *Crockford* (1980–2, 1987–8).
[33] J. Ecton, *Thesaurus* (1763), 403.
[34] Cf. J. Buckler, watercolours in W.A.S. Libr., vols. vi. 6; viii. 67.
[35] Aubrey, *Topog. Coll.* ed. Jackson, 215; P.R.O., PROB 11/82, ff. 321v.–322v.

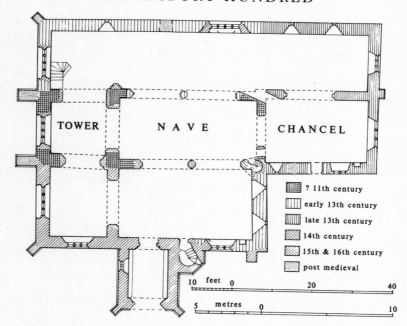

TOWER · N A V E · CHANCEL

? 11th century
early 13th century
late 13th century
14th century
15th & 16th century
post medieval

10 feet 0   20   40

5 metres 0   10

PLAN OF ALL SAINTS' CHURCH

en rood screen was moved to the north chapel in the later 20th century.[36]

Plate was apparently among property stolen from the church before 1550 since the church had none in 1553. In 1988 a chalice given in 1628 and two patens, one hallmarked for 1687, one for 1732, were held.[37] Three medieval bells, of which the second and third were cast in Gloucester, hung in the church. In 1821 there was a peal of five bells: the first and second were cast in 1633, the other three may have been the medieval bells recast. The entire ring was recast in 1858 by C. & G. Mears.[38] Registrations of baptisms and burials begin in 1659, those of marriages in 1663. No burial is recorded in the period 1680–94.[39]

NONCONFORMITY. That two parishioners were excommunicate and two others failed to attend church in 1674 suggests dissent.[40] One of the excommunicates failed to attend church in 1683[41] but his religious affiliation is unknown.

In 1773, 1800, and 1818 meeting houses for Independents were certified,[42] and an Independent meeting still flourished in 1833.[43] A chapel for Particular Baptists open beside the Cirencester–Malmesbury road c. 1840 was attended on Census Sunday in 1851 by 70 in the morning and 100 in the afternoon.[44] It closed between 1915 and 1920.[45]

Primitive Methodists, evangelized by William Sanger, certified a house in 1811.[46] A chapel was opened in Tetbury Lane between 1865 and 1867 and closed between 1939 and 1945.[47]

EDUCATION. A free school at Crudwell was founded by John, Lord Lucas (d. 1671), possibly between 1630 and 1649. The lords of Crudwell manor appointed the teacher. The school was endowed with 5 a., and the school buildings comprised a stone schoolroom and two adjoining cottages.[48] It may have been the school of industry in which six children were taught in 1803.[49] In 1818 the small number of pupils was given as the reason for not opening the school on weekdays: it was claimed, perhaps without justification, that attendance had been better between 1803 and 1818.[50] By 1833, when c. 18 attended, the school had become a day school, and it was then partly supported by the rector and some parents.[51] In 1846–7 a woman taught 30 children.[52] By a Scheme of 1856 the school's management was transferred to a board of trustees, and in 1857 a new school was built beside the old,[53] which was leased out. In 1859 average attendance was c. 60.[54] The school was affiliated to the National Society, and in 1871 was attended by 49 children on return day.[55] The average attendance, 107 in 1905–6, had declined to 73 by 1937–8.[56] New classrooms were built in

[36] T. E. Vernon, *Notes on All Saints, Crudwell* (Melksham, priv. print. 1962), 16.
[37] Above; Nightingale, *Wilts. Plate*, 196; inf. from the rector.
[38] Vernon, *All Saints, Crudwell*, 21; Walters, *Wilts. Bells*, 68; inf. from the rector.
[39] W.R.O. 1609/1–7; 1609/9. Bishop's transcripts for 1605–9, 1619–23, 1632–5, 1665–79, 1693 are ibid. Marriages 1663–1812 are printed in *Wilts. Par. Reg. (Mar.)*, ed. W. P. W. Phillimore and J. Sadler, iii. 73–88.
[40] W.R.O., D 1/54/6/1, no. 28.
[41] Ibid. D 1/54/10/1, no. 12.
[42] *Meeting Ho. Certs.* (W.R.S. xl), pp. 29, 55, 87.
[43] *Educ. Enq. Abstract*, 1034.

[44] P.R.O., HO 129/252/2/10/11; ibid. IR 29/38/93; IR 30/38/93.   [45] *Kelly's Dir. Wilts.* (1915, 1920).
[46] *Meeting Ho. Certs.* (W.R.S. xl), p. 69.
[47] *Harrod's Dir. Wilts.* (1865); *Kelly's Dir. Wilts.* (1867 and later edns.); W.R.O., G 7/760/165.
[48] *Endowed Char. Wilts.* (N. Div.), 373, 375–6; *V.C.H. Wilts.* iv. 406–7; P.R.O., C 3/452/68.
[49] *Poor Law Abstract, 1804*, 566–7.
[50] *Educ. of Poor Digest*, 1024.   [51] *Educ. Enq. Abstract*, 1034.
[52] Nat. Soc. *Inquiry, 1846–7*, Wilts. 4–5.
[53] P.R.O., ED 7/130, no. 94.   [54] *Acct. of Wilts. Schs.* 18.
[55] *Returns relating to Elem. Educ.* 420–1.
[56] *Bd. of Educ., List 21, 1908–9* (H.M.S.O.), 502; *1938*, 422.

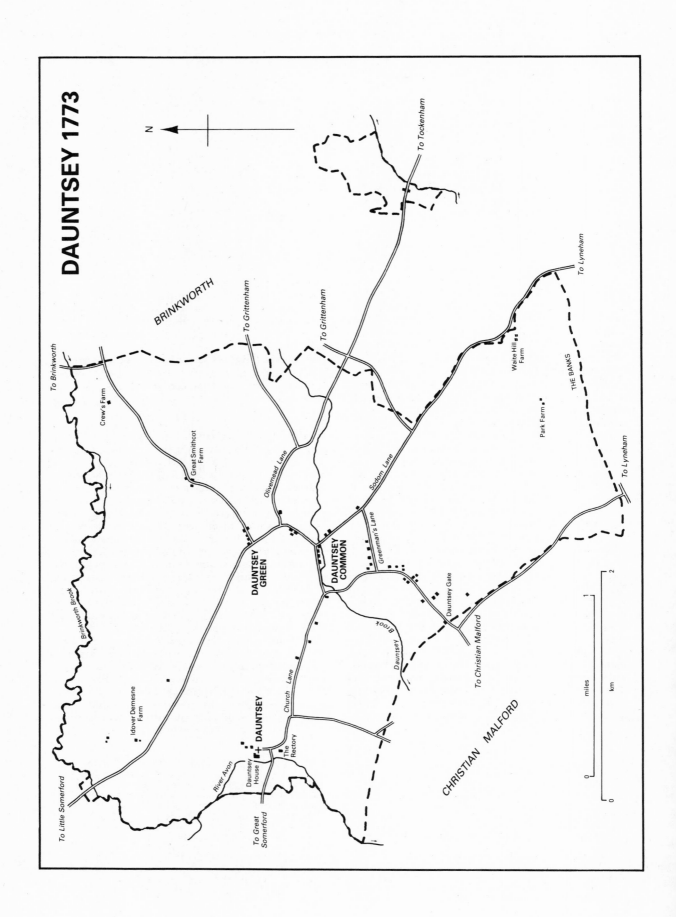

DAUNTSEY 1773

the 20th century. In 1985 the income of Crudwell Free School Foundation was £1,679 from the leasing of the land and cottages.[57] The 108 children on roll in 1989 were taught by six teachers.[58]

A school supported by J. R. Mullings was opened at Eastcourt in 1858.[59] It was a National school at which 30 children were taught in 1859 and 1871.[60] Average attendance declined from 36 in 1906–7 to 21 in 1921–2, and in 1923 the school was closed.[61]

CHARITIES FOR THE POOR. Numerous small benefactions were made for the poor, mainly in the 17th century[62] and most by members of the Earle family.[63] Giles Earle (will proved 1677) gave £100, and a Thomas Earle £50, to buy bread. In 1775 £582 was invested. In the earlier 19th century the income of £19 was distributed yearly in spring to all the poor. There was no distribution 1832–4 because the aged rector refused to make one. In 1905 £19 was spent on coal, and in 1954 coal for 51 old people was bought with £23.[64] Coal was last given in 1965, and in 1966 tea for pensioners was bought with £9 of the yearly income of £25. In 1972 a small part of the income was spent on tea, and in 1989 none. The income, £47 in 1989, was allowed to accumulate.[65]

DAUNTSEY

DAUNTSEY is a parish of scattered hamlets and farmsteads in the valley of the Bristol Avon, south-east of Malmesbury, north-east of Chippenham, and west of Wootton Bassett.[66] The parish makes a rectangle 4 km. by 3 km., with a south-eastern extension. A detached part to the east, 42 a., was transferred to Brinkworth parish in 1884, and another small area was transferred to Brinkworth between 1891 and 1901. Thereafter Dauntsey parish measured 1,318 ha. (3,258 a.).[67]

The parish developed from an estate called Dauntsey granted to Malmesbury abbey in 850. The boundaries of that estate, recorded in the late 12th century or the early 13th but probably surveyed earlier, coincided with those of all but the northern part of the modern parish.[68] The lands of Idover and Smithcot in the north were held with Dauntsey manor from the 12th century and the 13th respectively,[69] and, possibly at those dates, were added to the parish. The south-eastern extension brought into what was otherwise a lowland parish the scarp of the Corallian ridge which crosses north-east Wiltshire, and the detached portion, which is recorded as such only in the 19th century, may have been woodland assigned to the men of Dauntsey when other woodland in the parish was imparked in or before the 16th century.[70]

The Avon and its tributary Brinkworth brook mark the parish's western and northern boundaries with, respectively, Great Somerford and Brinkworth. Near the church, which is on its east bank, the main stream of the Avon, straightened probably in the 18th century either as a mill stream or for ornament, runs within the parish. West of it the boundary was marked by a smaller stream, perhaps following the original course of the Avon, until 1809 when it was defined on a straight course further west.[71] The name Dauntsey, in which an element possibly refers to an island or well watered land, is perhaps derived from the low island formed by the two courses of the river.[72] The south-eastern boundary, with Lyneham, runs along the edge of the Corallian ridge, there called the Banks. Between the Avon and the upland, part of the boundary near the river is straight and part follows a road; the straight part, with Christian Malford, continues a line which divides pairs of parishes further west and was possibly drawn when common land was inclosed. The long eastern boundary with Brinkworth is marked by a road in the south and is irregular in the north.

Dauntsey brook, also a tributary of the Avon, crosses the southern part of the parish. Oxford Clay outcrops throughout the parish, including the south-eastern extension, and is covered by alluvium and other river terrace deposits near the Avon, Brinkworth brook, and Dauntsey brook.[73] Nearly all the parish is flat; it is crossed by the 61 m. contour and is lowest near the Avon. The land reaches over 122 m. on the Banks.

The clay soils of the parish have long provided pasture, with meadow land beside the Avon and other streams. There has always been more grassland than arable in the parish.[74] In the 11th century Dauntsey, like neighbouring parishes, included large areas of woodland.[75] A park in the south-east, first recorded in the 16th century,[76] was described

[57] Char. Com. file.
[58] Inf. from the head teacher.
[59] W.R.O. 782/40.
[60] Acct. of Wilts. Schs. 18; Returns relating to Elem. Educ. 420–1.
[61] Bd. of Educ., List 21, 1908–9 (H.M.S.O.), 502; 1922, 359; 1927, 359.
[62] Except where stated, inf. from Endowed Char. Wilts. (N. Div.), 372–5.
[63] For the Earle fam., above, manors (Eastcourt).
[64] W.R.O., Char. Com., Crudwell.
[65] Char. Com. file; inf. from the rector.
[66] This article was written in 1986. Maps used include O.S. Maps 1/50,000, sheet 173 (1974 edn.); 1/25,000, ST

98, SU 08 (1959 edns.); 6″, Wilts. XIII–XIV (1887–8 and later edns.).
[67] P.R.O., IR 29/38/95; IR 30/38/95; Census, 1891, 1901.
[68] Arch. Jnl. lxxvi. 165–9, where, however, it is argued that boundaries described are those of the modern par.
[69] Below, manors.
[70] Below.   [71] W.R.O., EA/98.
[72] P. N. Wilts. (E.P.N.S.), 68.
[73] Geol. Surv. Map 1″, solid and drift, sheet 252 (1974 edn.); 1/50,000, drift, sheet 266 (1974 edn.).
[74] Below, econ. hist.
[75] V.C.H. Wilts. ii, pp. 60, 125, 144.
[76] Cal. S.P. Dom. 1595–7, 337; C. Saxton, Map of Wilts. (1576); P.R.O., DL 43/9/26.

in the mid 17th as having admirable oaks.[77] By the late 18th century it had become farmland[78] and most of the woodland in the parish had been cleared.[79] Between 1846 and 1885 c. 300 a. in the north-west around Dauntsey House became parkland and a lake was made west of the house and the main stream of the Avon.[80] Small areas of woodland were planted in the north in the 20th century.[81]

In the late 18th century, as presumably earlier, a road on an intricate north-east and south-west course through the parish, linking Brinkworth and Christian Malford, was crossed by others running north-west and south-east between Little Somerford and Tockenham and between Great Somerford and Lyneham. Another road to Lyneham left the Christian Malford road at Dauntsey Gate, later Swallett Gate, south-east of which it was the parish boundary.[82] South-east and south-west of Swallett Gate the roads were turnpiked in 1758 as part of the Swindon–Chippenham road. Although the trust was allowed to lapse, another was created in 1791.[83] The south-eastern part of the road was diverted to the east to avoid Bradenstoke village and to cross the escarpment on a lower gradient, presumably c. 1791; it was on its new course in 1815.[84] The older route remained in use as a minor road. The Swindon–Chippenham road through the parish was disturnpiked in 1879. The Little Somerford road west of its junction with the Brinkworth road and the Brinkworth road between that junction and Swallett Gate were turnpiked in 1809 with others leading east and south-east from Malmesbury. They were disturnpiked in 1876.[85] The south-east part of the Great Somerford to Lyneham road was called Sodom in 1884 and later Sodom Lane. In the later 20th century the north-west part of the road was called Church Lane, and the Tockenham road was called Olivemead Lane.[86] In the late 18th century lanes led to Grittenham in Brinkworth from Olivemead Lane and Sodom Lane.[87] From the mid 20th the east end of Sodom Lane, part of Olivemead Lane, and the lane from Olivemead Lane to Grittenham were used as farm roads.[88] An avenue running southeast from the gateway of Dauntsey House to Swallett Gate, partly along Church Lane, was planted in the mid 19th century.[89] In the later 20th it was called Mile Drive and was used as a public bridleway. Part of the London and south Wales motorway runs north-east and south-west across the parish and was opened in 1971.[90]

The Wilts. & Berks. canal was built east–west across the southern part of the parish and was opened c. 1801. A wharf was built near the parish's south-western boundary soon afterwards. The canal was closed in 1914;[91] by 1986 it had been drained but its course through the parish remained visible. The G.W.R. London–Bristol line which, in Dauntsey parish, ran parallel to and 200 m. north of the canal was opened in 1841.[92] Dauntsey station, near the parish boundary in Christian Malford, was opened for passenger traffic in 1868 and for goods traffic soon afterwards.[93] A branch line from the station to Malmesbury through the south-west part of the parish was open between 1877 and 1933.[94] Dauntsey station was closed in 1965.[95]

Taxation assessments of the 14th century and the 16th show Dauntsey to have been one of the wealthiest parishes of Malmesbury hundred.[96] In 1377 there were 111 poll-tax payers, a little above average for a rural parish of the hundred.[97] The population was 357 in 1801 but had fallen to 305 by 1811. Thereafter numbers rose until 1851, when the population was 623. In the late 19th century and the early 20th they fell; 357 people lived in the parish in 1921. Between 1951 and 1961 the population grew, presumably as a result of additional housing built in the 1950s.[98] In 1981 it was 456.[99]

Settlement in the parish has long been in scattered hamlets and farmsteads, several of which lie beside the Brinkworth to Christian Malford road. Few surviving buildings are older than the 18th century, and most of the older houses and farmsteads are of local brick.

The oldest settlement is presumably that where Church Lane crosses the Avon comprising the church, Dauntsey House, which is of 14th-century origin,[1] the former rectory house, and a house of the later 20th century. In the late 18th century the hamlet bore the name Dauntsey.[2] Glebe Farm, 200 m. south-east of the church, is on a site in use in the early 19th century;[3] a new farmhouse was built in the 1960s. Idover House, a little further east, was built between 1773 and 1820[4] and much extended in the early 20th century.[5]

The name Dauntsey was sometimes used in the 20th century of the settlement more usually called Dauntsey Green in the late 19th century and the 20th. About 1770 it consisted of two hamlets, Dauntsey Green, around the staggered junction of the road from Brinkworth to Christian Malford with the road from Little Somerford to Tockenham, and Dauntsey Common. At Dauntsey Green there were then two or three farmsteads or cottages. Little Smithcot Farm, at the northern junction of the two roads, was apparently built soon

[77] Aubrey, *Topog. Coll.* ed. Jackson, 216.
[78] W.R.O. 212A/27/21/2, lease, Peterborough to Sutton, 1793.
[79] *Andrews and Dury, Map* (W.R.S. viii), pl. 14.
[80] P.R.O., IR 30/38/95; O.S. Maps 6", Wilts. XIII–XIV (1887–8 edns.); W.R.O. 106, sale cat. of Meux estates, 3rd portion.
[81] O.S. Maps 6", Wilts. XIII–XIV (1887–8 and later edns.).
[82] *Andrews and Dury, Map* (W.R.S. viii), pl. 14.
[83] *V.C.H. Wilts.* iv. 260, 263, 270–1; *L.J.* xxix. 367; xxxix. 186.
[84] B.L. Maps, O.S.D. 169.
[85] *V.C.H. Wilts.* iv. 271; *L.J.* xlvii. 290.
[86] O.S. Map 6", Wilts. XIV (1887 and later edns.).
[87] *Andrews and Dury, Map* (W.R.S. viii), pl. 14.
[88] O.S. Map 1/25,000, SU 08 (1959 edn.).
[89] Ibid. 6", Wilts. XIV (1887 edn.); P.R.O., IR 30/38/95.

[90] Inf. from Co. Secretary, Co. Hall, Trowbridge.
[91] *V.C.H. Wilts.* iv. 273–4, 277.
[92] Ibid. 282.
[93] W.R.O. 1213/29.
[94] *V.C.H. Wilts.* iv. 288.
[95] C. R. Clinker, *Clinker's Reg. Closed Passenger Sta. 1830–1980,* p. 37.
[96] *V.C.H. Wilts.* iv. 301; *Taxation Lists* (W.R.S. x), 30, 53.
[97] *V.C.H. Wilts.* iv. 309.
[98] Ibid. 346; *Census,* 1961; below. [99] *Census,* 1981.
[1] Below, manors.
[2] *Andrews and Dury, Map* (W.R.S. viii), pl. 14.
[3] O.S. Map 1", sheet 34 (1828 edn.).
[4] C. Greenwood, *Map of Wilts.* (1820); *Andrews and Dury, Map* (W.R.S. viii), pl. 14.
[5] W.A.S. Libr., sale cat. xxxv, no. 52.

afterwards. The buildings of Dauntsey Common were around a square formed by the roads from Brinkworth to Christian Malford and from Great Somerford to Lyneham.[6] The east side of the square became part of Sodom Lane and the road across the south side was later called Greenman's Lane.[7] The c. 12 buildings in 1773 included a school and almshouse and, presumably, small farmsteads and cottages: most were on the north and south sides of the square.[8] Of those which survive, Evergreen Farm at the south-east corner dates from the early 18th century and Great Dairy Farm on the south side from that or an earlier date. In the 19th century building increased along the northern side and spread north to Dauntsey Green, forming a village street later known as the Green.[9] The new buildings included a new school and almshouse[10] and four pairs of estate cottages. Great Middle Green Farm, on the street, and White House Farm, east of the street on Olivemead Lane, both survive from the mid 18th century or earlier. Other estate cottages, a nonconformist chapel, and a house were built beside Greenman's Lane in the 19th century. In 1932 four pairs of council houses were built east of the school,[11] and houses and bungalows were built on both sides of the Green in the later 20th century. When the motorway was built between and roughly parallel to the Green and Greenman's Lane, the course of the road from Brinkworth to Christian Malford was moved slightly east and a bridge was built to carry it over the motorway. Sodom Lane was blocked, and that part of it north of the motorway was renamed Old Sodom Lane. Greenman's Lane was closed and a new road, called Sodom Lane, was made north of it linking the Lyneham and Brinkworth roads. The name Greenman's Lane was retained for the group of buildings which stood at the western end of the closed lane.[12]

Buildings, probably including several farmsteads, were scattered beside the Christian Malford road south of Greenman's Lane in the late 18th century. Good Monday's Farm, west of the road, is a brick house of early 18th-century origin, and a timber-framed cottage east of the road is of similar date. At the road's junction with the southern road to Lyneham, Dauntsey Gate was a small settlement in 1773.[13] It had been renamed Swallett Gate by the late 19th century when part of the hamlet was in Christian Malford parish. Several additional houses were built beside the Christian Malford road and in Dauntsey parish in the 19th century.[14] In 1938 two pairs of council houses, called St. John's, were built east of the road,[15] and in the 1950s an estate of 22 council houses, called St. James's, was built west of it. St. John's Farm, east of the junction with the Lyneham road, was rebuilt in 1976[16] on a site

which was in use in the late 18th century.[17]

By 1820 the Peterborough Arms had been built a little south of the bridge which carried the Swindon–Chippenham road over the canal.[18] In the later 19th century, probably after the opening of Dauntsey station, houses and farm and industrial buildings were erected nearby; about half lay in Christian Malford parish. The hamlet was known as Dauntsey Lock presumably from the opening of the canal and certainly from 1884.[19]

A group of small farmsteads built south-east of Dauntsey Common in the late 18th century or the early 19th[20] was called Sodom in 1884.[21] Bungalows, houses and, at the south end of the hamlet, a new farmstead were added in the late 20th century.

Outside the hamlets there were six or seven farmsteads in the parish in the later 18th century.[22] Most occupied sites which had possibly long been in use. Great Smithcot Farm may have been part of a larger settlement, perhaps nucleated around a chapel recorded at Smithcot in 1327 and 1474. In 1086 the estate called Smithcot included almost half the cultivated land of the later parish,[23] and the 111 poll-tax payers in 1377 included 21 of Smithcot.[24] Great Smithcot farmhouse consists of two parts, both of red brick with stone quoins. The older, probably of the later 17th century, is of two low storeys and attics. It has a symmetrical east entrance front of five bays and a short west service wing. The main doorway has been moved north by one bay. All the windows of the east front have moulded stone mullions. The south-west corner of the older building adjoins a taller two-storeyed block with a symmetrical west entrance front of five bays. The doorway has a broken segmental pediment and the windows have stone heads with decorative keystones. Moulded oak frames are visible where windows on the gables have been blocked, but the windows of the main front have sashes of the later 18th century. Within, the staircase, fireplaces, and three panelled rooms are of the early 18th century.

The 21 poll-tax payers recorded as of Smithcot in 1377 may have included occupants of other farmsteads in the northern part of the parish, among them those on the land called Idover. There were probably never more than one or two farmsteads on the Idover lands; in 1986 Idover Demesne Farm and Home Idover Farm survived as buildings of 18th-century or earlier origin. The site of Park Farm, on the escarpment in the southeast, may first have been used for a farmstead in the mid 16th century.[25] Crew's Farm in the northeast is of 18th-century or earlier origin, and Union Farm beside Church Lane and Waite Hill Farm on the escarpment may have been rebuilt in the late 18th or early 19th century: all three were

[6] *Andrews and Dury, Map* (W.R.S. viii), pl. 14; Greenwood, *Map of Wilts.*

[7] O.S. Map 6″, Wilts. XIV (1887 edn.).

[8] *Andrews and Dury, Map* (W.R.S. viii), pl. 14; below, educ.

[9] O.S. Maps 1″, sheet 34 (1828 edn.); 6″, Wilts. XIV (1887 edn.).

[10] See plate facing p. 61.   [11] W.R.O., G 7/132/17.

[12] O.S. Map 1/10,000, ST 98 SE. (1983 edn.).

[13] *Andrews and Dury, Map* (W.R.S. viii), pl. 14.

[14] O.S. Maps 1″, sheet 34 (1828 edn.); 6″, Wilts. XIV (1887 and later edns.).

[15] W.R.O., G 7/132/17.

[16] Inf. from Mrs. P. Hitchcock, St. John's Farm.

[17] *Andrews and Dury, Map* (W.R.S. viii), pl. 14.

[18] Greenwood, *Map of Wilts.*

[19] O.S. Map 6″, Wilts. XIV (1887 edn.).

[20] Ibid. 1″, sheet 34 (1828 edn.); *Andrews and Dury, Map* (W.R.S. viii), pl. 14.

[21] O.S. Map 6″, Wilts. XIV (1887 edn.).

[22] *Andrews and Dury, Map* (W.R.S. viii), pl. 14.

[23] Below, econ. hist., church.

[24] *V.C.H. Wilts.* iv. 309.

[25] P.R.O., DL 43/9/26.

standing in 1773.[26] Olivemead Farm near the eastern boundary was built in the mid 19th century;[27] extensive farm buildings were added in the later 20th.

MANORS AND OTHER ESTATES. In 850 King Ethelwulf granted to Malmesbury abbey 10 *mansiones* in Dauntsey.[28] The lands became *DAUNTSEY* manor, of which the abbey remained overlord until the Dissolution.[29]

In 1066 Alward held Dauntsey of Malmesbury abbey, apparently by lease. By 1086 the abbey had granted it as a knight's fee to Robert.[30] It apparently passed to Miles of Dauntsey, who was succeeded in turn by his son Miles and Miles's son Miles;[31] one of that name held the manor in the late 12th century.[32] In 1242–3 it was held by the youngest Miles's son Roger Dauntsey. It passed to Roger's brother Gilbert,[33] on whom it was settled for life in 1257 with remainder for life to a third brother Richard.[34] By 1275 it had passed to Richard's heir,[35] presumably his son Richard (fl. 1292).[36] Sir Richard Dauntsey, possibly the younger Richard's son, held the manor in 1331[37] and was succeeded after 1349[38] by his grandson Sir John Dauntsey (d. 1391). The manor passed in turn to Sir John's son Sir John[39] (d. 1405) and to that Sir John's son Sir Walter[40] (d. 1420). Sir Walter was succeeded by his sister Joan, wife of Sir John Stradling[41] (d. 1433),[42] later wife of John Dewale. From Joan (d. 1457) the manor passed in turn to her son Edmund Stradling[43] (d. 1461), Edmund's son John[44] (d. 1471), and John's posthumous son Edward[45] (d. 1487). Edward was succeeded by his sister Anne, wife of Sir John Danvers[46] (d. 1514).[47] From Anne (d. 1539) the manor passed to her grandson Silvester Danvers[48] (d. 1551) and to his son Sir John.[49] On Sir John's death in 1594 it was retained for her life by his relict Elizabeth,[50] who married Sir Edward Carey and died in 1630.[51] It passed in turn to her sons Henry Danvers, earl of Danby (d. 1644),[52] and Sir John Danvers, a regicide. Sir John (d. 1655) was succeeded by his son John, a minor.[53]

Dauntsey manor was among estates formerly Sir John Danvers's which were confiscated after the Restoration. In 1662 it was granted to James, duke of York,[54] and in 1685 he, as James II, settled it on Mary his queen.[55] The manor was resumed

by the Crown in 1690,[56] and in 1691 was granted to Charles Mordaunt, earl of Monmouth,[57] who in 1697 became earl of Peterborough. Charles (d. 1735) was succeeded by his grandson Charles Mordaunt, earl of Peterborough and of Monmouth (d. 1779), and by the younger Charles's son Charles, earl of Peterborough and of Monmouth (d. 1814),[58] who devised his estates to his niece Jane Bisset, later wife of the Ven. Maurice Fenwick. Jane (d. 1866)[59] had by 1840 conveyed Dauntsey manor to her son Mordaunt Fenwick,[60] who sold it in 1853 to C. W. Miles. In 1877 C. W. Miles and E. P. W. Miles sold it to Sir Henry Meux, Bt.[61] (d. 1883). Sir Henry was succeeded by his son Sir Henry (d. 1900) whose relict Valerie (d. 1910)[62] devised the manor to Ferdinand Marsham-Townshend.[63] He sold the estate, which then comprised c. 3,000 a. in Dauntsey parish, in lots in 1913 and 1914.[64]

BRASS OF SIR JOHN DANVERS AND HIS WIFE ANNE

[26] *Andrews and Dury, Map* (W.R.S. viii), pl. 14.
[27] Greenwood, *Map of Wilts.*; O.S. Map 6″, Wilts. XIV (1887 edn.). [28] Finberg, *Early Wessex Chart.* p. 73.
[29] P.R.O., SC 6/Hen. VIII/3986, rott. 100–1.
[30] *V.C.H. Wilts.* ii, p. 125.
[31] B.L. Add. MS. 15667, f. 38v. [32] *Reg. Malm.* i. 277.
[33] *Bk. of Fees*, ii. 732; B.L. Add. MS. 15667, f. 38v.
[34] *Cat. Anct. D.* iv, A 6769.
[35] *Rot. Hund.* (Rec. Com.), ii (1), 272–3.
[36] *Abbrev. Plac.* (Rec. Com.), 228; B.L. Add. MS. 15667, f. 38v.
[37] F. N. Macnamara, *Memorials of Danvers Fam.* 229; *Feet of F. 1327–77* (W.R.S. xxix), p. 28.
[38] Phillipps, *Wilts. Inst.* i. 46.
[39] *Feet of F. 1327–77* (W.R.S. xxix), p. 73; *Cal. Inq. p.m.* xvii, p. 21.
[40] *Cal. Inq. p.m.* xviii, p. 363.
[41] Aubrey, *Topog. Coll.* ed. Jackson, pedigree facing p. 217.
[42] P.R.O., C 139/68, no. 16.
[43] Ibid. C 139/163, no. 1; Aubrey, *Topog. Coll.* ed. Jackson, pedigree facing p. 217. [44] P.R.O., C 140/1, no. 12.
[45] Ibid. C 140/36, no. 21; Macnamara, *Danvers Fam.* 263.

[46] *Cal. Inq. p.m. Hen. VII*, i, p. 123.
[47] Aubrey, *Topog. Coll.* ed. Jackson, pedigree facing p. 217.
[48] P.R.O., C 142/62, no. 5.
[49] Ibid. C 142/94, no. 88. [50] Ibid. C 142/247, no. 100.
[51] Macnamara, *Danvers Fam.* 286.
[52] *Complete Peerage*, iv. 48–9; P.R.O., C 3/399/129.
[53] W.R.O. 130/24, deed, Danvers to Atkins, 1654; *D.N.B.*
[54] *Cal. S.P. Dom.* 1661–2, 428.
[55] Hist. MSS. Com. 56, *Stuart*, ii, p. 521.
[56] Ibid. 24, *12th Rep. VI, Ho. of Lords*, pp. 443–4; *L.J.* xiv. 421, 425.
[57] W.R.O. 212A/27/21/2, sched. of deeds.
[58] *Complete Peerage*, x. 499–504.
[59] Ibid. 504; J. Britton, *Beauties of Wilts.* iii. 75; Burke, *Land. Gent.* (1898), 123; P.R.O., PROB 11/1561, f. 392.
[60] Burke, *Land. Gent.* (1898), 123; J. C. Young, *Jnl.* (1871), 274.
[61] W.A.S. Libr., sale cat. xxviiiA, no. 14.
[62] Burke, *Peerage* (1907), 1151; *W.A.M.* xxxvii. 164.
[63] *W.A.M.* xxxviii. 524.
[64] W.A.S. Libr., sale cat. xxviiiA, no. 14; Wilts. Cuttings, xiv. 118.

Dauntsey House[65] was probably built for members of the Dauntsey family[66] and a tradition survives that their successors the Stradlings lived in it.[67] In 1344 a licence was granted to Roger Dauntsey for an oratory in Dauntsey manor.[68] The house was lived in by members of the Danvers family, although not always by lords of the manor, in the 16th century and the early 17th,[69] by Charles, earl of Peterborough and of Monmouth (d. 1814),[70] and by Sir Henry Meux (d. 1900) and his relict Valerie.[71] The oldest part of the house is an earlier 14th-century hall range running north and south, with a raised base cruck roof of three bays on rubble walls. In the early 17th century, and probably earlier, there was a chimney stack against the west wall and a stone-walled cross wing at the southern end. The plan of hall and cross wing was retained in the mid and later 18th century when the house was enlarged and faced with ashlar. The house was extended westwards, possibly by a distance equal to the length of an earlier west porch. The hall, into which a first floor had by then been inserted, was redecorated and the interior of the cross wing was reconstructed to provide a large drawing room. Early in the 19th century a stair hall, with a kitchen wing east of it, was built north of the hall, perhaps on the site of the medieval service rooms. More service rooms were built to the north, possibly in the late 19th century; a library built above them was removed in the mid 20th.[72] The house is approached through an arched gateway of late 18th-century style. North-east of the house is an extensive brick stable court, and west of it is a terrace, below which the Avon flows in a straight course probably made in the 18th century. The 19th-century lake is west of the house, most of the park to the north and east.

Dauntsey House and 365 a. were bought in 1913 by E. R. S. Richardson,[73] and sold in 1918 by G. S. Guiness to E. H. Brassey (d. 1946). The estate passed to Brassey's son Sir Hugh, who sold it in 1948 to Marigold Denison, countess of Londesborough. It was bought in 1952 by Peter Sturgis, who sold some of the land and bought other holdings in the parish. On his death in 1985 the estate passed to Mr. Julian Sturgis, who in 1987 held Dauntsey House and c. 300 a. in Dauntsey.[74]

Union farm, 160 a., was bought in 1913 by Ann Spooner.[75] After her death it was bought in 1919 by Wiltshire county council.[76] Great Middle Green farm, 179 a., was bought by W. J. Matthews in 1913.[77] It later belonged to E. F. Potter,[78] to John Downes,[79] and to G. F. Ashman who in 1931 sold it to the county council. The council also bought 88 a. of Crew's farm in 1914, and in 1986 it owned c. 370 a. in Dauntsey parish.[80]

A further c. 12 farms, the largest of which was c. 180 a., were sold in 1913–14:[81] since then they have generally descended separately although from 1942 to 1970 the London Brick Co. owned St. John's farm, Great Dairy farm, Scots Smith farm, and part of Good Monday's farm.[82] In the 1980s there were again c. 10 separately owned farms.[83]

SMITHCOT was held by Sawin in 1066, by Humphrey Lisle in 1086.[84] Overlordship of Smithcot manor presumably passed to Humphrey's daughter Adelize, wife of Reynold de Dunstanville,[85] and became part of the Dunstanvilles' barony of Castle Combe; Giles de Badlesmere, Lord Badlesmere (d. 1338), held the overlordship as part of that barony, and at the partition of his estates after his death it was allotted to his sister Maud and her husband John de Vere, earl of Oxford.[86] John (d. 1360) was succeeded by his son Thomas, earl of Oxford,[87] who was overlord of Smithcot at his death in 1371.[88] In 1412 Millicent, wife of Sir John Fastolf, and heir of the portion of the Badlesmere estates which included Castle Combe barony, was said to be overlord, and Smithcot was still part of the barony in 1573.[89]

In 1086 Elbert held Smithcot of Humphrey Lisle.[90] In 1242–3 the manor was held by Roger Dauntsey.[91] Thereafter it passed with Dauntsey manor to Anne (d. 1539), relict of Sir John Danvers; in 1536 she conveyed the reversion of Smithcot manor to her son William Danvers, on condition that her grandson Silvester Danvers might acquire it by exchange when he came of age in 1540.[92] Silvester held the manor at his death in 1551[93] and thereafter it again passed with Dauntsey manor. Great Smithcot farm, 195 a. in 1913,[94] belonged in 1927 to G. A. Potter[95] (d. 1941). He was succeeded by his son Mr. R. J. Potter, who with his sons Mr. M. J. Potter and Mr. J. R. Potter owned the farm in 1986.[96] Little Smithcot farm, 183 a. in 1913,[97] belonged to W. J. Rose in 1924[98] and to Mr. Derek Rose in 1986.[99]

IDOVER was held in 1166 and 1242–3 of the honor of Wallingford (Berks., later Oxon.). In 1242–3 Miles Niernut was mesne lord. Miles Dauntsey, lord of Dauntsey manor, held Idover

[65] See plate facing p. 140.
[66] Below.
[67] Aubrey, *Topog. Coll.* ed. Jackson, 218.
[68] W.R.O., D 1/2/3, ii, f. 61v.
[69] *Trans. Bristol and Glos. Arch. Soc.* l. 340, 345–6.
[70] *Complete Peerage*, x. 504.
[71] Burke, *Peerage* (1890), 945; W.A.S. Libr., sale cat. xxviiiF, no. 111.
[72] Inf. from Mr. D. Sturgis, Dauntsey Ho.
[73] Wilts. Cuttings, xiv. 118.
[74] Inf. from Col. Sir Hugh Brassey, Manor Farm, Little Somerford.
[75] W.A.S. Libr., sale cat. xxviiiA, no. 14.
[76] Inf. from Estates and Valuations Officer, Co. Hall, Trowbridge.
[77] Wilts. Cuttings, xiv. 118; W.A.S. Libr., sale cat. xxviiiA, no. 14.
[78] W.R.O., F 9, farm files, Great Middle Green farm.
[79] Ibid. G 7/515/3.
[80] Inf. from Estates and Valuations Officer.

[81] W.A.S. Libr., sale cat. xxviiiA, no. 14.
[82] Inf. from Mrs. P. Hitchcock, St. John's Farm.
[83] Inf. from owners and occupiers.
[84] *V.C.H. Wilts.* ii, p. 144.
[85] G. Poulett Scrope, *Castle Combe* (priv. print. 1852), 19.
[86] *Cal. Inq. p.m.* viii, pp. 137, 144, 146.
[87] *Complete Peerage*, x. 226.
[88] *Cal. Inq. p.m.* xiii, pp. 92–3.
[89] *Cal. Close, 1409–13*, 279–80; Poulett Scrope, *Castle Combe*, 166–70, 317.
[90] *V.C.H. Wilts.* ii, p. 144.
[91] *Bk. of Fees*, ii. 713.
[92] B.L. Add. Ch. 38881; P.R.O., C 142/62, no. 5.
[93] P.R.O., C 142/94, no. 88.
[94] W.A.S. Libr., sale cat. xxviiiA, no. 14.
[95] W.R.O., G 7/515/3.
[96] Inf. from Mrs. A. D. Potter, Great Smithcot Lodge.
[97] W.A.S. Libr., sale cat. xxviiiA, no. 14.
[98] W.R.O. 1608/7.
[99] Inf. from Mr. A. J. Capener, 91 Bradenstoke.

in 1166;[1] thereafter its lands passed with that manor. Idover was mentioned as a separate estate in the early 14th century,[2] but was afterwards absorbed by Dauntsey manor.

A rent of 3s. from Dauntsey was given to Amesbury priory in a charter confirmed in 1179.[3] No later reference to the rent has been found.

ECONOMIC HISTORY. In 1086 Robert's Dauntsey estate included land for 6 ploughteams. On the demesne were 2 teams and 2 servi; 10 villani, 11 coscets, and 3 cottars had 4 teams. Smithcot included a higher proportion of demesne. Although there was land for only 4 teams, there were 3 teams and 2 servi on the demesne, which was assessed at 2½ hides, and 3 villani, 4 bordars, and 1 coscet shared 2 teams. There were 12 a. of meadow and woodland ½ league square at Dauntsey, and 20 a. of meadow and woodland 4 furlongs long and 1 furlong broad at Smithcot.[4]

In the Middle Ages open fields and common pastures were presumably shared by the lords and tenants of the Dauntsey, Smithcot, and Idover estates. In the 13th century or earlier, however, much meadow land beside Brinkworth brook and the Avon was exclusive to Dauntsey manor.[5] Almost certainly a high proportion of the parish was pasture in the Middle Ages. In the mid 16th century only c. 550 a. were arable; the names of West and Hill fields are recorded. There were 800 a. or more of several pasture including the park in the parish's south-east corner and the pastures called Great Idover and Little Idover beside Brinkworth brook and the Avon. The remainder of the parish, about half of it, was common pasture.[6] The pastures were presumably used then, as later, for dairying and for fattening cattle.[7]

All the farms in the parish in the mid 16th century consisted of demesne or customary land of Dauntsey and Smithcot manors or of the rector's glebe, and presumably all included rights to feed animals on the common pastures. The demesne lands of the two manors were not then distinguished. The combined demesne included c. 500 a. with rights of common pasture c. 1550. In hand there were 280 a., of which 60 a. were arable in the open fields and the remainder lay in closes. Another 200 a. or more of inclosed demesne pasture were leased in five portions.[8]

Copyholds of the two manors were still distinct c. 1550. A total of 800 a., 370 a. in the open fields and 430 a. in closes of meadow and pasture, was held by 43 copyholders of Dauntsey manor. Most

holdings were of fewer than 20 a.; the largest was of 65 a. Only 25 copyholders had arable. The four copyholders of Smithcot manor held a total of 140 a., mostly arable.[9]

The open fields were inclosed apparently in the mid 17th century.[10] Inclosure of common pastures may have been in progress during the 17th century and the early 18th; most of what remained of Dauntsey common was inclosed in the 1760s.[11] In 1773 vestiges of the common survived as wide verges to the lanes in the centre of the parish.[12] In 1846 there were 46 a. of common;[13] the verges remained but were apparently not grazed in 1986. By the mid 18th century much arable had been converted to pasture. A visitor c. 1740 reported that the whole parish was used for grazing,[14] and in 1846 only 130 a. were arable.[15] Cattle fattened at Dauntsey had a high reputation in the mid 17th century,[16] and in the early 18th Dauntsey cheese was said to rival that from Cheddar (Som.).[17]

In the late 18th century there were between 20 and 25 farms in the parish. Most were worked from farmsteads at Dauntsey Green, beside Church Lane, and scattered in the north and east parts of the parish.[18] In 1846 there were 18 farms, of which three, all derived from demesne lands, were of more than 250 a. Park farm comprised 350 a., Great Idover farm and Little Idover farm 270 a. each. Most other farms measured between 100 a. and 200 a.[19]

The farms had changed little in size or number by the early 20th century.[20] From the 1920s, however, farms belonging to Wiltshire county council were broken up into small holdings. By 1941 the lands of Crew's, Great Middle Green, and Union farms had been divided into seven holdings, each of c. 50 a.[21] In 1987 there were five holdings, each of between 50 a. and 100 a.[22]

Most farms retained dairy herds in the late 19th century and the 20th, and from the 1870s beef cattle were reared. Between 1870 and 1940 there were usually between 800 and 950 cattle in the parish, of which over half were for milk. Numbers rose thereafter; over 1,800 cattle were kept in 1966. Sheep were also kept until c. 1950; the size of the adult flock fluctuated between 100 and 350. The area of arable in the parish declined from 343 a. in 1866 to 33 a. in 1936. More land was ploughed in the 1940s, and in 1966 there were again over 300 a. of arable.[23] In 1986 St. John's and Good Monday's farms were partly and Dauntsey House farm was chiefly arable, growing cereal and fodder crops.[24]

A mill at Dauntsey and another at Smithcot were

[1] Red Bk. Exch. (Rolls Ser.), i. 310; Bk. of Fees, ii. 727.
[2] Abbrev. Plac. (Rec. Com.), 314–15.
[3] V.C.H. Wilts. iii. 244; Cal. Chart. R. 1257–1300, 157–9.
[4] V.C.H. Wilts. ii, pp. 125, 144.
[5] Arch. Jnl. lxxvi. 169.
[6] P.R.O., DL 43/9/26.
[7] Below.
[8] P.R.O., DL 43/9/26.
[9] Ibid.
[10] Ibid. C 2/Jas. I/S 29/55; W.R.O. 130/24, deed, Danvers to Atkins, 1654; ibid. D 1/24/67/1.
[11] W.R.O., D 1/24/67/4.
[12] Andrews and Dury, Map (W.R.S. viii), pl. 14.
[13] P.R.O., IR 29/38/95.
[14] W.A.M. xxviii. 254.
[15] P.R.O., IR 29/38/95.
[16] Aubrey, Topog. Coll. ed. Jackson, 216.

[17] W.A.M. xxviii. 254.
[18] Andrews and Dury, Map (W.R.S. viii), pl. 14; W.R.O., A 1/345/134.
[19] P.R.O., IR 29/38/95; IR 30/38/95.
[20] W.R.O. 106, sale cat. of Meux estates, 3rd portion; W.A.S. Libr., sale cat. xxviiiA, no. 14.
[21] W.R.O., F 9, farm files, Great Middle Green farm, Union farm.
[22] Inf. from Estates and Valuations Officer, Co. Hall, Trowbridge.
[23] P.R.O., MAF 68/493, sheet 3; MAF 68/1063, sheet 2; MAF 68/2203, sheet 14; MAF 68/2773, sheet 9; MAF 68/3319, sheet 10; MAF 68/3814, no. 121; MAF 68/4182, no. 121; MAF 68/4552, no. 121; MAF 68/5004, no. 121.
[24] Inf. from Mrs. P. Hitchcock, St. John's Farm; Mr. F. W. Potter, Little Middle Green Farm; Mr. A. J. Capener, 91 Bradenstoke.

recorded in 1086.²⁵ A mill in the parish in 1487 and c. 1550²⁶ was presumably Smith's Mill, on the Avon north-west of Dauntsey House, which had been demolished by 1773.²⁷

In 1831, of 99 families in the parish, only 9 derived their income principally from a trade or craft.²⁸ From the early 19th century coal was brought to the parish by canal and unloaded at Dauntsey wharf.²⁹ In the late 19th century and early 20th there were usually two or three coal merchants.³⁰ Probably from the opening of the station for goods traffic c. 1870³¹ and certainly after the closure of the canal in 1914³² coal was brought to Dauntsey by train.

Clay for bricks may have been dug from a field east of the church in or before the late 17th century.³³ In the 1880s there were brickworks north and south of the railway line east of Dauntsey station. Those north of the line were disused in 1899 as were those south of it in 1922.³⁴

A milk depot had been built north of Dauntsey station by 1884.³⁵ In 1896–7 the Dauntsey Dairy Co. became part of Wilts. United Dairies, which supplied liquid milk to London.³⁶ The depot was closed probably in or soon after 1965 when the station was closed; in 1986 its site was used by several small businesses.³⁷

LOCAL GOVERNMENT.
Dauntsey and Smithcot were assessed separately for taxation from the 14th century to the 16th³⁸ and may have been separate tithings, but the two were not distinguished after the 16th century.

Records of spring and autumn courts of Dauntsey manor, at which customary tenants were admitted, survive for 1646–8.³⁹

In 1727–8 the overseers of the poor in Dauntsey parish spent £18 and gave monthly relief to five people. Those regularly relieved each received between 4s. and 12s. a month and occasional payments for rents. Other payments were for medical and funeral expenses; for a funeral in 1730 the overseers spent 10s. on the coffin, 3s. on ringing the bell, and 11s. 1½d. on ale, bread, cheese, tobacco, and pipes. By 1747–8 total expenditure had risen to £85 and the number regularly relieved to 10.⁴⁰ The custom of providing refreshments at funerals had lapsed by the 1760s, and the purchase of clothing and coal then accounted for a greater proportion of expenditure than before. In 1767–8

the overseers spent £226 and gave regular relief to 22 people.⁴¹ The cost of poor relief continued to rise until the early 19th century; £398 was spent and 40 adults received regular relief in 1802–3. Rates in Dauntsey were, however, then lower than in most parishes of Malmesbury hundred.⁴² From 1812 until the late 1820s both the cost of relief and, presumably, the number of the poor fell, with some fluctuations.⁴³ In the early 1820s poor relief paid to some labourers was replaced by leases of a few acres each at low rents from the farmers of Dauntsey.⁴⁴ In 1828 only £196 was spent on poor relief, by 1832 the sum had risen to £347,⁴⁵ and between 1833 and 1835 average annual expenditure on the poor was £257. Dauntsey became part of Malmesbury poor-law union in 1835⁴⁶ and of North Wiltshire district in 1974.⁴⁷

CHURCH.
The church at Dauntsey was claimed by Malmesbury abbey c. 1177. Since the abbey had already granted its Dauntsey estate in fee by 1086 and since the demesne of Dauntsey manor was later tithe free, it is possible that Dauntsey church was built before the Conquest and belonged to the abbey, and that the lord of the manor intruded the clerk against whom the abbey claimed the church c. 1177.⁴⁸ Then or later, certainly before 1263, the abbey gave up its claim to the church: the benefice became a rectory in the gift of the lord of the manor.⁴⁹ In 1961 the living was united with Brinkworth rectory.⁵⁰

Richard Dauntsey was patron in 1304,⁵¹ and lords of Dauntsey manor, or their trustees or executors, presented at most vacancies until the early 19th century.⁵² Rectors were presented by the king in 1405 and 1407,⁵³ for what reason is not known, and in 1465 William Lygon and his wife Elizabeth, formerly wife of Edmund Stradling, presented by a grant from Edmund's trustees.⁵⁴ In 1611 the king was patron by lapse, as was the bishop of Salisbury in 1757. Presentations were made by Robert Welborne in 1712 and by Henry St. John, Viscount Bolingbroke, in 1713, each by a grant of a turn.⁵⁵ After 1831 the advowson was apparently sold by trustees of Charles, earl of Peterborough and of Monmouth (d. 1814). In 1859 it was held by W. E. Elwell,⁵⁶ rector of Dauntsey 1859–75; after his death in 1880⁵⁷ it passed to his relict (d. by 1903).⁵⁸ In 1912 William, Eleanor, and Muriel Elwell conveyed it to Arthur Law,⁵⁹ rector of Dauntsey

²⁵ V.C.H. Wilts. ii, pp. 125, 144.
²⁶ Cal. Inq. p.m. Hen. VII, i, p. 123; P.R.O., DL 43/9/26.
²⁷ Andrews and Dury, Map (W.R.S. viii), pl. 14; W.R.O., EA/98.
²⁸ Census, 1831.
²⁹ V.C.H. Wilts. iv. 274.
³⁰ Kelly's Dir. Wilts. (1859 and later edns.).
³¹ W.R.O. 1213/29.
³² V.C.H. Wilts. iv. 277.
³³ Ch. Com., copy deed, no. 3335; W.R.O., D 1/24/67/2.
³⁴ O.S. Map 6″, Wilts. XIV (1887 and later edns.).
³⁵ Ibid.
³⁶ V.C.H. Wilts. iv. 225.   ³⁷ Local inf.
³⁸ V.C.H. Wilts. iv. 309; Sess. Mins. (W.R.S. iv), 109; Taxation Lists (W.R.S. x), 30, 53.
³⁹ P.R.O., C 116/273, pp. 1, 17, 33, 36, 56, 81.
⁴⁰ W.R.O. 1586/31.
⁴¹ Ibid. 1586/32.
⁴² Poor Law Abstract, 1804, 566–7.
⁴³ Poor Law Abstract, 1818, 498; Poor Rate Returns, 1816–21, 188; 1822–4, 228; 1825–9, 219.

⁴⁴ Wilts. Cuttings, i. 45.
⁴⁵ Poor Rate Returns, 1825–9, 219; 1830–4, 212.
⁴⁶ Poor Law Com. 2nd Rep. App. D, 559.
⁴⁷ O.S. Map 1/100,000, admin. areas, Wilts. (1974 edn.).
⁴⁸ Reg. Malm. i. 373–4; V.C.H. Wilts. iii. 218; above, manors; below. The freedom from tithes might, however, have arisen from a grant of tithes in Wilsford: below.
⁴⁹ Close R. 1261–4, 369; below.
⁵⁰ W.R.O. 1608/10.
⁵¹ Reg. Ghent (Cant. & York Soc.), ii. 626.
⁵² Phillipps, Wilts. Inst. i. 21, 24, 28, 41, 61, 63, 78, 107, 110, 123, 182, 186, 193, 199, 213; ii. 33, 57, 62, 74, 101.
⁵³ Ibid. i. 93; Cal. Pat. 1405–8, 300.
⁵⁴ Phillipps, Wilts. Inst. i. 155; Trans. Bristol and Glos. Arch. Soc. l, facing p. 326.
⁵⁵ Phillipps, Wilts. Inst. ii. 6, 51–2, 77.
⁵⁶ Rep. Com. Eccl. Revenues, 832–3; Kelly's Dir. Wilts. (1859).
⁵⁷ Alum. Oxon. 1715–1886, ii. 424.
⁵⁸ Kelly's Dir. Wilts. (1889, 1903); Crockford (1896).
⁵⁹ Ch. Com. file 52274.

1875–1915.[60] Law (d. 1923) devised the advowson to A. R. Law, rector of Dauntsey 1915–24, and E. C. Elwell.[61] They conveyed it in 1925 to the bishop of Bristol.[62] The bishop was patron of the united benefice from 1961.[63]

Dauntsey rectory was one of the richer livings in Malmesbury deanery in 1291, when it was assessed at £13 6s.[64] Its assessment was unchanged in 1535; if the figure was correct, its value was then about the average for the deanery.[65] Between 1829 and 1831 the rector received c. £350 yearly, an income close to the average for a Wiltshire living.[66]

In the late 17th century, as presumably earlier, tithes from the whole parish except the demesne of Dauntsey manor were due to the rector.[67] In 1846 1,197 a. were tithe free. The rectorial tithes were then valued at £400 and commuted.[68] By the late 13th century the rectors had also become entitled to tithes from land owned by members of the Dauntsey family in Wilsford in Swanborough hundred: those tithes were valued at £2 13s. 4d. in 1291.[69] They arose from 103 a. in Wilsford, from 114 a. after inclosure in 1808.[70] In 1843 they were valued at £52 and commuted.[71]

The rector had 40 a. of glebe in 1671[72] and 45 a. in 1887.[73] From 1698 to 1783 or longer the rector was also entitled to hay cut from a meadow in Great Somerford.[74] Most of the glebe was sold in 1919.[75] A rectory house standing in 1698 was probably that described in 1783 as ancient.[76] A new house of red brick, with its principal, northern front in Tudor style faced with ashlar, was built between 1829 and 1833 from designs by W. Strong. In 1869 it was extended and a new stable court and a high boundary wall were built. The house was sold c. 1957.[77]

A chapel at Smithcot in 1327[78] was called St. Anne's in 1347 and later. Between 1347 and 1387 lords of Smithcot manor presented chaplains. In 1390 and 1442 the bishop of Salisbury was patron by lapse.[79] No chaplain is recorded after 1442 and no reference to the chapel after 1474.[80] A chapel of Dauntsey church at 'West End' was referred to in 1763.[81] No such chapel or location is known, and the reference was possibly to the schoolroom later used for prayers.[82]

In 1304 Peter of Coleshill, rector of Dauntsey, was licensed to study at Oxford for three years and a curate was appointed to serve the parish.[83] In 1477 the rector, John Jones, received a dispensation to hold another benefice with Dauntsey in plurality.[84] Robert Davenant, rector 1663–74, was also a canon of Salisbury and had been sequestrated from West Kington rectory by 1654.[85] Joseph Trapp, a high church pamphleteer and the first professor of poetry at Oxford, held Dauntsey rectory from 1714 to 1722.[86] In 1783 a service was held at Dauntsey on Sundays alternately in the morning and the evening. Prayers were said twice daily in the school at Dauntsey Green and some additional weekday services were held in the church. Communion was celebrated at Christmas, Easter, and Whitsun.[87] On Census Sunday in 1851 the congregation at morning service numbered 146.[88]

The church of *ST. JAMES*, so called in 1763,[89] is mostly of rubble, in places rendered, with ashlar dressings. It has a chancel with a north chapel, an aisled nave with north and south porches, and a west tower. The nave was apparently built or rebuilt in the 12th century, and the aisles were apparently added in the 14th: the arcades, the porches, and the east window of the south aisle appear to be 14th-century. The 12th-century north and south doorways were reset in the walls of the aisles. The chancel, which is not divided from the nave, was enlarged and refenestrated in the 15th century and the early 16th. In the period 1630–2 the church was 'repaired and enlarged' for Henry, earl of Danby (d. 1644),[90] apparently in a debased 14th-century style. The chapel may have been built for Danby, whose tomb chest is in it, but is dated 1656:[91] its east window is in a style similar to that of the east window of the south aisle. The north and south windows of the aisles, which have cusped ogee lights with blank spandrels within a square frame, resemble the chapel's north windows: it is likely that the aisles are 14th-century and that they were refenestrated for Danby, but possible that they were built anew or rebuilt in the early or mid 17th century. The tower, in a plain Gothic style, was also built 1630–2.[92] Many 17th-century fittings survive, including the rood screen which incorporates some later 14th-century tracery, most of the pews in the nave, and, in the chancel, stalls which incorporate 15th-century bench ends. The church was restored in 1879,[93] in 1906 when the roofs of the nave and aisles were renewed,[94] and in 1932.[95] The tympanum of a rood screen of c. 1500, found in the mid 19th century,[96] remains in the church. Tomb chests commemorate Sir John Danvers (d. 1514), Anne Danvers (d. 1539), and Henry, earl of Danby; a tablet in the floor of the chancel commemorates Charles, earl of Peterborough and of Monmouth (d. 1814).

[60] *Crockford* (1926).
[61] Ibid.; Bristol R.O., EP/A/3/134.
[62] Ch. Com. file 52274; W.R.O. 1608/9.
[63] Inf. from the Revd. Canon C. L. Sutch, 18 Linden Road, Redland, Bristol.
[64] *Tax. Eccl.* (Rec. Com.), 189.
[65] *Valor Eccl.* (Rec. Com.), ii. 138.
[66] *Rep. Com. Eccl. Revenues*, 822–3.
[67] W.R.O., D 1/24/67/2.
[68] P.R.O., IR 29/38/95.
[69] *V.C.H. Wilts.* x. 212; *Tax. Eccl.* (Rec. Com.), 180.
[70] *Inclosure Awards* (W.R.S. xxv), p. 140.
[71] *Tithe Apportionments* (W.R.S. xxx), p. 104.
[72] W.R.O., D 1/24/67/1.
[73] *Glebe Lands Return*, H.C. 307, p. 52 (1887), lxiv.
[74] W.R.O., D 1/24/67/2; D 1/24/67/4.
[75] Ch. Com. file 86978.
[76] W.R.O., D 1/24/67/2; D 1/24/67/4.

[77] E. E. Dorling, *Wilts. Contemporary Biog.* ed. W. T. Pike (Pike's New Cent. Ser. xvi), 37; inf. from Mrs. L. Wild, Roboan Ho., Dauntsey.
[78] *Reg. Martival* (Cant. & York Soc.), i. 349.
[79] Phillipps, *Wilts. Inst.* i. 42, 46–7, 55, 71, 75, 133.
[80] W.R.O. 130/24, deed, Lynde to Fowler, 1474.
[81] J. Ecton, *Thesaurus*, 403; *W.A.M.* x. 275, 307.
[82] Below.
[83] *Reg. Ghent* (Cant. & York Soc.), ii. 867, 869.
[84] *Cal. Papal Reg.* xiii (2), 541.
[85] *Walker Revised*, ed. Matthews, 372; Phillipps, *Wilts. Inst.* ii. 33.
[86] *D.N.B.*
[87] *Vis. Queries, 1783* (W.R.S. xxvii), pp. 82–3.
[88] P.R.O., HO 129/252/1/10/15.
[89] Ecton, *Thesaurus*, 403.
[90] W.R.O. 1070/3.
[91] Date on arch.
[92] W.R.O. 1070/3.
[93] Ibid. 1608/12.
[94] Wilts. Cuttings, xvii. 29.
[95] W.R.O. 1608/12.
[96] *W.A.M.* iii. 14.

A chalice given in 1420[97] was perhaps that of 12 oz. retained by the parish in 1553 when 2 oz. of plate were taken for the king.[98] The parish had two chalices and two patens in 1783.[99] They were replaced, probably in 1823, by a chalice and a paten[1] which were still held, with another chalice and paten, by the parish in 1986.[2]

Three bells hung in the church in 1553. Of five bells there in 1783 two were of 1632, probably by Nathaniel Boulter, and one was of 1673. The other two were replaced or recast in 1848 by C. & G. Mears. One of the 1848 bells was recast in 1926 by Mears & Stainbank.[3] The three 17th-century bells and those of 1848 and 1926 hung in the church in 1986.[4]

There are registers of baptisms, marriages, and burials from 1653.[5]

NONCONFORMITY. In the late 17th century and early 18th several Quaker families lived in the parish.[6]

In 1783 there were said to be several Methodists.[7] A house was certified in 1827 for meetings of Wesleyan Methodists, and others in 1828 and 1839 for Primitive Methodists.[8]

Houses were certified for Independents in 1798, 1816, and 1817;[9] the meetings were addressed sometimes by Independent and sometimes by Baptist preachers.[10] An Independent chapel at Dauntsey Common, built in 1824 or 1825, was attended by 22 people on the morning of Census Sunday in 1851 and by 34 in the afternoon.[11] In 1863 a Strict Baptist church was founded. Thereafter the Baptists used the chapel, which was rebuilt as the Providence chapel, a small brick building, in 1875. It was closed in the 1960s[12] but was again in use in 1986.[13]

EDUCATION. By will proved 1645 Henry, earl of Danby, gave land in Dauntsey for a school and almshouse. The almshouse was to occupy the ground floor of the building, the schoolroom and accommodation for the schoolmaster the first floor. Lord Danby also gave land in Market Lavington to maintain the building and to pay the schoolmaster £16 a year. The master was to conform to the established church and to teach boys to read, write, and cipher, and girls to read. The building may have been standing in 1667, when disputes over the endowment were resolved by an agreement that a total of £50 a year should be paid to the school and almshouse.[14] Both were open in 1673.[15]

In 1818 Earl Danby's school had c. 40 pupils;[16] in 1833 numbers varied between 20 and 50 according to the demand for labour.[17] The building, timber-framed and with a bellcot, was in 1858 in poor repair and unsuitable for use as a school;[18] it was replaced between 1864 and 1866 by another on a neighbouring site. The new brick building comprised a teacher's house of two storeys from which single-storeyed wings extended east and west; the west wing was occupied by the school.[19] In the late 19th century the school usually had 60–70 pupils and two teachers.[20] Average attendance had fallen from 60 in 1909–10 to 39 by 1918–19 but was higher in the 1920s and 1930s.[21] In 1986 the school had 27 pupils on roll.[22]

The school received little or no income from Lord Danby's endowment from 1865 until 1905, when the Charity Commissioners ordered that part of the endowment should again be used for education.[23] A Scheme of 1981 required the income, then between £25 and £50, to be spent on benefits for the school not normally provided by the local education authority.[24]

A school in the parish, attended in 1833 by 40 girls,[25] was open in 1846.[26] It or another school was in 1858 attended by 20–30 children.[27] The school was open in 1865 but closed soon afterwards.[28]

CHARITIES FOR THE POOR. There was an almshouse with five or more residents in Dauntsey in 1420.[29]

By will proved 1645 Henry, earl of Danby, gave a site in Dauntsey and income, £50 a year from 1667, for a school and almshouse. The almshouse was to have six inmates, aged 50 or more, unable to support themselves, and preferably natives or residents of Dauntsey. Each was to receive £5 4s. a year and, if it could be afforded, clothing. The almshouse, like the school, was possibly open in 1667 and certainly was in 1673.[30] The almshouse occupied the east wing of the new building erected 1864–6. In 1905 there were eight residents, including two married couples;[31] in 1986 there were six

[97] Reg. Hallum (Cant. & York Soc.), p. 224.
[98] Nightingale, Wilts. Plate, 196.
[99] W.R.O., D 1/24/67/4.
[1] Nightingale, Wilts. Plate, 196.
[2] Inf. from Canon Sutch.
[3] Walters, Wilts. Bells, 69–71; W.R.O., D 1/24/67/4.
[4] Inf. from Canon Sutch.
[5] W.R.O. 1070/1–13. Bishop's transcripts for some earlier years are ibid.
[6] W.N. & Q. ii. 289, 426, 429; iv. 24; v. 223; vi. 134; vii. 133, 515.
[7] Vis. Queries, 1783 (W.R.S. xxvii), p. 83.
[8] Meeting Ho. Certs. (W.R.S. xl), pp. 113, 120, 148.
[9] Ibid. pp. 51, 78, 82.
[10] R. W. Oliver, Strict Bapt. Chapels Eng. (Strict Bapt. Hist. Soc.), v. 46.
[11] P.R.O., HO 129/252/1/10/16; date on bldg.
[12] Oliver, op. cit. 46; date on bldg.
[13] Local inf.
[14] Endowed Char. Wilts. (N. Div.), 377–9; P.R.O., PROB 11/194, f. 100.
[15] W.R.O. 1033, acct. bk. 1673–1805.

[16] Educ. of Poor Digest, 1025.
[17] Educ. Enq. Abstract, 1035.
[18] Acct. of Wilts. Schs. 19; Wilts. and Glos. Standard, 2 Nov. 1912.
[19] Endowed Char. Wilts. (N. Div.), 381; Wilts. Cuttings, xvi. 195; see above, plate facing p. 61.
[20] Returns relating to Elem. Educ. 420–1; Kelly's Dir. Wilts. (1867 and later edns.).
[21] Bd. of Educ., List 21, 1911 (H.M.S.O.), 547; 1919, 360; 1922, 359; 1936, 423.
[22] Inf. from the head teacher.
[23] Endowed Char. Wilts. (N. Div.), 382–3; Return of Non-Provided Schs. 21 n.   [24] Char. Com. file.
[25] Educ. Enq. Abstract, 1035.
[26] Nat. Soc. Inquiry, 1846–7, Wilts. 4–5.
[27] Acct. of Wilts. Schs. 19.
[28] Kelly's Dir. Wilts. (1865 and later edns.).
[29] Reg. Hallum (Cant. & York Soc.), p. 224.
[30] Endowed Char. Wilts. (N. Div.), 377–9; P.R.O., PROB 11/194, f. 100; above, educ.
[31] Endowed Char. Wilts. (N. Div.), 381, 383; Wilts. Cuttings, xvi. 195; see above, plate facing p. 61.

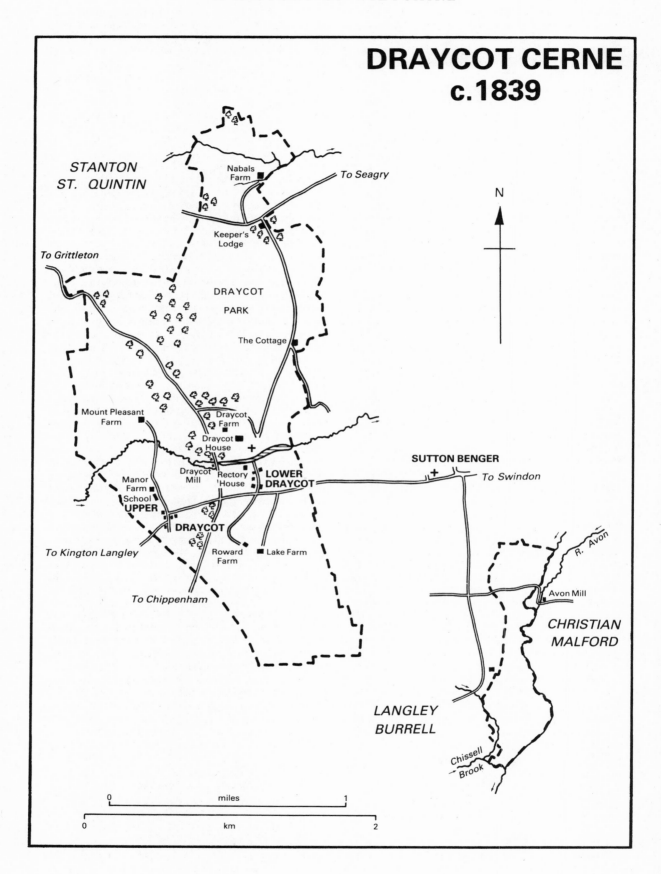

DRAYCOT CERNE
c.1839

residents.[32] From 1865 until 1905 most, if not all, of the income from the endowment was paid to the almshouse;[33] in 1905 the income was £62. Thereafter part of it was again paid to the school.[34]

Before 1837 Lady Catherine Bisset gave £833 to buy coal for the poor of Dauntsey parish. The income, c. £25 a year, and its use remained the same in the late 19th century and the early 20th.[35] In the 1960s the income was between £25 and £50 a year.[36]

DRAYCOT CERNE

DRAYCOT CERNE[37] is 5 km. NNE. of Chippenham.[38] The suffix Cerne is derived from the surname of the lords of the manor in the Middle Ages.[39] The parish included a detached portion, c. 90 a., between the eastern boundary of Sutton Benger and the west bank of the Bristol Avon, called Draycot Sutton in 1778:[40] it was transferred to Sutton Benger in 1884.[41] In the Middle Ages 81 a. of adjoining land to the north may have been among the lands of a hamlet or farmstead called Knabwell: the 81 a., Nabals farm, were extra-parochial until 1830 when they were added to Draycot Cerne parish. More of Knabwell's land may have been added to Stanton St. Quintin parish.[42] The boundary with Stanton St. Quintin was altered slightly in 1882.[43] The parish of Draycot Cerne, 1,015 a. (411 ha.), was added to Sutton Benger in 1934. The lands of the former parish north of the London and south Wales motorway became part of Seagry parish in 1971.[44]

A feeder of the Avon on the north-east, and, in the detached portion of the parish, the Avon itself, are the only natural features to have marked Draycot Cerne's boundaries. Its lands were divided from those of Kington Langley to the west before the mid 11th century.[45] Footpaths mark parts of the former east and west boundaries. Kellaways Clay and Oxford Clay outcrop over most of the former parish. There are outcrops of Cornbrash in the north and west, Kellaways Sand in the north-east, and, beside a stream flowing eastwards to the Avon, one of three to drain the former parish, Forest Marble in the west.[46] The land is undulating, highest, over 91 m., in the centre and north, lowest, below 61 m., in the flatter south. The Cornbrash favoured arable, but most of the parish was meadow and pasture and, in the centre, was for long parkland.[47]

The main Swindon–Chippenham road crosses the former parish: in 1727 it was turnpiked from Chippenham to the junction with the road from Draycot Cerne to Grittleton through Stanton St.

Quintin, in 1756 from that junction to Christian Malford, and in 1758 to Swindon. After 1727, possibly c. 1756, and certainly before 1773, when there were gates at each end, a new straight section was made south of the junction; west of it parts of the old road, which had several sharp bends, remain as a lane, a bridleway, and a track. The whole road was disturnpiked in the 1870s.[48] The road between Draycot Cerne and Grittleton was turnpiked in 1756 and disturnpiked in 1875.[49] The London and south Wales motorway was built across the former parish and opened in 1971.[50] South of it the road between Draycot Cerne and Stanton St. Quintin was diverted to join the Chippenham–Malmesbury road, and north of it ceased to be a through road. The road which followed the north boundary of Draycot park was called Scotland Hill in 1885.[51] In the detached part of the parish a road which led from that linking Chippenham, Langley Burrell, and Sutton Benger south-east to Avon Mill in Christian Malford, was diverted to run further east in 1778:[52] it was a track in 1987. The G.W.R. line from London to Bristol was constructed north-east and south-west across the same part of the parish and was opened in 1841.[53]

The sum at which Draycot Cerne was assessed for taxation in 1334 was among the lowest in Startley hundred.[54] There were 63 poll-tax payers in 1377.[55] Assessments for taxation in the 16th and earlier 17th century, often among the highest in Malmesbury hundred, reflected the wealth of members of the Long family who owned Draycot manor and lived in Draycot House.[56] The population rose from 141 in 1801 to 181 in 1841, declined to 158 in 1861, a decline attributed to there being no large household at Draycot House, rose in 1871 to 187, fell to 93 in 1921, and was 113 in 1931.[57] The population of the former parish may have been about the same in 1987.

In 1377 there were two settlements in the parish, and until the later 19th century there were two

[32] Inf. from Canon Sutch.
[33] W.R.O. 1033, acct. bk. 1804–1905.
[34] *Endowed Char. Wilts.* (N. Div.), 383–4; above, educ.
[35] *Endowed Char. Wilts.* (N. Div.), 385–6; Char. Com. file.
[36] Char. Com. file.
[37] This article was written in 1987.
[38] Maps used include: O.S. Maps 1″, sheet 34 (1828 edn.); 1/50,000, sheet 173 (1974 edn.); 1/25,000, ST 97–8 (1959 edns.); 6″, Wilts. XIII, XX (1888–9 and later edns.).
[39] *P.N. Wilts.* (E.P.N.S.), 69–70.
[40] W.R.O., A 1/316/12.
[41] *Census*, 1881; 1891.
[42] W.R.O. 2062/13, pp. 130–1; P.R.O., C 108/112/1, acct. bk. 1827–34; ibid. IR 29/38/103; IR 30/38/103; below, Stanton St. Quintin, introduction.
[43] *Census*, 1891.

[44] Ibid. 1931; 1971.
[45] *Arch. Jnl.* lxxvi. 253–5; *W.A.M.* lxxvii. 67–70.
[46] Geol. Surv. Map 1″, solid and drift, sheet 265 (1965 edn.).
[47] Below, econ. hist.
[48] *V.C.H. Wilts.* iv. 257, 267, 269–71; *L.J.* xxiii. 115; xxviii. 518; xxix. 367; *Andrews and Dury, Map* (W.R.S. viii), pl. 13.
[49] *V.C.H. Wilts.* iv. 260, 269; *L.J.* xxviii. 518.
[50] *Rep. Co. Surveyor, 1971–2* (Wilts. co. council), 3.
[51] O.S. Map 6″, Wilts. XIII (1888 edn.).
[52] W.R.O., A 1/316/12.
[53] *V.C.H. Wilts.* iv. 282.   [54] Ibid. 301.
[55] Ibid. 309.
[56] e.g. *Taxation Lists* (W.R.S. x), 53; P.R.O., E 179/199/356; below, manor.
[57] *V.C.H. Wilts.* iv. 323, 347.

nucleated groups of houses: Lower Draycot, apparently the larger in 1377 but removed in the 19th century, was between the church and the Swindon–Chippenham road, and west of it Upper Draycot was at a bend on the old course of that road.[58] Two farmsteads have stood in the south part of the former parish, and in the north part there has been scattered settlement from the 17th century.

Lower Draycot in 1773 and c. 1839 consisted of the rectory house and other houses east and west of the lane between the church and the main road.[59] An ornamental fishpond was formed in a feeder of the Avon as a feature of gardens laid out c. 1769 south of Draycot House;[60] in 1773 a bridge carried the lane over the pond, north of which the lane was then the main drive of Draycot House.[61] In 1808 or earlier and c. 1839 the main drive ran south-east from the Stanton St. Quintin road. Between c. 1839 and 1885 the land between the pond and the Swindon–Chippenham road was taken into the grounds of Draycot House, the rectory house and all the other buildings beside the lane were demolished, and gate piers, a gate, and a lodge were erected on the north side of the main road.[62] The lane again became the main drive of Draycot House. An avenue of Wellingtonias was planted along it and those on the east stood in 1987. The bridge across the pond was rebuilt in stone c. 1956.[63] A wall was built on the west and north sides of the park before 1870.[64] To the west the wall had gone by 1987 when the north part was ruinous. Gothic stone lodges were built on the east side of the Stanton St. Quintin road in 1869 and 1889.[65] A farmstead called Draycot Park Farm was built between them in the period 1885–99. Scotland Lodge, so called in 1885,[66] was built on the south side of Scotland Hill before 1773 and rebuilt in Gothic style in 1862.[67] A house called the Cottage stood in the east part of the park in 1773, and possibly in the 17th century.[68] A pair of rustic gabled cottages built on its site in 1858[69] was one house in 1987.

Upper Draycot is reached by an east–west section of the old Swindon–Chippenham road, called Day's Lane in 1987. In 1773 a few houses were on the south side of that road and others were on the west side of a lane leading north from it.[70] In the north part of the hamlet Manor Farm was built, possibly in the later 16th century, as an east–west range. A north–south range was built on the

north side at the east end in the 17th century, and in the 18th a pedimented doorcase was inserted on the south front and a new staircase was constructed. Stables north-west of the house were built c. 1924[71] and large farm buildings north of it in the period 1974–83.[72] The village school and an adjoining cottage which stood south of Manor Farm were incorporated after 1920 in a large stone house, in 1987 called the Grey House.[73] Cottages south of the school were replaced by three pairs of stone estate cottages built in Gothic style in the later 19th century.[74] Houses which stood c. 1839 on the south side of the old main road[75] were replaced in 1874, 1974,[76] and c. 1985.[77] On the north side a parish cemetery with a chapel, built of stone to the designs of J. F. Bentley, was opened c. 1883.[78]

A mill stood beside the Stanton St. Quintin road until the later 19th century.[79] Further north, a pair of stone estate cottages was built in 1904,[80] and two bungalows were built after 1972.[81] Mount Pleasant Farm, built to the west before 1808[82] at Parsonage barn, which stood in 1773,[83] was demolished between c. 1940 and 1987.[84] Nabals Farm, north of Scotland Hill, was standing in 1773,[85] was partly of stone rubble and partly timber-framed, and had a thatched roof.[86] The house was rebuilt, and its farm buildings were renewed, in the later 20th century.[87]

From the 18th century or earlier,[88] there have been only two farmsteads, Roward and Lake, in the south part of the parish. The east–west range of Lake Farm was built in the 17th century or earlier: c. 1800 that range was altered and re-roofed, and a short wing was added on the east end of the north side. Roward Farm, called Roward House and described as newly built c. 1637,[89] has a north–south range with stone-mullioned windows. It was enlarged in the 18th century and, westwards, in the earlier 19th when a new south entrance front was also constructed.

MANOR AND OTHER ESTATES. In 1066 Edric held the estate later called *DRAYCOT CERNE*. Geoffrey the marshal held it in 1084 or earlier and in 1086 by serjeanty. In 1086 the estate included a burgage in Malmesbury.[90] Geoffrey's heir, either his son or grandson, was Robert de Venoix,[91] in possession in 1130.[92] William de Venoix held Draycot in the years 1191–6,[93] and

[58] *V.C.H. Wilts.* iv. 309; P.R.O., IR 30/38/103; O.S. Map 6″, Wilts. XX (1889 edn.).
[59] *Andrews and Dury, Map* (W.R.S. viii), pl. 13; P.R.O., IR 29/38/103; IR 30/38/103.   [60] W.R.O. 1001/1A.
[61] *Andrews and Dury, Map* (W.R.S. viii), pl. 13.
[62] W.R.O. 1001/5; P.R.O., IR 30/38/103; O.S. Map 6″, Wilts. XX (1889 edn.).
[63] Inf. from Mr. J. E. Bent, Draycot Park Farm.
[64] W.R.O. 2062/21.   [65] Dates on hos.
[66] O.S. Maps 6″, Wilts. XX (1889 edn.), XX. NE. (1901 edn.).
[67] *Andrews and Dury, Map* (W.R.S. viii), pl. 13; date on ho.
[68] *Andrews and Dury, Map* (W.R.S. viii), pl. 13; *W.A.M.* lxxiv/lxxv. 76–7, 79, 82–8.   [69] Date on ho.
[70] *Andrews and Dury, Map* (W.R.S. viii), pl. 13.
[71] W.R.O., G 3/760/593.
[72] O.S. Maps 1/50,000, sheet 173 (1974 edn.); 1/10,000, ST 97 NW. (1983 edn.).
[73] Below, educ.; W.R.O. 1043/6, p. 40.   [74] Dates on hos.
[75] P.R.O., IR 30/38/103.   [76] Dates on hos.

[77] Inf. from Mr. R. Couzens, 9 the Close.
[78] W.R.O. 1093/21, deed and bldg. specifications, 1883.
[79] Below, econ. hist.   [80] Date on bldg.
[81] O.S. Maps 1/50,000, sheet 173 (1974 edn.); 1/10,000, ST 97 NW. (1983 edn.).
[82] W.R.O. 1001/5; 2062/13, pp. 44–5.
[83] *Andrews and Dury, Map* (W.R.S. viii), pl. 13.
[84] Inf. from Mr. Couzens.
[85] *Andrews and Dury, Map* (W.R.S. viii), pl. 13.
[86] W.R.O. 1043/6, photo. at p. 104.
[87] O.S. Maps 6″, ST 98 SW. (1960 edn.); 1/10,000, ST 98 SW. (1983 edn.).
[88] *Andrews and Dury, Map* (W.R.S. viii), pl. 13.
[89] P.R.O., C 112/53/2, deed, 1637.
[90] *V.C.H. Wilts.* ii, pp. 74–5, 167, 212; *V.C.H. Hants,* i. 430–1; ii. 518.
[91] *V.C.H. Hants,* ii. 518; *Complete Peerage,* xi, App. E, 123–4.
[92] *Pipe R.* 1130 (H.M.S.O. facsimile), 22.
[93] Ibid. 1191 & 92 (P.R.S. n.s. ii), 88, 297; 1195 (P.R.S. n.s. vi), 207; *Chanc. R.* 1196 (P.R.S. n.s. vii), 62.

BRASS OF SIR EDWARD OF CERNE
AND HIS WIFE ELLEN

frey of Cerne in 1242–3[3] and in the years 1250–5 by Geoffrey's son[4] Philip. From Philip's son Henry of Cerne (d. 1296), who held it in 1275 or earlier, the manor passed in the direct male line to John[5] (d. 1327), John[6] (d. 1344), and John[7] (d. 1346). From the third John, the manor passed to his brother Edward,[8] later Sir Edward, of Cerne (d. 1393), to Sir Edward's relict Ellen (d. 1418), and to Sir Edward's son Edward[9] (d. 1419). The manor was held for life by Edward's relict Isabel[10] (fl. 1438). The reversion was settled in 1438 by John Herring, a descendant of Geoffrey of Cerne, on William Rangebourne (d. 1450) for life with remainder to John Long.[11]

From John Long (d. 1478), who was of Draycot in 1452, the manor passed from father to son, to Thomas[12] (knighted 1501, d. 1508), Sir Henry[13] (d. 1556), Sir Robert[14] (d. 1581), and Sir Walter[15] (d. 1610). From Sir Walter, whose disinheritance of his eldest son gave rise to the legend of a ghostly hand preventing the writing of a deed of disinheritance, Draycot passed to his eldest son by his second marriage, Sir Walter Long[16] (d. 1637). The manor was sequestered in 1645 from that Sir Walter's son James, later Sir James Long, Bt., a royalist, and restored to him in 1649.[17] From Sir James (d. 1692) the manor, except Draycot House, park, and other lands settled for life on his relict Dorothy (d. 1710),[18] passed in turn to his grandsons Sir Robert Long, Bt. (d. 1692), Sir Giles Long, Bt. (d. 1697), and Sir James Long, Bt. (d. 1729). The reunited estate descended in the direct male line to that Sir James's son Sir Robert Long, Bt. (d. 1767), Sir James Long, from 1784 Tylney-Long, Bt. (d. 1794), and Sir James Tylney-Long, Bt. (d. 1805).[19] John Long (d. 1478) and six of his successors as lord of the manor represented Wiltshire constituencies in parliament.[20]

Catherine Long, the sister of Sir James (d. 1805), inherited Draycot Cerne manor and in 1812 married William Wellesley-Pole, from 1812 Pole-Tylney-Long-Wellesley, and from 1845 earl of Mornington. She was succeeded in 1825 by her son William Pole-Tylney-Long-Wellesley, from 1845 styled Viscount Wellesley, who became earl of Mornington in 1857. William, earl of Mornington (d. 1863), devised the manor to his cousin Henry Wellesley, Earl Cowley (d. 1884), from whom it passed in the direct male line to William, Earl Cowley (d. 1895), and Henry, Earl Cowley (d. 1919). In 1920 Henry's son Christian, Earl

his heir Robert de Venoix held it in 1197.[94] Robert held it by serjeanty of marshalcy in the years 1210–12,[95] and possibly before 1214, certainly before 1220, had been succeeded by his son John.[96] Members of the St. Germain family unsuccessfully claimed the estate from members of the Venoix family in 1197 and 1220–1.[97] John de Venoix, presumably another, was succeeded in 1260 by his son John,[98] whose overlordship was last mentioned in 1275.[99] The manor was said to be held of the king in chief in 1393.[1]

In 1228 John de Venoix subinfeudated Draycot to Henry of Cerne.[2] The manor was held by Geof-

[94] *Feet of Fines*, 1196–7 (Pipe R. Soc. xx), p. 145.
[95] *Red Bk. Exch.* (Rolls Ser.), ii. 482, 488.
[96] *Rot. de Ob. et Fin.* (Rec. Com.), 532; *Pat. R. 1216–25*, 262.
[97] *Feet of Fines*, 1196–7 (Pipe R. Soc. xx), p. 145; *Bracton's Note Bk.* ed. Maitland, iii, pp. 414–15.
[98] *V.C.H. Hants*, ii. 518.
[99] *Rot. Hund.* (Rec. Com.), ii (1), 272.
[1] *Cal. Inq. p.m.* xvii, p. 139.
[2] *Cal. Chart. R. 1226–57*, 67.
[3] *Bk. of Fees*, ii. 743.
[4] Ibid. ii. 1178; *Rot. Hund.* (Rec. Com.), ii (1), 235; P.R.O., C 139/87, no. 41.
[5] P.R.O., C 139/87, no. 41; *Rot. Hund.* (Rec. Com.), ii (1), 272; *Wilts. Inq. p.m. 1242–1326* (Index Libr.), 210.
[6] *Wilts. Inq. p.m. 1327–77* (Index Libr.), 6–7.
[7] Ibid. 158.
[8] *Cal. Inq. p.m.* ix, pp. 82–3.
[9] Ibid. xvii, p. 139; *Wilts. Inq. p.m. 1327–77* (Index Libr.),

319; P.R.O., C 138/38, no. 33.
[10] P.R.O., C 138/45, no. 31; C 139/87, no. 41.
[11] Ibid. CP 25(1)/257/63, no. 3; *W.A.M.* iii, pedigree facing p. 178; *V.C.H. Hants*, iv. 419 n.
[12] *Hist. Parl., Commons, 1439–1509*, 550–1; P.R.O., C 140/65, no. 13. For the Long fam., Burke, *Commoners*, iii. 211–18, which this acct. corrects; G.E.C. *Baronetage*, iii. 258–9.
[13] *Hist. Parl., Commons, 1439–1509*, 552.
[14] P.R.O., C 142/110, no. 167.
[15] Ibid. C 142/197, no. 95.
[16] Ibid. C 142/334, no. 65; J. Aubrey, *Miscellanies* (1721), 75–6.
[17] *Wilts. Inq. p.m. 1625–49* (Index Libr.), 237–41; *Cal. Cttee. for Money*, ii. 623–4.
[18] P.R.O., C 112/53/1, agreement and settlement 1639–40, altered settlement 1642.
[19] W.R.O., A 1/345/156.
[20] *Hist. Parl., Commons, 1439–1509*, 550–2; 1509–58, ii. 546; 1660–90, ii. 757–8; 1715–54, ii. 224; 1754–90, iii. 52–3.

Cowley,[21] sold Draycot House and park, *c.* 600 a., to Philip Ashworth.[22] In 1923 Herbert Dixon (cr. Baron Glentoran 1939, d. 1950) owned them.[23] Lord Glentoran sold that estate in 1946 to a syndicate of farmers, led by S. W. Maundrell, which sold the land in portions.[24]

A manor house stood in 1399 when Ellen of Cerne was licensed to employ a chaplain to serve an oratory in it.[25] The stone house may have been altered or rebuilt for John Long (d. 1478), whose parents' coat of arms was depicted in the oriel window of the hall.[26] Draycot House, so called in 1695,[27] was *c.* 1542 described as a 'fair manor place' and stood in a park.[28] The Long family lived in the house and its successor from the mid 15th century to the earlier 19th. The appearance in the house of the date 1574 and the coats of arms of Sir Henry Long (d. 1556) and Sir Robert Long (d. 1581) suggest some later 16th-century alterations. The gabled south entrance front was of four bays *c.* 1670. A two-storeyed porch, built for Sir Walter Long's father-in-law, James Ley, earl of Marlborough (d. 1629), was in the westernmost bay, and, on the ground floor, the oriel window of the hall was in the second bay from the east.[29]

That house was replaced in 1784 by another built of stone[30] to plans drawn up in 1769 for Sir James Long.[31] The new house[32] had a south-east garden front of 13 bays: the five central bays projected and were of three storeys surmounted by a pediment; the four bays on each side were of two storeys with attics concealed by parapets. The principal rooms were in the north-east part of the house.[33] The north-east front was also of two storeys with attics and a parapet, and it had a segmental bay of two storeys at each end. Terraces from which steps led down to formal gardens ran the length of both those principal fronts. A north-west wing, added in 1864 to the designs of R. J. Withers,[34] was of three storeys. The house, except the cellars, was demolished *c.* 1955.[35] Stone from it was used to adapt a north–south range of outbuildings as a house, called Draycot House, for Mr. E. J. Bent *c.* 1956. West of that house a large square stone stable block of *c.* 1864[36] and farm buildings survived in 1987.

Draycot House was bought *c.* 1950 by Mr. Bent. The largest portion of land, *c.* 200 a. in Draycot park, was bought before 1955 by J. N. Green, from whom it passed before 1963 to J. R. Pinniger. Mr. Bent bought it from a Mr. Trent in 1973–4 and owned it in 1987.[37] In 1920 the remainder of Draycot Cerne manor was sold to B. Crundell, who immediately sold it in portions.[38] Roward farm, 63 a., was sold, possibly *c.* 1920, to Arthur Newman,[39] from whom it was bought in 1930 by R. L. Ward. Some of its lands were sold *c.* 1966 and incorporated in Lake farm. Mr. R. C. Ward owned the remainder in 1987.[40] Lake farm, 130 a., was bought by Clifford Windell, the owner in 1939.[41] W. T. Greenhill owned it in 1955, and in 1987 members of the Greenhill family owned the 300-a. farm.[42] Manor farm, 79 a., was bought, possibly *c.* 1920, by Sir Hugh Levick, who sold it between 1924 and 1927 to P. E. Hawkins.[43] In 1986–7 Hawkins's son Mr. P. E. Hawkins sold the farm, then of 128 a., to Mr. Richard Hawker.[44] Mount Pleasant farm, 93 a., was sold in portions.[45]

In 1242–3 Ela Longespée, countess of Salisbury, held ½ knight's fee at Knabwell.[46] The overlordship of *NABALS* passed with the earldom of Salisbury and was last expressly mentioned in 1349.[47] In 1382 and 1491 the estate was said, inexplicably, to be held of the abbot of Malmesbury.[48]

The estate called Nabals was held of the countess of Salisbury in 1242–3 by Amice, relict of William of Knabwell, and by his coheirs.[49] One heir may have been Eve, wife of Richard of Lea, who in 1250 conveyed 2 yardlands, which became Nabals farm, to Robert de la Mare[50] (d. 1272). The lands descended in the direct male line to Peter de la Mare (d. 1292), Robert de la Mare[51] (d. 1308), Peter de la Mare (d. 1349), who was granted free warren in them in 1318, and Sir Robert de la Mare[52] (d. 1382).[53] Sir Robert was succeeded by his relict Maud (d. 1405)[54] and daughter William, the wife of Sir John Roches. From William (d. 1410)[55] the estate passed to her daughter Elizabeth, the wife of Sir Walter Beauchamp,[56] to Sir Walter (d. 1430), and to his and Elizabeth's son Sir William (d. 1457), from 1449 Lord St. Amand.[57] In 1477 Lord St. Amand's

[21] *Complete Peerage*, iii. 480–2; ix. 240–1; Burke, *Peerage* (1959), 560–1; P.R.O., IR 29/38/103.

[22] W.R.O. 1043/6, pp. 9–16; Wilts. Cuttings, xiv. 111.

[23] Burke, *Peerage* (1959), 942–3; *Kelly's Dir. Wilts.* (1923).

[24] Ch. Com. file 21559/2; inf. from Mr. J. E. Bent, Draycot Park Farm.

[25] W.R.O., D 1/2/6, f. 148v.

[26] Aubrey, *Topog. Coll.* ed. Jackson, 232; Burke, *Ext. & Dorm. Baronetcies* (1838), 320.

[27] P.R.O., E 134/7 Wm. III Trin./20.

[28] Leland, *Itin.* ed. Toulmin Smith, i. 133.

[29] Aubrey, *Topog. Coll.* ed. Jackson, 232–3, pl. xxi; Burke, *Ext. & Dorm. Baronetcies* (1838), 321; *Complete Peerage*, viii. 489.

[30] W.R.O. 1043/6, pp. 5, 11.

[31] Ibid. 1001/1A.

[32] See plate facing p. 188.

[33] P.R.O., C 108/112/2.

[34] W.R.O. 1001/6.

[35] Jackson-Stops & Staff, *Vanishing Hos. of Eng.* 58.

[36] P.R.O., IR 29/38/103; IR 30/38/103; O.S. Map 6″, Wilts. XX (1889 edn.); W.R.O. 1001/6; inf. from Mr. Bent.

[37] Inf. from Mr. Bent; W.R.O., G 3/516/1 (2); G 3/516/2 (2).

[38] Wilts. Cuttings, xiv. 116.

[39] W.R.O. 1043/6, p. 17; *Kelly's Dir. Wilts.* (1920 and later edns.).

[40] W.R.O., G 3/516/1 (2); G 3/516/2 (2); inf. from Mr. R. C. Ward, Roward Farm.

[41] *Kelly's Dir. Wilts.* (1923 and later edns.); W.R.O. 1043/6, p. 19.

[42] W.R.O., G 3/516/1 (2); G 3/516/2 (2); inf. from Mrs. B. Greenhill, Lake Farm.

[43] *Kelly's Dir. Wilts.* (1923 and later edns.); W.R.O. 1043/6, p. 20; ibid. G 3/516/1 (2); G 3/516/2 (2).

[44] Inf. from Mrs. E. J. Bent, Draycot Ho.

[45] Inf. from Mr. R. Couzens, 9 the Close; W.R.O. 1043/6, p. 23.

[46] *Bk. of Fees*, ii. 722.

[47] *Wilts. Inq. p.m.* 1242–1326 (Index Libr.), 192; *Cal. Inq. p.m.* v, pp. 61–2; ix, p. 309.

[48] *Cal. Inq. p.m.* xv, pp. 215–16; *Cal. Inq. p.m. Hen. VII*, i, p. 313.

[49] *Bk. of Fees*, ii. 722.

[50] P.R.O., CP 25(1)/251/17, no. 5.

[51] *Wilts. Inq. p.m.* 1242–1326 (Index Libr.), 60, 192.

[52] *Cal. Inq. p.m.* v, pp. 61–2; ix, p. 309; *Cal. Chart. R. 1300–26*, 391.

[53] *Cal. Inq. p.m.* xv, pp. 215–16.

[54] Ibid. xviii, p. 352. The descent from Maud to Wm. and from Wm. to Eliz. Roches corrects that given in *V.C.H. Wilts.* x. 87.

[55] P.R.O., PROB 11/2A, f. 173.

[56] *Cal. Pat. 1408–13*, 265–6; *Cal. Close, 1409–13*, 138–9.

[57] *Complete Peerage*, xi. 301–2; P.R.O., C 139/49, no. 36, rot. 6; C 139/164, no. 18, rott. 9–10.

relict Elizabeth, wife of Sir Roger Tocotes, conveyed the estate to her son Sir Richard Beauchamp (from 1491 Lord St. Amand, d. 1508), whose estates passed to John Baynton (d. 1516), great-grandson of Elizabeth, wife of Sir Walter Beauchamp.[58]

Nabals farm afterwards passed, possibly like Charlton Tantum manor, to Sir Henry Long who died holding it in 1556,[59] and it afterwards descended in the Long family with Draycot Cerne manor. In 1920 Nabals farm, 100 a. in Draycot Cerne, Sutton Benger, and Stanton St. Quintin, was offered for sale as part of the Draycot estate.[60] It was owned in 1955 by L. Haines,[61] who in 1979 sold the farm, 50 a., to Mr. G. T. Ridout, the owner in 1987.[62]

ECONOMIC HISTORY. Draycot was a 5-hide estate which in 1086 included demesne, with 4 *servi* and 2 ploughteams, and had on it 7 *villani* and 10 coscets with a total of 3 teams. There were 40 a. of meadow, and the pasture was 2 furlongs long and 1 furlong broad.[63]

From 1257, in return for pasture rights granted to Sutton Benger tenants in the detached portion of Draycot Cerne, each Sutton team at three days' notice ploughed ½ a. in Draycot's open fields.[64] The demesne of Draycot manor in 1296 included 160 a. of arable, 30 a. of highly valued meadow, and pasture worth 10s. yearly. In 1344 it included 240 a. of arable, of which 66 a. were inclosed and worth 4d. an acre yearly; of the 174 a. in the open fields, 100 a. were worth 2d. an acre and 74 a. were worth 1d. an acre. There were in addition 51 a. of demesne meadow and 40 a. of inclosed demesne pasture.[65] Besides the demesne and the glebe, in 1250 there were within the manor three small estates and a fourth holding of pasture.[66] Nabals farm in 1308 included c. 60 a. of arable, 1 a. of meadow, and pasture,[67] and in 1382 was apparently all pasture.[68] Customary tenants of the manor paid rents totalling 6s. 8d. in 1296.[69] Before 1393 Sir Edward of Cerne, without licence, freed four Draycot neifs and their families.[70]

Common husbandry prevailed in the parish in 1511,[71] and in the early 17th century Home and South were open fields,[72] possibly south of the Swindon–Chippenham road. The main period of inclosure may have been the mid 17th century: the glebe, with only 8 a. of c. 50 a. inclosed in 1632, was entirely several in 1678.[73]

Roward farm was created c. 1625, probably at an inclosure, as a 19-a. farm. In 1637 it had a new farmhouse and was of 22 a., mostly inclosed

from South field.[74] Lake farm may also have been created at an early 17th-century inclosure. In 1647 it comprised inclosed arable, formerly in Home field, and meadow land and was held by lease for £41 a year.[75] In 1651 and presumably earlier the demesne was held in portions by leases.[76] It was in two farms in 1731: Draycot or Home farm was 212 a., of which 143 a. were arable, 37 a. were pasture, and 32 a. were meadows; the second farm, 248 a., included c. 200 a. which were formerly, and were again later, parkland. Lake farm was 115 a. in 1731, another farm, possibly Manor, was 65 a., five farms, including Roward, were of 20–50 a., and there were 10 smallholdings.[77]

In 1808 Draycot or Home farm, 212 a., had 107 a. of arable, 94 a. of pasture, and 8 a. of meadows; in 1839 it had 216 a. of which 84 a. were arable and the rest pasture; and in 1851 it was an arable and pasture farm of 180 a. It was worked in 1808 and 1851 from Draycot Farm north-west of Draycot House. By 1808 the acreage of Roward farm had doubled to c. 41 a. Its acreage in 1839 was 78 a., and c. 93 a. added from Draycot farm before 1872 again more than doubled Roward farm, which in 1872 also had 13 a. in Kington Langley. Lake farm increased from 131 a. of meadow and pasture in 1808 to 162 a., mostly pasture, in 1839. Between 1851 and 1872 c. 29 a. in Sutton Benger were added to the farm. Manor was a pasture farm of 58 a. in 1808 and of 68 a. in 1839 and 1851. A further 12 a. were added to it before 1872. Nabals farm had 84 a. in 1794 and 1808, 81 a. in 1839 when it was pasture, and 81 a. in 1851 and 1872.[78]

In the 19th century some land in the parish, 71 a. in 1808, c. 90 a. in 1839, and c. 34 a. in 1851, were in farms based in Sutton Benger. The parish in 1839 contained c. 760 a. of pasture, of which c. 200 a. were in Draycot park, and c. 140 a. of arable were worked in a four-field rotation.[79] There were 215 a. of arable in 1876, but thereafter arable farming declined and in 1936 no land was ploughed. In 1867 corn, mostly wheat, was grown on half the arable and leguminous and fodder crops on the remainder. After c. 1876 corn crops were usually grown on two thirds. Most of the parish has been meadow and permanent pasture in the 19th and 20th centuries. The acreage on which grasses were grown in rotation, 104 a. in 1876, was 12 a. in 1936. In the same period the proportion of the grassland which was mown increased from a quarter to a third. There were on average c. 200 cows, c. 120 sheep, and c. 60 pigs in the years 1867–1936.[80]

There were six farms based in the parish c. 1920.

[58] *Cal. Inq. p.m. Hen. VII*, i, pp. 304, 306, 313; *Complete Peerage*, xi. 303; *V.C.H. Wilts.* vii. 181.
[59] P.R.O., C 142/110, no. 167; above, Charlton, manors.
[60] W.R.O. 1043/6, p. 110.
[61] Ibid. G 3/516/1 (2); G 3/516/2 (2).
[62] Inf. from Mrs. G. T. Ridout, Nables Farm.
[63] *V.C.H. Wilts.* ii, p. 167.
[64] B.L. Add. MS. 15667, f. 76 and v.
[65] *Wilts. Inq. p.m.* 1242–1326 (Index Libr.), 210; 1327–77 (Index Libr.), 158.
[66] *Bk. of Fees*, ii. 1224–5.
[67] *Cal. Inq. p.m.* v, pp. 61–2.
[68] Ibid. xv, pp. 215–16.
[69] *Wilts. Inq. p.m.* 1242–1326 (Index Libr.), 210.
[70] *Cal. Close*, 1392–6, 208.
[71] P.R.O., SC 2/208/28.

[72] Ibid. C 112/53/1, rental, 1647; W.R.O., D 1/24/80/1.
[73] Aubrey, *Nat. Hist. Wilts.* ed. Britton, 104; W.R.O., D 1/24/80/2; D 1/24/80/4.
[74] P.R.O., C 112/53/2, deeds, 1625, 1637.
[75] Ibid. C 112/53/1, rental, 1647.
[76] Ibid. C 112/53/1, rental, 1651.
[77] W.R.O. 970/1. For the parkland, below.
[78] W.R.O. 969/2; 1001/2; 1001/5; 2062/13, pp. 16–23, 130–1; 2062/14, ff. 1, 6, 14–17; 2062/15, ff. 6–10, 12–13; P.R.O., IR 29/38/103; IR 30/38/103.
[79] W.R.O. 1001/5; 2062/13, pp. 96–7; 2062/14, ff. 14, 21; P.R.O., IR 29/38/103; IR 30/38/103.
[80] P.R.O., MAF 68/151, sheet 2; MAF 68/493, sheet 5; MAF 68/1063, sheet 4; MAF 68/1633, sheet 5; MAF 68/2203, sheet 13; MAF 68/2773, sheet 3; MAF 68/3319, sheet 3; MAF 68/3814, no. 29.

Draycot Park farm was nominally of 607 a. but included woodland and parkland, and the parkland was leased in portions to other farmers in the parish. Lake, 130 a., Manor, 79 a., Roward, 63 a., and Nabals, 100 a. including land outside the parish, were dairy farms. Only on Mount Pleasant farm, 93 a. including former glebe, was farming mixed.[81] In 1987 only Manor farm was a dairy farm. The lands of Roward farm were leased for the grazing of beef cattle, on Lake farm beef cattle were reared and corn was grown, Draycot Park was an arable farm, and Nabals was a mixed farm.[82]

Most men in Draycot Cerne were farm labourers in 1831.[83] No trade or craft seems to have flourished in the parish.[84]

Land in the parish had been imparked by c. 1542.[85] In 1639–40 Draycot park included a lower park and an upper park.[86] It had been impaled by c. 1680 and remained so in 1769.[87] In 1731 the c. 200 a. of parkland were used for agriculture,[88] but were again parkland in 1827 and were grazed by deer in the 19th and early 20th century.[89] Before 1920 the parkland was leased in portions for grazing.[90]

In 1086 there was woodland 4 furlongs long and 2 furlongs broad.[91] Nabals farm included 4 a. of woodland in 1808 and 8 a. in 1920. In 1808 there were only 6 a. of woodland in Draycot park.[92] Trees, mainly oaks, were planted north of Draycot House in the 19th century and the park contained plantations of c. 55 a. in 1839, of c. 70 a. in 1880, and of 126 a. in 1920.[93] Much woodland was cut after 1946, and little remained in 1987.[94]

There was a mill at Draycot in 1086.[95] In 1296 a water mill could be used only in winter.[96] Three water mills formed part of Draycot Cerne manor in 1344,[97] and a mill remained part of the manor until the later 19th century. From the 17th century or earlier there was apparently a single mill,[98] that on the west side of the Stanton St. Quintin road driven by a tributary of the Avon. It ceased to work apparently between 1868 and 1872 and was demolished before 1885.[99]

LOCAL GOVERNMENT. Courts for Draycot Cerne manor were held from 1296[1] or earlier to 1848.[2] The only extant records are for 1511, 1647–50, 1652, and 1758–1848. At a court held in 1511 common husbandry was regulated, and

the ringing of pigs and the repair of cottages were ordered.[3] From 1647 or earlier, although no lord is known to have received a grant of leet jurisdiction, the court was called view of frankpledge with court baron. Between 1647 and 1652 it may have been held only once a year, in spring, to transact a mixture of leet and manorial business: deaths of customary tenants were recorded, customary holdings were surrendered and new tenants were admitted, the repair of roads, ditches, watercourses, and cottages was enjoined, and tithingmen were elected.[4] Courts with the same title were held twice a year in the period 1758–71, and in the period 1772–1848 once a year in autumn. Early 19th-century courts were marked by the giving of a dinner, probably at Sutton Benger, by the lord of Draycot to the tenants. The only business was the election of tithingmen, and, from 1820, of haywards, and provision for the repair of roads and bridges.[5]

Vestry meetings, at which overseers of the poor and churchwardens were elected and poor rates were set, were held from the earlier 19th century.[6] Sums spent on poor relief rose from £89 in 1775–6 to £125 in 1802–3 when 50, a third of the population, received outdoor relief. In each of the years 1813–15 c. £170 was spent on relieving an average of 16 paupers continuously and 6 occasionally. Although Draycot Cerne then spent less than most parishes in Malmesbury hundred, its paupers were relieved comparatively generously.[7] Average sums of £165 in the years 1816–21, £84 in 1822–4, £93 in 1825–9, £102 in 1830–4, and £114 in 1834–6, were spent.[8] The parish maintained a poorhouse in the early 1830s[9] and in 1830 employed a surgeon to attend paupers. In 1831 parishioners agreed to give, for each £20 at which their lands were rated, a day's work to an unemployed labourer.[10] Draycot Cerne became part of Chippenham poor-law union in 1835,[11] and, as part of Sutton Benger, part of North Wiltshire district in 1974.[12] A burial board was formed in 1883 to administer the parish burial ground and chapel opened in that year.[13]

CHURCH. A church stood at Draycot Cerne in the later 12th century.[14] The rectory was united with the vicarage of Seagry in 1939 and severed from it in 1954.[15]

[81] W.R.O. 1043/6, pp. 9–17, 19–20, 23, 110; below, church.
[82] Local inf.
[83] *Census*, 1831.
[84] *Kelly's Dir. Wilts.* (1848 and later edns.); Bristol R.O., EP/V/4/68.
[85] Leland, *Itin.* ed. Toulmin Smith, i. 133.
[86] P.R.O., C 112/53/1, agreement and settlement, 1639–40.
[87] Aubrey, *Topog. Coll.* ed. Jackson, 235; W.R.O. 1001/1A.
[88] Above.
[89] P.R.O., C 108/112/1, acct. bk. 1827–34; ibid. IR 29/38/103, and altered apportionment, 1880; IR 30/38/103; photo. of c. 1908 in Co. Libr. Headquarters, Trowbridge.
[90] W.R.O. 1043/6, pp. 9–16.
[91] *V.C.H. Wilts.* ii, p. 167.
[92] W.R.O. 1001/5; 1043/6, pp. 9–16; 2062/13, pp. 14–15, 130–1.
[93] Ibid. 1043/6, pp. 9–16; P.R.O., C 108/112/1, acct. bk. 1827–34; ibid. IR 29/38/103, and altered apportionment, 1880; IR 30/38/103.
[94] Inf. from Mr. J. E. Bent, Draycot Park Farm.
[95] *V.C.H. Wilts.* ii, p. 167.
[96] *Wilts. Inq. p.m.* 1242–1326 (Index Libr.), 210.
[97] *Wilts. Inq. p.m.* 1327–77 (Index Libr.), 158.
[98] P.R.O., C 112/53/2, deed, 1638; W.R.O. 970/1; 1001/5; 2062/14, f. 7.
[99] P.R.O., IR 29/38/103, and altered apportionment, 1880; IR 30/38/103; O.S. Map 6", Wilts. XX (1889 edn.); W.R.O. 969/2.
[1] *Wilts. Inq. p.m.* 1242–1326 (Index Libr.), 210.
[2] W.R.O. 2062/29, pp. 117–18.
[3] P.R.O., SC 2/208/28.
[4] Ibid. C 112/53/1, ct. rolls.
[5] Ibid. C 108/112/1, acct. bk. 1827–34; W.R.O. 2062/29.
[6] W.R.O. 1093/12; 1093/19–20.
[7] *Poor Law Abstract*, 1804, 566–7; *1818*, 498–9.
[8] *Poor Rate Returns*, 1816–21, 188; *1822–4*, 228; *1825–9*, 219; *1830–4*, 212.
[9] P.R.O., C 108/112/1, acct. bk. 1827–34.
[10] W.R.O. 1093/20.
[11] *Poor Law Com. 2nd Rep.* App. D, 558.
[12] O.S. Map 1/100,000, admin. areas, Wilts. (1974 edn.).
[13] W.R.O. 1093/21; above, introduction.
[14] *Reg. St. Osmund* (Rolls Ser.), i. 260–1.
[15] Ch. Com. files 21559/2; NB 5/72.

The church was the subject c. 1170 of rival gifts made by Ralph de St. Germain and Robert de Venoix, possibly him who held the manor in 1130, to Salisbury chapter. Robert claimed to give a pension of 10s. from the church, and Ralph claimed to give the church itself.[16] Although c. 1180 Salisbury chapter presented Reynold, the nephew of Ralph, as rector,[17] the right of the Venoix family to present rectors prevailed and in 1228 John de Venoix granted the advowson to Henry of Cerne.[18] The advowson descended like Draycot Cerne manor, and the lords presented.[19] The king presented in 1345 because John of Cerne (d. 1346) was a minor,[20] and Edward of Cerne (d. 1419) presented in 1410 and 1412–13.[21] The king's presentee in 1452 was evidently not instituted because in the same year John Long presented a rector who was.[22] By grant of a turn the Revd. Jeremiah Awdry presented in 1850.[23] The advowson passed with the manor to Christian, Earl Cowley, who transferred it to B. Crundell in 1921. Crundell immediately sold it to the A.M.A. Syndicate Ltd., from whom it was bought in 1923 by Herbert Dixon, later Baron Glentoran. In 1939 Lord Glentoran became entitled to present for the united benefice of Seagry with Draycot Cerne at the second and third of each three turns. In 1947 he transferred the advowson to S. W. Maundrell (d. 1963), whose executors in 1966 transferred it to the bishop of Bristol, the patron in 1987.[24]

The rectory was worth £7 in 1535,[25] £50 in 1650.[26] In the years 1829–31 its average income of £234 made it one of the poorer livings in Malmesbury deanery.[27]

By 1678 tithes from demesne land had been compounded for £20 a year.[28] It was presumably for such tithes that the rector received a composition of £146 in 1832.[29] In 1839 the tithes were valued at £280 and commuted.[30]

Before 1225 the rector held 1 yardland, possibly given by a member of the Venoix family.[31] It was confirmed to the rector in 1256.[32] In the 1550s the glebe included a rectory house which was ruinous.[33] The glebe measured c. 50 a. in the 17th century[34] and earlier 19th,[35] 55 a. in the later 19th.[36] The rectory house, which in 1839 stood on the west side of the lane south of Draycot House, was demolished when in 1879 the rector gave it with 14 a. north of the Swindon–Chippen-

ham road in exchange for 19 a., on which a new stone rectory house of three storeys and a basement was built, south of the road.[37] Part of the glebe, 34 a. called Mount Pleasant farm, was sold to William, Earl Cowley, in 1894 when it was added to the Draycot estate.[38] The 19 a. were sold later.[39] After 1950 the incumbent lived in Kington Langley Vicarage[40] and Draycot Cerne Rectory was sold in 1952.[41]

In 1304 the rector, Henry of Cerne, was licensed to study for two years.[42] Curates are known to have assisted the rector or to have served the cure in the years 1550–3, 1601–9, 1650, 1675–6, 1725, 1757, and 1848–50. Two or more became rectors.[43] John Rand, rector from 1631, was sequestered in 1650.[44] The minister intruded in his place received £12 a year in 1650, Rand's wife £13, and the assistant curate £25.[45] Rand was restored in 1662, and in that year he complained that a churchwarden prevented him from wearing a surplice and neglected to supply bread and wine for communion. The parish then lacked the Book of Homilies and Jewell's Apology. Because there was no flagon, Rand used a jug or 'vinegar glass' for the consecration of communion wine.[46] Daniel Fettiplace, rector 1712–35, was also rector of Yatesbury.[47] Francis West, rector 1779–1800, in 1783 held two services each Sunday and some weekday services. He administered communion at Christmas, Easter, and Whitsun to an average of 20 communicants. West was also rector of Dauntsey, curate of Kellaways, and occasionally did duty at Seagry.[48] Although the living was a meagre one, the presence of the Long family at Draycot House attracted in the 18th century and early 19th incumbents such as Edward Ernle, later styled Sir Edward Ernle, Bt., rector 1746–60,[49] and Andrews Windsor, rector 1800–12, a brother of Catherine, Lady Tylney-Long (d. 1823), and son of Other Windsor, earl of Plymouth.[50] Henry Barry, rector 1812–50, was also rector of Upton Scudamore.[51] He lived in Draycot Cerne and in 1832 held two services each Sunday and services on holy days. In 1850–1 an average congregation of 15 attended the Sunday services. From 1954 and in 1987 the rectory was held in plurality with the vicarage of Kington Langley.[52]

The church of ST. JAMES, so called in the later 19th and the 20th century,[53] was called All Saints'

[16] Reg. St. Osmund (Rolls Ser.), i. 260–1.
[17] Sar. Chart. and Doc. (Rolls Ser.), 42.
[18] Cal. Chart. R. 1226–57, 67.
[19] Phillipps, Wilts. Inst. (index in W.A.M. xxviii. 219); Reg. Ghent (Cant. & York Soc.), ii. 633; Clerical Guide (1822, 1829); Clergy List (1859 and later edns.); Crockford (1896 and later edns.).
[20] Cal. Pat. 1343–5, 529.
[21] Reg. Hallum (Cant. & York Soc.), pp. 27, 46, 57–8.
[22] Phillipps, Wilts. Inst. i. 143–4, 149.
[23] Bristol R.O., EP/A/3/142/3.
[24] Ibid. dioc. rec., registrar's bdle. 99, Draycot Cerne; Ch. Com. file 21559/1–2.
[25] Valor Eccl. (Rec. Com.), ii. 137.
[26] W.A.M. xli. 6.   [27] Rep. Com. Eccl. Revenues, 832–3.
[28] W.R.O., D 1/24/80/4.   [29] Ch. Com. file, NB 5/72.
[30] P.R.O., IR 29/38/103.   [31] Pat. R. 1216–25, 594.
[32] P.R.O., CP 25(1)/251/18, no. 30.
[33] W.R.O., D 1/43/1, f. 22; D 1/24/80/4.
[34] Ibid. D 1/24/80/1–2; D 1/24/80/4.
[35] Ibid. 2062/13, pp. 44–5; P.R.O., IR 29/38/103; IR 30/38/103.
[36] W.R.O. 969/3, deed, 1881.

[37] Ibid. 969/37; P.R.O., IR 18/10990; IR 29/38/103 and altered apportionment; IR 30/38/103.
[38] W.R.O. 969/3, deeds, 1881, 1894.
[39] Kelly's Dir. Wilts. (1939); inf. from Assistant Sec., Dioc. Bd. of Finance, Church Ho., 23 Gt. Geo. Street, Bristol.
[40] Crockford (1947 and later edns.).
[41] Bristol R.O., dioc. rec., registrar's bdle. 98, Draycot Cerne.
[42] Reg. Ghent (Cant. & York Soc.), ii. 868.
[43] W.R.O., D 1/43/1, ff. 22, 130; ibid. bishop's transcripts, bdle. 1; ibid. 1093/1; Bristol R.O., EP/V/4/68.
[44] Walker Revised, ed. Matthews, 379.
[45] W.A.M. xli. 6.   [46] W.R.O., D 1/54/1/6.
[47] Alum. Oxon. 1500–1714, ii. 494.
[48] Ibid. iv. 1526; Vis. Queries, 1783 (W.R.S. xxvii), 92–3.
[49] Phillipps, Wilts. Inst. ii. 72, 79; G.E.C. Baronetage, iii. 157.
[50] Phillipps, Wilts. Inst. ii. 101; Alum. Oxon. 1715–1886, iv. 1587; Clerical Guide (1822); Burke, Peerage (1959), 1796.
[51] V.C.H. Wilts. viii. 87.
[52] P.R.O., HO 129/253/4/5/6; Ch. Com. file, NB 5/72.
[53] Kelly's Dir. Wilts. (1867); O.S. Map 6″, Wilts. XX (1889 edn.); Crockford (1935).

in the later 12th century,[54] St. Peter's in 1763 and 1915.[55] It comprises a chancel, a nave with north chapel and south porch, and a west tower.[56] On the west wall of the chancel the weathering for the chancel roof of the 12th-century church survives, and it suggests that parts of the nave walls are also 12th-century. A small chancel arch which was enlarged in 1848 was possibly of the 12th century or earlier.[57] The chancel was rebuilt and enlarged in the early 13th century, and, apart from the construction in the 14th century of a canopied tomb recess in the north wall over a 13th-century effigy of a knight, was not altered thereafter. In the early 14th century a south doorway and two north windows, and in the 15th century a south window, were inserted in the nave. In the later 15th century the porch, which has two pairs of three-light openings on the east and west, and the tower were built. The upper stage of the tower was later rebuilt, perhaps in the 17th century. In 1692 a mortuary chapel for members of the Long family was built against the north doorway of the nave.[58] A west gallery which hid the tower arch c. 1850 had been removed by c. 1863 when a new west window was constructed. The north chapel was rebuilt in 1865. At about the same time the nave and chancel roofs were reconstructed, a new window was inserted in the nave, and the nave was repewed.[59] Monuments which commemorate members of the Cerne and Long families include, in the chancel, a memorial brass to Sir Edward of Cerne (d. 1393) and his wife Ellen (d. 1418), and the painted altar tomb of Sir Thomas Long (d. 1508).[60] Traces of wall paintings survived in the chancel in 1585.[61]

In 1891 the parish had a chalice, paten cover, paten, and flagon of 1702 given by Dame Dorothy Long (d. 1710).[62] The chalice and paten survived in 1987.[63] The tower in 1987 contained a bell cast in 1808 by James Wells of Aldbourne.[64] Registrations of baptisms and burials begin in 1691, of marriages in 1692.[65]

NONCONFORMITY. There were Quakers living in Draycot Cerne in the later 17th century and the 18th.[66] They were described as numerous in 1669 but in 1676 there were only seven.[67]

EDUCATION. In 1704 Dame Dorothy Long (d. 1710) and Dame Anna Mason gave a yearly income of £5 for a schoolmaster to teach poor children in Draycot Cerne. A school was built, possibly c. 1786 by Sir James Tylney-Long, Bt. (d. 1794).[68] It was well run in 1808.[69] A master taught 10 boys there in 1818. Sir James's relict Catherine then supported a girls' school, which may have been held in the same building.[70] The schools merged and in 1833, besides 10 supported by the charity income, other children were taught.[71] The two teachers who taught 18 children in 1846–7[72] were perhaps the parish clerk and his wife who in 1858 taught c. 20 children.[73] There were c. 30 pupils in 1868–9 when it was claimed that few boys in the parish were unable to read and write.[74] The school was closed c. 1903[75] and thereafter Draycot children went to school in Sutton Benger and Kington Langley.[76]

CHARITIES FOR THE POOR. Dame Dorothy Long (d. 1710) and Dame Anna Mason in 1704 gave a yearly income of £2 for the poor.[77] In 1782 Martha Angel, Sir James Tylney-Long, Bt., and Charles Long each gave £10 for the poor. In the 1960s the income of the combined charities, c. £2 yearly, was allowed to accumulate and bread was bought for the poor. The income was added to that of Rachel Long's charity in the 1980s.

Dorothy Long and Anna Mason in 1704 gave £5 a year to apprentice poor children from the charity school. In the early 19th century a pupil was apprenticed every three years, and in the early 20th boys were apprenticed to the head carpenter of the Draycot estate. In the later 20th century the income was allowed to accumulate and in 1986 money was given for a student to buy books.

By will proved 1781 Rachel Long gave £3 a year for the poor. That, and £1 yearly of unknown origin, was spent on coal for 29 people in 1832. In 1905 coal bought with the £4 was given to each poor householder in Draycot Cerne at Christmas. The income was allowed to accumulate in the 1960s and 1980s, and coal was occasionally distributed.

54 Reg. St. Osmund (Rolls Ser.), i. 260; Sar. Chart. and Doc. (Rolls Ser.), 42.
55 J. Ecton, Thesaurus, 403; Clergy List (1915).
56 Description based partly on J. Buckler, watercolour in W.A.S. Libr., vol. vi. 7.
57 Soc. Antiq. MS. 817, v, p. 200.
58 W.R.O. 1093/1.
59 Soc. Antiq. MS. 817, v, p. 200.
60 Above, manor.
61 W.R.O., D 1/43/6, f. 32v.
62 Nightingale, Wilts. Plate, 217.
63 Inf. from Mr. T. Couzens, 9 the Close.
64 Walters, Wilts. Bells, 79, which gives the date 1803; inf. from Mr. Couzens.
65 W.R.O. 1093/1–7; 2041/1–5; bishop's transcripts for

1601–9, 1619–23, 1666, 1668–9, and 1675–9 are ibid.
66 Ibid. 1093/1; W.N. & Q. v. 224, 454; vi. 82–3.
67 G. L. Turner, Orig. Rec. iii. 812.
68 Char. Donations, H.C. 511, pp. 1354–5 (1816), xvi (2).
69 Lamb. Palace Libr., MS. 1732.
70 Educ. of Poor Digest, 1025; G.E.C. Baronetage, iii. 259.
71 Educ. Enq. Abstract, 1036.
72 Nat. Soc. Inquiry, 1846–7, Wilts. 6–7.
73 Acct. of Wilts. Schs. 22.
74 2nd Rep. Employment of Children and Women in Agric. 1867 [4202], p. 248, H.C. (1868–9), xiii.
75 W.R.O. 1093/12.
76 Endowed Char. Wilts. (N. Div.), 476.
77 Section based on ibid. 473–8; Char. Donations, 1354–5; Char. Com. files; inf., for 1980s, from Mr. T. Couzens.

FOXLEY

FOXLEY[78] is 4 km. WSW. of Malmesbury.[79] The parish measured c. 735 a. in 1871.[80] It included a detached field of 6 a. to the east, and, from 1832, affixed to its south-east corner a total of 16 a. of Malmesbury common then allotted to the lord of Foxley manor and to the rector of Foxley.[81] In 1884 a small detached part of Norton parish, which separated Foxley from its own detached land, and the whole of Bremilham parish, apart from its detached pieces, were added to Foxley parish, thereafter 1,135 a.[82] (459 ha.). In 1934 the whole of that parish was transferred to Norton parish.[83]

Foxley was a parish of regular shape and was mostly bounded by prominent features. The northern boundary was marked by the Sherston branch of the Bristol Avon and the south part of the eastern boundary by a tributary of the river. The south-eastern boundary was marked partly by the same tributary and partly by an ancient road, the south-western partly by another tributary and another ancient road, and the whole of the north-western by the Roman Foss Way. Most of those boundaries had apparently been fixed by c. 1100.[84]

The land of the former Foxley parish slopes gently from c. 100 m. at the south-west corner to below 76 m. on the Avon in the north-east. Apart from the Avon and its eastern tributary three streams flow across it from west to east before joining to form a tributary of the Avon. Cornbrash outcrops over most of the former parish. The streams have exposed narrow bands of clay and deposited others of alluvium. Between the streams, the Cornbrash is covered by patches of Kellaways Clay in the north and south, and by small areas of gravel in the north and of head deposits in the south.[85] The predominantly flat, well drained land favours agriculture: there was much meadow land beside the streams[86] and the soils of the Cornbrash are suitable for growing cereals.[87] The Kellaways Clay in the north has long been wooded, and a walled park was made in the north-west:[88] parts of the wall survived in 1986. The polo ground of the Beaufort Hunt Polo Club was in the south-west corner of the parish in the earlier 20th century.[89]

Where it was the boundary of Foxley parish the Foss Way was for most of its length a green lane in 1986. The south-western end was from 1760 or earlier part of a route from Norton to Easton Grey[90] and was later made up. The Norton to Easton Grey road, part of the south-western boundary of Foxley parish, was called Narrow or Small Way in the 10th or 11th century, later Tetbury Way. The lane crossing the south of Foxley parish, and forming part of its south-east boundary, seems likely to have been the ancient Borough Way,[91] and from 1773 or earlier was called Honey Lane.[92] Two other roads cross the parish, each on the course which it followed in 1760.[93] An east–west road linking Foxley and Bremilham with Malmesbury and Sherston was part of the main Oxford–Bristol road in the later 17th century,[94] but had been superseded by 1756 when the Malmesbury–Sherston road further north was turnpiked.[95] The Malmesbury–Sherston road through Foxley is linked with Honey Lane by a short north–south road, probably the road called King's Way in the 10th or 11th century. That and the Malmesbury–Sherston road have wide verges, and where they meet near Foxley church the verges widen further to form a triangular village green.

Where the Foss Way crosses the Avon, Foxley parish may have included a small part of the Roman settlement called White Walls.[96] Foxley, first mentioned in 1086,[97] has never been more than a small village. Early 14th-century taxation assessments were low,[98] the figure of 12 poll-tax payers in 1377 was the 19th lowest in the county, the parish had fewer than 10 households in 1428,[99] and 16th-century taxation assessments were also low.[1] In 1801 the population was 50. With fluctuations it had risen to 73 by 1881. The enlargement of 1884 added 31 to the population, which was 96 in 1891 and 108 in 1901. By 1931 it had fallen to 61.[2] In 1986 the population of the former Foxley parish may have been c. 35.

Foxley's church and rectory house, and almost certainly its early farmsteads, were built near the stream which forms part of the east boundary. In 1675 there were buildings west of the church on both sides of the Malmesbury–Sherston road as far as a sharp bend in the road[3] where the farmhouse which became the manor house stands. That

[78] A map of the par. is below, s.v. Norton.
[79] This article was written in 1986. Maps used include, O.S. Maps 6″, Wilts. VIII, XII–XIII (1888–9 edns.); 1/25,000, ST 88 (1958 edn.); 1/50,000, sheet 173 (1974 edn.).
[80] *Census*, 1871.
[81] P.R.O., IR 29/38/123; IR 30/38/123; W.R.O., EA/142.
[82] *V.C.H. Wilts.* iv. 348; O.S. Maps 6″, Wilts. VIII, XIII (1888–9 edns.); W.R.O., Bremilham and Norton tithe awards.
[83] *V.C.H. Wilts.* iv. 355 n.
[84] *Arch. Jnl.* lxxvi. 221–3; lxxvii. 46; P.R.O., IR 30/38/123.
[85] Geol. Surv. Map 1″, solid and drift, sheet 251 (1970 edn.).
[86] P.R.O., IR 29/38/123; IR 30/38/123.
[87] R. S. Barron, *Geol. Wilts.* 40.
[88] B.L. Maps, M.T. 6e., 1 (2); below, econ. hist.
[89] *Shell Guide Wilts.* (1935), 39–40; *Kelly's Dir. Wilts.* (1939); W.R.O., G 7/505/1; inf. from Countess Badeni, Norton Manor, Norton.
[90] B.L. Maps, M.T. 6e., 1 (2).
[91] The names Small Way and King Way on O.S. Map 6″,

Wilts. XIII. NW. (1925 edn.) follow attributions by G. B. Grundy in *Arch. Jnl.* lxxv. 72–4. The attribution, by T. R. Thomson and B. J. Wallis on maps in W.A.S. Libr., of the name Borough Way to Honey Lane and of the name King's Way to a third road (below) seem more likely to be correct. The names are from *Arch. Jnl.* lxxvi. 221–3. For Tetbury Way, below, Norton, introduction.
[92] *Andrews and Dury, Map* (W.R.S. viii), pl. 13.
[93] B.L. Maps, M.T. 6e., 1 (2).
[94] J. Ogilby, *Brit.* (1675), pl. 79.
[95] *V.C.H. Wilts.* iv. 257, 260; *L.J.* xxviii. 581.
[96] *V.C.H. Wilts.* i (1), 68; *W.A.M.* xxxviii. 249.
[97] *P.N. Wilts.* (E.P.N.S.), 70.
[98] *V.C.H. Wilts.* iv. 301; P.R.O., E 179/196/8.
[99] *V.C.H. Wilts.* iv. 309, 312, 314.
[1] *Taxation Lists* (W.R.S. x), 29, 53; P.R.O., E 179/197/155.
[2] *V.C.H. Wilts.* iv. 348.
[3] Ogilby, *Brit.* pl. 79.

house was enlarged, possibly in the 1680s,[4] and farm buildings were erected north of it. By 1760 a new stretch of road had been made to cut the corner and take traffic away from the manor house. The rectory house, glebe farm buildings, a small farmstead, and a small house then stood near the church, west of it were Foxley Manor and farm and other buildings, three cottages stood beside the road between the church and Foxley Manor, and two cottages stood beside Honey Lane.[5] There were 13 houses in the parish in 1811,[6] and the pattern of settlement had changed little by 1986. Near the church, part of a large barn behind the rectory house had been converted for residence, and there were 20th-century farm buildings on the site of the small farmstead. East of them, south of the Malmesbury–Sherston road, the small house standing in 1760 was extended in red brick in the 19th century. Nearby a pair of cottages was built between 1883 and 1899[7] and a pair of council houses in 1944.[8] The stone farm buildings near Foxley Manor were not used after 1978: a barn was made into a house after 1982, and another was being converted in 1987.[9] Other buildings near Foxley Manor in 1986 included a small, apparently early 19th-century house and a building possibly surviving from an oxyard which stood south-west of the house in the 18th century.[10] Of the buildings beside the road between the rectory house and Foxley Manor in 1760 only an apparently 18th-century cottage at the west end survives. The others were replaced in the 19th century by a school[11] and a pair of cottages. A cottage built on the verge of Honey Lane in the earlier 19th century replaced one standing in 1760; the other cottage beside Honey Lane in 1760 was demolished between 1899 and 1921.[12]

MANOR AND OTHER ESTATES. Aldret held Foxley in 1066. Roger of Berkeley held it in 1084 and in 1086, when the estate included a house in Malmesbury,[13] later with an obligation to repair part of the town wall.[14] By 1089 Roger had given his daughter and rights over the estate to the abbey of Shaftesbury (Dors.). What rights he gave may later have been disputed: a title to the Foxley estate was confirmed to the abbey in 1089 by William II,[15] in 1121–2 by Henry I, before whom the abbess proved it against Alfred of Foxley,[16] in 1136 by King Stephen,[17] and in 1371,[18] but Roger or

his descendants may have retained or recovered the lordship in demesne. The abbey was no more than overlord in 1242–3[19] and 1275:[20] its overlordship was referred to in the 16th[21] and 17th centuries.[22] The lordship of *FOXLEY* manor may have descended with Eldersfield manor (Worcs.) from Roger's nephew William of Berkeley (fl before 1147) to William's son William (fl. 1195) and to the younger William's son Robert (fl 1210–12),[23] and in 1242–3 belonged to Simon of Eldersfield.[24] Simon was possibly the husband of Parnel de la Mare,[25] and thereafter Foxley manor descended in the de la Mare family, members of which held Hardwick manor in Eldersfield and Rendcomb manor (Glos.).[26]

Robert de la Mare, then bailiff of Startley hundred, may have held Foxley manor in 1255. William de la Mare held it in 1275:[27] he was presumably the Sir William de la Mare (fl. 1294) who held both Foxley and Hardwick[28] and the William de la Mare (d. by 1296), Parnel de la Mare's son, who held Rendcomb manor.[29] Foxley manor belonged to John de la Mare in 1334[30] and he, a namesake, or namesakes possibly held it in 1332[31] and 1361.[32] Robert de la Mare and John de la Mare of Hardwick may have owned it in 1365 and 1417 when, respectively, they each presented a rector.[33] John de la Mare, possibly the same, held the manor in 1428 when it was assessed as $\frac{1}{2}$ knight's fee and said to have been formerly Richard of Stamford's.[34] In the 1430s the manor was held by feoffees, among whom was John de la Mare (d. by 1462) of Rendcomb,[35] and in 1457, when he presented a rector, possibly by William de la Mare of Hardwick.[36]

By 1485 Foxley manor had been acquired by John Moody of Eldersfield.[37] It was held in 1495 by his son Edmund, on whose death in 1509 it passed to his relict Elizabeth.[38] In 1535 Edmund's son John held the manor[39] which passed on his death in 1549 to his son John, then a minor.[40] In 1583 John Moody, with Anthony Webb or Richmond and Anthony's son Roger, possibly his son-in-law and grandson, sold Foxley manor to Anthony Hinton[41] who held it until his death in 1599.[42] In 1600 Hinton's son Thomas sold it to John Ayliffe of Grittenham in Brinkworth.[43]

The manor passed with Grittenham manor from John Ayliffe (d. 1631) to Sir George Ayliffe (d. 1643), John Ayliffe (d. 1645), and George Ayliffe (d. 1713) whose relict Judith held it until her death

[4] Below, manor.
[5] B.L. Maps, M.T. 6e., 1 (2).
[6] W.R.O. 592/1.
[7] O.S. Maps 6″, Wilts. XIII (1888 edn.), XIII. NW. (1900 edn.).
[8] W.R.O., G 7/360/7.
[9] Inf. from Maj. A. R. Turnor, Foxley Manor.
[10] B.L. Maps, M.T. 6e., 1 (2); P.R.O., IR 30/38/123.
[11] Below, educ.
[12] O.S. Map 6″, Wilts. XIII. NW. (1900, 1925 edns.).
[13] V.C.H. Wilts. ii, pp. 154, 212.
[14] Reg. Malm. i. 137; W.A.M. xlviii. 80.
[15] Cal. Pat. 1370–4, 72.
[16] Reg. Regum Anglo-Norm. ii, p. 346.
[17] Ibid. iii, no. 818.
[18] Cal. Pat. 1370–4, 72.
[19] Bk. of Fees, ii. 743.
[20] Rot. Hund. (Rec. Com.), ii (1), 272.
[21] P.R.O., C 142/24, no. 26.
[22] Wilts. Inq. p.m. 1625–49 (Index Libr.), 176.
[23] V.C.H. Worcs. iv. 77.
[24] Bk. of Fees, ii. 743.

[25] V.C.H. Glos. vii. 221.
[26] Ibid.; V.C.H. Worcs. iv. 79. V.C.H. Glos. x. 181 may be wrong to identify Hardwick as Hardwicke (Glos.).
[27] Rot. Hund. (Rec. Com.), ii (1), 239, 272.
[28] Reg. Malm. ii. 155; V.C.H. Worcs. iv. 79.
[29] V.C.H. Glos. vii. 221.
[30] Phillipps, Wilts. Inst. i. 30.
[31] P.R.O., E 179/196/8.
[32] Phillipps, Wilts. Inst. i. 54.
[33] Ibid. 59; Reg. Chichele (Cant. & York Soc.), iii. 426.
[34] Feud. Aids, v. 235.
[35] Phillipps, Wilts. Inst. i. 123, 126–7, 129; V.C.H. Glos. vii. 221.
[36] Phillipps, Wilts. Inst. i. 148.
[37] Ibid. 169; Wilts. Pedigrees (Harl. Soc. cv/cvi), 135.
[38] P.R.O., C 142/24, no. 26.
[39] Valor Eccl. (Rec. Com.), ii. 122.
[40] P.R.O., C 142/92, no. 112.
[41] Ibid. CP 25(2)/240/25 & 26 Eliz. I Mich.; Wilts. Pedigrees (Harl. Soc. cv/cvi), 155, 207.
[42] P.R.O., C 142/257, no. 85.
[43] W.R.O. 11/3.

in 1716.[44] It passed to their son John (d. 1722)[45] and to their daughter Judith (d. 1737) who devised it to her cousin Susanna Strangways, wife of Thomas Horner.[46] Susanna settled it, from her death in 1758, on her daughter's brother-in-law Henry Fox,[47] from 1763 Baron Holland of Foxley.[48] Foxley manor passed from Lord Holland (d. 1774) to his son Stephen, Lord Holland (d. 1774), and was held by Stephen's relict Mary until her death in 1778. It descended to Stephen's son Henry,[49] Lord Holland, then a minor, who took the surname Vassall in 1800. After the death of Lord Holland in 1840 and of his relict Elizabeth in 1845 the manor passed to their son Henry Fox, Lord Holland (d. 1859). He devised it to his wife Mary (d. 1889) and she to his nephew Leopold Powys[50] who took the additional surname Fox in 1890. On Fox-Powys's death in 1893 Foxley passed to his nephew Thomas Powys, Baron Lilford (d. 1896), whose heir was his son John, Lord Lilford (d. 1945).[51]

In 1902 the land was sold by Lord Lilford to W. W. Turnor of Pinkney Park. Turnor was succeeded in 1931 by his grandson Maj. A. R. Turnor, the owner of Foxley farm, 700 a., and Foxley Manor in 1986.[52]

The oldest parts of Foxley Manor to survive are a long east–west range and a short north wing at its east end, both built in the early 17th century. Those parts may have been the **L**-shaped building to adjoin which a tall late 17th- or early 18th-century house was built.[53] The new house was possibly built for George Ayliffe, who moved to Foxley in 1688,[54] and was standing in 1760.[55] In 1775 Mary, Lady Holland, planned to improve the house and to use it in summer, and members of the Fox family apparently lived in it in 1781.[56] The house was a farmhouse in the 19th century. The new part had apparently been completely demolished by 1844.[57] The main range of the old house was extended westwards in the early 19th century and a long service wing was added west of the north wing in the later 19th century. Further additions were made when it was restored c. 1920.[58]

Thomas de Mandeville and his wife Alice conveyed 1 yardland in Foxley to Walter de Rysum and his wife Alice in 1314.[59] It may have been the small estate in Foxley which passed from Thomas Bremilham to his son John and to John's son Richard (d. s.p. c. 1557). Richard was succeeded by his grandnephew Thomas Nicholas and great-grandnephew Robert Shipton.[60] The estate

was possibly that, later called *PLAYER'S* farm, settled in 1639 by Edmund Hart on the marriage of his son Robert. In 1666 Robert's relict Margaret surrendered the estate to Edmund's grandson Robert Hart, who held the reversion.[61] The land passed, presumably by purchase, to Timothy Player (d. 1677 or 1678) who devised it to his wife Mary (fl. 1707) for life and afterwards to his son Robert (fl. 1738).[62] It passed to Robert's son Timothy who in 1760 sold Player's farm, 80 a., to Henry Fox.[63] It thereafter descended with Foxley manor.

Malmesbury abbey held land in Foxley for which, at the Dissolution, the lessee paid 5s.[64] It was possibly the land, 2 a. c. 1840,[65] later owned by the burgesses of Malmesbury and given by them to Mary, Lady Holland, in an exchange in 1872.[66]

ECONOMIC HISTORY. Foxley was assessed as 2 hides in 1066. In 1086 there was demesne of 1 hide on which were 2 ploughteams and 3 *servi*; on the remaining land 4 *villani* and 3 coscets had a total of 3 teams, and there were a mill, 4 a. of meadow, and 8 a. of pasture.[67] Domesday Book ascribed no woodland to Foxley, a name which implies that woodland was then or formerly nearby,[68] and the theory that much of Malmesbury abbey's extensive woodland was in Foxley, where the abbey held little land and there were 5 teams on land for 4,[69] seems untenable. Foxley Grove was c. 12 a. in 1760,[70] 15 a. c. 1840,[71] and 18 a. in 1986.[72] There was no direct reference to a mill after 1086, but Old Mills was in the 18th century the name of a field beside the Avon,[73] and in the Middle Ages, when it belonged to Malmesbury abbey,[74] may have been the site of a mill.

In the later 13th century the lord of Foxley manor and four others holding land in Foxley surrendered to Malmesbury abbey their rights to feed animals in common on heath land.[75] That may have been to restrict the Foxley animals to a particular part of what was later called Malmesbury common, and in 1760 rights to feed cattle from sunrise to sunset in the corner of the common adjoining Foxley, c. 45 a., was claimed for the inhabitants of Foxley.[76] In 1783 the rector claimed similar rights for sheep and the right to cut furze.[77] When the common was inclosed in 1832 the lord of Foxley manor was allotted 15 a. and the rector 1 a. of that land.[78]

There may have been open fields and common pasture in Foxley parish in the Middle Ages. The

[44] Above, Brinkworth, manors.
[45] W.R.O. 11/5–6; mon. in church.
[46] W.R.O. 11/8; 592/1; J. Hutchins, *Dors.* ii. 663.
[47] W.R.O. 11/11; Hutchins, *Dors.* ii. 663.
[48] For the Hollands, *Complete Peerage*, vi. 541–5.
[49] W.R.O. 11/154.
[50] Ibid. 11/161; *Complete Peerage*, vi. 545.
[51] Burke, *Peerage* (1959), 1374–5; *Kelly's Dir. Wilts.* (1895).
[52] Inf. from Maj. A. R. Turnor, Foxley Manor; Wilts. Cuttings, xvii. 90, 95.
[53] Watercolour attributed to T. Hearne in possession of Maj. Turnor; see plate facing p. 220.
[54] P.R.O., E 126/16, f. 29.
[55] B.L. Maps, M.T. 6e., 1 (2).
[56] Hist. MSS. Com. 42, *15th Rep.*, Carlisle, pp. 457, 751.
[57] e.g. P.R.O., IR 29/38/123; IR 30/38/123.
[58] Inf. from Maj. Turnor.
[59] *Feet of F.* 1272–1327 (W.R.S. i), p. 86.

[60] P.R.O., C 3/167/52.
[61] W.R.O. 1269/18.
[62] Ibid. 11/138; 11/141.
[63] Ibid. 11/150–1.
[64] *Valor Eccl.* (Rec. Com.), ii. 121–2.
[65] P.R.O., IR 29/38/123; IR 30/38/123.
[66] W.R.O. 11/168.
[67] *V.C.H. Wilts.* ii, p. 154.
[68] Ibid. p. 11; *P.N. Wilts.* (E.P.N.S.), 70; Ekwall, *Eng. Place-Names* (1960), 186.
[69] *W.A.M.* xlviii. 538; *V.C.H. Wilts.* ii, p. 154.
[70] B.L. Maps, M.T. 6e., 1 (2).
[71] P.R.O., IR 29/38/123; IR 30/38/123.
[72] Inf. from Maj. Turnor.
[73] B.L. Maps, M.T. 6e., 1 (2).
[74] Above, manor.
[75] *Reg. Malm.* ii. 155–6, 159, 161–3.
[76] B.L. Maps, M.T. 6e., 1 (2).
[77] W.R.O., D 1/24/97/3.
[78] Ibid. EA/142.

apparently open fields referred to in the surrenders to Malmesbury abbey may have been there,[79] open field in the parish was referred to in 1572,[80] and North field, South field, and Foxley heath were referred to in 1608. The two fields had been divided into closes by 1608, but the rector claimed rights to feed in common on the heath 2 horses and 8 cattle in summer and 50 sheep in winter.[81] The heath may have been south of the Sherston road west of the village, where there may have been common pasture in 1675[82] and fields were called Horseleaze and Cowleaze in 1760.[83] Bounded by the Sherston road, the Foss Way, and the Avon, Foxley park, c. 150 a., had been walled by 1675.[84] South of the Sherston road west of Foxley Manor lines of trees gave the appearance of parkland to more fields:[85] they may have been planted when the house was enlarged and the common pasture was inclosed, possibly in the 1680s.[86] The rector had no right to common pasture in Foxley in 1698.[87] By 1760 all the parkland had been converted to agriculture. Foxley green, c. 2 a., was then open pasture.[88] It remained so in 1986 but neither it nor the verges of the lanes was then used to feed animals.

The inclosure of land in Foxley may have been unimpeded because there were few farms. There are unlikely to have been more than two or three besides the demesne farm in the 16th and 17th centuries.[89] In 1690 the demesne, which was not leased, was a mixed farm: 66 a. of cereals, 2 a. of vetches, and 6 a. of peas were grown, there were 45 a. of meadows, and 14 cows, 14 calves, 400 sheep, and 7 pigs were kept.[90] The three or more other farms then in the parish were smaller.[91] In the 18th century there were three farms, Foxley, Player's, 80 a., and the glebe, 95 a. after 1728.[92]

In 1760 the parish, including the former parkland, lay divided by hedges into c. 65 fields: most of the park north of the Sherston road was then arable. The parish was about two thirds arable, a third meadow and pasture. There were c. 7 a. or more of orchards. Player's farm was worked from buildings beside the lane north-east of the church: its land was a strip beside the parish boundary north and south of the buildings. The glebe included farm buildings beside the rectory house: most of the old glebe lay together in the south-west part of the parish, most of the new was along the southern parish boundary. Foxley farm was worked from the buildings north of Foxley Manor and an oxyard south-west of it.[93]

The parish included 440 a. of arable, 264 a.

of meadow and pasture, and the 15 a. of woodland c. 1840. Foxley farm was 574 a., of which 553 a. were in a total of 26 fields, and Player's farm was 58 a.[94] From 1780 or earlier to c. 1862 c. 90 a. of the glebe were worked with Foxley farm,[95] and from 1842 Player's was added to Foxley farm, then 700 a.[96] Foxley remained the principal farm in the parish until c. 1920.[97] In 1863 the land beside the eastern boundary formerly Player's farm was given to the rector in exchange for the glebe in the west part of the parish,[98] and the glebe was thereafter cultivated separately from Foxley farm.[99] Arable was laid to pasture in the mid 19th century: in 1867 there were 279 a. each of grass and arable and a further 131 a. of grass sown in rotation. In the later 19th and earlier 20th century the grassland of Foxley farm was mainly for rearing sheep, with some cattle for beef. In the later 19th century cereals were grown on about two thirds of the arable.[1]

Foxley farm was 630 a. in 1910.[2] By 1927 it had been divided: 256 a. continued to be worked, as Manor farm, from the buildings near Foxley Manor, and 280 a. were worked with Cowage farm based in Bremilham. Other Foxley land had apparently been added to other farms worked from outside the parish.[3] The 280 a. were later worked as a separate farm from the buildings near Foxley church formerly part of Player's farm.[4] Sheep rearing continued in the parish until c. 1950.[5] From 1953 the whole of Foxley farm, 700 a., was worked by the owner. Cattle were kept until 1977, for milk before and for beef after 1974. In 1986 Foxley was an arable farm of 588 a. on which wheat, barley, and rape were grown in large fields: 112 a. of grassland were leased for summer grazing. The farm was worked mainly from new buildings near the church.[6] In 1986 cattle were grazed on the pastures south of Honey Lane and beside the eastern boundary stream.

LOCAL GOVERNMENT. The parish habitually appointed a single overseer. In 1719 and 1720 a total of £28 was spent on the poor: most was given in monthly doles, but in both years coal was given.[7] Between 1736 and 1752 the most spent in a year was £10, the least £2. Doles were given to a woman from 1736 to 1749: miscellaneous expenses included payments for funerals and clothing.[8] Expenditure was £14 in 1775–6, c. £11 a year 1783–5, £27 in 1802–3 when five adults were relieved continuously and two occasionally, and

[79] *Reg. Malm.* ii. 155–6.
[80] W.R.O. 88/1/72.
[81] Ibid. D 1/24/97/1.
[82] Ogilby, *Brit.* pl. 79.
[83] B.L. Maps, M.T. 6e., 1 (2).
[84] Ogilby, *Brit.* pl. 79; *Andrews and Dury, Map* (W.R.S. viii), pl. 16.
[85] B.L. Maps, M.T. 6e., 1 (2).
[86] Above, manor.
[87] W.R.O., D 1/24/97/2.
[88] B.L. Maps, M.T. 6e., 1 (2).
[89] *Taxation Lists* (W.R.S. x), 53.
[90] P.R.O., E 126/16, f. 29 and v.
[91] Ibid. E 134/3 & 4 Wm. and Mary Hil./5; W.R.O., D 1/24/97/2; ibid. 11/139.
[92] B.L. Maps, M.T. 6e., 1 (2); W.R.O., D 1/24/97/3; ibid. 11/16.
[93] B.L. Maps, M.T. 6e., 1 (2); P.R.O., IR 29/38/123; IR 30/38/123; W.R.O., D 1/24/97/3; ibid. 11/16. For the glebe, below, church.
[94] P.R.O., IR 29/38/123; IR 30/38/123.
[95] W.R.O., A 1/345/184; ibid. 11/158.
[96] Ibid. 11/161.
[97] Ibid. Inland Revenue, val. reg. 9; ibid. G 7/515/5.
[98] Ibid. 11/166.
[99] Ibid. A 1/345/184.
[1] P.R.O., MAF 68/151, sheet 3; MAF 68/550, sheet 2; MAF 68/1120, sheet 9; MAF 68/1690, sheet 11; MAF 68/2260, sheet 14; MAF 68/2830, sheet 10; MAF 68/3373, sheet 10.
[2] W.R.O., Inland Revenue, val. reg. 9.
[3] Ibid. G 7/515/5; *Kelly's Dir. Wilts.* (1927).
[4] Inf. from Maj. Turnor.
[5] P.R.O., MAF 68/3373, sheet 10; MAF 68/4589, no. 131; MAF 68/5055, no. 131.
[6] Inf. from Maj. Turnor.
[7] W.R.O. 592/1.
[8] Ibid. 592/4.

£16 in 1814–15 when two adults were relieved continuously.[9] It reached a peak of £62 in 1819–20, but in the 1820s and 1830s, at an average of c. £45, was very low even for a parish of Foxley's size. In 1835 Foxley joined Malmesbury poor-law union.[10] In 1974 it became part of North Wiltshire district.[11]

CHURCH. Foxley church was standing in the 12th century or earlier.[12] It may have originated as a chapel served from Malmesbury abbey since in 1291 it was called a chapel[13] and about then a pension from it was owed to the abbey,[14] but there is no later mark of Foxley's dependence on another church. The living was a rectory in 1300[15] and remained one. An Order in Council of 1874 authorized the union of Foxley and Bremilham rectories:[16] they were united in 1893 when the rector of Foxley was appointed rector of Bremilham.[17] The united benefice was in 1986 united with the benefice of Sherston Magna with Easton Grey and Luckington with Alderton.[18] Although Foxley and Bremilham were to remain separate parishes under the Order in Council of 1874, presumably because Bremilham church had long been closed Foxley with Bremilham was considered a single parish in 1986.[19]

In 1334, and apparently in 1361 and 1365 when, respectively, John de la Mare and Robert de la Mare presented, the advowson was held with Foxley manor.[20] Robert Oughtred presented in 1388 and John Poulton and Richard Webb jointly in 1416, by what right is obscure. In the period 1417–57, when there were eight presentations, the advowson apparently passed with the manor: John de la Mare of Hardwick presented in 1417, John de la Mare, possibly the same, in 1420 and 1435, and William de la Mare in 1457; the four other presentations, in 1432, 1435, 1437, and 1439, were by feoffees who held the manor and included John de la Mare of Rendcomb. From 1485, when John Moody presented, to 1902 the advowson did pass with the manor. In 1575 Christopher Twinhoe presented by grant of a turn,[21] in 1840 the Crown presented after the incumbent was promoted to a bishopric, and in 1862 the university of Oxford presented because Mary, Lady Holland, was a Roman Catholic.[22] After Foxley and Bremilham rectories were united the owner of the advowson of Foxley had the right to present at two of every three vacancies of the united benefice.[23] John, Lord Lilford (d. 1945), remained patron and presented in 1902.[24] No presentation after 1893 by a patron claiming the third turn is known. Lord Lilford's right passed to his brother Stephen, Lord Lilford (d. 1949).[25] In 1946 the university of Oxford presented because Stephen, Lord Lilford, was a Roman Catholic, and in 1951 and 1953 that Lord Lilford's executors presented. The Crown, patron of Corston with Rodbourne, with which Foxley with Bremilham was held in plurality, presented in 1963.[26] From 1986 George Powys, Lord Lilford, the successor of Stephen, Lord Lilford, was a member of the board of patronage for the benefice of Sherston Magna, Easton Grey, Luckington, Alderton and Foxley with Bremilham.[27]

As might be expected for so small a parish the rectory was not highly valued in 1291[28] or 1535,[29] but the exemption of the rector from taxation in 1545 on grounds of poverty[30] seems likely to have depended on more than the low value of the living. In 1650 the living was, at £50, more highly valued.[31] In 1728 it was augmented: Judith Ayliffe (d. 1737) gave land worth £400 on receiving £200 from Queen Anne's Bounty.[32] Thereafter the living was well endowed for such a parish.[33] In the earlier 19th century the rector compounded with his patron, the lord of Foxley manor, for the whole income of the benefice at £261, a sum found to exceed the true value of the living.[34]

The rector was entitled to all the tithes from the whole parish: in 1841 they were replaced by a rent charge of £189.[35] In 1341 the rector had 1 yardland and 5 a. of meadow.[36] In 1608 the glebe was c. 50 a. with pasture rights, in 1698 and 1704 c. 54 a. At the augmentation of 1728 the rector was given 36 a. of Foxley manor. In 1783 the glebe was 94 a.,[37] to which 1 a. inclosed from Malmesbury common was added in 1832.[38] Lands were exchanged between the rector and the lord of the manor in 1863.[39] The glebe was 94 a. in 1887:[40] 37 a. were sold in 1903 and 48 a. in 1920.[41] There was a house on the glebe in 1341,[42] and it was repaired in the 1380s.[43] It presumably stood on the site of the later rectory house near the west end of the church. The present house is L-shaped, consisting of a south block and a long back wing to the east. The south end of the wing is apparently medieval: the wing was extended northwards in the 16th century or early 17th. In 1729 the south end of the house was demolished and replaced by

[9] Poor Law Abstract, 1804, 566–7; 1818, 498–9.
[10] Poor Rate Returns, 1816–21, 188; 1822–4, 228; 1825–9, 219; 1830–4, 212; Poor Law Com. 2nd Rep. App. D, 559.
[11] O.S. Map 1/100,000, admin. areas, Wilts. (1974 edn.).
[12] Below.
[13] Tax. Eccl. (Rec. Com.), 189.
[14] V.C.H. Wilts. iii. 221.
[15] Reg. Ghent (Cant. & York Soc.), ii. 842.
[16] Lond. Gaz. 15 May 1874, p. 2576.
[17] Ch. Com. file, NB 5/137C, pt. 1; Bristol R.O., EP/A/1/6, pp. 33, 47.
[18] Ch. Com. file, NB 5/137C, pt. 1.
[19] Ibid.; Lond. Gaz. 15 May 1874, p. 2576; above, Bremilham, church.
[20] Phillipps, Wilts. Inst. i. 30, 54, 59; above, manor.
[21] Phillipps, Wilts. Inst. (index in W.A.M. xxviii. 221); Reg. Chichele (Cant. & York Soc.), iii. 426; above, manor.
[22] Complete Peerage, vi. 545; Bristol R.O., EP/A/3/155.
[23] Lond. Gaz. 15 May 1874, p. 2576.
[24] Bristol R.O., EP/A/1/6, p. 114.
[25] Burke, Peerage (1967), 1514.

[26] Bristol R.O., EP/A/3/155; inf. from Dioc. Registrar; Maj. A. R. Turner, Foxley Manor.
[27] Burke, Peerage (1967), 1512; Ch. Com. file, NB 5/137C, pt. 2.
[28] Tax. Eccl. (Rec. Com.), 189.
[29] Valor Eccl. (Rec. Com.), ii. 138.
[30] Taxation Lists (W.R.S. x), 29.
[31] W.A.M. xli. 6.
[32] C. Hodgson, Queen Anne's Bounty (1864), p. cxliii; W.R.O., D 1/24/97/3; Ch. Com. file, NB 5/82.
[33] Rep. Com. Eccl. Revenues, 834–5.
[34] Ch. Com. file, NB 5/137C, pt. 1.
[35] P.R.O., IR 29/38/123.
[36] Inq. Non. (Rec. Com.), 165.
[37] W.R.O., D 1/24/97/1–3.
[38] Ibid. EA/142.
[39] Ibid. 11/66.
[40] Glebe Lands Return, H.C. 307, p. 53 (1887), lxiv.
[41] Ch. Com. file 49475; W.A.S. Libr., sale cat. xvii, no. 64.
[42] Inq. Non. (Rec. Com.), 165.
[43] W.R.O., D 1/2/5, ff. 224v.–225.

a new block with a south entrance front of five bays.[44] Possibly about then, a stair and service block was built in the angle between the old wing and the new block. In 1783 the house, with walls and roofs of stone, had seven rooms on the ground floor, six on the first floor, outbuildings, and near it a farmyard.[45] In the early 19th century a small extension was built at the west end of the south block, and the house was partly refitted. The house was the glebe house of the united rectory[46] until it was sold, with the remaining 9 a. of glebe, in 1946.[47] Thereafter it was again partly refitted.

In 1300 the rector, William Martin, was licensed to visit Rome on condition that he appointed a chaplain to serve the church.[48] In 1417 William Scurion exchanged with Robert Benett the chaplaincy of Arundel's chantry in Canterbury cathedral for Foxley rectory.[49] Rectors may have been resident for much of the 17th century:[50] Richard Jeane (d. 1628) was also rector of Bremilham.[51] William Hart, rector 1645–78,[52] was approved of by parliamentary commissioners in 1650.[53] In 1662 the church was in poor repair and lacked the Book of Common Prayer, the Book of Homilies, Jewell's *Apology*, and a surplice.[54] John Stumpe, rector 1679–1726 and rector of Bremilham to 1681,[55] was from 1689 vicar of Sutton Benger. George Ayliffe, lord of Foxley manor, refused to pay tithes from 1689 on the grounds that Foxley became vacant when Stumpe was inducted to Sutton Benger because it was valuable enough to be under the provisions of the Act of 1529 restricting plurality, but by Exchequer decree was ordered to pay.[56] Hart and Stumpe were both said to have held a service every Sunday,[57] but from 1698 or earlier Stumpe appointed a succession of curates to serve Foxley. The last, Simon Crook,[58] was rector from 1726 to 1763:[59] in the period 1727–9 the living was augmented, the rectory house was largely rebuilt,[60] and new plate and a bell were given.[61] In 1783 the rector, Seth Thompson, was vicar of Thatcham (Berks.), where he lived, and the curate also served Hullavington. The curate held a service every Sunday and communion thrice yearly.[62] In 1801 the curate was also curate of Hullavington and of Norton.[63] Philip Shuttleworth, rector from 1824 until he became bishop of Chichester in 1840, was warden of New College, Oxford, and not resident: his curate held a service every Sunday.[64] In 1851 the curate, who was vicar of Hullavington, claimed that two services were held each Sunday with congreg-

ations averaging 53.[65] From 1893 or earlier parishioners of Bremilham attended Foxley church.[66] From 1899 to 1946 the rectors were also vicars of Norton:[67] in 1903 the rector, who lived at Foxley, held communion thrice monthly at Foxley and a service there every Sunday.[68] From 1951 to 1983 Foxley with Bremilham was held in plurality with the vicarage of Corston with Rodbourne.[69]

Foxley church is undedicated. It stands on a low circular mound, is built of rubble and ashlar, and consists of a chancel, a nave with north transeptal aisle and south porch, and a west tower.[70] Its small size suggests that the nave was built in the 12th century or earlier, and a plain 12th-century font is in the church. A north aisle with an arcade of three bays was built in the early 13th century, and the chancel, as suggested by its width, may have been rebuilt in the 13th century. In the 14th century the chancel was refenestrated and a north chapel was added to it. The tower was built in the 17th century. The aisle and the north chapel were demolished, probably in the late 17th century when the transeptal aisle was built to incorporate the centre and eastern bay of the arcade: 14th-century windows were reset in the new aisle and where the opening between the chancel and chapel was blocked. A monument records that the chancel was paved for the first time in 1708.[71] Also in the earlier 18th century the porch, in a simple classical style, was built, and much of the south wall of the nave was rebuilt: one, or possibly two, 15th-century windows were reset in the new wall. A west gallery was removed in 1902 or 1903 and the church was generally restored at intervals in the period 1902–33.[72]

Foxley is rich in plate which includes a silver-gilt cup made in 1572, a paten cover bearing the date 1606, and a silver-gilt set of chalice, paten, and flagon made by Paul Lamerie and given in 1727 by Judith Ayliffe (d. 1737).[73] In the late 18th century the plate was sometimes lent to Bremilham.[74] The church has one bell. It was renewed in 1729 when the same Judith Ayliffe gave a bell cast by Abraham Rudhall. That bell, which was cracked, was placed in Bremilham church and replaced by the Bremilham bell, possibly in 1923.[75]

The registers of baptisms and burials begin in 1713 and are complete. Those of marriages begin in 1715 and are lacking for 1753–85.[76]

NONCONFORMITY. The certifying in 1799 of

[44] W.R.O., D 1/61/1B, pp. 8–9.
[45] Ibid. D 1/24/97/3.
[46] *Crockford* (1898 and later edns.).
[47] Inf. from Lt.-Col. J. H. Pitman, Foxley Ho.
[48] *Reg. Ghent* (Cant. & York Soc.), ii. 842.
[49] *Reg. Hallum* (Cant. & York Soc.), p. 80.
[50] W.R.O., bishop's transcripts, bdle. 1.
[51] *Subscription Bk. 1620–40* (W.R.S. xxxii), pp. 18, 40, where Jeane is called Faine. Cf. Phillipps, *Wilts. Inst.* i. 228; *Wilts. Inq. p.m. 1625–49* (Index Libr.), 72.
[52] Phillipps, *Wilts. Inst.* ii. 21, 35.
[53] *W.A.M.* xli. 6.
[54] W.R.O., D 1/54/1/1, no. 67.
[55] Phillipps, *Wilts. Inst.* ii. 33, 36–7, 60.
[56] *W.N. & Q.* ii. 60–1; P.R.O., E 126/16, ff. 29, 66v.; Spiritual Persons Act, 21 Hen. VIII, c. 13, s. 9.
[57] P.R.O., E 134/4 Wm. and Mary East./15.
[58] W.R.O., D 1/51/1, ff. 21v., 47, 66, 133v., 170v.
[59] Phillipps, *Wilts. Inst.* ii. 60, 80.
[60] Above.   [61] Below.

[62] *Vis. Queries, 1783* (W.R.S. xxvii), p. 105.
[63] P.R.O., HO 67/23, nos. 58, 63, 103.
[64] *D.N.B.*; Ch. Com. file, NB 5/137C, pt. 1.
[65] P.R.O., HO 129/252/2/13/16; HO 129/252/2/15/20.
[66] W.R.O. 11/175; above, Bremilham, church.
[67] Bristol R.O., EP/A/1/6, pp. 33, 97, 114; EP/A/3/155; EP/A/7/3.
[68] *Kelly's Dir. Wilts.* (1903 and later edns.); W.R.O. 592/4D.
[69] *Crockford* (1957–8 and later edns.); *Bristol Dioc. Dir.* (1983 and later edns.); Bristol R.O., dioc. rec., registrar's bdle. 98, Foxley; Ch. Com. file, NB 5/137C, pt. 2; inf. from Dioc. Registrar.
[70] Description based on J. Buckler, watercolour in W.A.S. Libr., vol. vi. 28 (1809).
[71] Mon. in church.   [72] Bristol R.O., EP/J/6/2/128.
[73] Nightingale, *Wilts. Plate*, 197.
[74] *Vis. Queries, 1783* (W.R.S. xxvii), p. 43.
[75] Walters, *Wilts. Bells*, 91; W.R.O. 592/1; 592/4E.
[76] W.R.O. 592/1–3. Bishop's transcripts for earlier periods and for some of the missing entries are ibid.

a room for Independent meetings[77] is the only evidence of dissent in Foxley.

EDUCATION.

In 1818 there was a school for 18 children,[78] but it may have been that held on Sundays which was the only school in the parish in 1833.[79] A school held in the church was attended by 15 children on weekdays in 1846.[80] In 1858 a total of 16 Foxley and Bremilham children attended a school in a cottage in Bremilham:[81] that may have been the school attended by seven children in 1871.[82] A small school was held in the 1880s in a cottage in Foxley.[83] A school and schoolhouse were built in Foxley in 1894.[84] The school was attended by children from Norton and received money from the Anne Jacob and J. E. Jackson charities.[85] The average attendance was highest, at 32, in 1906, lowest, at 17, in 1913 and 1914. The school was closed in 1932.[86] In 1902 the rector furnished a room at the rectory house as a reading room and night school, then open three nights a week.[87]

CHARITY FOR THE POOR.

John Ayliffe (d. 1631) required his heirs to give 40s. a year for quarterly distribution to the poor of Foxley. There is no evidence that any did so.[88]

GARSDON

GARSDON parish,[89] a short distance east of Malmesbury,[90] originated as an estate apparently given to Malmesbury abbey in 701.[91] In 1934 the parish, 1,128 a. (457 ha.), was added to Lea and Cleverton parish.[92]

The streams which marked the western boundary of the parish and the western part of the southern may have been boundaries of the estate given to Malmesbury abbey, and the stream to the south, Woodbridge brook, was that called Garesburn until the late 13th century.[93] As in the case of its neighbour Charlton, Garsdon's eastern boundary in 1225 may have been the western boundary of Braydon forest which ran roughly north and south between Swatnage wood in Charlton and Woodbridge brook: such a boundary would have been east of the site of Park Farm. In 1228 the forest was extended west to Garsdon's western boundary stream, in 1279 reduced to its 1225 boundary, and in 1300 reduced to an area well to the east of Garsdon.[94] After 1630, when Braydon forest was inclosed, its purlieus, apparently the land between the boundaries of 1279 and 1300, were inclosed by the lords of manors near the forest. After dispute in 1632, land was conceded to Garsdon by Thomas Howard, earl of Berkshire, lord of the manor of both Charlton and of Garsdon's eastern neighbour Brinkworth, and possibly by other lords.[95] Garsdon was allotted 275 a. near the village of Minety (then Glos.): although it belonged to the lord of Garsdon manor until the late 18th or early 19th century that land, most of which was Minety farm in the early 19th century, was not added to Garsdon parish.[96] The c. 200 a. east of the 1279 boundary which became part of Garsdon parish were possibly conceded by Lord Berkshire, who is unlikely to have had land near Minety. Garsdon's boundary with Charlton was changed slightly c. 1882.[97]

The grassy hill which gave Garsdon its name[98] is a north-west and south-east ridge, rising from 76 m. near the church to 110 m. at the eastern boundary, and was a backbone for the former parish. The lowest land is in the south-west corner around the confluence of the two boundary streams, which are tributaries of the Bristol Avon. A third stream flows west through the former parish to join Woodbridge brook. Alluvium has been deposited in the south-west corner, and in the north-west corner Cornbrash outcrops. Elsewhere Kellaways Clay and Oxford Clay outcrop and there are areas of Kellaways Sand south-east and north-east of the church.[99]

The Cornbrash favours arable, but much of Garsdon parish was for long pasture. In the 18th century, as presumably earlier, the arable was scattered in the south and west and there were extensive meadows beside the streams.[1] In the early 18th century there were coppices near the western boundary and south-east and south-west of the church.[2] Much of the timber was cut c. 1750 and, although some new planting took place soon afterwards,[3] thereafter woodland in the parish was sparse.[4]

[77] Meeting Ho. Certs. (W.R.S. xl), p. 54.
[78] Educ. of Poor Digest, 1027.
[79] Educ. Enq. Abstract, 1037.
[80] Nat. Soc. Inquiry, 1846–7, Wilts. 6–7.
[81] Acct. of Wilts. Schs. 10.
[82] Returns relating to Elem. Educ. 420–1.
[83] Kelly's Dir. Wilts. (1885, 1889).
[84] P.R.O., ED 7/130, no. 130.
[85] Endowed Char. Wilts. (N. Div.), 482; below, Norton, educ.
[86] Bd. of Educ., List 21, 1919 (H.M.S.O.), 361; 1922, 360; 1927, 360; 1932, 408; P.R.O., ED 2/18423.
[87] W.R.O. 592/4D.
[88] Endowed Char. Wilts. (N. Div.), 481; W.R.O., wills, archd. Wilts., 1635, Ayliffe.
[89] A map of the par. is below, s.vv. Lea and Cleverton.

[90] This article was written in 1986. Maps used include O.S. Maps 1/50,000, sheet 173 (1974 edn.); 1/25,000, ST 98 (1959 edn.); 6″, Wilts. VIII–IX (1888–9 and later edns.).
[91] Below, manor.   [92] V.C.H. Wilts. iv. 352 n.
[93] Ibid. 444; P.N. Wilts. (E.P.N.S.), 11.
[94] V.C.H. Wilts. iv. 444–5; above, Charlton, introduction.
[95] W.N. & Q. vii. 453–4; above, Brinkworth, manors; Charlton, introduction, econ. hist.
[96] W.N. & Q. vii. 6; W.R.O. 212A/5130.
[97] O.S. Map 6″, Wilts. VIII (1889 edn.); W.R.O., tithe award; Census, 1891.   [98] P.N. Wilts. (E.P.N.S.), 59.
[99] Geol. Surv. Map 1″, solid and drift, sheet 252 (1974 edn.).
[1] Below, econ. hist; W.R.O. 88/7/4/1; 135/1.
[2] W.R.O. 135/1.   [3] Ibid. card index for 1742/393.
[4] Ibid. tithe award; O.S. Maps 6″, Wilts. VIII–IX (1888–9 and later edns.).

In the late 17th century the main Oxford–Bristol road ran east and west through the parish.[5] The bridge carrying it across the western boundary stream was called Milbourne bridge in the late 18th and early 19th,[6] Tanner's bridge from the late 19th century.[7] The road may have been of less importance by 1756 when a more northerly road through Charlton was turnpiked.[8] A plan of 1819 to replace part of the turnpike road by a new road running south-west to Garsdon Mill was not carried out.[9] In the early 18th century as in the late 20th the east–west road was crossed west of the church by a north–south road running between Charlton and Lea, and was left east of the church by a road leading north-east towards Charlton and Hankerton.[10] The old Oxford–Bristol road follows the ridge in the east part of the former parish. That length of road or a group of buildings beside it was called Park Lane in the late 18th century;[11] the road was so called in the late 19th century and later.[12] At its east end it is crossed by a lane which marked much of the eastern boundary of the parish.

In 1377 Garsdon had 55 poll-tax payers,[13] a high figure for a small rural parish. A tax assessment suggests that the parish was prosperous in the late 16th century.[14] In 1801 the population numbered 143. The number had risen to 234 by 1831, but declined for much of the rest of the century. Between 1891 and 1901 numbers rose from 141 to 162; thereafter they fell again. In 1931, the last date for which separate figures are available, 119 people lived in the parish;[15] it is unlikely that more lived in the former parish in 1986.

Garsdon village is on the ridge along the main east–west road between Garsdon Manor and the junction with the Charlton and Hankerton road. The church is north of the road, Garsdon Manor and the rectory house south of it. Several cottages along the main road south-east of the junction in 1720[16] had been demolished by 1773.[17] Church Farm was built on their site between 1773 and 1813.[18] Buildings on the south side of the main road were demolished or replaced in the mid or late 19th century,[19] and a Sunday school was built near the church in 1886.[20]

From the 18th century or earlier the parish contained scattered settlement and several hamlets. In 1720 there were buildings west of the village near Tanner's bridge;[21] 19th-century cottages stood there in 1986. Garsdon Mill, north-west of the village, may have been on its present site from the 13th century.[22] Between 1773 and 1813 two houses were built west of the Charlton–Lea road near the northern boundary:[23] the hamlet was called Noah's Ark in 1827[24] and later. In the 20th century two bungalows and farm buildings were added east of the road. Park Farm stands on the site of buildings which were beside Park Lane in 1720, but none of its buildings appears older than the 19th century. Further east there were several cottages near the western edge of Upper common in 1720; Hill Farm and Greenhill Farm stand there, each with a farmhouse apparently of the 19th century. A farmstead and cottages beside the Charlton and Hankerton road north-east of the village were standing in 1720[25] on land called Hazell Heath in 1773.[26] The farmhouse, called Garsdon Heath Farm in 1828[27] and later, was rebuilt in the late 18th century or the early 19th. A nonconformist chapel and two cottages were built north-east of it in the mid 19th century.[28] A few houses were built on scattered sites in the former parish in the later 20th century.

MANOR. In 701 King Ine apparently gave to Malmesbury abbey 5 *manentes* at Garsdon.[29] Ulueva held *GARSDON* in 1066. She may have held it as a tenant of the abbey, but it was later claimed that Queen Maud gave it to the abbey in 1081. Malmesbury abbey held Garsdon in 1086[30] and retained it until the Dissolution. In 1543 the Crown granted Garsdon manor to Richard Moody.[31] Richard (d. 1550)[32] settled the manor for life on his wife Catherine, later wife of William Basely. On her death in 1556 it passed to Richard's son Richard[33] (d. 1612). The younger Richard was succeeded by his son Sir Henry[34] (cr. a baronet 1622,[35] d. 1629), whose son Sir Henry[36] sold it in 1631 to Sir Laurence Washington.[37] Sir Laurence (d. 1643)[38] was succeeded in turn by his son Laurence (d. 1661)[39] and Laurence's daughter Elizabeth, who in 1671 married Sir Robert Shirley, Bt. (from 1677 Lord Ferrers, from 1711 Earl Ferrers). Earl Ferrers (d. 1717)[40] devised Garsdon manor to Laurence Shirley, his tenth son,[41] who died in 1743. Laurence's son Laurence became Earl Ferrers in 1745.[42] He sold the manor in 1758 to Paul Methuen[43] (d. 1795).

[5] J. Ogilby, *Brit.* (1675), pl. 79.
[6] *Andrews and Dury, Map* (W.R.S. viii), pl. 17; O.S. Map 1″, sheet 34 (1828 edn.).
[7] O.S. Map 6″, Wilts. VIII (1889 and later edns.).
[8] *V.C.H. Wilts.* iv. 257, 269; below, Malmesbury, introduction.
[9] W.R.O., A 1/370/22HC.
[10] Ibid. 135/1.
[11] *Andrews and Dury, Map* (W.R.S. viii), pl. 17.
[12] O.S. Map 6″, Wilts. IX (1888 and later edns.).
[13] *V.C.H. Wilts.* iv. 309.
[14] *Taxation Lists* (W.R.S. x), 51.
[15] *V.C.H. Wilts.* iv. 349.
[16] W.R.O. 135/1.
[17] *Andrews and Dury, Map* (W.R.S. viii), pl. 17.
[18] Ibid.; W.R.O. 135/16.
[19] W.R.O., tithe award; O.S. Maps 6″, Wilts. VIII–IX (1888–9 and later edns.).
[20] Date on bldg.
[21] W.R.O. 135/1.
[22] Below, econ. hist.
[23] *Andrews and Dury, Map* (W.R.S. viii), pl. 17; W.R.O. 135/16.
[24] Malmesbury Turnpike Roads Act, 14 & 15 Vic. c. 76 (Local and Personal).
[25] W.R.O. 135/1.
[26] *Andrews and Dury, Map* (W.R.S. viii), pl. 17.
[27] O.S. Map 1″, sheet 34 (1828 edn.).
[28] W.R.O. 135/16; ibid. tithe award; below, nonconf.
[29] Finberg, *Early Wessex Chart.* p. 70; *V.C.H. Wilts.* ii, p. 4.
[30] *V.C.H. Wilts.* ii, pp. 90, 126.
[31] *L. & P. Hen. VIII*, xviii (1), p. 257.
[32] *Cal. Pat.* 1550–3, 35.
[33] *W.N. & Q.* viii. 389; Aubrey, *Topog. Coll.* ed. Jackson, 243; P.R.O., C 142/92, no. 114.
[34] P.R.O., C 142/333, no. 7.
[35] *Cal. S.P. Dom.* 1619–23, 356.
[36] *Wilts. Inq. p.m.* 1625–49 (Index Libr.), 155.
[37] *W.N. & Q.* vii. 5.
[38] *W.A.M.* viii. 11.
[39] E. P. Shirley, *Stemmata Shirleiana* (1873), 173.
[40] *Complete Peerage*, v. 329–31.
[41] Shirley, *Stemmata Shirleiana*, 189.
[42] *Complete Peerage*, v. 336.
[43] W.R.O. 88/7/2/20.

Methuen was succeeded by his son Paul (d. 1816), whose son Paul (cr. Baron Methuen 1810)[44] sold it in 1843 to Thomas Howard, earl of Suffolk and of Berkshire.[45] The manor passed with Charlton manor and the titles to Charles Howard, earl of Suffolk and of Berkshire,[46] who between 1934 and 1939 sold Garsdon Manor and Manor farm to A. S. Butler and his wife Lois. In 1945 the Butlers sold the house and farm, c. 350 a., to E. H. and E. E. Higgins; E. E. and I. R. Higgins sold the land in 1977[47] to the Refuge Assurance Company, the owner in 1986. Mr. D. Allen owned Garsdon Manor and 5 a. in 1986.[48]

Garsdon Manor[49] was in the early 16th century and probably earlier used by the abbot of Malmesbury as a lodging.[50] It was probably occupied by members of the Moody and Washington families in the later 16th century and the 17th.[51] The oldest part of the house is the east–west back range which has an early 14th-century raised base cruck roof of four bays. Most of the supporting walls have been rebuilt or repaired but the lower courses and a mutilated buttress on the south side are apparently medieval. The roof of that range appears to have covered an upper room but surviving floor levels are the result of alterations. Another range of building, running north from the older range's eastern end, incorporates four 16th-century windows, some of which have been reset. That newer range was shortened, probably in the mid 19th century when buildings between the house and the road north of it were demolished.[52] A three-storeyed block was built on the south side of the 14th-century range at its eastern end apparently in the early 17th century. Its thick internal ground floor walls may, however, be part of an earlier building. The principal room on its first floor has an elaborate chimney piece and a ceiling decorated with strapwork. The house was altered and a new staircase made in the late 19th century.

The remaining lands of Garsdon manor, c. 750 a., passed with the titles from Charles, earl of Suffolk and of Berkshire (d. 1941), to his son Michael, who sold them in 1945. Church farm, 164 a., was bought by R. E. Organ, whose daughter Miss M. Organ owned it in 1986.[53] Park farm and Garsdon Heath farm, c. 300 a. each, were owned in 1986 by F. L. Lewis & Sons and by Mr. D. G. Topp respectively.[54]

ECONOMIC HISTORY. In 1086 there was land for 6 ploughteams at Garsdon. On the demesne of 1½ hide there were 2 teams and 6 *servi*; 5 *villani* and 5 coscets had a total of 3 teams. There were

10 a. each of meadow and pasture, and woodland ½ league long and 2 furlongs broad.[55]

The soils in parts of the parish favoured arable, and early tillage may have been in open fields, but there is no direct evidence of such fields. Whitehill green, east and south-east of Garsdon Manor, was a common pasture until the 17th century;[56] and north-east of the village the Heath, c. 10 a., was a common pasture which adjoined a namesake in Charlton.[57] The lord and tenants of Garsdon manor shared with many others grazing rights in Braydon forest and its purlieus.[58] They were excluded from the forest when it was inclosed in 1630[59] and from all but their own allotments of the purlieu c. 1633.[60] The grassland in the eastern part of the parish was apparently inclosed by the lord of the manor except for 30 a. near the eastern boundary, Upper common, assigned for use by the tenants in common.[61] The Heath was inclosed between 1821 and 1839; 22 a. of Upper common were inclosed after 1839.[62]

In 1210 stock on the demesne of Garsdon manor included 16 oxen, 1 draught beast, and 6 cows; tenants paid rents totalling 16s.[63] In 1535 the demesne was held on lease, as were two holdings of pasture, one of 40 a. and one much smaller, presumably several and perhaps formerly part of the demesne.[64] All or part of those pastures and part of Whitehill green were imparked in the early 17th century.[65] The park, roughly square with the manor house in the north-west corner, was walled and in 1678 measured 200 a. Other demesne lands, all several, were then held as farms of 90 a. and 273 a.[66] Although still walled, by 1721 the 200 a. had been disparked and divided into two holdings;[67] parts of the wall were still standing in 1757.[68] The demesne lands, including the former park and land in Lea, comprised 750 a. in 1759 and were held as seven farms;[69] the largest included 112 a. of arable, 81 a. of meadow, and 86 a. of pasture in 1766.[70]

Garsdon manor had less copyhold land than demesne. Two copyholders held a total of 56 a. in 1759, when 380 a. of former copyhold land were held on leases by five tenants.[71] By 1776 all copyholds had been converted to leaseholds.[72]

In the late 18th century and the early 19th the farms in the parish became fewer and larger. In 1776 there were farms of 337 a., 264 a., 171 a., and 137 a., and five of between 20 a. and 100 a.[73] In 1821 there were only four farms, all compact. Manor farm, 337 a., occupied the western part of the parish, and Park farm, also 337 a., the south-eastern part; the lands of Church farm, 173 a., lay mainly north of the church and those

[44] *Complete Peerage*, viii. 680–1.
[45] W.R.O. 1742/429.
[46] Above, Charlton, manors.
[47] *Kelly's Dir. Wilts.* (1939); W.R.O., G 7/505/1; sale cat. in Nat. Bldgs. Rec.
[48] Inf. from Mr. D. Allen, Garsdon Manor.
[49] See plate facing p. 93.
[50] P.R.O., SC 6/Hen. VIII/3986, rot. 130.
[51] Aubrey, *Topog. Coll.* ed. Jackson, 241–3; Ogilby, *Brit.* pl. 79.
[52] W.R.O., tithe award; O.S. Map 6″, Wilts. VIII (1889 edn.).
[53] Inf. from Miss M. Organ, Church Farm.
[54] Local inf.
[55] *V.C.H. Wilts.* ii, p. 126.
[56] P.R.O., C 2/Jas. I/M 3/41.

[57] W.R.O. 88/7/4/5; above, Charlton, econ. hist.
[58] W.R.O. 88/10/52; above, Charlton, econ. hist.
[59] W.R.O. 100.
[60] *W.N. & Q.* vii. 453–4.
[61] W.R.O. 88/7/4/5.
[62] Ibid. 135/16; ibid. tithe award.
[63] *Interdict Doc.* (Pipe R. Soc. N.S. xxxiv), 23.
[64] *Valor Eccl.* (Rec. Com.), ii. 121; P.R.O., C 3/120/43.
[65] P.R.O., C 2/Jas. I/M 3/41.
[66] *W.N. & Q.* vii. 5–6; W.R.O. 135/1.
[67] W.R.O. 54/72; 135/1.
[68] Ibid. card index for 1742/393.
[69] Ibid. 88/7/4/1.
[70] Ibid. 2478, survey of Garsdon, 1766.
[71] Ibid. 88/7/4/1.
[72] Ibid. 88/7/4/3.   [73] Ibid.

of Garsdon Heath farm, 170 a., east of it.[74] In 1759 and 1839 there were c. 700 a. of meadow and pasture, c. 300 a. of arable.[75]

In the 1860s and 1870s there were 700–750 a. of pasture and 200–300 a. of arable; the principal crop was wheat. In 1866 there were c. 200 sheep, 188 cattle including 83 cows, and 77. pigs.[76] The area of pasture increased, numbers of cattle and pigs rose, and the size of the flock decreased in the late 19th century.[77] Between 1906 and 1936 there were usually more than 300 cattle and 200 pigs, fewer than 100 sheep. Nearly the whole parish was pasture, with some arable in the north and west.[78] By the 1980s the area of arable had increased, mostly in the west; cereals and rape were grown. The pastures were still mainly used for dairy cattle.

There were two mills at Garsdon in 1086.[79] Records of a water mill in the parish survive from the early 13th century;[80] from the 16th century, as presumably earlier, it was part of Garsdon manor.[81] Probably in 1228 and certainly in 1720 the mill stood on the parish's western boundary.[82] It was used in 1950 for the preparation of animal feed,[83] and in 1986 was a private house. The building comprises an apparently 18th-century western range of two storeys with attics, and a 19th-century eastern extension of three storeys.

There were weavers in Garsdon in the late 16th century and the early 17th.[84] In 1766 there was a tanyard west of the village beside the bridge to which it later gave a name.[85] From 1855 or earlier bricks, tiles, and pottery were fired in a kiln west of Garsdon Heath Farm. In the 1880s and 1890s the brickworks was owned by J. E. Ponting, a Malmesbury ironmonger.[86] It had been closed by 1910.[87] Probably in the mid 19th century a quarry was opened on the Cornbrash near the parish's north-western corner, where there was a lime kiln; another was opened further east in the 1880s. Quarrying had apparently ceased by 1911.[88]

LOCAL GOVERNMENT. Courts were held for Garsdon manor in the 16th century[89] as, presumably, at other times, but none of their records survives.

Apparently in the early 17th century a cottage was built at the expense of the wealthier inhabi-

tants for the poor of Garsdon. Its use as an almshouse was confirmed in 1659.[90] It was perhaps one of four cottages a little east of Garsdon Manor which were held by the overseers of the poor in 1821.[91] The cottages had been demolished by 1839.[92]

Poor rates in Garsdon parish in the early 19th century were close to the average for Malmesbury hundred. Expenditure on the poor had risen from £30 in 1776 to £180 by 1812–13 when 16 people received permanent and 51 occasional relief.[93] Thereafter the cost of poor relief fluctuated, reaching peaks of £242 in 1817–18 and £268 in 1830–1.[94] In the period 1833–5 the average annual expenditure was £114. Garsdon became part of Malmesbury poor-law union in 1835[95] and of North Wiltshire district in 1974.[96]

CHURCH. There was a church at Garsdon in 1265.[97] Although in 1340 Malmesbury abbey was licensed to appropriate it,[98] the living remained a rectory. By the mid 16th century Lea church had been annexed to Garsdon rectory;[99] Garsdon and Lea and Cleverton were considered a united benefice in the earlier 20th century.[1] In 1987 the benefice of Garsdon, Lea and Cleverton, and Charlton was created.[2]

From 1298 or earlier Malmesbury abbey held the advowson of Garsdon. Until the Dissolution the abbot presented all known rectors but one; in 1511 the king presented, perhaps because the recently elected abbot had not then been confirmed.[3] After the Dissolution the advowson passed with Garsdon manor. John Purie in 1612, William Palmer and Elizabeth Herne together in 1640, and J. D. King in 1763 each presented a rector by grant of a turn.[4] In 1843 Thomas, earl of Suffolk and of Berkshire, sold the advowson to Joseph Neeld.[5] By 1859 it had passed, presumably by sale, to Henry Gale.[6] In 1869 Gale himself was presented to the rectory by the Revd. W. W. Gale and J. W. P. Gale. In 1877 J. W. P. Gale presented T. S. Gray, who in turn presented his successor, R. W. Hay, in 1895.[7] By 1905 the advowson had passed to Hay's wife Margaret.[8] In 1922 she sold it to the Church Association Trust,[9] later the Church Society Trust. The trust and the bishop of Bristol became joint patrons of

[74] W.R.O. 88/7/4/5; 135/16.
[75] Ibid. 88/7/4/1; ibid. tithe award.
[76] P.R.O., MAF 68/73, sheet 11; MAF 68/74, sheet 10; MAF 68/493, sheet 3.
[77] Ibid. MAF 68/1063, sheet 7; MAF 68/1633, sheet 6.
[78] Ibid. MAF 68/2203, sheet 14; MAF 68/2773, sheet 9; MAF 68/3319, sheet 10; MAF 68/3814, no. 140; [1st] Land Util. Surv. Map, sheet 104.
[79] V.C.H. Wilts. ii, p. 126.
[80] Close R. 1227–31, 103.
[81] L. & P. Hen. VIII, xviii (1), p. 527.
[82] Close R. 1227–31, 103; W.R.O. 135/1.
[83] W.R.O., F 12, corresp. file, Avon Silk Mills.
[84] Sess. Mins. (W.R.S. iv), 136; P.R.O., STAC 8/11/13.
[85] W.R.O. 2478, survey of Garsdon, 1766; above, introduction.
[86] Kelly's Dir. Wilts. (1855 and later edns.); O.S. Map 6", Wilts. VIII (1889 edn.).
[87] W.R.O., Inland Revenue, val. reg. 11.
[88] Kelly's Dir. Wilts. (1867 and later edns.); O.S. Map 6", Wilts. VIII (1889 and later edns.).
[89] Valor Eccl. (Rec. Com.), ii. 121; P.R.O., C 1/1025, no. 34.

[90] Hist. MSS. Com. 55, Var. Coll. i, p. 136.
[91] W.R.O. 88/7/4/5; 135/16.
[92] Ibid. tithe award.
[93] Poor Law Abstract, 1804, 566–7; 1818, 498–9.
[94] Poor Rate Returns, 1816–21, 189; 1822–4, 228; 1825–9, 219; 1830–4, 212.
[95] Poor Law Com. 2nd Rep. App. D, 559.
[96] O.S. Map 1/100,000, admin. areas, Wilts. (1974 edn.).
[97] Reg. Malm. i. 417.
[98] Cal. Pat. 1338–40, 431.
[99] Phillipps, Wilts. Inst. i. 219; below, Lea and Cleverton, church.
[1] Ch. Com. file 85095; ibid. NB 5/85.
[2] Inf. from Ch. Com.
[3] Phillipps, Wilts. Inst. i. 1, 9, 31, 56–7, 79, 129, 139, 154, 189–90; V.C.H. Wilts. iii. 225.
[4] Phillipps, Wilts. Inst. i. 214, 217, 219, 229; ii. 7, 20, 31, 45, 53, 61, 81, 99.
[5] W.R.O. 415/272, f. 41.
[6] Kelly's Dir. Wilts. (1859).
[7] Bristol R.O., EP/A/3/162.
[8] Ch. Com. file, NB 5/85.
[9] Ibid. 85095.

The north part of High Street

Air view from the south in 1975

MALMESBURY

Oaksey: Oaksey Park House, demolished 1956–7

Malmesbury: the south front of Milbourne House in 1965

Garsdon: the south front of Garsdon Manor

Oaksey: Oaksey Moor House, demolished 1966

Garsdon, Lea and Cleverton, and Charlton in 1987.[10]

A pension of 10s. paid from Garsdon church to Malmesbury abbey was confirmed in 1265.[11] In 1291 the abbey's income from the church was in the form of a portion of tithes worth 10s.[12] In 1535 the abbey took 10s. and the abbey's chamberlain took tithes worth 3s. 4d. The rectory was then valued at £10 9s. 8d., a little above the average for a living in Malmesbury deanery.[13] About 1830, however, the combined income of c. £350 from Garsdon parish and Lea and Cleverton parish was only about the average for a Wiltshire benefice.[14]

The rector was presumably entitled to all the tithes of the parish subject to the portion due to Malmesbury abbey. By the early 19th century tithes on 92 a., part of Park farm, had been replaced by an annual payment of £5 4s. In 1839 the tithes and the payment were valued at £170 and replaced by a rent charge.[15]

In 1341 the rector held 1 yardland and 1 a. of meadow.[16] There were said to be 10 a. of glebe in 1608[17] and 18 a. in the late 17th century and the early 19th.[18] In 1822 by an exchange 16 a. of glebe were replaced by 12 a. around the rectory house.[19] The glebe house recorded in 1671[20] was perhaps that of stone standing in 1783.[21] A new house, built in 1815, has a tall two-storeyed central block with east and west wings,[22] and was much enlarged in the late 19th century. It was sold in 1950,[23] probably with the 12 a. of glebe.

Nicholas of Stratton, rector 1309–17, was licensed in 1311 to be absent from the parish for a year to study;[24] he was later the subject of actions for debt.[25] Charges made in 1553 against the rector, Thomas Harmer, that he did not hold services at a reasonable hour or say the Lord's Prayer daily, as required, and that quarterly sermons had not been preached, may indicate that he opposed the Edwardian reformation;[26] he was deprived in 1553 or 1554.[27] John Herne, rector 1640–70,[28] was said to have been sequestrated and imprisoned during the Interregnum.[29] He had recovered the living by 1662 but the church then had no surplice and some prescribed books were missing.[30] Joseph Simpson, rector 1763–97, and T. A. Methuen, rector 1814–69, both held other benefices and were not resident.[31] During their incumbencies Garsdon was served by curates,[32] one of whom John

Davis, curate c. 1780, helped to found a Congregational church in Malmesbury.[33] In 1783 a service was held in Garsdon each Sunday, in the morning in winter and in the afternoon in summer. Communion was celebrated at Christmas, Easter, and Whitsun, and there were c. 10 communicants.[34] On Census Sunday in 1851 a congregation of 37 attended the single, morning, service.[35] From 1950 the rector lived at Lea,[36] and between 1974 and 1987 Garsdon with Lea and Cleverton was served by a priest-in-charge.[37]

ALL SAINTS' church, so called in 1763,[38] is built of coursed rubble with ashlar dressings and has a chancel with north vestry, a nave with south porch, and a west tower. Only the tower dates from before 1856.[39] Before that date the plan of the church, which consisted of a chancel, a nave with south porch, and the tower, was apparently 13th-century or earlier. The chancel and nave each had windows of the 14th and 15th centuries, and the porch was of the 15th century or the early 16th. The lower stage of the tower was built in the 15th century, the upper in the 16th.[40] The undivided nave and chancel built in 1856 to designs by Coe & Goodwin are taller and wider than their predecessors[41] and have windows in 15th-century style.

In 1553 the parish kept a chalice weighing 11 oz., and 2½ oz. of plate were taken for the king.[42] By will proved 1687 Eleanor, Lady Pargiter, formerly wife of Laurence Washington (d. 1661), gave two chalices, a flagon, and a paten. The 17th-century pieces were lost in the late 18th century or the early 19th but were recovered c. 1820[43] and were still held by the parish in 1986.[44]

There were four bells in the church in 1553. A medieval bell and one recast in 1586 were the only bells to hang there in the late 17th century. They were replaced c. 1880 by a ring of eight tubular bells by Harrington, Latham, & Co.,[45] which remained in the church in 1986.[46]

There are registers of baptisms, marriages, and burials from 1682.[47]

NONCONFORMITY. In 1662 William Midge and his son William were presented for failing to receive communion at Easter. The elder William refused to pay the Easter offering; the younger

[10] Inf. from Ch. Com.
[11] Reg. Malm. i. 417.
[12] Tax. Eccl. (Rec. Com.), 189.
[13] Valor Eccl. (Rec. Com.), ii. 119, 138.
[14] Rep. Com. Eccl. Revenues, 834–5.
[15] W.R.O., tithe award.
[16] Inq. Non. (Rec. Com.), 166.
[17] W.R.O., D 1/24/100/1.
[18] Ibid. D 1/24/100/2; D 1/24/100/4.
[19] Ibid. D 1/3/1/7.
[20] Ibid. D 1/24/100/2.
[21] Ibid. D 1/24/100/3.
[22] Ibid. D 1/61/5/21.
[23] Inf. from the priest-in-charge, Lea.
[24] Reg. Ghent (Cant. & York Soc.), ii. 714, 898; Reg. Martival (Cant. & York Soc.), ii. 226.
[25] Reg. Martival (Cant. & York Soc.), iii. 10–11, 15, 20–1, 24, 29, 31, 36–7, 42; Cal. Close, 1313–18, 312.
[26] W.R.O., D 1/43/1, f. 133.
[27] Phillipps, Wilts. Inst. i. 217.
[28] Ibid. ii. 20, 31.
[29] Walker Revised, ed. Matthews, 373.
[30] W.R.O., D 1/54/1/1, no. 50.

[31] W.N. & Q. ii. 224; Phillipps, Wilts. Inst. ii. 99; Vis. Queries, 1783 (W.R.S. xxvii), p. 109; V.C.H. Wilts. x. 31.
[32] Vis. Queries, 1783 (W.R.S. xxvii), pp. 109–10; Educ. of Poor Digest, 1027; Kelly's Dir. Wilts. (1848 and later edns.).
[33] Vis. Queries, 1783 (W.R.S. xxvii), p. 109; V.C.H. Wilts. iii. 132.
[34] Vis. Queries, 1783 (W.R.S. xxvii), p. 109.
[35] P.R.O., HO 129/252/1/7/10.
[36] Inf. from the priest-in-charge.
[37] Ch. Com. file, NB 5/85.
[38] J. Ecton, Thesaurus (1763), 403.
[39] Pevsner, Wilts. (2nd edn.), 254.
[40] J. Buckler, watercolour in W.A.S. Libr., vol. vi. 8; B.L. Add. MS. 36410, f. 16v.
[41] Pevsner, Wilts. (2nd edn.), 254; Aubrey, Topog. Coll. ed. Jackson, 243; Buckler, watercolour in W.A.S. Libr., vol. vi. 8.
[42] W.A.M. xii. 368.   [43] Nightingale, Wilts. Plate, 198–9.
[44] Inf. from the priest-in-charge.
[45] Walters, Wilts. Bells, 92.
[46] Inf. from the priest-in-charge.
[47] W.R.O. 525/1–5. Bishop's transcripts for some earlier and missing years are ibid.

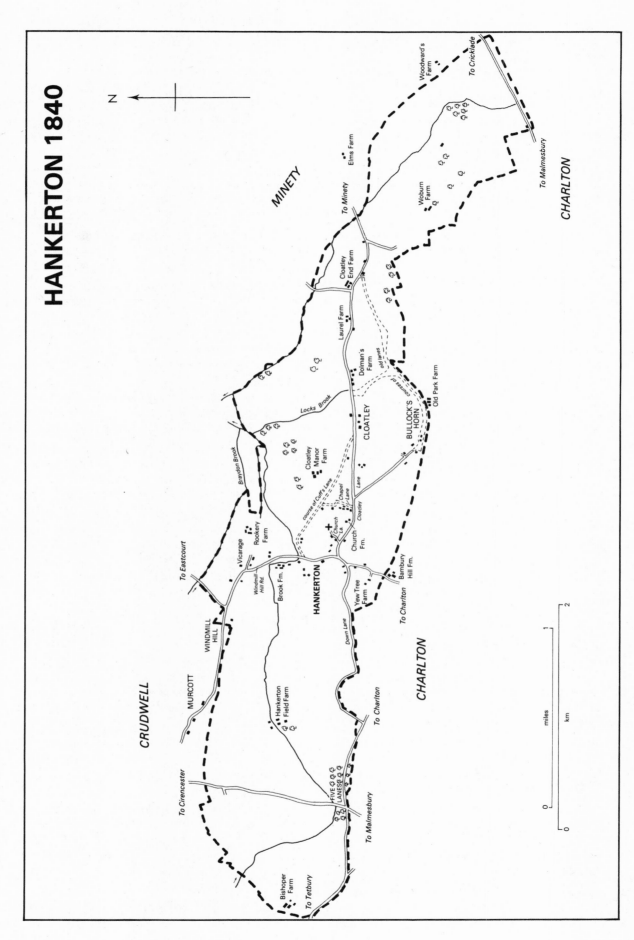

HANKERTON 1840

N

CRUDWELL

MURCOTT

MINETY

WINDMILL
HILL

To Cirencester

To Eastcourt

Vicarage

Windmill
Hill Rd.

Rookery
Farm

Brook Fm.

Braydon Brook

Locks Brook

HANKERTON

Down Lane

Hankerton
Field Farm

Church La.

Church
Fm.

course of Cuff's Lane

Chapel
Lane

CLOATLEY

Cloatley
Manor
Farm

Laurel Farm

Dolman's
Farm

old lanes

Cloatley
End Farm

To Minety

Elms Farm

Woburn
Farm

Woodward's
Farm

To Cricklade

To Malmesbury

CHARLTON

Cloatley
Lane

BULLOCK'S
HORN

courses

Old Park Farm

Yew Tree
Farm

Bambury
Hill Fm.

To Charlton

CHARLTON

To Charlton

FIVE
LANES

To Malmesbury

Bishoper
Farm

To Tetbury

miles

km

0   1   2

0

described the Prayer Book as popery.[48]

No other evidence of dissent in the parish has been found before 1827, when a house was certified for Methodist meetings.[49] In 1860 Primitive Methodists built the Jubilee chapel at Garsdon Heath.[50] It was still in use in 1986.[51]

EDUCATION. There may have been a day school at Garsdon in the 1840s.[52] By 1858 children from Garsdon attended the school in Lea.[53]

CHARITY FOR THE POOR. By will proved 1643 Sir Laurence Washington gave 12d. a week from Garsdon manor to buy bread for or to be given in cash to the poor of the parish. In the 18th century the rent from 3 a. of the manor was apparently used for doles or clothing. By 1834 the charity had been lost.[54]

HANKERTON

HANKERTON church is 5 km. north-east of Malmesbury.[55] The long and narrow parish, 891 ha. (2,203 a.), runs east–west and contains Hankerton village and the hamlets of Cloatley and Bullock's Horn: in the Middle Ages Moredon may have been another hamlet.[56] Hankerton manor was part of Malmesbury abbey's Crudwell estate, the church was dependent on Crudwell's,[57] and Hankerton was probably late in becoming a parish.

To the west, Hankerton's north and south boundaries were fixed early and appear to have been little changed. The northern, with Eastcourt and Murcott, both in Crudwell, may have been on or near its present course in the early Middle Ages when both Eastcourt's and Murcott's followed Braydon, otherwise Swill, brook:[58] part of Hankerton's later boundary with Crudwell followed Braydon brook and its feeders and, for short distances, roads. The southern, with Charlton, was defined possibly c. 1100[59] and was later marked by a road. The western boundary of Braydon forest in 1225 may have been the eastern boundary of Hankerton, as it apparently was of Charlton and Garsdon to the south and of Crudwell to the north. It ran, possibly almost due north, from Swatnage wood in Charlton to Braydon brook following the stream which was called Locks brook in 1225 and 1809. Braydon forest was extended westwards and took in Hankerton village in 1228, was reduced to its 1225 boundaries in 1279, and was reduced further in 1300.[60] The purlieus of the forest, apparently the land between the boundaries of 1279 and 1300, were open pastures and woods used in common by the lords and tenants of manors near the forest, but particular parts were claimed for, and perambulated by, each manor.[61] Until the 1540s Hankerton and Cloatley were parts of a single estate[62] and until c. 1580 parishioners of Hankerton perambulated part of the purlieus claimed for both Hankerton and Cloatley. For most of their length the northern and southern boundaries of that part seem to have been similar to the later boundaries of the parish, but towards the east end they both turned southwards and met at Charlham oak on Shire ditch.[63] About 1580 the lord of both Hankerton and Charlton, to deprive Cloatley of part of the purlieus, ordered the men of Charlton to perambulate what had formerly been perambulated by the parishioners of Hankerton. To keep it the men of Cloatley perambulated the same part of the purlieus. Probably soon after the dispute was heard in the Exchequer in 1595,[64] but possibly after the forest and purlieus were inclosed in the 1630s,[65] both the north and south boundaries of Hankerton were cut off at the Cricklade–Malmesbury road and the triangle to the south, formed by that road, Shire ditch, and a line from Charlham oak to Stonehill wood in Charlton, became Charlton land.[66] Only minor changes were later made to Hankerton parish boundaries. Those with Crudwell on Windmill Hill and with Charlton along the Cricklade–Malmesbury road were defined at inclosure in 1809,[67] and in 1882 a small part of Charlton was transferred to Hankerton.[68]

West of Hankerton village are outcrops of limestone and clay of the Forest Marble and, immediately west of the village, of Cornbrash: the land, over 100 m. in the west, slightly lower nearer the village, is almost flat. East of the village are outcrops of Kellaways Clay and Oxford Clay and, around Bullock's Horn, of Kellaways Sand: the land, c. 110 m. in the east, 90 m. near the village, is almost as flat as in the west. Virtually the whole parish drains to the Thames. Tributaries of Braydon brook flowing from each end of the parish meet in the middle north-east of the village, where they are joined by Locks brook and there are extensive deposits of alluvium.[69] A stream flowing south

[48] W.R.O., D 1/54/1/1, no. 50.
[49] Meeting Ho. Certs. (W.R.S. xl), p. 113; W. C. Tonks, Victory in the Villages, facing p. 40.
[50] Harrod's Dir. Wilts. (1865); O.S. Map 6″, Wilts. VIII (1889 edn.).
[51] Inf. from the priest-in-charge.
[52] Endowed Char. Wilts. (N. Div.), 485–6.
[53] Acct. of Wilts. Schs. 25; below, Lea and Cleverton, educ.
[54] Endowed Char. Wilts. (N. Div.), 485–6.
[55] This article was written in 1988. Maps used include O.S. Maps 1″, sheet 34 (1828 edn.), sheet 157 (1968 edn.); 1/50,000, sheet 173 (1974 edn.); 1/25,000, ST 99, SU 08–09 (1959 edns.); 6″, Wilts. VIII–IX (1888–9 edns.).
[56] Below.

[57] Ibid. manors, church.
[58] Arch. Jnl. lxxvii. 113, 115.
[59] Ibid. 11.
[60] V.C.H. Wilts. iv. 444–5; W.R.O., EA/132; above, Charlton, introduction; Crudwell, introduction; Garsdon, introduction.
[61] P.R.O., E 178/2408; W.R.O. 88/10/52.
[62] Below, manors. [63] Cf. above, Charlton, map.
[64] P.R.O., E 134/37 Eliz. I East./13.
[65] Above, Charlton, econ. hist.
[66] Cf. ibid. Charlton, map.
[67] W.R.O., EA/132. [68] Census, 1891.
[69] Geol. Surv. Maps 1″, solid and drift, sheets 251 (1970 edn.), 252 (1974 edn.).

to Charlton may have risen in Hankerton parish in the 16th century.[70] Hankerton's open fields were west of the village, its common pastures were north of the church and on clay south-east of the church. Most of the clay to the east was open pasture until the 1630s and little has ever been ploughed.[71] In several places west of the village the limestone has been quarried.[72] To the east John Aubrey thought, apparently mistakenly, that the parish could yield both fuller's earth and saltpetre.[73]

West of Hankerton village, where the open fields were, there was no road in the parish until the later 18th century[74] when the road from Cirencester (Glos.) to Malmesbury, turnpiked in 1778 and disturnpiked in 1874,[75] was made across it. The lanes follow the parish boundaries. From the north end of the village one led to Crudwell: the lane leading from it towards Eastcourt was on its present course in 1773.[76] From the south end of the village the road called Down Lane in 1585,[77] in the course of which is a semicircular detour, leads to Tetbury (Glos.). It was crossed by the Cirencester–Malmesbury road at a junction called Five Lanes. The Tetbury road was turnpiked west of Five Lanes in 1798,[78] east of Five Lanes to its junction with a new road from Charlton in 1808.[79] Both east and west parts were disturnpiked in 1876. On the grassland east of Hankerton village the Cricklade–Malmesbury road, turnpiked in 1756 and disturnpiked in 1876,[80] crosses the parish, and the lanes were more numerous. Cloatley Lane, called Locks Brook Road in 1809, led across the former purlieus to Minety and there were offshoots to the south. The lanes were wide and in 1809 the offshoots were inclosed and allotted as farmland.[81] The road to Bullock's Horn became a footpath in the 20th century,[82] and in 1988 that hamlet was approached by road only from the south. Where it runs straight across the former common pasture immediately east of the village Cloatley Lane may have been remade at inclosure in 1809.

In 1377 Hankerton had 61 poll-tax payers and Cloatley 33; Moredon, probably a hamlet in the parish, had 20. Those figures show the parish to have been one of the more populous of the hundred.[83] In 1676 there were 190 adults in the parish.[84] The population was 286 in 1801. It had risen to 413 by 1831 when 325 lived in Hankerton tithing and 88 in Cloatley, and reached a peak of 417 in 1841 when Hankerton had 340 inhabitants and Cloatley 77. The decrease to 371 in the period 1841–51, when Hankerton's population declined by 62, was attributed to lack of housing and to several families leaving the parish. From 393 in 1861 the population of the parish had fallen to 252 by 1901, between 1901 and 1951 it fell to 217,[85]

and in 1961 reached a low point of 178. In the period 1971–81, when new houses were built, it rose from 194 to 289.[86]

Hankerton village is almost certainly the oldest settlement in the parish. Its farmsteads and cottages were loosely grouped in lanes around the church. To the west the lane linking Hankerton and Charlton, called Windmill Hill Road in 1809,[87] forms a village street. North of the church Cuff's Lane ran between the street and Cloatley Lane. The east end of Cuff's Lane was stopped at inclosure in 1809 and the west end has largely gone out of use. In the 19th century Chapel Lane was formed between its middle and Cloatley Lane.[88] The pre-inclosure pattern of settlement could be clearly seen in 1988. In all parts of the village the older buildings were set back behind what until 1809 were the wide verges of lanes used for pasture in common: they are all of apparently local stone. Beside the village street to the north Brook Farm is a later 18th-century farmhouse with extensive farm buildings, south of it is an 18th-century cottage, and east of it are a small farmhouse much enlarged in the 1980s and a small 18th-century farmhouse. Further south Yew Tree Farm is an early 18th-century farmhouse near which is an early 18th-century cottage. Beside the west part of Cuff's Lane is a farmhouse of the 17th century or earlier, and beside the centre part a 19th-century cottage. North and south of Cloatley Lane are small 18th-century houses, and beside Chapel Lane, near what was the west edge of a common pasture until 1809, two cottages standing in 1809 survive. The north end of the village is possibly the site of Moredon. There Rookery Farm is a late 18th-century farmhouse, west of it Hankerton Priory is the old vicarage house,[89] and west of that are two cottages, apparently one of the 17th century and one of the 18th. From the mid 19th century to the mid 20th, while the population was declining, there was little new building in the village, and some buildings which were standing in 1840[90] were demolished. A school was built in Church Lane and a nonconformist chapel with a small cottage in Chapel Lane.[91] Some pre-1809 house sites were re-used in the 20th century, but the former verges between the older houses and the roads were the sites of much 20th-century housing. Those at the junction of the village street and Cloatley Lane were used for six council houses in 1948[92] and four old people's bungalows in 1962,[93] and several other houses and bungalows were built beside Cloatley Lane in the later 20th century. Follyfield, an estate of c. 35 houses, was built east of the village street in the early 1970s,[94] in 1988 five houses were being built on the site of Church Farm, and several other later 20th-

[70] W.R.O. 88/2/22, view 7 Apr. 27 Eliz. I.
[71] Below, econ. hist.
[72] W.R.O. 88/2/49; 212A/33/4, deed, Warneford to earl of Berks., 1693; ibid. Inland Revenue, val. reg. 7.
[73] Aubrey, *Topog. Coll.* ed. Jackson, 244–5.
[74] *Andrews and Dury, Map* (W.R.S. viii), pls. 16–17.
[75] *V.C.H. Wilts.* iv. 257, 269; *L.J.* xxxv. 436; 14 & 15 Vic. c. 76 (Local and Personal).
[76] *Andrews and Dury, Map* (W.R.S. viii), pl. 17.
[77] W.R.O. 88/2/22, view 7 Apr. 27 Eliz. I.
[78] Ibid. 88/5/46/3; *L.J.* xli. 655.
[79] *W.A.M.* xlii. 619; W.R.O. 88/5/46/3.
[80] *V.C.H. Wilts.* iv. 269; *L.J.* xxviii. 581; 14 & 15 Vic. c.

[76] (Local and Personal).
[81] W.R.O., EA/132.
[82] O.S. Maps 1″, sheet 157 (1940, 1968 edns.).
[83] *V.C.H. Wilts.* iv. 309–10.
[84] *Compton Census*, ed. Whiteman, 128.
[85] *V.C.H. Wilts.* iv. 321, 329.
[86] *Census*, 1961; 1971; 1981; below.
[87] Evidence of 1809 is from W.R.O., EA/132.
[88] O.S. Map 6″, Wilts. VIII. NE. (1900 edn.).
[89] Below, church. [90] W.R.O., tithe award.
[91] Below, nonconf., educ.
[92] W.R.O., G 7/505/1. [93] Ibid. G 7/360/10.
[94] Ibid. 1227, min. of par. council, 1961–75; local inf.

century houses were in the village. West of the village Bishoper Farm was built c. 1725,[95] and Hankerton Field Farm, where the farmhouse was rebuilt in the earlier 20th century, was probably built shortly before 1808.[96] A pair of estate cottages beside the Cirencester–Malmesbury road was built in the early 20th century.

The cottages and small farmsteads of which Cloatley hamlet may have consisted from the 13th century to the mid 16th[97] may have been beside Cloatley Lane east of its junction with Cuff's Lane, where a hamlet, consisting of only three cottages or houses south of the wide verge, was called Cloatley in 1773.[98] After the verges were allotted in 1809[99] a house was built on the north side of the road.[1] In 1988 that house, with a commercial garage, a later 20th-century bungalow, and one of the cottages on the south side survived. Cloatley Manor was built on low land east of Hankerton church in the Middle Ages.[2] After the purlieus were inclosed three new farmsteads were built beside Cloatley Lane east of the hamlet: the farmhouses of Dolman's Farm and Laurel Farm are clearly 17th-century; that of Cloatley End Farm has a late 18th-century front. At the east end of Cloatley Lane a few cottages include one of the early 19th century. At the eastern edge of Hankerton's common, a short distance west of Cloatley hamlet, three cottages stood in 1809.[3] One, possibly 18th-century, became the nucleus of Common End Farm, a house with later 20th-century extensions and farm buildings. Near the east end of the parish a cottage on inclosures called Woburn had been taken down by 1569.[4] A house and farm buildings there in 1840 were probably erected in the early 19th century:[5] none survives. In the early 19th century buildings were also on the site of Purlieus Farm beside the Cricklade–Malmesbury road and divided by the boundary with Charlton:[6] none of that date survives. An electricity substation was built on the boundary with Charlton in 1970.[7]

Bullock's Horn was named as a settlement site in the early 18th century,[8] and several cottages, most built in a wide lane leading east from Hankerton's common, stood there in 1773.[9] Six cottages and a house were there in 1840.[10] All four houses there in 1988, much altered, may survive from 1840.

MANORS AND OTHER ESTATES. Before the Conquest Hankerton, which was not mentioned

in Domesday Book, is likely to have been part of Malmesbury abbey's Crudwell estate and, lying between the abbey and Crudwell, may, like Crudwell, have been an early endowment.[11] It is also likely that the 10 cassati at Hankerton given by King Edward to the abbey in an exchange in 901[12] were the lands of Cloatley. The abbey held Hankerton and Cloatley until the Dissolution, each as part of its Crudwell estate.[13]

In 1552 the Crown granted HANKERTON manor, without Cloatley, to John Dudley, duke of Northumberland, in an exchange,[14] and in 1553 Northumberland sold it to Sir James Stumpe[15] (d. 1563), the owner of Charlton manor. Hankerton manor descended with Charlton to Stumpe's daughter Elizabeth (d. 1585) and her husband Sir Henry Knyvett (d. 1598), to the Knyvetts' daughter Catherine, wife of Thomas Howard, earl of Suffolk, and in the Howard family and with the earldoms of Suffolk and Berkshire to Michael Howard, earl of Suffolk and of Berkshire from 1941.[16] In 1840 Thomas, earl of Suffolk and of Berkshire, owned 1,125 a. in the parish.[17] About 1959 Lord Suffolk sold the eastern part of the manor, Church farm, Common End farm, part of Old Park farm based in Charlton, and Purlieus farm: in 1988 he owned c. 800 a. in the parish.[18]

In 1542 the Crown granted CLOATLEY manor to William Sharington[19] who in 1543 sold it to John Warneford[20] (d. 1558). The manor passed to Warneford's son John[21] (d. 1620) and to that John's son Thomas[22] (d. 1639) who settled it in 1627 on the marriage of his son Edmund[23] (d. 1649).[24] After Edmund's death the manor was held by his relict Margaret (will proved 1693) and at her death passed to his son Sir Edmund Warneford (d. 1700), who devised it to his son Edmund. In 1706 Edmund Warneford sold the manor to Giles Earle[25] (d. 1758), lord of the neighbouring manor of Eastcourt. It passed with Eastcourt to Giles's son William (d. 1774), and to William's son Giles who divided Cloatley manor c. 1806.[26] The manor house, Manor farm, and woodland, a total of 177 a. in 1840,[27] were bought by Joseph Pitt and remained part of the Eastcourt estate until 1919. They belonged successively to Pitt, J. R. Mullings (d. 1859), Joseph Mullings (d. 1860), A. R. Mullings (from 1877 A. R. Randolph, d. 1885), and J. R. Randolph.[28] In 1919 Randolph sold them to the tenant A. T. Hislop (d. 1968), who devised them to his brother and sister. In 1986 his sister Dorothy Hislop and the executors of his brother

[95] Ibid. 88/2/37B.
[96] Ibid. 88/10/7, survey of Hankerton Field farm, 1808; below, econ. hist.
[97] Reg. Malm. i. 150–3; P.R.O., SC 6/Hen. VIII/3986, rot. 122.
[98] Andrews and Dury, Map (W.R.S. viii), pl. 17.
[99] W.R.O., EA/132.
[1] Ibid. tithe award.
[2] Below, manors.
[3] W.R.O., EA/132.
[4] P.R.O., REQ 2/73/36.
[5] Andrews and Dury, Map (W.R.S. viii), pl. 17; C. Greenwood, Map of Wilts. (1820); O.S. Map 1", sheet 34 (1828 edn.); W.R.O., tithe award.
[6] W.R.O., tithe award.
[7] Inf. from Property Services Manager, C.E.G.B., Bedminster Down, Bridgwater Road, Bristol.
[8] W.R.O. 88/2/37B.
[9] Ibid. EA/132; Andrews and Dury, Map (W.R.S. viii), pl. 17.

[10] W.R.O., tithe award.   [11] Above, Crudwell, manors.
[12] Finberg, Early Wessex Chart. pp. 78–9.
[13] Reg. Malm. i. 148–53; Valor Eccl. (Rec. Com.), ii. 120.
[14] Cal. Pat. 1550–3, 369.
[15] Ibid. 258; P.R.O., CP 25(2)/65/533, no. 23.
[16] Above, Charlton, manors.
[17] W.R.O., tithe award.
[18] Local inf.; inf. from Mr. A. Witchell, Messrs. Humberts, 10 St. Mary Street, Chippenham.
[19] P.R.O., C 66/720, mm. 17–18; C 66/738, m. 17.
[20] Ibid. C 54/434, nos. 47–8.
[21] Ibid. C 142/141, no. 11.   [22] Ibid. C 142/380, no. 129.
[23] Wilts. Inq. p.m. 1625–49 (Index Libr.), 435–7; W.R.O. 1553/23.
[24] W.A.S. Libr., mon. inscriptions, Highworth, f. 8.
[25] W.R.O. 54/48; 1553/23; P.R.O., PROB 11/414, f. 191 and v.; PROB 11/456, ff. 297–298v.
[26] W.R.O., A 1/345/196; above, Crudwell, manors.
[27] W.R.O., tithe award.
[28] Ibid. A 1/345/196; above, Crudwell, manors.

A. C. Hislop[29] (d. 1986) sold the house and 146 a. to Mr. M. Thornbury, who owned that estate in 1988.[30] Cloatley Manor consists of an east–west hall range with, as east and west wings, the two stone cross wings of a substantial medieval house. The west, at the upper end of the hall, has a roof of arch-braced collars with elaborate wind braces below the purlins and may originally have been of one storey. The east, a two-storeyed service wing at the lower end of the hall, has a plainer roof with braced collars. Both wings are probably of 14th-century origin. Between them the long hall range, entered through a two-storeyed south porch, was rebuilt in the late 16th century. Both ground- and first-floor rooms retain some original plaster decoration, and at the north-west corner a wooden newel stair, possibly older than the present hall, gives access to the upper floor of the west wing. The roof of the hall range was renewed in the late 18th or early 19th century. After 1986 the house, which had become dilapidated, was extensively restored. The farm buildings near it include a 17th-century dovecot, a stable of 1706, and a barn of 1707. East and west of the house parts of a moat survive.

The other farms sold by Earle c. 1806 were Woburn, Dolman's, Laurel, and Cloatley End. Woburn farm, 203 a. in 1840, was bought by Christopher Cole; it became the main part of Elms farm based in Minety, and it has remained part of that farm. Jonathan Cole owned it in 1854[31] and 1873,[32] and in 1897 John Cole's trustees owned it.[33] In 1910 it belonged to Henry Hathaway,[34] in 1926 to Percy Manners.[35] In 1947 Elms farm, 160 a., was bought by M. H. Crocker and his wife, and Mrs. Crocker owned it in 1989. In 1968 Purlieus farm, c. 145 a., was bought by the Crockers' son Mr. P. H. Crocker, the owner in 1989.[36] After c. 1806 Dolman's, Laurel, and Cloatley End farms, a total of c. 310 a., usually descended separately,[37] but in the early 20th century Murray Shirriff owned all three.[38]

An estate called MOREDON seems to have originated in a grant of ¼ knight's fee, possibly demesne land, by Malmesbury abbey to William of Crudwell c. 1150.[39] William of Hankerton apparently held it in 1242–3,[40] as did John of Hankerton in the later 13th century.[41] It was possibly the estate conveyed by John Brown to Roger

Joliffe or Beaumond in 1365[42] and settled by Joliffe or Beaumond in 1367,[43] and possibly that held by Richard Urdley and his wife Margaret in 1388 and 1394.[44] The estate later seems to have been divided. An estate called Urdley's passed from Thomas Warneford (d. 1539), a freeholder in Hankerton in 1510, to his son John (d. 1558),[45] and with Cloatley manor to Sir Edmund Warneford who sold it in 1693 to Thomas, earl of Berkshire (d. 1706).[46] It belonged to Lord Berkshire's daughter Lady Frances Winchcombe in 1706[47] and later to George White.[48] A second portion was apparently sold by Richard Urdley's descendant Alison or Alice Parfet and her husband Thomas Hasard to John Hibberd in 1440,[49] and it descended in the Hibberd family. William Hibberd, who held it in 1539,[50] died holding it in 1560[51] and was succeeded by his son John (fl. 1605), who held Moredon in 1590. John's son Edmund[52] held it in 1606,[53] but its later descent is uncertain. It may have been the estate, held by John Cooper in 1616,[54] which on the death of Richard Cooper c. 1627 passed to John Machell (fl. 1644).[55] George Machell may have held it at his death c. 1684 when it passed to Richard Stacey.[56] George White held both Moredon and Urdley's in the earlier 18th century. His land descended to his son John (d. c. 1774) and to John's son John,[57] who in 1793 and 1809 exchanged lands with John, earl of Suffolk and of Berkshire.[58] John White's estate, ROOKERY farm, 102 a., was held in 1840 by, presumably another, John White,[59] and in 1868, when land was exchanged with Charles, earl of Suffolk and of Berkshire, by J. M. White.[60] In 1874 White (fl. 1883) sold the reversion to G. W. White (d. 1892).[61] In 1910 J. White owned the land,[62] in 1921 G. W. White sold most of it to Joseph Chivers,[63] and in 1951 Chivers sold it to Harold Sheppard whose relict, Mrs. A. Webb, owned it in 1988.[64]

A small estate in Hankerton was acquired by Bradenstoke priory before and in 1232.[65] Before the Dissolution some of the land was apparently granted freely to St. Bartholomew's hospital, Gloucester. At the Dissolution the priory's land passed to the Crown.[66] In 1541 it was granted to Sir Thomas Seymour[67] (cr. Baron Seymour 1547, d. 1549), who was attainted,[68] and in 1550 to Sir Walter Mildmay.[69] It was bought soon afterwards

[29] Princ. Regy. Fam. Div., 1969, will of A. T. Hislop; sale cat. 1986.
[30] Inf. from Mr. M. Thornbury, Cloatley Manor.
[31] W.R.O., A 1/345/196; ibid. tithe award; ibid. Minety tithe award.   [32] Ibid. 374/130/41.
[33] Ibid. 281/6; Wilts. Cuttings, vii. 113.
[34] W.R.O., Inland Revenue, val. reg. 7.
[35] Ibid. G 7/501/1.
[36] Inf. from Mr. P. H. Crocker, Home Farm, Minety.
[37] W.R.O., A 1/345/196; ibid. EA/132; ibid. G 7/501/1; G 7/505/1–3; ibid. tithe award; ibid. 374/130/41; 556/3; Kelly's Dir. Wilts. (1848 and later edns.).
[38] W.R.O., Inland Revenue, val. reg. 7.
[39] Reg. Malm. i. 453–7.   [40] Bk. of Fees, ii. 733.
[41] Reg. Malm. ii. 346–8.
[42] Feet of F. 1327–77 (W.R.S. xxix), p. 129.
[43] Cal. Close, 1364–8, 369.
[44] Feet of F. 1377–1509 (W.R.S. xli), pp. 23, 37.
[45] P.R.O., C 142/141, no. 11; ibid. E 318/Box 19/994, rot. 7; ibid. PROB 11/26, f. 111 and v.; ibid. SC 6/Hen. VIII/3986, rot. 103d.; W.R.O. 130/25, lease, Warneford to Dix, 1510.
[46] W.R.O. 212A/33/4, deed, Warneford to earl of Berks., 1693.

[47] Endowed Char. Wilts. (N. Div.), 218.
[48] W.R.O. 1301/4, deed, White to White, 1775.
[49] Feet of F. 1377–1509 (W.R.S. xli), p. 114; P.R.O., C 1/17, no. 174.
[50] P.R.O., SC 6/Hen. VIII/3986, rot. 103d.
[51] W.R.O. 88/2/33, view 12 Oct. 2 Eliz. I.
[52] Ibid. 88/2/43; P.R.O., C 3/94/25; C 3/273/40.
[53] W.R.O. 88/2/49.   [54] Ibid. 88/2/47.
[55] Ibid. 88/2/24, views 17 Sept. 3 Chas. I, 2 Oct. 20 Chas. I.
[56] Ibid. 88/3/2, ct. papers, 1684–5.
[57] Ibid. 1301/4, deeds, White to White, 1775.
[58] Ibid. 88/5/8; ibid. EA/132.   [59] Ibid. tithe award.
[60] Ibid. 1301/4, exchange, 1868.
[61] Ibid. 374/130/35; 1301/4, deed, White to White, 1874; W.A.S. Libr., sale cat. xvi, no. 20.
[62] W.R.O., Inland Revenue, val. reg. 7.
[63] W.A.S. Libr., sale cat. xvi, no. 20.
[64] Inf. from Mr. D. J. Sheppard, Rookery Ho.
[65] Bradenstoke Cart. (W.R.S. xxxv), pp. 78–9.
[66] Valor Eccl. (Rec. Com.), ii. 123, 489–90.
[67] L. & P. Hen. VIII, xvi, p. 462.
[68] Complete Peerage, xi. 637–9.
[69] Cal. Pat. 1549–51, 177.

by John Warneford[70] who added it to Cloatley manor. The hospital kept its land, 36 a. in 1840,[71] until between 1910 and 1926.[72]

Malmesbury abbey took the corn tithes from the parish from 1222 until the Dissolution[73] and they were granted by the Crown with Hankerton manor in 1552.[74] They descended with the manor and belonged to Thomas, earl of Suffolk and of Berkshire, in 1840, when those arising from his own land were deemed merged and those from other lands were valued at £15 and commuted.[75]

ECONOMIC HISTORY. Hankerton and Cloatley were each a part of Crudwell manor in the Middle Ages, but their lands were distinguished;[76] in a survey of them after the Dissolution the distinction was clarified.[77] To the west Hankerton's lands included common pastures and large open fields; east of them on the clay Cloatley's, presumably colonized later, apparently included little land used in common.[78] East of Locks brook and a line from its source to Swatnage wood in Charlton both Hankerton and Cloatley had rights to feed animals in common in the open woodlands and pastures of Braydon forest and its purlieus until the 1630s.[79]

HANKERTON. In the mid 12th century Malmesbury abbey may have alienated some of its demesne in Hankerton[80] and in the later Middle Ages it clearly had little there. In the early 16th century the demesne farm was called Hall Court. Other holdings were also small. In the later 13th century and the early 16th c. 30 yardlands were shared among 20–25 customary tenants and a few freeholders.[81] Isolated references to cultivation at Hankerton in the Middle Ages[82] suggest that by the mid 16th century the arrangement of open fields, inclosed land, and common pastures and meadows had long been little changed. The arable was in three fields, West, Middle, and Home, all west of the village, and the common pastures east and south of the village were called the Moors. Meadow land called lot mead was in the open fields, presumably most beside the tributary of Braydon brook crossing the parish from the west, and there were other common meadows, presumably beside that tributary and another stream north and north-east of the village. A meadow called New mead north-east of the church was used in common.[83]

Apparently in the 1570s, soon after Charlton Park was built and part of West field in Charlton was inclosed,[84] the neighbouring West field in

Hankerton was partly or wholly inclosed:[85] c. 90 a. were inclosed, another 63 a. may have been, closes of c. 5–10 a. were added to copyholds, and some land was converted to pasture.[86] There was no open West field in 1616.[87] Exchanges of plots in and inclosures of three common meadows, including New mead, were authorized in 1577,[88] and most meadow land had been inclosed by 1606.[89] There had been two other inclosures by the early 17th century: north of the village Moor down or Moredon, c. 100 a., was inclosed and divided into a few closes for the lord of the manor and a freeholder;[90] south of the village Down Hill was divided into the Down, 10 a., and smaller closes for the copyholders.[91] There were also small inclosures around the village.[92] In 1616 a total of 416 a. of arable was in Home field and Middle field: the 35 furlongs had 802 strips. The fields also contained 35 a. of lot mead in small pieces which were cut simultaneously. The arable was shared among 29, the meadow among 24.[93] The Moors were then 60 a. and Windmill Hill was a smaller common pasture. Inclosures at Hankerton totalled c. 450 a. In the later 16th century and early 17th Hall Court farm was c. 92 a. and a freehold may have been c. 100 a. All the copyholds were smaller: 3 were over 50 a., 4 were between 25 a. and 50 a., and 15 were under 25 a. The Down was part of Bambury Hill farm based in Charlton but all Hankerton's other land was presumably worked from the village.[94]

Hankerton's part of the purlieus of Braydon forest was presumably inclosed with Charlton's by the lord of the manor, Thomas, earl of Berkshire, in 1631,[95] and part of it was assigned to Cloatley in 1633.[96] By an agreement of 1634 the copyholders and freeholders of Hankerton were allotted 120 a. of the purlieus at the east end of the parish as a common and Lord Berkshire kept the rest: Lord Berkshire undertook to build a small house for the overseer of the common but there is no evidence that he did so. The agreement also sanctioned the inclosure of two meadows as demesne and use of the fallow field for meadow land, and excluded tenants of demesne land from the Moors.[97] In 1635 the copyholders and freeholders were stinted at 1 horse, 2 cattle, and 4 sheep on the new common for each yardland held.[98]

Small farms and common husbandry persisted at Hankerton until the late 18th century. Husbandry was regulated in the manor court where officers to oversee it were appointed.[99] A new third

[70] P.R.O., E 318/Box 32/1784.
[71] W.R.O., tithe award.
[72] Ibid. Inland Revenue, val. reg. 7; ibid. G 7/501/1.
[73] Sar. Chart. and Doc. (Rolls Ser.), 119–20; Valor Eccl. (Rec. Com.), ii. 118.
[74] P.R.O., E 318/Box 32/1820, rot. 2d.
[75] W.R.O., tithe award.
[76] Reg. Malm. i. 148–53; Valor Eccl. (Rec. Com.), ii. 120.
[77] P.R.O., E 134/37 Eliz. I East./13; ibid. SC 6/Hen. VIII/3986, rott. 103d., 121–2.
[78] Below.
[79] V.C.H. Wilts. iv. 444–5; above, introduction; above, Charlton, introduction.
[80] Reg. Malm. i. 453–7.
[81] Ibid. 148–51; P.R.O., SC 6/Hen. VIII/3986, rot. 121.
[82] Reg. Malm. ii. 275–6, 346–8.
[83] W.R.O. 88/2/21, views 21 Sept. 1575, 18 Mar. 1577; for New mead ibid. EA/132.

[84] Above, Charlton, manor, econ. hist.
[85] W.R.O. 88/2/21, views 13 Oct. 14 Eliz. I, 1 Apr. 21 Eliz. I.
[86] Ibid. 88/2/49.   [87] Ibid. 88/2/47.
[88] Ibid. 88/2/21, view 26 Sept. 1577.
[89] Ibid. 88/2/49.
[90] Ibid.; 88/2/45; P.R.O., SC 6/Hen. VIII/3986, rot. 121d.
[91] W.R.O. 88/2/22, ct. 26 Apr. 28 Eliz. I; 88/2/49.
[92] Ibid. 88/2/49.
[93] Ibid. 88/2/24, view 4 Apr. 8 Chas. I; 88/2/47.
[94] Ibid. 88/2/43; 88/2/49; for Bambury Hill farm, above, Charlton, econ. hist.
[95] Above, Charlton, econ. hist.
[96] W.R.O. 88/9/11; 177/22, deed, Warneford to Lattimer, 1646.
[97] Ibid. 88/9/1H.
[98] Ibid. 88/2/24, view 4 Apr. 11 Chas. I.
[99] Below, local govt.

arable field was marked out and in 1693 the fields were Home, Mersell (later Quarry), and Murcott,[1] but piecemeal inclosure apparently continued.[2] About 1800 the open fields, west of the village, may have been no more than c. 325 a. South-east of the village Home common was c. 70 a., north of the village Lower common was c. 35 a. and Windmill Hill common was c. 5 a., and further east the 120 a. allotted in 1634 were still a common pasture. Over 500 a. of Hankerton land were in closes of which the average size was no more than c. 5 a.[3] About 1725 Bishoper farm, 169 a., was created with land in Brokenborough and Charlton and 79 a. in closes at the west end of Hankerton.[4] In the late 18th century it was c. 529 a., including 124 a. in Hankerton, and by then another holding had grown to over 400 a., but there remained a number of small farms.[5]

As part of the improvement of his whole Wiltshire estate John, earl of Suffolk and of Berkshire, initiated many changes in Hankerton between c. 1790 and c. 1810. Hankerton Field farm was created and, following an exchange of lands between Lord Suffolk and John White in 1793, the three open fields were inclosed by bringing nearly all of each into separate farms. In 1808 Hankerton Field farm, 373 a., included the whole of both Murcott and Quarry fields.[6] The common pastures were inclosed in 1809 under an Act of 1808. A small allotment was made for every dwelling in the parish but most of the Hankerton commons, including that allotted in 1634, was allotted to Lord Suffolk and leased as farmland.[7] Brook farm, including most of Home field, was the largest of only a few farms based in the village; Bishoper farm, 355 a. in 1809, then had c. 165 a. in Hankerton.[8] A further exchange between Lord Suffolk and John White in 1809 left Rookery a compact farm of 102 a. north of the village.[9] Intending to improve drainage, roads, and buildings on the farms and to promote tillage by providing threshing machines, Lord Suffolk invited farmers from Northumberland and Scotland and found new tenants for about half his Hankerton land in 1809.[10]

CLOATLEY. An assart in the purlieus may have been added to Cloatley's lands in the mid 12th century,[11] but those lands were never extensive. In the later 13th century Malmesbury abbey had 13 tenants at Cloatley, some of whom apparently held very little. One or more held a Monday land. In 1540 the lands of only 2 of c. 10 tenants were referred to as yardlands, and the holdings were clearly very small.[12] Although there may earlier have been open field there is no evidence of it after 1540, but pasture and woodland adjoining the purlieus were claimed for Cloatley in the later 16th

century and were presumably used in common.[13] Four closes called Woburn, assarted in the purlieus, were part of Cloatley manor in the mid 16th century when they were mostly meadow land.[14]

After dispute, 120 a. of the purlieus near the east end of the parish were allotted to Cloatley to replace feeding rights in Braydon forest and the purlieus in 1633. They were divided equally between the lord of the manor and the tenantry: the tenants' 60 a. were for use in common.[15] Much of Cloatley's land may have been in the lord's hand from the mid 16th century,[16] and later the largest farm was worked from the manor house.[17] From the 17th century two farmsteads, later called Dolman's and Laurel, stood east of the hamlet, as did a third, Cloatley End, from 1773 or earlier.[18] Manor farm and the three farms worked from those buildings were the only ones based in Cloatley tithing in the early 19th century.[19] Each was apparently compact and, from when they were sold c. 1806,[20] without rights of common pasture. Those rights were apparently sold c. 1806 with the land called Woburn. Under the Act of 1808 the owner of Woburn farm, which was worked with Elms farm based in Minety, was allotted 123 a. in 1809.[21]

In 1840 there were 1,585 a. of grassland and 514 a. of arable in the parish. The part with the most arable remained that between the Cirencester–Malmesbury road and Hankerton village. To the west Bishoper farm was 407 a., including 170 a. in Hankerton, and Hankerton Field farm was 274 a. Based in the village Brook farm was 219 a. and Church farm 85 a. From Rookery Farm 172 a. in the parish were worked. To the east Manor was a pasture farm of 160 a. leased to the tenant of Bishoper farm; Dolman's farm, 137 a., included buildings at Bullock's Horn; Laurel farm was 89 a.; and Cloatley End farm was 79 a. Much land in the east and south was worked mainly from outside the parish: Elms farm included the old Cloatley common and land and buildings at Woburn, 239 a.; Woodward farm, based in Minety, included 29 a.; Summerhouse farm, based in Charlton, included 59 a. of the former Hankerton common in the purlieus; and two other farms based in Charlton, Old Park and Bambury Hill, included respectively 82 a. and 67 a. of Hankerton land.[22]

Between 1840 and 1939 arable farming in the parish declined further. There may have been less than 400 a. of arable in 1887 and no more than 200 a. in the 1930s. Cows, other cattle, sheep, and pigs were all kept.[23] Bishoper, Hankerton Field, and Brook remained the largest farms based in the parish. In 1926 Bishoper was 422 a. of which 171 a. were in Hankerton, Hankerton Field farm

[1] W.R.O. 212A/33/4, deed, Warneford to earl of Berks., 1693.   [2] Ibid. 88/2/37B.
[3] Ibid. 88/2/56–7; ibid. EA/132; Andrews and Dury, Map (W.R.S. viii), pls. 16–17.
[4] W.R.O. 88/2/37B.   [5] Ibid. 88/2/57.
[6] Ibid. 88/2/56–7; 88/5/8; 88/10/7, survey of Hankerton Field farm, 1808.   [7] Ibid. EA/132; ibid. tithe award.
[8] Ibid. 88/2/56; 88/10/9.
[9] Ibid. EA/132; ibid. tithe award.
[10] Ibid. 88/10/9; V.C.H. Wilts. iv. 88.
[11] Reg. Malm. i. 454.
[12] Ibid. 150–3; ii. 42; P.R.O., SC 6/Hen. VIII/3986, rot. 122.

[13] P.R.O., E 134/37 Eliz. I East./13.
[14] Ibid. C 66/738, m. 17; C 142/141, no. 11.
[15] W.R.O. 88/9/11; 177/22, deed, Warneford to Lattimer, 1646.
[16] P.R.O., C 142/141, no. 11.
[17] W.R.O., tithe award.
[18] Above, introduction; Andrews and Dury, Map (W.R.S. viii), pl. 17.
[19] W.R.O., tithe award.
[20] Above, manors.
[21] W.R.O., EA/132; below.   [22] W.R.O., tithe awards.
[23] P.R.O., MAF 68/1120, sheet 16; MAF 68/3850, no. 141; [1st] Land Util. Surv. Map, sheet 104.

was 304 a., and Brook 272 a. Other farms then based in the parish included Manor, 156 a., Rookery, 122 a. and other land in Crudwell, Dolman's, 136 a., Laurel, 90 a., and Cloatley End, 81 a. By 1926 Church farm had shrunk and Common End farm, 49 a. in 1926, had grown; Purlieus farm, 121 a., had been established on the old Hankerton purlieus; and Woburn, 63 a., had become a separate farm.[24]

After 1939 arable and stock farming both greatly increased. In 1977 there were 710 a. of arable and 901 cattle on farms based in the parish.[25] In 1988 c. 300 a., all arable, were in hand as part of Lord Suffolk's Charlton Park estate. Of the tenanted farms Bishoper, 458 a., was arable and dairy, Brook, 272 a., was arable.[26] Rookery, 120 a., was a mainly dairy farm.[27] East of Hankerton village much grassland was not intensively farmed. Further east the c. 300 a. of Elms farm and Purlieus farm were used with Home farm, Minety, and land in Charlton for dairy farming. A large dairy was built on Purlieus farm in 1969.[28]

Although Hankerton parish included much land which was within Braydon forest and its purlieus it was not well wooded. In 1840 several small woods totalled 23 a.,[29] and there was little more woodland in 1988.

A windmill stood on or near Windmill Hill in the later 13th century[30] and later 17th.[31] Its site, which may have been in Hankerton or Crudwell, is not known.

Few non-agricultural trades have flourished in Hankerton. References to a weaver in 1568,[32] a clothyard in 1700,[33] and a wool comber in 1710[34] are evidence of a local cloth industry. Bricks were made near Cloatley hamlet in the early 19th century.[35]

LOCAL GOVERNMENT. In the Middle Ages Malmesbury abbey's tenants in both Hankerton and Cloatley attended the abbey's courts held at Crudwell. To judge from the fact that they rendered cert money separately Hankerton and Cloatley were then separate tithings,[36] as they were later.[37] After the Dissolution the right to hold views of frankpledge and manor courts for Hankerton and Cloatley was granted separately with the respective manors.[38] For Hankerton, where copyhold tenure and open fields long survived, records exist in abundance; for Cloatley no court record survives.

From the mid 16th century to the mid 17th view of frankpledge with a court of the manor for Hankerton was usually held twice a year:[39] it may have been annual 1570–6. Leet jurisdiction was exercised throughout the period. In the early part the view proceeded on presentments of the tithingman, affirmed and supplemented by those of a jury, from the 1580s solely on the jurors' presentments. Bakers, tapsters, and butchers were presented; brawlers and players of prohibited games were punished; felony by tenants, including murder in 1571[40] and 1629,[41] was reported; in 1580 three were presented for not having bows and arrows for archery as required by a statute of 1542 which was invoked;[42] the lack of a rook net, required by statute, was presented in 1570 and 1573, and in 1574 a new rook net was displayed in court;[43] and an oath of allegiance was occasionally administered.[44] In 1583 a suspected thief and in 1586 a thief were punished in the stocks,[45] and in 1626 three men were forbidden to keep greyhounds.[46] By the 1620s, when a woman was required to find a male deputy,[47] the office of tithingman apparently rotated among the tenants. Under the jurisdiction of the manor court the homage presented normal business such as the deaths of tenants and dilapidated buildings, and increasingly the courts made orders to regulate the use of the open fields and common pastures and penalized misuse. Overstocking and inadequately maintained gates, boundaries, and watercourses were most frequently presented. A reeve, a hayward who was paid a salary by the tenants,[48] an agrarian watchman ('agrophilax'), and overseers of the fields were appointed.[49] Unlicensed undertenants were prohibited and in the 1640s orders made to prevent tenants introducing to the parish any thought likely to need relief.[50] The courts also heard pleas between tenants, settling some by agreement, some by arbitration, and some by wager of law.[51]

From the later 17th century to the early 19th the principal business of the courts was to make rules for husbandry.[52] From the 1670s the court, usually called view of frankpledge with court baron, was annual, and from then its records survive mainly in the form of a warrant from the steward ordering the tithingman or the constable to convene the court, a list of those who ought to attend handed in by the tithingman, and the bill of presentments drawn up by the foreman of the jury. A single body acted as homage and jury and little was done under leet jurisdiction. Old orders governing the use of the open fields and common

[24] W.R.O., G 7/501/1.
[25] P.R.O., MAF 68/5556, no. 141.
[26] Inf. from Mr. A. Witchell, Messrs. Humberts, 10 St. Mary Street, Chippenham.
[27] Inf. from Mr. D. J. Sheppard, Rookery Ho.
[28] Inf. from Mr. P. H. Crocker, Home Farm, Minety.
[29] W.R.O., tithe award.
[30] Reg. Malm. ii. 347–8.
[31] W.R.O. 88/2/26, view 11 Apr. 1672.
[32] P.R.O., REQ 2/73/36.   [33] W.N. & Q. ii. 552.
[34] W.R.O. 88/3/2, letter of attorney, 1710.
[35] Ibid. tithe award.
[36] P.R.O., SC 6/Hen. VIII/3986, rot. 122.
[37] W.R.O., A 1/345/195–6.
[38] P.R.O., C 66/738, m. 17; ibid. E 318/Box 32/1820, rot. 2d.
[39] Para. based on W.R.O. 88/2/21–5; 88/2/29; 88/2/33.
[40] Ibid. 88/2/21, view 26 Sept. 13 Eliz. I.

[41] Ibid. 88/2/24, view 14 Apr. 5 Chas. I.
[42] Ibid. 88/2/21, view 22 Sept. 22 Eliz. I; 33 Hen. VIII, c. 9.
[43] W.R.O. 88/2/21, views 30 Sept. 12 Eliz. I, 2 Oct. 15 Eliz. I, 22 Sept. 16 Eliz. I; 24 Hen. VIII, c. 10; 8 Eliz. I, c. 15.
[44] W.R.O. 88/2/24, views 15 Sept. 6 Chas. I, 14 Apr. 13 Chas. I.
[45] Ibid. 88/2/22, views 7 Mar. 1582, 30 Mar. 28 Eliz. I.
[46] Ibid. 88/2/24, view 27 Sept. 2 Chas. I.
[47] Ibid. view 19 Apr. 2 Chas. I.
[48] Ibid. 88/2/21, view 13 Oct. 14 Eliz. I.
[49] Ibid. 88/2/24, view 21 Sept. 1 Chas. I.
[50] Ibid. view 21 Apr. 18 Chas. I; 88/2/25, view 10 Oct. 22 Chas. I.
[51] Ibid. 88/2/21, views 28 Mar. 22 Eliz. I, 24 Oct. 1581; 88/2/22, view 30 Mar. 28 Eliz. I.
[52] Para. based on ibid. 88/2/14–16; 88/2/26–7; 88/3/2.

pastures were repeated or varied and new ones made, officers were appointed to supervise such use, orders to repair boundaries, gates, and watercourses continued to be made, and sometimes a common fund was raised to repair boundaries.[53] In the later 18th century most presentments were of rules to be observed rather than particular transgressions or nuisances, but they were not stereotyped. In 1799, for example, orders restricted the amount of furze to be cut, turf dug, and geese, cattle, and sheep kept on the commons.[54] After inclosure in 1809[55] fewer orders were made but matters such as nuisances and encroachments on the waste, the feeding of unmarked cattle in the lanes, and the need to repair the common pound continued to be presented.[56] For much of the period courts baron were also held to witness surrenders of and admittances to copyholds.

By deed of 1554 Thomas Walton, the lessee of Crudwell rectory estate, gave a church house in Hankerton to relieve poverty and repair highways. In 1671 it was being leased for £2 a year,[57] but its later history is obscure.

The parish spent £67 on poor relief in 1775–6, an average of £119 in the years 1782–5, and £232 in 1802–3 when 27 adults and 36 children were relieved permanently and 17 occasionally. Spending was below average for a parish of its size in 1814–15, when £105 was spent and 18 adults were permanently relieved,[58] and remained so until the mid 1820s. Over £300 was spent in 1824–5 and between 1828–9 and 1833–4, and over £400 in 1829–30: those sums were above average for such a parish.[59] Hankerton joined Malmesbury poor-law union in 1835[60] and became part of North Wiltshire district in 1974.[61]

CHURCH. Hankerton church was built as a chapel of Crudwell church in or before the early 12th century. By 1222 a vicarage of Hankerton had been ordained.[62] The vicar had cure of souls but the church remained dependent on Crudwell[63] until 1445 when a graveyard at Hankerton was licensed.[64] In 1954 the vicarage was united with the vicarage of Charlton with Brokenborough; in 1987 it instead became part of a new benefice with Ashley, Long Newnton (both now Glos.), Crudwell, and Oaksey.[65]

Until the Reformation all known presentations of vicars of Hankerton were by rectors of Crudwell:[66] the rector's right was tested and confirmed in 1379[67] and 1410.[68] Thomas Walton, while lessee of the Crudwell rectory estate, presented in 1552, and in 1600 Robert Beale presented a vicar under the lease to Walton.[69] In the later 16th century the lord of Hankerton manor, who owned the corn tithes,[70] claimed the advowson, and in 1590 the right to present at two of every three turns,[71] but did not present. An incumbent was appointed in 1647,[72] in 1662 the rector of Crudwell was called vicar of Hankerton,[73] and c. 1663 the new rector of Crudwell apparently appointed a vicar.[74] In 1699 the rector of Crudwell presented himself as vicar,[75] in 1717 the same rector presented his son,[76] in 1723 the rector of Crudwell was presented as vicar by his mother,[77] and in 1763, after that vicar's death, the bishop collated by lapse to Hankerton the man who became rector of Crudwell the same year.[78] The next rector presented himself as vicar of Hankerton in 1785,[79] as did his own successor in 1839.[80] That rector presented a vicar of Hankerton in 1855 and 1864.[81] In 1898, with the bishop's consent, Georgina, the wife of H. K. Adkin, later Knight-Adkin, rector of Crudwell, bought the advowson, and in 1903 presented Adkin to be vicar; in 1910 she again presented. In 1920 she transferred the advowson to the bishop of Bristol, who shared with the Crown the patronage of the united benefice of 1954–87, and with others the patronage after 1987. In 1961 the archbishop of Canterbury presented by lapse.[82]

The vicarage, worth £8 10s. in 1535,[83] £45 in 1650,[84] and £269 c. 1830, was of average wealth for the deanery.[85] In the later 12th century and earlier 13th the rector of Crudwell may have been entitled to all the tithes of Hankerton. When the corn tithes were appropriated by Malmesbury abbey in 1222 the remaining tithes may already have been an endowment of the vicarage,[86] as they were later.[87] By 1582 the tithe from meadow land in the open fields, apart from demesne meadow, had been replaced by a meadow of 1½ a.[88] The vicar's tithes were valued at £280 in 1840 and commuted.[89] The rector of Crudwell had 1 yardland of glebe in Hankerton.[90] From 1410 or earlier the vicar had a house,[91] and in the 17th century a house and 5 a.[92] The rector's yardland was transferred to the vicar, presumably in the 18th century, and there were 17 a. of glebe in 1840.[93] The vicarage

[53] W.R.O. 88/3/2, ct. papers, 1713.
[54] Ibid. ct. papers, 1799.
[55] Above, econ. hist.
[56] W.R.O. 88/3/2, ct. papers, 1826.
[57] Ibid. D 1/24/104/2.
[58] *Poor Law Abstract, 1804*, 566–7; *1818*, 498–9.
[59] *Poor Rate Returns, 1816–21*, 189; *1822–4*, 228; *1825–9*, 219; *1830–4*, 212.
[60] *Poor Law Com. 2nd Rep.* App. D, 559.
[61] O.S. Map 1/100,000, admin. areas, Wilts. (1974 edn.).
[62] *Sar. Chart. and Doc.* (Rolls Ser.), 119–20; below.
[63] *Reg. Hallum* (Cant. & York Soc.), pp. 142–3, where Hankerton is wrongly identified as Hannington.
[64] W.R.O., D 1/2/10, f. (2nd foliation) 71.
[65] Ch. Com. file, NB 5/3B.
[66] Phillipps, *Wilts. Inst.* (index in *W.A.M.* xxviii. 221).
[67] W.R.O. 88/1/10A.
[68] *Reg. Hallum* (Cant. & York Soc.), pp. 142–3.
[69] Phillipps, *Wilts. Inst.* i. 215; ii. 1; W.R.O. 88/1/10A.
[70] Above, manors.
[71] *W.N. & Q.* viii. 446–8; W.R.O. 88/2/43.
[72] W.R.O. 88/1/10A.

[73] Ibid. D 1/54/1/1, no. 58.
[74] Ibid. D 1/24/104/2; ibid. 88/1/10A; *W.N. & Q.* vii. 549.
[75] Phillipps, *Wilts. Inst.* ii. 43, 45.
[76] Ibid. 54; W.R.O. 2050/1.
[77] Phillipps, *Wilts. Inst.* ii. 55, 58; *Complete Peerage*, vii. 72–5.
[78] Phillipps, *Wilts. Inst.* ii. 81.
[79] Ibid. 91, 93.
[80] Bristol R.O., EP/A/1/4.
[81] *Clergy List* (1859, 1866).
[82] Ibid. (1915); *Crockford* (1907 and later edns.); Ch. Com. file, F 6007; ibid. 82199; ibid. NB 5/3B.
[83] *Valor Eccl.* (Rec. Com.), ii. 136.
[84] *W.A.M.* xli. 7.
[85] *Rep. Com. Eccl. Revenues*, 836–7.
[86] *Sar. Chart. and Doc.* (Rolls Ser.), 119–20.
[87] W.R.O., D 1/24/104/1.
[88] Ibid. 88/2/21, view 22 May 24 Eliz. I.
[89] Ibid. tithe award.
[90] Ibid. 88/2/22, view 7 Mar. 1582; 88/2/49; *Sar. Chart. and Doc.* (Rolls Ser.), 119–20.
[91] *Reg. Hallum* (Cant. & York Soc.), p. 143.
[92] W.R.O., D 1/24/104/1–2.
[93] Ibid. tithe award.

house, later called Hankerton Priory, and 6 a. were sold in 1903.[94] The house has small north and east ranges, each with moulded beams and apparently of the earlier 16th century: c. 1830 a taller block was built in the angle of the two ranges, and in 1903 the house was extended westwards and northwards to designs by H. S. de Bertodano.[95] A new vicarage house was built in 1905–6, also to designs by de Bertodano:[96] that house was sold in 1954.[97]

In the Middle Ages c. 4 a. for an obit and 1 a. for a light in the church were given.[98] In 1662 there was no surplice, Book of Homilies, or copy of Jewell's *Apology* in the church. The minister, who used the Elizabethan prayer book before the Restoration, was not licensed to preach: he was probably John Hopkins, vicar from c. 1663.[99] In the 18th century, when the rector of Crudwell was usually vicar of Hankerton, curates were often employed, and from 1782 to 1785, when he was instituted as vicar, the rector, James Wiggett, was himself curate.[1] In 1783 he held a Sunday service every week, celebrated communion four times a year, and catechized.[2] From 1785 to 1855 and from 1903 to 1909 the rector of Crudwell was again vicar.[3] In 1910 communion was celebrated 64 times and matins were said daily; in 1938 communion was celebrated 31 times, 23 times in 1950.[4] The church was served by priests-in-charge from 1945 to 1954.[5]

In 1706 Lady Frances Winchcombe gave a rent charge from land in Hankerton to provide Bibles and prayer books for poor children of Hankerton and other parishes. Hankerton's share, £1 a year, was given to the Sunday school in the 19th century[6] and spent on books in the early 20th.[7] From 1979 the charity was administered with the parish's eleemosynary charities.[8]

The church of *HOLY CROSS*, so called in 1763,[9] consists of a chancel, a nave with north aisle and south porch, and a west tower. The tower is of ashlar, the remainder of stone rubble with ashlar dressings. On its outside wall the nave has an early 12th-century animal-head stop on each side of the south doorway, and the whole nave is probably of that date. The aisle and porch were built in the early 13th century, and the chancel arch is early 14th-century. Apart from the triple lancet at the east end of the aisle, all the windows were renewed in the 15th century or early 16th, and the tower bears a date stone for 1531. The chancel was severely dilapidated in 1553[10] and, since in 1585 it was said to have been down 30

or more years,[11] was presumably demolished about then. In the early 19th century the east end of the nave was screened.[12] A new chancel was built in 1904.[13] The shouldered south doorway, matching a blocked north doorway, has been given a two-centred head, and building in the angle formed by the tower and aisle removed. Inside the church a wall tablet by Joseph Nollekens was put up in 1775 to commemorate the Earle family, and in the churchyard is the base of a stone cross.

The church had no plate in 1553. A cup with a paten cover, dated 1577, was given later[14] and belonged to the parish in 1988.[15] Of the four bells in the church in 1553 three survive. The present tenor is probably of the period 1300–50, the treble was cast by Thomas Jefferies c. 1530–40 and (iii) by Henry Jefferies c. 1540–50, and (ii) was cast in 1613 by a Purdue, probably at Bristol by Roger Purdue.[16] The registers begin in 1699 and, apart from 1719–21, are complete.[17]

NONCONFORMITY. There was dissent in Hankerton in the 1660s and 1670s:[18] in 1676 a papist and eight protestant nonconformists lived in the parish.[19] Independent meeting houses were certified in 1775 and 1800, a Calvinistic Methodist meeting house in 1809, and other meeting houses for dissenters in 1831 and 1833.[20] The Rehoboth chapel for Strict Baptists was built in 1837.[21] The pastor in the mid 19th century, William Beard, achieved prominence in the sect as the founder of a Strict Baptist chapel in Birmingham in 1854.[22] On Census Sunday in 1851 his two services at Hankerton were attended by 100 and 120.[23] Services were held only occasionally c. 1968[24] and the chapel was closed in 1971.[25]

EDUCATION. There was apparently no school in the parish until 1827 when the wife and daughter-in-law of Thomas, earl of Suffolk and of Berkshire, began to pay for 25 children to be taught. The school, attended by 35 in 1833, was presumably in Hankerton tithing. Another school, presumably in Cloatley tithing, may also have been started c. 1827. In 1833 it was attended by 15, of whom 6 were paid for by a daughter of Joseph Pitt, the owner of Manor farm.[26] A National school was built c. 1850–2 and was well run in 1858 when 40–50 were taught.[27] Average attendance was 42 in 1876,[28] 28 in 1902,[29] 35 in 1906–7, and 18 in

[94] Ch. Com. file, K 9109.
[95] Plans in Hankerton Priory.
[96] W.R.O., D 1/11, Hankerton, 1906.
[97] Ch. Com. file 95738.
[98] *Cal. Pat.* 1548–9, 187, 324.
[99] *W.N. & Q.* vii. 549; W.R.O., D 1/54/1/1, no. 58.
[1] W.R.O., D 1/48/4; ibid. bishop's transcripts, bdles. 2–3.
[2] *Vis. Queries, 1783* (W.R.S. xxvii), pp. 81, 114.
[3] Phillipps, *Wilts. Inst.* ii. 93; *Clergy List* (1859 and later edns.); *Crockford* (1896 and later edns.); W.R.O. 2050/2; Bristol R.O., EP/A/3/133.
[4] W.R.O. 2050/7–9.   [5] Ibid. 2050/2.
[6] *Endowed Char. Wilts.* (N. Div.), 499, 501; above, Charlton, church.
[7] W.R.O., Char. Com., Hankerton.
[8] Below, charities.
[9] J. Ecton, *Thesaurus* (1763), 403.
[10] W.R.O., D 1/43/1, f. 135.   [11] Ibid. D 1/43/6, f. 33A.
[12] *Gent. Mag.* lxxvi (1), 209.
[13] Bristol R.O., EP/A/22/1/77.

[14] Nightingale, *Wilts. Plate*, 200.
[15] Inf. from Mr. R. G. Ferris, 18 Follyfield.
[16] Ibid.; Walters, *Wilts. Bells*, 95.
[17] W.R.O. 2050/1–6. Bishop's transcripts for 1607–9, 1619–23, 1632–5, and 1666–79 are ibid.
[18] Ibid. D 1/54/1/1, no. 58; D 1/54/6/1, no. 37; Williams, *Cath. Recusancy* (Cath. Rec. Soc.), 283–4, 298, 348.
[19] *Compton Census*, ed. Whiteman, 128.
[20] *Meeting Ho. Certs.* (W.R.S. xl), pp. 30, 55, 64, 126, 133.
[21] Ibid. p. 145; P.R.O., HO 129/252/2/9/10.
[22] R. W. Oliver, *Strict Bapt. Chapels Eng.* (Strict Bapt. Hist. Soc.), v. 30 and pl. 12; *V.C.H. Warws.* vii. 442.
[23] P.R.O., HO 129/252/2/9/10.
[24] Oliver, op. cit. 30.   [25] Inf. from Mr. Ferris.
[26] *Educ. of Poor Digest*, 1027; *Educ. Enq. Abstract*, 1038; above, manors.
[27] *Acct. of Wilts. Schs.* 25; W.R.O., F 8/205/4.
[28] *Return of Public Elem. Schs. 1875–6* [C. 1882], pp. 282–3, H.C. (1877), lxvii.
[29] W.R.O., F 8/220/1.

1921–2. The school was closed in 1922 and re-opened in 1930. The numbers attending it were again small,[30] however, and in 1966 it was again closed.[31]

CHARITIES FOR THE POOR. By will proved 1748 Mary Panting gave £10 to the second poor of Hankerton parish. That sum was added to £42, the donor of which is unknown, and invested as the Poor's Money. In the late 18th century the income was £1 15s. 6d. and sums of c. 2s. were given away every few years. In the 20th distribution was quinquennial: in 1903 c. 2s. 6d. was given to each of 19 married couples, 6 widows, 3 widowers, and 1 spinster.[32] In 1924 money was given to 33 families.[33]

In 1848 Hannah Ludlow gave 5 a. in Hankerton to provide payments each year to six male, married, agricultural labourers over 50 among the second poor of the parish. In 1905 c. £11 was given away.[34] In 1931 the payments were of £1 16s. 9d. After the Second World War the beneficiaries were reduced to five and the sixth share of the money was paid to a repair fund.[35] Five parishioners shared £13 in 1960, £60 in 1971.[36]

By Scheme of 1979 the Poor's Money, Hannah Ludlow's, and Lady Frances Winchcombe's charities were administered jointly to relieve need generally in Hankerton parish. Hannah Ludlow's 5 a. were then being leased for £200 a year and the three charities had £496 stock.[37] In the late 1980s the income of c. £200 a year was used to help old people.[38]

HULLAVINGTON

HULLAVINGTON church is 6 km. SSW. of Malmesbury and 9 km. NNW. of Chippenham.[39] The parish, 4 km. from north to south and 7 km. from east to west, contains Hullavington village, Bradfield hamlet, and the site of the former hamlet of Surrendell. In 1084 Surrendell was in Dunlow hundred and was later a tithing of that hundred which was absorbed by Chippenham hundred:[40] references to a road called the Hundred way[41] and to a field and farmsteads called Dunley[42] suggest that the meeting place of Dunlow hundred was in the tithing. Hullavington parish was 3,255 a. (1,317 ha.) until 1884 when 49 a. of Norton at its north-east corner were transferred to it.[43] At its south-west corner 216 a. were transferred to Grittleton in 1934, and in 1989 the parish was 1,249 ha. (3,087 a.).[44]

For more than half its length the parish boundary follows roads and streams: the Roman Foss Way marked the western boundary, Gauze brook part of the southern and a small part of the northern. Hullavington's boundaries were recited in no early charter that survives, but references to the streams dividing Hullavington from Grittleton and Norton and to the road dividing Hullavington from Corston in Malmesbury in early recitals of the boundaries of those other places[45] suggest that they are early, and the Foss Way is likely to have been an early boundary of Hullavington as it was of Norton and Grittleton.[46] A road marked the whole boundary between Hullavington and Surrendell, Gauze brook most of that between Hullavington and Bradfield.[47]

The parish slopes gently downwards from west to east. The highest point is 126 m. in the south-west corner, the lowest below 76 m. in the north-east corner. Clay of the Forest Marble outcrops in the higher west part of the parish, Cornbrash across the centre, and Kellaways Clay in the lower north-east part. Kellaways Sand outcrops as a low ridge north-east of Hullavington village. Gauze brook has deposited a narrow strip of alluvium across the parish and more in the north-east corner.[48] The Kellaways Clay favours pasture, the Cornbrash tillage; the clay in the west has been used for both. Hullavington's open fields were on Cornbrash south and east of the village, on clay north-west of it.[49] Bradfield's land was mainly Cornbrash and Kellaways Clay, Surrendell's entirely clay of the Forest Marble. Some of the flat land south-east of Hullavington village was used for an airfield in the mid 20th century.[50]

The Malmesbury–Chippenham road, called Kingway c. 1100,[51] crosses the eastern corner of the parish. Many lanes link Hullavington village with its fields and neighbours, and their pattern has changed little since the mid 18th century.[52] Hullavington Street, West Field Lane leading south from it, and Down Lane leading north from it may have been parts of a Corston–Grittleton

[30] W.R.O., F 8, corresp. file for Hankerton sch.; *Bd. of Educ., List 21, 1908* (H.M.S.O.), 503; *1922*, 360; *1927*, 360; *1932*, 408; *1936*, 424.
[31] W.R.O., list of primary schs. closed since 1946.
[32] Ibid. wills, archd. Wilts., 1748, Panting; *Endowed Char. Wilts.* (N. Div.), 498–500.
[33] W.R.O., Char. Com., Hankerton.
[34] *Endowed Char. Wilts.* (N. Div.), 501–3.
[35] W.R.O., Char. Com., Hankerton.
[36] Ibid. 1227/2; 1227, par. council min. 1961–75.
[37] Char. Com. file. For Winchcombe's, above, church.
[38] Inf. from Mr. Ferris.
[39] This article was written in 1989. Maps used include O.S. Maps 1/50,000, sheet 173 (1974 edn.); 1/25,000, ST 88, ST 98 (1958–9 edns.); 6", Wilts. XII–XIII (1888–9 and later edns.).

[40] *V.C.H. Wilts.* ii, p. 205; iv. 298; v. 3.
[41] Eton Coll. Mun. 4/7.
[42] T. Gore, 'Syntagma Genealogicum' (MS. in V. & A. Mus., microfilm copy in W.R.O.), p. 211; W.R.O. 212B/3551; below.
[43] *Census*, 1891; O.S. Map 1/2,500, Wilts. XIII. 5 (1900 edn.); W.R.O., tithe award.
[44] *V.C.H. Wilts.* iv. 350; *Census*, 1971.
[45] For the road, O.S. Map 1", sheet 34 (1828 edn.).
[46] *Arch. Jnl.* lxxvi. 221, 223, 252; lxxvii. 45.
[47] W.R.O. 1553/101.
[48] Geol. Surv. Maps 1", solid and drift, sheets 251 (1970 edn.), 265 (1965 edn.).   [49] Below, econ. hist.
[50] Below.
[51] *Arch. Jnl.* lxxvii. 45.
[52] W.R.O. 1553/101.

road but, if so, the northern end, which may have been the lane called Corston Lane in 1592, had gone out of use by the mid 18th century.[53] The Street and Down Lane make a crossroads with Bradfield Lane, leading from Norton and Easton Grey, and Topsail Lane, so called in 1764, which divides into branches leading north-east and, as Tining Lane, south-east to the Malmesbury–Chippenham road.[54] In 1756 the Malmesbury–Chippenham road was turnpiked,[55] and in 1820 West Field Lane, Hullavington Street, and Topsail Lane and its north-east branch to the Malmesbury–Chippenham road were turnpiked to form a link between that road and a Draycot Cerne to Grittleton turnpike road south of the parish:[56] all the turnpike roads in Hullavington parish were disturnpiked in 1874.[57] At the north-west corner of the parish the Hullavington–Sherston road apparently followed the parish boundary until, presumably at inclosure c. 1611,[58] a new straight section, Town Leaze Lane, was made on the south-west; and at the time of further inclosure c. 1670 a new road, presumably Oarhedge Lane or Dean Bottom Lane, was made for carrying tithes from Surrendell to Hullavington.[59] Three lanes in the west have gone out of use: in 1764 neither Oarhedge Lane nor Dean Bottom Lane reached Surrendell,[60] in the early 19th century a road from Alderton and Luckington to Leigh Delamere across the south-west corner of the parish was closed,[61] and Pig Lane, leading from Sherston towards Leigh Delamere and marking the boundaries between Surrendell's land and Hullavington's and Hullavington and Grittleton parishes, has become impassable near Surrendell Farm where it has never been made up. For nearly the whole of its length on Hullavington's west boundary the Bath–Cirencester section of the Foss Way was made up as part of a Sherston to Yatton Keynell road. The road leading towards Castle Combe along the parish's south-east boundary between the Malmesbury–Chippenham and Draycot Cerne to Grittleton roads went out of use after the road through Hullavington Street was turnpiked in 1820.[62]

In 1903 the main London and south Wales railway was opened across Hullavington parish with, north of the village, a station with a siding and a weighbridge.[63] Hullavington station was closed to passengers in 1961 and entirely in 1965.[64]

A long barrow south-west of Surrendell Farm, and what may have been a cromlech to the east, are the only prehistoric remains to have been found in the parish.[65] Settlement was nucleated, and Hullavington is a street village. In the Middle Ages Bradfield and Surrendell seem to have been hamlets but later were single farmsteads; several other farmsteads were built in the west part of the parish, but there has been little new settlement away from

the village in the east. With 177 poll-tax payers the parish was populous in 1377.[66] The population rose rapidly in the early 19th century, from 395 in 1801 to 708 in 1851, and reached a 19th-century peak of 734 in 1871. It had fallen to 543 by 1891, was inflated to 823 by the presence of c. 275 building the railway line in 1901, and reached a 20th-century low point of 478 in 1921. The population was reduced by c. 20 when part of the parish was transferred to Grittleton, but in the 1950s and 1960s new housing in Hullavington village and on the airfield led to a rapid increase, from 600 in 1951 to 1,123 in 1971. The population was 1,021 in 1981.[67]

HULLAVINGTON church is near the middle of the Street on the west side. The church and Hullavington manor belonged to the abbey of St. Victor-en-Caux (Seine Maritime) in the earlier Middle Ages and Court House north-west of the church is presumably on the site of the chief messuage of the manor. The abbey had a priory in England, and between the mid 12th century and the early 15th monks may sometimes have lived in the chief messuage.[68] Its buildings were in poor condition in 1416: rooms and a chapel on the east side of the hall, a room on the west side of the hall, the kitchen, an east gatehouse, and a great barn and other farm buildings were all said to be unroofed or to have collapsed.[69] Either those dilapidations were exaggerated or much had been repaired by 1443 when the hall was said to be well built. It still incorporated a chapel, had rooms and a kitchen to the north, a granary to the south, and a gatehouse.[70] Court House has been adapted from a medieval building of which one two-centred timber doorway survives. The house has a central cross passage with the hall south of it. In the early 17th century, when the house was lived in by Thomas Ivy,[71] an upper floor and a chimney stack were built in the hall and a north crossing and, to the south, an east cross wing were added or rebuilt. A two-storeyed east porch was built, probably in the later 17th century. In the early or mid 18th century, when it was lived in by the Jacob family,[72] a room in the south wing was panelled, a rear projection containing a new staircase was built, and much of the house was refenestrated. The whole house was reroofed in the 18th century. An upstairs room contains reset early 17th-century oak panelling.

The pattern of settlement in Hullavington Street suggests early planning. On both sides copyhold farmhouses faced the Street and behind them were farm buildings and small inclosures of pasture; on each side the north–south boundaries of the plots joined to make long clear boundaries parallel to the Street. Those boundaries were possibly fixed in the 1440s when hedges were planted at

[53] Ibid.; Eton Coll. Mun. 4/175.
[54] W.R.O. 1553/101.   [55] L.J. xxviii. 526.
[56] Ibid. liii. 154; W.R.O., A 1/370/24.
[57] V.C.H. Wilts. iv. 269; 14 & 15 Vic. c. 76 (Local and Personal).   [58] Eton Coll. Mun. 4/235.
[59] P.R.O., E 134/12 Wm. III East./2.
[60] W.R.O. 1553/101.
[61] Ibid. tithe award; O.S. Map 1", sheet 34 (1828 edn.).
[62] C. Greenwood, Map of Wilts. (1820); O.S. Map 6", Wilts. XIII (1888 edn.).
[63] W.A.M. lxxiv/lxxv. 176.

[64] C. R. Clinker, Clinker's Reg. Closed Passenger Sta. 1830–1980, p. 66.
[65] W.A.M. xliii. 227; Aubrey, Topog. Coll. ed. Jackson, 115.
[66] V.C.H. Wilts. iv. 308–9.
[67] Ibid. 325, 350; Census, 1971; 1981.
[68] Below, manors. The suggestion, in V.C.H. Wilts. iii. 394, that monks lived at Bradfield is implausible.
[69] Cal. Inq. Misc. vii, pp. 300–1.
[70] Eton Coll. Mun. 4/96.
[71] W.A.M. xix. 262; below, manors.
[72] J. Badeni, Wilts. Forefathers, 76–7; below, manors.

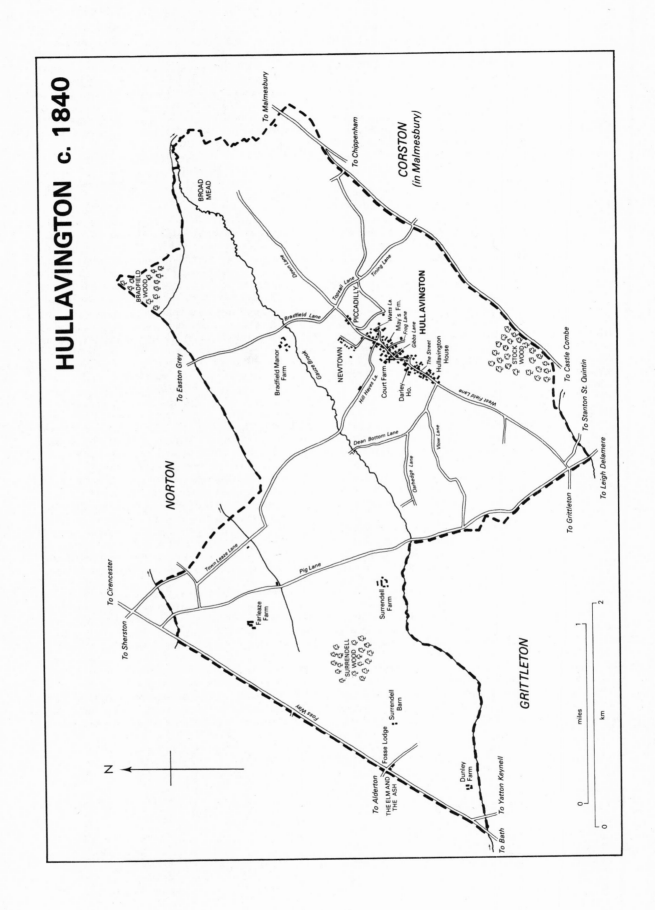

HULLAVINGTON c. 1840

east and west Townsend,[73] presumably to separate the fields from the farmyards behind the Street. That was the pattern of settlement in 1764 and it remained visible in 1989. Court House, the demesne farmhouse, and May's Farm, possibly the farmhouse of a large freehold, were apparently the only substantial houses behind the Street in 1764.[74] May's Farm is a 17th-century stone house, L-shaped and gabled, with an 18th-century rear extension: the house has end chimneys which may have replaced a central chimney, and its main west front has been much altered. Of the farmhouses facing the Street in 1764 about nine survive: characteristically they are of local stone, with roofs of stone slates, and gabled, and nearly all seem to have been built in the 17th century. Two other large houses were built in the Street between 1764 and 1840, Darley House on the west side near the church, and Hullavington House on the east side near the south end; in the same period the vicarage house was enlarged.[75] Darley House was restored in 1914.[76] The Star, on the west side, and the Queen's Head, a possibly 18th-century building on the east side, were open as public houses in 1819[77] and 1989. About 1900 the Star was rebuilt, and in 1903 the Queen's Head was refronted.[78] Few cottages earlier than 1700 survive in the Street, but many cottages and small houses of the 18th and 19th centuries are on both sides. Eton College (Bucks.) was lord of Hullavington manor[79] and in 1935 and 1936 Eton College Housing Society built Jubilee Cottages,[80] two terraces of four angled to look like a crescent, and there has been other 20th-century infilling. A church house was built on the east side of the churchyard facing the Street[81] between 1504 and 1535. In the 19th century it was an inn called the Plough,[82] closed by 1877, and it was demolished in the late 19th century.[83]

Until the later 20th century all Hullavington's land was worked from buildings in the Street,[84] on each side of which lanes led between the houses to the farm buildings behind. In 1764 a few houses and cottages stood in the lanes, especially Watts Lane, where an early 18th-century house survives, and Frog Lane,[85] and in the earlier 19th century a nonconformist chapel was built in each of three of them.[86] After the Second World War new housing was built on the pasture closes behind both sides of the Street and at the north end. On the west side 22 council houses were built in Greens Close in 1950, 4 council bungalows in Hill Hayes Lane in 1956[87] and 14 in Latimer c. 1976,[88] and a total of c. 60 private houses and bungalows in Parklands and Mere Avenue in the late 1960s. On the east side 4 council houses were built in Watts Lane in 1956,[89] and in the 1970s and 1980s small groups of larger private houses were built in Royal Field Close, Frog Lane, and Watts Lane, and larger groups north of Watts Lane and near the south end of the Street. Farm buildings behind the Street were still in use only on the east side at the north end in 1989: others to survive, especially in the centre on the west side, had been converted for residence.

A short distance north of the village a small house was built in a back lane west of the Street in the late 18th century. In the early 19th century cottages, one of which is dated 1829, were built in the lane, and in 1840 a nonconformist chapel and c. 10 cottages were there.[90] More small cottages had been built by 1885 when the settlement was called Newtown, more were built in the late 19th century or early 20th,[91] and in 1937 eight council houses were built.[92] The building of houses at the north end of Hullavington village after 1945 joined Newtown to the main part of the village. Also a short distance north of the village a small group of cottages on the waste from 1764 or earlier[93] was called Piccadilly in the later 19th century:[94] a pair of late 19th-century cottages was on the site in 1989.

Until the 20th century the only cottages away from the village were a few in Hill Hayes Lane where several of the 19th and 20th centuries survive. Three cottages were built near Hullavington station c. 1903, and in the later 20th century four houses were built near Bradfield Manor Farm and four bungalows at a market garden beside the Malmesbury–Chippenham road. R.A.F. Hullavington was opened in 1937.[95] The airfield included c. 159 a. south and south-east of Hullavington village but most of the runways were in Malmesbury parish and most of the offices in Stanton St. Quintin. Two pairs of hangars were erected in Hullavington parish, and near Hullavington village, to which Frog Lane connected them, 94 houses were built in Wellington Place in the period 1955–7.[96]

At the crossroads north of the village a cemetery, in the charge of a parochial burial committee, was opened in 1922[97] and a telephone exchange was built in 1939.[98] In Hill Hayes Lane a new village hall was built in 1971.[99]

BRADFIELD. It is likely that Bradfield was a hamlet in the early Middle Ages, when Bradfield manor apparently had customary tenants, and in 1377 Bradfield had 21 poll-tax payers. In the later 15th century, however, Bradfield manor house and its

[73] Eton Coll. Mun. 4/98, view 30 Sept. 1445.
[74] W.R.O. 1553/101; below, manors.
[75] W.R.O. 1553/101; ibid. tithe award; below, church.
[76] Eton Coll. Mun. 286/2.
[77] W.R.O., A 1/370/24.
[78] Date on bldg.
[79] Below, manors.
[80] Eton Coll. Mun. 353/1; dates on bldgs.
[81] Watercolour in possession of Mrs. J. Giles, 1 Gibbs Lane; see plate facing p. 108.
[82] Eton Coll. Mun. 4/233; 49/228.
[83] Ibid. 118/2, sale partic. 1877; O.S. Maps 6″, Wilts. XIII (1888 edn.), XIII. SW. (1900 edn.).
[84] Below, econ. hist.
[85] W.R.O. 1553/101.

[86] Below, nonconf.
[87] W.R.O., G 7/505/1.
[88] Ibid. A 1/355/469/2; A 1/355/474/2.
[89] Ibid. G 7/505/1.
[90] Ibid. tithe award; O.S. Map 1″, sheet 34 (1828 edn.).
[91] O.S. Maps 6″, Wilts. XIII (1888 and later edns.).
[92] W.R.O., G 7/505/1.
[93] Ibid. 1553/101.
[94] O.S. Map 6″, Wilts. XIII (1888 edn.).
[95] C. Ashworth, Action Stations, v. 104. More about the sta. is below, Stanton St. Quintin, introduction.
[96] Inf. from Defence Land Agent, Durrington.
[97] W.R.O. 1675/1.
[98] Ibid. G 7/505/1.
[99] Char. Com. file.

farmstead were almost certainly the only buildings there.[1] In 1989 a pair of mid 19th-century cottages and a later 20th-century bungalow were the only others, but the nearby buildings between them and the old Hullavington station again gave Bradfield the appearance of a hamlet.

SURRENDELL was presumably a hamlet in 1249 when it had a church and five men living there were named,[2] and was probably a group of farmsteads near the site of the present Surrendell Farm. A reference to Surrendell street in 1316,[3] however, may not have been to a village street. Surrendell had 37 poll-tax payers in 1377.[4] A new manor house was built between 1545 and 1575, and in the early 17th century, probably shortly before 1631 and apparently to replace the former chief messuage which stood in 1577, Surrendell Farm was built.[5] From the 17th century new farmsteads stood elsewhere and the hamlet may have consisted of only the church, manor house, farmhouse, and farm buildings. The church was in ruins in the late 17th century,[6] and the manor house was demolished c. 1871 when a fireplace was taken from it for use elsewhere.[7] The manor house stood near and to the west of Surrendell Farm: a drawing of part of what survived in the mid 19th century shows a gabled range of the earlier 17th century with mullioned and transomed windows.[8] Surrendell Farm consists of a single range of two storeys and attics and has three large gables to its north and south elevations and ovolo-moulded stone-framed windows. A large granary was built against the east end in the 18th century. Beside Pig Lane a pair of cottages was built in the earlier 20th century[9] and rebuilt as a house in the later 20th.

Farleaze Farm, north of Surrendell Farm, is a **T**-shaped house of the earlier 17th century with additions of the later 18th and of c. 1930. Its farm buildings include a stone barn of the late 18th or earlier 19th century. North of it a pair of cottages was built in the early 20th century[10] and another pair in 1946.[11] North-west of Farleaze Farm a farmstead called Kingsthorns standing in 1736[12] was taken down soon after 1820.[13] Dunley Farm was in the west corner of the parish in 1773:[14] the farmhouse was presumably Dunley House, so called in 1688.[15] Part of a ruined building is all that remains on its site. In 1842 a new farmstead, East Dunley Farm, was built north-east of it.[16] Also west of Surrendell Farm a barn and a small house were built in the 18th century, before 1773:[17] the house was later extended in brick.

Fosse Lodge, a Gothic lodge with an octagonal turret, was built in 1835 at the Elm and the Ash on the Foss Way near the site of a chapel in Grittleton parish.[18]

The population of Surrendell tithing was 26 in 1801, 41 in 1841, and 23 in 1851.[19]

MANORS AND OTHER ESTATES. Hullavington belonged to Earl Harold in 1066, and after the Conquest may have been given to Roger Mortimer. Roger's son Ralph held it in 1084 and 1086.[20] Ralph was succeeded by his son Hugh (d. 1148 × 1150) and in turn by Hugh's sons Roger (d. by 1153) and Hugh (d. 1180–1). One of the Hugh Mortimers gave HULLAVINGTON manor to the abbey of St. Victor. That the donor mentioned his brother Roger in the charter suggests that he was the younger Hugh.[21] The overlordship apparently descended in the Mortimer family like that of Bradfield manor,[22] but was not expressly mentioned after 1275.[23]

By 1194–5, when a monk was killed at Hullavington, the abbey of St. Victor may have had a cell there.[24] Later it had a priory sometimes called after Hullavington and sometimes after Clatford in Preshute where it also held an estate, and the prior represented the abbot as owner of Hullavington manor.[25] Although not expressly mentioned after 1338[26] the manor was among the possessions of Clatford priory in the king's hands 1338–60 and 1369–1414 because of the war with France: the king usually appointed the prior as keeper. When the alien priories were suppressed in 1414 the manor was among possessions granted to Queen Joan (d. 1437), relict of Henry IV, as dower and in 1439 to Humphrey, duke of Gloucester, for life. In 1441 Henry VI granted the reversion to Eton College, and in 1443 Humphrey surrendered the lands of the former priory to the college.[27] From 1443 to 1958 Eton College held Hullavington manor[28] which was expressly confirmed to it in 1444.[29] A house in Malmesbury was held with Hullavington in 1086:[30] it was one of the houses in respect of which an obligation to repair part of the town wall was imposed.[31] Eton College owned a house in High Street until 1652 or later.[32]

In 1568 Eton College leased the demesne lands and, with minor exceptions, the whole lordship of the manor to Giles Ivy:[33] at intervals and for large fines it renewed the lease on almost the same terms until 1866.[34] Leases passed from Giles (d. 1592)[35] to his son Thomas[36] (d. 1642),[37] to George

[1] V.C.H. Wilts. iv. 309; below, econ. hist.
[2] Crown Pleas, 1249 (W.R.S. xvi), p. 191; below, church.
[3] W.R.O. 312/6, no. 50.   [4] V.C.H. Wilts. iv. 308.
[5] 'Syntagma Genealogicum', pp. 162–3, 202, 272; below, manors.
[6] Aubrey, Topog. Coll. ed. Jackson, 114–15.
[7] Soc. Antiq. MS. 817, vii, f. 74v.; W.R.O. 1621/29.
[8] Badeni, Wilts. Forefathers, 84 and pl. 6; drawing by J. E. Jackson in W.A.S. Libr.
[9] O.S. Maps 6", Wilts. XII. SE. (1900, 1923 edns.).
[10] Ibid. 6", Wilts. XII. NE. (1900, 1923 edns.).
[11] W.R.O., G 7/760/198.
[12] Ibid. 312/7, lease, Jacob to Hughes, 1736.
[13] Greenwood, Map of Wilts.; O.S. Map 1", sheet 34 (1828 edn.).   [14] Andrews and Dury, Map (W.R.S. viii), pl. 13.
[15] W.R.O. 212B/3551.
[16] Inf. from Mr. H. R. G. Penny, 153 Queen's Crescent, Chippenham.

[17] Andrews and Dury, Map (W.R.S. viii), pl. 13; W.R.O., tithe award.
[18] Andrews and Dury, Map (W.R.S. viii), pl. 13; date on bldg.
[19] V.C.H. Wilts. iv. 350.
[20] Ibid. ii, p. 152.
[21] Eton Coll. Mun. 4/1; Complete Peerage, ix. 266–72.
[22] Below.   [23] Rot. Hund. (Rec. Com.), ii (1), 272.
[24] Rot. Cur. Reg. (Pipe R. Soc. xiv), 84.
[25] V.C.H. Wilts. iii. 393–4; Reg. Malm. i. 177.
[26] Cal. Close, 1337–9, 398.   [27] V.C.H. Wilts. xii. 173.
[28] Eton Coll. Mun. 4/96; below.   [29] Rot. Parl. v. 81.
[30] V.C.H. Wilts. ii, p. 152.   [31] Reg. Malm. i. 137.
[32] Eton Coll. Mun. 4/198.   [33] Ibid. 4/188.
[34] Ibid. 4/27–36; 4/38–9; 4/41; 4/43; 4/45; 4/47; 4/50; 4/52; 4/54–5.
[35] B.L. Eg. MS. 3128.   [36] P.R.O., REQ 2/37/123.
[37] Soc. Antiq. MS. 817, vii, f. 72v.

HULLAVINGTON
The church house in 1877

MALMESBURY
St. John's bridge and St. John's almshouse in 1809

OAKSEY
All Saints' church in 1809

HULLAVINGTON
St. Mary's church in 1809

Ivy (d. 1676),[38] to George's son Thomas,[39] and to that Thomas's son St. John.[40] In 1691 St. John Ivy mortgaged the lease to Thomas Jacob, and Jacob may have entered on the lands in 1696 when Margaret Ivy, relict of St. John's father Thomas, conveyed her life interest to him.[41] Jacob (d. 1730) was succeeded by his son John (d. 1742).[42] John's relict Anne held the lease until her death in 1762 when it passed to his cousin John Jacob (d. 1776). It passed in turn to that John's sisters Anne Jacob (d. 1787) and Mary Clutterbuck (d. 1790). Mary's heir was her nephew Robert Buxton[43] (cr. a baronet 1800).[44] In 1809 Buxton, who took the surname Jacob, contracted to sell the lease to William Chandler (d. 1821): the purchase money was paid but the conveyance not completed. In 1825 Buxton and Chandler's nephews S.B. Chancellor and Cornelius Chancellor sold it to John Christie who in 1829 sold it to Joseph Neeld[45] (d. 1856). Leases passed as part of Neeld's Grittleton estate from him to his brother Sir John Neeld, Bt.[46] The last lease of the lordship of the manor expired in 1885. Thereafter, until 1952, Eton College leased only the demesne, 453 a. in 1885, to Neeld and successive owners of the Grittleton estate as annual tenants.[47] From 1829 Joseph and Sir John Neeld, as lords farmer, granted copyholds of the manor, other than cottages, only to their own trustees.[48] In 1885 Sir John held c. 1,124 a. by copy,[49] and with his freehold land held c. 2,500 a. in the parish.[50] The copyhold was converted to leasehold,[51] and by exchange and sale in 1928 Eton College in effect sold the freehold of c. 250 a. to Sir Audley Neeld.[52] In 1952 the college ended L. W. Neeld's lease of the demesne and bought his lease of the former copyhold, a total of 1,320 a. between the Street and Pig Lane and in the north-east corner of the parish.[53]

In 1958 Eton College sold its land to a syndicate of farmers who bought the land which they occupied.[54] Court farm, 509 a., was bought by George Edwards and Miss E. E. Edwards: in 1975 their executors sold it, then 444 a., to Mr. T. G. Butler, the owner in 1989.[55] Newman's and Gardener's farm, 437 a., was bought by Mr. R. L. Hawker, who owned Gardener's farm in 1989.[56] Green's farm, 178 a., was bought by Mr. W. J. Greenman (d. 1988), whose executors owned it in 1989,[57] and the Green farm, 56 a., by B. W. Greenman

and Mr. H. W. Greenman, the owner in 1989.[58] Blick's farm, 71 a., was bought by N. T. Woodman: c. 1961 most of it was bought by Mr. L. J. Irvine, the owner in 1989.[59] In the north-west corner of the parish 59 a. were bought by Col. W. H. Whitbread and, with c. 100 a. of Newman's and Gardener's farm bought from Mr. R. L. Hawker,[60] added to Farleaze farm. In 1974 Col. Whitbread sold the 160 a. to Mr. J. H. Richards: the land was later sold in two portions.[61]

The Mortimers or the abbey of St. Victor granted c. 10 yardlands in Hullavington as freehold. Before 1203 a hide descended from Hugh of Hullavington to his son Ralph.[62] In the later 13th century and early 14th members of the Hullavington, Royle, French, Stur, Clatford formerly Preshute, and Peckinghill families were freeholders.[63] In 1370 Henry Eyre may have owned one of the freeholds,[64] and in 1402 Agnes, daughter of Henry Sodbury, conveyed what may have been a second to Eyre's son Nicholas.[65] Henry Eyre, presumably another, died holding 4 yardlands in 1424 and was succeeded by his son Nicholas,[66] who in 1461 settled land on his daughter Elizabeth Smith and her son John.[67] Elizabeth, then called Elizabeth Eyre, held the 4 yardlands at her death in 1466 when she was succeeded by her son John Eyre or Smith.[68] In 1521 John, then called John Eyre, sold an estate in Hullavington to Thomas Horton of Iford in Westwood.[69] A holding still belonged to the Royles in the 15th century: in 1423 Isold Royle died holding 2 yardlands and was succeeded by Agnes Royle,[70] and before c. 1442 John Royle died holding 2 yardlands. John's land was held by his relict Agnes and her husband Walter Brinkworth and passed to his son Thomas,[71] whose daughters Edith, wife of John Prior, and Lettice, wife of Thomas Squire, sold it to Thomas Horton in 1508.[72] In 1524 Horton (d. 1530) founded a chantry in Bradford church and endowed it with a tenement and 55 a. in Hullavington.[73] The rest of his Hullavington estate was held by his relict Mary[74] (will proved 1544) and passed to his nephew Thomas Horton (d. 1549)[75] who in 1549 bought the chantry's lands from the Crown.[76] That Thomas's relict Margery (d. 1564) held his lands: they passed to his son Edward (d. 1603), who held $5\frac{1}{2}$ yardlands in Hullavington in 1578, but from 1588 to 1599 or longer

[38] W.N. & Q. viii. 235.
[39] W.R.O., wills, archd. Wilts., 1676, admin. of Geo. Ivy.
[40] P.R.O., E 134/12 Wm. III East./2.
[41] W.R.O. 312/7; 312/10, deed, Ivy to Jacob, 1691.
[42] Ibid. 312/10, will of Thos. Jacob; ibid. bishop's transcripts, bdle. 2; mon. in church.
[43] Soc. Antiq. MS. 817, vii, f. 73v.
[44] J. Foster, Baronetage (1882), 96.
[45] W.R.O. 1305/114, abstr. and suppl. abstr. of title.
[46] Burke, Peerage (1890), 1017; Eton Coll. Mun. 179/5, val. 1865.
[47] Eton Coll. Mun. 286/2; ibid. JB 11/1/20. For the Neelds, below.
[48] Eton Coll. Mun. 179/5, progress notes, 1843.
[49] Ibid. 179/5, val. 1865; 286/2; W.R.O., Inland Revenue, val. reg. 13.
[50] Below.
[51] 12 & 13 Geo. V, c. 16, s. 133; Eton Coll. Mun. 323/1.
[52] Eton Coll. Mun. 114/6, award, 1928.
[53] Ibid. JB 11/1/20.
[54] For all the sales of 1958, ibid.
[55] Inf. from Mr. T. G. Butler, Hullavington Ho.
[56] Inf. from Mr. R. L. Hawker, Gardener's Farm.
[57] Local inf.
[58] Inf. from Mr. H. W. Greenman, Lawn Farm.
[59] Inf. from Mr. L. J. Irvine, Buckland Farm, Norton.
[60] Inf. from Mr. Hawker.
[61] Inf. from Mr. J. H. Richards, Lord's Wood Farm, Sherston.
[62] P.R.O., CP 25(1)/250/2, no. 39.
[63] W.R.O. 312/6.
[64] Ibid. 312/6, no. 29.
[65] Ibid. 312/6, no. 37.
[66] Eton Coll. Mun. 4/94, ct. 4 Oct. 1424.
[67] W.R.O. 312/6, deed, Eyre to Smith, 1461.
[68] Ibid. 312/6, no. 31; Eton Coll. Mun. 4/116, view 4 Oct. 1466.
[69] W.R.O. 312/6, no. 42.
[70] Eton Coll. Mun. 4/94, ct. 7 Oct. 1423.
[71] Ibid. 4/96; W.R.O. 312/6, no. 47.
[72] W.R.O. 312/6, nos. 12, 24.
[73] V.C.H. Wilts. vii. 26; P.R.O., E 301/58, no. 43.
[74] Eton Coll. Mun. 4/125.
[75] V.C.H. Wilts. xi. 226; Wilts. Pedigrees (Harl. Soc. cv/cvi), 87-8.
[76] Cal. Pat. 1548-9, 249.

they belonged to Edward's nephew William Horton.[77] Between 1599 and 1611 they were bought by Thomas Ivy,[78] and thereafter, later with other freeholds, they descended with the lease of Hullavington manor until 1885 when Sir John Neeld owned them.[79]

A yardland held in 1578 by William Chadderton[80] passed with Bradfield manor to Simon James.[81] It passed to Simon's son Giles (d. 1640), who left a wife Mary and as heir an infant son Woodland,[82] to Giles's daughter Mary and her husband Richard Lewis[83] (fl. 1702),[84] and to Richard's son Thomas who sold it to Thomas Jacob, the lessee of Hullavington manor, in 1707.[85]

Richard Gore (d. 1583), lord of Surrendell manor,[86] held 3 yardlands in Hullavington. In 1575 he sold 1 yardland to Robert Punter[87] who held it in 1599:[88] the land was held by James Punter in 1611,[89] Robert Punter in 1652,[90] and James Punter in 1660 and 1674.[91] Before 1696 James sold it to Joseph Beames whose son Roger sold it to Thomas Jacob in 1723.[92] Gore's other land in Hullavington was sold in 1593 by his son Edward to Thomas Lyte,[93] and James Lyte held it in 1611.[94] It was acquired by Henry, son of Simon James, was bought from him by his brother Giles,[95] and was part of the 83 a. sold by Thomas Lewis to Thomas Jacob in 1707.[96]

In 1766 the freeholds which passed with the lease of Hullavington manor were said to total 260 a., but they may have been no more than c. 150 a.: they included nearly all the land granted by the Mortimers or the abbey of St. Victor.[97] Sir John Neeld, Bt. (d. 1891), was succeeded in turn by his sons Sir Algernon (d. 1900) and Sir Audley (d. 1941).[98] By exchange and purchase in 1928 Sir Audley acquired another c. 250 a. from Eton College and concentrated his freehold, c. 400 a., south and south-east of the Street.[99] In the period 1937–40 he sold 94 a. to the state for Hullavington airfield.[1] His heir was his second cousin L. W. Inigo-Jones (d. 1956) who assumed the surname Neeld in 1942[2] and between 1941 and 1948 sold May's farm, 167 a., to C. E. Banwell.[3] In 1951 Banwell sold 64 a. to the state.[4] May's farm, c. 110 a. east of its buildings, was later bought by Mr. V. J. Rawlins, and sold by him, without its buildings, to Mr. J. Eavis, the owner in 1989, who added it to Manor farm based in Corston.[5] The Neelds' remaining land, south of Hullavington village and including Stock wood, was also sold, and 70 a. south-west of Stock wood belonged in 1989 to Bishop Bros. as part of Wood Barn farm based in Stanton St. Quintin.[6]

BRADFIELD belonged to Bristwi and Elwi in 1066. Like Hullavington it may have been given to Roger Mortimer and in 1086 Edward held it of Ralph Mortimer.[7] The overlordship descended with Hullavington manor to Hugh Mortimer (d. 1180–1). Hugh was succeeded by his son Roger (d. c. 1214), and by Roger's sons Hugh (d. 1227) and Ralph (d. 1246), who was overlord in 1242–3.[8] The overlordship passed in the direct male line to Roger Mortimer (d. 1282), Edmund, Lord Mortimer (d. 1304), Roger, earl of March (d. 1330), Edmund, Lord Mortimer (d. c. 1332), and Roger, earl of March (d. 1360), and with the earldom of March until it was merged in the Crown in 1461.[9] In 1547 Richard Scrope claimed the overlordship as part of his manor of Castle Combe,[10] possibly because the lord of Bradfield manor held other land of which Scrope was overlord,[11] and in 1616 the overlordship of John Scrope was acknowledged.[12] In 1622, when the lord of the manor was a minor, however, the Crown disputed Scrope's claim and itself claimed the overlordship as part of the earldom of March.[13]

In 1194 Philip of Knabwell may have held an estate at Bradfield,[14] and in 1236, when 2½ yardlands at Bradfield were conveyed to him, Walter of Raddington may have held another.[15] In 1242–3 William of Raddington held ¾ knight's fee and Amice, relict of William of Knabwell, and her partners held ½ knight's fee.[16] William of Raddington held his land in 1248.[17] In 1304 Robert Russell held land in Bradfield, possibly the whole manor,[18] and John Russell (fl. 1318–32)[19] may have held it. It belonged to Robert Russell in 1348,[20] John Russell in 1370,[21] Robert Russell in 1398–9.[22] In 1428 Walter Everard held the manor.[23] In the period 1445–66 it belonged to John Russell (d. c. 1472)[24] whose heir is said to have been John Collingbourne.[25] In 1476 it was settled on William Collingbourne[26] (executed 1484),[27] and

[77] V.C.H. Wilts. xi. 226; Wilts. Pedigrees (Harl. Soc. cv/cvi), 88; Eton Coll. Mun. 4/143; 4/156; 4/170; 4/187–8; 4/190.
[78] Eton Coll. Mun. 4/190; 4/194.
[79] Below. [80] Eton Coll. Mun. 4/187.
[81] Ibid. 4/170; below.
[82] Wilts. Inq. p.m. 1625–49 (Index Libr.), 310; P.R.O., C 142/392, no. 109.
[83] Eton Coll. Mun. 4/179; 4/198. [84] W.R.O. 436/27.
[85] Ibid. 1305/114, abstr. of title to freehold. [86] Below.
[87] 'Syntagma Genealogicum', p. 159.
[88] Eton Coll. Mun. 4/190. [89] Ibid. 4/194.
[90] Ibid. 4/198. [91] Ibid. 4/179; 4/198B.
[92] Ibid. 4/200; W.R.O. 1305/114, abstr. of title to freehold.
[93] 'Syntagma Genealogicum', p. 202.
[94] Eton Coll. Mun. 4/194.
[95] Wilts. Inq. p.m. 1625–49 (Index Libr.), 310, 312.
[96] Eton Coll. Mun. 4/179; W.R.O. 1305/114, abstr. of title to freehold.
[97] W.R.O. 4/210; below.
[98] Burke, Peerage (1924), 1667; Who Was Who, 1941–50, 838.
[99] Eton Coll. Mun. 114/6, award, 1928; above.
[1] Inf. from Defence Land Agent, Durrington.
[2] Burke, Land. Gent. (1952), 1868–9; W.R.O. 1655/8.
[3] Eton Coll. Mun., JB 11/1/4, sale cat. 1948.
[4] Inf. from Defence Land Agent, Durrington.

[5] Inf. from Mr. J. Eavis, Manor Farm, Corston, Malmesbury; Mr. V. J. Rawlins, May's Farm.
[6] Inf. from Bishop Bros., Wood Barn Farm, Stanton St. Quintin.
[7] V.C.H. Wilts. ii, p. 152.
[8] Complete Peerage, ix. 266–76; Bk. of Fees, ii. 711, 729.
[9] Complete Peerage, viii. 433–54; ix. 276–85; Cal. Inq. p.m. iv, p. 163; x, p. 537; P.R.O., C 139/18, f. 26.
[10] P.R.O., C 142/85, no. 79.
[11] Aubrey, Topog. Coll. ed. Jackson, 248.
[12] P.R.O., C 142/392, no. 109; B.L. Add. Ch. 18383.
[13] W.A.M. ii. 142, 289; Soc. Antiq. MS. 817, vii, f. 70v.; P.R.O., C 142/401, no. 88.
[14] Rot. Cur. Reg. (Pipe R. Soc. xiv), 75.
[15] P.R.O., CP 25(1)/250/10, no. 88.
[16] Bk. of Fees, ii. 711, 722, 729.
[17] Crown Pleas, 1249 (W.R.S. xvi), pp. 159–61.
[18] Cal. Inq. p.m. iv, p. 163. [19] W.R.O. 312/6, nos. 35, 39.
[20] Feet of F. 1327–77 (W.R.S. xxix), p. 90.
[21] W.R.O. 312/6, no. 29. [22] Cal. Inq. p.m. xvii, p. 455.
[23] Feud. Aids, v. 235.
[24] W.A.M. xxxvi. 103; Eton Coll. Mun. 4/98, view 30 Sept. 1445; 4/116, view 4 Oct. 1466.
[25] W.A.M. ii. 284; xxxvi. 104; V.C.H. Wilts. xi. 242.
[26] Cal. Close, 1476–85, p. 15.
[27] J. Gairdner, Richard the Third, 189.

in 1485 Richard III granted Bradfield and other lands to Edmund Chadderton for William's heirs, his daughters Margaret, wife of George Chadderton, and Joan, wife of James Lowther. Bradfield was assigned to the Chaddertons[28] and passed to their son Edmund (d. 1545) and to Edmund's son William,[29] who had daughters Margaret, wife of Simon James, Anne, wife of John Wright (d. 1585), and Edith, wife of George Best. William Chadderton (d. 1599) apparently settled the manor, after the death of him and his wife Bridget (d. 1597), on his daughters in portions.[30] In 1586 Simon James bought the Chadderton life interest in two thirds of the manor,[31] in 1594 apparently bought Anne Wright's portion,[32] and before 1596 may have bought Edith Best's.[33] On Simon's death in 1616 the whole manor passed to his son

manor, and it passed in the Hooper family.[36] In 1910 it belonged to representatives of William Hooper,[37] and, then 423 a., was offered for sale thrice in the period 1915–17.[38] In 1928 it belonged to C. H. Brown.[39] In 1932 it was bought from H. L. Storey by J. Branston who was succeeded by his son J. E. J. Branston and by his grandson Mr. J. E. Branston, the owner in 1989.[40]

With few interruptions Bradfield manor house was apparently lived in by its owners from the early 14th century or earlier to the early 18th.[41] The house has a main east–west range of six bays, formerly with a two-storeyed porch near the centre of the south side[42] giving access to a cross passage. East of the passage is a two-bayed hall with traceried two-light windows of the 15th century. In the early 17th century a chimney stack was built

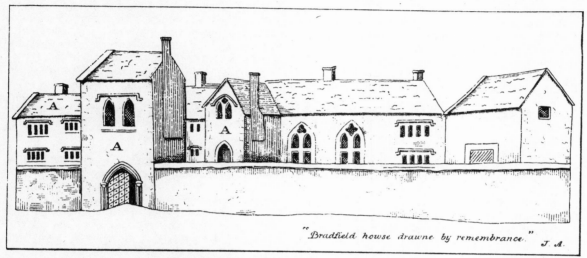

"Bradfield howse drawne by remembrance."   J. A.

BRADFIELD MANOR HOUSE IN THE 17TH CENTURY
(the parts marked A were destroyed before 1861)

Edmund[34] (d. 1620) whose heir was his son Richman, a minor. It was held by Edmund's relict Margaret[35] (fl. 1664) and his son Edmund (d. by 1675) whose relict Anne held it. Edmund and Anne had a daughter Margaret, an idiot. About 1677 Anne (d. 1701) married the naturalist William Cole (d. 1701) on whom the manor was settled. Cole's heir was his daughter Anne, wife of Gilbert Cale, and that Anne's was her daughter Anne (d. 1753), wife of the Revd. Anthony Whistler (d. 1719), of Whitchurch (Oxon.), and of Samuel Walker, rector of Whitchurch and possibly of North Stoke (Som.), who held the manor until his death in 1768. Bradfield manor may have been sold c. 1771 by Anne's son John Whistler, like land in Corston in Malmesbury. It was apparently bought by John Hooper, lord of North Stoke

behind the hall and a ceiling was inserted. About then, probably for Simon James, a large four-storeyed parlour block was built at the north-east corner. A two-storeyed north kitchen wing was built at the west end of the main range in the 18th century.

SURRENDELL belonged to Alwi in 1066. Like Hullavington and Bradfield it may have been given to Roger Mortimer, and in 1086 Ralph Mortimer was overlord.[43] From then until 1461 the overlordship descended like that of Bradfield.[44]

In 1086 Richard held Surrendell of Ralph.[45] From the earlier 13th century to the late 14th Surrendell manor descended in the Middlehope family: Richard Middlehope held it as 1 knight's fee in 1242–3,[46] William Middlehope held it in 1281,[47] and William Middlehope, possibly

[28] Cal. Pat. 1476–85, 542; W.N. & Q. ii. 50; P.R.O., C 1/259, no. 10.
[29] P.R.O., C 1/967, nos. 8–9; C 142/85, no. 79.
[30] Ibid. CP 25(2)/240/21 Eliz. I East.; CP 25(2)/240/25 & 26 Eliz. I Mich.; ibid. PROB 11/68, f. 182; ibid. REQ 2/274/15; Cat. Anct. D. v, A 12822; W.N. & Q. ii. 51; viii. 543.
[31] P.R.O., CP 25(2)/241/28 Eliz. I East.; ibid. REQ 2/37/123.
[32] Ibid. CP 25(2)/242/36 Eliz. I East.; CP 43/45, rot. 56.
[33] Ibid. REQ 2/274/15.   [34] Ibid. C 142/392, no. 109.
[35] Ibid. C 142/401, no. 88.
[36] Ibid. C 10/303/33; Aubrey, Topog. Coll. ed. Jackson,

248–9; D.N.B. s.v. Wm. Cole; Eton Coll. Reg. 1698–1752, ed. R. A. Austen-Leigh, 354; J. Collinson, Hist. Som. i. 135; W.R.O. 490/206, abstr. of title; ibid. A 1/345/225; Eton Coll. Mun. 4/210; below, Corston, manor.
[37] W.R.O., Inland Revenue, val. reg. 13.
[38] Eton Coll. Mun. 286/2.   [39] W.R.O., G 7/501/1.
[40] Inf. from Mr. J. E. Branston, Bradfield Manor Farm.
[41] e.g. Aubrey, Topog. Coll. ed. Jackson, 248–9.
[42] Ibid. pl. xxiv.   [43] V.C.H. Wilts. ii, p. 152.
[44] Bk. of Fees, ii. 729; Cal. Inq. p.m. iv, p. 163; x, p. 537; xvii, p. 455.   [45] V.C.H. Wilts. ii, p. 152.
[46] Bk. of Fees, ii. 729.   [47] Collectanea (W.R.S. xii), p. 90.

another, in the period 1304–25.[48] Alice, relict of William Middlehope, claimed dower in Surrendell in 1327.[49] Thomas Middlehope held the manor in 1342,[50] William Middlehope in 1398–9.[51] In 1428 John Skey and William Pedworth held the lands formerly Thomas Middlehope's,[52] and in 1448 John, son and heir of Thomas Skey of North Nibley (Glos.), settled a moiety of Surrendell manor on himself and his wife Joan.[53] From the later 15th century to the later 16th the manor descended in the Hamlin family: Thomas Hamlin held it in 1463,[54] Alexander Hamlin in 1502–3.[55] John Hamlin (d. by 1576) held the manor in 1545,[56] and in 1567 settled it, after his own death, on his sons William, John, and Nicholas in thirds.[57] In the period 1576–8 Richard Gore (d. 1583) bought land from all three, and in 1594 Richard's son Edward bought the manor house and other land from John. Edward Gore (d. 1622) settled the whole manor of Surrendell on the marriage of his son Charles in 1621. From Charles (d. 1649) and his wife Lydia (d. 1655) it passed to their son, the antiquarian Thomas Gore (d. 1684). Charles bought additional land in Surrendell from Roger Kilbury's son Roger in 1648 and Thomas from the younger Roger and the elder Roger's relict Anne, wife of Edward Webb, in 1654.[58] Thomas devised Surrendell manor to his son Thomas (d. 1697)[59] but his relict Mary (d. 1718) apparently held it for life.[60] It passed to Thomas's and Mary's granddaughter Elizabeth Gore (d. 1743), wife of William Hedges (d. 1757), and to Elizabeth's son Thomas Hedges (d. 1782), who devised it to James Montagu (d. 1790), the husband of his sister Eleanor (d. 1786). James was succeeded by his son James (d. 1797) who devised Surrendell to his nephew G. C. Montagu. By order of Chancery, Surrendell farm, 397 a. in 1840, was sold to Thomas Burne in 1804; the rest of the estate, Farleaze farm and Dunley farm, respectively 157 a. and 200 a. in 1840, was sold by Montagu and his son F. C. Montagu in 1827–8 to Joseph Neeld[61] (d. 1856). In 1810 Burne settled Surrendell farm on his son the Revd. W. W. Burne (d. 1858) who devised it to his nephew the Revd. T. B. Lancaster: in 1863 Lancaster sold it to Neeld's trustees.[62] Surrendell, Farleaze, and Dunley, later East Dunley, farms descended with other freehold and leasehold land in the parish as part of the Grittleton estate, which passed from L. W. Neeld to his nephew Mr. R. W. Inigo-Jones (later Mr. R. W. Neeld). East Dunley farm, 250 a. including

land in other parishes, and c. 110 a. adjoining it, formerly part of Surrendell farm, belonged to Mr. Neeld's son Mr. M. R. Neeld in 1989.[63]

Farleaze farm was sold c. 1930 to Mrs. E. C. Millais[64] and in 1934 belonged to H. R. Millais.[65] In 1946 or earlier it belonged to C. E. D. Cooper,[66] from whom it was bought in the mid 1950s by Col. W. H. Whitbread,[67] the owner of the farmhouse and c. 50 a. in 1989. In 1974 Col. Whitbread sold 100 a. to Mr. J. H. Richards, the owner in 1989, who added it to Lord's Wood farm based in Sherston.[68] In the 1970s Mr. R. W. Neeld sold c. 211 a. of Surrendell farm to Mr. V. J. Rawlins who in 1984 sold that land to Sir Mark Weinberg, the owner in 1989.[69]

Hullavington church and the *RECTORY* estate passed with Hullavington manor from the abbey of St. Victor to the Crown, and in 1443 to Eton College.[70] The land of the church and the land of the manor were not distinguished, and sometimes the demesne land of the manor was described as the rector's glebe.[71] In 1320 the rectory estate included all tithes of the parish, except those arising from the vicar's glebe,[72] but later only those of corn and hay.[73] In 1841 the demesne, estimated at 467 a., was tithe free. The tithes of corn and hay from the remainder of the parish were then valued at £455 and commuted.[74]

ECONOMIC HISTORY. HULLAVINGTON. In 1086 Ralph's 20-hide estate had 14 demesne hides, with 4 ploughteams and 8 *servi*, and 19 *villani* and 8 coscets with 6 teams. There were 12 a. of meadow and 10 a. of pasture. The estate had land for 14 teams, and apparently the uncultivated land was then demesne.[75] It may later have been assigned to freeholders or customary tenants for cultivation and in the 13th century, when Hullavington was fully cultivated, freehold and customary land greatly exceeded demesne.[76]

It is likely that the demesne of Hullavington manor, if not already several, was inclosed in the 12th century when the manor was given to the abbey of St. Victor, and in the 16th century virtually all the demesne lay inclosed and virtually all the free and customary land was open.[77] The demesne was devoted to sheep-and-corn husbandry in 1292 when 200 sheep and 24 oxen were on it.[78] It may have remained in hand until the alien priories were suppressed in 1414, and in 1416 the farm buildings were reported to have been

---

[48] *Cal. Inq. p.m.* iv, p. 163; W.R.O. 469/1; B.L. Add. Ch. 7740.
[49] P.R.O., CP 40/269, rot. 45; CP 40/270, rot. 52; CP 40/273, rot. 104d.; CP 40/274, rot. 80d.
[50] *Bradenstoke Cart.* (W.R.S. xxxv), pp. 63–4.
[51] *Cal. Inq. p.m.* xvii, p. 455.   [52] *Feud. Aids,* v. 253.
[53] *Feet of F. 1377–1509* (W.R.S. xli), p. 127.
[54] Eton Coll. Mun. 4/114, ct. 18 Aug. 1463.
[55] P.R.O., C 1/263, no. 25.
[56] *Taxation Lists* (W.R.S. x), 27.
[57] B.L. Add. Ch. 7071; P.R.O., CP 25(2)/239/9 Eliz. I Trin. no. 380.
[58] 'Syntagma Genealogicum', pp. 160, 162–3, 202, 218–20, 239, 294, 296, 320–1; P.R.O., C 142/203, no. 37; W.R.O. 1909/1; ibid. 2105.
[59] W.R.O. 212A/37/6, will of Thomas Gore, 1683; ibid. 2105.
[60] Aubrey, *Topog. Coll.* ed. Jackson, pedigree facing p. 47; P.R.O., E 134/12 Wm. III East./12.
[61] Aubrey, *Topog. Coll.* ed. Jackson, pedigree facing p. 47;

Burke, *Commoners* (1833–8), ii. 54; W.R.O. 1305/112, abstr. of title; ibid. tithe award.
[62] W.R.O. 1305/112, conveyance, Lancaster to Jones, 1863.
[63] Above; Burke, *Land. Gent.* (1952), 1868–9; inf. from Mr. H. R. G. Penny, 153 Queen's Crescent, Chippenham.
[64] W.R.O., G 7/501/1.
[65] Ibid. G 7/505/1.   [66] Ibid. G 7/760/198.
[67] Ibid. G 7/505/2; Eton Coll. Mun., JB 11/1/20.
[68] Local inf.; inf. from Mr. Richards.
[69] Inf. from Mr. Rawlins; Sir Mark Weinberg, Cole Park, Malmesbury.
[70] Eton Coll. Mun. 61/RR/A/10; above; below, church.
[71] Eton Coll. Mun. 179/5, progress notes, 1843.
[72] *Reg. Martival* (Cant. & York Soc.), ii. 286–7.
[73] Eton Coll. Mun. 4/188.
[74] W.R.O., tithe award.
[75] *V.C.H. Wilts.* ii, p. 152.
[76] Eton Coll. Mun. 14/184.
[77] Ibid. 4/188; above, manors.
[78] Eton Coll. Mun. 14/184.

much neglected.[79] In 1336–7 *c.* 110 a. were sown,[80] probably more in 1386–7 when 69 qr. of wheat, 45 qr. of barley, 2 qr. of dredge, and 41 qr. of malt were sold. In the later 14th century much of the livestock was brought from Clatford.[81] From 1442 or earlier the demesne was leased:[82] in 1538 it measured 320 a.,[83] 340 a., excluding woodland, in 1588.[84]

In the 13th and 14th centuries the open fields of Hullavington were extensive: East and West were apparently the largest, North field was smaller. The meadow land was used in common and some of it, including 6 a. of demesne, was in the open fields.[85] In 1292 the vicar held 2 yardlands, seven freeholders a total of *c.* 10 yardlands, and bondmen *c.* 45 yardlands. Later evidence shows each yardland to have included 20–30 a. of arable. Of the bondmen 10 held 2 yardlands each, 24 held 1 yardland each, the smith held ½ yardland, and 9 were cottagers. Labour services were numerous: each cottager, for example, was required to bring his whole family to autumn bed-rips.[86] Sheep-and-corn husbandry continued on the open lands throughout the 15th and 16th centuries. In 1588 East field was 540 a., West field 632 a.: in them the strips averaged *c.* ½ a., and 1,313 sheep, at the rate of 25 to 1 yardland, could be pastured.[87] The only inclosure was in the 1440s when hedges were planted around Stock wood and at east and west Townsend.[88] In the early 15th century men of Hullavington and Corston may have fed sheep on parts of each other's fallow,[89] an arrangement which had ended by the early 16th,[90] and a similar arrangement between Hullavington and Surrendell may have ended *c.* 1463.[91] In 1588 there were 58 a. of common meadows of which the largest was Broad mead beside Gauze brook north-east of the village: in them the copyholders and freeholders held lots, which were sometimes staked. Town leaze, 163 a. north-west of the village, and the Down, 92 a. north-east of the village, were common pastures for a total of 224 cattle, 2 beasts in each to 1 yardland. Closes in and around the village totalled 50 a. All those lands, *c.* 54 yardlands, were shared in 1588 by 24 copyholders, 6 freeholders, and the vicar: the largest holdings were William Horton's freehold, 5½ yardlands including 118 a. of arable, and a copyhold of 4 yardlands including 97 a. of arable.[92]

In 1558 Eton College licensed the copyholders to exchange among themselves strips of arable and lots of meadow,[93] and in the early 17th century was petitioned to permit inclosure of the common pastures and the worst parts of the open fields and further consolidation of holdings in the fields and meadows. The inconvenience of working scattered lands[94] may have been greater than elsewhere because the fields of Hullavington were so large. Under an agreement of 1611 Town leaze, the Down, and the outsides of East field and West field, presumably those parts furthest from the village, were divided, allotted, and inclosed, and holdings in the meadows were consolidated:[95] 196 a. of East field and 260 a. of West field were inclosed, and 356 a. of open arable were left in each. Most allotments of pasture were of 5–10 a.[96] Between the mid 17th century and the mid 18th most of the remaining arable was inclosed by agreement. Between 1652 and 1674, possibly *c.* 1670, 176 a. were inclosed, mostly in East field;[97] a further 143 a. had been inclosed by 1696 when the remaining 393 a. of open arable were in four fields;[98] and 221 a. were inclosed as tynings between 1696 and 1753 to leave only 71 a. of open field.[99] In the early 18th century clover was sown in the open fields and those sowing it could fold three sheep for each acre sown instead of one;[1] by *c.* 1770 many inclosures had been laid to grass.[2] In 1764 and 1840 there were 5 a. of open field north-east, 28 a. south-west, and 12 a. west of the village.[3] All may not have been inclosed until the early 20th century when the college bought some remaining strips.[4] Broad mead was still common in 1840 when it was apparently 31 a., and there may have been 10 a. more of common meadow north of the village.[5]

Until the later 20th century nearly all Hullavington's land was worked from buildings in the Street. The largest farm, 364 a. including 182 a. of arable in 1652, was the demesne,[6] later called Court farm: between 1652 and 1764 other land was added to Court farm and, presumably to avoid paying tithes to the vicar, was called demesne.[7] Other farms became fewer and larger. In 1840 the Hullavington part of the parish was about half arable and half grassland, and was in *c.* 10 farms of which six were of less than 100 a. The pattern of earlier inclosure still showed: the closes of Surrendell in the west, Bradfield in the north, and Court farm west and south-east of the village, all made before 1600, were larger than those made after 1611 from Town leaze, the Down, East field, and West field.[8] That distinction was scarcely visible in 1989.

Between 1840 and 1887 more arable was converted to grassland[9] and between *c.* 1910 and *c.* 1939 sheep farming was replaced by dairying.[10] After 1939 arable farming, especially for cereals, increased,[11] and in 1989 Hullavington's land was apparently more arable than grassland. In 1928

[79] *Cal. Inq. Misc.* vii, pp. 300–1.
[80] Eton Coll. Mun. 4/18.
[81] Ibid. 4/211–12.
[82] Ibid. 61/RR/A/10.
[83] Ibid. 4/128.
[84] Ibid. 4/188.
[85] Ibid.; W.R.O. 312/6, nos. 3, 27, 30, 45, 50.
[86] Eton Coll. Mun. 4/187; 14/184.
[87] Ibid. 4/187–8.
[88] Ibid. 4/98, view 30 Sept. 1445; 61/RR/A/18.
[89] Ibid. 4/94, ct. 21 Jan. 1423.
[90] Ibid. 4/234D.
[91] Ibid. 4/114, ct. 18 Aug. 1463; below.
[92] Eton Coll. Mun. 4/129; 4/188; P.R.O., E 301/58, no. 43; W.R.O., D 1/24/113/1; for the location, ibid. tithe award.
[93] Eton Coll. Mun. 4/143.

[94] Ibid. 4/92A–B.
[95] Ibid. 4/235.
[96] Ibid. 4/188; 4/198.
[97] Ibid. 4/198; 4/199B; P.R.O., E 134/12 Wm. III East./2.
[98] Eton Coll. Mun. 4/200.
[99] Ibid. 4/206.
[1] W.R.O. 312/3, view 25 Oct. 1703.
[2] Eton Coll. Mun. 4/240B.
[3] W.R.O. 1553/101; ibid. tithe award.
[4] Eton Coll. Mun. 323/1.
[5] W.R.O., tithe award.
[6] Eton Coll. Mun. 4/198.
[7] Ibid.; W.R.O. 1553/101; below, church.
[8] W.R.O., tithe award; for Bradfield and Surrendell, below.
[9] W.R.O., tithe award; P.R.O., MAF 68/1120, sheet 9.
[10] P.R.O., MAF 68/2260, sheet 14; MAF 68/2830, sheet 10; MAF 68/3373, sheet 10; MAF 68/3850, sheet 124.
[11] Ibid. MAF 68/4219, no. 124; MAF 68/4589, no. 124.

seven farms were based in the Street: Court, 508 a., May's, 417 a., Gardener's, 221 a., Newman's, 152 a., Beanfield, 92 a., Green's, 69 a., and Blick's, 40 a.[12] May's farm lost land used for the airfield and was otherwise made smaller.[13] The other farms were reorganized in 1954. In 1958 Court was a dairy and stock farm of 509 a., Newman's and Gardener's a dairy farm of 437 a., Green's a dairy and mixed farm of 178 a., Blick's a similar farm of 71 a., and the Green a dairy farm of 56 a.[14] Court and Gardener's were the main farms in 1989 when large new buildings were erected for them in, respectively, Down Lane and Vlow Lane. Court was largely an arable farm of c. 450 a., and Newman's an arable and dairy farm of c. 350 a.[15] Little land was then worked from farm buildings in or near the Street: May's farm was worked from Corston and other land from Sherston, Norton, and Stanton St. Quintin. In the north-west Town Leaze farm was a small stock farm.[16]

Apparently in the later 13th century the abbot of St. Victor, with the assent of his Hullavington freeholders, built a new water mill in a common pasture,[17] presumably on Gauze brook, and in 1292 Hullavington manor included two water mills.[18] In 1337 both were feeble,[19] and there is no later evidence of them. In 1448 a toft was called Old Mill,[20] and Old mills, a field bounded by Gauze brook north of the village,[21] may mark the site of the mills.

In the early 1970s a market garden with large greenhouses was set up in the north-east corner of the parish beside the Malmesbury–Chippenham road.[22] There was a malthouse in the late 18th century and early 19th,[23] a coal merchant was based at the station from 1903,[24] and a garage was in the Street in the later 20th century, but no trade has ever been prominent in the village.

BRADFIELD. More than half Edward's 2½-hide estate at Bradfield was demesne in 1086. The estate had 2 ploughteams, 3 villani, 2 coscets, and 12 a. of meadow.[25] References to land at Bradfield assessed as yardlands suggest that there may have been open fields in the Middle Ages,[26] and in the 16th century the names of the two large arable closes, East field and West field, may echo those of earlier open fields.[27] Also in the Middle Ages Bradfield manor may have included land held by customary tenants.[28] In the late 16th century, however, the whole manor was in hand and lay inclosed, and the transition is most likely to have been made in the late 15th century. In 1583 the

land was a single farm, then estimated as 448 a. including a total of 180 a. in East field and West field, 59 a. of meadow, and 177 a. of pasture.[29] Those acreages may have been overestimates: later Bradfield Manor farm was 425 a., and it remained a single farm in 1989. In 1840, when 281 a. were arable, it was more arable than pasture;[30] in 1916, when 326 a. were grassland, it was more pasture than arable;[31] and in 1989 half was for dairying and half for growing cereals.[32]

SURRENDELL. In 1086 Richard's 5-hide estate at Surrendell had 2½ hides in demesne with 2 ploughteams and 4 servi, 12 villani and 3 bordars had 4 teams, and there were 7 a. of meadow. The land was fully cultivated.[33] In the Middle Ages Surrendell had open field,[34] and presumably common pasture for cattle: Far leaze to the north may have been such a pasture. In 1327–8 four holding 1 yardland each were apparently customary tenants of Surrendell manor[35] and, since the manor comprised over 700 a.,[36] there may have been more tenants. In 1463 Thomas Hamlin, lord of Surrendell manor, was accused of sowing 60 a. of barley in an open field of Surrendell when, with an open field of Hullavington, the field should have been fallow and used together by men of Surrendell and Hullavington.[37] Common husbandry and customary tenure may not have survived at Surrendell long after that: there is no later evidence of either.

In the later 16th century the lease of a sheephouse and 60 a., staked out of Broad leaze, suggests that a new farm was created,[38] in the early 17th century a new farmhouse at Surrendell and Farleaze Farm were built,[39] and Dunley House was probably a farmhouse in the later 17th century.[40] The closes of Surrendell manor in 1665 included 17 over 20 a. and their names suggest that then or formerly many were used for cattle rearing.[41] About 1670, however, much pasture was ploughed up.[42] By 1736 the land of Surrendell had been divided among three farms, Surrendell in the centre worked from the early 17th-century farmhouse and a barn west of it, Kingsthorns or Farleaze to the north worked from two groups of farm buildings, and Dunley to the south worked from the farmstead in the south-east corner of the parish.[43] The buildings called Kingsthorns were removed in the early 19th century.[44] In 1840 Surrendell farm was 397 a. including 240 a. of pasture, Farleaze farm was 157 a. including 112 a. of pasture, and Dunley farm was 200 a. including 105 a. of arable.[45] Farleaze was held with 29 a. in Alderton.[46] From 1842 Dunley was worked from the

[12] W.R.O., G 7/501/1.
[13] Above, manors.
[14] Eton Coll. Mun., JB 11/1/20.
[15] Inf. from Mr. T. G. Butler, Hullavington Ho.; Mr. R. L. Hawker, Gardener's Farm.
[16] Local inf.
[17] Eton Coll. Mun. 4/5.
[18] Ibid. 14/184.
[19] Ibid. 4/18.
[20] Ibid. 4/102.
[21] W.R.O., tithe award.
[22] Local inf.
[23] Eton Coll. Mun. 4/56; 179/5, terrier, 1834.
[24] Kelly's Dir. Wilts. (1903 and later edns.).
[25] V.C.H. Wilts. ii, p. 152.
[26] Rot. Cur. Reg. (Pipe R. Soc. xiv), 75; Reg. Martival (Cant. & York Soc.), ii. 287; P.R.O., CP 25(1)/250/10, no. 88.
[27] Cat. Anct. D. v, A 12822.
[28] Feet of F. 1327–77 (W.R.S. xxix), p. 90.
[29] Cat. Anct. D. v, A 12822.
[30] W.R.O., tithe award.
[31] Eton Coll. Mun. 286/2.
[32] Inf. from Mr. J. E. Branston, Bradfield Manor Farm.
[33] V.C.H. Wilts. ii, pp. 152–3.
[34] Eton Coll. Mun. 4/114, ct. 18 Aug. 1463.
[35] P.R.O., CP 40/269, rot. 45; CP 40/273, rot. 104d.
[36] W.R.O., tithe award.
[37] Eton Coll. Mun. 4/114, ct. 18 Aug. 1463.
[38] W.R.O. 335/161.
[39] 'Syntagma Genealogicum', pp. 275–6; above, introduction.
[40] W.R.O. 212B/3551.
[41] Ibid. 1909/1.
[42] P.R.O., E 134/12 Wm. III East./2.
[43] Andrews and Dury, Map (W.R.S. viii), pl. 13; W.R.O. 312/7, lease, Jacob to Hedges, 1736.
[44] Above, introduction.
[45] W.R.O., tithe award.
[46] Ibid. Alderton tithe award.

new farmstead north-east of the old one.[47] In 1928 Surrendell farm was 393 a., Dunley, then East Dunley, 134 a., and Farleaze 156 a.[48] In 1989 nearly all the land was arable and none of the farmsteads was used for farming. About 211 a. of Surrendell farm were worked from Malmesbury; the rest of Surrendell farm, with East Dunley farm which was mainly used for dairying until the 1980s, a total of c. 360 a., was worked for its owner by contractors;[49] and part of Farleaze farm was used to keep horses, and the rest was worked from Sherston as part of an arable and dairy farm.[50]

The parish was sparsely wooded although Hullavington, Bradfield, and Surrendell each had a wood. Hullavington's, 8 a., was mentioned in Domesday Book.[51] Later it was Stock wood, south of the village; in 1443 and 1588 it was said to be 20 a.,[52] but in the mid 18th century, when 3 a. were cut yearly, it was 39 a.[53] In 1840 and 1989 it was 40 a.[54] Bradfield wood, in the north corner of the parish, was called the Heath in 1583.[55] In 1840 and 1989 it was 23 a.[56] Surrendell wood was 29 a. in 1665 and 1840,[57] 30 a. in 1989. Between 1840 and 1885 trees were planted on 54 a. along the south and west boundaries in the south-west corner of the parish:[58] that woodland stood in 1989.

LOCAL GOVERNMENT. The tithingman of Hullavington attended the tourns or views of frankpledge for Startley and Malmesbury hundreds; the Surrendell tithingman did so for Chippenham hundred.[59] Hullavington tithing seems to have included Bradfield. In the courts held for Hullavington manor in the early 15th century Queen Joan did not exercise leet jurisdiction, although the assize of ale was enforced and some courts were called view of frankpledge. The courts dealt mainly with admittances to copyholds, dilapidated buildings, the maintenance of the lord's rights over the bondmen and tenants, and problems arising from husbandry in common.[60] In 1443 the king granted to Eton College the fixed payments made for Hullavington at hundred courts[61] and, under a general grant of liberties,[62] the college began to hold view of frankpledge for Hullavington manor and to deny the bailiff of Malmesbury hundred entry on the manor.[63] The abbot of Malmesbury sent two men to a view of frankpledge at Hullavington in 1457 to demand, presumably in vain, that Hullavington should attend the Martinmas and Hocktide views of frankpledge for Startley hundred.[64] From 1443 to 1568 and after 1885 the college held courts for Hullavington; from 1568 to 1885 the lord farmer held them.[65]

In the period 1443–77 a view was held with a manor court twice yearly. The view proceeded on presentments of the tithingman affirmed and added to by a jury, and sometimes an aletaster presented. Those perpetrating assaults, a scold, a gossip, and unsworn boys over 12 were presented, and stray animals and nuisances such as the diversion of a watercourse or flooding of a road were reported. At the courts surrenders of and admittances to copyholds were performed, dilapidations were recorded, orders were made to affect common husbandry, and tenants sometimes impleaded each other. Occasionally manor courts were held at other times.[66] In the period 1531–94 the view with the manor court was still held twice a year.[67] It sometimes proceeded as earlier, but at other times only the jurors presented. In the later 16th century the courts were at their busiest. Additional leet business included the presentment of butchers, bakers, tapsters, and millers, the players of unlawful games, and those breaking a statute of 1571[68] by failing to wear woollen caps on Sundays and holy days. In 1558 the court ordered all males between 7 and 60 to practise archery on Sundays.[69] Constables, tithingmen, and aletasters were chosen. The court's orders to alter and enforce the rules of common husbandry and to maintain gates, hedges, and ditches were also more numerous, and men were appointed expressly to prevent pigs being kept unringed and pastures being overstocked with sheep. In the period 1650–1902 the view and manor court was usually held yearly in October, and it proceeded on presentments of men acting as both jurors and homage. Less leet business was done but throughout the period, more frequently in the 18th century, the courts ordered public nuisances and nuisances affecting agriculture to be amended. The use of land still commonable was regulated and orders to hedge and ditch inclosed land were frequently made. Repairs to houses, farm buildings, bridges, and gates were ordered, and in the 19th century inclosure of waste land, opening a quarry without licence, and removing a wall were all presented. A constable, a tithingman, and a hayward were chosen each year by rotation. Although its importance may have declined such business was done by the courts until 1902. Copyhold business was done in the annual court and at other times until the tenure was abolished, and as late as 1882 a court, after adjourning to consider, deprived a widow of a copyhold for unchastity.[70]

From the 1680s or earlier the parish had two overseers of the poor. Between 1689 and 1744 they usually spent between £15 and £20 a year, only occasionally over £20. In most years more than half was spent on monthly doles to between two

[47] Above, introduction.   [48] W.R.O., G 7/501/1.
[49] Inf. from Mr. V. J. Rawlins, May's Farm; Mr. H. R. G. Penny, 153 Queen's Crescent, Chippenham.
[50] Inf. from Mr. J. H. Richards, Lord's Wood Farm, Sherston.
[51] V.C.H. Wilts. ii, p. 152.
[52] Eton Coll. Mun. 4/96; 4/188.
[53] Ibid. 4/240B; W.R.O. 1553/101.
[54] W.R.O., tithe award.   [55] Cat. Anct. D. v, A 12822.
[56] W.R.O., tithe award.   [57] Ibid.; ibid. 1909/1.
[58] Ibid. tithe award; O.S. Map 6", Wilts. XII (1889 edn.).
[59] Reg. Malm. i. 275; W.A.M. xiii. 117; above, Malmesbury hund.

[60] Eton Coll. Mun. 4/93–4; 63/120.
[61] Ibid. 61/RR/A/10.   [62] Rot. Parl. v. 50.
[63] Eton Coll. Mun. 4/98, view 18 Sept. 1443.
[64] Ibid. 4/110.
[65] For leases of the manor, above, manors; for their terms e.g. Eton Coll. Mun. 4/188.
[66] Eton Coll. Mun. 4/96–100; 4/102–22.
[67] Ibid. 4/124–9; 4/132–9; 4/142–5; 4/147–77; 63/90.
[68] 13 Eliz. I, c. 19.
[69] Eton Coll. Mun. 4/143.
[70] Ibid. 4/178–82; ibid. Hullavington ct. bks. 1740–66, 1776–97, 1798–1836, 1837–82, 1882–1923; W.R.O. 312/1; 312/3; 2454.

and six paupers; other payments were for clothes, fuel, rent, and occasionally a funeral.[71] Expenditure rose in the mid and later 18th century, to £145 in 1775–6 and £242 in 1802–3: 28 adults were relieved continuously and 18 occasionally in 1802–3.[72] In the early 19th century the vestry resolved to provide a parish workhouse[73] but apparently did not do so. In 1812–13, at a cost of £357, 27 were relieved continuously and 14 occasionally.[74] Between then and 1835 Hullavington's expenditure on the poor remained between £200 and £400, about normal for a parish of its size.[75] In 1835 the parish joined Malmesbury poor-law union,[76] and in 1974 became part of North Wiltshire district.[77]

CHURCH. Either Ralph Mortimer (fl. 1086) or, more likely, his son Hugh (d. 1148 × 1150) gave Hullavington church to the abbey of St. Victor.[78] In the late 12th century the church had a chapel at Surrendell[79] and then or later possibly another at Bradfield.[80] It is possible that monks living at Hullavington served the church in the 12th century[81] but by 1240 a vicarage had been ordained.[82] The vicarage was united with the benefice of Stanton St. Quintin and Grittleton with Leigh Delamere and with the vicarage of Norton in 1976.[83]

The abbey of St. Victor was patron in 1240[84] and the advowson passed with Hullavington manor to the Crown and to Eton College.[85] In 1344, when the priory was in his hands, the king successfully claimed the advowson against the prior of Hullavington, who had presented in 1343, and the prior's nominee was expelled.[86] In the period 1297–1440 the prior presented 4 times, the king 21 times, and, in 1411, 1417, and 1430, Queen Joan thrice. Some of those presented by the king may not have been instituted. After 1443 Eton College made all presentations except that of 1465 by St. George's chapel, Windsor, with which the college was temporarily united.[87] The advowson was reserved from leases of Hullavington manor and rectory estate.[88] From 1976 the college was entitled to present for the united benefice at one turn in three.[89]

The vicar complained in 1240 that his portion was inadequate:[90] it was small in 1291 when the vicarage was valued at £4 6s. 8d.[91] Between 1320 and 1588 the vicarage was augmented with tithes,[92] and between 1443 and 1491 Eton College aug-

mented it with a yearly income of 53s. 4d., the total value of royal revenues granted to the college in 1443.[93] The living, valued at £6 13s. in 1535, remained poor.[94] In 1599 it was valued at £26 13s. 4d.,[95] in 1650 at £45:[96] parliament gave the incumbent £25 in 1649.[97] In 1719 the vicarage was augmented by £400, of which £200 was given by Queen Anne's Bounty, and c. 30 a. in Kington St. Michael were bought,[98] but its net income of £194 c. 1830 shows it to have remained of below average wealth for a living in Malmesbury deanery.[99]

Between 1320 and 1588 all tithes from the whole parish apart from Eton College's demesne, and except those of corn and hay, were transferred from the rectory estate to the vicarage.[1] In the early 19th century the vicar was accepting moduses totalling £7 16s. for the tithes from Surrendell. In 1841 the vicar's tithes were valued at £165 and commuted.[2]

The vicar held 2 yardlands in 1292–3.[3] In 1320 his endowment was a house, those yardlands, 4 a. of arable which parishioners had given for processional candles, and ½ yardland in each of Bradfield and Surrendell which inhabitants of those places had given for services.[4] Because it was discovered that, apparently much earlier, they had been granted without the licence of the lord of the manor, 2 a. were withdrawn from the church in 1448.[5] There is no evidence that the vicar long retained the ½ yardland at Bradfield, and by 1565 the lord of Surrendell manor had taken back the ½ yardland at Surrendell.[6] In 1588 the vicar held the house and 2 yardlands in Hullavington, 49 a. with pasture rights; although he claimed them he held neither of the ½ yardlands.[7] In 1652, after some land was inclosed, the glebe was 58 a.;[8] in 1783, when only 3½ a. remained open, it was 55 a. in Hullavington,[9] and in 1840 it was 53 a.[10] The c. 30 a. in Kington St. Michael were sold in 1921.[11] Eton College bought small parts of the glebe in Hullavington in the 1920s,[12] and the diocesan board of finance owned c. 33 a. in 1989.[13] In 1783 the Vicarage was a large house of stone with adjacent farm buildings on the south side of the churchyard.[14] It was apparently built in the 17th century, and in the early 19th was L-shaped. In 1828 the east range including the front was greatly altered and a new block was built on the south side.[15]

Surrendell church was mentioned in 1179.[16]

[71] W.R.O. 415/12.   [72] Poor Law Abstract, 1804, 566–7.
[73] W.R.O. 1622/20.   [74] Poor Law Abstract, 1818, 498–9.
[75] Ibid.; Poor Rate Returns, 1816–21, 189; 1822–4, 228; 1825–9, 219; 1830–4, 312; Poor Law Com. 2nd Rep. App. E, 406–7.   [76] Poor Law Com. 2nd Rep. App. D, 559.
[77] O.S. Map 1/100,000, admin. areas, Wilts. (1974 edn.).
[78] Eton Coll. Mun. 4/1; above, manors.
[79] Eton Coll. Mun. 47/96.   [80] Below.
[81] Above, introduction, manors.
[82] Eton Coll. Mun. 47/95.   [83] Ch. Com. file, NB 5/143B.
[84] Eton Coll. Mun. 47/95.
[85] Phillipps, Wilts. Inst. (index in W.A.M. xxviii. 222).
[86] Cal. Pat. 1343–5, 141, 295; 1345–8, 347; P.R.O., C 260/55, no. 44B.
[87] Phillipps, Wilts. Inst. (index in W.A.M. xxviii. 222); Cal. Pat. 1377–81, 412, 595; 1385–9, 485; 1388–92, 333; 1408–13, 148; 1413–16, 144; V.C.H. Bucks. ii. 167.
[88] e.g. Eton Coll. Mun. 49/233.
[89] Ch. Com. file, NB 5/143B.   [90] Eton Coll. Mun. 47/95.
[91] Tax. Eccl. (Rec. Com.), 189.
[92] Reg. Martival (Cant. & York Soc.), ii. 286–7; Eton Coll.

Mun. 4/188.
[93] Eton Coll. Mun. 61/RR/A/10; P.R.O., SC 6/Hen. VII/1473; above, local govt.   [94] Valor Eccl. (Rec. Com.), ii. 136.
[95] Eton Coll. Mun. 4/190.   [96] W.A.M. xli. 7.
[97] W. A. Shaw, Hist. Eng. Ch. ii. 548.
[98] C. Hodgson, Queen Anne's Bounty (1864), p. cccxxxvi; Vis. Queries, 1783 (W.R.S. xxvii), p. 124; W.R.O., D 1/24/113/3.   [99] Rep. Com. Eccl. Revenues, 838–9.
[1] Reg. Martival (Cant. & York Soc.), ii. 286–7; Eton Coll. Mun. 4/188.
[2] W.R.O., tithe award.   [3] Eton Coll. Mun. 14/184.
[4] Reg. Martival (Cant. & York Soc.), ii. 287.
[5] Eton Coll. Mun. 4/103.   [6] Ibid. 4/26A–B.
[7] Ibid. 4/188.   [8] Ibid. 4/198.
[9] W.R.O., D 1/24/113/3.   [10] Ibid. tithe award.
[11] Ch. Com. file, NB 5/97.   [12] Eton Coll. Mun. 323/1.
[13] Inf. from Deputy Dioc. Sec., Dioc. Bd. of Finance, Church Ho., 23 Gt. Geo. Street, Bristol.
[14] W.R.O., D 1/24/113/3.
[15] Ibid. 1483/11; Soc. Antiq. MS. 817, vii, f. 70.
[16] Eton Coll. Mun. 47/96.

The vicar held the ½ yardland at Surrendell to meet the cost of serving it, and from 1320 was required to provide a chaplain.[17] Eton College paid for two windows in the chancel to be made and glazed in 1444.[18] The lord of Surrendell manor's resumption of the ½ yardland was because, he claimed in 1565, the sacraments were not being administered in the chapel,[19] but, perhaps to support his claim to the land, the vicar christened children at Surrendell in 1563 and 1566.[20] The church was dilapidated in the later 17th century, and in the later 19th nothing of it survived.[21]

There may have been a chapel at Bradfield in the later 13th century,[22] and the vicar was given the ½ yardland at Bradfield to serve what in 1320 was called Bradfield chantry.[23] In the later 17th century John Aubrey mentioned a chapel within the curtilage of Bradfield manor house: he presumably referred to a separate building but did not mark one as a chapel on his drawing of the manor house, and no remains of one survived in the later 19th century.[24] Another report infers that the chapel was the lower part of a tower of the manor house,[25] but that has not been verified.

A mass in the parish church to celebrate St. Mary had been endowed by 1268, possibly by Nicholas of Preshute;[26] by 1272 a light on St. Peter's altar had been endowed for the souls of Nicholas's relatives Mabel Wynsum and William of Clatford;[27] a light on St. Mary's altar had been endowed by c. 1300, and a chaplain served the altar in 1298;[28] and in 1320 the vicar was made responsible for services at the altar of a chantry in the church.[29] Nothing more is known of such endowments and services. In 1448 the vicar, John Mandeville, resigned after being presented in the manor court for assault and housebreaking.[30] In the later 14th century and earlier 15th, when the king was usually patron, most incumbencies were short and began and ended by exchange.[31] Later incumbencies were longer: Laurence Banks was vicar from 1512 to 1550 or later. His successor, Robert Ward, was deprived in 1553, when there was no copy of the Articles in the church, or 1554,[32] but he again or a namesake was vicar from 1565[33] or earlier to 1599. John Stanley, instituted in 1636,[34] was replaced before 1649 by William Latimer (d. 1657), vicar of Malmesbury from 1633.[35] In 1744 the vicar, Giles Emly, held a service every Sunday, two every other Sunday.[36] Walter Adlam, vicar 1753–91,[37] was assisted by

a curate in the 1750s.[38] In 1783 he was himself curate of Foxley: at Hullavington he held a service every Sunday, celebrated communion thrice a year, and catechized after Whitsun.[39] Curates served the church in the period 1790–1820 when the vicar was Alexander Radcliffe, also vicar of Titchfield (Hants) and of St. Clement's, Sandwich (Kent).[40] William Carter, vicar 1827–64, held morning and afternoon services on Sundays in 1851:[41] he too was curate of Foxley.[42] By will proved 1690 Ayliffe Green gave the vicar £1 a year for a sermon on St. Thomas's day (21 December): the £1 continued to be paid until the later 20th century when the income of the charity was allowed to accumulate.[43]

The church was called St. Mary Magdalene's in 1408[44] but by 1763 had been dedicated to *ST. MARY* the Virgin.[45] It is built of stone rubble with ashlar dressings and has a chancel with north chapel, an aisled nave with south porch and north organ chamber, and a west tower. The nave was presumably unaisled until the later 12th century when both aisles were built, the north before the south. The chancel, which is not structurally separate from the nave, is also of 12th-century origin. The chapel, to which it is joined by a two-bay arcade, was built early in the 13th century, and the north aisle was rebuilt then to the same, greater, width as the chapel. The old north doorway of the aisle was reset. The porch was built in the 13th century and the tower in the 14th. Some windows were renewed in the 15th century, and in the 17th dormers were made on the south side of the nave and the two south aisle windows were carried up into hipped gables.[46] A gallery was built in 1834.[47] In 1871–2 the church was extensively restored to designs by A. W. Blomfield: the tower was taken down and the chancel, the south side of the nave, and the south aisle restored. A new tower was built to Blomfield's designs in 1880,[48] and in 1907 the north part of the church was restored, and the organ chamber built, to designs by C. E. Ponting.[49] In 1917 a 14th- and 15th-century wooden screen between the chapel and the north aisle was taken down.[50] The church retains late medieval bench ends, part of a medieval chasuble,[51] and, in the chapel, a tablet to Simon James (d. 1616). At the entrance to the churchyard from the village street a lych gate was erected in 1897.[52]

The parish has a silver cup hallmarked for 1735

[17] *Reg. Martival* (Cant. & York Soc.), ii. 287.
[18] Eton Coll. Mun. 61/RR/A/18.
[19] Ibid. 4/26A–B.   [20] B.L. Eg. MS. 3128, ff. 7B–8.
[21] Aubrey, *Topog. Coll.* ed. Jackson, 114–15.
[22] W.R.O. 312/6, no. 3.
[23] *Reg. Martival* (Cant. & York Soc.), ii. 287.
[24] Aubrey, *Topog. Coll.* ed. Jackson, 248–9, pl. xxiv; above, p. 111.   [25] Soc. Antiq. MS. 817, vii, f. 70v.
[26] *Bradenstoke Cart.* (W.R.S. xxxv), pp. 74–5.
[27] Ibid. p. 74; Eton Coll. Mun. 4/3, nos. 2, 4.
[28] W.R.O. 312/6, nos. 4, 27.
[29] *Reg. Martival* (Cant. & York Soc.), ii. 287.
[30] Phillipps, *Wilts. Inst.* i. 139; Eton Coll. Mun. 4/103.
[31] Phillipps, *Wilts. Inst.* (index in *W.A.M.* xxviii. 222); *Cal. Pat.* 1377–81, 412, 595; 1385–9, 485; 1388–92, 333; 1408–13, 148; 1413–16, 144.
[32] Phillipps, *Wilts. Inst.* i. 190, 216; W.R.O., D 1/43/1, ff. 22v., 130v.
[33] Eton Coll. Mun. 4/26A–B. A Robert Ward, vicar, was said to have d. before 28 Mar. 1553: ibid. 4/138.
[34] Phillipps, *Wilts. Inst.* ii. 1, 18.

[35] *W.A.M.* xlii. 556; *W.N. & Q.* vii. 549.
[36] W.R.O., D 1/51/5, f. 18.
[37] Phillipps, *Wilts. Inst.* ii. 75, 96.   [38] W.R.O. 1622/8.
[39] *Vis. Queries, 1783* (W.R.S. xxvii), p. 124.
[40] Phillipps, *Wilts. Inst.* ii. 96; *Alum. Oxon. 1715–1886,* iii. 1169; *Clerical Guide* (1829); W.R.O., bishop's transcripts, bdle. 3; Soc. Antiq. MS. 817, vii, f. 70.
[41] *Rep. Com. Eccl. Revenues,* 838–9; P.R.O., HO 129/252/2/15/20; mon. in church.   [42] P.R.O., HO 129/252/2/13/16.
[43] *Endowed Char. Wilts.* (N. Div.), 576–7; Char. Com. file.
[44] *Reg. Hallum* (Cant. & York Soc.), p. 4.
[45] J. Ecton, *Thesaurus* (1763), 404.
[46] J. Buckler, watercolour in W.A.S. Libr., vol. vi. 29; see above, plate facing p. 109; photo. in church.
[47] W.R.O. 1483/5.
[48] Ibid. 1622/22; *Kelly's Dir. Wilts.* (1939); Soc. Antiq. MS. 817, vii, ff. 70, 74; Bristol R.O., EP/J/6/2/142.
[49] *W.A.M.* xxxv. 518; Bristol R.O., EP/J/6/2/142.
[50] Badeni, *Wilts. Forefathers,* 78; W.R.O. 1622/21; photo. in church.   [51] *W.A.M.* xxx. 351–2; *Arch. Jnl.* i. 330.
[52] Wilts. Cuttings, xvii. 30.

which Thomas Jacob (d. 1730) gave by will. There is also a paten hallmarked for 1732.[53]

In 1553 there were three bells and a sanctus bell, later only two bells. A new bell, cast by Abraham Rudhall in 1705, was hung in 1707. When the new tower was built in 1880 the other bell was replaced by one cast then by John Warner & Sons.[54] Those two bells hung in the church in 1989.[55]

The registers begin in 1557: entries to 1599 were copied by the vicar, John Moore, instituted in 1599.[56] Burials are not recorded for 1636–54 and 1662–95, baptisms for 1641–57 and 1662–94, and marriages for 1644–95.[57]

NONCONFORMITY.

Quaker families lived at Hullavington from 1660 to 1832 or later, members of the Bullock family throughout the period.[58] Those of Hullavington excommunicated 1663–5, and still excommunicate in 1674, were almost certainly Quakers.[59] The society had opened a burial ground in the parish by 1747, and in 1753 also had a meeting house[60] which was later said to have been built in the 17th century.[61] The Quaker society at Hullavington was one of only seven active in Wiltshire in 1800, and had ceased to meet by 1820.[62]

Five meeting houses for Independents were certified between 1796 and 1803,[63] and a small stone chapel in Gothic style was built at Newtown in 1821.[64] Registers of baptisms survive for the period 1825–36.[65] Three services were held on Census Sunday in 1851 with an average congregation of 56: the church was then said to be for a union of Independents and Baptists,[66] and in 1910 was for General Baptists.[67] It had been closed by 1928.[68]

A Baptist chapel was founded in 1839,[69] and the small Mount Zion chapel was built of stone rubble in Gibbs Lane for Particular Baptists in 1843.[70] On Census Sunday in 1851 the three services were attended by an average of 35.[71] John Greenman (d. 1866) gave by will £110 to endow the chapel: a cottage was bought and, in 1897, sold.[72] Two meetings each Sunday were held c. 1968,[73] and meetings were held in the chapel until 1989.[74]

A chapel in Watts Lane for Primitive Methodists may have been the second chapel certified in 1843. Three services were held in it on Census Sunday in 1851 with an average congregation of 60.[75] The small chapel, of stone rubble with red-brick dressings, was improved in 1858.[76] It was closed in the mid 1980s.[77]

EDUCATION.

By will proved 1690 Ayliffe Green endowed an eleemosynary, sermon, and education charity for Hullavington.[78] In the earlier 18th century children attended a school at Hullavington which received £3 a year from the charity, a gift said to induce other contributions to the school.[79] The £3 was paid to a mistress to teach six children to read; in 1818 the parish wanted greater means to educate its children.[80] In 1832 a day school for 6 boys and 6 girls was started, and in 1833 another school, for 20 boys and 19 girls, was built on the east side of the Street. The £3 was given for the free teaching of 10 children in the larger school:[81] both were National schools. In 1846–7 a total of 71 children attended.[82] The larger school was enlarged in 1870.[83] In 1871, when the smaller was for the children of dissenters, a total of 100 attended.[84]

In 1887, when the National school may have been the only one in the parish and was undersubscribed, a school board was formed.[85] Between then and the mid 20th century the income from Green's charity, usually a little less than £3, was spent on prizes.[86] Average attendance was 114 in 1902.[87] It had risen to 131 by 1908–9 but thereafter declined until in 1937–8 it was 47.[88] New housing in the village after the Second World War brought about a rise, to 159 in 1970 when a new school was built on the west side of the Street.[89] The old school building remained in use until 1987.[90] In 1988 the new school had 96 pupils.[91]

CHARITY FOR THE POOR.

By will proved 1690 Ayliffe Green gave £1 a year to the second poor of Hullavington. In the early 20th century doles of 2s. or 4s. were given on St. Thomas's day (21 December); later the gifts were of 10s. In the 1960s and 1970s the charity's income was allowed to accumulate.[92]

[53] Nightingale, *Wilts. Plate,* 200; inf. from Mrs. J. Giles, 1 Gibbs Lane.
[54] Walters, *Wilts. Bells,* 107; W.R.O. 1622/20.
[55] Inf. from Mrs. Giles.
[56] B.L. Eg. MS. 3128; Phillipps, *Wilts. Inst.* ii. 1.
[57] W.R.O. 1622/1–12; bishop's transcripts for some of the missing periods are ibid.
[58] *W.N. & Q.* ii–vii, *passim.*
[59] Williams, *Cath. Recusancy* (Cath. Rec. Soc), 71.
[60] *W.N. & Q.* v. 552; Eton Coll. Mun. 4/206.
[61] *Vis. Queries, 1783* (W.R.S. xxvii), p. 124.
[62] *V.C.H. Wilts.* iii. 136.
[63] *Meeting Ho. Certs.* (W.R.S. xl), pp. 45, 51, 56, 59; *W.A.M.* lxi. 66.
[64] *Meeting Ho. Certs.* (W.R.S. xl), p. 94, where the attribution of the chapel to Baptists seems incorrect.
[65] P.R.O., RG 4/2233.
[66] Ibid. HO 129/252/2/15/22.
[67] W.R.O., Inland Revenue, val. reg. 13.
[68] Ibid. G 7/501/1.
[69] *V.C.H. Wilts.* iii. 138 n.
[70] *Meeting Ho. Certs.* (W.R.S. xl), p. 158; R. W. Oliver, *Strict Bapt. Chapels Eng.* (Strict Bapt. Hist. Soc.), v. 33 and facing pl.
[71] P.R.O., HO 129/252/2/15/23.

[72] W.R.O. 630/1, deed, Seager to Chappell, 1866.
[73] Oliver, op. cit. 33.
[74] Inf. from Mrs. Giles.
[75] *Meeting Ho. Certs.* (W.R.S. xl), p. 155; P.R.O., HO 129/252/2/15/21.
[76] Soc. Antiq. MS. 817, vii, f. 71.
[77] Inf. from Mrs. Giles.
[78] P.R.O., PROB 11/402, f. 241v.
[79] T. Cox, *Magna Brit.* vi (1731), 199.
[80] *Vis. Queries, 1783* (W.R.S. xxvii), p. 125; *Educ. of Poor Digest,* 1029.
[81] *Educ. Enq. Abstract,* 1039; *Endowed Char. Wilts.* (N. Div.), 576.
[82] Nat. Soc. *Inquiry, 1846–7,* Wilts. 6–7.
[83] W.R.O. 782/57.
[84] *Returns relating to Elem. Educ.* 420–1.
[85] Eton Coll. Mun. 286/2.
[86] *Endowed Char. Wilts.* (N. Div.), 567; W.R.O. Char. Com., Hullavington; Char. Com. file.
[87] W.R.O., F 8/220/1.
[88] *Bd. of Educ., List 21, 1910* (H.M.S.O.), 507; *1938,* 423.
[89] W.R.O., F 8/220/1.
[90] Wilts. Cuttings, xxx. 316.
[91] Inf. from Chief Educ. Officer, Co. Hall, Trowbridge.
[92] *Endowed Char. Wilts.* (N. Div.), 576–7; W.R.O., Char. Com., Hullavington; Char. Com. file.

LEA AND CLEVERTON

Lea village is 2.5 km. ESE. of Malmesbury, and Cleverton hamlet is 2 km. ESE. of that.[93] Lea and Cleverton is one of very few Wiltshire parishes called by the names of two settlements, and it has only one church, at Lea. By the mid 16th century the church was served by the rector of Garsdon;[94] in 1608 and 1671 the churchwardens of Lea entitled the glebe terriers Lea and Cleverton,[95] and in a visitation book of 1680 the bishop entered Lea and, erroneously, Cleverton as two chapels served by the rector of Garsdon. Although that entry was later corrected[96] the chapelry was called Lea and Cleverton in subsequent diocesan records[97] and that was the parish name in the 19th century;[98] it is unlikely that the name was used to distinguish Lea from Leigh Delamere in the same deanery.

To the south-west the parish embraced an island of Little Somerford parish, 5 a.: under an Act of 1882 that was transferred to Lea and Cleverton and a small area of Lea and Cleverton was transferred to Little Somerford.[99] Lea and Cleverton parish thereafter measured 1,778 a. (720 ha.). Garsdon parish was added to it in 1934 and increased its area to 1,176 ha. (2,908 a.).[1] The simplicity of the parish boundaries in the 19th century suggests that they may be ancient. The western is marked by the Bristol Avon, much of the northern and eastern by its tributary Woodbridge brook which was a boundary *c.* 1100, and the southern ran near or along the Swindon–Malmesbury road. The inclusion of *c.* 70 a. west of the Avon within the boundaries in 1840 was apparently a mistake.[2]

Two streams flow northwards across the parish to Woodbridge brook. The highest land, 100 m., is on the southern boundary, the lowest, 70 m., is beside the Avon, and the relief is gentle. Kellaways Clay outcrops in the west part of the parish, Kellaways Sand between the two streams, and Oxford Clay extensively in the east. Alluvium flanks the eastern stream, Woodbridge brook, and the Avon, and glacial drift covers the highest land to the south.[3] Most of the land has long been pasture,[4] and the name Lea may indicate that the parish was formerly well wooded.[5]

The main Swindon–Malmesbury road, in 1773 as later, entered the parish across Cow bridge: it was turnpiked in 1809, disturnpiked in 1876.[6] In 1773 a road led north from it through Lea to Charlton. An east–west road from Milbourne in Malmesbury parish crossed the Charlton road at

the south end of Lea, followed a winding course to Cleverton, and crossed Woodbridge brook by the bridge now called Wood bridge. West of Lea it was called Crab Mill Road in 1807, later Crab Mill Lane; between Lea and Cleverton it was called Cresswell Lane from the 1880s. Another road left it at Cleverton and led south to the main road. All those roads remained in use in the later 20th century, although Crab Mill Lane was then principally a farm road. North of Lea in 1773 a road ran east from the Charlton road, and from it two others ran south to Cleverton. In 1807 only the western road to Cleverton was in use, though both were used in 1887;[7] in 1989 the east–west road was a private drive. A Bristol–Cirencester canal across the parish was proposed in the late 18th century but not built.[8] The railway line to Malmesbury opened in 1877 crossed the parish near the Avon.[9]

In 1377 Lea had 40 poll-tax payers, Cleverton 55. The population of the parish rose rapidly in the early 19th century, from 252 in 1801 to 446 in 1841, when 330 lived in Lea tithing, 116 in Cleverton. Insufficient housing was said to have caused its fall to 414 between 1841 and 1851. It had risen to 494 by 1871 but thereafter declined, with some fluctuations. The steepest fall was from 414 in 1921 to 377 in 1931.[10] After 1970 the population of the enlarged parish was much increased by new housing; of 695 inhabitants in 1981,[11] the great majority lived in Lea village.

LEA. The village stands in the west part of the parish on sandy soil. It was called the Lea from the 13th century to the later 18th.[12] The church is at the junction of the Charlton road and Cresswell Lane. East of it Manor Farm is a gabled stone farmhouse of the late 17th or early 18th century: it may have been built to a **T**-shaped plan but is now square. South-west of the church Brill's Court was a large house in the 17th century: in the early 19th century it was replaced by a small farmhouse[13] which was later much extended. Between Manor Farm and Brill's Court, near the church, another farmhouse is of 18th-century origin.

West of the church Crab Mill Lane and the road approaching the village from the south had wide verges with a small green, Lea green, at their junction, and in 1773 buildings stood along the north side of the green, now the east end of Crab Mill Lane. Most were replaced in the 19th century or

---

[93] This article was written in 1989. Maps used include O.S. Maps 1/50,000, sheet 173 (1974 edn.); 1/25,000, ST 98 (1959 edn.); 6″, Wilts. VIII–IX, XIII–XIV (1887–9 and later edns.).
[94] Below, church.
[95] W.R.O., D 1/24/132/1–2.
[96] Ibid. D 1/48/1.
[97] Ibid. D 1/51/1.
[98] *V.C.H. Wilts.* iv. 352.
[99] *Census*, 1891; W.R.O., tithe award.
[1] *V.C.H. Wilts.* iv. 352 n.; *Census*, 1951.
[2] W.R.O., tithe award; ibid. Malmesbury tithe award; *Arch. Jnl.* lxxvii. 53.
[3] Geol. Surv. Map 1″, solid and drift, sheets 251 (1970 edn.), 252 (1974 edn.).

[4] Below, econ. hist.
[5] *P.N. Wilts.* (E.P.N.S.), 61.
[6] *Andrews and Dury, Map* (W.R.S. viii), pl. 14; *L.J.* xxviii. 581; *V.C.H. Wilts.* iv. 271.
[7] *Andrews and Dury, Map* (W.R.S. viii), pls. 14, 17; O.S. Maps 6″, Wilts. VIII–IX, XIII–XIV (1887–9 edns.); W.R.O. 1553/104.
[8] *W.A.M.* xlii. 399.
[9] *V.C.H. Wilts.* iv. 288.
[10] Ibid. 309, 321, 352.
[11] *Census*, 1981.
[12] *P.N. Wilts.* (E.P.N.S.), 61; *Andrews and Dury, Map* (W.R.S. viii), pl. 17.
[13] J. Britton, *Beauties of Wilts.* iii. 69.

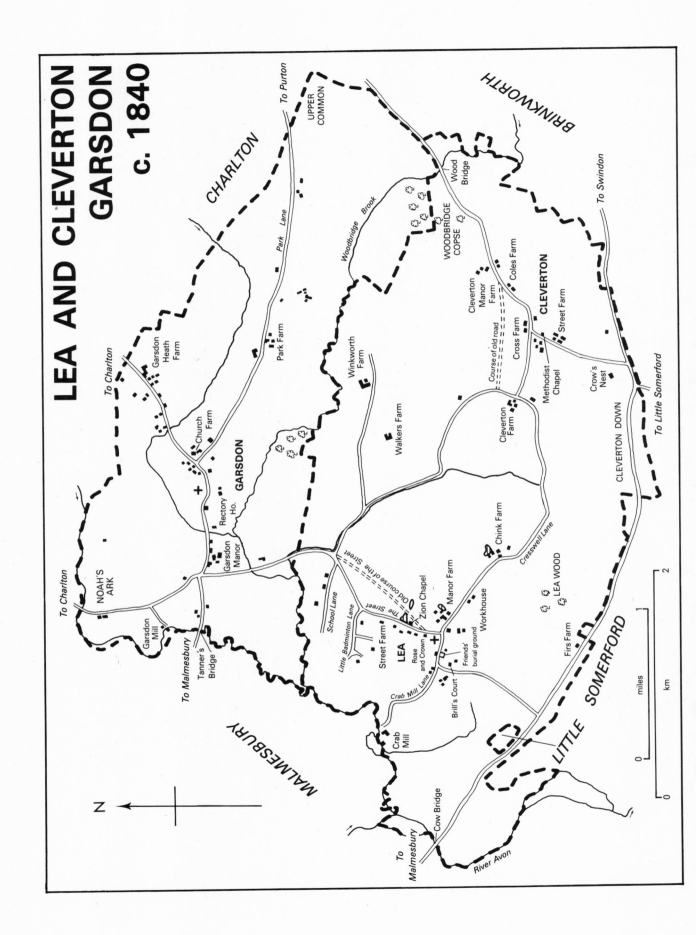

LEA AND CLEVERTON GARSDON c. 1840

N

CHARLTON

MALMESBURY

BRINKWORTH

LITTLE SOMERFORD

To Purton

UPPER COMMON

To Swindon

Wood Bridge

Woodbridge Brook

WOODBRIDGE COPSE

Coles Farm

CLEVERTON

Street Farm

Cleverton Manor Farm

Cross Farm

Course of old road

Methodist Chapel

Crow's Nest

To Little Somerford

CLEVERTON DOWN

Park Lane

Garsdon Heath Farm

Park Farm

Church Farm

GARSDON

Rectory Ho.

Garsdon Manor

Winkworth Farm

Walkers Farm

Cleverton Farm

Chink Farm

Cresswell Lane

LEA WOOD

Firs Farm

To Charlton

NOAH'S ARK

Garsdon Mill

Tanner's Bridge

To Malmesbury

To Charlton

School Lane

Little Badminton Lane

Street Farm

LEA

The Street

Old course of the Street

Zion Chapel

Rose and Crown

Friends' burial ground

Manor Farm

Workhouse

Brill's Court

Crab Mill Lane

Crab Mill

To Malmesbury

Cow Bridge

River Avon

miles
km
0
1
2

the 20th. Most of Lea green was used as a recreation ground in the later 20th century. Scattered houses were also along Cresswell Lane in 1773. North of the church in 1773 farmsteads and houses stood on the edges of the roughly triangular Lea lower common.[14] A few buildings survive from that date including Street Farm, Merton Farm, and some at the west end of Little Badminton Lane and in School Lane. When the common was inclosed in 1806 School Lane was made along its northern edge, Little Badminton Lane was made across it, and the Charlton road, later called the Street, was remade on a more westerly course.[15]

In the early 19th century much of the village was rebuilt, but its extent had changed little by 1840.[16] In the Street a nonconformist chapel was built in the early 19th century and a school in the later. The Rose and Crown inn, mentioned in 1788,[17] was at the southern end of the Street, rebuilt in 1891,[18] and open in 1989. The Old Inn, mentioned in 1822 and 1827,[19] may also have been in Lea village. A pond, east of the Street in 1840, had been drained by 1885.[20] A few more houses were built in the Street in the later 19th century but, apart from a village hall of 1934,[21] there was little further building until the later 20th century. A rectory house and some private houses in the Street and 14 council houses in St. Giles's Close at its north end were built in the 1950s and 1960s. In the 1970s and 1980s over 100 houses were built; there was infilling in the Street, School Lane, and Crab Mill Lane, 33 houses and bungalows were built in Pembroke Green west of the church, and 8 houses south of Little Badminton Lane.

West of the village Crab Mill stood on Woodbridge brook from the 15th century or earlier.[22] East of the village Walkers Farm and Chink Farm were standing in 1773;[23] Chink Farm was rebuilt c. 1800, Walkers was demolished between 1840 and 1885.[24] Winkworth Farm was built soon after 1773 on a raised site east of Walkers Farm;[25] it was much altered in the 19th century and cottages and a bungalow were built west of it in the 20th. Firs Farm was built beside the main road south of the village between 1807 and 1840,[26] and in the late 19th century Lea House, a large brick and stone villa, was built south of the road near Cow bridge. Several other houses were built beside the road and in the 1930s six pairs of council houses, Lea Crescent, were built at its junction with the road to the village.[27]

CLEVERTON in 1773 was a loose group of c. 12 farmsteads and cottages in Cresswell Lane and lanes leading north and south from it.[28] At the junction with the southern lane a cross standing in the late 18th century had been removed by 1840.[29] In the east part of Cresswell Lane a group of buildings was called Old Hill in 1773;[30] a lane linking Old Hill to the northern lane went out of use between 1807 and 1828.[31] Two farmsteads survive from 1773, Street Farm in the southern lane and Cleverton Manor Farm on the north side of Cresswell Lane at Old Hill. Between 1773 and 1802 Coles Farm was built south-west of Cleverton Manor Farm.[32] It and Cleverton Farm, further west in Cresswell Lane, were rebuilt and Cross Farm, on the site of the cross, was built in the early 19th century. In 1832 a nonconformist chapel, presumably on the site of a later chapel north of Street Farm, was built.[33] Between 1840 and 1885 a farmstead beside the northern lane north of Cleverton Farm was demolished,[34] but otherwise the hamlet has been little changed since 1840.

South of the hamlet the Swindon–Malmesbury road had very wide verges called Cleverton down.[35] Of two buildings north of the verge in 1773[36] one, called the Crow's Nest in 1828,[37] was an inn in 1865 and may have been earlier; it was closed between 1931 and 1939.[38] A 20th-century bungalow is on the site of the other. Cleverton down was inclosed in 1806,[39] and a new inn, the Traveller's Rest, was built beside the road between 1840 and 1885.[40] It was closed between 1915 and 1921[41] and the site was used for Lovett Farm. To the west Hill Field Farm was built in the earlier 20th century behind the line of the old verge.

MANORS AND OTHER ESTATES. The lands of Lea and Cleverton were probably held by Malmesbury abbey before the Conquest and may have been part of its large estate called Brokenborough c. 1100.[42] By the later 13th century the abbey had alienated some lands in the parish; it then had an estate called Cleverton[43] and perhaps a separate estate called Lea.

After the Dissolution the Crown granted the abbey's whole estate in the parish to Richard Moody in 1540.[44] As LEA AND CLEVERTON manor the estate passed with Garsdon manor from Moody (d. 1550) in turn to his relict Catherine[45] (d. 1556) and son Richard[46] (d. 1612), to Sir Henry Moody, Bt.[47] (d. 1629), and to Sir Henry's son Sir Henry,[48] who sold Lea and Cleverton manor to Henry Danvers, earl of Danby, in 1634.[49] Danby (d. 1644) devised it with Malmesbury

[14] Andrews and Dury, Map (W.R.S. viii), pls. 14, 17.
[15] W.R.O., EA/70; ibid. 1553/104.   [16] Ibid. tithe award.
[17] Ibid. 524/16.   [18] Date on bldg.
[19] W.R.O., A 1/326/3.
[20] Ibid. tithe award; O.S. Map 6", Wilts. VIII (1889 edn.).
[21] Date on bldg.
[22] P.R.O., SC 6/1054/20; below, econ. hist.
[23] Andrews and Dury, Map (W.R.S. viii), pls. 14, 17.
[24] O.S. Map 6", Wilts. VIII (1889 edn.); W.R.O., tithe award.
[25] W.R.O. 2057/P 1/1.
[26] Ibid. 1553/104; ibid. tithe award.
[27] Ibid. G 7/132/16.
[28] Andrews and Dury, Map (W.R.S. viii), pl. 14.
[29] W.R.O. 2057/P 1/1; ibid. tithe award.
[30] Andrews and Dury, Map (W.R.S. viii), pl. 14.
[31] O.S. Map 1", sheet 34 (1828 edn.); W.R.O. 1553/104.

[32] Andrews and Dury, Map (W.R.S. viii), pl. 14; W.R.O. 2057/P 1/1.
[33] Below, nonconf.
[34] O.S. Map 6", Wilts. XIV (1887 edn.); W.R.O., tithe award.   [35] W.R.O., tithe award.
[36] Andrews and Dury, Map (W.R.S. viii), pl. 14.
[37] O.S. Map 1", sheet 34 (1828 edn.).
[38] Harrod's Dir. Wilts. (1865); Kelly's Dir. Wilts. (1931, 1939).   [39] Below, econ. hist.
[40] O.S. Map 6", Wilts. XIII (1888 edn.); W.R.O., tithe award.
[41] Kelly's Dir. Wilts. (1915, 1921).
[42] Arch. Jnl. lxxvii. 52–3.   [43] Reg. Malm. i. 184–7; below.
[44] L. & P. Hen. VIII, xv, p. 410.
[45] P.R.O., C 142/92, no. 114; above, Garsdon, manor.
[46] P.R.O., C 142/131, no. 200.   [47] Ibid. C 142/333, no. 7.
[48] Wilts. Inq. p.m. 1625–49 (Index Libr.), 151–5.
[49] P.R.O., C 104/87, deed, Moody to Danby, 1634.

manor to his nephew Henry Danvers. After Danvers's death in 1654 his estates were shared by his sisters Elizabeth and Anne. Anne (d. 1659), wife of Sir Henry Lee, Bt. (d. 1659), was succeeded by her daughters Eleanor, wife of James Bertie, earl of Abingdon, and Anne, wife of Thomas Wharton, marquess of Wharton. A moiety of Lea and Cleverton manor was probably among estates allotted to the younger Anne at her marriage in 1673.[50] Elizabeth and her husband Robert Danvers held the other moiety in 1672[51] but had apparently conveyed it to the Whartons by 1685.[52] In 1705 Lord Wharton sold the whole manor, except apparently Westfield farm, to Thomas Boucher[53] (d. 1708), who was succeeded by his son Thomas (fl. 1749). The younger Thomas's daughter Julia or Judith married William FitzWilliam,[54] who held the manor in 1774[55] and 1780. By 1789 it had passed to William's grandnephew Richard FitzWilliam, Viscount Fitz-William (d. 1816),[56] who devised it to his kinsman Sidney Herbert (cr. Baron Herbert of Lea and d. 1861). Herbert, who in 1840 held c. 750 a. in the parish, was succeeded by his son George, Baron Herbert, who in 1862 became earl of Pembroke and of Montgomery. The manor, increased by purchase to c. 1,050 a., passed to Reginald Herbert, earl of Pembroke and of Montgomery,[57] who in 1916 and 1917 sold it in portions.[58]

Manor farm, 188 a., was bought in 1917 by J. Sellwood[59] and held in 1923 and 1939 by H. J. Sellwood.[60] It apparently belonged to the Sellwood family until 1973[61] and was later broken up.[62] John Newman bought Winkworth farm, 233 a., in 1917.[63] It passed to his kinsman George Newman (d. 1975) whose sons Mr. Anthony Newman and Mr. Timothy Newman owned it in 1989.[64] Cleverton farm, 150 a., was bought in 1916 by Frederick Smith,[65] who sold it in 1939 to Jesus College, Oxford. In 1971 the college sold it to Mr. Anthony Webb who with his son Mr. Paul Webb owned the farm in 1989.[66]

WESTFIELD farm was owned by Lord Wharton in 1685[67] and apparently retained in 1705. Between then and 1780, when it belonged to Jacob Bouverie, earl of Radnor, it may have passed with the main part of Whitchurch and Milbourne manor in Malmesbury or with Southfield farm in Milbourne. Lord Radnor sold Westfield farm c. 1820 either to John Howard, earl of Suffolk and of Berkshire (d. 1820), or to John's son Thomas, earl of Suffolk and of Berkshire,[68] who in 1840 held

133 a. in Lea and Cleverton parish.[69] The lands passed with Charlton manor and the titles, presumably to Michael Howard, earl of Suffolk and of Berkshire from 1941. In 1989 they probably belonged to Mr. R. G. Baker.[70]

A manor of *LEA*, of which Malmesbury abbey was overlord in 1439,[71] apparently consisted of land subinfeudated by the abbey. Richard Parfet held $\frac{1}{8}$ knight's fee in Lea in 1242–3 and perhaps after 1260, William of Hankerton held $\frac{1}{4}$ knight's fee, probably also in 1242–3,[72] and Robert, son of Pain of Lea, held $\frac{1}{2}$ hide and 1 yardland in the later 13th century.[73] In 1340 Ralph of Combe conveyed Lea manor to Sir John Mauduit, Mauduit conveyed it to John Moleyns, husband of his daughter Gille,[74] and Moleyns was granted free warren in the demesne lands.[75] The manor was confiscated in 1341 but restored to Moleyns in 1345.[76] On his death in 1360 it passed to Joan (d. 1369), relict of his son John and then wife of Sir Michael Poynings (d. 1369), and in 1369 to the elder John Moleyns's son Sir William (d. 1381),[77] whose relict Margery held it at her death in 1399. Margery was succeeded by her grandson Sir William Moleyns[78] (d. 1425), whose relict Margery held Lea manor at her death in 1439. It passed to her granddaughter Eleanor Moleyns, later wife of Sir Robert Hungerford, Lord Hungerford and Moleyns (attainted 1461, d. 1464).[79] In 1460 Robert and Eleanor conveyed Lea with other manors to trustees to raise money for Robert's ransom from Aquitaine. Eleanor sued for its return in 1461 but may not have recovered it until after 1464. In 1472 she and her husband Sir Oliver Manningham (d. 1499) settled it on themselves for life with reversion to Eleanor's son Sir Walter Hungerford (d. 1516) in tail and with remainder to her granddaughter Mary Hungerford, *suo jure* Baroness Botreaux, Hungerford, and Moleyns (d. c. 1533), who married first Edward Hastings, Lord Hastings (d. 1506), and secondly Sir Richard Sacheverell (d. 1534).[80] Sir Walter's rights were apparently ignored in 1499 and the manor passed to Mary's son George Hastings, Lord Hastings (cr. earl of Huntingdon 1529, d. 1544), who retained it after arbitration between him and Sir Walter's grandson Walter, Lord Hungerford, in 1535. Lea manor passed to George's son Francis, earl of Huntingdon (d. 1560), and to Francis's son Henry, earl of Huntingdon,[81] who sold Lea manor in parcels between 1571 and 1581. The lordship was bought in 1575

[50] W.R.O. 88/8/3; below, Malmesbury, manors.
[51] P.R.O., C 104/86/1, order, Danvers v. Lee, 1672.
[52] W.R.O. 88/8/44.
[53] P.R.O., CP 25(2)/979/4 Anne Mich.
[54] Burke, *Ext. & Dorm. Peerages* (1883), 214; W.R.O. 490/480.
[55] P.R.O., CP 25(2)/1446/14 Geo. III East.
[56] Burke, *Ext. & Dorm. Peerages* (1883), 215; W.R.O., A 1/345/261.
[57] *Complete Peerage*, vi. 445–6; x. 429–50; W.R.O., tithe award.
[58] W.R.O. 2057/R 113–14; W.A.S. Libr., sale cat. x, no. 17.
[59] W.R.O. 2057/R 114.
[60] *Kelly's Dir. Wilts.* (1923, 1939).
[61] Wilts. Cuttings, xxvii. 155.
[62] Inf. from Mr. N. Haines, Manor Farm.
[63] W.R.O. 2057/R 113–14.
[64] Inf. from Mrs. A. Newman, Winkworth Farm.
[65] W.R.O. 2057/R 113–14.

[66] Inf. from Mr. A. Webb, Cleverton Farm.
[67] W.R.O. 88/8/44.
[68] Ibid. A 1/345/261; below, Malmesbury, manors.
[69] W.R.O., tithe award.
[70] Above, Charlton, manors; local inf.
[71] P.R.O., C 139/94, no. 52.
[72] *Bk. of Fees*, ii. 716; *Reg. Malm.* i. 17; ii. 389.
[73] *Reg. Malm.* i. 17, 247–8.
[74] *Feet of F.* 1327–77 (W.R.S. xxix), pp. 61–4; *Complete Peerage*, ix. 39.
[75] *Cal. Chart. R.* 1327–41, 468.
[76] *Cal. Pat.* 1343–5, 543.
[77] *Complete Peerage*, ix. 39; *Cal. Inq. p.m.* xii, pp. 389–90, 393.
[78] *Cal. Inq. p.m.* xvii, p. 427.
[79] *Complete Peerage*, ix. 41–3; P.R.O., C 139/94, no. 52.
[80] *Complete Peerage*, vi. 620–5; Hist. MSS. Com. 78, *Hastings*, i, p. 303; P.R.O., C 1/28, no. 111.
[81] Hist. MSS. Com. 78, *Hastings*, i, pp. 309–10; *Complete Peerage*, vi. 654–7.

by William Drewet,[82] perhaps a trustee of Richard Moody, and in 1581 Huntingdon conveyed the lordship and some land of the manor to Moody,[83] who merged them with Lea and Cleverton manor.

Several other estates in Lea are known to have been parts of Lea manor, as others, not traced before the 17th century, may have been. In 1572 Lord Huntingdon sold an estate in Lea, including a manor house, to Henry Cheever[84] (d. by 1591), who was succeeded by his son Jeremy.[85] Sir Henry Moody (d. 1629) bought part of Cheever's estate and added it to Lea and Cleverton manor;[86] the rest, including the house, passed from Jeremy Cheever (d. 1622) to his son Robert.[87] Lands in Lea bought in 1571 from Lord Huntingdon by Thomas Rich,[88] and sold by Rich to Jeremy Cheever, were also held by Robert Cheever in 1623.[89] No later record of the Cheevers' holding has been traced.

Lands bought from Lord Huntingdon in 1571 by Robert Golding (fl. 1580)[90] passed to Golding's son Thomas (d. 1610) and to Thomas's son Robert.[91] By 1695 another Thomas Golding had sold the estate, c. 80 a., to John Jacob.[92] Lands sold by Lord Huntingdon in 1571 to Philip Watts or Gibbs[93] were probably also among c. 270 a. in the parish settled by Jacob (d. 1705) on the marriage of his son John.[94] The younger John (d. 1728 or 1729) devised thirds to his daughters Anne (d. 1787), Mary (d. 1790), later wife of James Clutterbuck, and Elizabeth, later wife of John Buxton.[95] Mary's portion passed c. 1788 to her nephew Robert Buxton (cr. a baronet 1800). That and Elizabeth's portion were apparently bought from Robert by Richard, Viscount FitzWilliam, who held them in 1790 and added them to Lea and Cleverton manor.[96] Anne's portion, later called Chink farm, also passed to Robert Buxton. In 1839 Sir Robert was succeeded by his son Sir John (d. 1842), who held c. 130 a. in the parish and was succeeded by his son Sir Robert.[97] In 1860 the farm was owned by Sidney Herbert.[98] It passed with Lea and Cleverton manor to Reginald, earl of Pembroke and of Montgomery, who sold it in 1917 to A. Shewring (d. by 1923).[99] H. J. Shewring owned the farm in 1939,[1] and it belonged to a member of the Shewring family in 1989.[2]

An estate in Lea, perhaps formerly Lord Huntingdon's, was held in 1625 and 1630 by Thomas Hungerford[3] and may have been that held in the

earlier 17th century by Anthony Hungerford which included a house called *BRILL'S COURT* and, after purchases by Anthony, 76 a. Brill's Court may have been acquired by Henry, earl of Danby, lord of Lea and Cleverton manor, but it apparently passed like Rodbourne manor in Malmesbury parish to Eleanor, countess of Abingdon, and Montagu Bertie, earl of Abingdon, and like Grange farm in Malmesbury to Edmund Estcourt, who held it in 1752, and Edmund Gale.[4] In 1840 James Bailey held the house and 30 a.; Gale's heirs held the rest of the estate, Walkers farm, 77 a.[5] The farm was later merged with Lea and Cleverton manor.[6]

In 1780 John Weeks owned the farm later called Cleverton Manor farm. He was succeeded c. 1802 by William Weeks,[7] who in 1840 held 129 a. in the parish.[8] A William Weeks held the farm in 1854[9] and 1865,[10] E. R. Case in 1910,[11] and W. A. Sellwood in the 1920s.[12] In 1965 it was bought by Mr. F. E. Durston, who sold the farmhouse and 75 a. to Mr. and Mrs. Fittes.[13]

Land in Lea and Cleverton, 74 a. in 1840,[14] was apparently sold by Sir Henry Moody with Garsdon manor in 1631. It descended as part of Garsdon manor, with which it was sold in 1843 by Paul Methuen, Baron Methuen, to Thomas, earl of Suffolk and of Berkshire, until c. 1945.[15]

Malmesbury abbey owned great tithes in the parish in 1248[16] and at the Dissolution.[17] By grants of 1540 and 1543 the abbey's tithes were acquired by Richard Moody,[18] and they descended with Lea and Cleverton manor. By 1840 the great tithes from that manor and most other land in the parish had been merged. From c. 300 a. the great tithes, belonging to Sidney Herbert, were valued at £35 and commuted.[19]

ECONOMIC HISTORY. There was an open field at Winkworth in the 13th century.[20] Burton field in the west part of the parish was apparently open in the 16th century,[21] and Westfield, which had been inclosed by the 17th century,[22] may earlier have been open. All are likely to have been on the sandy soils around Lea village. All or part of the field at Winkworth was inclosed in the later 13th century.[23] Most holdings in the parish consisted chiefly of inclosed meadow and pasture in the 16th century,[24] and there is no later reference

[82] C. Cross, *Puritan Earl*, 309.
[83] P.R.O., CP 25(2)/240/23 & 24 Eliz. I Mich.
[84] Ibid. CP 25(2)/239/14 & 15 Eliz. I Mich.
[85] Ibid. C 78/84, no. 3.
[86] *Wilts. Inq. p.m.* 1625–49 (Index Libr.), 151–5.
[87] P.R.O., C 142/399, no. 140.
[88] Ibid. CP 25(2)/239/13 Eliz. I Hil.
[89] Ibid. C 2/Jas. I/C 7/37.
[90] Ibid. CP 25(2)/239/13 Eliz. I East.; *Cal. Pat.* 1578–80, p. 267.
[91] P.R.O., C 142/341, no. 23.   [92] W.R.O. 312/9.
[93] Cross, *Puritan Earl*, 309.
[94] W.R.O. 312/9; 1655/8.
[95] Ibid. 11/344; 529/61; *V.C.H. Wilts.* ix. 169–70; above, Hullavington, manors; below, Norton, manor.
[96] W.R.O., A 1/345/261.
[97] W.R.O., tithe award; below, Norton, manor.
[98] W.R.O., A 1/345/261.
[99] Ibid. 2057/R 114; ibid. G 7/510/2.
[1] *Kelly's Dir. Wilts.* (1939).   [2] Local inf.
[3] P.R.O., C 2/Jas. I/M 3/41; ibid. C 104/85/1, deed, Moody to Couper, 1630.

[4] Aubrey, *Topog. Coll.* ed. Jackson, 251; W.R.O. 161/51; below, Malmesbury, manors; Rodbourne, manor.
[5] C. Greenwood, *Map of Wilts.* (1820); W.R.O., tithe award.
[6] W.A.S. Libr., sale cat. x, no. 17.
[7] W.R.O., A 1/345/261.   [8] Ibid. tithe award.
[9] Ibid. A 1/345/261.   [10] *Harrod's Dir. Wilts.* (1865).
[11] W.R.O., Inland Revenue, val. reg. 11.
[12] Ibid. G 7/510/2; G 7/515/5.
[13] Inf. from Mr. F. E. Durston, 5 Pembroke Green.
[14] W.R.O., tithe award.
[15] Ibid. 1742/429; above, Garsdon, manor.
[16] *Reg. Malm.* i. 411.
[17] *Valor Eccl.* (Rec. Com.), ii. 118.
[18] *L. & P. Hen. VIII*, xv, p. 410; xviii (1), p. 360.
[19] W.R.O., tithe award.
[20] *Reg. Malm.* ii. 140–1.
[21] P.R.O., C 78/84, no. 3; ibid. REQ 2/243/71.
[22] Ibid. C 104/85/1, deed, Moody to Hungerford, 1617.
[23] *Reg. Malm.* ii. 140–2.
[24] P.R.O., C 2/Eliz. I/W 7/25; ibid. REQ 2/102/40; REQ 2/105/57; REQ 2/243/71.

to open-field cultivation. Men of Cleverton had a common meadow near the field at Winkworth in the 13th century.[25] In the 18th century, as presumably earlier, there was grazing on Lea lower common, 59 a., south of Lea village on Lea upper common, 57 a., on Cleverton down, 30 a., and on scattered smaller greens.[26] Pasture rights in Braydon forest were claimed for the parcels of Lea manor sold in the 1570s,[27] and successfully in 1606 for Lea and Cleverton manor.[28] About 1631, after the forest was inclosed, rights to feed animals on Moonsleaze common, c. 280 a., part of the purlieus in Purton parish, were allotted to replace those wider rights.[29] By an award of 1733 under an Act of 1732 c. 175 a. of Moonsleaze common were allotted to replace the grazing rights of those owning land in Lea and Cleverton;[30] it is unlikely that the allotted land was added to a farm based in Lea or Cleverton.

There were 25 tenants on Malmesbury abbey's Cleverton estate in the late 13th century: two paid rents amounting to almost half the total, and nine were described as acremen.[31] No demesne was mentioned then, and in the mid 16th century there was said to be none,[32] but in 1630 there were 39 a. of demesne. What the abbey alienated in the earlier Middle Ages may have been demesne land. In 1630 a total of 722 a. of Lea and Cleverton manor was held by 33 tenants for lives; only four had holdings of more than 50 a., the largest being 79 a.[33] Westfield was a holding of 140 a. in 1617,[34] of 102 a. in 1685 when it included a small area recently ploughed and 22 a. of meadow.[35] The demesne of Lea manor was leased in the 1430s[36] and in 1554, when it included some open arable and pasture for 100 sheep.[37] There were copyholds of the manor in the mid 16th century.[38] In 1675 c. 270 a. formerly part of Lea manor may have been a single farm, of which probably less than a third was arable,[39] and, if so, that was almost certainly the largest farm in the parish. The farm held with Brill's Court was 76 a. of meadow and pasture in 1752.[40]

In 1340 the lord of Lea manor was licensed to impark a wood and 100 a. of meadow and pasture,[41] but there is no evidence that he did so. In the early 17th century a small area near the parish's northern boundary was taken into the park around Garsdon Manor;[42] by 1721 it had been disparked.[43]

The common pastures in the parish were inclosed in 1806 under an Act of 1805. A total of 192 a. was divided into small fields, the largest of which was c. 10 a., and many allotments were of green lanes and of the verges of lanes.[44] West of Lea village Westfield, 104 a. on which farm buildings stood c. 1800 but not in 1810, and north-east of the village 73 a. near the boundary with Garsdon were worked respectively from Southfield Farm in Malmesbury parish and from Garsdon in the early 19th century.[45] Five farms of over 100 a. were based in the parish in 1840, Winkworth, 287 a., Manor, 158 a., Street farm in Cleverton, 132 a., Cleverton Manor, 129 a., and Chink, then called Cresswell Lane, 118 a. There were eight farms of between 30 a. and 100 a. No more than a fifth of any of the larger farms was arable; the parish contained c. 1,300 a. of pasture, c. 300 a. of arable, and 10 a. of wood.[46]

In the 1850s new buildings were erected on some larger farms,[47] perhaps as tillage increased. In 1863 Manor farm, 239 a., and Winkworth farm, 233 a., were both about a third arable.[48] There was, however, no more than 350 a. of arable in the parish in 1866; wheat was the main crop. By 1906 the area of arable had fallen to 123 a. The number of cattle, half of them dairy cows, rose from c. 300 in 1866 to nearly 600 in 1906, of sheep from c. 300 to 1,634.[49] Manor, over 400 a., was the largest farm in the 1890s,[50] Winkworth, 225 a., in the 1920s.[51] Before the Second World War the area of arable remained small, much of it on the sand east of Lea village, and the pasture was used less intensively; 505 cattle and 410 sheep were kept in 1926.[52] In 1973 Manor farm, 150 a., was a corn and stock farm;[53] in the 1980s some land in the parish went out of agricultural use,[54] and in 1989 most of the remainder was used for dairying and for breeding and fattening cattle.[55]

A wood called the Grove was part of Lea manor in the earlier 15th century.[56] In the late 18th and the early 19th there were several small woods in the parish; in 1840 the largest was Lea wood, 7 a., south of Lea village.[57] In the 1880s Woodbridge copse north-east of Cleverton hamlet was also c. 7 a., and a smaller wood was north of the hamlet.[58] Those three woods still stood in the later 20th century.

MILL. In 1421 Crabwell Mill was part of Lea manor.[59] Crab Mill, presumably on the same site, was built in the early 17th century. Sir Henry Moody held it at his death in 1629,[60] but it did

[25] Reg. Malm. ii. 141.
[26] Andrews and Dury, Map (W.R.S. viii), pls. 14, 17; W.R.O., EA/70; ibid. 2057/P 1/1.
[27] W.N. & Q. vi. 552, 554; vii. 210.
[28] P.R.O., C 104/85/1, claim to rights in Braydon forest.
[29] Ibid. E 134/13 Chas. II Trin./5; W.A.M. xlvi. 184. For Braydon forest, cf. above, Charlton, introduction, econ. hist.
[30] W.R.O., A 1/200/3, rott. 7–8; ibid. 1553/104.
[31] Reg. Malm. i. 184–7.
[32] P.R.O., REQ 2/14/97.
[33] Ibid. C 104/85/1, deed, Moody to Couper, 1630; above, manors.
[34] Wilts. Inq. p.m. 1625–49 (Index Libr.), 152; P.R.O., C 104/85/1, deed, Moody to Hungerford, 1617.
[35] W.R.O. 88/8/44, deed, Wharton to Gunter, 1685.
[36] P.R.O., SC 6/1054/21.
[37] Ibid. REQ 2/243/71.
[38] Ibid. C 2/Eliz. I/W 7/25; ibid. REQ 2/105/57.
[39] W.R.O. 312/9.
[40] Ibid. 161/51.
[41] Cal. Chart. R. 1327–41, 468.

[42] P.R.O., C 2/Jas. I/M 3/41; ibid. C 104/87, deed, Prynne to Osborne, 1632.
[43] Above, Garsdon, econ. hist.   [44] W.R.O., EA/70.
[45] Ibid. 490/1041; 1553/40; ibid. tithe award.
[46] Ibid. tithe award.   [47] Ibid. 971/1.
[48] Ibid. 2057/S 177.
[49] P.R.O., MAF 68/73, sheet 11; MAF 68/74, sheet 9; MAF 68/1063, sheet 7; MAF 68/2203, sheet 14.
[50] W.R.O. 2057/R 113.
[51] Ibid. G 7/515/5.
[52] [1st] Land Util. Surv. Map, sheet 104; P.R.O., MAF 68/3319, sheet 10.
[53] Wilts. Cuttings, xxvii. 155.
[54] Inf. from Mr. N. Haines, Manor Farm.
[55] Inf. from Mr. A. Webb, Cleverton Farm; Mrs. A. Newman, Winkworth Farm.
[56] P.R.O., SC 6/1054/20–1.
[57] W.R.O. 1553/104; 2057/P 1/1; ibid. tithe award.
[58] O.S. Maps 6", Wilts. VIII–IX, XIII (1888–9 edns.).
[59] P.R.O., SC 6/1054/20.
[60] Wilts. Inq. p.m. 1625–49 (Index Libr.), 151.

not descend with Lea and Cleverton manor and in 1840 was owned by William Baker.[61] In 1848 Baker apparently had a flourishing trade, and in 1895 the mill was driven by both steam and water. Between 1927 and 1939 it went out of use.[62]

LOCAL GOVERNMENT. Until the Dissolution men of Lea and Cleverton manor may have attended Brokenborough court, at which Malmesbury abbey exercised leet jurisdiction. Courts were held at Lea for Lea and Cleverton manor in the 1540s and in 1550; apart from the granting of copyholds it is not clear what business was done.[63] In 1340 view of frankpledge in his manor of Lea was granted with other liberties to John Moleyns.[64] Courts were held from the earlier 15th century or earlier until the 1550s. In 1486–7 and 1510–14 a view of frankpledge and court was held twice a year. The tithingman of Lea attended and he or the homage presented dilapidations and minor nuisances such as blocked ditches.[65] From the late 16th century courts for Lea and Cleverton manor and for Lea manor may have been held together. In 1629 the lord was said to have view of frankpledge in Lea manor,[66] but the last recorded courts, described as courts for Lea and Cleverton manor and held yearly between 1646 and 1648, dealt only with tenurial matters.[67] In the 17th century Lea and Cleverton each had a tithingman.[68]

In the 18th century poor relief was administered by a pair of overseers acting for the parish as a whole. In 1741 permanent relief was given to five parishioners and £26 was spent. Occasional payments were for clothing, food, and coffins, to pay rents, and to the sick. In 1761 there were seven regular recipients of relief and £65 was spent. In 1788 the vestry held on lease all or part of the Rose and Crown inn,[69] presumably to house paupers, and in 1806 there was a building in Cresswell Lane called a workhouse;[70] no record has been found of its inmates. Expenditure had risen to £78 by 1776 and to £288 by 1803, when 28 adults and 41 children were permanently relieved and the parish rate was a little above the average for Malmesbury hundred.[71] Between 1810 and 1835 the cost of poor relief fluctuated, rising from £297 in 1828 to a peak of £575 in 1831. Between 1833 and 1835 the average annual expenditure was £301. Lea and Cleverton parish became part of Malmesbury poor-law union in 1835[72] and of North Wiltshire district in 1974.[73]

CHURCH. A church at Lea may have been served by chaplains appointed by Malmesbury abbey, which owned the great tithes in 1248,[74] and apparently remained a chapel. By the mid 16th century it had been annexed to Garsdon rectory.[75] A proposal of 1650 to separate Lea and Cleverton from Garsdon[76] came to nothing.[77] In the earlier 20th century Garsdon and Lea and Cleverton were considered a united benefice[78] and in 1987 the rectory of Garsdon with Lea and Cleverton was united with Charlton vicarage.[79]

Rectors of Garsdon took small tithes from all Lea and Cleverton parish except 77 a. which were mostly held with Garsdon manor and tithe free.[80] The tithes were valued at £30 in 1650[81] and at £188 in 1840, when they were commuted.[82] The rector had 37 a. of glebe in Lea and Cleverton parish in 1608, presumably then as in 1783 with rights of common pasture.[83] Those rights were replaced by an allotment of 8 a. in 1806,[84] and in 1919 the glebe, 45 a., was sold.[85] A house on the glebe in 1608 was probably that of two storeys each of two rooms which stood south of the church in 1671.[86] The clerk's house, presumably that house, was burned down in 1752[87] and there was no glebe house in 1783.[88] In 1950 a new house for the rector of Garsdon was built north of Lea church.[89]

In the Middle Ages a cottage, 2½ a. in Lea and Cleverton parish, and a rent of 20d. were given for lights, including St. Giles's, in Lea church.[90] Curates who served the church in the later 16th century may have lived in the parish, but from then until the 20th century no clergyman is known to have been resident. It was reported in 1553 that no quarter sermon had been preached,[91] in 1556 that ornaments necessary for the restored mass were missing,[92] and in 1585 that the church needed repair.[93] In 1662 the churchwardens promised to provide a surplice with all speed.[94] In 1783 according to long standing practice Sunday services were held at Lea in the morning in spring and summer, in the afternoon in autumn and winter. Communion was celebrated at Christmas, Easter, and Whitsun; there were 10 communicants.[95] On Census Sunday in 1851 a congregation of 108 attended the afternoon service.[96]

ST. GILES'S church was probably so called in the later 16th century[97] as it was in 1763.[98] It had a chancel and nave, perhaps undivided and both apparently of the 14th century, a south porch, and a 15th-century west tower.[99] Except for the tower

[61] W.R.O., tithe award.
[62] *Kelly's Dir. Wilts.* (1848 and later edns.).
[63] P.R.O., REQ 2/14/97; REQ 2/102/40; above, Brokenborough, local govt.
[64] *Cal. Chart. R. 1327–41*, 468.
[65] P.R.O., REQ 2/105/57; ibid. SC 2/208/28; SC 2/209/57, rot. 2 and d.; SC 6/1054/20–1.
[66] *Wilts. Inq. p.m. 1625–49* (Index Libr.), 151.
[67] P.R.O., C 116/273, pp. 4, 15, 56.
[68] *Early-Stuart Tradesmen* (W.R.S. xv), p. 6; Hist. MSS. Com. 55, *Var. Coll.* i, p. 156.
[69] W.R.O. 524/15.
[70] Ibid. EA/70.
[71] *Poor Law Abstract, 1804*, 566–7.
[72] *Poor Rate Returns, 1816–21*, 189; *1825–9*, 219; *1830–4*, 212; *Poor Law Com. 2nd Rep.* App. D, 559.
[73] O.S. Map 1/100,000, admin. areas, Wilts. (1974 edn.).
[74] *Reg. Malm.* i. 411.
[75] Phillipps, *Wilts. Inst.* i. 219; W.R.O., D 1/43/1, f. 24v.
[76] *W.A.M.* xli. 7.

[77] Phillipps, *Wilts. Inst.* (index in *W.A.M.* xxviii. 217, s.v. Garsdon).
[78] Ch. Com. files, NB 5/85; 85095.
[79] Inf. from Ch. Com.
[80] W.R.O., tithe award.   [81] *W.A.M.* xli. 7.
[82] W.R.O., tithe award.
[83] Ibid. D 1/24/132/1; D 1/24/132/3.   [84] Ibid. EA/70.
[85] W.A.S. Libr., sale cat. xv, no. 16.
[86] W.R.O., D 1/24/132/1–2.
[87] *Vis. Queries, 1783* (W.R.S. xxvii), p. 109.
[88] W.R.O., D 1/24/132/3.
[89] Inf. from the rector, Lea.   [90] P.R.O., E 178/3092.
[91] W.R.O., D 1/43/1, ff. 24v., 133v.
[92] Ibid. D 1/43/2, f. 19.
[93] Ibid. D 1/43/6, f. 33A.   [94] Ibid. D 1/54/1/1, no. 48.
[95] *Vis. Queries, 1783* (W.R.S. xxvii), p. 109.
[96] P.R.O., HO 129/252/1/13/21.   [97] Ibid. E 178/3092.
[98] J. Ecton, *Thesaurus* (1763), 403.
[99] J. Buckler, watercolour in W.A.S. Libr., vol. vi. 8; see below, plate facing p. 237.

the church was rebuilt to a larger scale in 1879, to a design by G. J. Phipps,[1] in coursed rubble and an early 14th-century style. It has a chancel with north vestry and a nave with north aisle and south porch.

Plate weighing 2½ oz. was confiscated and a chalice of 10½ oz. left in the church in 1553. All the church's plate was destroyed when the clerk's house was burned down in 1752. Plate given in the 19th century remained in 1989.[2]

There were four bells in 1553. Two new bells were cast in 1622 and, although in 1662 there was said to be no bell in the church, survived to the 20th century. Two more were cast in the 1660s and another in 1670; all five were by members of the Purdue family.[3] In 1978 four of the bells were unsound and removed:[4] one of 1663 remained in the church in 1989.[5]

Parish registers were destroyed in the fire of 1752.[6] Registers of baptisms and burials survive from 1751 and of marriages from 1754.[7]

NONCONFORMITY.
In 1662 seven or more parishioners attended what was probably a Quaker meeting.[8] A Friends' society for Lea and Brinkworth, recorded in 1678, acquired a burial ground west of the church in 1691.[9] There was a Quaker family in the parish until the 1720s and Quakers were buried there until the 1750s[10] or later. In 1883 and later the burial ground was a garden.[11]

A house in Lea was certified in 1797 for Independent meetings, as was another in 1802. By 1808 the congregation had become Calvinistic Methodists and had built the Zion chapel on the east side of the Street.[12] Independents worshipped there in 1851, when morning service on Census Sunday was attended by 133 people and evening service by 140.[13] The chapel was rebuilt in stone and a plain style in 1861.[14] It was used by Congregationalists between 1885 and 1939[15] and by Baptists in 1989.

A house at Cleverton was certified in 1735 for Presbyterian meetings and another in 1828 for Primitive Methodist meetings.[16] A Primitive Methodist chapel was built there in 1832. At the morning, afternoon, and evening services held on Census Sunday in 1851 congregations averaged 54.[17] A new chapel, small and of stone with brick dressings, was built in 1874[18] and was open in 1989.

EDUCATION.
There was no school in the parish in 1818 although the poor were said to desire one.[19] In 1833 there were two schools, attended by a total of 22 children.[20] One may have been that at Lea which in 1846 was affiliated to the National Society and attended by 43 children;[21] the other may have been the day and boarding school attended by 15 children in 1858 but not recorded thereafter. Children from outside the parish also attended the National school in 1858. It was then a small thatched building with one room[22] and in 1871 was severely overcrowded.[23] In 1873 a new school with a teacher's house was built at Lea to serve Lea, Cleverton, and Garsdon.[24] Attendance fell from 94 to 39 between 1906 and 1919, and was 42 in 1936.[25] The buildings were extended in 1976, and in 1989 there were 110 children on roll.[26]

CHARITIES FOR THE POOR.
By will proved 1722 Edward Mills gave £40 to the poor of Lea and Cleverton; 2 a. in Stratton St. Margaret were bought and the rent presumably distributed. The land was sold in 1814. The income of the charity, c. £6, was distributed among poor parishioners at Christmas in the later 19th century and the earlier 20th.[27] In 1950 there were 79 beneficiaries.[28] In 1989 the income, £5, was given for a Christmas party for elderly parishioners.[29]

At inclosure in 1806 allotments totalling 3 a. were made for the poor. In 1905 the lands were shared by 41 parishioners as garden allotments;[30] 1½ a. was used as allotments in 1989.[31]

[1] Ch. Guide (1988).
[2] Nightingale, Wilts. Plate, 199–200; W.R.O., D 1/24/100/3; inf. from the rector.
[3] Walters, Wilts. Bells, 120; W.R.O., D 1/54/1/1, no. 48.
[4] Ch. Guide (1988).
[5] Inf. from the rector.
[6] Vis. Queries, 1783 (W.R.S. xxvii), p. 109.
[7] W.R.O. 524/1–4; bishop's transcripts for some earlier dates are ibid.
[8] Ibid. D 1/54/1/1, no. 48.
[9] Ibid. tithe award; V.C.H. Wilts. iii. 116, 118.
[10] W.N. & Q. vi. 82, 132–3.
[11] W.R.O. 854/43, lease, Soc. of Friends to Slade, 1883.
[12] Meeting Ho. Certs. (W.R.S. xl), pp. 48, 58, 64.
[13] P.R.O., HO 129/252/2/13/18.
[14] Date on bldg.
[15] Kelly's Dir. Wilts. (1885 and later edns.).
[16] Meeting Ho. Certs. (W.R.S. xl), pp. 23, 120.
[17] P.R.O., HO 129/252/2/13/17.
[18] Date on bldg.
[19] Educ. of Poor Digest, 1031.
[20] Educ. Enq. Abstract, 1041.
[21] Nat. Soc. Inquiry, 1846–7, Wilts. 8–9.
[22] Acct. of Wilts. Schs. 25.
[23] Returns relating to Elem. Educ. 420–1.
[24] P.R.O., ED 7/130, no. 166.
[25] Return of Non-Provided Schs. 24; Bd. of Educ., List 21, 1911 (H.M.S.O.), 549; 1919, 362; 1936, 425.
[26] Inf. from the head teacher.
[27] Endowed Char. Wilts. (N. Div.), 645–6; W.R.O. 1247/9.
[28] W.R.O., Char. Com., Lea and Cleverton.
[29] Inf. from Mrs. D. Miles, 1 St. Giles's Close.
[30] Endowed Char. Wilts. (N. Div.), 646–7.
[31] Inf. from Mrs. Miles.

MALMESBURY

THE TOWN of Malmesbury stands on a steep hill almost encircled by the Tetbury and Sherston branches of the Bristol Avon.[32] The streams, flowing eastwards, come within 200 m. of each other at the town's north-western corner, diverge, and meet at its southern end.[33] The word Malmesbury was perhaps derived from the name of Mailduib, an Irish monk or hermit who may have settled on or near the town's site in the mid 7th century. Mailduib is said to have gathered around him a school which became the nucleus of the monastery later known as Malmesbury abbey.[34] A tradition was current in the abbey in the 14th century that Mailduib's settlement lay beneath a fortified place, called either Bladon or by the Saxon name Ingelbourne, which had been constructed by a heathen British king, had once been a thriving town, but was in Mailduib's time little frequented.[35] Malmesbury's naturally defensible site may have been that of a stronghold in an earlier period, but the tradition cannot be substantiated. Between the 7th century and the 11th the abbey was granted many estates near Malmesbury, including the lands, surrounding the town, which became Malmesbury and Westport parishes.[36] The two parishes may have been formed early: there was a church at Westport in the late Saxon period and the site of St. Paul's, the medieval parish church of Malmesbury, in or adjacent to the abbey precinct perhaps indicates a similarly early origin. The parishes were closely associated: the settlement called Westport formed a suburb of the town, and what became Malmesbury borough included part of that settlement and had most of its common land in Westport parish.[37]

Malmesbury parish comprised most of the town, but not the abbey precinct and the part in Westport parish, and lands north, east, and south of it. Within the parish were the villages or hamlets of Milbourne, Whitchurch, and Blick's Hill to the east, Burton Hill immediately south of the town, and Corston and Rodbourne further south. A settlement called Filands, north of the town, lay mainly in Westport parish.[38] The name of another, Walcot, in either Westport or Malmesbury parish may indicate an early settlement site or proximity to the town walls; the only references to it are from the late 13th century.[39] From the 14th century or earlier there was a chapel, dependent on St. Paul's church, at Corston and another at Rodbourne.[40] Each chapelry was a tithing: although neither relieved its own poor, both Corston and Rodbourne were thus separate from Malmesbury in some ecclesiastical and administrative matters.

The main part of the following article deals with all Malmesbury parish except Corston and Rodbourne, with the abbey precinct which was apparently considered extraparochial until the 18th century when it relieved its own poor,[41] and with the history of the town including some aspects of that part of it which lay in Westport parish. Corston and Rodbourne are dealt with in separate accounts at the end of the article.

Malmesbury parish, including the abbey precinct, Corston, and Rodbourne, measured 10 km. from north to south and at its widest, south of the town, 5 km. from east to west. It narrowed where crossed by the two branches of the Avon, and 360 a. to the north were attached to the rest of the parish by a neck of land north-east of the town. Further north again c. 20 a. in two parcels were detached, one surrounded by lands of Brokenborough parish and one between Brokenborough and Charlton; north of Milbourne village were c. 10 a., parcels of Westport and Charlton parishes, enclosed by Malmesbury lands.[42] The boundary of the 360 a. with Charlton was marked by a stream, but the boundaries with Brokenborough and Westport were irregular: that irregularity, and the existence of islands of other parishes in Malmesbury and of Malmesbury in other parishes, may be the result of inclosure and allotment of land shared by several parishes, of basing parish boundaries on the ownership of land with which tithes were merged after the Reformation, or of both. Further south the parish's eastern boundary was marked by the Avon, its tributary Woodbridge brook, and another tributary, while a tributary of the Sherston Avon marked part of the western boundary. Elsewhere the parish boundary was marked by few natural features, but on the western side of the town it may have followed part of the town wall and in other places was marked by roads. The boundaries of Rodbourne and Corston were surveyed in the late 11th century or early 12th when the road dividing Corston and Hullavington was mentioned and the Avon was Rodbourne's boundary with Little Somerford.[43] That last boundary was diverted west from the Avon, its natural line, at an agreed inclosure in 1281.[44] In the early 1630s, after the disafforestation of Braydon forest in 1630 and disputes with other landowners, the lord of Whitchurch and Milbourne manor was allotted 104 a. of the purlieus c. 6 km. east of the parish:[45] that allotment, Milbourne common, was part of Malmesbury parish in 1839.[46]

In the period 1882–4 the detached parts of

[32] See plate facing p. 92.
[33] This article was written in 1987–9. Maps used include O.S. Maps 1/50,000, sheet 173 (1974 edn.); 1/25,000, ST 88, ST 98–9 (1958–9 edns.); 6", Wilts. VIII, XIII (1888–9 and later edns.).
[34] The hist. of Malmesbury abbey is related in V.C.H. Wilts. iii. 210.   [35] Eulogium Hist. (Rolls Ser.), i. 225–6.
[36] Finberg, Early Wessex Chart. pp. 70–3, 100, 105–6; above, Brokenborough, introduction; below, manors; below, Westport, manors.

[37] Below, Westport, introduction, econ. hist., church.
[38] Ibid. introduction.
[39] Reg. Malm. ii. 120–1, 358–9; P.N. Wilts. (E.P.N.S.), 277.
[40] Below, Corston, church; Rodbourne, church.
[41] Ibid. local govt. (par. govt.).
[42] W.R.O., tithe award.
[43] Arch. Jnl. lxxvii. 43–6, 88–90.
[44] Reg. Malm. ii. 219–20.
[45] V.C.H. Wilts. iv. 406; W.R.O., EA/34; ibid. 88/10/52.
[46] W.R.O., tithe award.

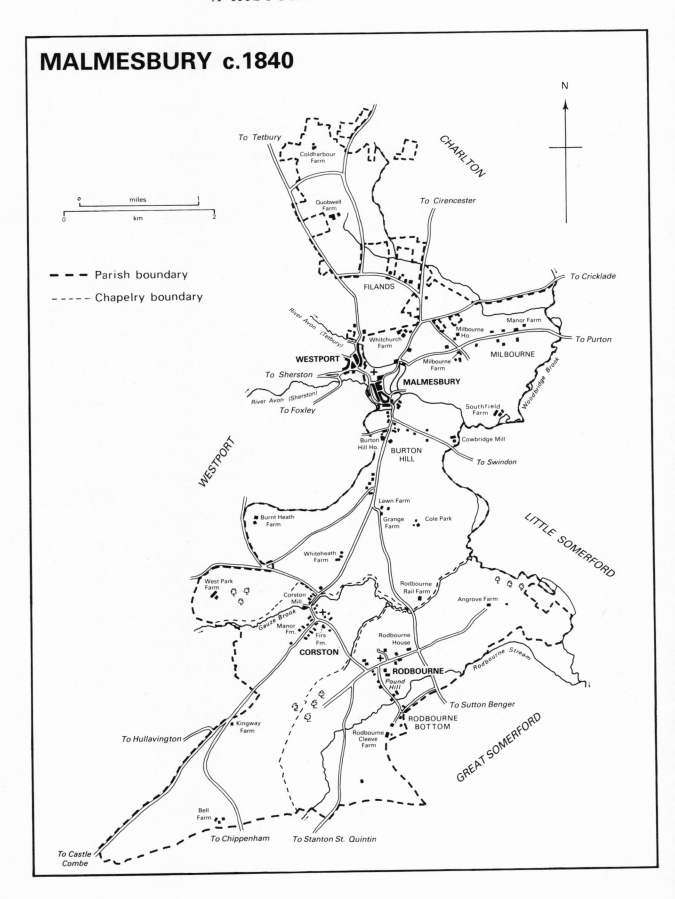

MALMESBURY c.1840

N

miles

km

- **– – –** Parish boundary
- **- - - -** Chapelry boundary

To Tetbury

Coldharbour Farm

CHARLTON

To Cirencester

Quobwell Farm

To Cricklade

FILANDS

Manor Farm

River Avon (Tetbury)

Milbourne Ho.

To Purton

Whitchurch Farm

MILBOURNE

WESTPORT

Milbourne Farm

To Sherston

MALMESBURY

River Avon (Sherston)

Woodbridge Brook

To Foxley

Southfield Farm

Burton Hill Ho.

Cowbridge Mill

WESTPORT

BURTON HILL

To Swindon

Lawn Farm

Burnt Heath Farm

Grange Farm

Cole Park

LITTLE SOMERFORD

Whiteheath Farm

West Park Farm

Corston Mill

Rodbourne Rail Farm

Angrove Farm

Gauze Brook

Manor Fm.

Firs Fm.

Rodbourne House

Rodbourne Stream

CORSTON

RODBOURNE

Pound Hill

To Sutton Benger

Kingway Farm

RODBOURNE BOTTOM

GREAT SOMERFORD

To Hullavington

Rodbourne Cleeve Farm

Bell Farm

To Castle Combe

To Chippenham

To Stanton St. Quintin

Malmesbury parish to the north were transferred to Brokenborough, Milbourne common was transferred to Brinkworth, and the detached parts of Westport and Charlton embraced by Malmesbury parish were transferred to Malmesbury; north of the town there were also small changes to the boundaries with Westport and Charlton.[47] In 1885, after losing c. 100 a. in the changes of 1882–4, Malmesbury parish measured 5,333 a. (2,160 ha.), of which Corston and Rodbourne were a total of c. 2,500 a.[48] In 1886 Malmesbury municipal borough was created; it contained 178 a. formerly part of Malmesbury, Westport, and Brokenborough parishes.[49] In 1894 the reduced Malmesbury parish was renamed St. Paul Malmesbury Without parish; to it was added in 1896 all Westport parish outside the borough.[50] In 1981 it measured 2,903 ha. (7,173 a.).[51] In 1984 small areas were exchanged between that parish and Brokenborough, and some land was transferred from it to Malmesbury parish.[52] Thereafter St. Paul Malmesbury Without measured 2,699 ha. (6,669 a.).[53]

From the confluence of its Sherston and Tetbury branches the Avon flows south-east across the old Malmesbury parish, turning south near the eastern boundary. The name Ingelbourne was applied to the Tetbury branch in the 11th or 12th century and in the later 15th, and to the Sherston branch in the later 13th; it may also have been used for a stream rising south-west of the town.[54] Most of the tributary streams cross the parish from west to east. Gauze brook flows north-east across the southern half of the parish to join the Avon on the eastern boundary, and further south is a parallel stream, formerly called the Rodbourne; the names were in use c. 1100, when both streams were boundaries of Rodbourne, and perhaps much earlier.[55] The town stands on a steep sided outcrop of Cornbrash, above 76 m. Elsewhere the steepest slopes in the parish are around Rodbourne village. Nowhere does the land rise much above 90 m. and in the north and south-west it flattens out at that height. Kellaways Clay outcrops over most of the parish and there are small areas of Oxford Clay. Kellaways Sand outcrops near Rodbourne, and there are outcrops of clay of the Forest Marble beside the Avon and in the extreme north. In the lower parts of the parish, especially between the town and Corston village, Cornbrash outcrops. Alluvium has been deposited by the Avon and its main tributaries, and deposits of sand and gravel are in several places north of the town.[56]

Although the well watered clay soils favour pasture rather than tillage, open fields on the clay lay south of Milbourne village and in the north.

The Cornbrash favours arable and the open fields near Corston village were on both the Cornbrash and clay. Most of the land between Gauze brook and the town was pasture and parkland from an early date. What became Cole park, beside the Avon south of the town, was wooded in the Middle Ages, but later there was little woodland in the parish. In the 19th century and the 20th there were quarries near Corston village and on the outskirts of the town, and the clay in the southern part of the parish was used for making bricks.[57] From 1935 the plateau in the south-western corner has been part of R.A.F. Hullavington.[58]

In the later 17th century the Oxford–Bristol road ran east and west through Milbourne village, Malmesbury, and Foxley crossing the Tetbury Avon by a stone bridge at the town's north-east corner.[59] The main road south from the town has always been that through Corston to Chippenham, called Kingway c. 1100 when it may have been on roughly its present course.[60] To the north the Tetbury (Glos.) road also served until 1778 as a link from Cirencester (Glos.) to Malmesbury and Chippenham, before 1743 via the Foss Way, thereafter alternatively on a turnpike road to Tetbury.[61] In 1756 the Tetbury–Malmesbury and Malmesbury–Chippenham roads were turnpiked to complete a Chippenham–Cirencester turnpike road via Tetbury. By then the Oxford–Bristol road may already have declined in importance and, east of the town, the more northerly Cricklade–Malmesbury road and, west of the town, the more northerly Malmesbury–Sherston road were turnpiked.[62] The road through Milbourne remained in use as a minor road. A more direct Cirencester–Malmesbury road was completed across Hankerton parish and turnpiked in 1778.[63] Another road, which left the Chippenham road south-east of the town, crossed the Avon by Cow bridge, and led to Wootton Bassett and Swindon, was in use in 1773 and turnpiked in 1809.[64] The Chippenham, Cirencester, and Tetbury roads were disturnpiked in 1874, the Cricklade, Swindon, and Sherston roads in 1876.[65] In 1973 the Cirencester–Chippenham road was diverted to bypass the town to the east.[66] There were few minor roads in the north part of the parish in the late 18th century. One, linking the Tetbury and Cirencester roads, was still in use in the late 20th century; since 1973 it has assumed greater importance by taking Chippenham–Tetbury traffic away from the town. Another, running north-west from the linking road east of and parallel with the Tetbury road,[67] was in use in 1842 but not in 1885.[68] South of the town in the late 18th century lanes led east and south-east from the Chippenham road to Sutton

---

[47] *Census*, 1891.

[48] O.S. Maps 6", Wilts. VIII, XIII (1888–9 edns.); W.R.O., tithe award.

[49] W.R.O., F 2/141.

[50] *Census*, 1901.   [51] Ibid. 1981.

[52] For Malmesbury par. in 1984, below.

[53] Inf. from Chief Assistant (Environment), Dept. of Planning and Highways, Co. Hall, Trowbridge.

[54] *Arch. Jnl.* lxxvii. 46; *P.N. Wilts.* (E.P.N.S.), 51; *Reg. Malm.* i. 122; W.R.O. 88/1/16.

[55] *Arch. Jnl.* lxxvii. 88, 90; *P.N. Wilts.* (E.P.N.S.), 7, 51–2.

[56] Geol. Surv. Maps 1", solid and drift, sheets 251 (1970 edn.), 252 (1974 edn.).

[57] Below, agric.; ibid. Corston, econ. hist.; Rodbourne, econ. hist.

[58] Inf. from Defence Land Agent, Durrington.

[59] J. Ogilby, *Brit.* (1675), pl. 79.

[60] *Arch. Jnl.* lxxv. 74.

[61] *Andrews and Dury, Map* (W.R.S. viii), pls. 16–17; *V.C.H. Wilts.* iv. 257, 268; *L.J.* xxvi. 241.

[62] *V.C.H. Wilts.* iv. 257, 269; *L.J.* xxviii. 526, 581.

[63] Above, Hankerton, introduction.

[64] *Andrews and Dury, Map* (W.R.S. viii), pl. 16; *L.J.* xlvii. 581.

[65] *V.C.H. Wilts.* iv. 269, 271; 36 & 37 Vic. c. 90.

[66] Inf. from Chief Assistant (Environment), Dept. of Planning and Highways.

[67] *Andrews and Dury, Map* (W.R.S. viii), pl. 16.

[68] W.R.O., tithe award; O.S. Map 6", Wilts. VIII (1889 edn.).

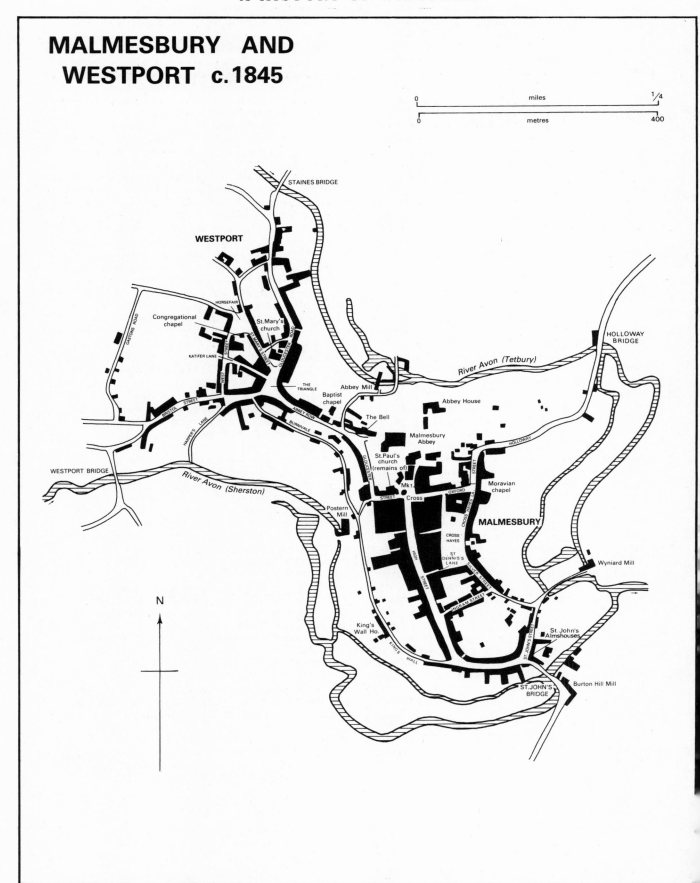

MALMESBURY AND
WESTPORT c.1845

STAINES BRIDGE

WESTPORT

HORSEFAIR

Congregational
chapel

St.Mary's
church

HOLLOWAY
BRIDGE

KATIFER LANE

River Avon (Tetbury)

THE TRIANGLE

Abbey Mill

Baptist
chapel

Abbey House

The Bell

Malmesbury
Abbey

Moravian
chapel

St.Paul's
church
(remains of)

HOLLOWAY

WESTPORT BRIDGE

River Avon (Sherston)

Mkt.
Cross

OXFORD

MALMESBURY

Postern
Mill

Wyniard Mill

CROSS
HAYES

ST
DENNIS'S
LANE

N

King's
Wall Ho.

St. John's
Almshouses

Burton Hill Mill

ST.JOHN'S
BRIDGE

Benger, to Rodbourne village, and to a road between Rodbourne and Stanton St. Quintin; they were crossed by others running north-east and south-west. Lanes led south-west from the Chippenham road 1 km. south of the town and west from it at the north end of Corston village to Malmesbury common in Westport parish, and further south one led west to Hullavington and another south-west along the parish boundary towards Castle Combe.[69] The road towards Castle Combe went out of use in the 19th century after a road through Hullavington village was turnpiked, but the road to Hullavington, part of that turnpike road, remains in use.[70] In the late 20th century the Sutton Benger road and that leading to it from Corston village were the only public metalled roads east of the Chippenham road, and Common Road, leading west from the north end of Corston village, was the principal route to Malmesbury common.

A canal between Bristol and Cricklade passing south-east of the town was planned in the late 18th century but not built.[71] A railway line through Malmesbury was proposed in 1864 but there was no service to the town until 1877 when a branch from the G.W.R. line at Dauntsey was opened. The new line skirted the town to the north-east, a tunnel was made under Holloway, and a small station was built east of the Tetbury Avon north of the abbey church. Part of the Bristol & South Wales railway was built across the south part of the parish in 1903, and in 1933 a spur was built to connect the Malmesbury branch to that line at Little Somerford; the southern half of the branch was then closed. Passenger services to Malmesbury ceased in 1951,[72] and goods services in 1963 when the station was closed.[73]

Despite the literary tradition of early settlement within the parish, little archaeological evidence of human activity in prehistoric times has been found. Some artifacts of the Iron Age and later have been found in the town and in the south part of the parish. On Cam's Hill south-east of the town are rectangular and circular prehistoric enclosures measuring 0.5 ha. and 0.25 ha. respectively.[74]

In 1377 a total of 556 poll-tax payers lived in Malmesbury, in other villages in the parish, and, probably, in the suburb of Westport.[75] The population of the parish was 1,571 in 1801. Between then and 1851 it increased steadily to reach a peak of 2,581, and between 1851 and 1891 it declined. The sharpest fall, from 2,543 in 1861 to 2,306 in 1871, was ascribed to the emigration of labourers to work in the oilfields of Ohio (U.S.A.). In 1891, the last date for which figures are available, 2,263 people lived in what had been Malmesbury parish.[76] In 1981 the population of Malmesbury St. Paul Without parish was 1,993.[77] In 1773 and 1842, as presumably earlier, settlement was concentrated in the town and in Milbourne, Corston, and Rodbourne villages. There was a group of buildings at Burton Hill and

scattered farmsteads in most parts of the parish.[78] The histories of the villages, hamlets, and farmsteads in the parish, apart from those of Corston and Rodbourne, which are dealt with separately, are described below after the account of the town.

TOWN HISTORY. The town which grew up around Malmesbury abbey had probably become a local trading centre by the late 9th century. At about that time it was included with three other places in Wiltshire in the list of fortified centres known as the Burghal Hidage: 1,200 hides were assigned to defend the fort which may therefore have had 1,650 yd. of wall. Moneyers worked at Malmesbury from the mid 10th century and coin evidence suggests that the town was one of the most important in the county in the early 11th. Its eminence was confirmed by Domesday Book, in which it was referred to as a borough, placed at the head of the entry for Wiltshire, and described in more detail than any other borough in the county, although it was not necessarily the largest or most prosperous. Within the borough in 1086 the king had 26 *masurae hospitate*, possibly houses let at rent, and 25 *masurae* exempt from geld, perhaps occupied by the king's servants; each *masura* may have consisted of more than one house. A further 22¾ *masurae* were held by other lords; in addition 8 or 11 burgesses of Malmesbury and 5½ houses in the borough were mentioned elsewhere in the survey as appurtenant to rural estates. Thus, although smaller than many others, the borough may have had in it 100 or more households. The mint in Malmesbury was the only one of perhaps five in Wiltshire to be mentioned in Domesday Book.[79] Between the 11th and the 16th centuries Malmesbury's importance in the county declined, although it was still highly assessed for tax in 1334 and was apparently populous in 1377.[80] In the later Middle Ages it was notable chiefly for its abbey and for its cloth industry, which was to remain a source of its prosperity until the mid 18th century. From the 18th century it was principally a local centre for commerce, manufacture, and administration.[81]

Before the Conquest Malmesbury was required to give to the king 20s. for his fleet when he went on an expedition by sea or a man for each five of its hides, probably three men, when he went on an expedition by land. Such a requirement suggests that Malmesbury was already a privileged borough.[82] A guild merchant had rights and lands and presumably played some part in the town's government in the 13th century. The burgesses' privileges, including exemption from certain dues, and lands, later called King's Heath or Malmesbury common, were confirmed in 1381 when the burgesses made the implausible claim that they had been granted by King Athelstan. The governing body was known from the 16th century or earlier as the alderman and burgesses.[83] In the 16th

[69] *Andrews and Dury, Map* (W.R.S. viii), pls. 13–14.
[70] Above, Hullavington, introduction.
[71] *W.A.M.* xlii. 399.
[72] *V.C.H. Wilts.* iv. 281, 288.
[73] C. R. Clinker, *Clinker's Reg. Closed Passenger Sta. 1830–1980*, p. 92; see below, plate facing p. 172.
[74] *V.C.H. Wilts.* i (1), 84, 100, 269; *W.A.M.* lxviii. 138–9.
[75] *V.C.H. Wilts.* iv. 309.

[76] Ibid. 324, 352–3.
[77] *Census*, 1981.
[78] *Andrews and Dury, Map* (W.R.S. viii), pls. 13, 16–17; W.R.O., tithe award.
[79] *V.C.H. Wilts.* ii, pp. 15–23, 113–25.
[80] Ibid. iv. 296, 309.   [81] Below, trade and ind.
[82] *V.C.H. Wilts.* ii, pp. 22–3.
[83] Below, local govt. (boro. govt.).

century the borough presumably included all the land within the town walls, except that within the abbey precinct, and an area in Westport beyond the walls. The extension of the borough boundary across the neck of land linking Malmesbury and Westport may have been to bring within the borough the markets and settlements which had grown up outside the confined area of the town; a Thursday market granted in 1252 was for Westport, and both the Triangle and Horsefair in Westport, within the borough boundary, may have been the sites of markets or fairs.[84] In the late 13th century the walled part of the town within Malmesbury parish was called Bynport to distinguish it from Westport: the name was still in use in the 16th century.[85] The alderman and burgesses may have exercised rights over the abbey site from the Dissolution, but the precinct was not formally included in the borough until 1685.[86] The earliest map showing the borough boundary is of 1831. The east, south, and south-west boundaries were the two branches of the Avon, and the north was a ditch then called Warditch. The north-western, between the Tetbury road and the Sherston Avon and taking in part of Westport, was in places marked by streets but followed an indirect line and for much of its distance no prominent feature. Approximately a third of the borough lay in Westport parish.[87]

In 1831 it was proposed to extend the borough boundary where each of four main roads entered the town. There is no evidence that extensions were made, but the urban sanitary district formed in 1872 took in an area greater than the 1831 borough, and its boundaries were those of the municipal borough created in 1886.[88] In 1894 the municipal borough was divided into the civil parishes of the Abbey, Malmesbury St. Paul Within, Westport St. Mary Within, and Brokenborough Within. The Abbey and Malmesbury St. Paul Within included the parts of the town formerly in Malmesbury parish. The other two were those parts of Westport and Brokenborough parishes brought into the urban sanitary district in 1872: they were merged as Westport St. Mary Within in 1897.[89] In 1934 a further 25 a. of Brokenborough parish on the west side of the town were added to the borough. The three civil parishes within the borough were then merged as a new Malmesbury parish,[90] to which was added in 1956 part of a built up area in Brokenborough and St. Paul Malmesbury Without.[91] In 1974 Malmesbury lost its borough status,[92] and in 1984 Malmesbury parish was extended west, north, and east, bringing more housing within it and increasing its area from 93 ha. (230 a.) to 283 ha. (699 a.).[93]

In 1547 the adult population of the town of Malmesbury, presumably its suburbs, was estimated at 860, the third largest total for a town in Wiltshire.[94] In 1801 the population of the town, apparently defined as the borough, was 1,107. It rose steadily to 1,624 in 1861, and in 1891 the municipal borough had 2,964 inhabitants, of whom 1,348 lived in that part of it which had been in the old Malmesbury parish. Numbers fell until 1931, when the borough had 2,334 inhabitants. The population of the enlarged borough was 2,510 in 1951;[95] in 1971, after further enlargement, it was no more than 2,610 and in 1981 Malmesbury parish had a population of 2,591.[96]

The chief buildings of the town stood in Malmesbury parish on the peninsula formed by the two branches of the Avon. At the northern end, on the highest ground, was the abbey. In the 1130s, when he held Malmesbury abbey and a lease of the borough from the Crown, Roger, bishop of Salisbury, built at Malmesbury a castle which reportedly encroached on a graveyard within a stone's throw of the abbey church.[97] Its site was probably west of the church, either that occupied in the late 20th century by the eastern range of the Old Bell hotel, formerly called Castle House,[98] or further west, beyond the lane which bounded the hotel. Another suggested site, east of the abbey church and encroaching on the monks' graveyard,[99] offered little command of the western approach to the town where the natural barriers were weakest. In 1215 the Crown granted the keeping of the castle to Malmesbury abbey, which in 1216 was licensed to demolish it and build on its site.[1] A document, apparently compiled by the abbey in the later 13th century, lists obligations to repair 26 sections of the town's wall, presumably its whole length. Those required to repair the wall, including the abbey itself in eight sections, were apparently the owners of the plots in the borough adjoining the respective sections. The correlation between the owners and the holders of the *masurae* listed in Domesday Book has given rise to the suggestion that the walls and the obligation existed in 1086, but it has been more plausibly suggested that although the wall was referred to in the document as the king's wall the obligations were imposed or defined only after the abbey acquired the castle. The stone wall may therefore also have been built by Roger in the 1130s.[2] Roughly parallel with the rivers, it may have followed the lines of earlier defences, possibly those of the later 9th century. The wall was still standing in the earlier 16th century but was then said to be very feeble.[3] It probably suffered further damage during the Civil War[4] and by c. 1800 had largely disappeared.[5] The eastern and south-eastern line of the wall was marked in the later 20th century by the boundaries of the plots behind Cross Hayes Lane, Silver Street, and Ingram Street, and the western by

[84] Below, trade and ind. (mkts. and fairs).
[85] *Reg. Malm.* i. 121; *L. & P. Hen. VIII*, xix (2), p. 414; *Eng. P. N. Elements* (E.P.N.S.), i. 36.
[86] *Cal. S.P. Dom.* 1685, p. 54.
[87] S. Hudson, *Hill Top Town*, 119–21; Soc. Antiq. MS. 817, ix, f. 1.
[88] *V.C.H. Wilts.* iv. 352; v. 258; O.S. Maps 6″, Wilts. VIII, XIII (1888–9 and later edns.); Soc. Antiq. MS. 817, ix, f. 1.
[89] *Census*, 1901.
[90] Ibid. 1931; *V.C.H. Wilts.* iv. 352.
[91] *Census*, 1951; 1961.
[92] *Local Govt. in Eng. and Wales* (H.M.S.O. 1974), 117.

[93] Inf. from Chief Assistant (Environment), Dept. of Planning and Highways.
[94] *W.A.M.* vii. 3.
[95] *V.C.H. Wilts.* iv. 352–3.
[96] *Census*, 1971; 1981.
[97] Wm. of Malmesbury, *Gesta Regum Angl.* (Rolls Ser.), ii. 484; below, manors.
[98] *W.A.M.* li. 187.
[99] *Memorials of Old Wilts.* ed. A. Dryden, 148.
[1] *Rot. Chart.* (Rec. Com.), 213, 222.
[2] *E.H.R.* xxi. 98–105, 713–23.
[3] Leland, *Itin.* ed. Toulmin Smith, i. 131.
[4] Below.
[5] J. M. Moffatt, *Hist. Malm.* 100–1.

paths parallel with and above the lanes called Burnivale and King's Wall. To the north the wall may survive as the garden wall of the Old Bell; east of the Old Bell the town wall was the outer wall of the abbey buildings which extended to the edge of the steep slope above the river. In the late 13th century there were at least four gates; the east gate was across the Oxford road, there called Holloway; Wyniard gate was a little gate at the south end of what became Silver Street; the south gate was at the southern end of High Street; and the postern

late 18th century.[6] In the late 20th century one jamb of the east gate survived in Holloway, and the rounded plan of the house at the junction of King's Wall and High Street may have reflected that of the west side of the south gate.

The plan of the town within the walls had largely been established by the late 13th century and had changed little by the late 20th. The extent of the abbey precinct was marked by the southward diversion of the old Oxford–Bristol road around three sides of a rectangle, near the south-western

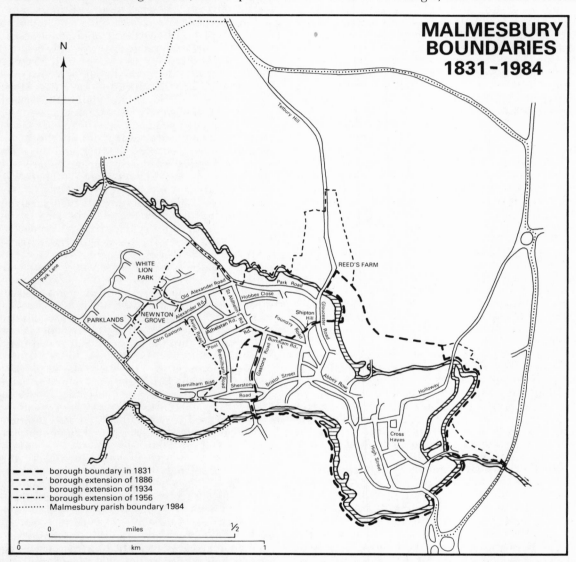

MALMESBURY BOUNDARIES 1831-1984

- – – borough boundary in 1831
- – – – borough extension of 1886
- –·–·– borough extension of 1934
- –··–··– borough extension of 1956
- ········· Malmesbury parish boundary 1984

gate was at the junction of King's Wall and Burnivale. A fifth, west, gate was mentioned in the earlier 13th century and may be identified with the bar in Westport recorded later in the century. It was presumably across what became Abbey Row, at or near the castle site, and foundations opposite nos. 31 and 33 Abbey Row have been identified as those of the gate. The gates were all ruinous in the early 16th century. The east gate and the postern gate were not, however, removed until the

corner of which stood St. Paul's church. The precinct may have been extended south to those boundaries either in the 12th century, when the abbey church was rebuilt, or by William of Colerne, abbot from 1260, in whose time the abbey buildings were much enlarged.[7] Apart from the abbey church and the undercroft of Abbey House, the most substantial monastic building surviving in the late 20th century was the central east–west range of the Old Bell hotel. The range, of two

[6] W.A.M. li. 187–90; Reg. Malm. i. 118, 121, 127, 129; ii. 71; inf. from Mr. M. Green, English Heritage, Fortress

Ho., 23 Savile Row, Lond.
[7] V.C.H. Wilts. iii. 220; below, churches.

storeys each divided into two rooms by a central chimney stack, was probably built in the 13th century to incorporate the abbot's lodging. The names of streets in the town are recorded in a rental of the late 13th century or the early 14th. High Street, called *magna strata*, presumably then as later formed the town's spine, running south from the abbey to the confluence of the two branches of the Avon; East Street was probably a parallel street following the line of the later Cross Hayes Lane and Silver Street. The streets were joined by lanes running east and west; Philip's Lane may have been the eastern part of the Oxford–Bristol road which skirted the abbey precinct, known from the 17th century as Oxford Street, and Griffin's Lane further south apparently became St. Dennis's Lane. The name of Ingram's Lane survives as Ingram Street. A market place adjacent to High Street may have been that within the abbey precinct, opposite the north end of High Street, where an octagonal vaulted market cross was built in the 15th century, or Cross Hayes which was mentioned in the rental and was presumably then as later an open space. King's Wall lay along the outside of the west part of the wall; further north a chapel, which became known as the Hermitage and was demolished in the early 19th century, stood in Westport parish between the lane later called Burnivale and the town wall. In the late 13th century the name Burnivale was apparently used for all or some of that part of the town which lay within Westport parish. At the southern end of the town Nethewall was the area between the wall and the lower parts of High Street and Silver Street,[8] below which Mill or St. John's bridge carried the Chippenham road across the river. St. John's hospital[9] had been built there by the 13th century; a blocked doorway of *c.* 1200 and other medieval stonework were incorporated into the south-west front when the hospital was rebuilt as almshouses probably in the 17th century.[10] Other buildings of medieval origin which survived in the late 20th century stood on or near the boundary of the abbey precinct. A building which became the Green Dragon inn, north-west of the market cross, incorporated a stairway perhaps of the 14th century; near the south-eastern corner of the precinct Tower House, which was extended in the 17th century and later, incorporated a later medieval roof with arch-braced collars; no. 8 Gloucester Street, formerly the White Lion inn, had a courtyard plan and may be of 16th-century origin. Mills were built beside the rivers on the outskirts of the town; in the later Middle Ages they occupied sites north of the abbey, below the postern gate, and beside Mill bridge and Wyniard, later Goose, bridge. In the late 13th century or the early 14th the Tetbury Avon was crossed by the Oxford–Bristol road over St. Leonard's, later Holloway, bridge and by the Tetbury road over Theyn, later Staines, bridge.[11]

The abbey church survived the Dissolution and replaced the ruined St. Paul's as the parish church of Malmesbury.[12] Other monastic buildings were used as workshops in the 1540s,[13] but most were probably demolished in the mid or late 16th century. In 1561 buildings in the borough were said to be in great decay;[14] the description presumably refers to the former abbey. A proposal by William Stumpe, the purchaser of the abbey site, to build a row or rows of weavers' houses north-east of the abbey church[15] apparently came to nothing. In the later 16th century, however, Stumpe's son Sir James built Abbey House there.[16] The house has a half **H** plan with two storeys and gabled attics: its central, northern, range is over a 13th-century undercroft, and it has short wings to the south. The undercroft, the vaulted roof of which was demolished, was partly filled to form a basement. There was a hall on the ground floor of the central range, in the east wing were parlours, and in the west wing kitchens and service rooms. A turret, housing a newel stair, was built in the angle between the hall and the east wing, and the main south front had a low porch bearing the arms of Stumpe and his wife Isabel Baynton.[17] There was probably a walled forecourt south of the house, and a re-used 12th-century arch, which survived in the late 20th century, was incorporated in the south part of the wall in line with the porch. In the early 19th century a low wing extended eastwards from the house and a long two-storeyed range ran south from the west wing; both were probably of 17th-century origin.[18] The western extension was demolished, probably in the early 20th century when the eastern extension was replaced by a two-storeyed wing with attics similar in style to the original building. In 1636 there were *c.* 60 houses within the former precinct and most of the inhabitants were poor.[19]

Abbey House is the only large house to have survived from the late 16th century or the early 17th. No. 9 Oxford Street is a gabled house of stone with a late 16th-century roof and is said to have been used as a guildhall.[20] Partly timber-framed buildings with jettied first floors survive at nos. 6 and 10 Gloucester Street, no. 9 High Street, and in the gabled southern wing of the King's Arms in High Street. No. 6 Oxford Street, sometimes called Manor House, has an elaborate early 17th-century staircase rising through three storeys. Houses in Abbey Row were said to have been destroyed in the Civil War, perhaps during Sir William Waller's capture of the town in 1643, and there may have been other destruction arising from the military occupation of Malmesbury,[21] but it is not possible to identify areas of post-war reconstruction. The main range of the King's Arms is probably late 17th-century, as is the substantial building later subdivided into nos. 5 and 7 High Street. The Old Brewery, north-east of the market cross, bears the date 1672 on a gable, and the much

8 *Reg. Malm.* i. 117–33; *P. N. Wilts.* (E.P.N.S.), 49; below, Westport, church. For High Street, see above, plate facing p. 92; below, plate facing p. 236. For the mkt. cross and Cross Hayes, see below, plates facing p. 189.
9 See plate facing p. 108.
10 *V.C.H. Wilts.* iii. 340–1.
11 *Reg. Malm.* ii, p. xxxiii; below, trade and ind. (mills).
12 Below, churches.
13 Leland, *Itin.* ed. Toulmin Smith, i. 132.
14 P.R.O., E 301/26/153, no. 40.
15 Leland, *Itin.* ed. Toulmin Smith, i. 132.
16 See plate facing p. 45.   17 *W.N. & Q.* viii. 444–5.
18 J. Buckler, watercolour in W.A.S. Libr., vol. vi. 36.
19 *Wilts. Q. Sess. Rec.* ed. Cunnington, 117–18.
20 Hudson, *Hill Top Town,* 17.
21 Moffatt, *Hist. Malm.* 30 n.; below.

restored frontage of no. 46 High Street has a date stone for 1671. Stone was the normal building material by that time, but the chimneys of nos. 5 and 7 High Street are of red brick and have diagonally set shafts. Away from the centre of the town a number of smaller houses are of one storey and attics with large gables rising from the main elevation; examples are no. 3 Back Hill south of Silver Street, no. 66 High Street, and no. 10 St. John's Street.

The eastern block of King's Wall House, west of King's Wall and in Westport parish, was built, probably soon after 1700, with an ashlared front of three bays and three storeys and a shell hood over the entrance. It was extended westwards and northwards shortly afterwards and the new sections were given old-fashioned mullion and transom windows. Other substantial houses of the early and mid 18th century include Cross Hayes House, which is dated 1728 and has an ashlar front of three bays with rusticated end pilasters and a moulded cornice, and no. 32 Cross Hayes, which has a front of five bays surmounted by a small central pediment. Smaller 18th-century houses are behind modern shop fronts, and no. 36 High Street has a date stone for 1763. Unusually for Malmesbury no. 10 High Street has a brick façade, apparently 18th-century, but its elaborate stone architraves and parapet were added or renewed in the later 19th century and its original form is uncertain. In the last quarter of the 18th century and the early years of the 19th much new building took place in the town. The mill by St. John's bridge was replaced by a cloth factory c. 1790.[22] No. 25 Abbey Row, dated 1798, has a front of three bays and three storeys with a projecting architrave, a pilastered doorcase with broken pediment, rusticated quoins, and a moulded cornice below a narrow parapet. St. Michael's House, near the market cross, has a plainer elevation of similar proportions and bears the date 1790. No. 63 High Street is of two storeys with attic dormers and a Doric doorcase. It has a front of mixed rubble and brick, perhaps the result of alterations to an earlier building, and was probably rendered. Roughcast elevations are still common on buildings of the later 18th century and early 19th, among them no. 27 Abbey Row, dated 1811, and buildings along the east side of Cross Hayes Lane. Many more buildings, which in the late 20th century had exposed rubble walls, were probably once so treated. At the southern end of High Street[23] and in St. John's Street and Silver Street are cottages, usually of two storeys with stone-slated roofs and brick stacks, which were probably built or altered in the early 19th century.

New building in the town centre after c. 1825 was chiefly commercial or institutional. The northern part of Cross Hayes was the site of a town hall and a nonconformist chapel, and another nonconformist chapel stood nearby in Oxford Street. Two schools and a Roman Catholic church were built on the east side of Cross Hayes; the former teacher's house on the same side of Cross Hayes bears the dates 1851 and 1857 and is in baroque style. A hospital was built north of the market cross,[24] and houses in High Street were refronted or rebuilt as shops and banks. No. 44 High Street has a narrow front of three storeys with a shaped attic gable and is of bright red brick with moulded brick decorations characteristic of c. 1900. There was little new building in the part of the town which had been in the old Malmesbury parish in the 20th century. After the closure of the station in 1962 factories, a fire station, and an ambulance station were built on and near its site, and new houses were built north of its site in the 1970s and 1980s. Part of the town was designated a conservation area in 1971; the conservation area was extended in 1987.[25]

Most of the 19th-century population increase was achieved by greater density of occupation in the town where there was little space for building on new sites. On the outskirts the union workhouse was built in Brokenborough parish[26] and cottages were built east of Wyniard Mill beyond the borough boundary in the earlier 19th century, and throughout the 19th century and the early 20th the town continued to expand into Westport.[27] Between the early 1930s and the late 1960s the built-up area of Malmesbury extended further westwards[28] on land which, until 19th- and 20th-century boundary changes, was principally in Brokenborough parish and partly in Bremilham and Westport. Between 1931, when lands called Pool Gastons and Gastons were bought by Malmesbury borough council, and 1941 c. 60 council houses were built in Pool Gastons Road and Athelstan Road. The former workhouse was converted into council houses in 1936 and 1938.[29] Another 125 council houses were built between 1946 and 1956 in Alexander Road, Avon Road, Hobbes Close, and Corn Gastons.[30] A school and a swimming pool were built,[31] and another c. 40 council dwellings were later built in Newnton Grove and near the swimming pool. The Parklands estate, built on land transferred from Brokenborough to Malmesbury parish in 1984, included c. 55 houses and bungalows in 1958; in the late 1960s c. 84 more houses, bungalows, and sheltered homes were built.[32] Also in the 1960s the c. 100 private houses in White Lion Park, north of Parklands, were built, and in place of the converted workhouse, Bremilham Rise, a row of 27 council houses, was built. Accommodation for old people was later built in the grounds of Burnham House in Burnham Road. The town was extended northwards in the 1980s when c. 250 private houses were built east of Tetbury Hill as Reed's Farm.

In the Middle Ages the knight's fees held of Malmesbury abbey apparently constituted an honor for which courts may have been held, and courts for Startley, possibly Chedglow, and Malmesbury hundreds were held at Malmesbury.

---

[22] Below, trade and ind.
[23] See plate facing p. 236.
[24] Below, local govt. (boro. govt.), public services, Rom. Catholicism, prot. nonconf., educ.
[25] Inf. from Chief Assistant (Environment), Dept. of Planning and Highways.
[26] Above, Brokenborough, introduction.

[27] C. Greenwood, *Map of Wilts.* (1820); O.S. Map 6″, Wilts. VIII (1889 edn.).   [28] See plate facing p. 92.
[29] W.R.O., G 21/132/4; G 21/132/6; G 21/132/21.
[30] Ibid. G 21/132/2–5.
[31] Below, public services, educ.
[32] W.R.O., G 7/360/10; above, Brokenborough, introduction.

Assizes were occasionally held at Malmesbury in the 13th century, as were quarter sessions in the late 14th and the 15th. Private sessions allegedly held improperly in the town in 1614 may have been petty sessions;[33] no later reference to quarter sessions held there has been found. In 1927 and for much of the 20th century a bishop suffragan of Malmesbury was appointed to assist in the diocese of Bristol.[34]

Malmesbury was directly involved in the civil wars of both the 12th century and the 17th. After the arrest of Roger, bishop of Salisbury, in June 1139, the castle was taken by King Stephen, lost on 7 October of that year to Robert FitzHubert, and recaptured a fortnight later; whether Robert held it for himself or for the Empress Maud is not clear. In 1144 Malmesbury was attacked by William of Dover, a supporter of Maud, besieged by Robert, earl of Gloucester, her brother, and relieved by the king. In that year, presumably at a time when she hoped that her supporters would take and hold Malmesbury, Maud granted the borough to Humphrey de Bohun with the provision that no new fortification should be made there.[35] William of Dover renewed his attack in 1145 but, although he captured the castellan, the garrison remained loyal to Stephen. The castle changed hands in 1153 when it was captured by Henry of Anjou after a confrontation, but no battle, with Stephen's army. The presence of a garrison was apparently unwelcome to the monks; in 1151 Pope Eugenius III required the soldiers not to trouble the abbey, and c. 1173 Alexander III empowered the abbot to excommunicate any of the garrison who harmed the monks.[36]

At the outbreak of war in 1642 Malmesbury apparently held to the parliamentary side and the committee for Wiltshire met there. The town submitted to the royalists on 3 February 1643, the day following Prince Rupert's capture of Cirencester, but on 23 March it was taken by Sir William Waller for parliament. Sir Edward Hungerford was appointed governor but changed his allegiance and surrendered the town to the royalists on 5 April. Malmesbury may have changed hands twice more before 24 May 1644 when Col. Edward Massey recaptured it for parliament. From then until the late summer or autumn of 1646 a garrison numbering perhaps 1,000 men was kept in the town. A petition was submitted to the county committee, probably early in 1645, complaining of the cost of the garrison to the locality and of its inadequacy as a defence against royalist raids; the petition may have had its result in the new regulations for the garrison issued in July 1645. The garrison had probably been disbanded by November 1646,[37]

but other smaller forces were stationed at Malmesbury in 1649 and 1651, and, when renewed disturbances threatened after the Restoration, in 1661 and 1663.[38] The Restoration itself was celebrated in Malmesbury, according to John Aubrey, with 'so many and so great volleys of shot' that part of the abbey tower fell the following night.[39]

Beside St. John's there may have been two medieval hospitals in the town; their sites are not known. In 1245 protection was granted to the brethren of St. Anthony's hospital,[40] and Hugh Mortimer, perhaps he who died c. 1180, apparently confirmed another hospital in Malmesbury to the monks of St. Victor-en-Caux (Seine Maritime).[41]

In 1540 there were inns in Malmesbury called the Crown, the Lamb, the Griffin, and, perhaps, the Red Cross.[42] The Griffin, in High Street, was still open in 1751,[43] but had closed by 1809;[44] no reference to the other three signs after 1540 has been found. In 1592 seven licences to sell ale in the town were granted[45] and in 1620 there were 12 alehousekeepers in the parish including two in Burton Hill.[46] There were between 17 and 20 inns and alehouses within the borough, including the part of it in Westport parish, in the mid 18th century. The number had fallen to 11 by 1827,[47] but had risen to 17 by 1875 perhaps as a result of the expansion of brewing in the town. The total had fallen again to 12 by 1927.[48] Among the oldest houses were the White Lion in Gloucester Street, first recorded in 1618,[49] the King's Arms in High Street, open in the late 17th century,[50] the Old Bell, called the Castle in 1703[51] and the Bell in 1798,[52] and the George in High Street, open in 1823.[53] The White Lion and the George closed after 1955;[54] the Bell, then the Old Bell hotel, and the King's Arms remained open in 1988. Other public houses in the town in 1988, apart from those in Westport, were the Borough Arms in Oxford Street and the Old Greyhound and the Rose and Crown in High Street.

The *Wiltshire and Gloucestershire Standard* was published in Malmesbury from 1837 until 1840, when the place of publication was moved to Cirencester.[55] A monthly *Malmesbury Journal* was started in the summer of 1841 but only two editions were published,[56] and seven or more editions of a weekly *Malmesbury Free Press* appeared in 1867.[57]

Malmesbury's Horticultural and Floral Society was founded c. 1870[58] and in the earlier 20th century held an annual show near Arches Farm in what had been Westport parish.[59] It was disbanded c. 1930.[60] The masonic lodge of St. Aldhelm met in Malmesbury from 1901 and in 1906 the Royal

---

[33] *V.C.H. Wilts.* v. 19–20, 35, 63–4, 93; above, Malmesbury hund.

[34] *Cat. Rec. Bristol Dioc.* comp. I. M. Kirby, 178.

[35] *V.C.H. Wilts.* iii. 216–17; *Anct. Chart.* (Pipe R. Soc. x), 45–6.

[36] *V.C.H. Wilts.* iii. 217; R. H. Luce, *Hist. Malm.* 25–7; Wm. of Malmesbury, *Gesta Regum Angl.* (Rolls Ser.), ii. 548, 556.

[37] *Accts. of Parl. Garrisons* (W.R.S. ii), 27–36.

[38] *Cal. S.P. Dom.* 1649–50, 353; 1651, 371; 1660–1, 478; 1663–4, 301.   [39] Aubrey, *Topog. Coll.* ed. Jackson, 255.

[40] *Cal. Pat.* 1232–47, 459.

[41] *Complete Peerage*, ix. 268; Eton Coll. Mun. 4/1.

[42] *L. & P. Hen. VIII*, xv, p. 551; P.R.O., SC 6/Hen. VIII/3986, rott. 96–98d.

[43] W.R.O. 212B/4000.   [44] Ibid. 212B/4274.

[45] *Sess. Mins.* (W.R.S. iv), 150.

[46] *Early-Stuart Tradesmen* (W.R.S. xv), pp. 29–30.

[47] W.R.O., A 1/326/1–3.

[48] *Kelly's Dir. Wilts.* (1875, 1927).

[49] W.R.O. 177/23, deed, Alright to Thorner, 1618.

[50] Aubrey, *Topog. Coll.* ed. Jackson, 262.

[51] W.R.O. 212B/3908.

[52] Ibid. 212B/4201.

[53] Ibid. A 1/326/1.   [54] Ibid. G 21/516/4.

[55] *W.A.M.* xl. 66–9.

[56] *Malm. Jnl.* 30 July 1841; 28 Aug. 1841.

[57] *Malm. Free Press*, 18 May 1867.

[58] W.R.O. 815/24.   [59] Ibid. 815/26.

[60] Hudson, *Hill Top Town*, 154.

Arch Chapter of St. Aldhelm was formed.[61] There was a town brass band in 1895,[62] but in 1945 its instruments were sold.[63] A new band had been formed by 1988.[64] The Athelstan cinema was built north of the market cross in 1935; it had 333 seats[65] and was closed c. 1973.[66] There was a bowling green north of Holloway in 1831.[67] A bowling club had been started in the town by 1923;[68] from 1948 or earlier it had greens by Goose bridge.[69] There was a cricket club in 1895; clubs for football, hockey, and tennis were founded after the First World War. The hockey club had been disbanded by 1927.[70] In 1988 the football and tennis clubs had grounds west of Tetbury Hill and the cricket club a ground north of the former station.

In 1837 Joseph Poole of Malmesbury owned a travelling show, which was later managed by his sons. As the Poole Brothers they developed the 'myriorama', an arrangement of backcloths and mirrors, which was used to illustrate topical events. In the 1890s they toured widely in England and Wales from a base in Westport where the scenery was painted.[71]

In 1980 the town celebrated the supposed 1100th anniversary of the granting of a charter by King Alfred.[72] The date 880 was given as that of the town's charter in a book published in or after 1951 in which the grant attributed by the burgesses in 1381 to Athelstan was apparently ascribed to Alfred;[73] the date 880 was later repeated in a history of Malmesbury.[74]

St. Aldhelm joined the monastic community at Malmesbury as a young man, became abbot, probably in 675, and was from 705 until 709 bishop of Sherborne (Dors.). He was buried in Malmesbury and miracles were worked at his shrine there. William of Malmesbury (d. c. 1143) records the tradition that John Scotus Erigena, the philosopher, lived at the abbey in the late 9th century and was murdered there by his pupils. William himself spent most of his life in the monastery at Malmesbury.[75]

BURTON HILL or Burton was a small suburb of Malmesbury immediately south of the town beside the Chippenham road. In the later 13th century its buildings probably included the hospital of St. Mary Magdalene.[76] Part of the hospital may have survived as a chapel which stood at the junction of the Chippenham and Swindon roads in 1540.[77] The chapel, used as a private house in

1768 and apparently in 1809,[78] was demolished in the early 19th century when a new house called Canister Hall was built on its site. The three-storeyed brick house was later called the Priory.[79] Burton Hill House was built south of the junction probably in the early 17th century. It was rebuilt in 1840 or 1842 to a design by C. R. Cockerell, the owner's brother, but part or all of the house was burned down in 1846. It was rebuilt again in the same year in a Tudor Gothic style, probably again designed by Cockerell,[80] and enlarged in the later 19th century and the 20th.[81] In the late 18th century a farmhouse, called Manor House in 1823, stood south-east of the junction; it was rebuilt in the later 19th century in Tudor style and from 1925 was used as a hospital.[82] A house later called the Beeches, another which became the Black Horse inn, open as such in 1822, and a turnpike cottage stood near the junction, and cottages were scattered south of Burton Hill House in 1773.[83] Between 1773 and 1828 there was much new building beside the Chippenham road north of the junction, presumably to house workers at the cloth mill built near St. John's bridge, and terraces of early 19th-century cottages survive there. Cottages were also built south of Burton Hill House, where a track ran south-west from the Chippenham road,[84] and a turnpike cottage was built there after 1842. Some cottages beside the Chippenham road had apparently been demolished by 1842.[85] In the mid and later 19th century houses in Burton Hill were built or rebuilt for members of Malmesbury's landed, commercial, and professional families.[86] A police station north of the hospital was built later.[87] The Priory and the Black Horse were demolished, probably in 1973 when a roundabout was built at the southern end of the Malmesbury bypass.[88] West of the roundabout 27 council houses and 12 maisonettes were built shortly afterwards,[89] and in the 1980s an estate of c. 50 private houses was built north of Burton Hill House.

COWBRIDGE is a settlement which has spread north-westwards from Cowbridge Mill on the Avon along the Swindon road towards Burton Hill. In 1773 only the mill, on a site used since the 13th century or earlier, and a large house beside it were standing.[90] Cottages were built beside the road west of the mill in the early 19th century.[91] Cowbridge House beside the mill was rebuilt c. 1853,[92] a farmhouse north of it was probably built

[61] V.C.H. Wilts. iv. 389.
[62] Kelly's Dir. Wilts. (1895).
[63] W.R.O., G 21/119/3.
[64] Local inf.
[65] W.R.O., F 12, corresp. file, Athelstan cinema.
[66] Inf. from Curator, Athelstan Mus.
[67] Glos. R.O., D 674B/P 73.
[68] Kelly's Dir. Wilts. (1923).
[69] Town Guide (1948).
[70] Kelly's Dir. Wilts. (1895 and later edns.).
[71] Hudson, Hill Top Town, 112–13; W.A.M. xliii. 108–9; Kelly's Dir. Wilts. (1885, 1895).
[72] W.A.M. lxxiv/lxxv. 133.
[73] W. B. Faraday, Eng. and Welsh Boroughs, 15.
[74] B. Hodge, Hist. Malm. (1968), 4.
[75] V.C.H. Wilts. iii. 211–14, 217.
[76] Ibid. 341; Reg. Malm. i. 119.
[77] Leland, Itin. ed. Toulmin Smith, i. 133.
[78] Buckler, watercolour in W.A.S. Libr., vol. vi. 34; see below, plate facing p. 173.
[79] W.R.O. 1165/1, deeds, Dewell to Robins; photo. in Nat. Bldgs. Rec.

[80] W.N. & Q. viii. 433 and facing pl.; D. Watkin, Life of C. R. Cockerell, 253.
[81] See plate facing p. 141.
[82] Andrews and Dury, Map (W.R.S. viii), pl. 16; Kelly's Dir. Wilts. (1927); W.R.O. 212A/38/37/161.
[83] Andrews and Dury, Map (W.R.S. viii), pls. 13, 16; W.R.O., A 1/326/3.
[84] Andrews and Dury, Map (W.R.S. viii), pl. 13; O.S. Map 1″, sheet 34 (1828 edn.).
[85] W.R.O., tithe award.
[86] Kelly's Dir. Wilts. (1848 and later edns.).
[87] Below, public services.
[88] Inf. from Chief Assistant (Environment), Dept. of Planning and Highways.
[89] Inf. from Property Maintenance Manager, Dept. of Housing and Property Services, N. Wilts. District Council, Bewley Ho., Marshfield Rd., Chippenham.
[90] Reg. Malm. i. 176–7; Andrews and Dury, Map (W.R.S. viii), pl. 16.
[91] O.S. Map 1″, sheet 34 (1828 edn.); W.R.O., tithe award.
[92] Below, manors.

then, and the Knoll, another large house 500 m. west of it, is of similar date. In the 1880s a new vicarage house was built north-west of the Knoll.[93] From 1939 Cowbridge House and mill were incorporated into a factory;[94] the old buildings were extended and new workshops and offices built. In Cowbridge Crescent, west of Cowbridge House, 12 houses and 26 prefabricated bungalows were built by the local authority in, respectively, 1941 and 1948 partly to house workers from the factory.[95] Most of those dwellings were later replaced and more houses built in the 1970s and 1980s.

MILBOURNE was a settlement in the Middle Ages but for that period little documentary and no architectural evidence of it survives. In the later 17th century Milbourne was described as a 'discontinued' village on the Oxford–Bristol road,[96] indicating that its farmsteads were then, as in the later 18th century, scattered along the road which formed the village street.[97] The wide verges of the road were common pastures until the earlier 19th century,[98] and the older houses stand well back from the road. The oldest to survive are at the western end, near the junction of the street with Moochers Lane, later Milbourne Lane, which leads north-west to the Cricklade road. Milbourne House, north of the junction, incorporates an east–west range possibly of the late 16th century.[99] In the earlier 17th century a cross wing at the west end and a rear kitchen wing at the east end were added. Extensive 20th-century alterations included the addition of a bay window on the main south front and the fitting of 18th century panelling. Milbourne Farm, south of the junction, is of 17th-century origin. East of those houses are cottages and farmsteads built in the 18th century or earlier, and the village's eastern end was marked in 1773, as in the later 20th century, by Manor Farm,[1] an early 18th-century stone house of three bays. There was little new building in the 19th century. A row of four cottages on the north side of the village street bears the date 1901, there was infilling north of the street in the 1930s, and 12 semidetached houses were built at the north end of Milbourne Lane c. 1938.[2] In the later 20th century there was more infilling on the north side of the street, houses were built on the west side of Milbourne Lane, and two private estates of bungalows and houses were built, Monks Park on the common pasture south of the street, and Milbourne Park west of Milbourne Lane. When the bypass was built in 1973 the street was closed west of the village and Milbourne Lane became the principal western approach to the village.

WHITCHURCH. There was a settlement, prob-
ably including a chapel, at Whitchurch in the 13th century.[3] Perhaps in the late 17th century and certainly in the late 18th Whitchurch comprised a single farmstead. Before 1670 the chapel was incorporated into Whitchurch Farm; its 'steeple' was demolished c. 1675.[4] Parts of a late medieval building survive as the western end of the long 17th-century domestic range. That range was altered in the 18th century when a small central pediment above a pedimented porch was added to the north front and much of the interior was refitted. At the centre of a range of brick buildings north-west of the house is a square tower dated 1797. A garage, a small farmstead, several houses, and a water tower were built north of Whitchurch, later Whychurch, Farm beside the Cirencester road in the late 19th century and the 20th.

OTHER SETTLEMENT. The abbot of Malmesbury had a lodge, which may have been in use in the 13th century[5] and was standing in 1540, in Cowfold park.[6] Its site was presumably that of the mansion called Cole Park built south of the town from the later 16th century.[7] A grange in Cowfold park in the early 16th century[8] is likely to have been on the site of either Lawn Farm or Grange Farm, neighbouring farmsteads north-west of Cole Park. Lawn Farm, perhaps used as one of two lodges for officers of the royal stud farm in Cole park in the earlier 17th century,[9] is an L-shaped 17th-century house within which survive parts of two cruck trusses; it was extended and refronted in the early 19th century. The farmhouse of Grange farm was rebuilt in the 1820s.[10] West of Corston village there was a lodge in West park, presumably on the site of West Park Farm, in 1653.[11]

A building which stood north of Holloway bridge in 1773[12] may have been the Duke of York inn, open in 1822;[13] the inn was rebuilt in the 1960s. Cottages were built north-east of it in the 18th century and the 19th; with some 20th-century buildings they formed the hamlet known in the later 20th century as Blick's Hill.

Most outlying farmsteads in the old Malmesbury parish occupy sites which were in use in the 18th century and probably earlier. Farmsteads on the sites of those later called Whiteheath, north of Corston village, Rodbourne Rail, south of Cole Park, and Burnt Heath, north-west of Whiteheath, were standing in 1729, 1770, and 1773 respectively.[14] Quobwell Farm and Coldharbour Farm, north of the town, were built in the mid 18th century and Southfield Farm, south of Milbourne village, was built between 1773 and 1802.[15] Lower West Park Farm was built on a new site north of West Park Farm between 1842 and 1885,[16] and the Coopers' Arms, beside the Tetbury road

[93] Below, churches.   [94] Ibid. trade and ind.
[95] W.R.O., G 7/760/149; G 7/760/219.
[96] Ogilby, Brit. (1675), pl. 79.
[97] Andrews and Dury, Map (W.R.S. viii), pls. 16–17.
[98] W.R.O. 900/12.   [99] See plate facing p. 93.
[1] Andrews and Dury, Map (W.R.S. viii), pl. 17.
[2] W.R.O., G 7/760/101.
[3] Reg. Malm. ii. 120–1.
[4] Aubrey, Topog. Coll. ed. Jackson, 267; Andrews and Dury, Map (W.R.S. viii), pl. 16.
[5] Rot. Hund. (Rec. Com.), ii (1), 230, 272.
[6] Leland, Itin. ed. Toulmin Smith, i. 133; P.R.O., SC 6/Hen. VIII/3986, rot. 116.

[7] Below, manors.
[8] P.R.O., SC 6/Hen. VIII/3986, rot. 116.
[9] Ibid. LR 2/301, f. 233.
[10] W.R.O. 161/52, sale partic. of Grange farm.
[11] P.R.O., LR 2/301, f. 256.
[12] Andrews and Dury, Map (W.R.S. viii), pl. 16.
[13] W.R.O., A 1/326/3.
[14] Ibid. 568/30, deed, Scrope to Young, 1729; 161/26/2; Andrews and Dury, Map (W.R.S. viii), pl. 13.
[15] Andrews and Dury, Map (W.R.S. viii), pl. 17; W.R.O. 900/12.
[16] W.R.O., tithe award; O.S. Map 6", Wilts. XIII (1888 edn.).

north-west of Quobwell Farm, was open as an inn in 1875[17] and converted to a farmhouse after 1927.[18]

MANORS AND OTHER ESTATES. The *BOROUGH* of Malmesbury belonged to the king in 1086. He then received the third penny; the remaining two thirds were held at farm by Walter Hosed. Of 73¾ *masurae* 52, probably including 10 formerly held by Earl Harold, were held by the king, 4½ were held by Malmesbury abbey, and the remainder by 15 different lords.[19]

Hugh, provost of Malmesbury, paid £20 for the farm of the borough in 1130.[20] Between 1136 and 1139 King Stephen granted the lordship of the borough to Roger, bishop of Salisbury, his justiciar, who had taken possession of Malmesbury abbey in 1118. The lordship presumably reverted to the Crown after the bishop's disgrace and death in 1139.[21] In 1144 Maud granted it to Humphrey de Bohun but the grant may not have taken effect.[22] The borough was apparently part of the dowry of Berengaria, wife of Richard I, which was withheld from her by John presumably from Richard's death in 1199.[23] In 1204 John granted the borough to his queen, Isabel, as dower,[24] and in 1215 he gave it in fee farm to Malmesbury abbey.[25] The abbey held it until the Dissolution for £20 a year.[26] The alderman and burgesses held it at fee farm from 1566 until 1598 or later.[27]

By 1628 lordship of the borough had been granted, under the name of *MALMESBURY* manor, to Henry Danvers, earl of Danby[28] (d. 1644),[29] who devised it to his nephew Henry Danvers. From Henry (d. 1654) the manor passed in moieties to his sisters Elizabeth and Anne.[30] Elizabeth (d. 1709) and her husband Robert Danvers, formerly Villiers (d. 1674), held her moiety in 1673.[31] Anne (d. 1659), wife of Sir Henry Lee, Bt. (d. 1659), was succeeded by her daughters Eleanor, later wife of James Bertie, Baron Norreys (cr. earl of Abingdon 1682), and Anne, later wife of Thomas Wharton (Baron Wharton from 1696, cr. earl of Wharton 1706, cr. marquess of Wharton 1715).[32] The settlement made on the Whartons' marriage in 1673 provided for the division of Anne Lee's estates; the Whartons' portion probably included her moiety of Malmesbury manor. The settlement was later disputed[33] but in 1685 Thomas and Anne Wharton held both Anne Lee's and Elizabeth Danvers's moieties.[34] On Wharton's death in 1715 the manor passed to his son Philip, marquess of Wharton (cr.

duke of Wharton 1718, d. 1731), whose estates were confiscated when he was outlawed for treason in 1729. In 1733 the estates were settled on trustees for payment of his debts and afterwards for his sisters and coheirs, Jane, wife of Robert Coke, and Lucy (d. *s.p.* 1739), wife of Sir William Morice, Bt.,[35] and in 1743 were sold on Jane's behalf. Malmesbury manor was bought by Sir John Rushout, Bt.[36] Sir John was succeeded in 1775 by his son Sir John (cr. Baron Northwick 1797, d. 1800), whose relict Rebecca[37] retained the manor until her death in 1818.[38] She devised it to her younger son the Revd. George Rushout-Bowles.[39] George was succeeded in 1842 by his son George Rushout (Baron Northwick from 1859, d. 1887), whose relict Elizabeth may have held the manor until her death in 1912;[40] the reversion was sold in lots in 1896. The manor then comprised *c.* 80 a. in the town.[41]

The lands which became Malmesbury parish were probably held by Malmesbury abbey from its foundation, but the copies of charters granting them are suspect. The monks claimed to have received an estate called Malmesbury, the site of the abbey, by a grant of 675 from Bishop Leutherius and Rodbourne and Corston by a grant of 701 from King Ine. The boundaries of an estate of 100 hides called Brokenborough, said to have been confirmed to the abbey by King Edwy in 956, were surveyed in the 11th century or the 12th when they included all of what became Malmesbury parish and other lands.[42] In 1066 Gilbert and Godwin each held an estate of 1 hide said to be in Malmesbury; those estates were held by the bishop of Coutances and by Chetel respectively in 1086.[43] The later history of those estates has not been traced, and from 1086 to 1539 Malmesbury abbey owned virtually the whole parish apart from the borough.

Malmesbury abbey claimed to have been granted the estate later called *COWFOLD* as part of the Brokenborough estate by King Edwy in 956, but is likely to have held it much earlier. Between 1066 and 1086, when it was part of the Brokenborough estate, the abbey apparently granted it for knight service.[44] It later recovered it and by the early 13th century had imparked part of it. In the late 13th century the Cowfold estate apparently included the abbey's Corston land.[45] Cowfold passed to the Crown at the Dissolution, when Corston was a separate estate, and in 1548 as Cowfold manor was granted to Edward Seymour, duke of Somerset.[46] The manor presumably escheated on his attainder in 1552.[47] In 1556 lands at Cow-

[17] *Kelly's Dir. Wilts.* (1875).
[18] W.R.O., G 7/515/9.
[19] *V.C.H. Wilts.* ii, pp. 21–2, 113, 115.
[20] *Pipe R.* 1130 (H.M.S.O. facsimile), 16.
[21] *Reg. Regum Anglo-Norm.* iii, no. 784; *D.N B.*
[22] *Anct. Chart.* (Pipe R. Soc. x), 45–6; above, introduction.
[23] *Cal. Papal Reg.* i. 33.
[24] *Rot. Chart.* (Rec. Com.), 128.   [25] Ibid. 213.
[26] *Valor Eccl.* (Rec. Com.), ii. 119, 122.
[27] P.R.O., E 310/26/154, nos. 6, 8.
[28] *Wilts. Inq. p.m.* 1625–49 (Index Libr.), 432.
[29] *Complete Peerage*, iv. 48–9.
[30] P.R.O., C 104/86/1, order, Danvers v. Lee, 1672.
[31] Ibid. CP 25(2)/746/25 Chas. II Trin.; *Complete Peerage*, x. 687–8.
[32] *Complete Peerage*, ix. 649; xii (2), 606–8; Aubrey, *Topog. Coll.* ed. Jackson, pedigree facing p. 217.

[33] P.R.O., C 104/86/1, bill, Wharton v. Rochester.
[34] Ibid. CP 25(2)/806/1 Jas. II East.
[35] *Complete Peerage*, xii (2), 607–14.
[36] W.R.O. 212B/2207.
[37] *Complete Peerage*, ix. 751–2.
[38] W.R.O. 212B/4264; 212B/4298.
[39] P.R.O., PROB 11/1609, f. 232.
[40] *Complete Peerage*, ix. 752; W.R.O. 212B/4318.
[41] W.R.O. 622/1.
[42] Finberg, *Early Wessex Chart.* pp. 69–70, 91; *Arch. Jnl.* lxxvii. 42–54; above, Brokenborough, introduction, manor.
[43] *V.C.H. Wilts.* ii, pp. 122, 162.
[44] Finberg, *Early Wessex Chart.* pp. 91, 105–6; *V.C.H. Wilts.* ii, pp. 88, 125–6.
[45] *Close R.* 1234–7, 126; *Reg. Malm.* i. 176–7, 203.
[46] *Cal. Pat.* 1548–9, 27–8; below, Corston, manor.
[47] *Complete Peerage*, xii (1), 63.

fold, probably part of the manor, were granted to the hospital of the Savoy, London, on its refoundation;[48] they were restored to the Crown by exchange in 1558.[49] In 1560 or earlier Cowfold grange and c. 80 a. were granted to Edward Welsh;[50] the greater part of the estate, c. 650 a., was retained by the Crown.[51]

Between 1653 and 1656 the Crown's Cowfold estate was sold as COLE PARK to Hugh Audley[52] (d. 1662),[53] who was succeeded by his nephew Robert Harvey.[54] In 1694 the estate, 520 a., was settled on Robert's grandson John Harvey (d. 1712),[55] who was succeeded by his son Audley.[56] In 1725 Cole park was held by another John Harvey[57] (fl. 1767),[58] in 1770 by another Audley Harvey.[59] Audley (d. 1774)[60] devised it for life to his daughter Sarah (fl. 1783), wife of John Lovell, with remainder to her son Peter Lovell.[61] From Peter (d. 1841) it passed in turn to his son Peter (d. 1869) and the younger Peter's son Peter (d. 1909), whose relict Rosalind[62] (d. 1945) devised it to her grandnephew Capt. A. D. C. Francis. In 1945 Capt. Francis sold the house called Cole Park, the parkland, and Rodbourne Rail farm, a total of 120 a., to J. F. Fry.[63] The house and parkland were sold by Fry in 1954 to Frank and Avril Darling, by the Darlings in 1955 to Mr. E. J. M. Buxton. In 1978 Mr. Buxton sold Cole Park and 8 a. to C. L. McMiram, from whom they were bought in 1980 by Sir Mark Weinberg, the owner in 1987.[64] Mr. P. Roberts bought Lawn farm, c. 270 a., from Capt. Francis c. 1977 and remained the owner in 1987.[65]

The moated site of Cole Park may be that of the abbot of Malmesbury's lodge.[66] A lodge for the royal stud in the park stood there in the late 16th century and the early 17th.[67] A tall red-brick range of the mid or later 16th century,[68] which formed most of the north-east part of the house in the later 20th century, was probably a wing of a house whose main range lay to the north-west. A plan to rebuild the house c. 1625, when Sir George Marshall, lessee of the stud, received £100 of £500 promised for the construction of a new lodge,[69] may have had little effect. The house was described c. 1650 as 'a very fair brick building' of two storeys with a large courtyard and a moat.[70] In the late 17th century a large staircase was built at the south-western corner of the wing, and the hall, immediately north-west of the staircase, was altered or rebuilt. Additions were made, probably then, north-east and south-west of the hall to create a new north-western entrance front. That front and the south-west front were refaced in the later 18th century, perhaps in 1775–6 when building work at the house was recorded[71] and minor additions, apparent from dark headers in the brickwork, were being made to the 16th-century part of the house. The north-west side of that part was refaced in the later 19th century and its north-east end was rebuilt with an oriel overlooking the moat in 1981. About then ground-floor additions were made south-east of the wing and much of the inside of the house was altered and redecorated. The moat, surviving in 1987, is almost square and has walled sides and a paved floor. New buildings of the 18th century include a stable and a coach house flanking an entrance court north-west of the house.

The estate granted to Edmund Welsh in 1560 was later called GRANGE farm. Sir James Stumpe held it at his death in 1563;[72] thereafter it passed with Rodbourne manor to Walter Hungerford (d. 1754).[73] By 1752 Hungerford had sold Grange farm to Edmund Estcourt[74] (d. 1758).[75] It passed to Estcourt's relict Anna Maria (d. c. 1783) and daughter Anne, who apparently held jointly, and in 1766 was settled on the daughter's marriage to William Earle (d. 1774). Anne Earle (d. 1776) devised the farm to William Edwards her son perhaps by Earle. In 1787 Edwards sold it to Edmund Wilkins (d. 1804), who devised it to his nephew Edmund Gale (d. 1819). Gale's heirs sold the farm in 1829 to Peter Lovell[76] (d. 1841), and Lovell's relict Charlotte (d. 1854)[77] devised it to their sons Peter, Frank, and Willes. Peter Lovell apparently bought his brothers' shares of the farm c. 1855;[78] thereafter it passed with Cole Park to Capt. A. D. C. Francis, who held the farm, c. 200 a., in 1987.[79]

WEST PARK, c. 150 a., was held with Cole Park until 1653[80] but by 1694 had been sold separately.[81] Its owners in the late 17th century and the earlier 18th have not been traced. It was held by Richard Watts c. 1770[82] and by the heirs of John Watts in 1780.[83] In 1789 it was sold,[84] probably to George Garlick, the owner in 1790. Garlick and another George Garlick held West park in 1820; by 1827 it had passed to a Mrs. Garlick and Isaac Berry.[85] In 1839 Mary Berry held West park, 139 a.[86] It was owned by Michael Hulbert

[48] Cal. Pat. 1555–7, 544, 546.
[49] Ibid. 1557–8, 361.
[50] W.N. & Q. iv. 456; below.
[51] P.R.O., LR 2/301, f. 236.
[52] Ibid.; W.R.O. 161/49, settlement, 1656.
[53] D.N.B.
[54] W.R.O. 161/49, settlement, 1656.
[55] Ibid. 161/34, settlement, 1694; ibid. tithe award; Burke, Land. Gent. (1937), 1412.
[56] W.R.O. 161/34, will of John Harvey.
[57] Ibid. 161/28/2.
[58] Ibid. 161/53, lease, Harvey to Keynes, 1767.
[59] Ibid. 161/26/3.
[60] W.N. & Q. viii. 442.
[61] M. Masson, Cole Park (priv. print. 1985), 45; W.R.O. 161/34, will of Audley Harvey.
[62] Burke, Land. Gent. (1937), 1412.
[63] Masson, Cole Park, 70; inf. from Capt. A. D. C. Francis, the Grange, Corston.
[64] Inf. from Messrs. Nabarro Nathanson, 50 Stratton Street, Lond.
[65] Inf. from Capt. Francis.
[66] Above, introduction.
[67] P.R.O., LR 2/191, f. 132; LR 2/301, f. 232; below, agric.
[68] See plate facing this page.
[69] Hist. MSS. Com. 23, 12th Rep., Coke, i, p. 184.
[70] P.R.O., LR 2/301, f. 232.
[71] Masson, Cole Park, 40–1.
[72] P.R.O., C 142/135, no. 1.
[73] Below, Rodbourne, manor.
[74] W.R.O. 161/48, deed, Ratcliffe and Knipe to Wilkins, 1787.
[75] W.N. & Q. viii. 436.
[76] J. Badeni, Wilts. Forefathers, 109; W.R.O. 161/52, abstr. of title; below, Little Somerford, manor.
[77] Burke, Land. Gent. (1937), 1412.
[78] W.R.O. 161/43, abstr. from will of Charlotte Lovell; 161/134, letter, Stone to Lovell, 1855.
[79] Inf. from Capt. Francis.
[80] P.R.O., LR 2/301, f. 233.
[81] W.R.O. 161/34, settlement, 1694.
[82] Ibid. 490/1112.
[83] Ibid. A 1/345/274.
[84] P.R.O., CP 25(2)/1447/29 Geo. III East.
[85] W.R.O., A 1/345/274.
[86] Ibid. tithe award.

MALMESBURY
Cole Park from the north-east

DAUNTSEY
The west front of Dauntsey House

The south front of Cowbridge House, built *c.* 1853

Burton Hill House, built from the 1840s

MALMESBURY

in 1865,[87] by Henry Wellesley, Earl Cowley, in 1910,[88] and by W. W. West in 1912.[89] By 1927 the estate had been divided into smaller holdings.[90]

Malmesbury abbey's lands at Burton Hill were a distinct estate in the 13th century and at the Dissolution.[91] As the manor of Burton or *BURTON HILL* they were granted by the Crown in 1552 to John Dudley, duke of Northumberland, who conveyed the manor in 1553 to Sir James Stumpe[92] (d. 1563). It passed to Stumpe's daughter Elizabeth, wife of Henry Knyvett.[93] In 1570 the Knyvetts conveyed the manor to William and George Wynter,[94] perhaps trustees for Sir Thomas Gresham who sold it to Edward Carey and William Doddington in 1574.[95] Carey and Doddington sold Burton Hill manor in 1577 to Adam Archard and Thomas Hall,[96] who in the same year sold several parts of it. The rest, still called Burton Hill manor, passed on Archard's death in 1588 to his son Nicholas.[97] In 1616 Nicholas sold the estate to Anthony Risby[98] (d. 1626), who devised it for sale; it then comprised *c.* 40 a.[99] In 1638 it was held by Zacharias Ward.[1] The estate was probably that described as Burton Hill manor which Thomas Ridler and his wife Anne held in 1724.[2] In 1748 Anne, then a widow, held it, perhaps jointly with her daughters Barbara Ridler and Anne, wife of William Pinn.[3] By 1782 it had passed to Joseph Cullerne,[4] who in 1794 sold it to Thomas Brooke. In 1800 Brooke sold the estate to Edmund Wilkins (d. 1804),[5] who devised it to Elizabeth Dewell and her sister Mary.[6] By will dated 1805 Elizabeth devised her interest in the estate for life to Mary (fl. 1809), with reversion to their nephew the Revd. Charles Dewell.[7] In 1823 the whole estate, then the house called the Manor House and 99 a., was settled on Charles.[8] On his death in 1828 it passed to his wife Sarah, later wife of W. R. Fitzgerald, and on her death in 1863 to Charles's nephew C. G. Dewell. In 1863 Dewell sold the estate to the Revd. Thomas Brindle and the Revd. William Brindle.[9] The lands were thereafter dispersed, the house later became part of the Burton Hill House estate, and the lordship was sold in 1867 to T. D. Hill.[10]

The manor house and *c.* 250 a. of Burton Hill manor were bought from Archard and Hall by Richard Cowche[11] (d. by 1588), who was suc-

ceeded in turn by his son Richard[12] (d. 1596) and Richard's son Richard[13] (d. 1611). The estate passed to the last Richard's nephew Richard Cowche,[14] who held it in 1638.[15] Before 1714 John Scrope bought *c.* 170 a. in Burton Hill from a Richard Cowche. As *WHITEHEATH* farm the lands had by 1720 passed to his son Richard, who was succeeded in turn by his son Richard (d. 1787) and Richard's son William, who sold the farm in 1810 to Giles Canter.[16] It was held in 1839 by Giles's son Joseph (d. 1865).[17] In 1910 and 1912 trustees of the Canter family held it;[18] by 1927 it had passed presumably by sale to M. H. Chubb,[19] who still held it in 1939.[20] In 1985 R. Alvis sold 103 a., comprising most of Whiteheath farm, to Mr. P. J. Pritchard, the owner in 1989.[21]

In 1577 Adam Archard and Thomas Hall sold lands of Burton Hill manor to Henry Grayle.[22] In 1612 Grayle and his son David bought *COWBRIDGE* Mill and other lands, also part of the manor, from Nicholas Archard.[23] Their holding comprised 20 a. and the mill in 1615.[24] In 1706 that estate was sold by George Forman to George Ayliffe,[25] whose son John sold it in 1715 to Walter Trimnell.[26] By will proved 1832 Daniel Young devised it to his daughter Elizabeth.[27] In 1839 the mill and Cowbridge farm, 38 a., were held by S. B. Brooke[28] (d. 1869) whose nephew, the Revd. Charles Kemble (d. 1874), devised it to his wife Charlotte (d. 1890) for life. In 1882 Charlotte settled the reversion of Cowbridge House and *c.* 50 a. on her son Stephen Kemble.[29] The estate was offered for sale in 1893[30] and 1894,[31] and was bought in 1899 by Baldomero de Bertodano[32] (d. 1921).[33] It was sold in 1923,[34] probably to Sir Philip Hunloke, the owner in 1927,[35] who sold it in 1938 to E. K. Cole Ltd.[36] In 1989 Cowbridge House belonged to AT & T Telecommunications UK Ltd.,[37] the farmland to Mr. K. F. Edwards.[38] The house was designed in 1853 by John Shaw with an Italianate south garden front. It had terraced gardens adjacent to it, and stood in a larger garden or small park with lawns and walks.[39]

Lands of Burton Hill manor bought from Archard and Hall in 1577 by Ralph Slifield[40] probably passed to Francis Slifield (d. 1620), who was succeeded by his brother Matthew.[41] By 1627 the lands had passed to Adam Peddington or Tuck

[87] Ibid. G 21/510/1.
[88] Ibid. Inland Revenue, val. reg. 9.
[89] Ibid. G 7/500/1.   [90] Ibid. G 7/515/9.
[91] *Reg. Malm.* ii. 221–3; *Valor Eccl.* (Rec. Com.), ii. 120.
[92] *Cal. Pat.* 1550–3, 258, 369; P.R.O., CP 25(2)/65/533, no. 23.
[93] P.R.O., C 142/135, no. 1.   [94] *Cal. Pat.* 1569–72, p. 180.
[95] W.R.O. 88/1/76.   [96] *Cal. Pat.* 1575–8, p. 274.
[97] P.R.O., C 142/218, no. 42.
[98] Ibid. CP 25(2)/371/14 Jas. I Mich.
[99] *Wilts. Inq. p.m.* 1625–49 (Index Libr.), 37–8.
[1] P.R.O., CP 25(2)/511/14 Chas. I Mich.
[2] Ibid. CP 25(2)/1079/10 Geo. I Mich.
[3] Ibid. CP 25(2)/1261/21 Geo. II East.; *V.C.H. Glos.* xi, 42 where a slightly different acct. of the fam. is given.
[4] W.R.O., A 1/345/273.
[5] Ibid. 212A/38/42/22.
[6] Ibid. 1165/1, deed, Dewell to Robins, 1809.
[7] Ibid. 212A/38/42/22.
[8] Ibid. 212A/38/37/16.   [9] Ibid. 212A/38/42/24/1.
[10] Ibid. 212A/38/40/5–6; below.
[11] *Cal. Pat.* 1575–8, pp. 502–4; P.R.O., C 142/326, no. 53.
[12] W.R.O. 568/62.
[13] P.R.O., C 142/247, no. 25.
[14] Ibid. C 142/326, no. 53.   [15] W.R.O. 568/62.

[16] Ibid. 212A/36/44, abstr. of title.
[17] Ibid. tithe award; below, Norton, manor.
[18] Ibid. Inland Revenue, val. reg. 9; ibid. G 7/500/1.
[19] Ibid. G 7/515/9.
[20] *Kelly's Dir. Wilts.* (1939).
[21] Inf. from Mr. P. J. Pritchard, Whiteheath Farm.
[22] *Cal. Pat.* 1575–8, p. 504.
[23] W.R.O. 212A/36/34, deed, Grayle to Gymer, 1613.
[24] Ibid. 212A/13, lease, Grayle to Forman, 1615.
[25] P.R.O., CP 25(2)/979/5 Anne Mich.
[26] W.R.O. 212A/36/34, deed, Ayliffe to Trimnell, 1715.
[27] Ibid. 803/19.   [28] Ibid. tithe award.
[29] Ibid. 663/8; 856/3; Wilts. Cuttings, xvii. 13.
[30] W.A.S. Libr., sale cat. i, no. 21.
[31] W.R.O. 130/78, sale cat.   [32] Wilts. Cuttings, xii. 201.
[33] *W.A.M.* xli. 307–8.   [34] *Country Life*, 9 June 1923.
[35] W.R.O., G 7/515/9.
[36] Ibid. F 12, corresp. file, E. K. Cole Ltd.
[37] Inf. from Mr. G. Halton, AT & T Telecommunications UK Ltd., Cowbridge Ho.
[38] Inf. from Mr. K. F. Edwards, Cowbridge Farm.
[39] Print in possession of AT & T Telecommunications UK Ltd.; see plate facing this page.
[40] *Cal. Pat.* 1575–8, p. 274.
[41] P.R.O., C 142/388, no. 71.

(d. 1628), whose estate of 24 a. and 4 yardlands in Burton Hill, including lands formerly belonging to a Slifield, was divided between his nephews Adam Peddington and John Peddington.[42] The estate may have been that bought from Robert and Margaret Tuck by Edmund Estcourt (d. 1758), who held other lands in Burton Hill.[43]

An estate of c. 50 a. in Burton Hill held by Anthony Clase in 1623[44] may have derived from that bought from Archard and Hall by John Young in 1577.[45] Clase (d. 1626) devised the estate to Christopher and Thomas Meade.[46] By 1678 it had passed to Anne, relict of the Revd. Nathaniel Ashe, in 1680 wife of Thomas Petty.[47] It was sold by Anne's daughter Anne Ashe to Matthew Smith in 1693.[48] Smith sold part of it to Edmund Estcourt[49] (d. 1717) and part in 1742 to Estcourt's cousin and heir Edmund Estcourt (d. 1758),[50] who held c. 100 a. in Burton Hill. Those lands passed with Grange farm to William Edwards who sold his Burton Hill estate in 1787 to Timothy Dewell (d. 1792). Dewell devised the estate, including *BURTON HILL HOUSE*, to his wife Elizabeth and his sister Mary Dewell. It was sold in 1792 to Francis Hill (d. 1828) and, after litigation over Hill's will, in 1833 to Simon and Isaac Salter. The Salters apparently sold the estate in parcels; the house and 35 a. had been bought by John Cockerell by 1839.[51] Between 1846 and 1849 Cockerell sold his estate to C. W. Miles[52] (d. 1892).[53] It passed in turn to Miles's sons C. N. Miles (d. 1918) and A. C. Miles (d. 1919),[54] after whose death the Burton Hill House estate, then c. 120 a., was broken up and sold.[55] Burton Hill House and some land in Malmesbury were probably then bought by H. L. Storey (d. 1933).[56] In 1945 the house and 16 a. were bought for use as a school for handicapped children by the Shaftesbury Society, the owner in 1987.[57]

BURNT HEATH farm, c. 80 a. north of West park, was held by Alexander Staples in 1585 and by George Staples in 1599.[58] Before 1766 the farm was bought from William Robins by William Earle[59] (d. 1774). It presumably passed with Grange farm to William Edwards and was probably sold in or after 1787.[60] In 1839 the farm, c. 60 a., belonged to Richard Perrett[61] and in 1865 to J. G. Lyne.[62] H. C. Lyne was the owner in 1910[63] and 1912.[64] The farm was sold in 1927, after the death of his relict.[65] It was bought in 1957 by Mr. A. R. Highman, the owner in 1989.[66]

Whitchurch was described as a manor in the mid 13th century,[67] and from the mid 16th the manor was usually called *WHITCHURCH* and (or with) *MILBOURNE*.[68] It passed from Malmesbury abbey to the Crown at the Dissolution and in 1545 was granted to Richard Moody[69] (d. 1550). It passed like Garsdon manor to Richard's relict Catherine Basely, to Richard Moody (d. 1612), and to Sir Henry Moody, Bt. (d. 1629).[70] In 1630 Sir Henry's relict Deborah surrendered her life interest to her son Sir Henry Moody,[71] who sold the manor, probably in 1630,[72] to Henry Danvers, earl of Danby, the owner in 1636.[73] From Danby (d. 1644) it passed with Malmesbury manor to Henry Danvers (d. 1654) and, possibly in portions, to Elizabeth, wife of Robert Villiers or Danvers, Anne, wife of Sir Henry Lee, Eleanor, wife of James Bertie, Baron Norreys, and Anne, wife of Thomas Wharton:[74] the whole manor was sold in or after 1681.[75] In 1684 the lordship and some of or all the lands belonged to George Hill who in 1707 sold them, as Whitchurch manor, to Francis Hayes, his mortgagee.[76] Hayes (d. in or before 1724) was succeeded by his son Charles[77] who sold the manor in 1729 to Jonathan Willis[78] (will proved 1732). Willis was succeeded by his daughter Sarah who sold it in 1762 to William Bouverie, Viscount Folkestone[79] (cr. earl of Radnor 1765, d. 1776). William's son Jacob, earl of Radnor,[80] sold it c. 1820 either to John Howard, earl of Suffolk and of Berkshire (d. 1820), or his son Thomas, earl of Suffolk and of Berkshire.[81] In 1839 Lord Suffolk owned c. 950 a., including most of the land around Milbourne and the 360 a. north of the town and almost detached from the rest of Malmesbury parish.[82] With Charlton manor and the titles it descended to Michael Howard, from 1941 earl of Suffolk and of Berkshire.[83] In 1987 Lord Suffolk retained most of the northern part of the estate, then in Quobwell farm, and lands north of Milbourne village. In 1978 Mr. R. A. Clarke bought Manor farm, Milbourne, 200 a., which he owned in 1987.[84]

Lands of Whitchurch and Milbourne manor were apparently sold separately in the late 17th century or the early 18th. They included 30 a. bought from Francis Hayes by Henry Croome (fl. 1717). Croome's daughter Rebecca sold the land in 1729 to Humphrey Woodcock (d. 1754), who

42 *Wilts. Inq. p.m.* 1625–49 (Index Libr.), 70–1.
43 W.R.O. 161/42, lease, Estcourt to Fothergill, 1764; below.
44 *Wilts. Inq. p.m.* 1625–49 (Index Libr.), 46–7.
45 *Cal. Pat.* 1575–8, p. 274.
46 *Wilts. Inq. p.m.* 1625–49 (Index Libr.), 46–7.
47 W.R.O. 118/97, deed, Petty to Tyte, 1680.
48 Ibid. 568/16, deed, Ashe to Smith, 1693.
49 Ibid. 161/48, deed, Ratcliffe to Wilkins, 1787.
50 *W.N. & Q.* viii. 435–6; Glos. R.O., D 1571/T 108, draft deed, Smith to Estcourt, 1742.
51 *W.N. & Q.* viii. 436–9; W.R.O., tithe award.
52 *W.N. & Q.* viii. 433; W.R.O. 700/137/5.
53 Wilts. Cuttings, xvii. 17.
54 *W.A.M.* xl. 202, 432.
55 W.R.O., G 7/150/2; G 7/500/1; G 7/515/9.
56 *W.A.M.* xlvi. 279–80.
57 Inf. from the head teacher, Burton Hill Ho. Sch.
58 W.R.O. 1269/17, deeds, Staples to Seede, 1585, Staples to Hobbes, 1599.
59 Ibid. 212A/38/52/2A.
60 Above.
61 W.R.O., tithe award.
62 Ibid. G 21/510/1.
63 Ibid. Inland Revenue, val. reg. 9.
64 Ibid. G 7/500/1.
65 W.A.S. Libr., sale cat. xx, no. 41E.
66 Inf. from Mrs. A. R. Highman, Burnt Heath Farm.
67 *Cal. Chart. R.* 1226–57, 400.
68 e.g. P.R.O., SC 6/Hen. VIII/3986, rot. 129.
69 *L. & P. Hen. VIII*, xx (2), p. 539.
70 *Wilts. Inq. p.m.* 1625–49 (Index Libr.), 152, 155; P.R.O., C 142/92, no. 14; C 142/131, no. 200; above, Garsdon, manor.
71 P.R.O., C 104/91/2, abstr. of title.
72 Ibid. CP 25(2)/509/6 Chas. I Mich.
73 *Wilts. Inq. p.m.* 1625–49 (Index Libr.), 206.
74 Above.
75 P.R.O., CP 25(2)/747/33 & 34 Chas. II Hil.
76 W.R.O. 88/8/15.
77 Ibid. 88/8/16.
78 Ibid. 88/8/19.
79 Ibid. 88/8/35.
80 *Complete Peerage*, v. 542–3; x. 717–18.
81 Ibid. xii (1), 479–80; W.R.O. 88/10/10.
82 W.R.O., tithe award.
83 Above, Charlton, manors.
84 Inf. from Mr. J. H. Guest, Quobwell Farm; Mr. D. W. Clarke, Marsh Farm; Mr. R. A. Clarke, Manor Farm, Milbourne.

devised it to his nephew Charles Williamson.[85] In 1756 Williamson bought 179 a., formerly part of the manor, from Frederick St. John, Viscount Bolingbroke.[86] Williamson's estate, including *SOUTHFIELD* farm, passed on his death in 1760 to his niece Sarah Kyffin and her husband Matthew Sloper. In 1770 Sloper sold it to William Bouverie, earl of Radnor,[87] and it again became part of Whitchurch manor. Southfield farm, 175 a. in 1839,[88] was owned by Mr. R. G. Baker in 1987.[89]

In 1717 Henry Croome held a further 26 a. formerly part of Whitchurch and Milbourne manor. The land was sold by another Henry Croome in 1741 to William Earle,[90] who bought 170 a. in Whitchurch and Milbourne from Henry Brooke in 1763.[91] Those lands passed with Grange farm to William Edwards, who in 1787 sold them to Richard Kinneir as *WHITCHURCH* farm.[92] Kinneir or a namesake held the farm in 1839.[93] In 1850 and 1852 it was offered for sale as a farm of 200 a.[94] The farmhouse and 75 a. belonged in 1865 to the Revd. E. E. Elwell.[95] Members of the Elwell family owned it in 1910 and 1927.[96] That farm and other lands, 156 a. in all, were bought in 1941 by John Weaver; 60 a., part of Milbourne farm, were added c. 1977, and in 1987 the farm, then called Whychurch, belonged to John's son Mr. Edward Weaver.[97]

Milbourne farm, presumably derived from Whitchurch and Milbourne manor, belonged in 1839 to Isaac Beak.[98] In 1910 Daniel Beak owned 103 a.,[99] and those and other lands, totalling 152 a., were owned in 1927 by William Spong (fl. 1931).[1] Some of the land became part of Whychurch farm;[2] the farmhouse and other land were bought c. 1987 by members of the Wickes family.[3]

The lands south-west of the town and mainly in Westport parish, which were held from the 13th century or earlier by the guild merchant and in 1989 by the warden and freemen of Malmesbury, included c. 50 a. in Malmesbury parish.[4]

Malmesbury abbey appropriated the parish church of Malmesbury in or after 1191,[5] and owned the *RECTORY* estate until the Dissolution. Thereafter most rectorial tithes passed with the estates from which they derived, but those from the Cowbridge estate were apparently owned separately from the land. In 1735 they were conveyed by Thomas Boucher, perhaps a trustee, to William Carey. In 1789 Carey's son William sold them to Samuel Brooke[6] (d. 1837), whose son

S. B. Brooke held both the estate and the tithes in 1839.[7] Rectorial tithes from the lands of Whitchurch and Milbourne manor passed with the manor to Sir Henry Moody, Bt. (d. 1629),[8] but he or a later lord of the manor apparently sold some. Between 1765 and 1774 tithes from part of the manor were bought by William Bouverie, earl of Radnor, lord of Whitchurch and Milbourne manor.[9] In 1839 all rectorial tithes in the parish were merged or held by the owners of the lands from which they arose.[10]

In 1232 Bradenstoke priory owned a house near one of the guildhalls in Malmesbury, and c. 1252 William Porter gave the priory a tenement in High Street.[11] In the mid and later 13th century Nicholas of Malmesbury gave a tenement in East Street, William Spicer gave a rent of 1s. from a tenement in East Street, and Andrew son of John of Malmesbury gave a rent of 3s.[12] The priory retained a small estate in Malmesbury until the Dissolution.[13]

In the Middle Ages small estates in Malmesbury also belonged to two chapels, St. Mary's, possibly the hospital of St. Mary Magdalene, and All Saints'.[14] At their dissolution in 1548 St. Mary's chantry in St. Paul's church had tenements in the town and 17 a. elsewhere in the parish, and St. Mary's chantry in Westport church included c. 4 a. and tenements in Malmesbury parish.[15]

St. John's hospital in Nethewall, said in 1389 to have been founded by the burgesses, in the late 13th century occupied a site which comprised lands formerly belonging to William Aldune and Thomas Purs and a parcel called *De Profundis*. In 1247 Walter Bodmin and his wife Emme gave two messuages to the hospital, the property of which was valued at 46s. in 1389. It was presumably dissolved and its lands confiscated by the Crown in the mid 16th century. John Stumpe acquired part of the property from John Marsh and William Marsh and part from John Herbert and Andrew Palmer. In 1580 Stumpe conveyed the whole to the alderman and burgesses of Malmesbury,[16] who maintained an almshouse in the former hospital from 1584 or earlier.[17]

AGRICULTURE. On the two small estates called Malmesbury in 1086 there was a total of 1½ plough-team, 5 bordars, 10 a. of meadow, and 3½ square furlongs of pasture. The bishop of Coutances had demesne of 3 yardlands. A vineyard was planted on a hill north of the abbey in the early 11th century; another, planted in the later 13th century,[18]

---

[85] W.R.O. 88/8/50; 88/10/15; above, Charlton, manors.
[86] W.R.O. 88/8/43.
[87] Ibid. 88/10/15.
[88] Ibid. tithe award.
[89] Local inf.
[90] W.R.O. 88/10/15.
[91] Ibid. 212A/38/52/2A.
[92] Ibid. 161/52, abstr. of title.
[93] Ibid. tithe award.
[94] Ibid. 88/10/10; 137/125/47.
[95] Ibid. G 21/510/1.
[96] Ibid. Inland Revenue, val. reg. 9; ibid. G 7/515/9.
[97] Inf. from Mr. E. Weaver, Whychurch Farm.
[98] W.R.O., tithe award.
[99] Ibid. Inland Revenue, val. reg. 9.
[1] Ibid. G 7/515/9; *Kelly's Dir. Wilts.* (1931).
[2] Above.
[3] Local inf.
[4] Below, Westport, manors, econ. hist.
[5] *Reg. Malm.* i. 374–5.

[6] W.R.O. 212A/36/34, deeds, Boucher to Carey, 1735, Carey to Brooke, 1789.
[7] Ibid. tithe award; above, Charlton, manors.
[8] *Wilts. Inq. p.m.* 1625–49 (Index Libr.), 151–5.
[9] W.R.O. 88/8/40.
[10] Ibid. tithe award.
[11] *V.C.H. Wilts.* iii. 281.
[12] *Bradenstoke Cart.* (W.R.S. xxxv), pp. 77–8.
[13] *Valor Eccl.* (Rec. Com.), ii. 123.
[14] *Cal. Pat.* 1572–5, pp. 408–9; 1575–8, pp. 25, 27; below, churches. The hist. of the hosp. of St. Mary Magdalene is related in *V.C.H. Wilts.* iii. 341.
[15] P.R.O., E 301/58, nos. 35–6; below, churches; ibid. Westport, church.
[16] *W.A.M.* xxix. 124. The hist. of St. John's hosp. is related in *V.C.H. Wilts.* iii. 340.
[17] W.R.O., D 1/43/5, f. 21; below, charities.
[18] *V.C.H. Wilts.* ii, pp. 122, 162; iii. 214, 221.

may have given its name to Wyniard Mill on the eastern edge of the town.[19] No later reference to viticulture has been found.

In the Middle Ages and later Malmesbury parish, apart from Corston and Rodbourne, included c. 650 a. to the south in Cole park and West park; c. 600 a. of agricultural land between the parks and the town were worked from farms based in or near Burton Hill, c. 500 a. east of the town were worked from farmsteads in or south of Milbourne, and c. 500 a. north and north-east were worked from Whitchurch or farmsteads north of it.[20]

PARKS. Part of Malmesbury abbey's estate called Cowfold was woodland in the late 12th century[21] and may then or soon afterwards have been imparked. In 1235 the abbot was given two bucks from Braydon forest for his park of Cowfold.[22] In the mid 15th century there was a second park, West park, presumably west of the Malmesbury–Chippenham road.[23] In 1535 the Cowfold estate included a park of 300 a., meadow land of 100 a. in closes, both in hand, and 40 a. of pasture and arable held by a tenant.[24] The tenanted land with other lands and the grange, later called Grange farm, c. 1550 comprised 78 a. including 4 a. in the open fields of Burton Hill.[25]

In the mid 16th century Cowfold, later Cole, park, 300 a., and West park, 200 a., accommodated a royal stud farm,[26] known as the race.[27] The stud was administered by a yeoman or groom of the race. The first may have been Ralph Bolton (fl. 1555–9), who was involved in a dispute when fences around Cowfold park were broken and cattle were driven in.[28] The title yeoman of the race was recorded in 1583, when Ralph Slifield, the yeoman, was commissioned to take for the stud forage of 40 qr. of oats from Wiltshire and another 40 qr. from Gloucestershire.[29] In the early 17th century the yeoman received a fee and a further 26s. 8d. for every colt raised. In 1621 there were also three servants and a farrier at the stud.[30] According to a report made before 1587 the site of the stud was unsuitable; the area was too small, and drainage and soil were poor. It was suggested that fodder should be produced in West park if that from the larger Cole park was insufficient. There were then 34 mares and 31 young horses in Cole park. By the 1590s numbers had fallen to 24 mares and 27 young horses, some of which had been carelessly bred. Walls and fences were in poor repair, and most of the great trees with which the park had been well supplied c. 1550 had been felled.[31] Cattle and sheep were kept in

the parks; in 1599 there were 85 cows and calves and 80 ewes.[32] Improvements were made in the early 17th century. In 1608–9 a stone wall was built around Cole park,[33] and in 1628 there were 37 mares and 35 young horses.[34] By 1628 the parks had been leased but the stud remained there, on payment of a fee to the lessee,[35] until c. 1630.[36]

By 1653 both parks had been disparked. About 500 a. in closes represented the former Cole park; c. 70 a. were meadow and some former pasture had been ploughed. Of the former West park, 166 a., some land was arable and 16 a. were wooded.[37] In the 18th and 19th centuries c. 200 a. around Cole Park were again parkland. The rest of the former park was in Wood farm, Lawn farm, and Rodbourne Rail farm in the early 18th century.[38] In the 1730s a three-year rotation was practised at Wood farm; clover was grown every third year.[39] In 1767 Lawn farm comprised 145 a. north of Cole Park, including 32 a. of arable.[40] In 1796 Rodbourne Rail farm comprised 119 a. south of Cole Park.[41] South of Lawn farm, Grange farm was 108 a. in 1764 when over half of it was arable.[42] What had been West park was apparently worked as a single farm until the early 19th century.[43] The lands of the two former parks were mostly pasture in 1839, except for 24 a. of wood east of West Park Farm.[44] In 1927 only c. 60 a. around Cole Park remained parkland. Lawn farm was then 229 a., Rodbourne Rail farm 188 a., Grange farm 99 a., and West Park farm 86 a.; there were also three smaller holdings in what had been West park.[45] In the later 20th century all but c. 8 a. of the park[46] was agricultural land: Lawn farm and Lower West Park farm were principally dairy farms but there was also some arable.[47]

BURTON HILL. Open arable fields of Burton Hill were the subject of an agreement between Malmesbury abbey and the lord of Bremilham manor in the early 13th century when the abbey proposed to cultivate temporarily inclosed parts of the fallow field. The lord of Bremilham and his tenants apparently held land and pasture in those fields, two of which were called Ham and Kemboro fields.[48] Kemboro field may have lain partly in Westport parish and was still open in the 17th century, when there were also fields called Shelfield and Burton field.[49] From the later 14th century part of the demesne pasture of Burton Hill was shared with one or more tenant.[50] The chief pastures of Burton Hill were presumably Burnt heath and Whiteheath to the south-west. Part of Burnt heath had been ploughed by the early 14th century,[51] and by the late 16th much of it had been

[19] P.N. Wilts. (E.P.N.S.), 53.
[20] For the areas, W.R.O., tithe award.
[21] Reg. Malm. i. 222.　　[22] Close R. 1234–7, 126.
[23] Eton Coll. Mun. 4/105.
[24] Valor Eccl. (Rec. Com.), ii. 120.
[25] P.R.O., LR 2/191, f. 132.　　[26] Ibid.
[27] B.L. Lansd. Ch. 46.
[28] Acts of P.C. 1554–6, 240; Cal. Pat. 1558–60, 172–3; P.R.O., STAC 4/4/56.
[29] B.L. Lansd. Ch. 46.
[30] Cal. S.P. Dom. 1611–18, 596; 1619–23, 231.
[31] C. M. Prior, Royal Studs, 13–23, 64–5; P.R.O., LR 2/191, f. 132.
[32] Hist. MSS. Com. 9, Salisbury, ix, p. 115.
[33] Cal. S.P. Dom. 1603–10, 496; P.R.O., E 178/4707.
[34] Prior, Royal Studs, 70.

[35] Cal. S.P. Dom. 1628–9, 389.　　[36] Ibid. 1629–31, 455.
[37] P.R.O., LR 2/301, ff. 232–59.
[38] W.R.O. 161/27/2; 161/28/1; 161/29/1.
[39] Ibid. 161/31/21.
[40] Ibid. 161/53, lease, Harvey to Keynes, 1767.
[41] Ibid. 161/134, lease, Lovell to Reynolds, 1796.
[42] Ibid. 161/42, lease, Estcourt to Fothergill, 1764.
[43] Ibid. A 1/345/274.　　[44] Ibid. tithe award.
[45] Ibid. G 7/515/9.　　[46] Above, manors.
[47] Inf. from Mr. P. Roberts, Lawn Farm; Mr. G. T. Warr, Lower West Park Farm.
[48] Reg. Malm. ii. 118, 185–6.
[49] Wilts. Inq. p.m. 1625–49 (Index Libr.), 46–7; below, Westport, econ. hist.
[50] Feet of F. 1327–77 (W.R.S. xxix), p. 148.
[51] Reg. Malm. ii. 151.

inclosed.[52] Much of Whiteheath was a several farm in the early 18th century.[53]

In the late 13th century Malmesbury abbey had 16 tenants, presumably customary, at Burton Hill.[54] In the mid 16th there were 12 customary tenants; 4 held a total of 5 yardlands, the others may have had smaller holdings. Works, including two days cutting and carting hay, had almost certainly been commuted by then. There were five leaseholders, excluding tenants of mills; one, with several pasture and 'lords lands' in Kemboro field, held what may have been the demesne.[55] In 1585 Burnt Heath was a several farm of c. 80 a.[56]

In the 17th and 18th centuries farms derived from Burton Hill manor numbered about five; most were smaller than 100 a., and the largest was Whiteheath farm. There were also holdings of only a few acres. Part of Whiteheath farm was arable but the smaller farms were chiefly pasture and meadow.[57] Part of Kemboro field had been inclosed by 1679[58] and part of Burton field by 1764; apparently the whole of Shelfield remained open.[59] By 1839 all arable had been inclosed and only a few acres of pasture, beside a track between Burnt Heath and Whiteheath farms, remained common. There were then c. 400 a. of pasture and c. 120 a. of arable around Burton Hill. Whiteheath, still the largest farm, was a compact holding of 147 a. west of the Chippenham road. There were seven farms of between 20 a. and 100 a., and c. 130 a. were in holdings smaller than 20 a.[60] In 1866 stock on all those farms included 65 cows, 57 other cattle, 140 sheep, and 70 pigs.[61] Most of the land around Burton Hill was pasture in the 1930s;[62] in the later 20th century farms remained small, dairying continued, but there was also some arable farming.[63] On Whiteheath farm, 103 a. in the 1980s, pedigree cattle were bred and in winter store lambs were kept.[64]

MILBOURNE. South field, south of Milbourne village and recorded in the early 17th century,[65] had probably been an open field, and the men of Milbourne had common grazing for horses and perhaps other beasts on c. 30 a. beside the village street.[66] They also had unrestricted grazing rights in Braydon forest and its purlieus: the nearest point at which their animals could enter the purlieus was c. 4 km. east of the village. Milbourne common, 104 a., allotted to them when the purlieus were inclosed in the early 1630s, remained a common pasture and they could feed c. 68 cattle on it. They may also have shared Lot meadow, which in 1792 comprised 15 a. south of the village.[67]

In 1630 the Milbourne portion of Whitchurch and Milbourne manor included a leasehold of 133 a., most of which was a pasture close called South-field and which may have been largely demesne. The manor also included 920 a. apparently held by copy; there were 4 holdings of over 50 a. each, 9 of between 20 a. and 50 a., and 18 smaller than 20 a. Most of the land was inclosed but 91 a., of which 28 a. were exclusive to copyholders, were still worked in common; whether the 91 a. were in Milbourne or Whitchurch is not clear.[68]

Lands south of Milbourne village were said in 1756 to have been recently inclosed.[69] Lot meadow and Milbourne common were inclosed in 1792 under an Act of 1790; allotments in Milbourne common were made to 10 landholders.[70] The Home common, beside Milbourne village street, was inclosed by an agreement of 1831.[71]

In 1802 Southfield farm, c. 170 a., was a compact holding south of the village worked from a farmstead recently built on a new site near the parish boundary. What became Manor farm, c. 130 a. east of the village, and what became Milbourne farm, c. 110 a. scattered around the village, were worked from farmsteads beside the street. There were over 300 a. of pasture, c. 75 a. of arable, and c. 50 a. of meadow.[72] On Southfield farm c. 1800 were 100 sheep, 40 cows and 18 young cattle, and 10 colts.[73] The former Milbourne common, held in parcels in 1802, was in 1839 all in the lord's hand, but there had been few changes in the size or number of farms.[74] In the early 20th century the lands were in three farms of c. 150 a. each;[75] there was arable north of the village but not elsewhere in Milbourne in the 1930s.[76]

WHITCHURCH. In the 17th century and probably earlier Whitchurch had fields called North and Coldharbour.[77] There was common pasture for beasts and sheep on Whitchurch marsh and Wallow marsh, north and north-west of Whychurch Farm, a total of 46 a. in 1792;[78] in the earlier 18th century haywards for the pastures were appointed at Whitchurch and Milbourne manor courts.[79]

Whitchurch farm, possibly demesne land, was held by lease in the early 17th century; it then comprised 174 a., perhaps including land outside the parish, and pasture rights in Whitchurch and Wallow marshes. Other leaseholds in the Whitchurch portion of Whitchurch and Milbourne manor were of no more than 30 a. each. All or part of Coldharbour field may have been open in 1695,[80] but open-field cultivation had probably ceased by the late 18th century. In 1792, under the Act of 1790, Whitchurch and Wallow marshes

[52] W.R.O. 1269/17, deed, Staples to Seede, 1585.
[53] Ibid. 212A/36/44, abstr. of title.
[54] Reg. Malm. i. 176–7.
[55] P.R.O., E 318/Box 32/1820; ibid. SC 6/Hen. VIII/3986, rot. 113.
[56] W.R.O. 1269/17, deed, Staples to Seede, 1585.
[57] Ibid. 212A/13, lease, Grayle to Forman, 1615; 568/30, lease, Scrope to Young, 1729; Wilts. Inq. p.m. 1625–49 (Index Libr.), 27–8, 46–7, 70–1.
[58] W.R.O. 212A/36/16, deed, Gastrell to Hart, 1679.
[59] Ibid. 161/42, lease, Estcourt to Fothergill, 1764.
[60] Ibid. tithe award.
[61] P.R.O., MAF 68/73, sheet 14.
[62] [1st] Land Util. Surv. Map, sheet 103.
[63] Inf. from Capt. A. D. C. Francis, the Grange, Corston; Mrs. A. R. Highman, Burnt Heath Farm.

[64] Inf. from Mr. P. J. Pritchard, Whiteheath Farm, Corston.
[65] Wilts. Inq. p.m. 1625–49 (Index Libr.), 152.
[66] W.R.O. 88/5/26B.
[67] Ibid. EA/34; ibid. 88/4/43; 88/10/52; ibid. tithe award; V.C.H. Wilts. iv. 406.
[68] P.R.O., C 104/85/1, deed, Moody to Cowper, 1630.
[69] W.R.O. 88/8/43.
[70] Ibid. EA/34.
[71] Ibid. 88/5/26B.
[72] Ibid. 88/5/47; 900/12.
[73] Ibid. 490/1041.
[74] Ibid. 88/5/47; 900/12; ibid. tithe award.
[75] Ibid. G 7/500/1; G 7/515/9.
[76] [1st] Land Util. Surv. Map, sheet 103.
[77] W.R.O. 149/104/3.
[78] Ibid. EA/34.
[79] Ibid. 88/5/47.
[80] Ibid. 149/104/3.

were inclosed and allotments in them were made to eight landholders.[81] In 1802 most of the Whitchurch portion of the manor lay in three compact farms. The most southerly, Whitchurch, 316 a. including 116 a. in Westport parish, was worked from buildings on a site north-east of Malmesbury which had long been in use; Quobwell, c. 290 a. north of Whitchurch, and Coldharbour, c. 65 a. further north, were worked from farmsteads probably built on new sites in the 18th century. Over 400 a. were pasture, less than 100 a. arable;[82] the extent and number of the farms had changed little by 1839.[83]

In the earlier 20th century Quobwell farm comprised c. 200 a., Coldharbour farm c. 100 a., and Whitchurch farm c. 75 a.; 50 a. were worked as part of Griffin's Barn farm based in Charlton parish.[84] North of Quobwell Farm was arable in the 1930s; most of the remaining land was then pasture.[85] In 1987 most of what had been Coldharbour farm was part of Quobwell, 311 a., and Griffin's Barn farms; Whitchurch was then c. 130 a. All were dairy and arable farms.[86]

TRADE AND INDUSTRY. The range of trades in Malmesbury in the mid 13th century is illustrated by the claim of the guild merchant to rights allegedly denied by the abbot of Malmesbury: that only its members might sell cloth, leather goods, fish, sheepskins, or hides within the borough, that no glover from outside Malmesbury might sell gloves made of horse skin, and that no wool merchant might trade with his own weights.[87] The outcome of the dispute is not known. Late 13th-century surnames also suggest that the leather and cloth trades were prominent[88] and there may have been a tannery near Postern Mill.[89] A fulling mill was recorded in the late 12th century[90] and the production of woollen cloth apparently remained Malmesbury's chief industry throughout the later Middle Ages.

In 1542 John Leland reported that 3,000 cloths were produced at Malmesbury yearly.[91] Wool was presumably bought at markets in north Wiltshire and Gloucestershire; a Malmesbury clothier bought yarn at Cirencester from a Northampton supplier.[92] Broadcloths from Malmesbury were sold in London in the early 16th century and the early 17th.[93] The most notable clothier in the town in the earlier 16th century was William Stumpe, who used the buildings of the dissolved monastery to house perhaps as many as 20 looms.[94] The names of nine Malmesbury clothiers of the later 16th century and the earlier 17th are known. Between them they apparently occupied most of the mills on the outskirts of the town. Wyniard Mill, Postern Mill, and Cowbridge Mill were all held by clothiers during that period. A new fulling mill beside St. John's bridge was built c. 1600 by Nicholas Archard, and William Hobbes, who then held Postern Mill, complained that the course of the Sherston branch of the Avon had been altered to his detriment.[95] Archard's business failed and he sold the fulling mill, Cannop's Mill, in 1622.[96] Malmesbury was still said to have 'a great name for clothing' c. 1650[97] but thereafter references to the industry are less frequent. There was still a dye house at Wyniard Mill in 1653,[98] a clothier and a silk weaver were in the town in 1687,[99] and some woollen manufacture was said to have continued until c. 1750.[1]

The woollen industry was revived c. 1790 when Francis Hill bought Cannop's Mill and built a new cloth mill, Burton Hill Mill, on its site. Hill chose Malmesbury, away from existing areas of cloth production, so that he could install modern machinery without opposition. The mill, which had been enlarged by 1803, used the spring loom or fly shuttle, powered by water, to produce superfine broadcloth. Hill also owned Postern Mill from 1793. Burton Hill Mill was closed c. 1825[2] and in 1831 was used as a corn mill.[3] It was reopened for cloth production by members of the Salter family in 1833[4] and by 1838 steam power had been introduced.[5] Woollen broadcloths were produced throughout the 1840s. Woollen cloth was also dyed and finished at Cowbridge Mill in the 1830s and 1840s.[6] Burton Hill Mill was bought c. 1850 by Thomas Bridget & Co. of Derby and converted to produce silk ribbon. The ownership, but not the use, of the mill changed several times in the later 19th century. In 1862 there were 56 power looms and 281 workers. Numbers employed were said to have risen to 400, perhaps an exaggeration, by 1867. In 1900 there were 150 employees: the mill was closed soon afterwards. It had reopened by 1923[7] and, with an interruption during the Second World War, continued to produce fancy silk and cotton goods until c. 1950.[8] For some years thereafter part of the building was used for dressing furs and skins.[9] The mill was used for the storage and sale of antiques in the 1970s[10] and as workshops for light engineering between 1980 and 1984, and in 1984 it was sold for conversion to flats.[11]

[81] W.R.O., EA/34.   [82] Ibid. 88/5/47; 900/12.
[83] Ibid. tithe award.   [84] Ibid. G 7/500/1; G 7/515/9.
[85] [1st] Land Util. Surv. Map, sheet 103.
[86] Inf. from Mr. J. H. Guest, Quobwell Farm; Mr. E. Weaver, Whychurch Farm.
[87] Reg. Malm. ii. 393–4.   [88] Ibid. i. 118–33.
[89] Medieval Arch. xxxi, p. 167.   [90] Reg. Malm. ii. 435.
[91] Leland, Itin. ed. Toulmin Smith, i. 132.
[92] V.C.H. Wilts. iv. 144.
[93] Ibid. 139–40; Early-Stuart Tradesmen (W.R.S. xv), p. 61.
[94] V.C.H. Wilts. iv. 146–7; G. D. Ramsay, Wilts. Woollen Ind. 17, 32–4.
[95] Cal. Pat. 1550–3, 259; 1575–8, p. 247; Early-Stuart Tradesmen (W.R.S. xv), p. 61; Wilts. Inq. p.m. 1625–49 (Index Libr.), 70, 431–2; Hist. MSS. Com. 55, Var. Coll. i, p. 98; P.R.O., E 134/3 Jas. I East./12.
[96] Wilts. Inq. p.m. 1625–49 (Index Libr.), 320.

[97] E. Leigh, Eng. Described, 208.
[98] P.R.O., E 317/Wilts. no. 39.
[99] Moffatt, Hist. Malm. 161; W.R.O. 212B/3889.
[1] Moffatt, Hist. Malm. 162.
[2] Ibid. 159–60; V.C.H. Wilts. iv. 167, 172; K. H. Rogers, Warp and Weft, 89; W.R.O. 1301/9, deed, Wilkins to Hill, 1793; see below, plate facing p. 172.
[3] Soc. Antiq. MS. 817, ix, f. 1v.
[4] V.C.H. Wilts. iv. 172 n.; J. Bird, Hist. Malm. 204.
[5] W.A.M. liv. 98.
[6] Pigot, Nat. Com. Dir. (1830), 805; (1842), 21–2; Kelly's Dir. Wilts. (1848); Hudson, Hill Top Town, 11.
[7] V.C.H. Wilts. iv. 177; Kelly's Dir. Wilts. (1859 and later edns.).
[8] W.R.O., F 12, corresp. file, Avon Silk Mills.
[9] Local inf.
[10] Hudson, Hill Top Town, 12.
[11] W.A.S. Libr., sale cat. xxix, no. 382; xxxii, no. 5.

Before Burton Hill Mill was opened lace making was one of the town's chief occupations. Many of the workers were women and were recruited to work in the mill, although they could earn more by making lace. In the 19th century the industry declined in the face of competition from machine-made lace,[12] but women and children continued to make pillow lace throughout the century.[13] In the 1830s and 1850s lace was sent from Malmesbury to Wales and Lancashire.[14] After 1900 there was a revival under the patronage of Mary Howard, countess of Suffolk and of Berkshire, and a Mrs. Jones one or both of whom opened a school in Malmesbury to teach lace making,[15] but little or no lace was made in the town after 1914.[16]

Gloves were still made at Malmesbury in the mid 17th century.[17] In the 18th century most of the trades practised there and not connected with textile production were those usual in a market town, and only a few may have been of more than local importance.[18] A firm of parchment makers, William Browning & Co., was recorded in the town in 1750, there was a glover in Westport in 1751, and parchment, gloves, and glue were all made c. 1800.[19]

There were two brewers and four maltsters in Malmesbury and Westport parishes in 1830.[20] In 1848 there were breweries in High Street and Cross Hayes; a third, later called Abbey brewery, was south of Abbey House. That in High Street was owned by Thomas Luce who in 1859, with a partner, had breweries in Cross Hayes and Westport; the latter was probably that later called Mill brewery, on the site of and incorporating Postern Mill. By 1867 he had been succeeded by C. R. Luce, who from c. 1875 owned both Abbey and Mill breweries.[21] In 1912, when there were 42 public houses tied to his breweries, he sold them to the Stroud Brewery Co.[22] Mill brewery was still in use in 1935–6,[23] but from 1941 was no longer used for brewing.[24] Abbey brewery may also have been closed c. 1940.[25] Esau Duck owned Cross Hayes brewery in 1875 and 1885. In 1895 and 1910 the brewery traded as Duck & Reed, in 1915 as Duck & Co.[26] In 1920, when it had 20 tied houses, it was taken over by the Stroud Brewery Co.; it may have been closed with Abbey brewery c. 1940.[27]

Edwin Ratcliffe opened a foundry, later known as Westport Ironworks, in the north-western part of the town c. 1870. Up to 12 men were employed in the late 19th century and the early 20th in making and repairing agricultural and other machinery.[28] There was an engineering workshop in the foundry buildings in 1988.

From 1877 or earlier bacon was cured in a factory belonging to Adye & Hinwood Ltd. in Park Road. In the 1930s much of the bacon was exported but later most was for home consumption. Some 500 pigs were killed weekly c. 1950, but the number had fallen to 200 by 1956.[29] The factory was closed c. 1965[30] and was demolished. West of it in Park Road from the mid 20th century was a slaughterhouse, used in 1987 by V. & G. Newman, and in 1987 the premises of Ready Animal Foods, pet food wholesalers, were nearby.

In 1923 Wilts. & Somerset Farmers Ltd. had a milk depot in Park Road.[31] The depot belonged c. 1950 to Wiltshire Creameries Ltd.; milk was treated there and up to 60 lb. of cheese produced daily.[32] The depot had been closed by 1974 and in 1986 its site was converted into small industrial units.[33]

The town was a local commercial centre in the 19th century. A bank was opened in St. Dennis's Lane after 1800, and in 1813 Thomas Luce became a partner in it. Luce was later the bank's sole proprietor and sold it in or after 1836 to the Wilts. and Dorset Banking Co. Ltd. The bank became part of Lloyds Bank Ltd. between 1911 and 1915. The North Wilts. Banking Co. took over the business of a smaller Malmesbury bank c. 1836, and its successor, the Capital and Counties Bank Ltd., had a branch in the town until 1915 or later.[34]

Two companies which were moved to Malmesbury shortly before and during the Second World War remained in the town after 1945. E. K. Cole Ltd., manufacturers of 'Ekco' radio, electrical, and electronic equipment, bought Cowbridge House in 1939 and built a factory adjacent to it.[35] In the 1940s and early 1950s radar equipment was produced and there were c. 1,000 employees. Domestic electrical goods were produced after 1958 and continued to be made after 1963 when E. K. Cole Ltd was absorbed into the Pye group of companies. From 1968 Pye-TMC Ltd. and from 1971 TMC Ltd. developed and produced telephone equipment on the site. New buildings were erected in 1975 and 1982. In 1987 AT & T and Philips Telecommunications UK Ltd. acquired the site jointly and in 1988 employed 400 people in research into and the development and manufacture of telephone transmission and switching systems.[36] In 1941 Linolite Ltd., originally makers of lighting fittings but then producing hose clips for use in aeroplanes and tanks, was moved from London to the former Mill brewery in Malmesbury. After 1945 the firm again produced lights, especially gas-filled tubes, and in 1952 employed c. 50 people. A new factory was built north of the town in 1985. In 1988 Linolite Ltd., then a subsidiary of the General Telephone

[12] V.C.H. Wilts. iv. 180–1; W.A.M. liv. 100.
[13] Kelly's Dir. Wilts. (1848 and later edns.).
[14] W.R.O. 988/2.
[15] Wilts. Cuttings, xvii. 17.
[16] Kelly's Dir. Wilts. (1915 and later edns.).
[17] Aubrey, Nat. Hist. Wilts. ed. Britton, 78–9.
[18] Wilts. Apprentices (W.R.S. xvii), passim.
[19] Ibid. pp. 35, 60; Moffatt, Hist. Malm. 162.
[20] Pigot, Nat. Com. Dir. (1830), 804–5.
[21] Kelly's Dir. Wilts. (1848 and later edns.).
[22] Wilts. Cuttings, xvii. 17; inf. from Mr. N. Redman, Whitbread & Co. plc, Chiswell Street, Lond. E.C. 1.
[23] W.R.O., G 21/516/2.
[24] Below.
[25] Inf. from Mr. Redman.

[26] Kelly's Dir. Wilts. (1875 and later edns.); W.R.O., Inland Revenue, val. reg. 9.
[27] Inf. from Mr. Redman.   [28] V.C.H. Wilts. iv. 196.
[29] Ibid. 222; Town Guide [c. 1950].
[30] Inf. from Curator, Athelstan Mus.
[31] Kelly's Dir. Wilts. (1923).
[32] Town Guide [c. 1950].
[33] Inf. from Direct Labour Organisation Manager, N. Wilts. district council, Parsonage Way, Chippenham.
[34] Hudson, Hill Top Town, 111; Kelly's Dir. Wilts. (1848 and later edns.).
[35] V.C.H. Wilts. iv. 204.
[36] Mass-Observation, War Factory, 6; inf. from Mr. G. Halton, AT & T Telecommunications UK Ltd., Cowbridge Ho.

and Electronics Corporation, employed 290 people.[37]

After the closure of the railway in 1962[38] several small factories were built on and near the site of the station. In 1988 sheet metal and traffic lights were among the goods produced.

MILLS. In 1066 Earl Harold held a mill at Malmesbury.[39] It may have stood, as did most of the mills recorded later, beside one or other branch of the Avon on or a little outside the borough boundary. Another, whose location is not known, was recorded in the 13th century, and in the late 13th century Malmesbury abbey had a mill on its Cowfold estate;[40] that mill was not afterwards mentioned.

A mill held in the 13th century by William of Westmill[41] may have been in Westport parish, perhaps below the postern gate where a mill stood apparently from the 12th century or the 13th.[42] Postern Mill, which belonged to Malmesbury abbey at the Dissolution, in 1539 incorporated a corn mill and a fulling mill;[43] the fulling mill may have been standing in 1605.[44] In 1610 Postern Mill and a possibly adjacent corn mill were sold with Wyniard Mill to Sir Peter Vanlore;[45] they may have been the two mills held by John Waite in 1702.[46] Waite and a namesake held one of the mills in 1725.[47] Postern Mill was in use, presumably as a corn mill, in 1830; it was bought by Thomas Luce in 1834 and converted to a brewery soon afterwards.[48]

'Schotesbure' Mill, which stood beside a road leading southwards from the town in the late 13th century or the earlier 14th,[49] was probably that east of St. John's bridge later held of Burton Hill manor and called Cannop's Mill.[50] In the late 13th century, as in the 16th, the bridge was called Mill bridge,[51] and the mill was standing near it in 1480.[52] Between 1535 and 1564 the millers were members of the Cannop family. In 1564 John Cannop was fined for overcharging.[53] From the early 17th century buildings on the site of the mill were used chiefly in the production of cloth.[54]

Cowbridge Mill, standing in the late 13th century,[55] also became part of Burton Mill manor.[56] Although it seems to have been principally a grist mill, it was held by clothiers in the early 17th century and the early 19th.[57] The mill and mill house

were rebuilt c. 1850. In 1875 and 1882 the mill was leased to a Malmesbury brewer.[58] Water power was still used in 1894;[59] by 1910 the mill had apparently been converted to generate electricity for Cowbridge House.[60]

A mill beside the abbey garden in 1535[61] was presumably Abbey Mill, north of the abbey church. It was part of Malmesbury manor in the 18th century and the early 19th, and was leased with Abbey House;[62] in 1808 the tenant was a brewer.[63] The mill was probably in use in 1910 but closed soon afterwards.[64]

Wyniard Mill north of St. John's bridge was also standing in 1535.[65] It passed from Malmesbury abbey to the Crown at the Dissolution and was sold in 1610 to Sir Peter Vanlore, whose relict Catherine, then wife of Peregrine Pelham, held it in 1653.[66] It was bought by John Estcourt c. 1662,[67] and passed in the Estcourt and Dewell families, from 1717 with land in Burton Hill and Burton Hill House,[68] until it was sold in 1865.[69] In 1535 and 1585 the mill was leased to members of the Stumpe family and may have been used for cloth production. In 1585 it was said to require extensive repairs.[70] On its site in 1653 were two corn mills and a dye house;[71] repairs costing £100 were made to either one of or both the mills c. 1662.[72] In the 19th century millers at Wyniard Mill usually followed an additional trade, in 1839, 1848, and 1867 that of brewer or maltster, in 1859 that of millwright, and in 1885 those of timber merchant and builder. Water and steam powered the mill in 1895; it probably passed out of use shortly afterwards.[73]

A water mill, part of Whitchurch and Milbourne manor in 1539,[74] perhaps stood by the Tetbury Avon north-east of the town. It passed by exchange from Sir Henry Moody, lord of the manor, to Thomas Howard, earl of Suffolk, in 1614.[75] It may have been standing in 1720[76] but was not in use in 1802.[77]

MARKETS AND FAIRS. Malmesbury was a market town until the mid 20th century but as such never seems to have been as popular as Chippenham, Tetbury, or Cirencester, all within 17 km. of it. In the Middle Ages market and fair tolls were taken by Malmesbury abbey[78] and later passed as part of Malmesbury manor to George Rushout, Baron

[37] V.C.H. Wilts. iv. 204; inf. from Mr. P. J. Sear, Managing Director, Linolite Ltd., Malmesbury.
[38] Above, introduction.
[39] V.C.H. Wilts. ii, p. 115.   [40] Reg. Malm. i. 131, 174–5.
[41] P.R.O., CP 25(1)/250/9, no. 48.
[42] Inf. from Mr. C. K. Currie, 15 Claudeen Close, Swaythling, Southampton.
[43] P.R.O., SC 6/Hen. VIII/3986, rott. 96–98d.
[44] Ibid. E 134/3 Jas. I East./12.
[45] Ibid. E 317/Wilts. no. 39.
[46] Ibid. CP 25(2)/979/1 Anne Mich.
[47] Ibid. CP 25(2)/1079/11 Geo. I Hil.
[48] Pigot, Nat. Com. Dir. (1830), 805; (1842), 21; W.R.O. 1301/9, deed, Thomas to Luce, 1834.
[49] Reg. Malm. ii. 230.
[50] P.R.O., C 142/495, no. 60; ibid. E 318/Box 32/1820.
[51] Ibid. SC 6/Hen. VIII/3986, rot. 112; Reg. Malm. ii, p. xxxiii.   [52] W. Worcestre, Itin. ed. J.H. Harvey, 283.
[53] Valor Eccl. (Rec. Com.), ii. 120; W.R.O. 88/2/13.
[54] Above.   [55] Reg. Malm. i. 176–7.
[56] P.R.O., E 318/Box 32/1820.
[57] Wilts. Inq. p.m. 1625–49 (Index Libr.), 93; Pigot, Nat. Com. Dir. (1830), 805.

[58] Kelly's Dir. Wilts. (1875); W.R.O. 856/3.
[59] W.R.O. 130/78, sale cat.
[60] Ibid. Inland Revenue, val. reg. 9.
[61] Valor Eccl. (Rec. Com.), ii. 119.
[62] W.R.O. 212B/3970; 212B/4157.
[63] Ibid. 212B/4264.
[64] Ibid. Inland Revenue, val. reg. 9; Kelly's Dir. Wilts. (1907 and later edns.).
[65] Valor Eccl. (Rec. Com.), ii. 121.
[66] P.R.O., E 317/Wilts. no. 39.
[67] Ibid. E 134/25 Chas. II Trin./4.   [68] Above, manors.
[69] W.R.O. 212A/38/29.
[70] Valor Eccl. (Rec. Com.), ii. 121; P.R.O., E 310/26/154, no. 30.
[71] P.R.O., LR 2/301, ff. 261–3.
[72] Ibid. E 134/25 Chas. II Trin./4.
[73] Kelly's Dir. Wilts. (1848 and later edns.); W.R.O., tithe award.
[74] P.R.O., SC 6/Hen. VIII/3986, rot. 129.
[75] W.R.O. 130/1B, deed, Millard to Clerke, 1671.
[76] P.R.O., CP 25(2)/1078/7 Geo. I Mich.
[77] W.R.O. 88/5/74.
[78] Reg. Malm. i. 134.

Northwick (d. 1887), whose trustees sold them in 1896 to the borough council.[79] Probably from then until 1941 the markets were administered by a committee of the council.[80]

Until 1223 a Saturday market was held partly within and partly outside a graveyard, presumably that of St. Paul's church. Thereafter it was to be held in the New Market,[81] perhaps the area within the abbey precinct where the market cross was built in the 15th century. The market was confirmed by the borough charter of 1635.[82] For much of the 19th century, when it was held in Abbey Row, the area either around the market cross or west of the abbey church, meat and other provisions were sold at it. It ceased c. 1890.[83]

A cattle market, held at first on the last Tuesday and later on the last Wednesday of each month, was started c. 1790. Like the Saturday market it was held in Abbey Row in the 19th century. In the 1840s and 1850s the market was not held between March and May.[84] It had become a general market by 1950,[85] but a monthly cattle market was again held, on land near the railway station, between 1956 and 1966.[86]

In 1252 Malmesbury abbey was granted a Thursday market to be held in Westport,[87] but no such market is known to have been held. Between 1900 and 1945 a general market was held on Wednesdays in Cross Hayes.[88] References to a pig market in the 1760s and 1770s,[89] and to a corn market in High Street, perhaps at the north end near the market cross, in 1809,[90] imply that those markets were sometimes held in the town.

William I granted to Malmesbury abbey a fair on three or five days including St. Aldhelm's day, 25 May. A five-day fair was granted or confirmed by William II, and extended by Maud to eight days, including the three days before the feast and the four days after it.[91] In 1252 the abbey was also granted a yearly fair on its manor of Whitchurch for three days at the feast of St. James, 25 July.[92] St. Aldhelm's fair was held on St. Aldhelm's mead south-west of the town,[93] and in the 16th century was said to have been so large that a company of soldiers was present to keep order.[94] It and St. James's fair were reduced to one day each and three other fairs, on 17 March, 17 April, and 17 October, were added by the borough charter of 1635.[95] One or more of the fairs may have been held in Horsefair, in Westport, first mentioned by name in the late 17th century;[96] in the 19th century the Triangle in Westport was also called Sheep Fair.[97] In the late 18th century and

the early 19th there were three fairs,[98] and between 1842 and 1867 yearly fairs, at which horses, cattle, and sheep were sold, were held on 28 March, 28 April, 5 June, and 15 December. By 1875 the fairs had ceased.[99]

LOCAL GOVERNMENT. The borough of Malmesbury may have had powers of self government from the early Middle Ages.[1] Outside the borough, Malmesbury parish seems likely to have contained several tithings, Burton Hill, Milbourne, Rodbourne, and Corston.[2]

BOROUGH GOVERNMENT. Malmesbury was probably already a privileged borough in 1086.[3] There was a guild merchant in the early 13th century: presumably in 1215 when it became fee-farmer of the borough,[4] and certainly before 1222, Malmesbury abbey excused members of the guild and other inhabitants of the borough from payment of certain scotales in return for a fine and an annual rent to be paid by the hand of the guild steward.[5] In the mid 13th century the guild comprised an alderman, 2 stewards, and 16 or more other members; the 19 apparently formed a body governing the borough and guild. In an exchange with the abbey in the mid 13th century the guildsmen surrendered part of Portmans heath and received Cooks heath, Broad croft and the assart which separated it from Cooks heath, and another assart on Burnt heath.[6] The lands presumably lay southwest of the town mainly in Westport parish, among those which belonged to the borough in the 16th century and were known from the early 17th as King's Heath.[7] The holding was of 700 a. in the early 19th century.[8] In the later 14th century there were in the borough, in addition to the guild, groups of men called half-hundreds and hundreds. In 1370 the half-hundreds were called Bynport and Westport; the hundreds were called Coxfort, Thornhill, Davids, Fishers, Glovers, and Taylors, names which suggest that the grouping was partly by trade. An agreement of that year, intended to make the assessment of the scotale fairer, required payment only from members of the guild, half-hundreds, and hundreds, and implied that those were the wealthier inhabitants. The half-hundreds and hundreds included members of the guild,[9] and it seems likely that each group had specified rights over the borough's lands.

The borough ascribed an early origin to its privileges. A charter of 1381 confirming them related

[79] W.R.O., G 21/150/10.
[80] Ibid. G 21/113/1-5.
[81] Rot. Litt. Claus. (Rec. Com.), i. 537.
[82] Luce, Hist. Malm. 102.
[83] J. Britton, Beauties of Wilts. iii. 89; Kelly's Dir. Wilts. (1848 and later edns.).
[84] Moffatt, Hist. Malm. 163; Pigot, Nat. Com. Dir. (1842), 20; Kelly's Dir. Wilts. (1859 and later edns.); Britton, Beauties of Wilts. iii. 89.
[85] Town Guide [c. 1950].
[86] Inf. from the town clerk, Malmesbury.
[87] Cal. Chart. R. 1226-57, 400.
[88] Inf. from the town clerk; see plate facing p. 189.
[89] W.R.O. 212B/4045; 212B/4129.
[90] Ibid. 212B/4274.
[91] Reg. Malm. i. 329; Reg. Regum Anglo-Norm. ii, nos. 494, 971.
[92] Cal. Chart. R. 1226-57, 400.

[93] Britton, Beauties of Wilts. iii. 89.
[94] Camden, Brit. (1806), i. 130.
[95] Luce, Hist. Malm. 102.
[96] Aubrey, Topog. Coll. ed. Jackson, 264.
[97] Glos. R.O., D 674B/P 73.
[98] Univ. Brit. Dir. v (1798), 115; Britton, Beauties of Wilts. iii. 89.
[99] Pigot, Nat. Com. Dir. (1842), 20; Kelly's Dir. Wilts. (1848 and later edns.).
[1] Above, introduction.
[2] Taxation Lists (W.R.S. x), pp. 48-50; W.R.O. 88/2/13; 88/2/40.
[3] Above, introduction.
[4] Ibid. manors.
[5] Reg. Malm. i. 446.
[6] Ibid. 150-65.
[7] P.R.O., E 178/5701.
[8] W.R.O., Westport tithe award.
[9] B.L. Add. Ch. 18182.

that King Athelstan confirmed privileges held in the time of his father, that he granted freedom from burghbote, brugbote, wardwyte, horngeld, and scot, and that he gave 5 hides of heath near Norton; the gift was described as a reward to the men of the town for their help in campaigns against the Danes.[10] The attribution of those actions to Athelstan may represent a tradition surviving in 1381 or an attempt to provide a title to rights and privileges long held. The 1381 charter was confirmed at various dates, lastly in 1604.[11]

Many of the functions of government normally performed by the corporation of a borough were retained in Malmesbury by the manor court,[12] and there is little evidence of the corporation's responsibility for the regulation of trade or the administration of justice before the 17th century. In the 16th century the corporation consisted of a company of 13 burgesses including an alderman and two stewards,[13] and three other companies, the twenty-four, the landholders, and the commoners. Every man who was born in the town, married to a woman born there, or resident for three or more years in what was described as an ancient tenement was eligible to become a commoner. He did so by entering one of the six hundreds; by 1600 the half-hundreds of Bynport and Westport had disappeared and Davids had become Davids Loynes hundred. Men apparently entered a hundred primarily to acquire rights to the common land. The companies were distinguished by the extent of their rights in King's Heath. The commoners had only grazing rights but the twenty-four, the landholders, and the burgesses, including the alderman, had in addition small several holdings.[14] In the mid 16th century some burgesses' places were vacant, apparently because their portions of King's Heath were poor. At the instigation of John Jewell, bishop of Salisbury, Cooks heath was inclosed and divided between four burgesses c. 1570; the full number of burgesses was thereupon restored.[15]

In the early 17th century the rights of the alderman and burgesses to inclosed lands, then totalling 100 a., were challenged by members of the other companies who claimed that the land should be common. In 1609 it was agreed that a representative of each of the four companies should be appointed to resolve the dispute. The four agreed that the alderman and burgesses should retain their closes on payment to the steward of £20 a year for the general benefit, that closes held by the twenty-four and the landholders should be retained by them, and that the remainder of the land, the greater part, should remain common under new regulations. The settlement was defined in ordinances published by a Chancery decree in 1610. An attempt was made in the same year, presumably by those who had earlier challenged the burgesses' rights, to have the decree dismissed, and in 1611 the burgesses' inclosures

were broken. At the annual meeting of the alderman and burgesses in the town hall in 1612 their opponents occupied the burgesses' benches and may have attempted to set up a rival form of government by 12 overseers selected from all members of the corporation, then called the free burgesses. During subsequent litigation it was claimed that government by the alderman and burgesses was an innovation of the 1560s, that previously government of the town was by a head bailiff, two constables, and wardsmen or assistants, elected annually at the court leet of Malmesbury manor, and that the ordinances of 1610 were drawn up without the knowledge of those who later opposed them.[16] The decree, however, seems to have remained in force from 1612, with the slight variation that there were four stewards, one from each company.[17]

A commission issued in 1631 to inquire whether King's Heath was Crown land which had been concealed may have been the product of further disputes within the borough or an attempt by the Crown to reclaim the freehold of the land. Perhaps to settle a dispute or remove uncertainty created by the commission, the borough obtained a new charter in 1635. The composition of the corporation was little changed. Thereafter the burgesses were called chief or capital burgesses and the twenty-four were called assistant burgesses, but the landholders and commoners were still so called. Membership of each company was for life; vacancies in each of the senior companies were to be filled by election from the immediately inferior company. The capital burgesses, of whom there were 12 in addition to the alderman, were to elect annually a lawyer as steward, later called the high steward, to advise them. The preamble of the charter referred to a need for better means of keeping the peace within the borough. The alderman, elected annually, was therefore to be a justice of the peace, the coroner, and the clerk of the market. A court was to be held every three weeks for civil cases, and the corporation, meeting in the common hall, was empowered to make regulations for the government and victualling of the borough, enforceable by fines. It was also allowed to appoint two serjeants-at-mace.[18]

Attempts by Charles II and James II to control parliamentary elections brought changes in the constitution of Malmesbury as of most boroughs. In or before 1668 the corporation defended a *quo warranto*, presumably successfully.[19] Another *quo warranto*, issued in 1684,[20] was not contested[21] and a new charter was granted to the borough in 1685. It provided for the capital burgesses to keep their number at 12 (beside the alderman) by choosing new burgesses to fill vacancies from members of the whole corporation, for the high steward, or in his absence the deputy steward, to act as a justice of the peace in addition to the alderman, and for the officers of the corporation to be removable by

[10] *Cal. Pat.* 1381–5, 54; *W.A.M.* lxxiv/lxxv, 135–6.
[11] Luce, *Hist. Malm.* 95.   [12] Below, manorial govt.
[13] P.R.O., STAC 8/130/3.
[14] Ibid. STAC 8/290/22.
[15] Ibid. C 33/115, f. 36; ibid. E 134/9 Chas. I Mich./75.
[16] Ibid. STAC 8/93/2; STAC 8/130/3; STAC 8/138/8; STAC 8/290/22; Luce, *Hist. Malm.* 98.

[17] *W.A.M.* xlvii. 323; Malmesbury boro. rec., ct. bk. 1600–1721.
[18] Luce, *Hist. Malm.* 101–2; P.R.O., E 134/9 Chas. I Mich./75.
[19] Malmesbury boro. rec., ct. bk. 1600–1721.
[20] B.L. Harl. MS. 6013, p. 38.
[21] Luce, *Hist. Malm.* 145.

the Crown. The precinct of the former abbey was for the first time expressly included within the borough.[22] In 1690 the constitution of 1635 was restored[23] and in 1696 a new charter was issued. It confirmed the liberties and franchises held under the charter of 1635, and the provisions of 1685 for the inclusion of the abbey precinct in the borough and the appointment of the high steward or his deputy as a justice.[24]

In the early 19th century the qualifications for becoming a commoner, then also known as a free burgess, were apparently a matter of dispute. An inquiry held in 1821 found that the right belonged to every resident of an entire tenement in the borough who was of age, married, and either the son of a commoner or married to a commoner's daughter.[25] In the 1840s the alderman and burgesses attempted to limit admission as commoners to those who lived in ancient tenements, apparently without success.[26] Complaints were made about the administration of justice in Malmesbury and the character of its alderman and burgesses in the 1830s,[27] but the constitution of the borough remained unchanged until 1886. It was then incorporated as a municipal borough, under the Municipal Corporations Act of 1882, with a mayor, four aldermen, and 12 councillors.[28] In 1974 the borough became part of North Wiltshire district.[29]

The principal borough court recorded from 1600 was held annually, usually on the Tuesday after Trinity Sunday in a room in the former St. John's hospital. In the 17th and 18th centuries it was presumably convened, as later, by the alderman; it is not clear how it proceeded. The principal business was probably the election of aldermen and stewards, but the elections are recorded only from 1613. New commoners were admitted to the hundreds on payment of a fine. Regulations were made for grazing on the part of King's Heath not inclosed, called Malmesbury common from the 18th century; those who broke the rules were fined. Until 1614 an account of rents received from those holding closes in King's Heath was presented regularly in the name of the alderman and stewards; thereafter accounts were only occasionally recorded. In the 19th century the alderman and stewards elected at the Trinity court were sworn at a Michaelmas court and other courts were held for the election of capital and assistant burgesses, the nomination of landholders, and the admission of commoners as need arose.[30] No record survives of the three-weekly court provided for by the charter of 1635.

Courts called borough sessions, at which the alderman and deputy steward presided, are recorded from 1712 to 1741. They were held yearly, usually in April or October, presumably in the same place as the borough court. Orders were made concerning the repair of roads and bridges, apprenticeships, and the setting of poor rates, and weights used in the markets were tested. From 1729 constables were appointed.[31] The borough sought the right to hold separate quarter sessions c. 1750,[32] apparently without success. Borough sessions were still held in 1876,[33] but presumably ceased in 1886.[34] From 1842 or earlier petty sessions for Malmesbury hundred were also held in the town.[35] Petty sessions continued to be held in Malmesbury; from 1973 they were held by Chippenham magistrates sitting in Malmesbury town hall fortnightly.[36] Between 1830 and 1854 the alderman exercised the right to act as coroner, granted in the 1635 and 1696 charters.[37] The borough was included in the North Wiltshire coroner's district in 1860.[38]

In the 13th century there were two guildhalls in the borough, one in Malmesbury parish and one in Westport parish.[39] After the Dissolution the corporation bought St. Paul's church and in 1542 used the east end as a town hall.[40] What was called the church house, presumably the east end of St. Paul's, was used for meetings in 1691 and, of the alderman and capital burgesses, in 1709.[41] In 1580 the alderman and burgesses bought the site of St. John's hospital.[42] The building was later used as almshouses, a school, and from 1616 the usual meeting place of the borough court.[43] No. 9 Oxford Street was owned by the corporation and may also have been used for meetings in the 18th century when it was called the Guildhall; such use had ceased by 1794.[44] A town hall was built in Cross Hayes in 1854 and enlarged in 1927.[45] It was used as the offices of the municipal borough council from 1886 and of the town council from 1974.[46]

In 1622 the corporation decided that each burgess should pay 5s. yearly to the alderman towards the cost of a dinner on the day of the borough court. The total allowance to the alderman was increased from £3 to £10 in 1652.[47] An allotment of land on King's Heath, known as the alderman's kitchen, later replaced the payments.[48]

In 1886 the borough lands, including Malmesbury common, were retained by the old corporation under a new name, the warden (later the burgesses) and freemen of Malmesbury. That body also became the trustees of several borough charities. The structure of hundreds and companies was retained and in 1988 three courts were

[22] *Cal. S.P. Dom.* 1685, pp. 64–5.
[23] Malmesbury boro. rec., ct. bk. 1600–1721.
[24] *Cal. S.P. Dom.* 1696, 433.
[25] *1st Rep. Com. Mun. Corp.* H.C. 116, App. 1, pp. 78–9 (1835), xxii (1).
[26] W.R.O. 1305/203.
[27] *1st Rep. Com. Mun. Corp.* p. 79; P.R.O., HO 52/27, no. 264; HO 52/31, no. 162.
[28] *Kelly's Dir. Wilts.* (1903); W.R.O., F 2/141.
[29] *Local Govt. in Eng. and Wales* (H.M.S.O. 1974), 117.
[30] Malmesbury boro. rec., ct. bks. 1600–1721, 1722–81, 1793–1868, 1868–1986; inf. from the clerk to the burgesses and freemen, 1 Market Lane; below, Westport, econ. hist.
[31] Malmesbury boro. rec., sessions order bk. 1712–41.
[32] Ibid. case for separate q. sess. c. 1750.
[33] *Rep. Com. Mun. Corp.* [C. 2490–1], p. 73, H.C. (1880), xxxi.

[34] W.R.O., F 2/141.
[35] Pigot, *Nat. Com. Dir.* (1842), 20.
[36] Inf. from the town clerk.
[37] Malmesbury boro. rec., coroner's rec. 1830–54.
[38] *Lond. Gaz.* 30 Oct. 1860, p. 3898.
[39] *Reg. Malm.* i. 121, 123; *Bradenstoke Cart.* (W.R.S. xxxv), p. 76.
[40] Leland, *Itin.* ed. Toulmin Smith, i. 131.
[41] Malmesbury boro. rec., ct. bk. 1600–1721.
[42] *V.C.H. Wilts.* iii. 341.
[43] Below, educ., charities; Malmesbury boro. rec., ct. bk. 1600–1721; see below, plate facing p. 221.
[44] W.R.O. 177/23, deed, Pinnell to Clarke, 1816.
[45] *Kelly's Dir. Wilts.* (1927); see below, plate facing p. 189.
[46] *Kelly's Dir. Wilts.* (1895); inf. from the town clerk.
[47] Malmesbury boro. rec., ct. bk. 1600–1721.
[48] *Endowed Char. Wilts.* (N. Div.), 695.

still being held yearly in the court room of St. John's almshouses to admit commoners, elect officers, and administer property.[49]

In the late 18th century a tradition existed that a common seal had been in use in the 1550s and had born the legend COMMUN[E] SIGILL[UM] BURG[I] DE MALMESBURY.[50] The borough arms, as depicted on a seal matrix cast in the late 16th century or the 17th, were an embattled castle or gateway flanked by two round towers and surmounted by a third from the dome of which flew a pennon; in base the waters of Avon, on each side a teazle or wheat plant; in chief a blazing star and crescent, and in the dexter chief three pellets. The matrix, 6.3 cm. in diameter, bears the legend SIGIL[LUM] COM[MUNE] ALD[E]R[MAN]I ET BUR-GEN[SIUM] BURGI DE MALMESBURY IN COM[ITATU] WILTS. A second matrix, 5.6 cm. in diameter, has the same device, except that the three pellets are in the sinister chief, and a similar legend, with the addition of the date 1615. Two smaller matrices, one perhaps of the early 17th century, bear reduced versions of the arms shown on the matrix of 1615 and of the undated legend.[51]

The borough possessed two silver-gilt maces, possibly of the mid 17th century, each 71 cm. long, and two silver maces, hallmarked for 1703, each 82 cm. long. A cross on the head of one of the older pair was renewed in brass. Both the seals and the maces were held by the warden and freemen from 1886 and remained in use in the later 20th century.[52]

In 1950 arms were granted to Malmesbury borough council: parted saltirewise argent and gules, a cross botony in chief a Saxon crown and in base an orb, all gold, on a chief sable a lion passant between a mitre and a crozier erect, all gold.[53]

MANORIAL GOVERNMENT. Malmesbury abbey claimed to be free of shire and hundred courts and to have other liberties in estates including Cowfold by a charter of 1065, but the relevant part of the charter, if not the whole, is almost certainly spurious.[54] The abbey nevertheless held those liberties in the mid 13th century for all its estates in Malmesbury parish.[55]

Records of views of frankpledge and other courts held for Malmesbury manor survive for several periods from the mid 16th century. From the mid 18th century the courts were described as courts leet and courts baron for the manor of Malmesbury and Westport. In the 1560s, in the late 1640s, and between 1750 and 1780 courts were usually held in spring and autumn each year.[56] Military activity prevented courts from being held in the early 1640s.[57] Many functions of town government were apparently performed in Malmesbury by the manor courts rather than or in addition to the borough courts. At the view held in 1561 bakers, butchers, and innkeepers were presented for breaches of the assize, and fines were imposed on those who had neglected to repair King's Wall;

whether the street of that name or part of the town wall needed repair is not clear. In the later 18th century the jurors at the court leet presented defaulters from the court, roads in need of repair, and rubbish and pigsties in Cross Hayes and High Street. In 1752 they reported the lack of a ducking stool. Constables were appointed from the 1750s. A court leet was held once a year from the 1780s; none was held after 1806. In 1561 offences by victuallers were also presented at the court baron. Later the court baron, at which the homage presented, dealt mainly with the tenure of copyhold premises in the town. From c. 1780 until 1914 courts were held irregularly, apparently at need.[58]

Courts and views held for Burton Hill manor were recorded with those for Rodbourne manor under the rubric of Cowfold manor with Rodbourne and Burton Hill for the years 1559, 1563–4, 1569, and 1571–3. The courts and views were held

THE BOROUGH SEAL, 1615

in spring and autumn yearly, probably at a house in Cole park. Between 1559 and 1564 and in 1573 views were held for Burton Hill at which a tithingman presented and a jury affirmed his presentments. Between 1569 and 1572 views were held jointly for Burton Hill and Rodbourne; there was a single jury but a tithingman from each presented. Burton Hill business included stray animals and overcharging by millers and a butcher. Courts baron for Burton Hill were held separately. The homage presented defaulters from the court, deaths of copyholders, and tenements in need of repair. The use of common pastures was regulated and, at the autumn court, a tithingman and a reeve were appointed.[59]

Courts leet and courts baron for Whitchurch and Milbourne manor are recorded for the years 1763–1816. The courts were usually held annually in autumn; additional courts were held to admit

[49] Malmesbury boro. rec., ct. bk. 1868–1986; *Town Guide* (1986).
[50] Moffatt, *Hist. Malm.* 132.   [51] *W.A.M.* xxviii. 43–4.
[52] Ibid. 42–4; inf. from the town clerk.
[53] C. W. Scott-Giles, *Civic Heraldry of Eng.* 386.
[54] *Reg. Malm.* i. 323; *V.C.H. Wilts.* ii, p. 88 n. 68.
[55] Above, Malmesbury hund.

[56] P.R.O., C 116/273, pp. 6–9, 16; ibid. SC 2/209/16; W.R.O. 212B/3977; 1165/3.
[57] Hist. MSS. Com. 55, *Var. Coll.* i, p. 110.
[58] *Wilts. Q. Sess. Rec.* ed. Cunnington, 159; P.R.O., C 116/273, pp. 6–9, 16; ibid. SC 2/209/16; W.R.O. 212B/3977; 1165/3–6.
[59] W.R.O. 88/2/7; 88/2/13; 88/2/21; 88/2/29.

copyholders. At the autumn court two haywards, one each for Milbourne common and Whitchurch marsh, were appointed. Orders were made for footpaths to be repaired and, in 1766, a new pound to be built; encroachments on waste ground were presented.[60]

PARISH GOVERNMENT. In 1632 those who lived in Cole park and West park were ordered to contribute to poor relief in the parish,[61] which was presumably administered without differentiating the town and the outlying parts. In 1636 it was reported that 60 houses within the precinct of the former abbey contained 47 persons needing relief; the implication was that the precinct was being treated as extraparochial but the parish should provide relief. Seven houses within the precinct were then in Westport parish.[62] Probably by 1760, however, and certainly by 1776 the Abbey had become a separate parish relieving its own poor.[63]

In 1642 £30 a week for six weeks was ordered to be collected from Malmesbury and parishes within 5 miles of it to relieve its poor, then affected by plague. Only £68 was collected and in 1646 the constables, churchwardens, and overseers were still seeking compensation for money spent during the epidemic.[64]

In the later 18th century the Malmesbury vestry set a rate and delegated its collection and the distribution of relief to 6 overseers, 2 for the town and 1 each for Burton Hill, Corston, Rodbourne, and Milbourne (presumably with Whitchurch). In 1779 John Chamberlain was appointed by the vestry to administer poor relief throughout the parish. From 1780, however, the six overseers again received and made payments. Relief in the parish, excluding Corston and Rodbourne, cost c. £150 in 1760–1. It was given regularly at a cost of £82 to 26 people; 22 apparently lived in the borough and 2 each in Milbourne and Burton Hill tithings. Occasional relief and other expenses cost £70; payments were made for clothing, bedding, rents, and funerals. In 1770–1 regular relief was given to 28 in the borough, 1 in Milbourne, and 3 in Burton Hill; in 1779–80 it was given to c. 40 in the borough, 6 in Milbourne, and 1 in Burton Hill.[65] In 1802–3 in Malmesbury parish, including Corston and Rodbourne, regular relief was given to 129 adults, some of whom were in the workhouse, and 168 children; 52 inhabitants and 107 people from outside the parish received occasional payments. The total cost was £972. During the next decade fewer people were relieved. In 1815 regular relief was given to 111 and occasional relief to 59. Costs, however, rose; £1,102 was spent on the poor in 1815.[66] A peak was reached in 1818 when £1,928 was spent. Thereafter expenditure fell until 1824,

when £1,086 was spent, and usually remained between £1,000 and £1,200 until 1835[67] when Malmesbury poor-law union was formed.[68]

In the later 18th century the east end of St. Paul's church housed some of the poor.[69] There was a workhouse in 1781,[70] which in 1803 had 46 inmates.[71] It was probably the building in Holloway held in 1805 by the churchwardens and overseers on a 21-year lease,[72] and may previously have been part of Jenner's almshouses.[73] In 1814 there were 23 inmates.[74] In 1825 a new poorhouse for the parish was built on the site of part of Jenner's almshouses at the junction of Oxford Street and Holloway; in 1834 the remaining almshouses also housed poor families placed there by the parish.[75] Such use presumably ceased when the union workhouse on the outskirts of the town in Brokenborough parish was opened in 1838.[76]

Poor relief in the Abbey parish cost £15 in 1775–6 and £30 in 1802–3, when four adults and four children were regularly relieved. Expenditure had risen to £50 by 1814, when seven people received regular relief. There is no record of occasional relief being given in the parish.[77] Between 1815 and 1835 the cost of poor relief was usually £35–£45; it was a little higher in 1816, 1820, and 1827–8, and lower in 1822–4.[78] The Abbey parish became part of Malmesbury poor-law union in 1835.[79]

PUBLIC SERVICES. Constables of Malmesbury were first recorded in the 1640s; it is not clear by whom they were appointed. In 1642 two constables complained to the justices at quarter sessions of the additional expense they had incurred during the plague of that year and in watching and warding, providing and mending arms, and attending and transporting prisoners. In 1644 a constable sought release from the office, in which he had served for three years apparently because manor courts had not been held. In 1646 a similar request was made by both constables, who claimed to have suffered great loss, particularly through plunder and imprisonment by royalist troops.[80] Between 1729 and 1741 two constables each for Malmesbury and Westport were appointed at the borough sessions, and from 1753 two constables for Malmesbury, two for Westport, and one for the Abbey parish at the manor court. Two sidesmen for Malmesbury and two for Westport were also sworn at the manor courts from 1753.[81]

From 1840 Malmesbury parish outside the borough was policed by the county constabulary.[82] The borough force was separate, presumably from c. 1840, until in 1887 it became part of the county constabulary.[83] A police station in the town belong-

[60] Ibid. 88/5/47.
[61] P.R.O., ASSI 24/20, f. 55v.
[62] Wilts. Q. Sess. Rec. ed. Cunnington, 117–19.
[63] Poor Law Abstract, 1804, 566–7; W.R.O. 1589/33.
[64] Hist. MSS. Com. 55, Var. Coll. i, pp. 108, 110.
[65] W.R.O. 1589/33.
[66] Poor Law Abstract, 1804, 566–7; 1818, 498–9.
[67] Poor Rate Returns, 1816–21, 188–9; 1822–4, 228; 1825–9, 219; 1830–4, 212–13.
[68] Poor Law Com. 2nd Rep. App. D, 559.
[69] Camden, Brit. (1806), i. 142. [70] W.R.O. 1589/34.
[71] Poor Law Abstract, 1804, 566–7.
[72] Moffatt, Hist. Malm. 99; W.R.O. 1589/46B

[73] Endowed Char. Wilts. (N. Div.), 677; below, charities.
[74] W.R.O. 1589/35.
[75] Endowed Char. Wilts. (N. Div.), 677.
[76] W.A.M. xlvii. 565.
[77] Poor Law Abstract, 1804, 566–7; 1818, 498–9.
[78] Poor Rate Returns, 1816–21, 188–9; 1822–4, 228; 1828–9, 219; 1830–4, 212–13.
[79] Poor Law Com. 2nd Rep. App. D, 559.
[80] Wilts. Q. Sess. Rec. ed. Cunnington, 159; Hist. MSS. Com. 55, Var. Coll. i, p. 110.
[81] Malmesbury boro. rec., sessions order bk. 1712–41; W.R.O. 212B/3977; 1165/3.
[82] W.R.O., F 5/100/1.   [83] Ibid. A 1/150/28, p. 628.

ing to the county police in 1844[84] was replaced in 1854 by a new building in Burnham Road.[85] A new station in Burton Hill was built c. 1955.[86]

The abbot of Malmesbury had a prison in the 12th and 13th centuries.[87] Prisoners were sent from the hundred courts to a gaol in Malmesbury in 1613,[88] and in 1682 the justices at quarter sessions ordered that a gaol be built there.[89] In 1831 a building east of the abbey gateway was used as the town prison.[90]

A fire brigade, formed in 1851, had a station in 1866, perhaps that in Ingram Street in use c. 1894. From 1907 to c. 1948 the brigade was based at the town hall. It was moved to a station in Gloucester Road c. 1948 and a new station was opened there in 1969.[91]

In 1798 an Act for paving the footways and for cleaning and lighting the streets of the borough[92] established a body of improvement commissioners, and in 1872 the town became an urban sanitary district under the authority of the same body.[93] Its duties apparently passed to the borough council in 1886.[94]

In 1835 it was proposed to supply gas to the town; a gasworks north of St. John's bridge may have been built then[95] and was standing in 1848.[96] The Malmesbury Gas & Coke Co. was vested in the South Western Gas Board in 1949.[97] Electricity was supplied to the town by the Western Electricity Distributing Corporation in 1923.[98] The Malmesbury Water Works Co. Ltd. built a pumping house in Holloway in or soon after 1864 and a water tower south-east of Abbey House probably at the same date. The waterworks was transferred to the borough in 1900.[99] Another water tower, to serve Malmesbury rural district and the borough, was built north of Whychurch Farm between 1947 and 1953[1] and was replaced by a new tower and pumping station in 1985.[2] In 1904 and 1920 proceedings were instituted by Wiltshire county council against the borough council to prevent the discharge of sewage into the Avon.[3] A sewage works was built north of Cowbridge Farm c. 1962.[4]

A cemetery and a mortuary chapel for Malmesbury and Westport parishes were opened on 1 ha. west of the Tetbury road in Westport in 1884.[5] A cottage hospital north of the market cross was opened in 1889 and rebuilt in 1897. It was transferred to the Manor House, Burton Hill, in 1925;[6]

that house, much extended, was still used as a hospital in 1988. An isolation hospital was opened on a site then in Brokenborough parish c. 1890. It was a wooden building with 6 beds in 2 wards, but without cooking apparatus, bath-house, or bath. The hospital was closed in 1933.[7]

In 1851 a mechanics' institute in Malmesbury had 92 members and a library of 900 books.[8] A library in the town was open on two evenings a week in 1926, and in 1935 was in the town hall. Thereafter it was moved several times; from 1972 it occupied part of the former Malmesbury Church of England school in Cross Hayes.[9] In 1931 the Athelstan Museum was opened in the town hall.[10] It was moved to a building in Gloucester Road c. 1970[11] but from 1979 was again in the town hall.[12]

Between 1931 and 1956 Malmesbury borough council built most of the new houses west of the town and the houses and prefabricated bungalows in Cowbridge Crescent. The council also built the swimming pool in Old Alexander Road opened in 1961. The Parklands estate was built for Malmesbury rural district council,[13] and North Wiltshire district council built the houses and maisonettes at Burton Hill.[14] In 1971 Wiltshire county council bought Burnham House as a residential home for the elderly, and later built the additional accommodation in its grounds.[15]

PARLIAMENTARY REPRESENTATION. Malmesbury returned burgesses to the parliament of 1275 and to a total of 74 parliaments before 1449; only New Salisbury, Wilton, and Marlborough of the boroughs in Wiltshire were more frequently represented. Until 1832 the borough usually had two M.P.s. The earliest surviving indentures are between the sheriff and the alderman and burgesses; in 1455 the borough's representatives were selected by the alderman and at least 13 burgesses.[16] The franchise had probably been restricted to the alderman and 12 other burgesses, later called the capital burgesses, by the late 16th century. The first record of an election by those 13 dates from 1640.[17] Conflicts over King's Heath and borough government in the early 17th century may have derived in part from attempts to extend the franchise,[18] but no complaint about electoral rights was recorded.

[84] W.R.O., F 5/100/1.
[85] Ibid. A 1/592, plan of police station, deed, Lloyd to Jacob, 1853.
[86] Inf. from Chief Constable, Police Headquarters, Devizes.
[87] Reg. Malm. ii. 318, 364.
[88] Acts of P.C. 1613–14, 92–3.
[89] W.A.M. xliv. 387.
[90] Glos. R.O., D 674B/P 73.
[91] Kelly's Dir. Wilts. (1903, 1907); TS. notes on fire brigade in Athelstan Mus.; inf. from the town clerk.
[92] L.J. xli. 655.
[93] V.C.H. Wilts. v. 258; W.R.O. 1269/16.
[94] Above, introduction.
[95] Inf. from Dr. H. Nabb, British Gas plc (South Western), Bristol; W.R.O. 1269/16.
[96] Kelly's Dir. Wilts. (1848); O.S. Map 6″, Wilts. VIII (1889 edn.).
[97] Inf. from Dr. Nabb.
[98] 'Malm. Electricity Special Order, 1923', Electricity (Supply) Acts, Special Orders (Min. of Transport).
[99] W.R.O., G 21/150/1.
[1] Ibid. G 21/127/1, p. 3; Hudson, Hill Top Town, 145.

[2] Inf. from Supply Controller, Wessex Water, Quay Ho., the Ambury, Bath.
[3] V.C.H. Wilts. v. 277, 327.
[4] Hudson, Hill Top Town, 151.
[5] Kelly's Dir. Wilts. (1939).
[6] Ibid. (1907, 1939); V.C.H. Wilts. v. 343.
[7] V.C.H. Wilts. v. 345; above, Brokenborough, introduction.
[8] J. W. Hudson, Hist. Adult Educ. 231.
[9] Inf. from Director, Libr. and Mus. Service, Co. Hall, Trowbridge.
[10] Wilts. Cuttings, xvii. 10.
[11] Hudson, Hill Top Town, 22.
[12] Inf. from the Curator, Athelstan Mus.
[13] Above, introduction; W.R.O., G 21/100/12.
[14] Inf. from the Property Maintenance Manager, N. Wilts. District Council, Bewley Ho., Marshfield Rd., Chippenham.
[15] Inf. from Property Services Dept., Co. Hall, Trowbridge.
[16] V.C.H. Wilts. v. 73, 75; W.A.M. xlvii. 177–258.
[17] Hist. Parl., Commons, 1660–90, i. 452.
[18] Above, local govt. (boro. govt.).

In the 15th century over half the borough's M.P.s whose names are known were residents of Malmesbury. In the mid 16th century leading clothiers were among the M.P.s. William Stumpe (d. 1552) sat in the parliaments of 1529 and 1547–52, and Matthew King in those of 1553–5 and 1558.[19] Sir James Stumpe was returned in 1555. A controlling interest in the borough's parliamentary elections apparently passed to Sir James's son-in-law Sir Henry Knyvett, who himself represented Malmesbury four times in the later 16th century, and later to Knyvett's son-in-law Thomas Howard, earl of Suffolk.[20]

For much of the 17th century at least one and sometimes both of Malmesbury's M.P.s were drawn from families with local interests: members of the Moody, Poole, Hungerford, Lee, Washington, and Estcourt families represented the borough.[21] Sir John Danvers, elected in place of Anthony Hungerford in 1645, was a signatory to Charles I's death warrant.[22] Elections were occasionally influenced by the earls of Berkshire, resident at Charlton Park, but more usually by members of the Danvers family and their heirs as lords of Malmesbury manor or by the holders of the post of high steward created by the borough charter of 1635. The high steward's influence presumably derived from his duty under the charter to advise the alderman and burgesses on all business concerning the borough. The post was held by members of the Estcourt family of Sherston Pinkney, in Sherston, between 1641 and 1659 and between 1671 and 1677.[23] Later high stewards were usually men of wider influence, often peers.[24]

A letter of 1684 refers to recent elections in Malmesbury as popular, but returns of that year do not indicate any increase in the number of electors. In 1689 Thomas Wharton, later marquess of Wharton and then lord of Malmesbury manor, took advantage of uncertainty over the borough charter to extend the franchise to assistant burgesses, landholders, and commoners; a total of 172 voted in the election of that year.[25] The old franchise was presumably restored in 1690 with the 1635 constitution of the corporation, and the franchise was not defined in the new charter of 1696. In the 1720s and 1730s a standard tariff, by which each of the 13 voters received £100 for a general election and £20 for the re-election of a member who had taken office, secured uncontested elections. In the mid 18th century Henry Fox (cr. Baron Holland 1763) and Henry Howard, earl of Suffolk and of Berkshire (d. 1779), competed for control of the borough. Fox, high steward from 1751 to 1760, proposed a compromise by which they shared both the representation and the electoral costs, paying each capital burgess a total of £30 a year and jointly providing for them two feasts each year.[26]

Lord Suffolk and his supporter Edmund Wilkins, a Malmesbury apothecary, were successively high steward 1762–9. Wilkins transferred his support to Fox and from 1769 to 1775 served as deputy high steward to Charles James Fox, who was M.P. for Malmesbury 1774–80. Wilkins was again high steward from 1775 to 1806. He controlled parliamentary elections by refining the system of annual pensions and reinforcing it by a bond of £500 entered by each capital burgess. Until 1789 he sold the borough at each election to the highest bidder; later he consistently supported government candidates. He was succeeded in control of the borough by Edmund Estcourt, who raised the pension to £50 yearly. Control of the borough's two seats was sold at least twice before 1832. The narrow franchise and the corruption and illiteracy of the burgesses were frequently attacked in the late 18th century and early 19th, and in 1796, 1802, 1806, and 1807 provided the grounds for petitions for elections to be overturned. The borough lost one seat in 1832,[27] and the remaining seat in 1884, when it was merged in the Chippenham division of the county.[28]

CHURCHES. In 1191 Malmesbury abbey was granted the right to appropriate the parish church, St. Paul's church 'in atrio monasterii', to endow lights in the abbey church.[29] By the mid 13th century a vicarage had been ordained.[30] Between 1650 and 1658 the vicarage was united with Westport vicarage[31] but the benefices were separated after 1660.[32] The vicarages and parishes were united under the name Malmesbury with Westport St. Mary in 1946, and in 1984 the new benefice and parish of Brokenborough was added.[33] Chapels at Corston and Rodbourne were dependent on St. Paul's church from the 14th century or earlier until 1881.[34]

The abbot of Malmesbury was patron of the vicarage presumably from its ordination and certainly from 1301. He presented at most vacancies until the Dissolution. The bishop of Salisbury may have collated a vicar in 1332, and in 1387 a vicar, who obtained the living by exchange, was apparently instituted without the abbot's consent. After the Dissolution the Crown presented[35] until 1866 when the advowson was sold to S. B. Brooke.[36] It passed with his Cowbridge estate to the Revd. Charles Kemble and to Charlotte Kemble[37] (d. 1890), who devised the advowson to her daughter Charlotte Kemble.[38] By 1907 the advowson had passed to the Church Trust Fund,[39] the patron of Malmesbury with Westport and Brokenborough in 1987.[40]

After a pension of £5 was paid to Malmesbury abbey the vicarage, worth £4 6s. 8d., was one of the poorer livings in Malmesbury deanery in

[19] *Hist. Parl., Commons,* 1439–1509, i. 711; 1509–58, i. 227; ii. 467–8; iii. 403–5; above, trade and ind.
[20] *Hist. Parl., Commons,* 1558–1603, i. 274–5.
[21] Ibid. 1660–90, i. 453; *W.A.M.* xlvii. 216–19.   [22] *D.N.B.*
[23] *Hist. Parl., Commons,* 1660–90, i. 453; Luce, *Hist. Malm.* 101.   [24] *V.C.H. Wilts.* v. 218.
[25] *Hist. Parl., Commons,* 1660–90, i. 453.
[26] Ibid. 1715–45, i. 348–9; 1754–90, i. 417–18.
[27] Ibid. 1754–90, i. 417–18; 1790–1820, ii. 422–4; *V.C.H. Wilts.* v. 219; see below, plate facing p. 221.
[28] *V.C.H. Wilts.* v. 311–12.

[29] *Reg. Malm.* i. 374–5.   [30] Ibid. ii. 75.
[31] *W.A.M.* xli. 5; *Cal. S.P. Dom.* 1658–9, 220.
[32] Phillipps, *Wilts. Inst.* ii. 27, 29–31.
[33] *Lond. Gaz.* 1 Nov. 1946, p. 5361; inf. from Ch. Com.
[34] Below, Corston, church; Rodbourne, church.
[35] Phillipps, *Wilts. Inst.* (index in *W.A.M.* xxviii. 225); *Clerical Guide* (1829); *Clergy List* (1859).
[36] Ch. Com. file 34228.   [37] Above, manors.
[38] Wilts. Cuttings, xvii. 13.   [39] Bristol R.O., EP/A/3/218.
[40] Inf. from Gen. Secretary, Church Pastoral Aid Soc., Falcon Ct., 32 Fleet Street, Lond.

1291;[41] probably excluding a pension of £4 to the abbey, it was valued at £8 in 1535, close to the average for the deanery.[42] About 1830 the vicar's net annual income was £265, average for a Wiltshire living.[43]

Tithes, apart from those of grain and hay, were due to the vicar from the whole parish except some demesne of Malmesbury abbey. In the mid 13th century offerings and tithes owned by St. John's hospital were replaced by 40d. and ½ lb. wax a year.[44] In 1839 a total of 823 a., mostly what had been Cole park and West park, was tithe free; moduses totalling 12s. were paid in place of vicarial tithes from a further 185 a., said to be former demesne of the abbey. The vicar's tithes were then valued at £430 and commuted.[45]

The vicar had a house, perhaps in King's Wall, c. 1300;[46] it is not known whether it was part of the glebe. In 1412 Edmund Dauntsey and John Thornbury endowed the vicarage with a house and 5 a.[47] In 1671 the glebe comprised 3½ a., a cottage, and a house.[48] The house, of one bay in 1704,[49] stood in Gloucester Street opposite St. Paul's church. In the earlier 19th century it was used as a shop and vicars lived in lodgings.[50] From c. 1882 incumbents lived in a house, then newly built beside the Swindon road, belonging to Westport vicarage.[51] A new vicarage house was built in Holloway, and that beside the Swindon road was sold, in 1969.[52]

Its name suggests that Whitchurch may have been the site of an early chapel. Such a chapel may have invoked St. James in 1252, when Malmesbury abbey was granted a St. James's fair on its land at Whitchurch.[53] In 1535 offerings made from or at Whitchurch to an image of St. James were taken by the abbey.[54] Alms were distributed in a chapel at Whitchurch by the abbey or by the lessee of its Whitchurch estate at mass on the eve and feast of St. James in the early 16th century.[55] After the Dissolution presumably no service was held in the chapel, which from the 1560s or earlier passed with Whitchurch manor.[56] By 1670 it had been incorporated in Whychurch Farm.[57] In 1268 Nicholas of Malmesbury gave land at Fowlswick in Chippenham for a chaplain to say masses for his parents in the chapel of 'la Charnere' in Malmesbury.[58] No other reference to the chapel has been found. All Saints' chapel stood in High Street, perhaps on the eastern side, in the late 13th century and in 1545.[59] In 1544 the Crown granted a house called 'St. White's hermitage' at Burton

Hill;[60] what, if any, ecclesiastical purpose the hermitage had before the Dissolution is not clear. In 1268 William Porter gave a rent of 1s. a year for a light in St. Paul's church.[61] A chantry was endowed at the altar of St. Mary in the church probably before 1300;[62] in 1388 the Crown presented a chantrist.[63] At the chantry's dissolution in 1548 its priest had an income of £6 11s. from Malmesbury and Westport and was described as a very honest poor man.[64]

Some parishioners apparently heard mass in the chapel of St. John's hospital until the mid 13th century, when attendance there was forbidden to all but those wearing the habit of the hospital.[65] In 1378 the vicar John Swan travelled to Rome for the sake of his conscience;[66] he resigned the living in that or the following year.[67] William Sherwood held the vicarage and a rectory in Oxford, and in 1477 was dispensed to hold a third living.[68] Richard Turner, vicar from 1535, in 1539 condemned the dissolution of the monasteries;[69] he seems to have suffered no penalty but had resigned the living by 1544.[70]

In the early 16th century parishioners may have attended services in the abbey church and St. Paul's fell into disrepair. In 1541 the nave of the church of the dissolved abbey was licensed as the parish church because St. Paul's had 'fallen even unto the ground'.[71] The former abbey church was then in the king's hand and in the keeping of William Stumpe.[72] In 1542 John Leland reported that the townsmen, among whom Stumpe was the chief contributor, had bought the church from the king.[73] Stumpe was probably then only the lessee of the site of the abbey; in 1544 he was granted the site by the Crown[74] and may then have given or sold the church to the parish.

There were said to be 860 communicants in Malmesbury and Westport parishes in 1548, and the Crown was then petitioned for assistant clergy to replace chantry priests who had formerly helped incumbents in both parishes.[75] John ApRice, vicar of Malmesbury from 1544 until c. 1564, had two other benefices and in 1556 no licence for plurality.[76] In 1551 the church had no copy of Erasmus's *Paraphrases* or Book of Homilies.[77] ApRice's successor John Skinner was deprived in 1564 or 1565,[78] for what reason is not known. In 1583 the vicar, James Steele, was alleged to have leased the vicarage and to have left the town.[79] In 1585, when he may still have been absent, the churchwardens complained that services were not

[41] *Tax. Eccl.* (Rec. Com.), 189.
[42] *Valor Eccl.* (Rec. Com.), ii. 137; P.R.O., E 123/7, f. 285v.
[43] *Rep. Com. Eccl. Revenues*, 840–1.
[44] *Reg. Malm.* ii. 75–8.
[45] W.R.O., tithe award.
[46] *Reg. Malm.* i. 121.
[47] *Cal. Pat.* 1408–13, 417.
[48] W.R.O., D 1/24/141/1.
[49] Ibid. D 1/24/141/2.
[50] Ch. Com. file 34228; ibid. NB 5/116B; Soc. Antiq. MS. 817, ix, f. 9; see below, p. 158.
[51] Ch. Com. file, NB 5/116B. [52] Ibid. 83703.
[53] *Cal. Chart. R.* 1226–57, 400.
[54] *Valor Eccl.* (Rec. Com.), ii. 119.
[55] P.R.O., E 315/102, ff. 28–9.
[56] Ibid. C 3/109/19.
[57] Aubrey, *Topog. Coll.* ed. Jackson, 267.
[58] *Reg. Malm.* ii. 125, 127.
[59] Ibid. ii. 340–1; P.R.O., E 318/Box 18/874.

[60] *L. & P. Hen. VIII*, xix (2), p. 414.
[61] *Reg. Malm.* ii. 113. [62] Ibid. i. 119; ii. 192–3.
[63] *Cal. Pat.* 1385–9, 511.
[64] P.R.O., E 301/58, no. 35.
[65] *Reg. Malm.* ii. 75–8. [66] *Cal. Close*, 1377–81, 528.
[67] Phillipps, *Wilts. Inst.* i. 63.
[68] *Cal. Papal Reg.* xiii (2), 596.
[69] *L. & P. Hen. VIII*, xiv (2), p. 351.
[70] Phillipps, *Wilts. Inst.* i. 210.
[71] *W.A.M.* i. 249.
[72] Ibid. viii. 587.
[73] Leland, *Itin.* ed. Toulmin Smith, i. 132.
[74] *L. & P. Hen. VIII*, xix (2), p. 414; P.R.O., E 318/Box 20/1074.
[75] P.R.O., E 301/58, no. 36.
[76] Phillipps, *Wilts. Inst.* i. 210, 221; W.R.O., D 1/43/2, f. 22.
[77] W.R.O., D 1/43/1, f. 23v.
[78] Phillipps, *Wilts. Inst.* i. 221–2.
[79] P.R.O., E 123/7, f. 285v.

MALMESBURY
The nave of the abbey church, built in the 12th century

The abbey church from the south

The west tympanum in the porch of the abbey church

MALMESBURY

held at the proper times and that there was no curate.[80]

In 1651 the alderman and burgesses granted to Robert Harpur, the vicar, rights of pasture on King's Heath as a mark of esteem.[81] In 1661 the bishop of Salisbury mentioned Malmesbury among places, whose incumbents were 'busy, turbulent' men, which he was unable to bring to good order; Simon Gawen was expelled from the vicarage in 1662.[82] Between 1643 and 1686 there were several cases of witchcraft in the town,[83] and Aubrey reported that seven or eight witches from Malmesbury were hanged in the 1670s.[84]

Vicars of Malmesbury received 20s. a year from each of three annual sermon charities, founded by Michael Wickes, Elizabeth Hodges, and Robert Cullerne in 1695, c. 1723, and in 1758 respectively. No payment was received from Hodges's charity in or after the late 19th century,[85] but payments from Wickes's and Cullerne's were still made in the late 20th.[86]

John Copson, vicar 1749 to c. 1786, was from 1765 also vicar of Kemble (now Glos.).[87] In 1783 he lived at Kemble and a curate, who was also curate of Ashley (now Glos.), served Malmesbury, including Corston and Rodbourne chapels. Services were then held at Malmesbury on Sunday afternoons and additionally at festivals and in Lent. Communion was celebrated four times a year and there were usually c. 50 communicants.[88] From 1879 until the benefices were united Malmesbury and Westport vicarages were held in plurality.[89]

ST. PAUL'S church was so called in 1191.[90] In 1542 all that remained of it was the west tower, then used as a house, and part of the east end, used as a town hall.[91] Reports in 1556 and 1585 that a church in Malmesbury needed repair[92] may refer to St. Paul's and, if they did, indicate some hope of its restoration as the parish church. Part of it may have continued in ecclesiastical use until the 1630s; there were said to have been marriages and sermons at St. Paul's until then.[93] The east end was probably used for meetings of the corporation until the 18th century,[94] and in the late 18th century was apparently a poorhouse.[95] When it was demolished in 1852 it was said to have long been used as a timber warehouse.[96] The tower was standing in 1988 and then as earlier housed bells rung for services in the abbey church.[97] It was built in the 14th century, of limestone rubble with ashlar dressings, and has three stages.

Before the Dissolution the abbey church[98] was apparently dedicated to St. Mary and St. Aldhelm.[99] In the early 20th century an additional or alternative dedication was to *ST. PETER AND ST. PAUL*.[1] In 1988 all four saints were invoked.[2] Nothing survives of the churches and other buildings of the abbey which stood before the 12th century.[3] Parts of the crossing, transepts, and nave[4] of the 12th-century church survive and footings found by excavation indicate a semicircular ambulatory at the east end. The surviving parts suggest that the church had arcades, a triforium, a clerestory, and a timber roof, and that the whole was built to one design in the later 12th century. The arcades were of nine bays and the transepts each of three bays; chapels probably extended eastwards from the outer bay of each transept.[5] The south doorway and porch were richly decorated with stone sculptures representing the apostles and scenes from the Old and New Testaments.[6] The cloister was to the north and was probably surrounded by other buildings although only one wall, to the east and presumably part of the chapter house, has been traced. Because the ground falls steeply north of the cloister, the dormitory and its undercroft seem likely to have run east–west. The vaulted 13th-century undercroft incorporated in Abbey House[7] may have been at the end of or beside the dormitory range. Another probably 13th-century range, incorporated in the Old Bell hotel west of the church,[8] may have been part of a building which, according to the usual plan of a monastery, consisted of the inner gatehouse and the abbot's lodging. By the 16th century, however, the abbot's lodging was apparently south-east of the church. Late 13th-century improvements and additions included alterations to the chapter house and the building of a new infirmary;[9] neither building survives. In the early 14th century the nave and transepts were vaulted and the clerestories altered and, at the west end, rebuilt. Flying buttresses were added to the nave to support the vault, the parapets of the nave and aisles were reconstructed, and the porch walls were made thicker, perhaps to support a tower. A first-floor room, but no tower, was built over the porch. A tower was built over the two western bays of the nave c. 1400. A central tower, perhaps built in the 12th century, was apparently heightened and topped with a tall spire of wood and lead in the later Middle Ages. It fell probably in the early 16th century.[10] The west tower was standing in 1660 but fell soon afterwards, destroying the south-west corner of the nave.[11] When the nave became the parish church a wall was built between it and the crossing. After the west tower fell a wall was built across the nave three bays from the west end. That wall had a window with wooden tracery which in

[80] W.R.O., D 1/43/6, f. 31AV.
[81] Luce, *Hist. Malm.* 99.
[82] *Calamy Revised*, ed. Matthews, 218.
[83] *W.A.M.* xxiv. 159–64; *Wilts. Q. Sess. Rec.* ed. Cunnington, 225.
[84] Aubrey, *Nat. Hist. Wilts.* ed. Britton, 121–2.
[85] *Endowed Char. Wilts.* (N. Div.), 672–3, 678–9.
[86] Ibid. 685, 688, 690; inf. from the vicar.
[87] Phillipps, *Wilts. Inst.* ii. 73, 93; *W.N. & Q.* viii. 225.
[88] *Vis. Queries, 1783* (W.R.S. xxvii), pp. 150–1.
[89] *Clergy List* (1892); *Crockford* (1907 and later edns.).
[90] *Reg. Malm.* i. 374–5.
[91] Leland, *Itin.* ed. Toulmin Smith, i. 171.
[92] W.R.O., D 1/43/2, f. 22v.; D 1/43/6, f. 31AV.
[93] Nightingale, *Wilts. Plate*, 203; Soc. Antiq. MS. 817, ix, f. 9.

[94] Above, local govt. (boro. govt.).
[95] Camden, *Brit.* (1806), i. 142.
[96] Soc. Antiq. MS. 817, ix, f. 3v.
[97] Below.   [98] See plate facing this page.
[99] *V.C.H. Wilts.* iii. 228.
[1] *Kelly's Dir. Wilts.* (1903, 1911).
[2] Inf. from the vicar.
[3] *V.C.H. Wilts.* iii. 228.   [4] See plate facing p. 156.
[5] *Archaeologia*, lxiv, pl. lxvi.
[6] *Jnl. Brit. Arch. Assoc.* [3rd ser.], xxviii. 40–54; see plate facing this page.
[7] Above, introduction.   [8] Ibid.
[9] *Archaeologia*, lxiv. 401–5.
[10] Leland, *Itin.* ed. Toulmin Smith, i. 131; *W.A.M.* xxxviii. 473.
[11] Aubrey, *Topog. Coll.* ed. Jackson, 255–6.

1823 was replaced by one in stone made to designs by H. E. Goodridge. A plaster vault, presumably imitating the surviving 14th-century vaulting, was then built over the western bays of the nave and a gallery and an organ were built against the west wall.[12] Major alterations since then include the extension of the south aisle and clerestory in

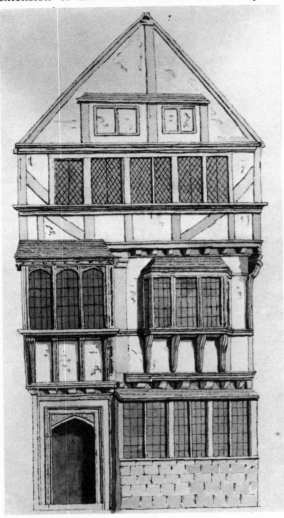

THE VICARAGE HOUSE IN 1790

1900,[13] the vaulting of the porch in 1905,[14] and the restoration of the upper room in 1912.[15] Between 1926 and 1928 the plaster part of the nave vault was renewed in stone and the gallery was removed.[16]

A chalice valued at 40s. was stolen from St. Paul's church in 1383 or 1384;[17] no other record survives of plate used in that church. Chalices of

1575 and 1631, the latter given in 1632, and a paten of 1702 belonged to the parish c. 1890.[18] That plate, a chalice of 1703, and other plate mainly of the late 19th century and the 20th, some from Westport church, belonged to the parish in 1988.[19]

In 1987 eight bells hung in the tower of St. Paul's. The oldest was one cast in Bristol c. 1500; one of 1610 was cast by a member of the Purdue family. A bell of 1640, perhaps cast by A. Hughes, and one of 1703 by William Cor were recast by Mears & Stainbank in 1910, and a bell of 1739 was recast in 1896 by Llewellins & James. Three new bells were cast in 1951 by Gillett & Johnston.[20]

Registers of baptisms, marriages, and burials survive from 1591.[21]

ROMAN CATHOLICISM. In 1865 a site in Cross Hayes was bought for a Roman Catholic church,[22] which was in the charge of Missionaries of St. Francis de Sales from 1867.[23] By 1876 that church had been replaced by a new stone building in a plain 14th-century style.[24] The former church was used as a school from 1876 or earlier until c. 1932.[25] By will proved 1923 C. J. Pollen gave the income from an invested sum, then £22 yearly, for the use of a Roman Catholic priest in Malmesbury.[26]

PROTESTANT NONCONFORMITY. Simon Gawen, ejected from Malmesbury vicarage in 1662, preached in the town until his death in 1672.[27] Other dissenting ministers in the town in the late 17th century included Henry Chandler, a Presbyterian recorded there in 1687,[28] and Samuel Clifford, formerly rector of East Knoyle, who preached in Malmesbury between 1695 and 1699.[29] Until the late 18th century nonconformity in the town was concentrated in the Westport part. In 1676 there were 5 nonconformists in Malmesbury, 18 in Westport;[30] in 1715 a Presbyterian minister in Westport was said to serve a congregation of 160;[31] and in 1783 the curate of Malmesbury reported that there were many dissenters of various denominations in the parish, but that their teachers lived elsewhere,[32] presumably in Westport.

An Anabaptist parishioner of Malmesbury refused to allow his child to be baptized in 1660[33] and in 1672 a house in Malmesbury may have been licensed for Baptist meetings.[34] A chapel was built in Westport parish, in Abbey Row on the boundary with Malmesbury parish, in or before 1695 and another built on the same site for Strict Baptists in 1802 was open in 1987.[35] Several Quaker families lived in Burton Hill

12 *Gent. Mag.* ii. 170 n.; Wilts. Cuttings, i. 154.
13 Bristol R.O., EP/J/6/2/164, pet. for faculty.
14 *W.A.M.* xxxviii. 479.
15 Bristol R.O., EP/J/6/2/164, faculty papers, 1912.
16 *W.A.M.* xliii. 498–9; Wilts. Cuttings, xi. 196–8.
17 *Proc. before Justices*, ed. B. H. Putnam (Ames Foundation), 387.
18 Nightingale, *Wilts. Plate*, 202.
19 Inf. from the vicar.
20 Walters, *Wilts. Bells*, 128–30; inf. from the vicar.
21 W.R.O. 1589/1–16.
22 Ibid. 212A/38/37/27.

23 *V.C.H. Wilts.* iii. 96.
24 J. Bird, *Hist. Malm.* 202.   25 Below, educ.
26 W.R.O., Char. Com., Malmesbury, 1.
27 *Calamy Revised*, ed. Matthews, 218.
28 Dr. Williams's Libr., Wilson MS. F i, p. 155.
29 *Calamy Revised*, ed. Matthews, 122.
30 *Compton Census*, ed. Whiteman, 128.
31 Dr. Williams's Libr., Wilson MS. F i, p. 155.
32 *Vis. Queries, 1783* (W.R.S. xxvii), p. 150.
33 Soc. Antiq. MS. 817, ix, f. 9.
34 *Meeting Ho. Certs.* (W.R.S. xl), pp. 174–5.
35 Below, Westport, nonconf.

between 1669 and 1750.[36] A house in Malmesbury parish, probably in Burton Hill, was certified in 1695 for Quaker meetings.[37] A Quaker Sunday school was opened in Malmesbury in 1827, and in 1833 had 50 pupils,[38] but there is no record of a meeting in the town.

Between 1739 and 1741 John Wesley preached three or four times in Malmesbury.[39] John Davis (d. 1796), chaplain of Lea and Cleverton and curate of Garsdon, held evangelical services in a cottage in the town[40] and some of his congregation may have become Methodists c. 1800.[41] In 1814 and 1825 Primitive Methodists met in the former Ebenezer chapel in Silver Street,[42] but they had no permanent church in the town until 1856 when a chapel was built in Bristol Street in Westport parish.[43] A chapel in the Triangle in Westport was open in 1987. Wesleyan Methodist services were held in the town hall from 1882 to 1886, when a chapel was opened in Cross Hayes.[44] The chapel had been closed by 1919.[45]

In 1745 John Cennick, a follower of George Whitefield, invited the Moravian Brethren to take charge of congregations in north Wiltshire founded by his preaching, including one in Malmesbury.[46] A Moravian church may have been in the town since 1742.[47] In 1770 a chapel was built near the junction of Oxford Street and Cross Hayes Lane. On Census Sunday in 1851 morning service was attended by 96 adults and 51 children; 122 adults attended evening service and a school was held in the afternoon.[48] The chapel was open in 1987. Registers of births and baptisms for the years 1827–40 and of burials 1826–40 survive.[49]

A cottage in Malmesbury certified in 1792 for Independent meetings[50] may have been used for John Davis's evangelical services.[51] Before 1800 two cottages in Silver Street were converted for use as the Ebenezer chapel by all or part of his congregation. In 1812 the congregation was united with that of Westport Congregational church, formerly the Presbyterian or Independent chapel, and the Ebenezer chapel was sold soon afterwards. A new meeting house was opened in Silver Street as a branch of the Westport church in 1836, and from 1841 was a separate church. The building was enlarged or rebuilt in 1848. On Census Sunday in 1851 the three services in the chapel, again called the Ebenezer chapel, were each attended by a congregation of between 150 and 200; attendance was said to be lower than usual.[52] In 1914, because there was no settled minister, it was proposed to reunite the chapel with Westport Congregational

church; the proposal was resisted by the Silver Street deacons,[53] apparently successfully. The chapel had been closed by 1974.[54]

Other meeting houses in Malmesbury were certified in 1825 and 1827, and in 1842 a hall was certified.[55] From 1948 meetings of an Assemblies of God Pentecostal church were held in the town; the church occupied a building in Silver Street from 1967 and was open in 1987.[56]

EDUCATION. A school may have been opened in the former hospital of St. John after the building was acquired by Malmesbury corporation in 1580.[57] The agreement of 1609 concerning the borough's government required that, of £20 paid annually by the alderman and burgesses for their inclosures on King's Heath, £10 should be paid to a schoolmaster.[58] From 1629 or earlier the payment was in the form of a rent charge on some of the inclosures.[59] The payment was confirmed by the borough charter of 1696. In 1695 Michael Wickes endowed the schoolmaster with an additional £10 a year from land in Great Somerford.[60] The school was apparently held in the part of the former hospital also used as a court room.[61] Instruction was free; in 1714 a master was dismissed for leaving the town and appointing a deputy who demanded fees.[62] There were 25 pupils in 1818,[63] and in 1858, when 50 pupils attended in wet weather and 20 in fine, the school was described by its master as little better than a refuge on a wet day.[64] In the late 19th century the school was attended only by sons of members of the corporation or freemen of Malmesbury. It was closed in 1890 and the warden and freemen of Malmesbury gave the rent charge to the National school provided that it accepted 20 sons of freemen. Payment of the rent charge to the school ceased on introduction of free elementary education in 1891.[65] Under a Scheme of 1910 the rent charge provided exhibitions at secondary schools or technical institutions for boys and girls resident in Malmesbury, preferably the children of freemen.[66] After 1890 occasional payments were made from Wickes's charity to schools in the town.[67]

In 1634 Robert Arch gave 11 a., mostly in Lea and Cleverton parish, for the general good of Malmesbury borough.[68] In 1818 the income of £55 was used for a school attended by c. 150 pupils.[69] By 1834 the income had fallen to £33. It then paid for a free school for 45 girls held in a room over

[36] W.N. & Q. ii. 290, 463, 519; iii. 228–9; iv. 212, 287; v. 224–5, 305, 515, 517, 550; vi. 82, 133–4.
[37] Meeting Ho. Certs. (W.R.S. xl), p. 5.
[38] Educ. Enq. Abstract, 1042.
[39] J. Wesley, Works (1872), i. 253, 259, 273, 299.
[40] V.C.H. Wilts. iii. 132.
[41] Moffatt, Hist. Malm. 159.
[42] Britton, Beauties of Wilts. iii. 90; G. L. Jenkins, Nonconf. in Malm. (1895), 26; below.
[43] Wilts. Cuttings, xxvii. 311; below, Westport, nonconf.
[44] Jenkins, Nonconf. in Malm. 49.
[45] W.R.O., G 21/160/2.
[46] V.C.H. Wilts. iii. 130–1.
[47] Jenkins, Nonconf. in Malm. 49.
[48] P.R.O., HO 129/252/2/6/4.
[49] Ibid. RG 4/2237.
[50] Meeting Ho. Certs. (W.R.S. xl), p. 40.
[51] Above.
[52] Jenkins, Nonconf. in Malm. 21–3, 27; P.R.O., HO 129/252/2/1/2.
[53] W.R.O. 1418/22.   [54] Wilts. Gaz. 10 Jan. 1974.
[55] Meeting Ho. Certs. (W.R.S. xl), pp. 108, 114, 154.
[56] Inf. from Mr. H. Latham, 4 Silver Street.
[57] W.A.M. liii. 123.
[58] P.R.O., STAC 8/290/22; above, local govt. (boro. govt.).
[59] W.A.M. liii. 123.
[60] Endowed Char. Wilts. (N. Div.), 672–3; below, charities.
[61] W.A.M. liii. 123; Endowed Char. Wilts. (N. Div.), 683.
[62] Malmesbury boro. rec., ct. bk. 1600–1721.
[63] Educ. of Poor Digest, 1032.
[64] Acct. of Wilts. Schs. 32.
[65] P.R.O., ED 49/8215; below.
[66] Char. Com. file.
[67] P.R.O., ED 49/8215.
[68] Endowed Char. Wilts. (N. Div.), 674.
[69] Educ. of Poor Digest, 1032.

the porch of the abbey church; lace making was among the subjects taught.[70] The school was open in 1873[71] but apparently closed soon afterwards. In 1908 the endowment was used for Malmesbury and Westport church schools,[72] and in 1911 provided scholarships for pupils from the town attending secondary schools.[73]

By will dated 1723 Elizabeth Hodges gave £30 yearly to schools in Malmesbury and other bequests to schools in nearby parishes. The provisions of the will were executed in 1730 when a Chancery decree ordered the foundation of a school for 15 boys.[74] The school's income and the number of its pupils were unchanged in 1846.[75] In 1869 the school was amalgamated with Westport Church of England school.[76] A Scheme of 1915 provided that the endowment should promote the education of children in the town by the award of exhibitions or other means. The annual income was between £10 and £15 in the 1960s.[77] In 1987 a share of the £67.50 given by the charity was received by schools in Malmesbury.[78]

A school for Malmesbury and Westport parishes was built in or before 1851 beside Sherston Road on a site then said to be in Westport parish,[79] but probably that in a detached part of Bremilham parish on which additional buildings, including a teacher's house, were erected in 1855–7. In 1857 it was attended by 63 boys and 34 girls.[80] From 1859 Westport Church of England school was a National school for boys only,[81] and in 1872 there were 247 pupils.[82] Another Church of England school for Malmesbury parish, built in 1857 in Cross Hayes, was for girls and infants.[83] In 1858 it had 220 pupils.[84] Average attendance at the two schools totalled 471 in 1909–10, 301 in 1921–2.[85] Both were closed in 1964 when a new primary school was opened in the old grammar school in Tetbury Hill.[86] A new school was built on the Tetbury Hill site in 1983; in 1988 it had 290 pupils on roll.[87]

A secondary school was opened in the town hall in 1896. It moved to new buildings on the west side of Tetbury Hill in 1903.[88] As Malmesbury grammar school it was attended by c. 240 in 1948.[89] A new school was built 750 m. north of it in 1964. A secondary modern school was built north of Sherston Road in Brokenborough parish in 1954;[90] it then had 450 pupils. The buildings of that school, the grammar school, and Westport Church

of England school were used by a comprehensive school known as Malmesbury school from 1971; in 1988 it had 809 pupils on roll.[91]

The Roman Catholic school, built in Cross Hayes in 1869,[92] using the former church by 1876,[93] run by Sisters of St. Joseph of Annecy from 1884,[94] was known as St. Joseph's school. In 1892 average attendance was 60;[95] numbers changed little before 1922.[96] A new school was built in Holloway in 1932–3; it had c. 90 pupils in 1935–6.[97] In 1988 there were 98 children on roll from Malmesbury, Brinkworth, Hullavington, Crudwell, and Sherston.[98]

Other schools in the town included one kept by J. M. Moffatt (d. 1802), minister of Westport Presbyterian chapel,[99] and one held by the three daughters of Thomas Milsome in 1806.[1] In 1830 there were five and in 1842 seven schools in addition to the endowed schools in the town; most were probably in Westport parish. They included two ladies' boarding schools in 1830; in 1842 one was in Burton Hill.[2] Burton Hill House was used as a private school during the Second World War. Since 1945 it has been a residential school for physically handicapped children. In 1987 there were 32 pupils.[3]

CHARITIES FOR THE POOR. From 1584 the alderman and burgesses were using the former hospital of St. John as an almshouse and possibly a school,[4] and from 1609 they gave £10 of the £20 paid for their inclosures on King's Heath to maintain five inmates of it; from 1629 or earlier the £10 was a rent charge on particular inclosures,[5] and in 1696 its payment was confirmed by the borough charter. From 1695 the almshouse also received £10 a year from Michael Wickes's charity. In the early 20th century it comprised three cottages, providing accommodation for six widows of freemen of Malmesbury.[6] Between 1927 and 1967 it was rarely full and was sometimes empty. It was converted to house three people and filled in 1967.[7]

In 1612 Thomas Cox gave the income from 40s. to be distributed to the poor of Malmesbury on Good Friday annually.[8] Nothing more is known of the bequest. In 1641 Robert Jenner built almshouses near the corner of Oxford Street and Holloway for eight people.[9] In 1643 he gave a rent

[70] *Endowed Char. Wilts.* (N. Div.), 674.
[71] P.R.O., ED 21/18532.
[72] Below.
[73] W.R.O., Char. Com., Malmesbury, 1.
[74] *Educ. of Poor Digest*, 1032.
[75] *Endowed Char. Wilts.* (N. Div.), 687–8; Nat. Soc. *Inquiry, 1846–7*, Wilts. 8–9.
[76] Glos. R.O., D 1571/R 44; below.
[77] Char. Com. file.
[78] Inf. from clerk to Eliz. Hodges Trust, Courtfield, Tetbury, Glos.
[79] W.R.O. 782/69; P.R.O., ED 7/131, no. 185.
[80] *Return of Non-Provided Schs.* 25; *Endowed Char. Wilts.* (N. Div.), 696; *Acct. of Wilts. Schs.* 48; P.R.O., ED 7/131, no. 185.
[81] *Kelly's Dir. Wilts.* (1859 and later edns.).
[82] P.R.O., ED 21/18532.
[83] *Endowed Char. Wilts.* (N. Div.), 696–7; date on bldg.
[84] *Acct. of Wilts. Schs.* 32.
[85] *Bd. of Educ., List 21, 1911* (H.M.S.O.), 550; *1922*, 361.
[86] Hudson, *Hill Top Town*, 31–2; below.
[87] Inf. from Chief Educ. Officer, Co. Hall, Trowbridge.

[88] Inf. from Mr. G. Allnatt, Malmesbury Sch.
[89] *Town Guide* (1948).
[90] Hudson, *Hill Top Town*, 31–2.
[91] Inf. from Mr. Allnatt. [92] P.R.O., ED 7/131, no. 96.
[93] Bird, *Hist. Malm.* 202. [94] *V.C.H. Wilts.* iii. 97.
[95] P.R.O., ED 7/131, no. 186.
[96] *Bd. of Educ., List 21, 1911* (H.M.S.O.), 550; *1914*, 552; *1919*, 362; *1922*, 361.
[97] Ibid. *1936*, 425; W.R.O., F 8, corresp. file, primary schs., special ser., Malmesbury R.C. St. Joseph's.
[98] Inf. from the head teacher, St. Joseph's Sch.
[99] *V.C.H. Wilts.* iii. 123 n.; *D.N.B.*
[1] W.R.O. 805/22.
[2] Pigot, *Nat. Com. Dir.* (1830), 805; (1842), 20.
[3] Inf. from the headmaster, Burton Hill Ho. Sch.
[4] W.R.O., D 1/43/5; above, educ.
[5] P.R.O., STAC 8/290/22; above, local govt. (boro. govt.).
[6] *Endowed Char. Wilts.* (N. Div.), 672–3, 684; below.
[7] *Almshos. Gaz.* lxx. 2–3; *Country Life*, 3 Dec. 1959; W.R.O., Char. Com., Malmesbury, 1.
[8] Soc. Antiq. MS. 817, ix, f. 9.
[9] W.R.O. 161/133, Sansum v. Jenner; 1589/28.

charge of £40 from Widhill manor in Cricklade for their upkeep and by will dated 1651 provided for the payment to continue. In the later 17th century and the early 18th actions were brought against his heirs for failure to pay the rent charge; payment ceased before c. 1740. Four of the almshouses were demolished in 1825 and the remainder in the later 19th century.[10]

In 1654 Henry Grayle gave a rent charge of £10 yearly from lands in Great Somerford to apprentice poor children of Malmesbury. In the 19th century two children were usually apprenticed each year. Three boys were apprenticed in 1904; beneficiaries were usually from the borough but sometimes from St. Paul Malmesbury Without.[11]

E. Waite (d. 1661) gave by will £3 a year to the poor of the borough and Burton Hill. By a deed of 1774 Anne Rowles gave two thirds of the income from £100 to the poor of Malmesbury parish. In the 1830s the income from the two charities was distributed together; each beneficiary received 6d. In 1904 Waite's charity was distributed separately; adults received 6d. each and children 3d.[12] No record has been found of payments after 1910.[13] By a Scheme of 1907 Rowles's charity was united with that of William Arnold. The combined income, then c. £17, was thereafter used to buy coal for elderly residents or widows in the borough and Burton Hill.[14] In the later 20th century the income was allowed to accumulate and few payments were made.[15]

In 1695 Michael Wickes gave the income from lands in Great Somerford for charitable purposes in Malmesbury, including payments to St. John's almshouse, the free school, and the vicar of Malmesbury. The residue was to be distributed as the trustees thought fit. There was apparently little residue until the school was closed in 1890.[16]

Thereafter the money was given to other Malmesbury institutions; in 1914 recipients of a total of £68 included the cottage hospital, the lying-in society, and the mayor's coal fund.[17]

Benefactions under the will of Elizabeth Hodges, dated 1723, included £10 yearly for poor housekeepers of Malmesbury. From 1820 equal payments were made to 20 of the second poor; beneficiaries were nominated for life. Similar payments were made in 1904.[18] The charity's income remained c. £10 in 1960.[19] In 1987 payments totalling £175 were made to poor residents of Malmesbury and of three other parishes named in the founder's will.[20]

By a deed of 1758 Robert Cullerne gave £17 10s. of a rent charge of £20 from lands in Lea and Cleverton to be given to the poor of Malmesbury (presumably the borough), of Burton Hill, and of Westport; each family was to receive 5s. annually. In 1904 payments were probably to individuals and each received 2s. 6d.,[21] in 1975–6 payments of 25p each were made to 87 applicants,[22] and similar payments were made in 1987.[23]

By will dated 1778 William Arnold gave the income from £400 to buy bread for the poor of Malmesbury. In 1904 the income, £14 8s. 4d., was used to buy bread for the poor of the borough and Burton Hill.[24] By a Scheme of 1907 the charity was united with that of Anne Rowles.[25]

May Moore (d. 1978) gave by will a house in Abbey Row and £10,000 to house and care for the elderly. In 1983 it was declared that the endowment should be used to provide grants, clothing, or travel for elderly residents within the boundaries of the former borough, and that an administrator should occupy the house. The yearly income was then c. £1,300.[26]

CORSTON

CORSTON was a village, chapelry, and tithing in the south-western corner of Malmesbury parish. In 1839 its lands measured c. 1,140 a. (461 ha.).[27] They may have been those of a 10-hide estate beside the 'Corsaburna', later called Gauze brook,[28] apparently the subject of a grant in 701.[29] In 1086 Corston was part of Malmesbury abbey's large estate called Brokenborough. Corston's boundaries had apparently been fixed by c. 1100 when all except its northern one were surveyed

with others of the Brokenborough estate; they may have been roughly those of c. 1840, when the northern boundary was a little north of Gauze brook, but few landmarks on them c. 1100 can now be traced.[30] In the later 13th century Corston was apparently part of the abbey's Cowfold estate,[31] but later may again have been a separate estate; possibly in the 12th century, certainly before 1341, a church was built there.[32]

In 1377 there were 46 poll-tax payers in Corston,

[10] *Endowed Char. Wilts.* (N. Div.), 677; above, local govt. (par. govt.).
[11] *Endowed Char. Wilts.* (N. Div.), 678, 689.
[12] Ibid. 678, 689–90.
[13] W.R.O., Char. Com., Malmesbury, 1.
[14] Ibid.; Char. Com. file; below.
[15] Inf. from Mr. T. Winch, Westport Granary.
[16] *Endowed Char. Wilts.* (N. Div.), 672–3, 685.
[17] W.R.O., Char. Com., Malmesbury, 1.
[18] *Endowed Char. Wilts.* (N. Div.), 675, 679–80, 688.
[19] Char. Com. file.
[20] Inf. from clerk to Eliz. Hodges Trust, Courtfield, Tetbury, Glos.
[21] *Endowed Char. Wilts.* (N. Div.), 678–9, 690.

[22] Char. Com. file.
[23] Inf. from Mr. J. A. G. Toogood, Forrester & Forrester, 59 High Street.
[24] *Endowed Char. Wilts.* (N. Div.), 679, 691.
[25] Above.
[26] Char. Com. file.
[27] W.R.O., tithe award.
[28] Finberg, *Early Wessex Chart.* p. 70; *V.C.H. Wilts.* ii, pp. 4, 88–9.
[29] Below, manor.
[30] *V.C.H. Wilts.* ii, p. 125; *Arch. Jnl.* lxxvii. 42–4, 88–90; W.R.O., tithe award; above, Brokenborough, manor.
[31] *Reg. Malm.* i. 174.
[32] *Inq. Non.* (Rec. Com.), 167; below, church.

a little below average for a place in Malmesbury hundred,[33] and Corston was of below average prosperity in the late 16th century.[34] Its population rose rapidly in the early 19th century, from 127 in 1801 to reach 171 in 1821 and 322 in 1851,[35] but had fallen to 304 by 1881.[36] Numbers increased again in the mid and late 20th century when married quarters were built for R.A.F. Hullavington and private and local authority houses were built in Corston village.[37]

The village lies beside Gauze brook at the north end of the chapelry. Its early focus may have been around a green where a road from Rodbourne joins the Malmesbury–Chippenham road; the church stands on rising ground in the north-eastern angle of the junction. In the early 18th century settlement extended north along the Malmesbury road to Gauze brook and Corston Mill, south to the farmstead later called Manor Farm, and east along the Rodbourne road to the farmstead later called Firs Farm.[38] Surviving buildings of that or earlier date include the possibly 17th-century Manor Farm, two stone cottages of 17th-century origin east of the main road, and the Hermitage, a 17th-century stone house south of the church. Only a few 18th-century cottages survive; some were rebuilt in the 19th century. The Radnor Arms west of the road was built and opened as an inn in the 1790s.[39] Firs Farm was largely rebuilt in the 19th century. The southern and eastern limits of the village remained unchanged until the 20th century. By 1828 settlement had spread north of Gauze brook to and beyond the boundary of the chapelry, mainly on the west side of the Malmesbury road.[40] There Newlands Cottage bears the date 1825; north of it Newlands Farm and Quarry House replaced other buildings in the later 19th century. The Bell inn, which stood west of the main road north of Gauze brook in 1881, had closed by 1899.[41] North of Gauze brook settlement also spread along Mill Lane in the mid and later 19th century when cottages and a nonconformist chapel were built west of the mill.[42] The Mill inn was open in 1910[43] and closed c. 1965.[44] Another chapel was built west and the vicarage house north of the church in the late 19th century; a reading room was built north-west of the church in 1904.[45] In 1933 three pairs of council houses were built 350 m. south-west of Manor Farm;[46] in the later 20th century a garage, on the site of a small group of gabled 17th-century cottages demolished in the 1960s,[47] and Kingway View, a row of bungalows, was built north of them. In the 1950s 22 council houses were built beside the Rodbourne road.

Manor Park, a private estate of eight houses and bungalows, was built north-east of Manor Farm in the 1970s. Elsewhere in the village there has been infilling in the late 20th century. The bridge carrying the Malmesbury–Chippenham road over Gauze brook was rebuilt in 1984.[48]

There was no substantial building in the chapelry outside the village in the early 18th century.[49] By 1773 a farmstead called the Bell had been built beside the boundary with Stanton St. Quintin south-west of the village. Another, Kingway, was built east of the Chippenham road south of the village between 1773 and 1828.[50] After its land was acquired for Hullavington airfield in 1935 Bell Farm was demolished and houses and other buildings for R.A.F. Hullavington were thereafter built on and around its site. They include 62 houses in Anson Place built in 1935–6 and 1948–9. In addition to the buildings the main north-east and south-west runway was built on the 115 ha. of Corston in the station, which also had land and buildings in Stanton St. Quintin and Hullavington.[51] Hangar Farm was built east of the Chippenham road near the airfield between 1959 and 1974.[52] The Plough, a small 19th-century stone building beside the Rodbourne road, was open as a public house in 1885;[53] it was closed in 1964.[54]

MANOR AND OTHER ESTATES. Corston seems to have been the 10-hide estate beside Gauze brook apparently granted by King Ine to Malmesbury abbey in 701.[55] Six hides in Corston, presumably the whole estate, were held of the abbey by Ranulph Flambard in 1086,[56] but later the abbey had no tenant in demesne. Corston passed to the Crown at the Dissolution[57] and in 1564 the manor of CORSTON was sold to Thomas Chadderton[58] (fl. 1567).[59] In 1569 it was bought from Thomas's creditors by his cousin William Chadderton,[60] who sold the lordship and most of the lands in 1573 to Sir Walter Hungerford.[61] Sir Walter (d. 1596)[62] was succeeded by his half-brother Sir Edward Hungerford (d. 1607),[63] whose relict Cecily, from 1608 wife of Francis Manners, from 1612 earl of Rutland, may have retained the manor until her death in 1653.[64] It was inherited by Sir Anthony Hungerford (d. 1657) and by his son Sir Edward,[65] who in 1682 conveyed the manor to his uncle Sir Giles Hungerford.[66] From Sir Giles (d. 1685) it passed like Stanton St. Quintin manor to his relict Margaret, to his son-in-law Robert Sutton, Baron Lexinton,

[33] V.C.H. Wilts. iv. 309.
[34] Taxation Lists (W.R.S. x), 52.
[35] V.C.H. Wilts. iv. 352.
[36] P.R.O., RG 11/2025; RG 11/2027.   [37] Below.
[38] W.R.O. 490/774.   [39] Ibid. 490/706.
[40] O.S. Map 1″, sheet 34 (1828 edn.).
[41] Ibid. 6″, Wilts. XIII (1888 edn.), XIII. NW. (1900 edn.); P.R.O., RG 11/2027.
[42] W.R.O., tithe award; O.S. Map 6″, Wilts. XIII (1888 edn.).
[43] W.R.O., Inland Revenue, val. reg. 9.
[44] Wilts. Cuttings, xxii. 277.
[45] Ch. Guide (1986).   [46] Date on bldg.
[47] Inf. from Co. Archivist, Co. Hall, Trowbridge.
[48] Date on bridge.   [49] W.R.O. 490/774.
[50] Andrews and Dury, Map (W.R.S. viii), pl. 13; O.S. Map 1″, sheet 34 (1828 edn.).

[51] Below, manor; O.S. Map 1/50,000, sheet 173 (1974 edn.); inf. from Defence Land Agent, Durrington.
[52] O.S. Maps 1/25,000, ST 98 (1959 edn.); 1/50,000, sheet 173 (1974 edn.).   [53] Ibid. 6″, Wilts. XIII (1888 edn.).
[54] Wilts. Cuttings, xxii. 277.
[55] Finberg, Early Wessex Chart. p. 70.
[56] V.C.H. Wilts. ii, p. 125.
[57] P.R.O., SC 6/Hen. VIII/3986, rot. 115.
[58] Ibid. E 318/Box 34/2307.
[59] Ibid. C 3/201/11.   [60] Ibid. REQ 2/178/30.
[61] Ibid. CP 25(2)/239/15 & 16 Eliz. I Mich. no. 742.
[62] Aubrey, Topog. Coll. ed. Jackson, 412.
[63] P.R.O., C 142/306, no. 160.
[64] Complete Peerage, xi. 262; W.R.O. 442/2.
[65] Aubrey, Topog. Coll. ed. Jackson, 412; E. M. Oliver, Memoirs of Hungerford Fam. (priv. print. 1930), 15.
[66] W.R.O. 490/73, abstr. of title, 1718.

and in the Bouverie family and with the viscountcy of Folkestone and the earldom of Radnor to Jacob, earl of Radnor (d. 1930).[67]

In 1905 Lord Radnor sold Manor farm, c. 330 a.,[68] probably to David Roberts, the owner in 1910[69] and 1912.[70] The farm was sold again in 1919,[71] and in 1927 belonged to Frank Sage.[72] In 1951 it was offered for sale as Manor farm, 155 a., and South Side farm, 143 a., by W. S. Tyler.[73] Since then those lands have been owned by members of the Eavis family, who held Manor farm, c. 330 a., in 1987.[74] Between 1910 and 1912 Lord Radnor sold Bell farm, 401 a., and 146 a., part of Lower Stanton farm based in Stanton St. Quintin, to Meredith Meredith-Brown (d. 1920), whose estate was broken up c. 1920. In 1919 or 1920 S. H. Jones bought Lower Stanton farm and 116 a. of Bell farm. Half those lands descended to his son Mr. S. Jones[75] who sold them as Hangar farm, 217 a., in 1989.[76] F. J. Huntley bought Bell farm in 1920, and in 1935 sold it to the state for Hullavington airfield.[77]

In 1575 William Chadderton sold the rest of Corston manor, c. 130 a. and rights of pasture, to Thomas Richman[78] (fl. 1576).[79] That estate was held c. 1580 by John Richman[80] (d. 1615), who was succeeded by his daughter Margaret, wife of Edmund James (d. 1620).[81] From Margaret (fl. 1664) it passed to her son Edmund James (d. by 1675) whose relict Anne married William Cole c. 1677. From Elizabeth, wife of Francis Goddard and a descendant of Margaret James's younger daughter, Cole bought the reversion of a moiety in 1691, and from Edward Brown, grandson of Margaret's elder daughter Margaret, he bought the reversion of the other in 1700. The manor descended with Bradfield manor in Hullavington to Cole's daughter Anne Cale and to her daughter Anne, wife of the Revd. Anthony Whistler (d. 1719). The Whistlers' son John[82] sold it in 1771 to William, earl of Radnor,[83] and it was reunited with the manor.

The rectorial tithes from Corston were due to Malmesbury abbey, passed to the Crown at the Dissolution,[84] and were probably all granted in 1606 to Laurence Baskerville, William Blake, and Roger Rogers,[85] perhaps for a member of the Bridges family. In 1622 John Bridges conveyed the tithes to Robert Bridges and his wife Elizabeth,[86] and in 1653 they were settled on Richard Bridges and his wife Eleanor. Richard was apparently succeeded in turn by his son George and by George's son George, who in 1731 sold the tithes to Richard Bromwich. By will proved 1753

Bromwich gave them to his wife Susannah (d. 1764), who devised them to her nephew John Melhuish. In 1791 Melhuish sold them to R. H. Gaby and Walter Gaby (d. c. 1811)[87] and in 1822 R. H. Gaby sold them to Jacob, earl of Radnor.[88] Thereafter they were merged.[89]

ECONOMIC HISTORY. In 1086 Ranulph Flambard's estate had land for 5 ploughteams, but only 3 teams worked it; 2 villani and 2 coscets had 2 teams, and 2 servi and a third team were apparently on the demesne. There were 10 a. of meadow, 15 a. of pasture, and woodland 3 furlongs long and 1 furlong broad.[90]

Customary tenants may have cultivated much of Corston's land in the late 13th century.[91] In the late 16th century almost two thirds of the lands were arable. There were fields called Ham, Up, and Broad lying respectively east, south, and west of Corston village. Another, West field, was in the south-west corner of the chapelry; the location of a fifth field, Old Lands, is not known. Most were presumably open fields, but all or part of Up field had been inclosed by the earlier 15th century. Most of the pasture lay in the south and beside the western boundary; there was presumably meadow land beside Gauze brook. Only c. 100 a. of pasture were common, and c. 200 a. of meadow and pasture were in closes; c. 60 a. of pasture, probably near the boundary with Hullavington, had been inclosed by the early 16th century. The tenants of both parts of Corston manor shared the common pasture; some also had grazing rights on 60 a. of King's Heath.[92]

The farm sold to Thomas Richman in 1575 was in 1574 a holding of 3 yardlands, including 34 a. of several pasture of which 12 a. had recently been inclosed, 90 a. of arable in the open fields, 6 a. of meadow, and rights of common pasture.[93] By 1691 most of the farm's arable had been converted to c. 160 a. of several pasture.[94] The copyholders of Corston owed cash payments instead of services of cutting and carrying hay from three meadows in Cole park,[95] and had earlier owed works of ploughing in Kemboro field in Burton Hill.[96] A leasehold comprised 98 a., including 80 a. of arable.[97]

By 1720 all Corston's lands had been inclosed.[98] Some were still copyhold in the late 18th century[99] but the larger holdings were probably leasehold. In 1800, by which date the two portions of the manor had been reunited, there were two large farms, of 354 a. and 409 a., and five of between

[67] Below, Stanton St. Quintin, manor.
[68] W.A.S. Libr., sale cat. xiv, no. 9.
[69] W.R.O., Inland Revenue, val. reg. 9.
[70] Ibid. G 7/500/1.   [71] W.A.S. Libr., sale cat. xiv, no. 9.
[72] W.R.O., G 7/515/9.
[73] W.A.S. Libr., sale cat. xxixC, no. 19.
[74] Inf. from Mr. J. Eavis, Manor Farm.
[75] W.R.O., Inland Revenue, val. reg. 9; ibid. G 7/500/1; G 7/515/9; below, Stanton St. Quintin, manor.
[76] Wilts. Times, 14 Jan. 1989.
[77] Inf. from Defence Land Agent, Durrington.
[78] W.R.O. 490/206, abstr. of title.
[79] Taxation Lists (W.R.S. x), 52.
[80] W.R.O. 442/1, f. 187v.
[81] P.R.O., C 142/350, no. 44; C 142/401, no. 88.
[82] W.R.O. 490/206, abstr. of title; above, Hullavington, manors.

[83] W.R.O. 490/206, deed, Whistler to earl of Radnor, 1771.
[84] Above, Malmesbury, manors.
[85] W.R.O. 490/13, abstr. of title.
[86] P.R.O., CP 25(2)/372/20 Jas. I Mich.
[87] W.R.O. 490/13, abstr. of title.
[88] Ibid. 490/213, deed, Gaby to earl of Radnor, 1822.
[89] Ibid. tithe award.
[90] V.C.H. Wilts. ii, p. 125.
[91] Reg. Malm. i. 174-7.
[92] W.R.O. 442/1; 490/206, deed, Chadderton to Richman, 1574; 490/774; Eton Coll. Mun. 4/94; 4/234D.
[93] W.R.O. 490/206, deed, Chadderton to Richman, 1574.
[94] Ibid. 490/206, deed, Goddard to Skermer, 1691.
[95] Ibid. 442/1.
[96] Reg. Malm. i. 186.
[97] W.R.O. 442/1.
[98] Ibid. 490/774.
[99] Ibid. 490/705.

20 a. and 60 a. each.[1] In 1839 Manor farm was 484 a., mainly in the north, and Bell farm was 455 a., mainly in the south. The chapelry was then half arable and half pasture; most of the arable was in the south and centre. There were 16 a. of wood beside the boundary with Rodbourne.[2] Coarse heath, 17 a. lying 700 m. south of the village, was worked as 60 allotments in 1834,[3] but not in 1839.[4] Pasture in Corston was used principally to graze sheep in the mid 19th century; there were over 1,100 in 1866.[5] In 1910 most of the land lay in four farms, Manor, 308 a., Bell, 401 a., Newlands, 119 a., and one of 146 a.[6] Manor farm was mainly pasture in the early 20th century.[7] It was later worked as two farms, in 1951 as Manor, 155 a., and South Side, 143 a., respectively northwest and south-east of the Malmesbury–Chippenham road. Both were mixed farms; there was more arable than pasture on Manor farm, more pasture than arable on South Side farm.[8] Thereafter the lands were again worked as a single farm. In 1987 Manor farm was a mixed holding; there was a dairy herd of 200, and wheat and barley were grown on c. 300 a., some of it in Hullavington parish.[9] Bell farm had been divided into holdings of 116 a. and 285 a. by 1927.[10] The larger portion, west of the Malmesbury–Chippenham road, went out of agricultural use in 1935.[11] The smaller, east of the road, was part of Lower Stanton farm; later, as part of Hangar farm, it was worked from a re-used hangar.[12]

There was a mill at Corston in 1086[13] and 1539.[14] A mill on Gauze brook was part of Corston manor in 1810.[15] It and the mill house were rebuilt in the early 19th century. The mill ceased working c. 1899.[16]

Stanton brickworks, east of the Malmesbury–Chippenham road 500 m. north of the boundary with Stanton St. Quintin, was probably open in 1861 and certainly in 1885; it was closed in the early 20th century.[17]

In 1834 there was a quarry, presumably for limestone, north of Corston church, and another at the north end of the village;[18] both had apparently been closed by 1885. Two more quarries were at the north end of the village, and another south of the brickworks, in 1899. By 1921 one of the quarries in the village had been closed.[19] The other and that near the brickworks remained open in 1927[20] but were disused in 1987.[21]

LOCAL GOVERNMENT. In the early 16th century and perhaps until the sale of the manor by the Crown in 1564, courts for Corston were held at a house in Cole park.[22] In 1561–2 the Crown held views of frankpledge and manor courts in spring and autumn.[23] Between 1712 and 1742 courts baron were usually held annually, in spring until 1718 and in autumn thereafter. From 1720 leet business was also transacted. A tithingman was appointed and the homage presented buildings to be repaired, watercourses to be cleaned, and the deaths of copyholders.[24] No court is recorded after c. 1790.[25]

Corston did not relieve its own poor, but in the later 18th century and the early 19th an overseer was appointed to deal only with Corston. In 1760–1 two people received regular relief totalling £7; occasional relief and other extraordinary costs amounted to £3. The number regularly relieved had risen to six by 1770–1, and £39 was spent on the poor in 1780–1.[26]

CHURCH. The shape of Corston church before it was rebuilt in the 19th century suggests that it was built in the 12th century.[27] A church at Corston may have been served from Malmesbury abbey until a vicarage of Malmesbury was ordained between 1191 and the mid 13th century, but none is recorded until 1341 when there was a chapel dependent on Malmesbury church.[28] Inhabitants of Corston had right of burial there in the 18th century,[29] and there is no evidence that they lacked it earlier. A recommendation in 1650 that Corston and Rodbourne should form a benefice[30] was apparently not implemented. In 1881 Corston with Rodbourne became a district chapelry, with an incumbent usually called a vicar. The advowson was assigned to Charlotte Kemble, patron of Malmesbury, and the vicar was apparently given part of the income of Malmesbury vicarage. In 1882 the advowson was given to the Crown in an exchange and the vicar's income was increased by £16 13s. 4d. from a private benefaction and by the same sum from the Ecclesiastical Commissioners.[31] A vicarage house was built in 1884.[32] The house was sold in 1985,[33] and in 1986 the benefice was united with the benefice of Great Somerford, Little Somerford, and Seagry: the Crown had the right to present at two of every five turns to the united benefice.[34]

Until 1881 vicars of Malmesbury usually appointed a curate to serve both Corston and Rodbourne churches.[35] In 1650 Simon Gawen served the two churches 'at the request of the greatest part of the inhabitants', who paid him tithes due

1 W.R.O. 490/707.
2 Ibid. tithe award.
3 Ibid. 1553/105.
4 Ibid. tithe award.
5 P.R.O., MAF 68/73, sheet 12.
6 W.R.O., Inland Revenue, val. reg. 9.
7 W.A.S. Libr., sale cat. xiv, no. 9.
8 Ibid. sale cat. xxixC, no. 19.
9 Inf. from Mr. J. Eavis, Manor Farm.
10 W.R.O., G 7/515/9.
11 Above, manor.
12 Wilts. Times, 14 Apr. 1989; local inf.
13 V.C.H. Wilts. ii, p. 125.
14 P.R.O., SC 6/Hen. VIII/3986, rot. 115.
15 W.R.O. 212A/27/48, survey of Corston.
16 O.S. Maps 6″, Wilts. XIII (1888 edn.), XIII. NW. (1900 edn.); Kelly's Dir. Wilts. (1899, 1903).
17 O.S. Map 6″, Wilts. XIII (1888 and later edns.); P.R.O., RG 9/1278.

18 W.R.O. 1553/105.
19 O.S. Map 6″, Wilts. XIII (1888 and later edns.).
20 W.R.O., G 21/501/1.
21 Local inf.
22 P.R.O., REQ 2/178/30.
23 Ibid. SC 2/209/16.
24 W.R.O. 212A/27/48, Corston manor ct. bk.
25 Ibid. 490/705.
26 Ibid. 1589/33.
27 Below.
28 Inq. Non. (Rec. Com.), 167; above, Malmesbury, churches.
29 W.R.O. 490/212.
30 W.A.M. xli. 5.
31 Lond. Gaz. 11 Jan. 1881, p. 120; ibid. 19 May 1882, p. 2350; Bristol R.O., EP/A/3/127; EP/A/4/2/3.
32 Ch. Com. file, NB 5/86c.
33 Ch. Guide (1986).
34 Ch. Com. file, NB 5/86c.
35 Cal. Pat. 1385–9, 237; W.N. & Q. vii. 548; Lond. Gaz. 10 Feb. 1882, p. 536; W.R.O., D 1/43/1, f. 23v.; Bristol R.O., EP/A/4/2/3.

to the vicar of Malmesbury.[36] In the late 18th century and the early 19th afternoon services were held on alternate Sundays at Corston.[37] The church was apparently served by the vicar of Malmesbury c. 1830.[38] On Census Sunday in 1851 a morning service at Corston was attended by 38 adults, a congregation said to be smaller than usual.[39] From 1951 the church with that at Rodbourne, was held in plurality with the benefice of Foxley with Bremilham; the incumbent usually lived at Corston.[40] After 1983 there was no resident incumbent.[41]

ALL SAINTS' church, so called in 1763,[42] is built of limestone rubble with ashlar dressings and has a chancel and a nave with north transept and south porch. Only the south doorway and the octagonal west bellcot, both of which are probably 15th-century, survive from the structure of a single-celled church which was rebuilt in 1881. The old church was a long narrow building, of similar size to the 12th-century nave of Rodbourne church.[43] A 15th-century screen, which divided the chancel and nave, a plain early 17th-century pulpit, and some wall tablets survive from its interior. The transept was added c. 1900 but other alterations which were proposed then, including the removal of a gallery, were not carried out until 1911 when the chancel was added.[44]

In 1553 plate weighing 2½ oz. was confiscated from Corston; a chalice weighing 8½ oz. was left. It was replaced in 1577 by another with paten cover for use at both Corston and Rodbourne. A paten of c. 1720, a flagon, and an almsdish were acquired by the chapels in the 19th century.[45] The chalice and the later plate were still held in 1987.[46]

There were two bells in 1553. A bell, said in 1927 to be ancient, and another, of 1884 by J. Warner & Sons,[47] were recast in 1930.[48] They hung in the church in 1986.[49]

NONCONFORMITY. A curate removed from Corston and Rodbourne in 1662, presumably for nonconformity, may have been the vicar of Malmesbury, Simon Gawen, or his nominee.[50] There were said to be many dissenters, including Quakers, in Corston and its neighbourhood in the late 17th century.[51]

A house at Corston was certified for Independent meetings in 1803[52] and a chapel was built north of the church in 1821. It was served in 1823 by John Evans, a minister from Malmesbury, who claimed that the congregation then numbered 200. In 1851 on Census Sunday 67 people attended the morning service, 127 the evening service.[53] The chapel was replaced by a new small Congregational chapel, of brick with stone dressings, built west of the church c. 1898; that chapel had been closed by 1921.[54] In 1825 a house at Corston was certified for meetings of Primitive Methodists.[55] The Zion chapel in Mill Lane was built in 1857[56] and opened in 1858 by Strict Baptists.[57] The small chapel, of stone rubble, had been closed by 1899.[58]

EDUCATION. There were two dame schools with a total of c. 20 pupils in Corston in 1858.[59] A school there in 1865[60] was presumably closed when the school at Rodbourne was extended to serve both villages in 1872.[61]

RODBOURNE

RODBOURNE is a village whose lands formed a long and narrow tithing and chapelry in the southeast corner of Malmesbury parish. The chapelry originated as an estate on the stream called Rodbourne given to Malmesbury abbey.[62] The stream was that south of Rodbourne village, joining the Avon at Great Somerford. The boundaries of Rodbourne's lands were described in the late 11th century or early 12th, when they were marked partly by the Rodbourne, Gauze brook, and the Avon.[63]

Little Somerford was given land west of the Avon in 1281,[64] but Rodbourne's other boundaries had apparently been changed little by 1839. The chapelry then comprised c. 1,350 a. (546 ha.).[65] Rodbourne had a church from the 12th century or earlier.[66]

In 1334 Corston and Rodbourne were assessed together for taxation at the above average sum of 56s. Rodbourne may then have been more prosperous than Corston and in 1377 had 69 poll-tax

[36] *W.A.M.* xli. 5.
[37] *Vis. Queries, 1783* (W.R.S. xxvii), p. 150; Ch. Com. file, NB 5/116B.
[38] *Rep. Com. Eccl. Revenues*, 840–1.
[39] P.R.O., HO 129/252/1/18/24.
[40] *Crockford* (1965–6 and later edns.); Ch. Com. file, NB 5/86c.
[41] *Ch. Guide* (1986).
[42] J. Ecton, *Thesaurus*, 404.
[43] *Ch. Guide* (1986); J. Buckler, watercolours in W.A.S. Libr., vol. vi. 32; see below, plate facing p. 237; below, Rodbourne, church.
[44] Bristol R.O., EP/J/6/2/110, pet. for faculty, corresp., consecration papers.
[45] Nightingale, *Wilts. Plate*, 195–6.
[46] Inf. from the rector, Great Somerford.
[47] Walters, *Wilts. Bells*, 66.
[48] *Kelly's Dir. Wilts.* (1939).   [49] *Ch. Guide* (1986).

[50] W.R.O., D 1/54/1/1, no. 70; above, church.
[51] Aubrey, *Topog. Coll.* ed. Jackson, 266.
[52] *Meeting Ho. Certs.* (W.R.S. xl), p. 59.
[53] P.R.O., HO 129/252/2/5/3; O.S. Map 6″, Wilts. XIII (1888 edn.); W.R.O. 1418/18, letter, Evans to Elliott.
[54] A. Antrobus, *Wilts. Congregational Union*, 45; O.S. Map 6″, Wilts. XIII. NW. (1925 edn.).
[55] *Meeting Ho. Certs.* (W.R.S. xl), p. 109.
[56] Date on bldg.
[57] R. W. Oliver, *Strict Bapt. Chapels Eng.* (Strict Bapt. Hist. Soc.), v. 33.
[58] O.S. Map 6″, Wilts. XIII. NW. (1900 edn.).
[59] *Acct. of Wilts. Schs.* 32.
[60] *Harrod's Dir. Wilts.* (1865).
[61] Below, Rodbourne, educ.
[62] Below, manor.
[63] *Arch. Jnl.* lxxvii. 88–90.
[64] *Reg. Malm.* ii. 219–20.
[65] W.R.O., tithe award.
[66] Below, church.

payers, well above the average for Malmesbury hundred.[67] It may have been less prosperous in the late 16th century.[68] In 1801 the population of the chapelry was 108. Numbers rose in succeeding decades, with some fluctuations, and reached a peak of 173 in 1851.[69] By 1881 they had fallen to 143,[70] and the decline apparently continued in the 20th century.

The buildings of Rodbourne village are strung out along a street behind wide verges which in 1773 opened out to form a central green on which the church stood. Settlement then extended northwards along lanes forming the green's eastern and western edges, and southwards along the road later called Pound Hill. The oldest buildings in the village are at its east and west ends; Rodbourne House to the east and a cottage to the west are of 17th-century origin. Some houses beside Pound Hill had been demolished by 1828; those which survived, on both sides of the Rodbourne stream, form a hamlet called Rodbourne Bottom. North of the stream Bottom Farm and south of the stream cottages and farm buildings were rebuilt in the 19th century. A cottage on the west side of Pound Hill bears the date 1836. By 1828 the lane on the west side of the green had been closed and the green made smaller. It and the wide verges east and west of it survived in the late 20th century, when trees stood on much of them. Between 1773 and 1828 cottages or farmsteads were built on the south side of the street between the church and Rodbourne House,[71] but some of them had been removed by 1842.[72] Much of the village was rebuilt in the mid 19th century by members of the Pollen family which owned Rodbourne manor; some buildings bear their arms or initials. Roman Cottage south of the street was built in 1845; Parsloe's Farm north of it was extended in 1852.[73] Both are of stone with dressings of local brick. Also on the south side of the street Manor Farm and a school were built in the mid 19th century. Thereafter little new building took place in the village; a house and a bungalow were built north of Rodbourne House in the late 20th century, and a water tower was built west of the church in 1951.[74]

There was a farmstead called Rodbourne Cleeve, 1 km. south of the church, in 1773[75] and probably earlier. Cleeve House was built on its site in 1899.[76] From 1970 until 1985 it was used as a children's home by Wiltshire county council.[77] Angrove Farm north-east of the village was built between 1828 and 1842.[78] Angrove Cottages, south-west of the farmstead, were built in the early 20th century to replace others east of the farmstead apparently demolished when the railway line was built in 1903.[79]

MANOR AND OTHER ESTATE. The 10 *manentes* of Rodbourne were apparently granted to Malmesbury abbey by King Ine in 701, although the abbey later claimed to have been given them as part of its Brokenborough estate in 956.[80] Rodbourne belonged to the abbey until the Dissolution.[81] In 1544 the Crown granted *RODBOURNE* manor to William Stumpe[82] (d. 1552). It passed to his son Sir James[83] (d. 1563) and to Sir James's daughter Elizabeth, wife of Henry Knyvett.[84] In 1573 Elizabeth and Henry conveyed the manor to Sir Giles Poole[85] (d. 1588). Poole was succeeded in turn by his son Sir Henry[86] (d. 1616) and Sir Henry's son Henry,[87] who sold it to Henry Danvers, earl of Danby, in 1642.[88] It passed with Malmesbury manor to the sisters of Henry Danvers (d. 1654), and with other Danvers lands may have been divided in 1673 when a moiety was probably assigned to Eleanor Lee, daughter of Danvers's sister Anne.[89] In 1683 Danvers's sister Elizabeth surrendered a moiety to James Bertie, earl of Abingdon, Eleanor's husband.[90] Abingdon was succeeded in 1699 by his son Montagu, earl of Abingdon,[91] who by 1720 had sold the whole manor to Walter Hungerford.[92] Walter (d. 1754) was succeeded by his nephew George Hungerford (d. 1764),[93] who devised a portion of Rodbourne to his wife Elizabeth and the rest to members of the Duke and Luttrell families.[94] On Elizabeth's death in 1816 all or part of the manor passed to her nephew Sir John Pollen, Bt., who held the whole manor in 1839.[95] From Sir John (d. 1863) the manor passed with the baronetcy to his nephew Richard (d. 1881), to Sir Richard's son Richard (d. 1918), and to that Sir Richard's sons Sir Richard (d. 1930) and Sir John.[96] About 1938 Sir John sold Angrove farm, 204 a. Thereafter the farm was held by members of the Palmer family until 1976 when it was bought by Mr. and Mrs. R. F. Parfitt, the owners in 1987.[97] The bulk of the estate passed from Sir John (d. 1959) to his kinsman Sir John Pollen, Bt., the owner in 1987.[98]

Rodbourne House, formerly the home of the Pollens, is apparently of early 17th-century origin and consists of a main east–west range. It was given a new south front and a west wing with a bow window at its north end in the later 18th century.

[67] *V.C.H. Wilts.* iv. 298, 309.
[68] *Taxation Lists* (W.R.S. x), 52.
[69] *V.C.H. Wilts.* iv. 352.
[70] P.R.O., RG 11/2025.
[71] *Andrews and Dury, Map* (W.R.S. viii), pl. 13; O.S. Map 1″, sheet 34 (1828 edn.).
[72] W.R.O., tithe award.
[73] Dates on bldgs.
[74] Inf. from Supply Controller, Wessex Water, Quay Ho., the Ambury, Bath.
[75] *Andrews and Dury, Map* (W.R.S. viii), pl. 13.
[76] Date on bldg.
[77] Inf. from Co. Secretary, Co. Hall, Trowbridge.
[78] O.S. Map 1″, sheet 34 (1828 edn.); W.R.O., tithe award.
[79] O.S. Map 6″, Wilts. XIII (1888 and later edns.); above, Malmesbury, introduction.
[80] Finberg, *Early Wessex Chart.* pp. 70, 91, 105–6; *V.C.H. Wilts.* ii, pp. 4, 88–9.

[81] P.R.O., SC 6/Hen. VIII/3986, rot. 112.
[82] Ibid. E 318/Box 20/1074.
[83] *W.N. & Q.* viii. 389, 394.
[84] Ibid. 446, 448.
[85] P.R.O., CP 25(2)/239/15 Eliz. I East. no. 695.
[86] Ibid. C 142/222, no. 45.
[87] Ibid. C 142/365, no. 153.
[88] Ibid. CP 25(2)/512/18 Chas. I East.
[89] Above, Malmesbury, manors.
[90] P.R.O., CP 25(2)/747/35 Chas. II Trin.
[91] *Complete Peerage*, i. 46.
[92] W.R.O. 130/76, survey, 1719–20.
[93] *W.N. & Q.* viii, pedigree facing p. 300.
[94] Aubrey, *Topog. Coll.* ed. Jackson, 280.
[95] Burke, *Peerage* (1931), 1905; W.R.O., tithe award.
[96] Burke, *Peerage* (1931), 1905–6.
[97] Inf. from Mrs. C. Parfitt, Angrove Farm.
[98] *Who Was Who, 1951–60*, 881; local inf.

In the early 19th century the interior was refitted and a little later rooms were added to the north in the angle between the main range and the wing. A tower was built east of that extension in 1859;[99] at a similar or slightly later date some chimneys were rebuilt with alternating bands of red brick and ashlar. A ground-floor extension in red brick was built across the whole of the south front in the late 19th century. The gardens were extended between 1842 and 1885, when the road beside the south front was moved 50 m. further south.[1]

After the Dissolution tithes of grain, hay, wool, and lambs, arising in Rodbourne, probably in the whole chapelry, passed with tithes from Corston to Robert Bridges (fl. 1622) and his wife Elizabeth.[2] They were apparently bought by Henry Poole and were merged with Rodbourne manor.[3]

ECONOMIC HISTORY. Intercommoning of pastures beside the Avon between Rodbourne and Little Somerford was ended by an agreement of 1281. Most of the pastures on the right bank were allotted to the men of Rodbourne, but the lord and tenants of Little Somerford also retained meadow land there.[4] Rodbourne's pastures beside the river were apparently several in the mid 16th century when the only common pasture in the chapelry was the Heath, c. 60 a. south of the village. Open arable fields were then called East, West, and Park.[5]

There is no record of demesne land at Rodbourne. In the mid 16th century 15 copyholders held between them $29\frac{1}{2}$ yardlands; none held more than 3 yardlands. Other holdings were of no more than a few acres each. Like those of Corston the tenants' obligations to cut and carry hay from Cole park and to plough in Kemboro field had been commuted for cash payments by the mid 16th century.[6]

There were still open fields in Rodbourne in the early 18th century,[7] but common cultivation had ceased by the early 19th.[8] The Heath, apparently common pasture in 1820,[9] had by 1839 been inclosed and ploughed. Most of the chapelry was grassland in 1839; there were c. 250 a. of arable and 57 a. of woodland, including Angrove wood, 18 a. near the Avon, and Bincombe wood, 31 a. south-west of Rodbourne village. There were seven farms of over 80 a. each; 166 a., including the woodland, was in the lord's hand. Farms of 152 a., 179 a., and 82 a. worked from farmsteads in the village, and Bottom farm, 173 a., worked from a farmstead south of the village, were scattered holdings. Angrove farm, 208 a. in the north-east corner of the chapelry, and Cleeve farm, 264 a. in the south-west corner, were compact.[10]

Totals of stock in the chapelry in 1866, including 213 cattle, 322 sheep, and 105 pigs,[11] suggest that farming remained primarily pastoral. In the earlier 20th century most of the land was worked in farms of 100–200 a. In 1910 a farm of 308 a., called Godwins, worked from the village, may have included land formerly in Cleeve farm, the buildings of which had been removed, but by 1927 it had been divided into smaller holdings. In 1910 Parsloe's farm and Manor farm were also worked from the village, Angrove farm and Bottom farm from outside it.[12] Then, as later in the century, dairying and sheep farming predominated. Cattle reared for beef replaced some dairy herds in the late 1970s.[13]

There was a brickworks at the west end of Rodbourne village in 1839. Then and in 1848 Richard Tanner made bricks and tiles there. In 1867 George Tanner also produced pipes, and in 1911 Robert Tanner made bricks and tiles, burned lime, perhaps on the same site, and owned a quarry. In the 1930s he also produced small bricks for fireplaces.[14] The brickworks was closed c. 1940.[15]

LOCAL GOVERNMENT. Views of frankpledge and courts for Rodbourne manor were held in May or June and in December in the years 1544–6. Jurors presented public nuisances, such as the disrepair of a lane and a road, and the arrival of stray animals, and the homage presented the death of copyholders. A tithingman and a reeve were elected.[16]

Between 1559 and 1573 views and courts for Rodbourne were recorded with those for Burton Hill manor. From 1569 to 1572 a single view was held for both and the tithingman of Rodbourne presented. Separate courts baron were held for Rodbourne at which the homage presented and the tithingman was elected.[17]

Rodbourne did not relieve its own poor, but like Corston had its own overseer in the later 18th century and early 19th. Regular relief was received by five people in Rodbourne in 1760–1 and 1770–1. The cost was £16 in 1760–1 when a further £10 was spent on occasional relief; in 1780–1 a total of £21 was spent.[18]

CHURCH. Rodbourne church was built or replaced in the 12th century,[19] and, until a vicarage of Malmesbury was ordained between 1191 and the mid 13th century, may have been served from Malmesbury abbey.[20] Inhabitants may have had right of burial, as those of Corston had,[21] but marriages probably took place in the mother church until 1873 when Rodbourne chapel was

[99] Date on bldg.
[1] W.R.O., tithe award; O.S. Map 6″, Wilts. XIII (1888 edn.).
[2] Above, Corston, manor; P.R.O., CP 25(2)/372/20 Jas. I Mich.
[3] P.R.O., CP 25(2)/512/18 Chas. I East.
[4] Reg. Malm. ii. 219–20.
[5] W.R.O. 88/2/4; cf. ibid. tithe award.
[6] Reg. Malm. ii. 186; P.R.O., E 318/Box 20/1074; above, Corston, econ. hist.
[7] W.R.O. 130/76, survey, 1719–20.
[8] Ibid. tithe award.
[9] Greenwood, Map of Wilts.
[10] W.R.O., tithe award.

[11] P.R.O., MAF 68/73, sheet 12.
[12] Kelly's Dir. Wilts. (1911); W.R.O., Inland Revenue, val. reg. 9; ibid. G 7/515/9.
[13] Inf. from Mrs. Parfitt.
[14] Kelly's Dir. Wilts. (1848 and later edns.); W.R.O., tithe award.
[15] Inf. from Mrs. S. Verity, Old Sch.
[16] W.R.O. 88/2/6.
[17] Ibid. 88/2/13; 88/2/29; above, Malmesbury, local govt. (manorial govt.).
[18] W.R.O. 1589/33.
[19] Below.
[20] Above, Malmesbury, churches.
[21] Ibid. Corston, church.

licensed for their performance.[22] The institutional history of the church from 1881, and aspects of the earlier life of the church, are described with those of Corston.[23]

In the late 18th century and the early 19th services were held in Rodbourne church on alternate Sunday afternoons.[24] On Census Sunday in 1851 an afternoon service was attended by 80 adults, a congregation which was said to be larger than usual.[25]

The church of the *HOLY ROOD*, so called in 1763,[26] is built of stone rubble with ashlar dressings and has a chancel and a nave with south porch, baptistry, and tower. The narrow nave is 12th-century and has two windows and two doorways of that date. Each doorway has a tympanum, the south carved with the tree of life, the north with a cross. Because it is small and almost square the chancel may also be 12th-century but otherwise its earliest feature is the late 13th-century east window. The chancel piscina is 14th-century and new windows were made in the south and west walls of the nave and the south wall of the chancel in the 15th century. The porch is of the later 15th century or the earlier 16th. The chancel was refitted in 1849, when a window in 14th-century style was made in its north wall. The tower and the baptistry which joins it to the porch were added in 1862;[27] there may earlier have been a bellcot. In 1865 glass designed by Ford Madox Brown and D. G. Rosetti and made by Morris & Co. was fitted in the east window. Extensive repairs, including the renewal of some roofs and the reflooring of the nave, were made in 1903.[28]

In 1553 a chalice weighing 7 oz. was left in Rodbourne and 2 oz. of plate were taken for the king.[29] Later plate was held jointly with Corston.[30]

A bell of 1654, probably cast at Bristol, hung at Rodbourne in 1987.[31]

NONCONFORMITY. A Quaker from Rodbourne was buried in 1669 and a Quaker family lived there in 1697.[32]

A house at Rodbourne was certified for Independent meetings in 1797.[33] An Independent chapel had been built by 1823 and on Census Sunday in 1851 an afternoon service in it was attended by 50 people.[34] No later reference to the chapel has been found.

EDUCATION. A school built at Rodbourne in 1851[35] was described as picturesque and commodious in 1858 when it had 20–30 pupils.[36] From 1872 or earlier the school was a Church of England school and served both Rodbourne and Corston;[37] it was extended in 1872 and 1893.[38] The number of pupils fell from 82 in 1872[39] to *c*. 65 in 1908; until the 1930s average attendance remained between 50 and 65.[40] The school was closed in 1971.[41] In 1947–8 Rodbourne House was used as a private day and boarding school attended by 42 boys.[42]

NORTON

NORTON is 5 km. south-west of Malmesbury.[43] On Speed's map of 1611 the name Coloparle, in error for Cole Park, was juxtaposed to the name Norton, and Cole Park, a house 2 km. SSE. of Malmesbury, was marked by no symbol.[44] As a result Norton was named on later maps as Norton Colepark or Norton Coleparle[45] and that addition to the name was adopted. It appeared in ecclesiastical reference books in the 18th century[46] and on census returns in the 19th.[47] The antiquary J. E. Jackson, vicar of Norton 1846–91, persuaded the bishop to drop the addition from the name of the benefice,[48] and it went out of use generally in the 20th century.

The parish, a shallow **V** in shape, had two detached portions, one to the north-east and one to the south-east. Both adjoin Malmesbury common: the northern, an area called Starvall, was perhaps assigned to the men of Norton in the Middle Ages to replace rights on the common, but the southern, which adjoins Bradfield wood in Hullavington, is more likely to have been ancient woodland, also assigned to Norton in the Middle Ages, and later cleared. Norton parish measured *c*. 990 a. (*c*. 401 ha.) in 1840 and was reduced to 928 a. (376 ha.) in 1884 when the detached areas were transferred to, respectively, Foxley and Hullavington.[49] In 1934 the whole of Foxley parish, which included Starvall and the main part of Bremilham parish, was transferred

[22] Bristol R.O., EP/A/23/8.
[23] Above, Corston, church.
[24] *Vis. Queries, 1783* (W.R.S. xxvii), p. 150; Ch. Com. file, NB 5/116B.
[25] P.R.O., HO 129/252/1/19/26.
[26] Ecton, *Thesaurus*, 404.
[27] *Wilts. Cuttings*, ix. 32.　　　　[28] *Ch. Guide* (1987).
[29] Nightingale, *Wilts. Plate*, 196.
[30] Above, Corston, church.
[31] Walters, *Wilts. Bells*, 163–4; inf. from the rector, Great Somerford.
[32] *W.N. & Q.* iv. 26; v. 225.
[33] *Meeting Ho. Certs.* (W.R.S. xl), p. 46.
[34] P.R.O., HO 129/252/1/19/27.
[35] Date on bldg.　　　　[36] *Acct. of Wilts. Schs.* 32.
[37] P.R.O., ED 21/18532.　　　　[38] Dates on bldg.

[39] P.R.O., ED 21/18532.
[40] *Bd. of Educ., List 21, 1910* (H.M.S.O.), 509; *1912*, 553; *1919*, 363; *1922*, 362; *1936*, 426.
[41] Inf. from the rector.
[42] W.R.O., F 12, corresp. file, Rodbourne Coll.
[43] This article was written in 1987. Maps used include O.S. Maps 6", Wilts. XII–XIII (1888–9 edns.); 1/25,000, ST 88, ST 98 (1958–9 edns.); 1/50,000, sheet 173 (1974 edn.).
[44] J. Speed, *Map of Wilts.* (1611).
[45] e.g. R. Blome, *Map of Wilts.* (1681).
[46] Phillipps, *Wilts. Inst.* ii. 98; W.R.O., D 1/48/4.
[47] *Census*, 1821.
[48] Soc. Antiq. MS. 817, ix, f. 57v.; for Jackson, below, church.
[49] *V.C.H. Wilts.* iv. 355; O.S. Map 6", Wilts. XIII (1888 edn.); W.R.O., tithe award.

to Norton parish[50] and increased it to 835 ha. (2,063 a.).

As might be expected of long established boundaries in an area of gentle relief Norton's followed streams and in several places roads which are apparently ancient. The modern boundaries were broadly similar to those of the main part of the parish recited in the 10th or 11th century when they followed the Roman Foss Way and roads called King's Way, Borough Way, and Narrow Way or Small Way. The more likely of two interpretations suggests that the road which divided Norton parish from Malmesbury common was King's Way, that Borough Way was the road which divided Norton from Foxley north-east of Norton village, and that Small Way was the road which divided those parishes north-west of Norton village.[51] The streams divide Norton from Foxley to the north and from Hullavington to the south.

Forest Marble clay outcrops in the west part of the old Norton parish, Cornbrash in the centre, and Kellaways Clay in the east. South-east of Norton village Kellaways Clay also forms an island in the Cornbrash. The land, at *c.* 100 m. above sea level, is nearly flat. It is drained north-eastwards by tributaries of the Sherston branch of the Bristol Avon, two of which meet near Norton village. The south-east boundary stream flows into Gauze brook which joins the Avon south of Malmesbury. In some places the streams have deposited small amounts of alluvium.[52] The small parish was rich in meadow land, the Cornbrash favours tillage, and the clays favour pasture.[53] Until the mid 20th century pastoral farming outweighed cultivation,[54] and, especially in the 19th century, there were many ponds.[55] East of the village part of Maidford farm, with lodges, long drives, and avenues, was given the appearance of a park in the later 19th century.[56]

The Bath–Cirencester section of the Foss Way was in 1987 a road for only one short stretch on the old boundary of Norton, and was derelict for most of its course there. No modern main road touches the parish. Four roads, from Easton Grey, Foxley, Sherston, and Hullavington, converge on the village. The first two meet at its north end at a ford. The Easton Grey road, Small Way, was often called Tetbury Way;[57] the Foxley road, possibly Borough Way, was called Honey Lane from 1773 or earlier.[58] Beside the Hullavington road the wide verges were used as gardens in the earlier 19th century.[59]

Norton was mentioned in the early 10th century.[60] Few prehistoric remains have been discovered in the old parish,[61] and Norton village has never been large or populous. There were only 23 poll-tax payers in 1377,[62] and 16th-century taxation assessments were low.[63] The population of the parish was 94 in 1801. From 89 in 1811 it rose to a peak of 123 in 1851. It had fallen to 101 by 1881 and to 99 by 1891 after the transfer of the detached portions, the northern with 4 inhabitants. The population was 117 in 1901, 85 in 1911, and 90 in 1931. After Foxley and Bremilham had been added to it, Norton parish had 170 inhabitants in 1951,[64] 123 in 1981.[65]

Norton is a small nucleated village lying on each side of the Sherston road in the centre of the parish. South of the road are the church and Manor (formerly Church) Farm, a farmhouse and buildings possibly on the site of those of the demesne of Norton manor.[66] Manor Farm has a tall early 17th-century west block to which a lower east range may have been attached. In the 1820s a new east range was built and the appearance of the south front of the house was unified by a central entrance beneath a pediment and by Venetian windows to the ground-floor rooms.[67] The farm buildings include a possibly 18th-century barn and a late 20th-century dairy. North of the road Norton Manor was built in 1623,[68] and Buckland Farm is another 17th-century farmhouse which was later extended. Near Buckland Farm and Norton Manor are large stone barns, one of which has been converted for residence. South of the road a row of several cottages is apparently 19th-century, a cottage was built in 1856,[69] a pair of estate cottages was built between 1900 and 1910,[70] another pair of estate cottages was built *c.* 1955,[71] and two private houses were built later. Near the ford at the north end of the village Elstubs was a house in the mid 17th century.[72] A row of four cottages was built on its site in the 19th century. Two rows of cottages and a small, apparently 18th-century, house were nearby in 1840.[73] The house was licensed as the Vine Tree in 1890:[74] it was a public house in 1987. In the late 19th century one of the rows of cottages was demolished;[75] the other was rebuilt as a house.

East of the village Maidford and Gorsey Leaze are farmsteads which may have stood in the 17th century. Maidford has a small farmhouse, possibly of 17th-century origin, near the centre of extensive buildings. North-east of it a barn is dated 1840 and there are later 20th-century farm buildings. South-west of it a large new house was built *c.* 1890[76] and extended to the west in the earlier 20th century and *c.* 1970. The farmhouse of Gorsey Leaze was rebuilt in 1877.[77] The farm buildings, most of which are 19th-century, incorporate an old two-storeyed building, possibly part of an older house. Another house was built nearby *c.* 1910.[78]

[50] *V.C.H. Wilts.* iv. 355; above, Bremilham, introduction; Foxley, introduction.
[51] *Arch. Jnl.* lxxvi. 221–3; cf. W.A.S. Libr., maps marked by T. R. Thomson and B. J. Wallis.
[52] Geol. Surv. Map 1", solid and drift, sheet 251 (1970 edn.).
[53] e.g. W.R.O., tithe award.   [54] Below, econ. hist.
[55] O.S. Map 6", Wilts. XIII (1888 edn.); W.R.O., tithe award.
[56] O.S. Maps 6", Wilts. XIII (1888 edn.), XIII. NW. (1900 edn.).
[57] e.g. W.R.O. 11/305 (1631).
[58] *Andrews and Dury, Map* (W.R.S. viii), pl. 13.
[59] W.R.O., tithe award.
[60] Finberg, *Early Wessex Chart.* pp. 83–4.
[61] *V.C.H. Wilts.* i (1), 93.   [62] Ibid. iv. 309.

[63] *Taxation Lists* (W.R.S. x), 29, 53.
[64] *V.C.H. Wilts.* iv. 355; above.
[65] *Census,* 1981.   [66] Below, econ. hist.
[67] Date stone on ho.   [68] Below, manor.
[69] Ibid. church.
[70] Inf. from Countess June Badeni, Norton Manor.
[71] W.R.O., G 7/505/1.   [72] Ibid. 11/310.
[73] Ibid. tithe award.
[74] Soc. Antiq. MS. 817, ix, f. 46v.
[75] O.S. Maps 6", Wilts. XIII (1888 edn.), XIII. NW. (1900 edn.).
[76] Ibid.; J. Badeni, *Wilts. Forefathers,* 125.
[77] Soc. Antiq. MS. 817, ix, f. 87v.
[78] O.S. Maps 6", Wilts. XIII. NW. (1900, 1925 edns.); inf. from Countess Badeni.

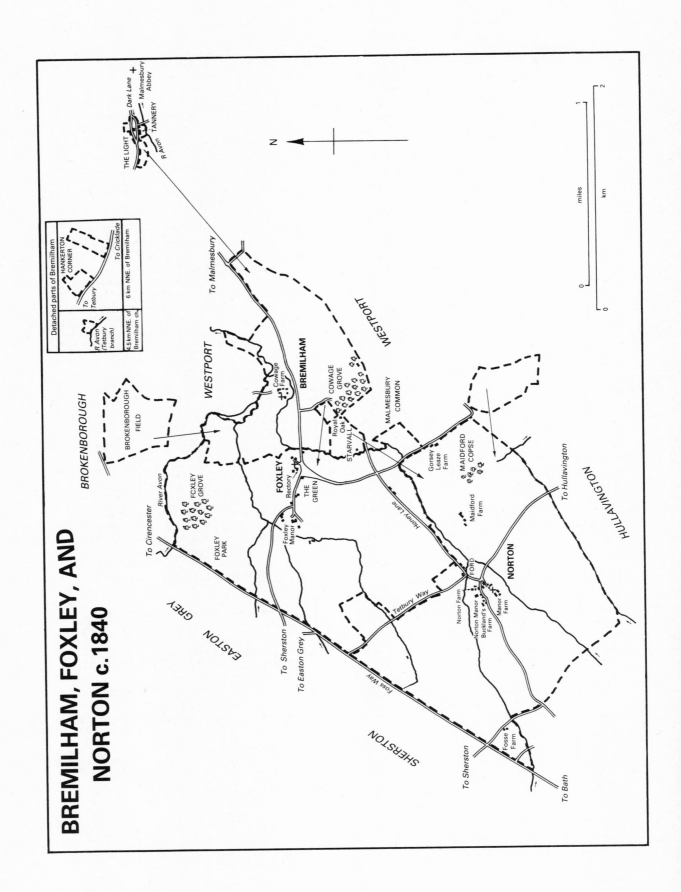

BREMILHAM, FOXLEY, AND
NORTON c.1840

THE LIGHT
Dark Lane
Malmesbury
Abbey
R Avon TANNERY

Detached parts of Bremilham
HANKERTON CORNER
To Cricklade
To Tetbury
To Bremilham
R Avon (Tetbury branch)
6 km NNE. of Bremilham
4.5 km NNE. of Bremilham ch.

N

miles
km

To Malmesbury

WESTPORT

WESTPORT

BROKENBOROUGH

BROKENBOROUGH FIELD

Cowage Farm

BREMILHAM

COWAGE GROVE

Royal Oak
STARVALL

MALMESBURY COMMON

River Avon

FOXLEY GROVE

FOXLEY PARK

FOXLEY
Rectory
THE GREEN

Foxley Manor

Gorsey Leaze Farm

MAIDFORD COPSE

Honey Lane

Maidford Farm

To Cirencester

EASTON GREY

To Sherston

To Easton Grey

Tetbury Way

FORD

Norton Farm
Norton Manor
Buckland's Farm
Manor Farm

NORTON

To Hullavington

HULLAVINGTON

SHERSTON

Fosse Way

To Sherston

Fosse Farm

To Bath

170

Dispersed settlement in the parish increased after the 17th century. West of the village Fosse may have been a farmstead in 1742,[79] as it was in 1773[80] and later. The farmhouse was rebuilt in the later 19th century. Beside the Foss Way near Fosse Farm a house called Little House stood in the 18th century.[81] A possibly 18th-century cottage at Starvall was a public house called the Royal Oak in 1875.[82] It remained open until c. 1925.[83] A barn stood west of that cottage in 1840:[84] extensive farm buildings called Highfield Farm were erected around its site in the later 20th century, and a new house was built near the Royal Oak in 1986. New buildings and a farmhouse were erected north-west of the village for Norton farm between 1900 and 1911.[85]

MANOR AND OTHER ESTATES. King Athelstan granted *NORTON*, containing 5 *mansae*, to Malmesbury abbey in the period 934–9.[86] The abbey kept it until the Dissolution.[87] In 1547 the Crown granted it to Sir John Brydges[88] (cr. Baron Chandos 1554, d. 1557),[89] and it was inherited in turn by his son Edmund, Lord Chandos[90] (d. 1573), and Edmund's son Giles, Lord Chandos (d. 1594).[91] Apparently in 1577 and 1589 Lord Chandos sold the manor in three portions.[92]

In 1589 Alexander Staples bought the demesne farmhouse, some demesne land, and land in the east part of the parish later Maidford farm and Gorsey Leaze farm, and in the same year Richard Estcourt (d. 1611) of Long Newnton (now Glos.) and his son Edmund bought farmsteads, land in the south part of the parish later Manor farm, land in the east part, and the detached part called Starvall.[93] Staples (d. 1590)[94] sold his land in 1589 to William Jones (d. 1610) and it passed in turn to Jones's son John[95] (d. 1611) and John's son William, a minor in 1611.[96] In 1615 Jones sold it to Edmund Estcourt.[97] The lordship of Norton manor and, apart from Norton farm in the west and north-west,[98] nearly all the land of the parish descended from Edmund Estcourt (d. 1651) of Sherston Pinkney in turn to his son Sir Thomas (d. 1683), Sir Thomas's son Sir Thomas (d. 1702), and that Sir Thomas's son Thomas (d. 1704) who devised the estate to his sister Elizabeth,

wife of Richard Cresswell.[99] In 1714 the Cresswells sold it to Sir Edward Gould (d. 1728) who devised it for life to his wife Frances (d. 1738) and afterwards to his grandnephew Edward Gould (d. c. 1775). That Edward was succeeded by his son Edward who in 1798 offered the estate for sale in portions.[1]

In 1798 Gorsey Leaze farm, 149 a. in 1840 including the parish's detached lands to the southeast, and the lordship of Norton manor were bought by Samuel Williams. In 1821 they were sold by Williams to William Whieldon, in 1823 by Whieldon to Charles Wilkins, and in 1824 by Wilkins to R. H. Gaby (d. 1829).[2] Gaby's heir was his nephew John Gaby (d. 1830), whose own heirs, his siblings Thomas and Mary Anne Gaby, sold the estate in 1830 to Joseph Neeld (d. 1856).[3] It passed as part of Neeld's Grittleton estate to his brother John (cr. a baronet 1859, d. 1891) and in turn to Sir John's sons Sir Algernon (d. 1900), and Sir Audley[4] (d. 1941).[5] Soon after 1910 Gorsey Leaze farm was bought, almost certainly from Sir Audley Neeld, by Hugh Raymond-Barker who c. 1925 sold it to A. S. C. Browne, the owner until c. 1937. From c. 1948 the farm belonged to K. J. Gagen whose son Mr. B. A. Gagen sold it in portions in the 1980s.[6] The farmhouse and 20 a. were sold in 1986.[7]

Manor farm, 305 a. in 1840,[8] was bought c. 1798 by William Walker[9] (d. 1830).[10] It passed to his sister Elizabeth Walker (d. 1833), who devised it to her brother-in-law Giles Canter for his life or widowerhood and thereafter to Giles's son Joseph.[11] In 1840 Joseph Canter owned the farm.[12] At his death in 1865 it passed to his daughter and her husband H. A. Neck. In 1872 Neck sold it to W. Matthews, a Bristol drysalter, who in 1877 sold it to John Bush.[13] In 1920 the farm was bought, apparently from Bush's relict, by W. E. Smith (d. 1939), whose trustees in 1940 sold it to Exeter College, Oxford. In 1954 and 1978 the college sold it in portions to Smith's grandson Mr. C. D. Smith, the owner in 1987.[14]

Maidford farm, 149 a. in 1840,[15] was bought c. 1798 by John Bennett[16] (d. 1819). Bennett was succeeded by his son John Bennett[17] (fl. 1840) and by the younger John's son J. D. G. Bennett, who was succeeded as owner in turn by his relict

[79] W.R.O. 312/11, will of John Jacob.
[80] *Andrews and Dury, Map* (W.R.S. viii), pl. 13.
[81] Ibid.; B.L. Maps, M.T. 6e., 1 (2).
[82] *Kelly's Dir. Wilts.* (1875); Soc. Antiq. MS. 817, ix, f. 48v.
[83] *Kelly's Dir. Wilts.* (1923, 1927), s.v. Foxley; local inf.
[84] W.R.O., tithe award.   [85] Inf. from Countess Badeni.
[86] Finberg, *Early Wessex Chart.* pp. 83–4, which revises the textual date 931.
[87] *Valor Eccl.* (Rec. Com.), ii. 120.
[88] *Cal. Pat.* 1547–8, 115.
[89] For the Brydgeses, *Complete Peerage*, iii. 126–7.
[90] P.R.O., C 142/114, no. 71.
[91] Ibid. C 142/163, no. 59.   [92] Below.
[93] W.R.O. 130/25, deed, Chandos to Staples, 1589; 212B/5141. For the location of the lands cf. ibid. tithe award; for Ric. Estcourt, Burke, *Land. Gent.* (1937), 710.
[94] Badeni, *Wilts. Forefathers*, 115.
[95] P.R.O., C 142/680, no. 30; Soc. Antiq. MS. 817, ix, f. 1.
[96] P.R.O., C 142/325, no. 187.
[97] Ibid. CP 25(2)/371/13 Jas. I Mich.
[98] Below.
[99] For the Estcourts, Burke, *Land. Gent.* (1937), 710–11. For the date 1683, P.R.O., PROB 11/373, ff. 248v.–249.

[1] W.R.O. 1305/205, abstr. of title, 1829. For dates of d., *V.C.H. Mdx.* vi. 181; *Musgrave's Obit.* iii (Harl. Soc. xlvi), 63; P.R.O., PROB 11/1013, ff. 6v.–7.
[2] W.R.O. 1305/205, abstr. of title, 1829; ibid. tithe award.
[3] Ibid. 1305/205, abstr. of conveyance, 1830.
[4] Ibid. A 1/345/309; ibid. 1305/294; Burke, *Peerage* (1924), 1667.
[5] *Who Was Who, 1941–50*, 838.
[6] *Kelly's Dir. Wilts.* (1911 and later edns.); W.R.O., Inland Revenue, val. reg. 13; ibid. G 7/505/1; inf. from Countess Badeni.
[7] W.A.S. Libr., sale cat. xlii, no. 42.
[8] W.R.O., tithe award.
[9] Ibid. 1305/205, abstr. of title, 1829; ibid. A 1/345/309.
[10] Mon. in church.
[11] Ibid.; W.R.O. 130/25, copy will of Eliz. Walker; Soc. Antiq. MS. 817, ix, f. 89v.
[12] W.R.O., tithe award.
[13] Ibid. 374/130/87; *Kelly's Dir. Wilts.* (1875); Soc. Antiq. MS. 817, ix, f. 89v.
[14] Inf. from the Librarian and Archivist, Exeter Coll., Oxf.; Countess Badeni; Bristol R.O., EP/A/22/1/92.
[15] W.R.O., tithe award.
[16] Ibid. A 1/345/309.
[17] For the Bennetts, inf. from Countess Badeni.

Marianne (d. 1882) and sons John (d. 1886) and Richard. In 1887 Richard Bennett sold the farm to Malcolm Macleod.[18] The estate was offered for sale in 1894[19] and may have been bought by W. W. Turnor of Pinkney Park who owned it in 1910.[20] Before 1928 Turnor sold it to W. H. Haydon[21] (d. 1930).[22] Before 1934 Haydon's executors sold it to H. J. Melville, who c. 1946 sold it to H. J. Blackborow.[23] In 1958 Blackborow sold the estate to Lt.-Col. E. G. V. Northey, who sold it to J. Salmond in 1966. Salmond sold it to C. Bunbury who sold it to Mr. D. Brown, the owner in 1987.[24]

Buckland farm, 83 a. in 1840, was bought c. 1798 by William Kilmister (d. 1847), the tenant of the adjoining Norton farm. Kilmister devised it to his nephew William Kilmister, on whose death in 1886 it passed to his daughter, the wife of W. A. Notley.[25] In 1910 Mrs. M. J. Notley owned the farm.[26] It was bought by Isita Wilson in 1917 and has since been part of Norton farm.[27]

In 1577 Giles, Lord Chandos, was licensed to alienate land in Norton to Thomas Best and Anthony Bonner and it is likely that Norton farm was sold in that year to Best,[28] who is known to have been a freeholder in Norton. Best and his widow Elizabeth had both died by 1607.[29] Norton farm was possibly bought by John Workman and in 1615 belonged to his son Thomas,[30] who in 1616 added to it a house and 2 a. bought from Edmund Estcourt.[31] Thomas Workman (d. 1650)[32] was succeeded by his son Richard who sold the farm to John Jacob in 1652.[33] Jacob (d. 1705) was succeeded by his son John (d. 1728 or 1729). That John's son John (d. 1776)[34] sold the land, almost certainly in 1749, to Henry Fox[35] (d. 1774), from 1758 the owner of the adjoining Foxley manor and from 1763 Baron Holland. Norton farm, 264 a. in 1840, passed with Foxley manor to Stephen, Lord Holland (d. 1774), to his relict Mary (d. 1778), to Henry, Lord Holland (d. 1840), to his relict Elizabeth (d. 1845), to Henry, Lord Holland (d. 1859), to his relict Mary (d. 1889), to Leopold Fox-Powys (d. 1893), to Thomas Powys, Lord Lilford (d. 1896), and to John, Lord Lilford (d. 1945).[36] In 1900 Lord Lilford sold it to C. H. Fenwick who in 1911 sold it[37] to trustees of William Wilson including his relict Isita Wilson (d. 1939). Buckland farm was later added to it. Norton farm passed to the Wilsons' son Noel who in 1967 conveyed it to his daughter June and her husband Count Jan Badeni, the owners in 1987.[38] Norton Manor[39] was built by Thomas Workman. The southern part, a main east–west range with a short back wing at each end, has on the south front a two-storeyed central porch decorated with classical pilasters and inscribed 1623. That was probably the full extent of the house in 1630 and 1631 when Workman settled separate parts of it on the marriages of, respectively, himself and his son Richard.[40] By 1652 a new north range had been built.[41] It abutted the wings and apparently left a small open courtyard between them. From the early 18th century the house was apparently tenanted, and the two parts may have been separately occupied, as they were later.[42] When Lord Holland visited the estate in 1856 he found the house in poor repair, but had the south range restored for his own occasional occupation. The extent of the restoration has been obscured by later alterations:[43] gables were possibly removed from the south front, the roof of the south range was possibly replaced by the present hipped roof, and a fireplace was lined with tiles bearing the letter H. The north range may have continued in use as a farmhouse and it kept its tall gables. After he bought the house in 1900 C. H. Fenwick reunited the two parts and added to, repaired, and altered it:[44] he demolished a small stair turret in the central court, which until then was otherwise roofed at first-floor level, and made the whole court a stair hall; he rearranged the rooms on both main floors behind the south front, extended the north part of the house, and added an entrance vestibule and bay windows on the east; and he improved the surroundings of the house by demolishing adjacent farm buildings. Barns and a dovecot east of the house were retained, and gardens were laid out to the south and west. A two-storeyed west porch was added to the house in 1925.[45]

John Jacob (d. 1742), the nephew of John Jacob (d. 1728 or 1729), owned a small farm, Fosse, in the south-west corner of the parish, presumably taken from Norton farm, and devised it to his cousin John Jacob (d. 1776). It passed in 1776 to that John's nephew Sir Robert Buxton, Bt. (d. 1839), and was inherited by Sir Robert's son Sir John (d. 1842), whose heir was his son Sir Robert (d. 1888).[46] The farm, 20 a. in 1840,[47] was sold to Joseph Neeld in 1852[48] and with Gorsey Leaze farm it remained part of the Grittleton estate. Between 1910 and 1928 it was bought by J. T. Hitchings.[49] In the later 20th century the land was bought by Mr. C. D. Smith and added to Manor farm.[50]

In 1222 Malmesbury abbey was licensed to

[18] Soc. Antiq. MS. 817, ix, ff. 87v.–90. Apparently in error John Bennett was recorded in 1840 as the tenant or mortgagee of his wife's sister-in-law Eliz. Walker (d. 1848): W.R.O., tithe award; ibid. 130/25, copy will of Eliz. Walker; inf. from Countess Badeni.   [19] W.R.O. 1409/243.
[20] Ibid. Inland Revenue, val. reg. 13.
[21] Ibid. G 7/501/1.   [22] W.A.M. xlv. 271.
[23] W.R.O., G 7/505/1; inf. from Countess Badeni.
[24] Wilts. Cuttings, xxi. 106; xxii. 376; inf. from Countess Badeni.
[25] W.R.O., tithe award; ibid. A 1/345/309; ibid. 374/130/87; Soc. Antiq. MS. 817, ix, f. 85v.; P.R.O., PROB 11/2069, ff. 263–4.   [26] W.R.O., Inland Revenue, val. reg. 13.
[27] Inf. from Countess Badeni.
[28] Cal. Pat. 1575–8, p. 265; W.R.O. 130/25, exemplification of recovery.
[29] P.R.O., C 2/Jas. I/R 15/28.
[30] Ibid. C 2/Jas. I/C 9/8; W.R.O. 11/310.

[31] W.R.O. 11/299.   [32] Ibid. 1655/7.
[33] Ibid. 11/310.
[34] Jacob pedigree compiled by J. E. Jackson: ibid. 1655/8.
[35] Soc. Antiq. MS. 817, ix, f. 81v.; B.L. Maps, M.T. 6e., 1 (2).
[36] Above, Foxley, manor; W.R.O., tithe award.
[37] W.R.O. 1734/2–4.   [38] Inf. from Countess Badeni.
[39] See plate facing p. 60.
[40] W.R.O. 11/305; 212A/27/47, agreement, Workman and Gore, 1630.   [41] Ibid. 11/310.
[42] Badeni, Wilts. Forefathers, 124.   [43] Ibid. 127.
[44] Plan by F. A. Lawson in possession of Countess Badeni.
[45] Badeni, Wilts. Forefathers, pl. 13.
[46] W.R.O. 312/11, will of John Jacob, 1742; 1655/8.
[47] Ibid. tithe award.
[48] Soc. Antiq. MS. 817, ix, f. 81v.
[49] W.R.O., Inland Revenue, val. reg. 13; ibid. G 7/501/1.
[50] Inf. from Countess Badeni.

The railway station in 1966

Burton Hill Mill *c.* 1965

MALMESBURY

Malmesbury: Burton Hill chapel in 1809

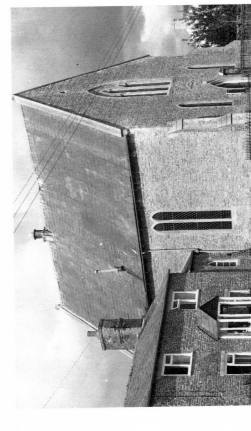

Brinkworth: Barnes Green chapel, built 1860

Westport: the Hermitage in Burnivale in 1809

Brinkworth: Callow Hill chapel, built 1889

appropriate Norton church.[51] It held it until the Dissolution.[52] The *RECTORY* estate apparently included 1 yardland and 4 a. of meadow in 1341.[53] That land was apparently absorbed by Norton manor and the estate later consisted of no more than tithes. It was granted with Norton manor in 1547,[54] and passed with the manor in the Brydges family,[55] to Alexander Staples,[56] and in the Jones, Estcourt, and Gould families.[57] In 1589 it was said to comprise all the great tithes from Norton.[58] Tithes were disputed in the period 1613–15 between the vicar and the lessee of the rectory estate: the vicar claimed great tithes from a small part of Norton farm and the lessee denied the vicar's right to any tithe from Norton.[59] The rectory estate thereafter seems to have consisted of the great tithes from nearly all the parish, and no small tithe.[60] The great tithes from the farms owned by members of the Estcourt and Gould families in the 17th and 18th centuries were merged with the farms,[61] and the farms sold *c.* 1798 were said to be tithe free.[62] In the early 18th century John Jacob (d. 1728 or 1729) held a lease of tithes, presumably those arising on his own land.[63] It is likely that Jacob or a successor bought those tithes since by the early 19th century the great tithes from Fosse farm and from the greater part of Norton farm had been merged with the land. In 1840 the tithes which had been the rectory estate, all belonging to the owners of the lands on which they arose, were valued at a notional £78 and commuted.[64]

ECONOMIC HISTORY. Norton had land for 8 ploughteams in 1086, and only 5 teams were on it. Of the 5 hides of its Norton estate Malmesbury abbey had in demesne 2½ hides on which there were 2 teams and 5 *servi*. On the other half of the estate 7 *villani* and 3 coscets had a total of 3 teams. There was pasture 2 furlongs by 1 furlong and a mill and 6 a. of meadow.[65]

The demesne may have been in hand in the early 13th century when, with a stock of 16 oxen, much of it may have been ploughed. The customary tenants, whose rents totalled £1 12s., presumably cultivated it.[66] In the later 13th century, when the abbey paid for new farm buildings at Norton, it may still have been in hand.[67] It is likely to have been worked from buildings near the church where the present Manor Farm stands. There were 24 tenants in the late 13th century: 4 or 5 may have

held as much as a yardland each and the remainder were apparently cottagers.[68] The only evidence of common husbandry at Norton in the Middle Ages is that of extensive pastures later divided.[69] Malmesbury abbey leased the whole manor and the rectory estate in 1512.[70]

All Norton's land lay in closes in the 16th century when most was meadow or pasture. Cattle rearing was apparently important then. Part of Starvall was tilled. By 1589 a pasture called Wye furlong, 150 a., had been divided into 3 closes; Greenhill had been divided into Homeward Greenhill, 11 a., and Great Greenhill, 36 a. subdivided into 3 closes; and New leaze and Luddocks had apparently been divided respectively into 6 and 3 closes.[71] Broad leaze, 50 a., and Galley hill and Ox leaze, 40 a. and 70 a. respectively and both bounded by the Foss Way, were all divided later.[72]

The north-west part of the parish was from the late 16th or early 17th century Norton farm,[73] worked until the early 20th century from Norton Manor.[74] The farm was *c.* 177 a. in 1631,[75] *c.* 244 a. in 1652.[76] In the early 18th century there were nine farms. The 636 a. of Norton manor was in seven farms: Maidford was 140 a., Gorsey Leaze 108 a., Manor 100 a., and Starvall 20 a., and the others were 102 a., 88 a., and 66 a. Gorsey Leaze and Starvall were held together in 1707 and later.[77] Fosse was a farm in 1742,[78] later of 20 a.;[79] Norton farm was 264 a. in 1749.[80] In the earlier 18th century most land was still meadow and pasture. Only about a fifth was arable and of that most, including 38 a. after burnbaking, was newly ploughed.[81] All the farms were worked from buildings in the village except Maidford, Gorsey Leaze, and Fosse. Of the six farms of Norton manor in 1780 Maidford and Gorsey Leaze were held together, a total of 256 a.; two made up Manor, a total of 185 a.; and two were held by John Buckland, a total of 192 a.[82]

In 1840 the parish contained *c.* 550 a. of meadow and pasture and *c.* 380 a. of arable. The farms were Manor, 299 a. in the south-west, Norton, 264 a., Maidford, 149 a., Gorsey Leaze, 149 a., Buckland, 83 a. between Manor and Norton farms, and Fosse, 20 a. The 20 a. of Starvall was not included in any of those farms. Arable exceeded meadow and pasture on Manor and Norton farms; in the east Maidford and Gorsey Leaze were predominantly grassland.[83] In the mid 19th century Maidford, Gorsey Leaze, and Starvall were sometimes

[51] *Sar. Chart. and Doc.* (Rolls Ser.), 120.
[52] P.R.O., SC 6/Hen. VIII/3986, rot. 120d.
[53] *Inq. Non.* (Rec. Com.), 165–6.
[54] *Cal. Pat.* 1547–8, 115.
[55] P.R.O., C 142/114, no. 71; C 142/163, no. 59.
[56] W.R.O. 130/25, deed, Chandos to Staples, 1589.
[57] e.g. ibid. 1305/205, abstr. of title, 1829; P.R.O., C 142/680, no. 30; ibid. CP 25(2)/371/13 Jas. I Mich.
[58] W.R.O. 130/25, licence to alienate, 1589.
[59] P.R.O., C 2/Jas. I/C 9/8.
[60] W.R.O., tithe award.
[61] Ibid. 130/25, deed, Estcourt to Ivye; Soc. Antiq. MS. 817, ix, f. 53.
[62] W.R.O. 1305/205, abstr. of title, 1829.
[63] Soc. Antiq. MS. 817, ix, f. 53.
[64] W.R.O., tithe award.
[65] *V.C.H. Wilts.* ii, p. 125.
[66] *Interdict Doc.* (Pipe R. Soc. N.S. xxxiv), 22.
[67] *Reg. Malm.* ii. 367.
[68] Ibid. i. 178–9.
[69] Below.
[70] P.R.O., SC 6/Hen. VIII/3986, rot. 120d.
[71] Ibid. C 3/88/41; C 3/107/17; ibid. REQ 2/34/56; REQ 2/228/15; W.R.O. 130/25, deed, Chandos to Staples, 1589; 212B/5141.
[72] W.R.O. 11/302; 11/305; 11/307; 11/309.
[73] Ibid. 11/302; above, manor.
[74] Below; inf. from Countess Badeni.
[75] W.R.O. 11/302.
[76] Ibid. 11/310.
[77] Ibid. 1305/205, abstr. of title, 1829; Soc. Antiq. MS. 817, ix, f. 53. For the identification of farms, cf. W.R.O., tithe award.
[78] W.R.O. 312/11, will of John Jacob, 1742.
[79] Ibid. tithe award.
[80] B.L. Maps, M.T. 6e., 1 (2); cf. W.R.O., tithe award.
[81] Soc. Antiq. MS. 817, ix, f. 53; B.L. Maps, M.T. 6e., 1 (2).
[82] W.R.O. 1305/205, abstr. of title, 1829.
[83] Ibid. tithe award.

held together, as were Manor and Norton.[84] In 1867 and 1877 grassland still exceeded arable and the farming was mixed.[85] Manor farm was two thirds arable in 1877,[86] Maidford less than a third arable in 1894.[87]

There were four main farms in the parish in the 20th century.[88] In the 1930s some nine tenths of the parish were under permanent grass.[89] Later there was more arable, and in 1987 the old parish was about half arable and half pasture. Norton farm, worked from the buildings erected outside the village in the period 1900–11, absorbed Buckland farm. It was not leased and Noel Wilson kept a herd of pedigree Herefordshire cattle on it. The farm, c. 380 a., was an arable and beef farm in 1987.[90] Manor farm, 303 a. in 1940,[91] continued to be worked from buildings near the church. It was an arable and dairy farm in 1987.[92] Maidford farm, 176 a. in 1958,[93] 152 a. in 1966,[94] was a dairy farm in 1987. Gorsey Leaze farm was worked by Jewish refugees in the Second World War. A dairy herd was later kept on it, and it was still grassland when it was broken up in the 1980s.[95] On the land called Starvall the extensive buildings of Highfield farm were erected in the later 20th century. In 1987 c. 200 a. of Malmesbury common was worked from them and they incorporated a dairy.[96]

Norton is sparsely wooded. In 1631 a coppice was said to have been newly planted.[97] Maidford Copse was 4 a. in 1707.[98] A further 3 a. were planted with trees between 1840 and 1877,[99] and another small area between 1921 and 1951.[1] There were c. 10 a. of woodland in the old parish in 1987.

LOCAL GOVERNMENT. In 1775–6 the parish spent £45 on poor relief, and between 1782 and 1785 an average of £57. By 1802–3, when 12 adults and 20 children were continuously relieved, expenditure had risen to £126. For a parish of Norton's size such figures were about average, but in 1812–13, when 24 adults were relieved continuously,[2] and in the period 1817–20, when over £200 a year was spent, spending on poor relief was apparently above average. In the 1820s and early 1830s it fluctuated between £81 and £166 and was again about average.[3] The parish joined

Malmesbury poor-law union in 1835,[4] and in 1974 became part of North Wiltshire district.[5]

CHURCH. Malmesbury abbey had a chapel at Norton in 1151.[6] In 1222 the abbey was licensed to appropriate it on condition that a vicarage was ordained,[7] and the church was being served by a vicar in 1283.[8] In 1976 the vicarage was united with the benefice of Stanton St. Quintin and Grittleton with Leigh Delamere and with the vicarage of Hullavington.[9]

The advowson of the vicarage belonged to Malmesbury abbey until the Dissolution.[10] The king presented in 1283 and 1332, for reasons which are not clear,[11] and in 1511 when the abbey was vacant;[12] the bishop collated by lapse in 1363;[13] and in 1533 Christopher Brown and Thomas Burnell presented by the abbey's grant.[14] The advowson was granted with Norton manor and the rectory estate to Sir John Brydges in 1547[15] and descended with them to his son Edmund, Lord Chandos, and to Edmund's son Giles, Lord Chandos.[16] Between 1589 and 1592 the advowson was acquired by Sir John Danvers, who presented in 1592[17] and died holding it in 1594.[18] In 1608 trustees of Sir John's son Henry, later earl of Danby, presented with the consent of Sir John's relict Elizabeth Carey.[19] No presentation between 1608 and 1675 is known. The advowson was, with Bremilham manor, referred to in deeds effecting the descent of Sir John Danvers's estate to Henry, earl of Danby (d. 1644), and to Sir John Danvers (d. 1655). There is no evidence that Sir John's trustees sold the advowson of Norton with Bremilham manor in 1656 to Sir Thomas Estcourt, lord of Norton manor and rectory,[20] and the advowson was referred to in later deeds of the Danvers and Wharton families, which retained the advowson of Bremilham.[21] In 1675 and 1680, however, Sir Thomas Estcourt presented, as his son Sir Thomas did in 1687:[22] in each case the vicar was also rector of Bremilham.[23] In 1713 the advowson was disputed between a trustee of Thomas Estcourt (d. 1704) and Thomas, earl of Wharton. Apparently because the three previous presentations had not been disputed, the trustee's claim was upheld,[24] and he presented in 1713.[25] The advowson was sold with Norton manor in 1714 and passed with

[84] W.R.O., A 1/345/309.
[85] P.R.O., MAF 68/151, sheet 3; MAF 68/550, sheet 1.
[86] W.R.O. 374/130/87.
[87] Ibid. 1409/243.
[88] Ibid. Inland Revenue, val. reg. 13.
[89] [1st] Land Util. Surv. Map, sheet 103.
[90] Inf. from Countess Badeni.
[91] Bristol R.O., EP/A/22/1/92.
[92] Inf. from Countess Badeni.
[93] Wilts. Cuttings, xxi. 106.   [94] Ibid. xxii. 376.
[95] Inf. from Countess Badeni.
[96] O.S. Map 1/25,000, ST 88 (1958 edn.); local inf.
[97] W.R.O. 11/302.
[98] Soc. Antiq. MS. 817, ix, f. 53.
[99] W.R.O., tithe award; ibid. 374/130/87.
[1] O.S. Maps 6", Wilts. XIII. NW. (1925 edn.); 1/25,000, ST 88 (1958 edn.).
[2] Poor Law Abstract, 1804, 566–7; 1818, 498–9.
[3] Poor Rate Returns, 1816–21, 189; 1822–4, 228; 1825–9, 219; 1830–4, 212.
[4] Poor Law Com. 2nd Rep. App. D, 559.
[5] O.S. Map 1/100,000, admin. areas, Wilts. (1974 edn.).
[6] Reg. Malm. i. 349.

[7] Sar. Chart. and Doc. (Rolls Ser.), 120.
[8] Cal. Pat. 1281–92, 74.
[9] Ch. Com. file, NB 5/143B.
[10] Phillipps, Wilts. Inst. (index in W.A.M. xxviii. 226).
[11] Cal. Pat. 1281–92, 74, where, in error, the king is said in 1283 to have presented sede vacante; Phillipps, Wilts. Inst. i. 28.
[12] Phillipps, Wilts. Inst. i. 189.
[13] Ibid. 57.   [14] Ibid. 203.
[15] Cal. Pat. 1547–8, 115.
[16] P.R.O., C 142/114, no. 71; C 142/163, no. 59.
[17] Phillipps, Wilts. Inst. i. 233; W.R.O. 130/25, deed, Chandos to Staples, 1589.
[18] P.R.O., C 142/247, no. 100.
[19] Phillipps, Wilts. Inst. ii. 5; Complete Peerage, iv. 48–9.
[20] W.N. & Q. viii. 211; P.R.O., CP 25(2)/526/4 Chas. I Trin.; CP 25(2)/527/8 Chas. I Trin.; CP 25(2)/616/1652 Trin.; above, Bremilham, manor.
[21] P.R.O., CP 25(2)/806/1 Jas. II East.; W.R.O. 212B/3917; above, Bremilham, church.
[22] Phillipps, Wilts. Inst. ii. 33, 36, 41.
[23] Below.   [24] W.R.O., D 1/2/14, f. 176.
[25] Phillipps, Wilts. Inst. ii. 52.

it until offered for sale in 1798.[26] In 1727 Robert Greenway presented, presumably by grant of a turn.[27] Robert Kilmister bought the advowson in 1802 and sold it in 1817 to Joseph Pitt.[28] In 1835 Pitt sold it to Joseph Neeld[29] and thereafter it descended with Gorsey Leaze farm to Sir Audley Neeld, Bt. (d. 1941).[30] It passed to Sir Audley's second cousin L. W. Inigo-Jones (d. 1956), L. W. Neeld from 1942, and in 1965 an executor of L. W. Neeld presented. In 1971 Neeld's executors transferred the advowson to his nephew R. W. Inigo-Jones (later R. W. Neeld), who since 1976 has had the right to present a candidate for the benefice of Stanton St. Quintin and Grittleton with Leigh Delamere, Hullavington, and Norton at every third turn.[31]

The vicarage, valued at 5 marks in 1535[32] and c. £20 in 1650,[33] was poor. It was augmented by lot with £200 from Queen Anne's Bounty in 1809–10.[34] With a yearly income of £80 c. 1830, it remained poor.[35] The vicar may have been entitled to tithes of hay and to small tithes in 1341.[36] After the dispute of 1613–15 between the vicar and the lessee of the rectory estate,[37] and presumably a compromise, the vicar was entitled to the great tithes from 49 a. and to the small tithes from the whole parish. His tithes were valued in 1840 at £100 and commuted.[38] The vicar had little glebe in the later 16th century, and in 1672 he had only two small pastures.[39] There was a small house on the glebe north-east of the church in 1783,[40] said c. 1833 to be unfit for residence.[41] In 1840 the vicar owned the house and no other glebe.[42] The house was rebuilt in 1856 and sold in 1956.[43]

In the 14th and 15th centuries most incumbencies were short, and no vicar is known to have remained more than 20 years.[44] There is no evidence that a vicar lived in the parish. Richard Cox, vicar from 1608 to 1650, when the county committee called him 'godly',[45] or later, may have done so, but from 1675 most vicars were pluralists and all apparently non-resident. John Stumpe, vicar 1675–80, was rector of Foxley and of Bremilham;[46] Edmund Wayte, 1680–7, was rector of Bremilham;[47] John Harris, 1687–1713, was rector of Easton Grey and of Bremilham; Timothy Millichamp, 1713–27, was rector of Long Newnton;[48] Thomas Hornidge, 1752–96, was vicar of Coaley (Glos.) and curate of Beverstone (Glos.), where

he lived;[49] Hornidge's son-in-law John Green, 1796–1837, lived at Hullavington and held curacies elsewhere;[50] W. S. Birch, 1837–46, was rector of Easton Grey and of Luckington.[51] Curates were often employed:[52] Simon Crook, curate 1716–18[53] or longer, also served Foxley,[54] and Thomas Jones, curate 1793–1805 or longer,[55] was also curate of Foxley and of Hullavington.[56] From 1846 to 1891 the Wiltshire antiquary J. E. Jackson, first editor of the *Wiltshire Archaeological Magazine*, was vicar. He was also rector of Leigh Delamere, where he lived.[57] From 1870 he often employed a curate to serve Norton.[58] His successor, C. T. Read, 1891–9, was also rector of Easton Grey,[59] and Read's successors G. L. Pitt, 1899–1902, and H. L. Warneford, 1902–46, were both rectors of Foxley with Bremilham.[60] From 1948 to 1973 the vicarage was held in plurality with Hullavington vicarage.[61]

In 1662 the church lacked a Book of Homilies and Jewell's *Apology*.[62] In 1783 no curate was employed and services were held on alternate Sundays by the vicar who lived at Beverstone. Communion was celebrated four times a year with seven or eight communicants. Children were catechized in summer.[63] The augmentation of 1809 was set aside because the vicar would not consent to hold a weekly service, and restored in 1810 when the question of duty was referred to the bishop. The vicar held two services on Sundays in 1832.[64] A service was held every Sunday in the afternoon in 1851: it was attended by 46 on Census Sunday.[65] In 1903 there were two services on every second and fourth Sunday of five, one on the other Sundays.[66] Few services were held in the church in 1987.

The church of *ALL SAINTS*, so called in 1763,[67] is of limestone rubble with ashlar dressings and consists of a chancel and a nave with north porch and incorporating a west vestry surmounted by a bellcot. The sizes of the chancel and the nave, both small, are little changed from the 12th century, and there is a later 12th-century font in the church. The east window is 13th-century, the west window and a blocked south doorway are 14th-century, and other windows are 15th- and 16th-century. The porch and the chancel roof are also 16th-century. In 1858 the west wall of the church was rebuilt and the bellcot was replaced by

[26] W.R.O. 1305/207, abstr. of title, 1835.
[27] Phillipps, *Wilts. Inst.* ii. 60.
[28] W.R.O. 1305/207, abstr. of title, 1835.
[29] Ibid. 1305/207, deed, Pitt to Neeld, 1835.
[30] Bristol R.O., EP/A/3/238.
[31] Burke, *Land. Gent.* (1952), 1868–9, where Sir Audley's date of d. is misprinted; Ch. Com. file, NB 5/143B; W.R.O. 1655/8.
[32] *Valor Eccl.* (Rec. Com.), ii. 137.
[33] *W.A.M.* xli. 7.
[34] Ch. Com. file, F 3528.
[35] *Rep. Com. Eccl. Revenues*, 842–3.
[36] *Inq. Non.* (Rec. Com.), 165.
[37] P.R.O., C 2/Jas. I/C 9/8.
[38] W.R.O., tithe award.
[39] Ibid. D 1/24/157/1–2.
[40] *Vis. Queries, 1783* (W.R.S. xxvii), p. 167; for the location, W.R.O., tithe award.
[41] *Rep. Com. Eccl. Revenues*, 842–3.
[42] W.R.O., tithe award.
[43] Ibid. 1655/8.
[44] Phillipps, *Wilts. Inst.* (index in *W.A.M.* xxviii. 226).
[45] Phillipps, *Wilts. Inst.* ii. 5; *W.A.M.* xli. 7.
[46] Phillipps, *Wilts. Inst.* ii. 33, 36; above, Foxley, church.
[47] Phillipps, *Wilts. Inst.* ii. 36, 41; W.R.O., D 1/48/2.

[48] Phillipps, *Wilts. Inst.* ii. 41, 52, 60; W.R.O., D 1/51/1.
[49] Phillipps, *Wilts. Inst.* ii. 74, 98; *Vis. Queries, 1783* (W.R.S. xxvii), p. 167; Soc. Antiq. MS. 817, ix, f. 65.
[50] Phillipps, *Wilts. Inst.* ii. 98; Soc. Antiq. MS. 817, ix, f. 65; Ch. Com. file, F 3528.
[51] Bristol R.O., EP/A/1/4 (1837, 1846); Soc. Antiq. MS. 817, ix, f. 65.
[52] W.R.O., bishop's transcripts, bdles. 2–3.
[53] Ibid. bdle. 2.   [54] Above, Foxley, church.
[55] W.R.O., bishop's transcripts, bdle. 3.
[56] P.R.O., HO 67/23, nos. 58, 63, 103.
[57] Bristol R.O., EP/A/3/238 (1846, 1891). For Jackson's life, J. Stratford, *Cat. of Jackson Coll.* 11–26; *D.N.B.*
[58] W.R.O. 1655/7–8.
[59] Bristol R.O., EP/A/3/238 (1891, 1899); *Crockford* (1898).
[60] Bristol R.O., EP/A/3/238 (1899, 1902); above, Foxley, church.
[61] Ch. Com. files 89557; NB 5/143B.
[62] W.R.O., D 1/54/1/1, no. 18.
[63] *Vis. Queries, 1783* (W.R.S. xxvii), p. 167.
[64] Ch. Com. file, NB 5/143B.
[65] P.R.O., HO 129/252/2/17/24.   [66] W.R.O. 592/4D.
[67] J. Ecton, *Thesaurus* (1763), 404.

another, made in 1854 for Grittleton House.[68] A 5-ft. high wall dividing the chancel and the nave was removed in 1866 when the present chancel arch was erected and the church was reseated. The chancel and the sanctuary were raised in 1902, and in 1910 they were panelled and the nave was reroofed.[69] The pulpit incorporates early 17th-century panelling.

The parish had a chalice of 8 oz. in 1553.[70] It was replaced in the later 16th century by a cup with a cover[71] which belonged to the parish in 1987.[72] A new silver paten was given in 1854.[73] The church had two bells in 1553.[74] In the mid 19th century there was a bell cast by James Burrough, probably in the mid 18th century.[75] It was rehung in 1926.[76] There was no parchment register in 1662.[77] New registers were begun in 1663.[78]

NONCONFORMITY. Several inhabitants of Norton in the late 17th century were Quakers,[79] and in 1798 a meeting house for Independents was certified.[80] There is no other evidence of dissent in the parish.

EDUCATION. Anne Jacob (d. 1710) gave by will £100, which was invested in a rent charge of £4 on an estate in Kenn (Som.), for teaching 12 children of poor inhabitants of Norton. The teacher nominated in the will may already have been teaching Norton children. The charity paid for teaching until 1816,[81] when a master taught 6–10 children,[82] but there was apparently no special school building. The income of the charity was lent informally from 1816 to 1834 when accumulated income of £68 was invested. From 1846 or earlier to 1890 the income was paid to a schoolmistress.[83] The school was attended by 8 in 1846–7,[84] by 12 in 1859 when the schoolroom was in the rebuilt house on the glebe,[85] and by 13 in 1871.[86] J. E. Jackson (d. 1891) gave by will £231 to raise the capital of Jacob's charity to £300, but from 1894, when a new school was built at Foxley, no school was held at Norton. The income from the Jacob and Jackson charities was given to Foxley school which was attended by Norton children.[87] Under a Scheme of 1905 prizes, bursaries, and outfits for those taking up a trade might be given. The two charities were merged by a Scheme of 1935, and secondary education and apprenticing thereby made the preferred objects.[88] In the 1970s and 1980s the income, £29, was used occasionally for grants to promote education. The rent charge from Kenn was redeemed in 1977.[89]

CHARITY FOR THE POOR. None known.

OAKSEY

OAKSEY village[90] is 9 km. north-east of Malmesbury.[91] A detached part of the parish, 95 a. lying to the south and almost surrounded by Minety, originated in land allotted to the men of Oaksey to replace pasture rights in Braydon forest.[92] It was transferred to Minety in 1884 and thereafter Oaksey measured 1,827 a. (739 ha.).[93]

Oaksey's boundaries follow streams and roads, and may therefore be ancient. They were described in 1591 when they were on their present course.[94] The whole of the southern boundary follows Swill brook and a tributary of it, the east part of the northern follows Flagham brook, and the eastern follows a straight road between the two brooks. The boundary with Minety to the south-east ceased to be a county boundary when that parish was transferred from Gloucestershire to Wiltshire in 1844,[95] but the northern and eastern boundaries, with Kemble, Poole Keynes, and Somerford Keynes, became the county boundary in 1896 when those parishes were transferred to Gloucestershire.[96]

Oaksey lies in the valley of the upper Thames, of which both Flagham brook and Swill brook are tributaries.[97] Kellaways Clay outcrops in the west and forms an east–west ridge, over 107 m., on which the village stands. North of the ridge limestone and clay of the Forest Marble outcrop, and south of it Cornbrash outcrops. Much land in the west was wooded and much has long been pasture

[68] W.R.O. 1655/8; Soc. Antiq. MS. 817, ix, f. 64.
[69] W.R.O. 1655/8.
[70] W.A.M. xii. 368.
[71] Nightingale, *Wilts. Plate*, 205.
[72] Inf. from the incumbent, Stanton St. Quintin.
[73] W.R.O. 1655/8.
[74] W.A.M. xii. 368.
[75] Walters, *Wilts. Bells*, 315–16; Soc. Antiq. MS. 817, ix, f. 64.
[76] W.R.O. 1655/8.
[77] Ibid. D 1/54/1/1, no. 18.
[78] Ibid. 1655/1–6. Bishop's transcripts for a few earlier years are ibid. The marriage reg. 1663–1812, with one exception, have been printed: *Wilts. Par. Reg. (Mar.)*, ed. W. P. W. Phillimore and J. Sadler, v. 147–50.
[79] *W.N. & Q.* ii. 289, 429; v. 223, 366.
[80] *Meeting Ho. Certs.* (W.R.S. xl), pp. 51–2.
[81] *Endowed Char. Wilts.* (N. Div.), 792–3.
[82] *Educ. of Poor Digest*, 1034.
[83] *Endowed Char. Wilts.* (N. Div.), 792; W.R.O. 1655/8.

[84] Nat. Soc. *Inquiry, 1846–7*, Wilts. 8–9.
[85] *Acct. of Wilts. Schs.* 36; above, church.
[86] *Returns relating to Elem. Educ.* 420.
[87] *Endowed Char. Wilts.* (N. Div.), 793–4; above, Foxley, educ.
[88] W.R.O., F 8, corresp. files, endowed chars., Norton.
[89] Char. Com. file.
[90] This article was written in 1986.
[91] Maps used include: O.S. Maps 1", sheets 34 (1828 edn.), 157 (1968 edn.); 1/50,000, sheet 173 (1974 edn.); 1/25,000, ST 99, SU 09 (1959 edns.); 6", Wilts. III–IV, IX (1885–8 and later edns.).
[92] Below, econ. hist.; for the area, P.R.O., IR 18/11109.
[93] *Census*, 1891; *Endowed Char. Wilts.* (N. Div.), 795.
[94] *W.A.M.* vi. 198.
[95] *V.C.H. Wilts.* iv. 354.
[96] Edmond Fitzmaurice, Baron Fitzmaurice, and W. L. Bown, *Boundaries of Admin. Co. of Wilts.* 9.
[97] Para. based on Geol. Surv. Map 1", solid and drift, sheet 252 (1974 edn.).

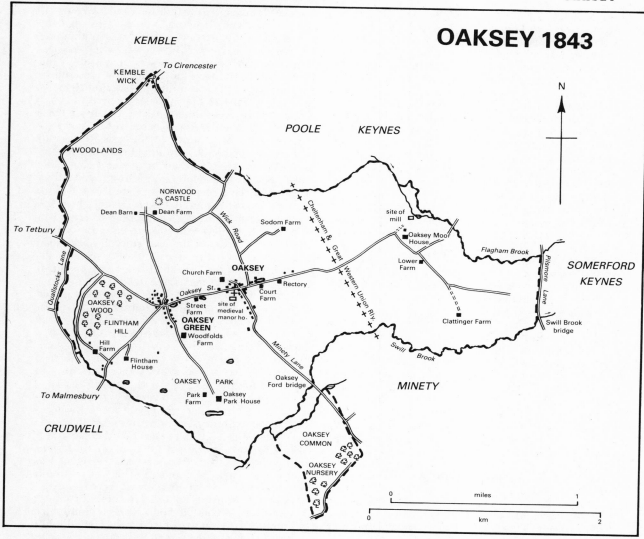

OAKSEY 1843

for dairy cattle and parkland.[98] In the east between Flagham brook and Swill brook gravel and alluvium have been deposited. Although some land there was ploughed in the earlier 19th century[99] most was and is meadow or pasture. The meadow in the south-east part was watered.[1] The snake's-head fritillary (*fritillaria meleagris*) was once abundant in the meadows and had the local name Oaksey lily.[2] Near Flagham brook gravel was extracted in the 1970s and three lakes were formed.[3] The highest point in the parish, 110 m., is in the south-west on Flintham Hill, the lowest, 85 m., in the south-east. There are small ponds in many fields throughout the parish.

The road from Somerford Keynes to Minety, which forms the eastern boundary, ran on its present course in 1591. It was called Pilsmore Lane in 1810. The Oaksey–Kemble road, Wick Road, was also on its present course where it marked the parish boundary in 1591. East of the church, Minety Lane led southwards: in 1591 it was carried

over Swill brook by Oaksey, later Oaksey Ford, bridge. Other lanes on their present courses in 1591 were that which formed the west part of the parish's north boundary and Quallstocks Lane, which declined in use in the earlier 20th century and was a footpath in 1986.[4] Oaksey Street, so called in 1609,[5] was part of a road from Somerford Keynes which entered the parish over Stockham bridge in 1591.[6] It ran along the ridge and at the west end of the village forked into branches leading north-west and south-west. A line constructed across the parish from Swindon to Kemble and Cirencester (Glos.) by the Cheltenham & Great Western Union Railway was opened in 1841 and transferred to the G.W.R. in 1844. The line was part of the main route from London to south and west Wales from 1850 to 1903. The road from Oaksey to Somerford Keynes was carried over the line on Oaksey bridge: a halt south of the bridge was opened in 1929[7] and closed in 1964.[8]

A Bronze-Age axe is the only prehistoric artifact

[98] Below, econ. hist.
[99] P.R.O., IR 29/38/211; IR 30/38/211.
[1] O.S. Map 6", Wilts. IV (1885 edn.).
[2] D. Gross, *Flora of Wilts*. 557; N. Rogers, *Wilts. Dialect*, 83.
[3] Inf. from Mrs. G. F. Raines, Lower Moor Farm.

[4] *W.A.M.* vi. 198; W.R.O. 529/87/16.
[5] P.R.O., REQ 2/389/16.
[6] *W.A.M.* vi. 198.
[7] *V.C.H. Wilts*. iv. 283, 289; Ch. Com. file 75717.
[8] C. R. Clinker, *Clinker's Reg. Closed Passenger Sta. 1830–1980*, p. 104.

found in the parish. A kiln, possibly Romano-British, for making bricks and tiles was found in the detached part of Oaksey now in Minety.[9] Norwood castle north of Dean Farm is possibly a Norman motte-and-bailey site.[10] In the early 14th century demesne cultivation and the number of tenant holdings increased, and from 1347 or earlier a large manor house was built in the parish. Presumably as a result the assessment of Oaksey for taxation in 1334 was the highest in Chedglow hundred. In 1377 Oaksey had 86 poll-tax payers, one of the higher numbers in the hundred. Economic decline in the intervening period[11] may have accounted for Oaksey's low assessment for taxation in 1545, 1576, and the earlier 17th century.[12] The population of the parish was 363 in 1801, had risen to 614 by 1841 when 46 of the inhabitants were labourers building the railway, and had fallen to 354 by 1901. Between 1901 and 1951 the population fluctuated between 308 and 362.[13] New housing between 1951 and 1961 led to an increase to 446, but between 1961 and 1981 there was a decrease to 409.[14]

Oaksey is a street village on a ridge, a form of settlement which suggests that it originated early. Its older buildings are of stone and rubble and many have Cotswold stone roofs. In 1975 part of it was designated a conservation area.[15]

The church stood in the 12th century on the south side of Oaksey Street.[16] The large manor house was built south of it. Only the foundations of the house remained c. 1593[17] and earthworks in a field marked its site in 1986. Also on the south side of the street a gabled 17th-century cottage west of the church was perhaps the church house which stood in 1609.[18] West of it a school was built in the mid 19th century,[19] a village hall was opened in 1921, and land south and east of the school was laid out as playing fields in 1950.[20] Further west on the south side of the street an 18th-century house has a decorative stone window lintel and other decoration in the manner of a carver's trial pieces, and Johnson's House, formerly Street Farm, is an early 18th-century house much altered c. 1980[21] with a derelict farmstead west of it. East of the church on the south side Court Farm incorporates in its north wing, where a doorway dated 1692 has been reset, part of a house of the later 17th century: the house was enlarged and extended southwards between 1843 and 1875.[22] To the east, the former Rectory is 18th-century.[23] Of the houses which stood on the north side of the street in 1773,[24] Tudor House is 17th-century. The main

east–west range has a central stack and a symmetrical south entrance front. A short north wing contains a 17th-century staircase, and west of that was a north service wing. The service wing was demolished, new north-west service rooms were built, and the house was extensively restored c. 1970.[25] Street Villa was built in the period 1872–83 for R. C. Warner as a farmhouse for Street farm.[26] A farmstead stands west of it. East of it six flats, four for old people and two for young couples, were built in the grounds of the new Rectory in 1978 for the Oaksey Charitable Trust, which Mr. J. R. Assheton established for general charitable purposes in England in 1972.[27] In a lane leading north from the street the Wheatsheaf was an inn in 1848[28] and 1986, and Church Farm, which has extensive farm buildings around it, was rebuilt in 1884 for R. C. Warner.[29] Four pairs of council houses were built on the east side of Wick Road in 1931[30] and in the 1970s and 1980s there was building on both sides of Oaksey Street and of the north end of Minety Lane.

Oaksey Green, where there may have been settlement in the later 12th century,[31] was a subsidiary settlement at the west end of Oaksey village where the street forked. The fork was called Earl's Corner. Nearly all the houses in the settlement in 1986 appear to be of the 19th and 20th centuries, but several may be on sites of those standing in 1773.[32] Woodfolds Farm to the south-east may have been built in the 18th century. It has a symmetrical west entrance front with a central doorway, gable chimneys, and a lower south range. The house was altered, restored, and enlarged for Gervas Huxley in the period 1938–41 to designs by Thomas Rayson.[33] An east service wing was extended c. 1972.[34] A nonconformist chapel built west of Earl's Corner in the mid 19th century[35] was a private house in 1986. In the period 1946–65 an estate of 46 council houses called Bendybow and sewage disposal works were constructed south of the street at Oaksey Green.[36]

In the east Oaksey Moor House was standing in 1773.[37] A new north–south range of three storeys and five bays was added on the west in the later 18th century. The west entrance front of the new range had a moulded stone cornice and parapet and a stone portico with a pediment and Tuscan columns. The house was demolished in 1966. Little Moor Cottage to the north was built before 1843.[38] South of the road to Somerford Keynes, Lower Moor Farm was standing in 1773[39] and may have been built in the 18th century. It was added

[9] V.C.H. Wilts. i (1), 90, 93.
[10] W.A.M. xlv. 137.
[11] Cal. Pat. 1345–8, 450; V.C.H. Wilts. iv. 298, 309; below, econ. hist.
[12] Taxation Lists (W.R.S. x), 29, 51; P.R.O., E 179/198/287; E 179/198/324; E 179/199/366.
[13] V.C.H. Wilts. iv. 320, 355.
[14] Census, 1961; 1971; 1981.
[15] Inf. from Co. Planning Officer, Co. Hall, Trowbridge.
[16] Below, church.
[17] Ibid. manor.
[18] P.R.O., REQ 2/389/16.
[19] Below, educ.   [20] Char. Com. files.
[21] W.R.O. 374/129/41; 560/1.
[22] P.R.O., IR 30/38/211; O.S. Map 6", Wilts. IV (1885 edn.).
[23] Below, church.
[24] Andrews and Dury, Map (W.R.S. viii), pl. 17.

[25] Inf. from Mr. J. R. Assheton, Tudor Ho.
[26] W.R.O. 392/13, deed, 1872, copy will of Robert Warner; below, manor.
[27] Char. Com. file; inf. from Mr. Assheton.
[28] Kelly's Dir. Wilts. (1848).
[29] E. Huxley, Gallipot Eyes, 48.
[30] Date on ho.
[31] W.A.M. liv. 227.
[32] Andrews and Dury, Map (W.R.S. viii), pl. 17.
[33] Country Life, 10 May 1941.
[34] Inf. from Mrs. N. Nicholls, Woodfolds Farm.
[35] Below, nonconf.
[36] W.R.O., G 7/516/1–3.
[37] Andrews and Dury, Map (W.R.S. viii), pl. 17.
[38] Pevsner, Wilts. (2nd edn.), 363; P.R.O., IR 30/38/211; photo. in possession of Mr. and Mrs. G. H. Baker, 14 Pittsfield, Cricklade; see above, plate facing p. 93.
[39] Andrews and Dury, Map (W.R.S. viii), pl. 17.

to in the 19th century and altered in 1947.[40] A cottage south-east of it was built c. 1946.[41] South of Lower Moor Farm, Clattinger Farm has a 17th-century north–south range in which older beams may be incorporated. A short west wing was built in the later 17th century, and c. 1783 an east wing was built and the north–south range was re-roofed.[42] South of the farmhouse, two ranges of cowsheds, one of which was still open-sided in 1986, may have been built in the 18th century, and possibly gave the farmhouse the name Stall House which it bore in 1773. East of Wick Road, Sodom Farm, so called c. 1959, was called Oaksey Farm in 1773,[43] Sodoms in 1828,[44] Sodhams or Lowfield c. 1843,[45] Lowfield in 1986. It was partly refitted in the early 19th century, and was altered and restored c. 1985.

In the north there had been settlement by 1573 on the manorial waste at Wick Green, called Kemble Wick in 1773.[46] The north-east part of the settlement was in Kemble parish. Houses of the 17th and 18th centuries stood in the Oaksey portion in 1986. South-west of Kemble Wick settlement had also taken place by 1773 at Woodlands, called Eame Cross in 1591 and also partly in Kemble.[47] Two 18th-century houses in Oaksey stood there in 1986. South-east of Woodlands, Dean Farm was built to an L-shaped plan for Benjamin Adamson in 1775 east of Dean barn, which stood in 1773 and 1986. The house was enlarged to form a square, given a mansard roof, and partly refitted in the early 19th century. It was altered in 1923.[48]

In the south-west Hill Farm was built on Flintham Hill in the 17th century. It was L-shaped, with a long range running south-east and north-west and a short north-east wing containing a staircase. Much of the inside of the house was refitted in the 18th century, and a north-west wing was built c. 1934 for Sir Geoffrey Lawrence to designs by E. J. T. Lutyens.[49] East of Hill Farm all or part of a house of the 18th century or earlier, standing in 1773,[50] was incorporated into the west part of Flintham House, which had been built by 1815;[51] on the east service rooms were built in the later 19th century. In the parkland in the south part of the parish[52] there was a lodge c. 1591 and from the early 17th century to 1956 a large manor house.[53] In the 17th century Park Farm was built west of it as a low range running north-west and south-east. A taller south-east block was built in 1761 for Benjamin and Alice Adamson.[54]

Steeplechases were held across its land in the early 20th century.[55]

MANOR AND OTHER ESTATES.

Beorhtric, a thegn, in 1086 held land at OAKSEY which his father had held in 1066. The estate was apparently bought after 1086 by Edward of Salisbury.[56] Like the manor of Wilsford in Swanborough hundred[57] it presumably passed to his daughter Maud, wife of Humphrey de Bohun, and to their son Humphrey (fl. 1131 × 1146):[58] Oaksey church was held by either that Humphrey or his father.[59] The manor descended to the younger Humphrey's son Humphrey (d. 1181),[60] whose relict Margaret de Bohun (d. 1201) held it at some time in the period 1189–99[61] for life or until her son Henry de Bohun (cr. earl of Hereford 1200, d. 1220) came of age. Henry forfeited his lands in 1217 for supporting the baronial party and Louis of France. The manor was granted to Robert FitzPayn but was restored to Henry in 1217 and after his death was held in dower by his relict Maud de Bohun.[62] In 1232 she exchanged Oaksey with her son Humphrey de Bohun, earl of Hereford (from 1236 also earl of Essex, d. 1275), and the manor afterwards descended with the earldoms to Humphrey's grandson Humphrey de Bohun[63] (d. 1298), to that Humphrey's son Humphrey[64] (d. 1322), and to that Humphrey's son John[65] (d. 1336). John was succeeded by his brother Humphrey[66] (d. 1361), and Humphrey by his nephew Humphrey de Bohun, earl of Hereford, Essex, and Northampton[67] (d. 1373),[68] whose relict Joan held Oaksey until her death in 1419.[69] When the Bohun estates were partitioned in 1421 Oaksey was allotted to Henry V, the son of Humphrey's and Joan's daughter Mary, and it was part of the duchy of Lancaster until the early 17th century. It was assigned in 1422 to Catherine, relict of Henry V, and in 1467 to Elizabeth, queen of Edward IV.[70] Henry VII resumed the manor in 1485.[71]

In 1347 Humphrey, earl of Hereford, was licensed to crenellate his house in Oaksey.[72] In the earlier 15th century the house had a hall with an east tower, a solar on the west, eight rooms on the south, and a ninth room and domestic offices on the north. Hall and tower were roofed with lead and other buildings with stone slates. The house included two chapels and a third stood within its precinct. A farmstead stood nearby.[73]

40 W.R.O., G 7/760/207.
41 Ibid. G 7/760/197.
42 Date on ho. and roof timbers.
43 Andrews and Dury, Map (W.R.S. viii), pl. 17; O.S. Map 1/25,000, ST 99 (1959 edn.).
44 O.S. Map 1", sheet 34 (1828 edn.).
45 P.R.O., IR 30/38/211.
46 Ibid. DL 1/88, f. 65; Andrews and Dury, Map (W.R.S. viii), pl. 17.
47 W.A.M. vi. 198; Andrews and Dury, Map (W.R.S. viii), pl. 17.
48 Andrews and Dury, Map (W.R.S. viii), pl. 17; Country Life, 6 July 1929; initials and date on ho.; below, manor.
49 W.R.O., G 7/760/22.
50 Andrews and Dury, Map (W.R.S. viii), pl. 17.
51 W.R.O. 374/587.
52 Below, econ. hist.
53 Ibid. manor.
54 W.R.O. 212A/27/28, p. 3; initials and date A/B A/1761 on S. front.
55 Huxley, Gallipot Eyes, 66–7.
56 V.C.H. Wilts. ii, pp. 110 n., 160.
57 Ibid. x. 207.
58 For the Bohun fam., Complete Peerage, vi. 457–77; xi. 373–4; Dugdale, Baronage, i. 178–80.
59 Below, church.
60 Rot. de Dominabus (Pipe R. Soc. xxxv), 5 n., 62.
61 Abbrev. Plac. (Rec. Com.), 14.
62 Rot. Litt. Claus. (Rec. Com.), i. 321, 423.
63 Cal. Inq. p.m. ii, p. 87; P.R.O., CP 25(1)/283/9, no. 93.
64 Cal. Inq. p.m. iii, p. 425.
65 Feud. Aids, v. 209.
66 Cal. Inq. p.m. viii, p. 27.
67 Ibid. xi, pp. 367–8.
68 Ibid. xiii, p. 132.
69 Cal. Close, 1369–74, 496; Feud. Aids, vi. 529.
70 Rot. Parl. iv. 135–7, 183–9; v. 628.
71 Ibid. vi. 347; P.R.O., DL 1/173, f. 27.
72 Cal. Pat. 1345–8, 450.
73 P.R.O., DL 29/652/10553; DL 29/653/10564; DL 43/14/

The buildings were often repaired in the 15th century,[74] but had been demolished by c. 1593.[75]

The Crown sold the park at Oaksey between 1596 and 1598. In 1598 it was owned by Mary, relict of Sir Thomas Heneage (d. 1595), chancellor of the duchy of Lancaster, and conveyed by her to Henry Nevill,[76] whose brother-in-law Sir Henry Poole owned it before 1612. In 1614 the Crown sold Oaksey manor to Sir Henry (d. 1632), from whom the reunited estate descended in the direct male line to Sir Nevill Poole[77] (d. c. 1660) and Sir Edward Poole (d. 1673). All the Pooles represented Wiltshire boroughs in parliament.[78] Sir Edward was apparently succeeded by his son Nevill Poole,[79] and Nevill by his son Henry, in possession 1687.[80] In 1716 Poole sold lands that became Oaksey Moor farm and Lower Moor farm, and in 1720 mortgaged the rest of the manor to Robert Westley (knighted 1744, d. 1745), to whom it passed on Poole's death in 1726.[81] Westley was succeeded by his son John (d. 1748), who devised the estate to his sister Alice, the wife of Benjamin Adamson (d. 1783).[82] From Alice, who died before 1773, it passed to her son Robert Adamson, M.P. for Cricklade 1784–5.[83] It comprised the whole parish except Oaksey Moor farm and Lower Moor farm, and Adamson sold it in portions in 1789–90.

Oaksey park, woodland, and the manor house later called Oaksey Park House, a total of 450 a., were bought in 1790 by James Harris, Baron Malmesbury (cr. earl of Malmesbury 1800, d. 1820). In 1800–1 the earl sold them to Francis Webb, who c. 1789 had bought PARK farm and other land from Adamson[84] and in 1795 had settled some of those lands on his daughter Frances and her husband Thomas Salisbury (d. 1810). Frances inherited the rest on her father's death in 1814,[85] and in 1843–4 she owned c. 600 a. in Oaksey parish.[86] From Frances Salisbury (d. 1862)[87] the estate passed to her daughters Sophia Salisbury (d. 1882) and Maria Salisbury (d. 1886).[88] They sold land north of Oaksey Street in 1872. The remainder of the estate[89] descended to their grandnephew Algernon Burnaby who in 1906 sold it to L. J. Baker (d. 1921). Baker's executors sold Oaksey wood in 1922, and in 1938 the remainder of the estate to A. H. Smith, who sold it in portions. Oaksey Park House and Park farm were bought by the Cotswold Bruderhof, a group of men and women who farmed in common. The Bruderhof sold them in 1941 to the Cirencester Benefit Society and the society in 1954 to Mr. James Woodhouse,[90] who also bought other land in the parish. In 1986 J. Woodhouse & Co. owned c. 440 a. in it including Park farm and the lands of Sodom farm.[91]

Before 1591 a lodge in the park was rebuilt for Sir Henry Knyvett, deputy keeper of the park. Oaksey Park House was built as the manor house in the early 17th century, possibly for Sir Henry Poole.[92] It was called Oaksey House in 1773,[93] Oaksey Manor in 1938. It had mullioned windows and a north-east entrance front of three storeys with twin gables. Additions, including a two-storeyed segmental entrance porch with a pyramidal roof, were made, apparently in the 18th and 19th centuries.[94] The house was a hotel in 1955–6,[95] and demolished in 1956–7.[96]

OAKSEY MOOR farm and LOWER farm, later Lower Moor farm, were bought in 1716 by John Oatridge (d. 1744), from whom they descended to his son Robert (d. 1754), and to Robert's daughter Anne. She, from 1773 the wife of the Revd. John Lloyd (d. 1807), settled the lands on herself and her husband. In 1808 she sold them to Richard Holtham (d. 1838),[97] whose successor John Holtham (d. 1887) in 1843–4 owned those two farms and other land, a total of 259 a.[98] Of that land, Lower Moor farm, c. 120 a., was owned in 1896 by W. W. B. Beach and J. Inskip,[99] in 1910 by Robert Bolton,[1] in 1927 by W. B. Wilson,[2] and from 1947 by M. Everleigh, who in 1960 sold the farm, then 106 a., to Mr. and Mrs. G. F. Raines, the owners in 1986.[3] Oaksey Moor or Upper Moor farm, then 95 a., and a 65-a. farm formed from its lands and called Little Moor, were owned in the period 1927–49 by F. G. Baker, whose son sold most of the land to D. J. C. Thomas c. 1963.[4]

CHURCH farm, 77 a., was bought c. 1789 by William Croome, who sold it in 1805 to Leonard Hawkins (d. 1819). Hawkins devised it to his relict Hester (d. 1841),[5] whose trustees sold the farm, 117 a., in 1843 to E. P. Warner (d. 1883).[6]

[74] P.R.O., DL 29/653/10564; DL 29/654/10577; DL 29/656/10616.
[75] Ibid. DL 4/35/33.
[76] Ibid. CP 25(2)/242/39 & 40 Eliz. I Mich.; ibid. DL 1/177, f. 26; Complete Peerage, xii. 126–7.
[77] Wilts. Inq. p.m. 1625–49 (Index Libr.), 148–50; P.R.O., C 66/2018, mm. 7–9; D. Rowland, Hist. and Geneal. Acct. of Fam. of Nevill, table III.
[78] Hist. Parl., Commons, 1558–1603, iii. 231; 1660–90, iii. 262; M. F. Keeler, Long Parl. 309–10; P.R.O., CP 25(2)/744/12 & 13 Chas. II Hil.
[79] P.R.O., CP 25(2)/745/22 Chas. II East.; ibid. PROB 11/344, ff. 177v.–178.
[80] Alum. Oxon. 1500–1714, iii. 1179; W.R.O. 130/25, view of frankpledge, 1687.
[81] W. A. Shaw, Knights of Eng. ii. 286; Musgrave's Obit. vi (Harl. Soc. xlix), 240; Sale of Hen. Poole's Estates, 5 Geo. II, c. 5 (Priv. Act); W.R.O. 392/9B, deed, 1790; P.R.O., PROB 11/614, ff. 23v.–24v.; below.
[82] W.N. & Q. vii. 131; Musgrave's Obit. i (Harl. Soc. xliv), 11; W.R.O. 667/1/1, copy will of John Westley.
[83] Hist. Parl., Commons, 1754–90, ii. 11; W.R.O. 392/9B, deed, 1790.
[84] Complete Peerage, viii. 358–61; W.R.O., A 1/345/312; ibid. 280/75/2.
[85] W.R.O. 667/1/5, deed, 1829.

[86] P.R.O., IR 29/38/211; IR 30/38/211.
[87] W.R.O. 392/13, deed, 1872.
[88] Huxley, Gallipot Eyes, 183.
[89] W.R.O. 374/130/89; 392/13, deed, 1872; 560/1.
[90] Ibid. 1008/9; ibid. G 7/515/7; Huxley, Gallipot Eyes, 183–4, geneal. tables.
[91] Inf. from Mrs. E. Huxley, Green End; Mr. J. Woodhouse, Park Farm.
[92] Wilts. Inq. p.m. 1625–49 (Index Libr.), 148–50; P.R.O., DL 42/115, f. 78.
[93] Andrews and Dury, Map (W.R.S. viii), pl. 17.
[94] Gent. Mag. lxxvi (1), pl. facing p. 212; see above, plate facing p. 93; W.R.O. 1008/9; 1579/30.
[95] W.R.O., G 7/516/2. [96] Ibid. 1579/30.
[97] Ibid. 374/582, deeds of Holtham's estate; 1579/1; 1579/11.
[98] Ibid. 1579/11; P.R.O., IR 29/38/211; IR 30/38/211.
[99] W.R.O. 281, sale cat. of Lower Moor farm, 1896.
[1] Ibid. Inland Revenue, val. reg. 5. [2] Ibid. G 7/515/7.
[3] Inf. from Mrs. G. F. Raines, Lower Moor Farm.
[4] W.R.O., G 7/515/7; G 7/516/1; G 7/516/3; inf. from Mrs. G. H. Baker, 14 Pittsfield, Cricklade.
[5] W.R.O. 280/75/1; 392/9C, deeds of Church farm; 1579/11; ibid. A 1/345/312.
[6] Ibid. A 1/345/312; ibid. 1579/11; 1579/27, pp. 6–8; P.R.O., IR 29/38/211; IR 30/38/211.

Warner's successor was his kinsman R. C. Warner (d. 1930),[7] and his a kinsman Frank Warner[8] (d. 1981).[9] The land, 105 a., passed to Frank Warner's relict Ruth (d. 1983), whose executors owned it in 1986.[10]

CLATTINGER farm, 131 a., was bought *c.* 1789 by Joseph Pitt. He sold it *c.* 1807 to William Hewer, whose relict Hannah succeeded him in it *c.* 1812. From Hannah Hewer the farm passed *c.* 1823 to Henry Jones, possibly a trustee, and *c.* 1824 it was owned by John Lucas (d. 1842 or 1843), whose trustees held it in 1843–4 and later.[11] Thomas Lucas owned the farm in 1910,[12] Walter Ody 1918–60, and Ody's son Mr. Harold Ody in 1986 when Clattinger farm was 154 a.[13]

COURT farm, 161 a., was bought in 1790 with Oaksey park by Lord Malmesbury. He sold it in 1800–1 to John Hawkins[14] (d. 1815),[15] who was succeeded by Thomas Hawkins[16] (d. 1848).[17] J. L. Hawkins owned the farm in 1870–1.[18] Arthur Rich (d. 1943), the owner in 1889, was succeeded by his nephew[19] Thomas Rich, from whom W. H. Wilson bought it *c.* 1952. Mr. Keith Wilson bought it from his father in 1957, added 45 a. to it *c.* 1962–3, and owned 140 a. in 1986.[20]

DEAN farm, 283 a., was also bought in 1790 by Lord Malmesbury,[21] who sold it to John Brooks in 1800–1. Brooks sold the farm in 1806–7 to William Henderson[22] (d. 1830), who devised it for his son Alfred (d. 1867) and for Alfred's children.[23] In 1877 Chancery ordered the farm to be sold. William Cole bought it in 1878 and owned it in 1888.[24] It was owned in 1910 by L. J. Baker[25] and 1923–31 by W. D. Phipps.[26] It was bought in 1931 by G. C. Todd (d. 1982), who settled the 270-a. farm on his son Mr. C. Todd and daughter Miss J. Todd, the owners in 1986.[27]

In 1789 David Miles bought a portion of Oaksey manor and in 1799 owned a farm of 80 a. in the south-west.[28] Part of the land became *HILL* farm, 38 a., which was owned in 1832–3 by William Stevens, 1842–4 by Mary Stevens, and in 1870–1 by a Mrs. Stevens, perhaps the same.[29] The Misses Wilton owned it in 1910[30] and sold it in 1919 to Geoffrey Lawrence (knighted 1932, cr. Baron Oaksey 1947, from 1959 Lord Trevethin, d. 1971), who bought Oaksey wood, 40 a., in 1922. His son John, Lord Trevethin and Oaksey, the steeplechase jockey and racing journalist, owned the farm, 120 a., and the wood in 1986.[31]

Most of *STREET* farm, 64 a., and *SODOM* farm, 96 a., were bought from Sophia and Maria Salisbury in 1872 by Robert Warner (d. 1883), and passed to his son R. C. Warner (d. 1930).[32] Street farm was bought after 1930 by G. C. Todd, who settled the farm, 75 a., on his son Mr. D. C. C. Todd, the owner in 1986.[33]

ECONOMIC HISTORY. In 1086 Oaksey was assessed as 6 hides and could support 6 ploughteams. On the demesne there were 10 *servi* with 2 ploughteams, and elsewhere 6 *villani* and 12 coscets had 4 ploughteams. There were 40 a. of meadow and 30 a. of pasture.[34]

The demesne in 1299 included 300 a. of arable, 80 a. of meadow worth only 1*s.* an acre because the land was poor, several pasture worth £2 6*s.* 8*d.*, and 6 a. of woodland.[35] Between 1299 and 1347 the demesne increased in size. In 1336 it included 360 a. of arable, 104 a. of meadow, 50 a. of pasture, and 110 a. of parkland and woodland which included Oaksey park.[36] In 1347 the demesne was 724 a., more than a third of the parish: it included 416 a. of arable, 107 a. of meadow, 74 a. of pasture, and 127 a. of woodland including the 96-a. park.[37] From *c.* 1347 or earlier there was a large house at Oaksey, presumably used by the earls of Hereford and Essex with their household, and the early 14th-century increase in the demesne may be associated with the use of Oaksey by the earls.[38] The demesne, except the park and woods, was leased from 1412 or earlier.[39] Afterwards the amount of arable was reduced, to 131 a. *c.* 1591, which is only partly accounted for by the increase to 180 a. and 129 a. respectively of the demesne pastures and meadows, and some arable may have been granted by copy. From 1438 or earlier until 1575 or later the demesne was leased to groups of tenants, varying from three to nine, who may either have worked the lands co-operatively or may have divided them and worked them with land held customarily. In 1575 the demesne was leased as a whole to a group of five men, who in 1591 were subletting it to 10 copyholders, including three of themselves.[40] Exceptionally, in the years 1469–78 a single lessee had the whole demesne.[41] It was apparently leased in the early 17th century.[42]

The early 14th-century expansion of the demesne was matched by an increase in the number of tenant holdings from 63 in 1299 to 88 in 1347. In 1299 there were 13 free tenants, of

[7] *W.A.M.* xlv. 271.
[8] Huxley, *Gallipot Eyes*, 48–9; W.R.O., G 7/516/1–3.
[9] Mon. in churchyd.
[10] Inf. from Miss M. Warner, Driftwood, Ham Lane, S. Cerney, Glos.
[11] W.R.O. 280/75/1; 1579/27, pp. 43–4; ibid. A 1/345/312; P.R.O., IR 29/38/211; IR 30/38/211.
[12] W.R.O., Inland Revenue, val. reg. 5.
[13] Ibid. G 7/515/7; G 7/516/1–3; inf. from Mr. H. W. Ody, Clattinger Farm.
[14] W.R.O. 280/75/1; ibid. A 1/345/312.
[15] Ibid. 1579/11.
[16] Ibid. 1579/27, pp. 22–3.
[17] Mon. in churchyd.
[18] W.R.O., A 1/345/312.
[19] *Kelly's Dir. Wilts.* (1889); Huxley, *Gallipot Eyes*, 29–30.
[20] Inf. from Mr. K. Wilson, Court Farm.
[21] W.R.O. 280/75/1; 667/1/4.
[22] Ibid. A 1/345/312.
[23] Ibid. 374/585; 1579/11.
[24] Ibid. 281, sale cat. 1888; 374/130/90.

[25] Ibid. Inland Revenue, val. reg. 5.
[26] Ibid. G 7/515/7; *Kelly's Dir. Wilts.* (1923 and later edns.).
[27] Inf. from Miss J. Todd, Dean Farm.
[28] W.R.O. 374/584, abstr. of title to Miles's lands.
[29] W.R.O. A 1/345/312; ibid. 1579/27, p. 10; P.R.O., IR 29/38/211; IR 30/38/211.
[30] W.R.O., Inland Revenue, val. reg. 5.
[31] Burke, *Peerage* (1959), 1707–8; *Debrett's Peerage and Baronetage* (1976), 875–6; inf. from Lord Oaksey, Hill Farm.
[32] W.R.O. 374/130/89; 392/13; 560/1; above.
[33] Inf. from Miss Todd.
[34] *V.C.H. Wilts.* ii, p. 160.
[35] *Wilts. Inq. p.m.* 1242–1326 (Index Libr.), 241–3.
[36] P.R.O., C 135/48, no. 2, rot. 18.
[37] Ibid. DL 43/9/29.   [38] Above, manor.
[39] P.R.O., DL 29/652/10553.
[40] Ibid. DL 42/115, ff. 69–79; R. C. Payne, 'Agrarian conditions on Wilts. estates of Duchy of Lanc., etc.' (Lond. Univ. Ph.D. thesis, 1940), 274, 282, 285–7.
[41] P.R.O., DL 29/656/10613–14.
[42] Ibid. DL 42/115, f. 75v.

whom 4 held 1 yardland each, 2 held ½ yardland each, and 7 held 5 a. or less each. The customary tenants included 10 yardlanders who each paid 5*d*. yearly and either worked for the lord throughout the year or paid ½*d*. a day between 29 September and 24 June; 18 ½-yardlanders paid 2*d*. each yearly and owed similar services; and 22 cottars paid a total of 18*s*. 5*d*. yearly. In 1347 of the 88 holdings, 9 were vacant; 16, of which 9 were held either by grant of the earls of Hereford and Essex or by copy, were considered free; a further 9 were yardlands, apparently of 25 a. each; 21 were ½-yardlands, and 33 were held by cottars. There were in addition 2 ¼-yardlanders and 3 tenants who held a few acres each, worked for the lord each Monday, and provided a man for a second day to complete unfinished work. As well as the usual harrowing and haymaking duties, in 1347 a total of 5,702 works was owed, 3,889 winter works, 618 summer works, 961 autumn works, 154 autumn boon-works, and 80 reaping duties.[43]

A decline in the number of tenant holdings during the 15th century was accompanied by a decline in rents after *c.* 1425.[44] The average net return received yearly by the lord also declined in the earlier 15th century but was afterwards steady, £32 in the years 1455–69, £38 in the years 1470–80.[45] In 1591 only *c.* 80 a. were held freely. Copyhold land comprised *c.* 187 a. of inclosed pasture, *c.* 111 a. of common meadows, and *c.* 230 a. of arable in the open fields. It was divided among 37 farms of which 10 also included demesne land. Eight were of between 50 a. and 100 a., the remainder of 50 a. or less.[46]

In the 1570s open arable lay in North, South, Down, and Town fields. South field was south of Oaksey Street and east of the park, and Town field was in the north abutting Poole Keynes.[47] Some arable was inclosed possibly between 1608 and 1671.[48] There was common pasture at Wick Green in 1573,[49] and meadow land in the eastern half of the parish in 1591.[50]

The tenants enjoyed common rights in woods and coppices in the parish,[51] and claimed pannage for the whole year in Flisteridge wood in Crudwell. In 1278 their claim was denied for the period 28 September to 11 November by Malmesbury abbey which impounded their pigs at Crudwell. With extreme violence the pigs were recaptured and returned to Flisteridge wood, but the lord of Oaksey shortly afterwards gave up Oaksey's claim to pannage in it for the disputed period.[52] Although the right to common pasture in Minety Moor and

Hawksbrook in Minety from 8 September to 2 February[53] was extinguished in 1531,[54] the tenants were still intercommoning in Minety in 1583.[55] The men of Oaksey also had the right to pasture cattle in Braydon forest and its purlieus.[56] The forest was inclosed in 1630,[57] and after dispute those rights were replaced by two separate allotments of *c.* 100 a. of the purlieus made in 1633 to the lord of Oaksey manor.[58] One, a triangle *c.* 5 km. south of Oaksey, was apparently inclosed and not used from Oaksey: it was later sold to the lord of Charlton manor and in Charlton parish.[59] The second was Oaksey common, the detached land of the parish.[60] It was used only for horses, bullocks, and dry cattle *c.* 1674 and was not stinted:[61] it was inclosed in 1802.[62]

Oaksey Moor and Lower Moor were farms *c.* 1716.[63] Dean farm, 214 a., was probably formed *c.* 1775.[64] In addition there were in 1787 Park farm, which had 172 a. in the parish, Court farm, 120 a., Clattinger farm, 131 a., a farm of 124 a. that became Street farm, three farms of *c.* 70 a. each, and two of less than 50 a.[65] Dean Farm in 1775 had a cheese store[66] and in 1800 Church farm was owned by a Cirencester cheese factor.[67] Woodfolds farm, *c.* 150 a., was a dairy farm in 1812.[68] In 1843–4 there were 16 farms in Oaksey of which only Dean, 255 a., and Park, 211 a., were large; Church, Clattinger, Court, Oaksey Moor, Street, and Woodfolds were of 100–160 a.; Sodom had 95 a.; and seven farms, including the glebe, had less than 55 a. All were mainly pasture farms, and the small amount of arable, 240 a., was scattered throughout the parish.[69]

There were 17–18 farms in the later 19th century.[70] In 1906, of the 18 farms 2 had over 300 a., 6 had 50–300 a., and 10 had 50 a. or less. In 1926 there were 12 farmers, of whom 7, at Clattinger, Lower Moor, Court, Church, Street, Park, and Dean farms,[71] had farms of 100–150 a. In 1956, of the 17 farmers, 1 had 500–700 a., 11 had 50–300 a., and 5 had less than 50 a. There were 12 farmers in 1976, of whom 5 had more than 50 ha.

In the later 19th century there remained much less arable than pasture. On a quarter to a third of the arable, fodder crops were grown, and on the remainder corn, chiefly wheat. Grasses grown in rotation increased from 77 a. in 1876 to 219 a. in 1896. On average, 580 cows and 300 pigs were kept in the period 1876–96. In 1876 there were over 1,000 sheep, perhaps an unusually large number: 420 were kept in 1886 and 176 in 1896.

[43] P.R.O., DL 43/9/29; Payne, 'Agrarian conditions', 82, 112, 230–3, 235, 237, 239; *Wilts. Inq. p.m.* 1242–1326 (Index Libr.), 241–3.
[44] *V.C.H. Wilts.* iv. 40–2.
[45] Payne, 'Agrarian conditions', 346, 355.
[46] P.R.O., DL 42/115, ff. 69–79.
[47] For the locations, ibid. DL 4/12/18; ibid. IR 29/38/211; IR 30/38/211.
[48] W.R.O., D 1/24/159/1–2.
[49] P.R.O., DL 1/88, f. 65.
[50] *W.A.M.* vi. 198.
[51] P.R.O., DL 29/652/10553; DL 43/9/29; DL 44/87.
[52] *Reg. Malm.* ii. 345–6, 396–7.
[53] P.R.O., DL 3/18, ff. 14–18.
[54] Ibid. DL 42/115, f. 78.
[55] Ibid. DL 1/128, f. 32.
[56] Ibid. DL 42/115, f. 77v.
[57] *V.C.H. Wilts.* iv. 406–7.
[58] W.R.O. 88/1/141.

[59] Above, Charlton, introduction, manors (Summerhouse farm).
[60] Above, introduction.
[61] P.R.O., E 134/26 Chas. II East./11.
[62] Ibid. C 54/7764, no. 10.
[63] Above, manor.
[64] W.R.O. 130/25, deed, 1775.
[65] Ibid. 280/75/1.
[66] *Country Life*, 6 July 1929.
[67] W.R.O. 392/9c, deed, 1800.   [68] Ibid. 212A/27/28.
[69] P.R.O., IR 29/38/211; IR 30/38/211.
[70] This and the following para. based on ibid. MAF 68/151, sheet 1; MAF 68/493, sheet 6; MAF 68/1063, sheet 15; MAF 68/1633, sheet 3; MAF 68/2203, sheet 5; MAF 68/2773, sheet 9; MAF 68/3319, sheet 10; MAF 68/3814, no. 144; MAF 68/4182, no. 144; MAF 68/4552, no. 144; MAF 68/5004, no. 144; MAF 68/5505, no. 144; MAF 68/5878, no. 144.
[71] W.R.O., G 7/515/7.

The arable acreage was only 71 a. in 1936, but thereafter increased and was 836 a. in 1966. Grasses were grown in rotation on 20 a. in 1936, 338 a. in 1976. The number of cows kept and the proportion of dairy cattle increased after 1906. Over 600 cattle were kept in the earlier 20th century. Although there were as many cattle 1956–76, fewer were dairy cattle. Dairying had declined further by 1986 when there was more arable than grassland.

In 1986 the land was in eight farms, of which Park, an arable farm, and Dean were the largest.[72] Dean and Street farms, c. 350 a., were worked together, included 180 a. on which corn was grown, and supported a herd of pedigree Guernsey cows and a flock of sheep.[73] Cattle were fattened on Clattinger farm[74] and Hill farm was used as grass keep and for grazing horses.[75] Court farm included 50 a. of arable and supported a herd of cows.[76] The 35 a. of Lower Moor farm from which gravel was extracted 1974–8 were in three lakes used for commercial trout fishing.[77]

Of the 266 men living in Oaksey in 1831, only 17 were tradesmen.[78] In the later 19th century a threshing machine owner lived in the parish, and a business called the Oaksey Direct Meat Supply flourished 1927–35.[79]

The 96-a. park created in the south part of the parish in the period 1299–1347 was surrounded by a wooden palisade and in 1347 contained 22 a. of pasture and 74 a. of woodland.[80] It was stocked with c. 100 beasts of the chase in 1419,[81] with c. 160 deer in 1591,[82] and may have included a rabbit warren c. 1453.[83] There was a ruinous lodge in the park in 1427.[84] In 1423 or earlier until 1595 or later the park was administered by keepers or parkers, of whom several were either senior officials of the duchy of Lancaster[85] or notable Wiltshire landowners. In the years 1469–81 John Ferris, demesne farmer of Oaksey, was also parker and lessee of the herbage and pannage of the park.[86] Other parkers included Sir Henry Long[87] (d. 1556),[88] and Henry Herbert, earl of Pembroke (d. 1601),[89] whose deputy Sir Henry Knyvett,[89] also a duchy official,[90] rebuilt the lodge before 1591.[91] Other officers included a walker, who in 1587 was accused of aiding and abetting a poacher.[92] In the

1660s the oaks in the park were accounted the best in Wiltshire.[93] Before 1787 its lands had become the nucleus of Park farm.[94]

The woodland was 1 league long and ½ league broad in 1086.[95] In 1347, besides the woodland in the park, the manor included demesne woods called Northwood, 27 a., and Clattinger, 7 a., and a customary wood called Westwood.[96] The woods, like the park, were excluded from leases of the demesne.[97] Clattinger wood was replanted c. 1537, and 16 a. of Westwood c. 1517. Westwood contained several large oaks c. 1543:[98] it was hedged before 1563. Also before 1563 Clattinger wood was assigned to the customary tenants, and the tenants hedged it.[99] Westwood, then a demesne wood, was leased in 1566.[1] Its 112 a. were in coppices in 1568.[2] More trees may have been planted in the later 16th century, and in 1591 there were 146 a. in Westwood, Northwood, and Clattinger wood, from all of which the copyholders were entitled to take timber for repairs.[3] Part of Westwood south of Oaksey Street, and all of Clattinger wood, in the east, and Northwood, in the north-west, were grubbed up before 1773,[4] and the woodland had further decreased by 1787.[5] Oaksey Nursery, a wood of 20 a., was planted over part of Oaksey common in 1810.[6] Other woodland, c. 40 a., was in Oaksey wood, perhaps a remnant of Westwood. Dean plantation was grown in the period 1843–75.[7] In 1986 there were 19 ha. of woodland in the parish.[8]

There was a mill at Oaksey in 1086.[9] A water mill was held freely by Robert Capell in 1299,[10] by Ralph of Shipton in 1347.[11] It was conveyed by Cecily Friend to John Twinhoe in 1474.[12] Agnes Flisteridge owned the mill in the period 1558–91,[13] Andrew Kettleby in 1591,[14] and Sir Henry Poole in 1632.[15] The mill, which stood north-east of Oaksey Moor Farm on a leat west of Flagham brook,[16] was demolished before 1773.[17] There was a windmill on the manor in 1299[18] and 1347.[19]

LOCAL GOVERNMENT. In 1255 or earlier the earl of Hereford and of Essex had view of frankpledge within Oaksey manor.[20] The earl in 1289

[72] Above, manor; inf. from Mr. J. Woodhouse, Park Farm.
[73] Inf. from Miss J. Todd, Dean Farm.
[74] Inf. from Mr. H. W. Ody, Clattinger Farm.
[75] Inf. from Lord Oaksey, Hill Farm.
[76] Inf. from Mr. K. Wilson, Court Farm.
[77] Inf. from Mrs. G. F. Raines, Lower Moor Farm.
[78] Census, 1831.
[79] Kelly's Dir. Wilts. (1859 and later edns.).
[80] Wilts. Inq. p.m. 1242–1326 (Index Libr.), 241–3; P.R.O., DL 43/9/29.
[81] P.R.O., DL 43/14/4.
[82] Ibid. DL 42/115, f. 78.
[83] Ibid. DL 29/654/10577.
[84] Ibid. DL 29/653/10564.
[85] Ibid.; DL 1/164, f. 16; DL 29/657/10621; Hist. Parl., Commons, 1558–1603, i. 512–13; Rot. Parl. vi. 347; R. Somerville, Hist. Duchy Lanc. i. 478.
[86] P.R.O., DL 29/656/10613; DL 29/657/10618.
[87] Ibid. DL 3/44, f. 70.
[88] Hist. Parl., Commons, 1509–58, ii. 543–4.
[89] Complete Peerage, x. 410–11; P.R.O., DL 1/173, f. 27.
[90] Hist. Parl., Commons, 1558–1603, ii. 420–3.
[91] P.R.O., DL 42/115, f. 78.
[92] Ibid. DL 1/140, f. 70.
[93] Aubrey, Topog. Coll. ed. Jackson, 276.
[94] W.R.O. 280/75/1.

[95] V.C.H. Wilts. ii, p. 160.
[96] P.R.O., DL 43/9/29.
[97] Ibid. DL 29/654/10590; DL 29/655/10603.
[98] Ibid. DL 3/44, f. 50 and v.
[99] Ibid. DL 44/87.
[1] Ibid. DL 1/75, ff. 4–6.
[2] Ibid. DL 4/11/29.
[3] Ibid. DL 42/115, ff. 76–77v.
[4] Andrews and Dury, Map (W.R.S. viii), pl. 17; W.R.O. 130/25, deed, 1775.
[5] W.R.O. 280/75/1.
[6] Ibid. 212A/27/28, p. 3.
[7] P.R.O., IR 29/38/211; IR 30/38/211; O.S. Map 6″, Wilts. IV (1885 edn.).
[8] Inf. from Lord Oaksey; Miss Todd.
[9] V.C.H. Wilts. ii, p. 160.
[10] Wilts. Inq. p.m. 1242–1326 (Index Libr.), 242–3.
[11] P.R.O., DL 43/9/29.
[12] Feet of F. 1377–1509 (W.R.S. xli), p. 153.
[13] P.R.O., DL 43/9/30.
[14] Ibid. DL 42/115, f. 70.
[15] Wilts. Inq. p.m. 1625–49 (Index Libr.), 148–50.
[16] P.R.O., DL 42/115, f. 69; O.S. Map 6″, Wilts. IV (1885 edn.).
[17] Andrews and Dury, Map (W.R.S. viii), pl. 17.
[18] Wilts. Inq. p.m. 1242–1326 (Index Libr.), 242–3.
[19] P.R.O., DL 43/9/29.
[20] Rot. Hund. (Rec. Com.), ii (1), 230.

also claimed by ancient right assize of bread and of ale, pillory, tumbril, and gallows.[21] Views were held twice yearly 1299–1538. Courts were held with the views in 1411.[22] Between 1523 and 1538 views and courts were held on the same day, their proceedings were undifferentiated in the records, and their business included the payment of cert money by the tithingman, the presentment of brewers who had broken the assize, of badly maintained boundaries, roads, and watercourses, and of encroachments on common land, and surrenders of, and admittances to, customary holdings. In 1532 the rector was presented for assault, and tenants were enjoined not to pasture animals in Overdean before 22 October.[23] Oaksey was called a liberty in the later 16th century.[24] Although the right to hold courts leet and view of frankpledge was conveyed with the manor in 1614,[25] none seems to have been held, and in 1700 and later manorial courts were apparently held only when copyhold business required it.[26]

In 1775–6 the parish spent £66 on its poor, an average of £91 a year 1783–5. It spent £280 in 1802–3 on 132 paupers, of whom 80 were children and 14 were relieved only occasionally. In the years 1813–15 an average of £340 was spent on permanent relief for an average of 34 paupers yearly and on occasional relief for another 33.[27] Oaksey's average yearly expenditure 1816–34 was generally among the lower in Malmesbury hundred: its maximum was £462 in 1820, its minimum £166 in 1828.[28] One or more poorhouse was maintained in 1787, 1812, and 1830–1.[29] The parish was included in Malmesbury poor-law union in 1835[30] and in North Wiltshire district in 1974.[31]

CHURCH. A church stood at Oaksey in the earlier 12th century.[32] The living was a rectory which in 1956 was united with the vicarage of Minety.[33] In 1987 Oaksey and Minety were severed and a new benefice was formed for Oaksey, Crudwell, and Hankerton, and Ashley and Long Newnton (both now Glos.).[34]

Either Humphrey de Bohun or his son Humphrey (fl. 1131 × 1146) gave the church and tithes of unbroken colts in Oaksey to Monkton Farleigh priory.[35] The priors presented rectors until the Dissolution. In 1313, apparently because the priory was the dependency of an alien house, the presentation was disputed between the prior, the earl of Hereford and of Essex, and John of Chippenham, and the bishop of Salisbury collated. The king presented in 1349 and 1421, and in 1481 Sir William Orchard presented by the prior's grant.[36] The Crown presented as patron in 1547,[37] and its apparent sale of the advowson in 1564 was ineffective.[38] The lessee of the rectory estate, Henry Chadderton,[39] presented rectors in 1569 and 1575 and the Crown presented in 1595.[40] When Oaksey manor was granted to Sir Henry Poole in 1614, the advowson was expressly reserved to the Crown.[41] In 1640 Kellaway Gridott and William Gridott presented,[42] whether by grant of a turn or as patrons is unknown.

Sir Edward Poole, lord of the manor, owned the advowson in 1670.[43] It passed with the manor,[44] and Benjamin Adamson presented rectors in 1760, 1765, and 1770.[45] Robert Adamson sold it to Giles Greenaway in 1791. Greenaway immediately sold it to Charles Howard, duke of Norfolk, who sold it to Thomas Ryder in 1802. Ryder (d. 1839) in 1808 presented as rector his son Edward, who succeeded him as patron. From Edward Ryder (d. 1857) the advowson passed to his daughter Adelaide Ryder. In 1857 she sold it to Lady (Harriet) Wetherell Warneford, who sold it in 1859 to J. R. Mullings. It descended like Eastcourt manor in Crudwell to Joseph Mullings, A. R. Mullings, and J. R. Randolph.[46] In 1921 Randolph transferred the advowson to the bishop of Bristol, who from 1956 was entitled to present alternately,[47] and from 1987 jointly at three of four turns.[48]

Before 1291 the prior of Monkton Farleigh gave up his right to the tithes of unbroken colts for a yearly pension of £1.[49] The pension had been increased to £2 by 1428.[50] In 1429 the prior instituted proceedings in King's Bench to compel the rector to pay it,[51] in 1444 required the rector to guarantee payment,[52] and in the early 16th century caused a rector to be imprisoned for refusing to pay it.[53] From the Dissolution to 1614 or later the rectors paid the pension to the Crown,[54] which afterwards granted it at fee-farm. The rector paid £2 to Sir Gerald Corbet, Bt., in 1943 and redeemed the pension in that year.[55]

The rector took all the tithes and in 1341 had a house, ½ yardland, and 8 a. of meadow.[56] The rectory was valued at £9 in 1535.[57] The glebe was

[21] P.R.O., JUST 1/1006, rot. 45.

[22] Ibid. DL 29/652/10553; DL 29/655/10592; DL 29/656/10609; DL 30/127/1907, ff. 76v.–77; Wilts. Inq. p.m. 1242–1326 (Index Libr.), 243.

[23] P.R.O., DL 30/127/1907, ff. 2–3v., 9–10, 12v.–13, 14v.–15v., 28v., 34v., 37–8, 59, 76v.–77.

[24] Extents for Debts (W.R.S. xxviii), p. 81; W.A.M. vi. 198–9.

[25] P.R.O., C 66/2018, mm. 7–9.

[26] W.R.O. 803/8.

[27] Poor Law Abstract, 1804, 566–7; 1818, 498–9.

[28] Poor Rate Returns, 1816–21, 189; 1822–4, 228; 1825–9, 219; 1830–4, 213; Poor Law Com. 2nd Rep. App. D, 559.

[29] W.R.O. 212A/27/28, p. 6; 280/75/1; 1579/28.

[30] Poor Law Com. 2nd Rep. App. D, 559.

[31] O.S. Map 1/100,000, admin. areas, Wilts. (1974 edn.).

[32] Dugdale, Mon. v. 26.

[33] Ch. Com. file 26346.

[34] Ibid. NB 5/3B.

[35] Dugdale, Mon. v. 24, 26.

[36] Phillipps, Wilts. Inst. (index in W.A.M. xxviii. 226); Reg. Ghent (Cant. & York Soc.), ii. 810–11; Cal. Pat. 1348–50, 286, 433; 1416–22, 314; V.C.H. Wilts. iii. 264–5.

[37] Phillipps, Wilts. Inst. i. 213.

[38] Cal. Pat. 1563–6, p. 13.

[39] P.R.O., DL 1/75, f. 6.

[40] Phillipps, Wilts. Inst. i. 224, 227, 234.

[41] P.R.O., C 66/2018, mm. 7–9.

[42] Subscription Bk. 1620–40 (W.R.S. xxxii), p. 67.

[43] P.R.O., CP 25(2)/745/22 Chas. II East.

[44] Phillipps, Wilts. Inst. ii. 41, 51; W.R.O. 374/584, deed, 1720.

[45] Phillipps, Wilts. Inst. ii. 79, 82, 85.

[46] Clergy List (1859 and later edns.); W.R.O. 374/589, deeds, 1791–1859, abstr. of title, 1802–59; above, Crudwell, manors.

[47] Ch. Com. file 26346.

[48] Ibid. NB 5/3B.

[49] Tax. Eccl. (Rec. Com.), 196.

[50] Feud. Aids, v. 281.

[51] Phillipps, Wilts. Inst. i. 112, 124; Cal. Pat. 1429–36, 8.

[52] P.R.O., E 326/8986.

[53] Ibid. C 1/599, no. 35.

[54] Ibid. C 66/2018, mm. 7–9.

[55] Ch. Com. file, K 10801.

[56] Inq. Non. (Rec. Com.), 166.

[57] Valor Eccl. (Rec. Com.), ii. 134.

increased from c. 15 a. in 1570[58] to 23 a. in 1608 and to 26 a. in 1671 after allotments of 3 a. and 4 a. to replace tithes from 38 a. and 37 a. respectively.[59] The yearly average value of the rectory was £400 1829–31.[60] The tithes were valued at £406 in 1843 and commuted. The 26 a. of glebe was reduced after 1843[61] to c. 20 a.,[62] but whether by alienation or more precise survey is unknown. The rector sold 5 a. in 1937 and the remaining 14 a. in 1941.[63]

The Rectory was rebuilt in the 18th century as a two-storeyed stone house with a south front of five bays, attics, and a stone-slated roof. It was altered, and east and west additions were built, in the early 19th century. The south elevation became the entrance front in 1869 when, to the designs of J. B. Bridges, a new staircase was built in the former north entrance hall and a central south doorway was made.[64] The house was sold in 1941 and a house on the north side of Oaksey Street was bought.[65]

A chantry chapel of St. Mary the Virgin stood near the church in the grounds of the manor house in 1361.[66] Its endowments in Oaksey included a cottage and land.[67] The advowson descended with the manor.[68] A priest who served the chapel in 1419 received 6s. 8d.: the chapel contained three bells, mass vessels, and vestments.[69] In 1442 its incumbent was called a warden.[70] The endowments, a house and 2 a., were valued at £2 6s. 8d. in 1535, and the chantry was dissolved in 1546.[71]

Parishioners of Minety attended Oaksey church in 1304 while their own church was under an interdict.[72] Roger Bragges was rector of Oaksey twice, 1465–78 and in 1509 or earlier. Robert Gerish, rector 1547–54, was also rector of Crudwell.[73] His successor was licensed to hold two benefices and in 1556 was admonished to attend to the state of the crucifix in Oaksey church.[74] John Mason, rector from 1575 to c. 1595,[75] did not reside 1583–91,[76] and in 1584 an old man was curate.[77] A curate assisted the rector in 1650.[78] Although the church lacked a Book of Homilies in 1662,[79] the cure seems to have been adequately served in the later 17th century.[80] Ralph Smith, rector 1770–1808, was curate of Minety before 1783. He lived in Oaksey 1770–81, from 1781 sometimes

in Cirencester. In 1783 he served only Oaksey, where he held two Sunday services in summer, a Sunday afternoon service in winter, and weekday services on the principal festivals. He administered the sacrament four times a year to c. 10 communicants.[81] Edward Ryder (d. 1857), rector 1808–57, was also from 1814 vicar of Wendens Ambo (Essex).[82] He lived at Oaksey and in 1832 held two Sunday services, at one of which he preached.[83] In 1850–1 average congregations of 80 and 50 respectively attended morning and afternoon services.[84] W. J. H. Faithfull (d. 1951), rector 1890–1920, was a lunatic from c. 1917. A commission in 1917 found that he had neglected his duties and a curate served Oaksey until 1920.[85] The rector of Oaksey was also curate of Minety 1950–6.[86]

The church of ALL SAINTS, so called in 1763,[87] is of ashlar and consists of a chancel with south chapel, a clerestoried nave with north porch and south aisle and porch, and a west tower.[88] The nave walls may survive from the 12th century. In the 13th the chancel was rebuilt, and the tower and a wide south aisle with a three-bayed arcade and south porch were built. The north porch with a statue of the Blessed Virgin Mary above the inner north doorway was erected in the earlier 14th century. In the earlier 15th an embattled clerestory of five bays was built. In the early 16th the aisle was extended to form the south chapel, and was given a new window and an embattled parapet; new windows were made in the north wall of the nave, an embattled third stage was built on the tower, stained glass was placed in some of the windows, and the south nave wall was decorated with paintings including figures of Christ and St. Christopher.[89] The church was pewed c. 1658.[90] It had a gallery in 1826[91] and two more were erected in 1858.[92] None survived in 1986. A new east window was inserted in 1862.[93] A carved fertility figure, possibly of the 12th century,[94] has been reset in the north wall of the nave east of the porch. The early 16th-century chancel screen, which stands lower than the doorway to the rood loft, may originally have been the screen of the chancel chapel. The church was restored under the direction of P. H. Thomas c. 1934.[95]

There was a chalice in the church in 1553. In 1986 the parish had an Italian silver chalice and

[58] P.R.O., DL 4/12/18.
[59] Ibid. IR 29/38/211; W.R.O., D 1/24/159/1–2.
[60] Rep. Com. Eccl. Revenues, 842–3.
[61] P.R.O., IR 29/38/211; IR 30/38/211.
[62] Glebe Lands Return, H.C. 307, p. 55 (1887), lxiv.
[63] Ch. Com. files, NB 5/119; 75717.
[64] Bristol R.O., EP/A/25/1.
[65] Ch. Com. files 75717; E 6623; K 10801.
[66] Wilts. Inq. p.m. 1327–77 (Index Libr.), 271; Cal. Pat. 1549–51, 403; P.R.O., DL 43/14/4; ibid. E 301/56, no. 40.
[67] P.R.O., SC 6/1056/15.
[68] Wilts. Inq. p.m. 1327–77 (Index Libr.), 371–2; Cal. Close, 1374–7, 25.
[69] P.R.O., SC 6/1056/15.
[70] W.N. & Q. vii. 260.
[71] Valor Eccl. (Rec. Com.), ii. 122; P.R.O., E 301/56, no. 40.
[72] V.C.H. Wilts. iii. 9.
[73] A. B. Emden, Biog. Reg. Univ. Oxf. to 1500, i. 247; 1500–40, 257.
[74] W.R.O., D 1/43/2, f. 23.
[75] Ibid. D 1/43/6, f. 32v.; Phillipps, Wilts. Inst. i. 227, 234.
[76] P.R.O., DL 42/115, f. 76v.
[77] W.R.O., D 1/43/5, f. 23.
[78] W.A.M. xli. 8.
[79] W.R.O., D 1/54/1/1, no. 63.
[80] Ibid. D 1/54/6/1, no. 31; D 1/54/10/1, no. 7; D 1/54/11/1, no. 41; D 1/54/12/1/Oaksey.
[81] Vis. Queries, 1783 (W.R.S. xxvii), pp. 169–70.
[82] R. Newcourt, Repertorium Eccl. Par. Lond. ii. 649; Alum. Cantab. 1752–1900, v. 394.
[83] Ch. Com. file, NB 5/119.
[84] P.R.O., HO 129/252/1/2/3.
[85] Crockford (1896 and later edns.); Huxley, Gallipot Eyes, 23–4; Ch. Com. files 26346; NB 5/119.
[86] Ch. Com. file, NB 5/119.
[87] J. Ecton, Thesaurus (1763), 403.
[88] Description based partly on J. Buckler, watercolour in W.A.S. Libr., vol. vi. 17 (1809); see above, plate facing p. 109.
[89] W.A.M. xlvii. 632–6; l. 101.
[90] W.R.O., D 1/54/1/1, no. 64.
[91] W. Cobbett, Rural Rides, ed. G. D. H. and M. Cole, ii. 418.
[92] W.R.O. 1579/18.
[93] Pevsner, Wilts. (2nd edn.), 362.
[94] W.A.M. xlvi. 391–2.
[95] W.R.O. 1579/21.

a communion set of plated metal given in 1862.[96] There were three bells in 1553. The tenor, cast at Worcester, hung in the church until 1773 when a new peal of six, cast by Thomas Rudhall of Gloucester, was hung.[97] The ring was recast by Taylor of Loughborough (Leics.) in 1960.[98] The registers are complete from 1670.[99]

NONCONFORMITY. Independents certified a room in Oaksey in 1802 and houses in 1821 and 1822.[1] Methodists certified a house in 1812.[2] Primitive Methodists from Brinkworth evangelized the village and in 1838 a house was certified.[3] The group in 1842 built, west of Earl's Corner, a chapel which on Census Sunday in 1851 was attended by congregations of 80, 101, and 86 at morning, afternoon, and evening services respectively.[4] The chapel was rebuilt in 1874[5] and closed c. 1956.[6]

EDUCATION. There were two small day schools in Oaksey in 1818:[7] 20 children were taught in them in 1833.[8] No day school was held in 1846–7.[9] A school was built in 1854 on the south side of Oaksey Street where 40–50 children were taught in 1858.[10] On return day in 1871 it was attended by 53 children.[11] An average of 54 children was taught in 1906–7. Average numbers were steady until 1913–14, fell to 39 in 1921–2, rose inexplicably to 61 in 1926–7, and fell to 37 in 1937–8.[12] R. C. Warner in 1929 paid for a large open-air classroom south of the school.[13] The 32 children on roll in 1986 had two teachers.[14]

CHARITIES FOR THE POOR. Sir Robert Westley (d. 1745) gave £50, and at other times John Archer gave £20 and others gave £30, for paupers who were not relieved by the parish. By 1834 the income, £3 10s., had not been distributed for many years, although one of the trustees gave money to be distributed each Christmas. In the early 20th century yearly income of £2 10s. was distributed every other year in February to all paupers not relieved by the parish: in 1904 small sums were received by 76 adults and 45 children.[15] Biennial distributions were made until 1932 or later.[16] In the 1970s the income was temporarily augmented by an anonymous benefactor and in December 1972 sums of 50p each were given to 15 people.[17] The £2 yearly income was being allowed to accumulate c. 1986.[18]

By will proved 1930 R. C. Warner gave money for public purposes in Oaksey. £1,000 stock was vested in Oaksey parish council by a Scheme of 1961. The yearly income was £45 c. 1965, £110 c. 1986. Some of it was given to maintain the church clock and for general parish expenses.[19]

SEAGRY

SEAGRY[20] is 8.5 km. north-east of Chippenham. The ancient parish, with which this article deals, measured 1,082 a. (437 ha.)[21] and in 1934 was added to Sutton Benger parish.[22] A new Seagry parish, 594 ha. (1,468 a.), was formed in 1971: it comprises all the land north of the London and south Wales motorway that had been in the parishes of Seagry, Draycot Cerne, and Sutton Benger.[23]

The parish was triangular. Its eastern boundary, with Christian Malford, was marked by the Bristol Avon, and its western, with Sutton Benger and Stanton St. Quintin, by a tributary of the Avon. Those boundaries with Christian Malford and Sutton Benger were recorded in the 11th or 12th century.[24] The straight northern boundary with Great Somerford, part of a line which also divides pairs of parishes east and west of Seagry, was possibly made at an early inclosure. The parish was almost flat: the highest land, Seagry Hill, 73 m., and the lowest, c. 50 m. beside the Avon, is in the south. Kellaways Clay and Kellaways Sand outcrop, and lighter sandy soils lie in the east, where more land has been ploughed. Alluvium and valley gravel have been deposited near the Avon, where the land was used as water meadows, and alluvium also lies beside the western boundary stream.[25]

The road between Sutton Benger and Great Somerford bisected Seagry and linked it to the

[96] Nightingale, Wilts. Plate, 205; inf. from Mr. B. N. Gibbs, Flintham Ho.
[97] Walters, Wilts. Bells, 149–50, 271.
[98] Inf. from Mr. Gibbs.
[99] W.R.O. 1579/1–11; bishop's transcripts for 1605–9, 1619–23, 1632, and 1666–9 are ibid.
[1] Meeting Ho. Certs. (W.R.S. xl), pp. 58, 93, 96.
[2] Ibid. p. 70.
[3] Ibid. p. 147.
[4] P.R.O., HO 129/252/1/2/4.
[5] Date on bldg.
[6] Glos. R.O., D 3931/2/12/4.
[7] Educ. of Poor Digest, 1034.
[8] Educ. Enq. Abstract, 1044.
[9] Nat. Soc. Inquiry, 1846–7, Wilts. 8–9.
[10] Acct. of Wilts. Schs. 36; P.R.O., ED 7/131, no. 213.
[11] Returns relating to Elem. Educ. 420–1.
[12] Bd. of Educ., List 21, 1908–38 (H.M.S.O.).

[13] W.A.M. xlv. 271.
[14] Inf. from Chief Educ. Officer, Co. Hall, Trowbridge.
[15] Endowed Char. Wilts. (N. Div.), 794–6.
[16] W.R.O., Char. Com., Oaksey.
[17] Char. Com. file.
[18] Inf. from Mr. Gibbs.
[19] Char. Com. file; inf. from Mr. Gibbs.
[20] This article was written in 1987.
[21] Maps used include O.S. Maps 1", sheets 34 (1828 edn.), 157 (1968 edn.); 1/50,000, sheet 173 (1974 edn.); 1/25,000, ST 97–8 (1959 edns.); 6", Wilts. XIII, XX (1888–9 and later edns.).
[22] Census, 1931.
[23] Ibid. 1971.
[24] Arch. Jnl. lxxvi. 256; lxxvii. 53–4.
[25] Geol. Surv. Maps 1", solid and drift, sheet 252 (1974 edn.), solid and drift, sheet 265 (1965 edn.); 1/50,000, drift, sheet 266 (1974 edn.); below, econ. hist.

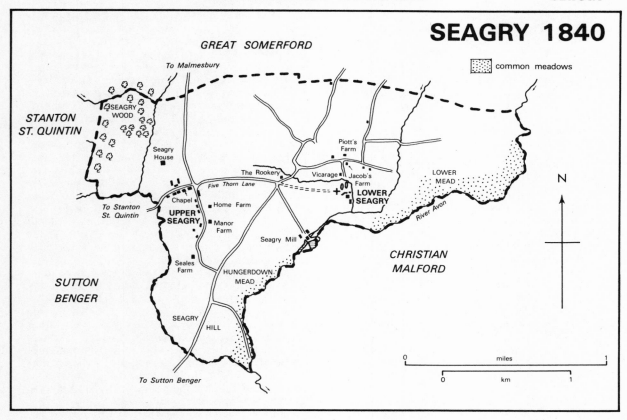

SEAGRY 1840

GREAT SOMERFORD

To Malmesbury

common meadows

STANTON
ST. QUINTIN

SEAGRY
WOOD

Seagry
House

Piott's
Farm

LOWER
MEAD

The Rookery

Vicarage   Jacob's
Farm

N

Five Thorn Lane

Chapel

To Stanton
St. Quintin

Home Farm

UPPER
SEAGRY

Manor
Farm

LOWER
SEAGRY

River Avon

CHRISTIAN
MALFORD

Seagry Mill

Seales
Farm

SUTTON
BENGER

HUNGERDOWN.
MEAD.

SEAGRY

HILL

To Sutton Benger

0   miles   1

0   km   1

Chippenham–Swindon road south of the parish. It was turnpiked in 1809 and disturnpiked in 1876.[26] In the south a lane branched from it to lead northwards to Malmesbury. The only east–west road, leading to Stanton St. Quintin, crossed both the Great Somerford and Malmesbury roads and between them was called Five Thorn Lane in 1885.[27] East of the Great Somerford road it led to Lower Seagry hamlet. A track running from the hamlet south-west to Seagry Mill in 1773[28] had by 1828 been replaced by a lane running south-east from the Great Somerford road.[29] When the London and south Wales motorway was built across the south part of the former parish and opened in 1971,[30] the road across Seagry Hill was diverted westwards over it.

An artifact of the Upper Palaeolithic Age and other artifacts possibly of the late Bronze Age have been found in the parish.[31] The assessment of Seagry for taxation in 1334 was among the lowest in Startley hundred. Of the two hamlets in the parish in 1377 Lower Seagry had 65 poll-tax payers, Upper Seagry 45.[32] Taxation assessments of the 16th and 17th centuries were among the lowest, showing that Seagry was among the poorest parishes in Malmesbury hundred.[33] There were 233 inhabitants in 1801, 231 in 1841 when 135 lived in Upper Seagry and 96 in Lower Seagry.

The population had increased to 263 by 1861, declined to 151 by 1881, and was 230 in 1931.[34] In 1981 most of the 251 people in the new parish of Seagry lived in Upper and Lower Seagry.[35]

Lower Seagry was called Nether Seagry from 1218 or earlier.[36] In 1720[37] and in 1987 settlement was around the church and around the junction of the lane running eastwards from the Great Somerford road with the lane to the church. The church stood in the 12th century.[38] The manor house of Lower Seagry may have stood south-east of it in 1447 or earlier on the site of Church Farm.[39] A barn of stone rubble with a stone-slated roof, a chimney, and a central carriageway was built between the church and that site in the 15th century. The Vicarage north of the church was made into three cottages c. 1940.[40] At the junction further north Jacob's Farm, which stood in 1761,[41] was replaced, apparently in the early 19th century, by a pair of cottages occupied as one house in 1987. On the north side of the lane leading to the Great Somerford road, Lower Seagry, formerly Piott's, Farm, was burned down in 1927. It was replaced c. 1928 by a large stone and brick house called Trinity Farm after 1940. A new single-storeyed farmhouse was built east of it in 1986. An early 19th-century farmhouse stands west of Trinity Farm.[42] New houses, mainly bungalows, were

[26] V.C.H. Wilts. iv. 257, 263, 271; L.J. xlvii. 290.
[27] O.S. Map 6″, Wilts. XIII (1888 edn.).
[28] Andrews and Dury, Map (W.R.S. viii), pl. 14.
[29] O.S. Map 1″, sheet 34 (1828 edn.).
[30] Rep. Co. Surveyor, 1971–2 (Wilts. co. council), 3.
[31] W.A.M. liii. 374; lxxix. 226–7.
[32] V.C.H. Wilts. iv. 301, 309–10.
[33] Taxation Lists (W.R.S. x), 29, 53; P.R.O., E 179/199/ 356; E 179/199/399; E 179/259/20.

[34] V.C.H. Wilts. iv. 357.
[35] Census, 1981.
[36] Rot. Litt. Claus. (Rec. Com.), i. 377.
[37] W.R.O. 1553/120.   [38] Below, church.
[39] Ibid. manors; Feet of F. 1377–1509 (W.R.S. xli), p. 125.
[40] W.R.O., G 3/760/1147.
[41] Ibid. 969/14, survey of Stratton's and Jacob's farms, 1761.
[42] Ibid. G 3/760/695; inf. from Mr. D. Selwood, Long Tyme; Mrs. E. J. Biggin, Trinity Farm.

built in the hamlet south of the lane to the Great Somerford road between 1972 and 1983.[43]

The hamlet of Upper Seagry, called Over Seagry in 1317,[44] grew up east and west of the Malmesbury road and mainly south of the Stanton St. Quintin road. On the west side of the Malmesbury road Seales Court, formerly Seales Farm, is at the south end of the hamlet.[45] North of it the Mount, a large red-brick house, was built c. 1897[46] and extended northwards c. 1905.[47] A western extension, possibly adapted from stables, was added later. On the east side of the road are Manor Farm, with extensive farm buildings, and the Chestnuts.[48] Beside the Stanton St. Quintin road a nonconformist chapel was built[49] and the New Inn was open in 1885[50] and 1987. Ten council houses were built south of the Stanton St. Quintin road and west of the Malmesbury road c. 1950,[51] and a new school was built there.[52]

Outside the hamlets two large houses were built. Seagry House was built north of the Stanton St. Quintin road, with a lodge and stables beside that road and a lodge beside the Malmesbury road;[53] near the stables Oak Hill House was built of stone in 1981, and in 1987 the stables were being made into dwellings.[54] In the south beside the Great Somerford road Hungerdown House was built for Guy Freemantle to designs by Maurice Chesterton in 1914,[55] in an 18th-century style of red brick and stone with a tiled roof. Also in 1914 brick stables north of the house were built to designs by H. B. Harrison.[56] The stables were made into a house in 1947.[57] At the east end of Five Thorn Lane the Rookery was built of stone in 1792 for Robert and Anne Vines to replace a house which stood in the earlier 18th century.[58] Nearby, at the junction of the Great Somerford road and the road to Lower Seagry, a school was built.[59] In the 20th century houses with farm buildings or stables were built on the north side of Five Thorn Lane, the east side of the Malmesbury road, and the west side of the Great Somerford road. At Seagry Hill in the south 11 council houses were built beside the Great Somerford road c. 1950.[60]

MANORS AND OTHER ESTATES. Two 5-hide estates were called Seagry in 1086, and in the Middle Ages there were two manors in the parish, each called Seagry.

In 1066 two thegns, who were free to choose their own overlord, held one of the estates, and

in 1086 two knights held it. In 1086 Durand of Gloucester was overlord of that estate,[61] which became one of the manors called *SEAGRY*. The overlordship passed to his son Roger (d. s.p. 1106) and his nephew Walter of Gloucester. From Walter's son Miles of Gloucester (cr. earl of Hereford 1141, d. 1143), the overlordship passed successively to his brothers Walter of Hereford, Henry of Hereford, and Mahel of Hereford. After Mahel's death, Seagry was allotted to his sister Margaret, wife of Humphrey de Bohun, passed to her son Humphrey de Bohun, and afterwards in the direct male line to Henry de Bohun (cr. earl of Hereford 1200, d. 1220), and thereafter with the earldom of Hereford.[62] After the death of Earl Humphrey in 1373,[63] the overlordship was allotted in 1384 to his daughter Mary, wife of Henry of Lancaster, earl of Derby (Henry IV).[64] Seagry was last expressly mentioned as a fee of the honor of Hereford in 1401–2.[65]

The estate held by the two knights may be identified with the land held by Alice Cockerell in the early 13th century and may have belonged to her father Ralph Cockerell. Before 1218 Alice, wife of Walter of Sherborne, gave 5 yardlands to her daughter Felice and Felice's husband William Chambers.[66] Alice gave 1 yardland to her daughter Isabel whose husband Alexander of Broom[67] may have conveyed it to Bradenstoke priory before 1232. William Chambers apparently sold land in Seagry to the priory before 1232,[68] and in 1236 he and Felice conveyed the 5 yardlands to the priory. Also in 1236 Alice, then the wife of John Chambers, gave the priory another yardland. The rest of Alice's land passed to her son Robert of Sherborne, who confirmed the conveyances to Bradenstoke priory.[69] In 1242–3 the priory and Robert each held ½ knight's fee in Seagry. The prior was undertenant of Robert's fee,[70] and in 1373 held the entire fee.[71] The priory held that manor of Seagry until the Dissolution.

The Crown sold the manor in 1559 to Francis, later Sir Francis, Walsingham.[72] In 1560 Walsingham sold it to Dorothy, relict of Sir William Stafford, she sold it in 1580 to Richard Drake,[73] and Drake sold it in 1585 to Edward, later Sir Edward, Hungerford[74] (d. 1607).[75] From 1596 to 1877 the manor descended like Corston manor in Malmesbury to Cecily, countess of Rutland, to Sir Anthony, Sir Edward, and Sir Giles Hungerford, to Robert Sutton, Baron Lexinton, and from 1718 with Stanton St. Quintin manor in the Bouverie

[43] O.S. Maps 1/50,000, sheet 173 (1974 edn.); 1/10,000, ST 98 SE. (1983 edn.).
[44] *Feet of F.* 1272–1327 (W.R.S. i), p. 98.
[45] Below, manors.
[46] W.R.O. 969/20, deed, Bayliffe to Mornington, 1900; ibid. G 3/760/8.
[47] Ibid. G 3/760/235.
[48] Below, manors.
[49] Ibid. nonconf.
[50] O.S. Map 6", Wilts. XIII (1888 edn.).
[51] Ibid. 1/25,000, 31/98 (1949 edn.); W.R.O., G 3/516/1 (2).
[52] Below, educ.
[53] Ibid. manors.
[54] Inf. from Mr. and Mrs. P. Head, Oak Hill Ho.
[55] W.R.O., G 3/760/403; Nat. Bldgs. Rec., sale cat. 1982.
[56] W.R.O., G 3/760/439.
[57] Ibid. G 3/760/1310.
[58] Ibid. A 1/345/355; ibid. 1553/120; 2096/2; date and initials V/RA on ho.

[59] Below, educ.
[60] O.S. Map 1/25,000, 31/97 (1949 edn.); W.R.O., G 3/516/1 (2).
[61] *V.C.H. Wilts.* ii, p. 148.
[62] Ibid. p. 108; *Bk. of Fees*, ii. 711, 722; for the Bohun fam., *Complete Peerage*, vi. 451–77.
[63] *Cal. Inq. p.m.* xiii, p. 139.
[64] *Cal. Close*, 1381–5, 512–15.
[65] *Feud. Aids*, vi. 632.
[66] *Rot. Litt. Claus.* (Rec. Com.), i. 377.
[67] *Civil Pleas, 1249* (W.R.S. xxvi), p. 103.
[68] *Cal. Chart. R.* 1226–57, 159–62.
[69] *Bradenstoke Cart.* (W.R.S. xxxv), pp. 70, 157–8.
[70] *Bk. of Fees*, ii. 711, 722.
[71] *Cal. Inq. p.m.* xiii, p. 139.
[72] *Cal. Pat.* 1558–60, 248.
[73] *Musgrave's Obit.* v (Harl. Soc. xlviii), 335; W.R.O. 490/1066, copy deed, 1580.
[74] P.R.O., CP 25(2)/241/27 Eliz. I Trin.
[75] Ibid. WARD 7/41, no. 44.

DRAYCOT CERNE
The south-east front of Draycot House

SEAGRY
Seagry House from the south-east

The 15th-century market cross in 1815, with St. Paul's church behind it

The town hall, built in 1854, and Cross Hayes *c.* 1900

MALMESBURY

family, later with the earldom of Radnor.[76] In 1877 Jacob, earl of Radnor, sold the land, Seales farm (202 a.) based in Upper Seagry and Seagry farm (77 a.) mainly in Lower Seagry[77] to Henry Wellesley, Earl Cowley (d. 1884). Those farms, as part of the Draycot Cerne estate, passed to William, Earl Cowley (d. 1895), Henry, Earl Cowley (d. 1919), and Christian, Earl Cowley.[78] Seales farm, then 86 a., was sold c. 1920[79] and several times after that.[80] Other land that was part of the larger Seales farm was bought by Wiltshire county council in 1920 and owned by it in 1987.[81] A house stood on the manor in 1559.[82] It may be represented by the west range of Seales Court, the roof of which has a central truss with arch braces between cruck principals. A cross wing was built on the east in the 17th century. Later in that century or in the 18th the east range was extended southwards at a lower height. In 1935 a north service wing was built and the east and west ranges were much altered.[83]

In 1066 Wiflet held 5 hides which became the second manor of *SEAGRY*, and in 1086 Drew Fitz-Pons held them.[84] The overlordship of the lands presumably passed to Drew's brother Richard, and to Richard's son Walter Clifford (d. 1190).[85] It presumably passed to Walter's sons, Richard (?d. *s.p.* 1199) and Walter Clifford (d. 1221).[86] That last Walter was succeeded by his sons Walter (d. 1263),[87] and Roger, who held it in 1275.[88]

Alexander of Seagry apparently held the manor of the first Walter Clifford in the later 12th century.[89] Simon of Seagry, perhaps Alexander's son, held it of Walter Clifford in 1242–3.[90] The Simon of Seagry who held it in 1275[91] was perhaps Simon's son. John of Seagry held it in 1316 and 1321.[92] The manor was held in 1362 by Thomas Drew and his wife Joan,[93] in 1374 by Thomas Drew, perhaps the same, and his wife Emme,[94] in 1384 and 1412 by Emme, and 1428–51 by another Thomas Drew.[95] The manor was allotted to Isabel, a daughter and coheir of Thomas and wife of John Mompesson (d. 1500). From John it descended to his grandson John Mompesson[96] (d. 1511) and to that John's son Edmund (d. 1553).[97] The manor was allotted in 1556 to Anne, a sister and coheir of Edmund and wife of William Wayte (d. 1561).[98] On Anne's death before 1571

the manor passed to her daughter Elizabeth (d. before 1576), wife of Richard, later Sir Richard, Norton[99] (d. 1592).[1] The manor descended in the direct male line to Sir Richard Norton (d. 1611), Sir Richard Norton, Bt. (d. 1645), and Sir Richard Norton, Bt. (d. 1652),[2] who sold it in portions in 1648.

The largest portion, called *LOWER SEAGRY* manor, was bought by Rebecca Stratton (d. 1678). She was succeeded by her son Thomas's relict, Anne Stratton (d. 1693), and by her son Robert Stratton (d. 1700).[3]

Robert Stratton devised land later called Stratton's farm or *CHURCH* farm to Anne Stratton (d. 1731), the daughter of Thomas and Anne Stratton, and to his grandnephew Robert Stratton in turn. Robert (d. 1758) devised the farm for sale.[4] It was owned in 1761 or earlier by Henry Fox (cr. Baron Holland 1763, d. 1774)[5] and descended with Grittenham manor in Brinkworth and the Holland title to Henry Fox, Baron Holland (d. 1859),[6] whose relict Mary in 1864 sold the farm to Henry Wellesley, Earl Cowley.[7] It descended with the Draycot Cerne estate to Christian, Earl Cowley, who sold the 151-a. farm c. 1920[8] to J. P. Godwin, the owner in 1939[9] and later. The farm was bought in 1947 by Provincial Estates Development (Bath) Ltd.,[10] and in 1958 by Mr. F. Newman who owned the 125-a. farm in 1987.[11] A medieval house on the manor may have stood south-east of the church. Church Farm was built on that site for Robert Stratton (d. 1758),[12] and was altered and extended in 1947 to designs by C. Godfrey. The west wall and the north wall west of the front door were rebuilt and both elevations were refenestrated. The gabled south elevation was extended southwards and a new doorway and windows were inserted in it.[13]

Other land of Lower Seagry manor was devised by Robert Stratton (d. 1700) to Robert Stratton (d. 1758), who in 1710 sold some of it at Upper Seagry to Joseph Houlton (d. 1731). Houlton enlarged his estate by purchase and settled it in 1723 on his son Nathaniel (d. 1754) and Nathaniel's wife Mary. Nathaniel also enlarged it by purchase and built Seagry House on it. Mary owned c. 330 a. in Seagry in 1766 and was succeeded in 1770 by Nathaniel's nephew John Houlton, who

[76] Above, Corston, manor; below, Stanton St. Quintin, manor.
[77] W.R.O. 969/16.
[78] Above, Draycot Cerne, manor.
[79] W.R.O. 1043/6, p. 99.
[80] *Kelly's Dir. Wilts.* (1921 and later edns.); inf. from Mrs. E. S. Hynes, Seales Ct.
[81] P.R.O., IR 29/38/230; IR 30/38/230; inf. from Estates and Valuations Officer, Co. Hall, Trowbridge.
[82] *Cal. Pat.* 1558–60, 248.
[83] W.R.O., G 3/760/884.
[84] *V.C.H. Wilts.* ii, p. 156.
[85] This descent of the Clifford fam. follows I. J. Sanders, *Eng. Baronies*, 35–6, and W. Dugdale, *Baronage*, i. 335–6.
[86] *Ex. e Rot. Fin.* (Rec. Com.), i. 59; B.L. Harl. Ch. 48. C. 25.
[87] *Bk. of Fees*, ii. 730; *Ex. e Rot. Fin.* (Rec. Com.), ii. 407–8.
[88] *Rot. Hund.* (Rec. Com.), ii (1), 272.
[89] *Bradenstoke Cart.* (W.R.S. xxxv), p. 68.
[90] Ibid. p. 69; *Bk. of Fees*, ii. 730.
[91] *Rot. Hund.* (Rec. Com.), ii (1), 272; *Bradenstoke Cart.* (W.R.S. xxxv), p. 70.
[92] *Feud. Aids*, v. 209; *Feet of F.* 1272–1327 (W.R.S. i), p. 107.
[93] *Feet of F.* 1327–77 (W.R.S. xxix), p. 122.

[94] Ibid. pp. 144–5; *Coll. Topog. et Gen.* vi. 358–9.
[95] *Feet of F. 1377–1509* (W.R.S. xli), pp. 14, 129; *Feud. Aids*, v. 236; vi. 538.
[96] *Geneal.* N.S. xiii. 149; *Cal. Inq. p.m. Hen. VII*, ii, pp. 317–18.
[97] P.R.O., C 142/26, no. 117; C 142/104, no. 123.
[98] *Wilts. Pedigrees* (Harl. Soc. cv/cvi), 132; *W.A.M.* xliii. 291–2; *V.C.H. Hants*, iii. 167.
[99] P.R.O. C 3/9/21; C 3/40/18; ibid. CP 25(2)/260/18 Eliz. I Hil.; ibid. PROB 11/53, ff. 192v.–193v.
[1] Ibid. C 142/233, no. 118.
[2] Ibid. WARD 7/45, no. 105; G.E.C. *Baronetage*, i. 195.
[3] *W.A.M.* xliii. 286, 293; P.R.O., CP 25(2)/512/24 Chas. I Mich.
[4] *W.A.M.* xliii. 286.
[5] W.R.O. 969/14; for the Fox fam., *Complete Peerage*, vi. 541–5.
[6] Above, Brinkworth, manors.
[7] W.R.O. 969/21.
[8] Ibid. 1043/6, p. 105; above.
[9] *Kelly's Dir. Wilts.* (1920 and later edns.).
[10] W.R.O., G 3/760/1323.
[11] Inf. from Mrs. E. Newman, Church Farm.
[12] *W.A.M.* xliii. 287.
[13] W.R.O., G 3/760/1323.

sold the estate in 1785 to Sir James Tylney-Long, Bt.[14] (d. 1794). The Seagry House estate passed with the Draycot Cerne estate to Sir James Tylney-Long, Bt. (d. 1805), Catherine Pole-Tylney-Long-Wellesley (d. 1825), William, earl of Mornington (d. 1863), and Henry, Earl Cowley (d. 1884), and with that estate and the Cowley title to Christian Wellesley[15] who owned c. 500 a. in the parish. In 1920 Lord Cowley sold most of the land,[16] including c. 150 a. to Wiltshire county council, the owner in 1987.[17] Other land, c. 40 ha., formerly part of the Seagry House estate, was owned in 1987 by Mr. P. J. Dickinson.[18] Lower farm, later Trinity farm, was sold in 1920 to E. F. Potter, from whom it passed in 1930 to D. Potter. In 1939 D. Potter sold it to Trinity College, Cambridge. J. B. Stafford bought it from the college in 1984,[19] and in 1984 sold it to A. J. Biggin & Son, the owner in 1987.[20]

Seagry House was retained by Lord Cowley, and the house was occupied until 1949 by Clare, relict of Henry, Earl Cowley (d. 1919).[21] It was built, possibly in 1740,[22] north of a small 17th-century gabled stone farmhouse.[23] The new house was of local stone with freestone dressings and a stone-slated roof.[24] It was of two storeys with attics concealed by a parapet. The main east front had five bays, of which the central three were surmounted by a triangular pediment containing in a cartouche arms[25] including those of Houlton.[26] Bays projected at the west end of both the north and south fronts. West of the 17th-century house and south-west of the 18th-century one, a long and low red-brick 18th-century range may have been stables. Additions of 1915 designed by Harold Brakspear united the three buildings as a single house.[27] An upper floor was built on part of those additions in 1929.[28] The 18th-century house and the 20th-century additions were demolished after a fire in 1949.[29] The 17th-century farmhouse and the 18th-century stable range, which had been mainly service rooms, were, with minor additions, made into a new Seagry House. The large stone stable block was built between 1828 and 1840,[30] and the two stone lodges in 1890.[31]

Another portion of the elder Robert Stratton's manor of Lower Seagry, c. 40 a., was the nucleus

of MANOR farm and was sold in 1702 by John Stratton to Charles Bayliffe[32] (d. 1735).[33] Manor farm passed to G. S. Bayliffe (d. 1813),[34] Henry Bayliffe (d. 1865), John Bayliffe (d. 1881), and J. S. Bayliffe,[35] who in 1900 sold it, then 168 a., to Henry, Earl Cowley.[36] The farm was part of the Draycot Cerne estate and, 73 a.,[37] was sold in 1921 to W. B. Hayward. It passed in 1967 to W. E. Hayward and in 1973 to his daughters Mrs. R. Kingston and Mrs. M. Gupwell. In 1987 Manor farm, c. 29 ha. (72 a.), was owned by Mr. and Mrs. Kingston.[38] Manor Farm was built of stone in the later 17th century[39] and has a twin-gabled west entrance front with stone-mullioned windows. A southern extension was built in the early 18th century.

A further portion of Robert Stratton's manor was owned in 1736 by John Hollis.[40] A house, later called Hide House, Home Farm, or the CHEST-NUTS, was built on it. The estate was owned in 1761 by Robert Hollis,[41] and descended to Robert Hollis (d. c. 1820), to that Robert's relict Elizabeth, and to his son William.[42] In 1870 William Hollis sold it to his daughter Elizabeth and her husband John Teagle.[43] In 1879 Teagle's trustees conveyed the house and 11 a. to his son William (d. 1913)[44] and sold c. 10 a. to Henry, Earl Cowley.[45] Lord Cowley bought William Teagle's portion in 1914.[46] The Chestnuts and 13 a. were sold in 1920,[47] and have since had several owners. The house was built in the early 18th century[48] of red brick with ornamental stone dressings. It is of two storeys with attics and dormers and the west entrance front has five bays of which the central one contains a doorway with a broken scroll pediment.

Seagry church was appropriated by Bradenstoke priory between 1194 and 1217.[49] In 1539 the REC-TORY estate comprised tithes and a house[50] and passed to the Crown, which sold it in 1560 to Richard Oakham.[51] Sir John Danvers (d. 1594), the owner in 1572, in 1594 settled the estate on himself and his wife Elizabeth (d. 1630).[52] Elizabeth's interest was barred and in 1612 Sir John's son Henry, Baron Danvers (cr. earl of Danby 1626, d. 1644), apparently owned the estate.[53] Lord Danby settled it in 1628 on his brother Sir

[14] W.R.O., A 1/345/355; ibid. 1553/120; W.A.M. xliii. 286–9, 297–9, 306–9; for the Houlton fam., W.N. & Q. vi, pedigree at pp. 272–3.
[15] Above, Draycot Cerne, manor.
[16] W.R.O. 1043/6, pp. 92, 95–7, 99–101, 104–6, 108, 116.
[17] Inf. from Estates and Valuations Officer, Co. Hall, Trowbridge.
[18] Inf. from Mr. P. J. Dickinson, the Paddocks.
[19] Inf. from Senior Bursar, Trinity Coll., Camb.
[20] Inf. from Mrs. E. J. Biggin, Trinity Farm.
[21] The Times, 10 May 1949 (obit.); Who Was Who, 1916–28, 237; Kelly's Handbk. (1924, 1948).
[22] J. B. Burke, Vis. of Seats and Arms (1853), ii, Vis. of Seats (1), 38.
[23] W.R.O. 1553/120.
[24] Ibid. 1043/6, p. 92.
[25] Jackson-Stops and Staff, Vanishing Hos. of Eng. 58; see above, plate facing p. 188.
[26] Burke, Vis. of Seats and Arms, ii, Vis. of Seats (1), 38.
[27] W.R.O., G 3/760/447.   [28] Ibid. G 3/760/736.
[29] The Times, 10 May 1949 (obit.).
[30] O.S. Map 1", sheet 34 (1828 edn.); P.R.O., IR 30/38/230.
[31] Dates on hos.
[32] P.R.O., C 54/4891, no. 11.
[33] Phillipps, Mon. Inscriptions N. Wilts. 126.
[34] Ibid.; W.R.O., A 1/345/355.

[35] P.R.O., IR 29/38/230; IR 30/38/230; W.R.O., A 1/345/355; for the Bayliffe fam. from 1848, W.R.O. 969/20, declaration, 1900.
[36] W.R.O. 969/20; 1409/272.   [37] Ibid. 1043/6, p. 100.
[38] Inf. from Mrs. R. Kingston, Sturmage Ho.
[39] The tablet on the porch, inscribed JH 1632, was taken from a ho. in Lower Seagry: W.A.M. xxiii. 76; inf. from Mr. D. Selwood, Long Tyme.
[40] Q. Sess. 1736 (W.R.S. xi), p. 43.
[41] W.A.M. xliii. 309–10.
[42] W.R.O., A 1/345/355; ibid. 109/445–6; P.R.O., IR 29/38/230; IR 30/38/230.
[43] W.R.O. 969/15, deed, 1870.
[44] Ibid. 374/130/111; 969/15, deeds, 1879, 1914; Soc. Antiq. MS. 817, x, f. 56.
[45] W.R.O. 969/20, deed, 1879.
[46] Ibid. 969/15, deed, 1914.
[47] Ibid. 1043/6, p. 97; Wilts. Cuttings, xiv. 116.
[48] W.A.M. xliii. 309–10.
[49] Bradenstoke Cart. (W.R.S. xxxv), p. 69.
[50] P.R.O., SC 6/Hen. VIII/3985, rot. 54d.
[51] Cal. Pat. 1558–60, 463.
[52] Phillipps, Wilts. Inst. i. 226; P.R.O., C 142/247, no. 100; for the Danvers fam., above, Dauntsey, manors; Malmesbury, manors.
[53] Complete Peerage, iv. 48–9; Phillipps, Wilts. Inst. ii. 6.

John Danvers (d. 1655), a regicide, and John's wife Elizabeth.[54] In 1661 the Crown, to which Sir John Danvers's property was forfeited, granted the estate to trustees of Sir John and his son Henry (d. 1654).[55] It was assigned after 1666 to Henry's niece Eleanor Lee (d. 1691) and her husband James Bertie, Lord Norreys (cr. earl of Abingdon 1682, d. 1699),[56] and was afterwards acquired by Eleanor's brother-in-law Thomas Wharton, Baron Wharton, and his wife Lucy. They sold it in 1705 to Thomas Boucher[57] (d. 1708), and Thomas's son Thomas sold it in 1749 to Robert Herbert (d. 1769). Herbert devised it to his nephew Henry Herbert (cr. earl of Carnarvon 1793, d. 1811), who was succeeded in turn by his son Henry, earl of Carnarvon (d. 1833), and that Henry's son Henry, earl of Carnarvon (d. 1849). In 1815 Lord Radnor bought the tithes arising from his own lands from Lord Carnarvon,[58] and in 1816 Lord Holland did the same.[59] In 1840 Lord Carnarvon's tithes were valued at £80, those which had been sold at £54 and £28 respectively, and all were commuted.[60]

ECONOMIC HISTORY.

Durand of Gloucester's 5-hide estate could support 4 ploughteams in 1086. There was 1 team on the 2 demesne hides, and on the other 3 hides there were 3 *villani* and 2 bordars with 3 teams. The meadow measured 40 a.[61] Later, as one of the manors called Seagry, the estate included a demesne farm based in Upper Seagry. In the 16th and 17th centuries members of the Adye family were lessees of the demesne farm, which in 1687 supported 150 sheep and 22 cows.[62] Copyholders paid rents totalling £1 8s. 8d. c. 1539.[63] Of the three leaseholders recorded c. 1609, one had a 112-a. farm with 92 a. of arable in the open fields, 8 a. of meadow or pasture, and 12 a. of coppices, and two had c. 30 a. each.[64] In 1840 all those demesne and tenant lands were in Seales farm, 202 a., based in Upper Seagry, and Seagry farm, 70 a., mainly in Lower Seagry.[65]

Drew FitzPons's 5-hide estate could also support 4 ploughteams in 1086. On the 2 demesne hides there was 1 team. On the other 3 hides there were 5 *villani*, 6 bordars, and 5 coscets. That there was only 1 team on the 3 hides suggests that they were not fully cultivated. There were 30 a. of meadow.[66] Later, as the other manor called Seagry, the estate included lands in all parts of the parish. In 1648 it comprised a demesne farm, later Church

farm, and 5 small copyholds:[67] the demesne farm was then 252 a.[68] In the 18th century the lands of the estate were mainly shared among Church farm, Piott's farm, two other farms based in Lower Seagry,[69] and Manor and another farm based in Upper Seagry.[70]

In the Middle Ages Upper and Lower Seagry may each have had its own open fields and may have shared a common meadow, Seagry meadow, so called in 1207.[71] The parish had North, East, and West fields in 1585[72] and Down field in 1648. Inclosure was apparently in progress in the 17th century: the 112-a. farm included 92 a. in the open fields c. 1609, but parts of North field had been inclosed by 1648 when the 252-a. farm included only 10 a. in open fields.[73] In 1656 more of North field and land in Down field and Clay Corner field, a total of 24 a., presumably open until then, were apportioned among various farms; and in 1663 a further c. 30 a. of Down field were allotted.[74] The open fields had all been inclosed by 1720.[75] Meadow beside the Avon, however, remained open. Hungerdown mead and Lower mead, a total of 124 a., were allotted and inclosed in 1883.[76] That land was still being watered in the earlier 20th century,[77] and in the later 20th century was still mainly open grassland.

In 1801 husbandry in Seagry was predominantly pastoral. Only 96 a. were arable: grain, mostly wheat, was grown on 67 a. and root crops for fodder on 29 a.[78] The tenant of Church farm in the earlier 19th century had to pay extra rent if he ploughed up pasture.[79] In 1840 there were 137 a. of arable in the parish: Seales farm had 40 a., Piott's 18 a., other farms less. There were 886 a. of pasture and 180 cows and 200 sheep were kept. Of the five farms based in Upper Seagry only Seales had more than 200 a.: the others were of 148 a., 133 a., 70 a., and 33 a. The three farms based in Lower Seagry were of 134 a., 118 a., and 58 a.[80]

The proportion of pasture to arable in Seagry changed little until c. 1886. Thereafter the small amount of arable decreased steadily and in 1933 only 36 a. were ploughed. Meadow and grass sown in rotation amounted to nearly half the grassland in 1876, a little over half in 1926, and about a third in 1933. An average of 280 cows and an average of 76 pigs were kept 1876–1933, an average of 76 sheep 1876–1906. In the period 1916–33 no sheep was kept.[81] Farming was still predominantly pastoral in 1987 and six farms were based

[54] P.R.O., C 104/84/1, mar. settlement, 1628; final concord, 1647.

[55] Ibid. C 66/2978, no. 20; ibid. PROB 11/246, ff. 224v.–225.

[56] Phillipps, *Wilts. Inst.* ii. 28; *Complete Peerage*, i. 45–6; W.R.O., D 1/54/6/1; D 1/54/15/1, no. 24.

[57] *Complete Peerage*, xii (2), 606–8; P.R.O., C 54/4952, no. 8.

[58] W.R.O. 490/480, abstr. of title; for the Herbert fam., *Complete Peerage*, iii. 46–8; *Musgrave's Obit.* iii (Harl. Soc. xlvi), 197.

[59] W.R.O. 11/130–1.   [60] P.R.O., IR 29/38/230.

[61] *V.C.H. Wilts.* ii, p. 148.

[62] W.R.O. 442/2, pp. 324–30; P.R.O., C 5/211/2.

[63] P.R.O., SC 6/Hen. VIII/3985, rot. 54d.

[64] W.R.O. 442/2, pp. 324–30.

[65] P.R.O., IR 29/38/230; IR 30/38/230.

[66] *V.C.H. Wilts.* ii, p. 156.

[67] W.R.O. 490/1066, final concord, 1585; copy notification, 1648.

[68] Ibid. 212B/6021.

[69] Ibid. 11/378/1, deed, Derham or Bailey to Jacob, 1752; 969/14, survey of Stratton's and Jacob's farms, 1761; *W.A.M.* xliii. 298–9.

[70] W.R.O., A 1/345/355; P.R.O., IR 29/38/230; IR 30/38/230.

[71] *Rot. Chart.* (Rec. Com.), 169–70.

[72] W.R.O. 442/2, p. 324.

[73] Ibid. 212B/6021; above.

[74] W.R.O. 2096/7.

[75] Ibid. 1553/120.

[76] Ibid. EA/193.

[77] O.S. Map 6″, Wilts. XIII. SE. (1925 edn.).

[78] P.R.O., HO 67/23/121.

[79] W.R.O. 856/1, deeds, Holland to Bailey, 1808; Holland to Godwin, 1824.

[80] P.R.O., IR 18/11135; IR 29/38/230; IR 30/38/230.

[81] Ibid. MAF 68/493, sheet 5; MAF 68/1063, sheet 4; MAF 68/1633, sheet 5; MAF 68/2203, sheet 14; MAF 68/2773, sheet 3; MAF 68/3319, sheet 3; MAF 68/3697, sheet 3.

in the former parish. On Trinity farm, 89 ha., a pedigree herd of Friesian cows was kept and *c.* 19 ha. of corn were grown,[82] the 50 ha. of Church farm were leased for grazing,[83] and Manor farm, *c.* 29 ha., was a dairy farm.[84] The *c.* 60 ha. owned by Wiltshire county council were in two small farms,[85] and corn was grown on the *c.* 56 ha. owned by Mr. P. J. Dickinson.[86]

In 1605 an inhabitant of Seagry bought wool in Gloucestershire to sell speculatively,[87] woollen cloth was fulled at Seagry Mill *c.* 1648,[88] Joseph Houlton (d. 1731), who bought land in Seagry from 1710, was a Trowbridge clothier,[89] and Robert Hollis (fl. 1761) of the Chestnuts was a woolstapler *c.* 1777.[90] In 1831 most men in Seagry were farm labourers. Nine described as tradesmen or artisans[91] may have worked outside the parish. Gravel was extracted *c.* 1947 by the Pyramid Sand and Gravel Co. from land east of Church Farm.[92] In 1958 a poultry farm was established by C. W. P. Head in the grounds of Seagry House to produce fertile eggs for hatching, and in 1987 chickens for egg production were reared for Mr. P. Head in buildings near Oak Hill House.[93]

The lessee of Bradenstoke priory's manor was obliged *c.* 1539 to plant 10 oaks or ashes and 20 willows yearly.[94] Woodland in Upper Seagry may have been grubbed up before 1648.[95] In 1840 all the woodland in the parish, 12 a. of plantations and 27 a. in Seagry wood, was in the north-west corner near Seagry House.[96] The woods in 1865 contained oak, ash, spruce, pine, and larch.[97] Some of the 62 a. of woodland said to be in Seagry in 1910 may have been in Great Somerford.[98] In 1920 there were *c.* 36 a. of woodland in the north-west part of the parish.[99]

In 1086 two mills were part of Drew FitzPons's estate.[1] One of them fell into disuse before 1207.[2] From 1648 a water mill and a fulling mill, presumably in the same building, were part of Lower Seagry manor.[3] Seagry Mill was part of Church farm in 1761[4] and passed with it until 1864 when Mary, Lady Holland, sold the mill to James Godwin.[5] It was owned in 1891 by members of the Godwin family,[6] became part of the Seagry House estate before 1910,[7] and in 1920 was offered for sale by Lord Cowley.[8] The mill, which had an undershot wheel, was demolished in 1950.[9] The mill house was built in the late 18th century and was refenestrated in the earlier 19th. A range of 19th-century cottages faces it.

LOCAL GOVERNMENT. Courts baron for the manor formerly Bradenstoke priory's were held twice yearly by the Crown *c.* 1539[10] and Sir Anthony Hungerford *c.* 1657, and courts baron were also held twice yearly for his manor by Sir Richard Norton *c.* 1647. The tenant of the demesne farm of each manor was obliged to provide for the officials who came to hold the courts.[11] None was held in the 18th century or later.[12]

By 1725 vestries dealt with all parish business and elected churchwardens, overseers of the poor, and surveyors of highways. In the 1850s the use of the common meadows and of the lanes for pasture was still regulated by the vestry.[13]

Between 1690 and 1708 average sums of £15 a year were spent on the poor.[14] Expenditure rose steadily throughout the 18th century and averaged *c.* £50 yearly 1775–85. By 1777 some paupers were accommodated in a parish house. Most received out relief, however, and in 1802–3 £169 was spent on permanent relief for 80 adults and children,[15] about a third of the population.[16] In the years 1813–15 on average 18 were relieved permanently and 35 occasionally.[17] Yearly expenditure of £200–£250 in the years 1816–36 was median for a parish in Malmesbury hundred. The parish became part of Chippenham poor-law union in 1835.[18] The new Seagry parish was included in North Wiltshire district in 1974.[19]

CHURCH. Between 1182 and 1193 Alexander of Seagry gave Seagry church to Bradenstoke priory. The priory appropriated it between 1194 and 1217, reserved a £2 pension from its revenues, and assigned the rest to a vicar.[20] The vicarage and the rectory of Draycot Cerne were united in 1939 and disunited in 1954.[21] In 1967 the vicarage was united with the benefices of Great Somerford and Little Somerford, and in 1986 the benefice of Corston with Rodbourne was added to form one benefice.[22]

The priors of Bradenstoke presented vicars until the Dissolution. In 1544 Richard Hughes presented by grant of a turn from the priory, and the Crown presented in 1545 and 1547. Although it was not expressly mentioned in the grant the

[82] Inf. from Mrs. E. J. Biggin, Trinity Farm.
[83] Inf. from Mrs. E. Newman, Church Farm.
[84] Inf. from Mrs. R. Kingston, Sturmage Ho.
[85] Inf. from Estates and Valuations Officer, Co. Hall, Trowbridge.
[86] Inf. from Mr. P. J. Dickinson, the Paddocks.
[87] *Early-Stuart Tradesmen* (W.R.S. xv), p. 53.
[88] W.R.O. 212B/6021.
[89] *V.C.H. Wilts.* vii. 138; above, manors.
[90] *W.A.M.* xliii. 309–10.   [91] *Census*, 1831.
[92] W.R.O., G 3/760/1318.
[93] Inf. from Mr. and Mrs. P. Head, Oak Hill Ho.
[94] P.R.O., SC 6/Hen. VIII/3985, rot. 54d.
[95] W.R.O. 212B/6021.
[96] P.R.O., IR 29/38/230; IR 30/38/230.
[97] W.R.O. 2062/31.
[98] Ibid. Inland Revenue, val. reg. 14.
[99] Ibid. 1043/6, p. 111.
[1] *V.C.H. Wilts.* ii, p. 156.
[2] *Rot. Chart.* (Rec. Com.), 169–70.
[3] W.R.O. 212B/6021.
[4] Ibid. 969/14, survey of Stratton's and Jacob's farms, 1761.

[5] Ibid. 969/14, deed, Holland to Godwin, 1864; above, manors.
[6] W.R.O. 969/14, deed, Godwin to Godwin, 1891.
[7] Ibid. Inland Revenue, val. reg. 14.
[8] Ibid. 1043/6, p. 116.
[9] Inf. from Mr. D. Selwood, Long Tyme.
[10] P.R.O., SC 6/Hen. VIII/3985, rot. 54d.
[11] *W.A.M.* xliii. 292; W.R.O. 490/481, deed, Hungerford to Adye, 1657.
[12] W.R.O. 335/184, ff. 13v.–14; 490/1066, letter, Powell to Radnor, 1754.
[13] Ibid. 2096/8; 2096/14.
[14] Ibid. 2096/7.
[15] Ibid. 2096/17; *Poor Law Abstract, 1804,* 566–7.
[16] *V.C.H. Wilts.* iv. 357.
[17] *Poor Law Abstract, 1818,* 498–9.
[18] *Poor Rate Returns, 1816–21,* 189; *1822–4,* 228; *1825–9,* 219; *1830–4,* 213; *Poor Law Com. 2nd Rep.* App. D, 558.
[19] O.S. Map 1/100,000, admin. areas, Wilts. (1974 edn.).
[20] *Bradenstoke Cart.* (W.R.S. xxxv), pp. 68–9.
[21] Ch. Com. files, NB 5/72; NB 5/86; 21559/2.
[22] Inf. from Ch. Com.

Crown presumably sold the advowson with the rectory estate to Richard Oakham in 1560. In 1572 Sir John Danvers owned the rectory estate and presented a vicar. The advowson descended with the rectory estate to Henry Herbert, earl of Carnarvon (d. 1849),[23] and then with the earldom[24] until 1927 when Henry Herbert, earl of Carnarvon, transferred it to Harrogate College Ltd. In 1939 Harrogate College was assigned the first of every three turns of presentation to the united benefice.[25] In 1967 the Martyrs Memorial and Church of England Trust, the successor of Harrogate College as patron, became entitled to present at the third of every four turns, and in 1986 to present jointly at the first, third, and fifth of every five turns.[26]

The vicarage was worth £5 in 1291.[27] In 1437 the arrangement under which Bradenstoke priory and the vicar shared the income was revoked. Thenceforth the priory took the entire income and paid the vicar £6 and a robe yearly.[28] That stipend had been increased to £8 by 1535.[29] None was paid in 1671.[30] The benefice was worth only £10 in 1650.[31] Although augmented in 1771 and 1774 with grants from Queen Anne's Bounty totalling £600,[32] the living remained poor, and in the years 1829–31 had an average income of £173.[33]

The vicar presumably took all the tithes until 1437.[34] He may have taken all except corn tithes in the 17th century.[35] He took the small tithes in 1704[36] and in the earlier 19th century. The vicarial tithes, which perhaps included hay tithes, were valued at £160 in 1840 and commuted.[37] The vicar had no glebe.[38] Bradenstoke priory provided a vicarage house in 1437,[39] and the vicar had a house north of the church in 1720.[40] In 1828 it was replaced by a new stone house, which was enlarged in 1852,[41] and sold in 1939.[42]

During the Middle Ages incumbencies were often short.[43] The benefice was vacant in 1561,[44] presumably because the vicar had been deprived for rejecting the Anglican settlement. The parish lacked the *Paraphrases* of Erasmus in 1585.[45] Edward Bridges, vicar 1627–66, was also rector of Bremilham and of North Wraxall.[46] Gilbert Lake, vicar from 1750, was also vicar of Westport.[47] Benjamin Rogers (d. 1802), vicar from 1762, lived at Rainscombe in North Newnton and usually employed a curate at Seagry. In 1783

Rogers asserted that he held no more than a single Sunday service at Seagry because his income from the benefice was small. The only weekday services were on Ash Wednesday and Good Friday. The sacrament was administered on Christmas day, Easter Sunday, and Whit Sunday to an average of 11 communicants. When neither Rogers nor a curate employed by him did duty at Seagry it was done by the rector of Draycot Cerne.[48] Arthur Edie, vicar from 1827, was also vicar of Rodbourne Cheney.[49] He, too, held only one service each Sunday.[50] On Census Sunday in 1851 a congregation of 70 attended the morning service and one of 69 the afternoon service.[51] C. H. Awdry, vicar 1854–78, augmented his income by taking pupils.[52] H. K. Anketell, vicar 1878–87, observed Ritualistic practices at services on Good Friday and Easter Sunday in 1879, and in 1880 introduced a robed choir.[53] From 1954 until 1967 the vicarage was held in plurality with the rectory of Stanton St. Quintin.[54]

The church of *ST. MARY*, so called in 1763,[55] in 1808 comprised a chancel and a nave with south chapel, south porch, and west bellcot.[56] The south chapel and the style of the east window and of windows in the south wall of the chancel suggest that the 12th-century church was either much altered or rebuilt in the 13th century. The church was rebuilt in 1849 on the same plan, and in a 13th-century style, to the designs of J. H. Hakewill.[57] Monuments including two 13th-century stone effigies, a 12th-century font, and a 15th-century rood screen were retained from the old church.[58]

Seagry church was apparently rich in plate in the Middle Ages. In 1553 the king's commissioners took 3½ oz. of plate and left 14 oz. A chalice hallmarked for 1811 and an 18th-century paten were bought from Lyneham parish in 1864 and held in 1987.[59] There were two bells in 1553, of which one was probably cast in Bristol. A new bell was cast in 1839 by C. & G. Mears and hung in the bellcot in 1987.[60] Registrations of baptisms, marriages, and burials begin in 1610. No baptism is recorded 1705–10 and no marriage 1711–29.[61]

NONCONFORMITY. Members of the Kerfoot

[23] Phillipps, *Wilts. Inst.* (index in *W.A.M.* xxviii. 229); above, manors.
[24] *Clergy List* (1859 and later edns.); *Crockford* (1896 and later edns.); *Complete Peerage*, iii. 46–8; Burke, *Peerage* (1959), 406–7; Bristol R.O., EP/A/3/269, deed, 1926.
[25] Ch. Com. files 21559/1–2.
[26] Ibid. NB 5/86c; inf. from Ch. Com.; Martyrs Memorial and Church of Eng. Trust, 32 Fleet Street, Lond.
[27] *Tax. Eccl.* (Rec. Com.), 189.
[28] W.R.O., D 1/2/9, ff. 65–6.
[29] *Valor Eccl.* (Rec. Com.), ii. 135.
[30] W.R.O., D 1/24/178/2.
[31] *W.A.M.* xli. 5.
[32] C. Hodgson, *Queen Anne's Bounty* (1864), pp. clxxi, cccxxxvi.
[33] *Rep. Com. Eccl. Revenues*, 846–7.
[34] W.R.O., D 1/2/9, ff. 65–6.
[35] Ibid. D 1/24/178/1.
[36] Ibid. D 1/24/178/3.
[37] P.R.O., IR 29/38/230.
[38] W.R.O., D 1/24/178/1–3.
[39] Ibid. D 1/2/9, ff. 65–6.
[40] Ibid. 1553/120.
[41] Soc. Antiq. MS. 817, x, f. 56.
[42] Ch. Com. file 21559/2.
[43] Phillipps, *Wilts. Inst.* (index in *W.A.M.* xxviii. 229).
[44] *V.C.H. Wilts.* iii. 33 and n.
[45] W.R.O., D 1/43/6, f. 32.
[46] *Subscription Bk. 1620–40* (W.R.S. xxxii), p. 18; *W.N. & Q.* vii. 547.
[47] *Alum. Oxon. 1715–1886*, iii. 809.
[48] Ibid. 1218–19; *V.C.H. Wilts.* x. 130; *Vis. Queries, 1783* (W.R.S. xxvii), pp. 187–8; W.R.O., bishop's transcripts, bdle. 3.
[49] *Rep. Com. Eccl. Revenues*, 846–7.
[50] Ch. Com. file, NB 5/86c/1.
[51] P.R.O., HO 129/253/4/7/9.
[52] *W.A.M.* xxxvi. 491.
[53] *Clergy List* (1881); Wilts. Tracts, ccx, no. 9; W.R.O. 2096/2.
[54] *Lond. Gaz.* 21 Dec. 1967, p. 14051; Ch. Com. file, NB 5/72.
[55] J. Ecton, *Thesaurus* (1763), 404.
[56] J. Buckler, watercolour in W.A.S. Libr., vol. vi. 31.
[57] Pevsner, *Wilts.* (2nd edn.), 463–4.
[58] Wilts. Tracts, ccx, no. 9, where the statement that the effigies are of a Walter Clifford and Isabel Mompesson is not supported by evidence.
[59] Nightingale, *Wilts. Plate*, 224; inf. from the rector, Great Somerford.
[60] Walters, *Wilts. Bells*, 194, 252; inf. from the rector, which corrects the date 1849 given ibid.
[61] W.R.O. 2096/1–3. Transcripts for 1605–9, 1707–9, 1716–18, and 1727–9 are ibid.

and Wheeler families were Quakers in the later 17th and earlier 18th century.[62] In 1669 a large meeting of 'fanatics', presumably including Quakers from other parishes, took place at Jasper Wheeler's house.[63] Six nonconformists were recorded in 1676.[64]

A small red-brick chapel for Primitive Methodists was built at Upper Seagry in 1825.[65] On Census Sunday in 1851 congregations of 103 and 120, which may have included people from outside Seagry, respectively attended the morning and evening services.[66] A Sunday service was still held at the chapel in 1986.

EDUCATION. Catherine, Lady Tylney-Long, in 1808 supported a school in Seagry.[67] It was apparently closed before 1818. A few children, whose parents paid for them, were then taught in another school.[68] A National school and schoolhouse were built of stone in 1850 beside the Great Somerford road between Upper Seagry and Lower Seagry.[69] In it 30–40 children were taught by an uncertificated mistress in 1858.[70] An average of 40 pupils was taught in 1906.[71] Numbers declined in the earlier 20th century and an average of only 15 attended in 1937–8.[72] After the building of council houses in Seagry c. 1950[73] numbers rose; the school was closed, and a new one was opened at Upper Seagry, in 1963. In it 58 children were taught by four teachers in 1987.[74]

CHARITY FOR THE POOR. None known.

GREAT SOMERFORD

GREAT SOMERFORD,[75] 5 km. south-east of Malmesbury on the Bristol Avon,[76] was called Somerford Mautravers from the later 13th century. From the 15th century the suffix, the surname of the lords of a manor in the parish, was gradually replaced by the prefix Broad or Great.[77] Both suffix and prefix distinguished Great Somerford from its smaller and less populous neighbour Little Somerford or Somerford Mauduit. The parish includes the hamlet of Startley. Under an Act of 1882 small parts of the parish were transferred to Little Somerford and Malmesbury.[78] Great Somerford thereafter measured 672 ha. (1,660 a.).

Most of the northern boundary is marked by the Avon and its tributary the Rodbourne stream. Failure to follow the river round the bend north of the village suggests that the Avon's course has changed. The stream, dividing Great Somerford from Rodbourne in Malmesbury, was a boundary in the late 11th century or early 12th.[79] To the east the boundary with Dauntsey followed what may have been an earlier course of the Avon until 1809, when it was redefined as a straight line west of it.[80] Elsewhere a road and a stream mark short stretches, but most of the west and south boundaries follow no prominent feature. The south is part of a line, presumably drawn at an early inclosure, which also marks the south boundary of Great Somerford's east and west neighbours.

Kellaways Clay, Oxford Clay, and Kellaways Sand outcrop in the parish, the clay mainly in the west, the sand mainly in the centre. To the east are extensive gravel terraces, and much alluvium has been deposited by the Rodbourne stream in the north-west and by the Avon in the north-east and south-east. The parish is almost flat. The highest land, c. 90 m., is in the north-west, the lowest, c. 60 m., at the south-east corner.[81] The extensive meadow land on the alluvium and the pasture on the clays have favoured animal husbandry in the parish, but tillage is also favoured by the gravel, and some of the clay has been ploughed.[82]

The parish is well served by lanes but no main road crosses it. The road between Little Somerford and Sutton Benger links Great Somerford village with the road from Malmesbury to Wootton Bassett and Swindon in the north and the Swindon–Chippenham road in the south. Its original course may have been across a ford north of the church, but in 1773 was further east across a bridge. The Avon was presumably bridged long before 1773; a new bridge, with a balustraded parapet, was built c. 1799.[83] The road was turnpiked in 1809 and disturnpiked in 1876.[84] Joining it in Seagry parish another north–south road, leading from Malmesbury, crosses the parish through Startley. An east–west road from Dauntsey ran through Great Somerford village to Startley, and in 1773 west of Startley towards Rodbourne.[85] In 1809, when that west part was no longer in use, the east part was made straight at inclosure.[86] A

[62] W.N. & Q. ii. 371, 427, 430; iii. 121; iv. 63; v. 223, 307.
[63] G. L. Turner, Orig. Rec. i, p. 107; ii, p. 1077.
[64] Compton Census, ed. Whiteman, 129.
[65] Meeting Ho. Certs. (W.R.S. xl), p. 110.
[66] P.R.O., HO 129/253/4/7/10.
[67] Lamb. Palace Libr., MS. 1732.
[68] Educ. of Poor Digest, 1036.
[69] P.R.O., ED 7/131, no. 238.
[70] Acct. of Wilts. Schs. 41.
[71] Return of Non-Provided Schs. 27.
[72] Bd. of Educ., List 21, 1908–38 (H.M.S.O.).
[73] Above, introduction.
[74] Inf. from Chief Educ. Officer, Co. Hall, Trowbridge.
[75] This article was written in 1988.

[76] Maps used include O.S. Maps 1", sheets 34 (1828 edn.), 157 (1968 edn.); 1/50,000, sheet 173 (1974 edn.); 1/25,000, ST 98 (1959 edn.); 6", Wilts. XIII (1888 edn.); 1/10,000, ST 98 SE., SW. (1983 edn.).
[77] Rot. Hund. (Rec. Com.), ii (1), 272; P.N. Wilts. (E.P.N.S.), 73–4; below, manors.
[78] Census, 1891.   [79] Arch. Jnl. lxxvii. 88–90.
[80] W.R.O., EA/98; above, Dauntsey, introduction.
[81] Geol. Surv. Maps 1", solid and drift, sheets 251 (1970 edn.), 252 (1974 edn.).   [82] Below, econ. hist.
[83] Andrews and Dury, Map (W.R.S. viii), pl. 14; V.C.H. Wilts. v. 250.
[84] V.C.H. Wilts. iv. 257, 263, 271.
[85] Andrews and Dury, Map (W.R.S. viii), pls. 13–14.
[86] W.R.O., EA/98.

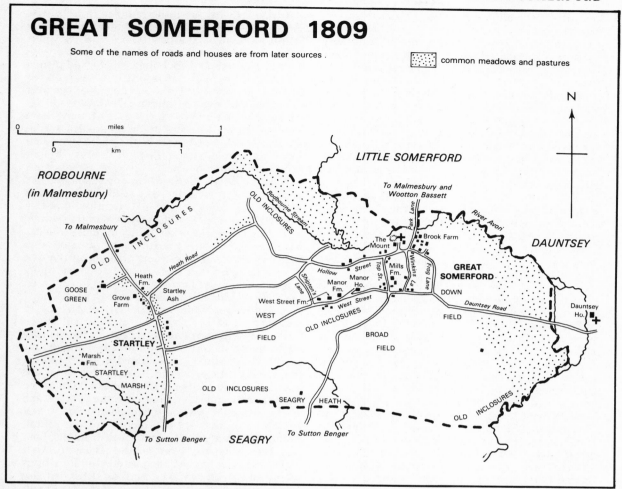

GREAT SOMERFORD 1809

Some of the names of roads and houses are from later sources.

common meadows and pastures

N

more northerly road that ran to Startley in 1773[87] was, except at either end, a rough track in 1988. The Malmesbury railway, to link Malmesbury with Dauntsey station on the G.W.R. line between London and Bristol, was built across the parish and opened in 1877. A station called Somerford, later Great Somerford, stood north of the village in Little Somerford parish. Line and station were closed in 1933,[88] and the line south of the station had been removed by 1949.[89]

Artifacts of the early and middle Bronze Age have been found in the parish.[90] In 1377 there were 92 poll-tax payers of Great Somerford, one of the higher totals for Malmesbury hundred, and only 10 of Startley.[91] Taxation assessments in the 16th and early 17th century suggest that the parish was prosperous. The fact that John Yew, the owner of two manors in the parish and a clothier, lived at Great Somerford, may account for a higher than usual assessment in 1571 and in 1576.[92] Between 1801 and 1841 the population increased from 358 to 556. It fluctuated little between 1841 and 1891, when it was 530, but afterwards fell. It was 421 in 1921, 448 in 1931. Thereafter the building of private and council houses caused it

to increase: it was 662 in 1971, 668 in 1981.[93]

In 1989 Great Somerford was a large village spread out mainly along the Little Somerford to Sutton Benger road, called Park Lane to the north, Top Street to the south, and along several streets east and west of that road. Some of the older buildings are timber-framed but most, and most 19th-century ones, are of stone. The village grew up on the south bank of the Avon presumably near the ford from which it took its name.[94] A mound near the river is possibly the site of a motte-and-bailey castle which may have been raised in the 12th century, and east of it the church was standing by the late 12th century. Fragments of 12th-century masonry have been found in the mound.[95] A house called the Mount was built south of the mound in the later 16th century and, east of the Mount, a timber-framed building was erected, possibly as a house, in the early 17th century. The rectory house was built south of the church in the early 17th century, and Brook Farm in the 16th century on the east side of Park Lane.[96] At the junction of Park Lane and Frog Lane a house called Bevis has a long north–south range which was originally timber-framed and of early 17th-

[87] *Andrews and Dury, Map* (W.R.S. viii), pls. 13–14.
[88] *V.C.H. Wilts.* iv. 288; C. R. Clinker, *Clinker's Reg. Closed Passenger Sta. 1830–1980*, pp. 56, 163.
[89] O.S. Map 1/25,000, 31/98 (1949 edn.).
[90] *V.C.H. Wilts.* i (1), 74.
[91] Ibid. iv. 310.
[92] *Taxation Lists* (W.R.S. x), 29, 49–50; *W.A.M.* xxxi. 288;

P.R.O., E 179/197/153; E 179/198/287; E 179/199/356; E 179/199/399; E 179/259/20; below, manors.
[93] *V.C.H. Wilts.* iv. 357; *Census*, 1971; 1981.
[94] *P.N. Wilts.* (E.P.N.S.), 73.
[95] *W.A.M.* xxxviii. 321; xlv. 88–9, 137; below, church.
[96] Below, manors, church.

century construction. At different dates the house was partly rebuilt in brick and stone. J. L. Osborn (d. 1940), a writer on Wiltshire topics, lived there 1910–24.[97] East of Bevis, a small symmetrically fronted farmhouse was built in the early 19th century, and on the south side of Frog Lane cottages were built of stone rubble in the late 18th. Further west, north of the junction of Top Street and Hollow Street, the Old Maltings was built in the early 19th century, and west of the junction, the Close is a house built in the early 17th century, extended south and west in the early 18th century, and much altered inside c. 1985. East of the junction a group of later 19th-century red-brick buildings includes a reading room erected in 1872 which became a chapel in 1882.[98] Mills Farm on the east side of Top Street was built in the 17th century,[99] and east of it and abutting Winkins Lane is a large barn of cruck construction. The Beeches, on the west side of Top Street, was built of stone in the later 19th century.[1]

In the 17th century or earlier farmsteads and cottages were built in West Street to form a group away from the main part of the village. The Manor House, Manor Farmhouse, and West Street Farm were all built in the 17th century,[2] and houses on both sides of the street incorporate timber framing and may have been built in the later 16th or earlier 17th century. West Street was diverted from the south to the north side of the Manor House between 1853 and 1885.[3]

Settlement began in Hollow Street after 1773.[4] The only older building, of the early 17th century, timber-framed, and partly rebuilt in brick, was apparently a farm building. Parsloe, formerly Church Farm, a small stone farmhouse, was built on the north side of the street c. 1800, in 1809 c. 10 houses and cottages stood beside the street,[5] and later a school was built. On the south side a pair of stone cottages with an east front of ashlar survives.

A house at the junction of Winkins Lane and Dauntsey Road was built of rendered stone with brick quoins in 1766.[6] In the 19th century the village developed southwards along Top Street and around its junction with West Street and Dauntsey Road. South-west of the junction the Volunteer inn was open in 1822,[7] and from 1836 to 1912 a friendly society met there.[8] Further south, on the east side of the road to Sutton Benger, the New Inn later the Masons Arms, was open from 1841 until c. 1968.[9] Outside the village, Downfield Farm south of Dauntsey Road was built of stone c. 1824 to designs by Charles Fowler.[10] A keeper's house was built at the level crossing in Dauntsey Road c. 1877. South of the village at Seagry Heath a farmstead was built c. 1850 and another c. 1912.[11]

Council and private houses were built in all parts of the village in the 20th century. In 1932 six, and in 1938 ten, council houses were built along Dauntsey Road, and a new school was later built there. In Winkins Lane 16 council houses were built in 1949–50 and six bungalows for old people in 1951, and in 1955 four council houses replaced two cottages north of Hollow Street. Further west along Hollow Street a residential caravan site was opened beside the Avon in 1964. Two bungalows were built on the east side of Shiptons Lane in the 1960s and, north-west of the junction of Top Street and West Street, 15 bungalows in Manor Park were built 1969–70.[12]

Near its eastern edge the common called Startley marsh was crossed by the road leading from Malmesbury. According to tradition Startley hundred courts met on the common in the Middle Ages.[13] East of the road the common formed a wide verge, extending north of the junction with the road from Great Somerford first on the east side of the road and then on the west, and there was a further area of common, called Goose Green in 1773,[14] to the north-west. There was settlement round the edges of the common in the 17th century and later: Heath Farm, east of the road at the north end of the settlement, is a small 17th-century stone house of one storey and attics which was raised to two storeys and altered in the 19th century; the Cottage, west of the road at the south end, is a small timber-framed house built in the 17th century and cased in brick in the 18th; Marsh Farm, which apparently stood in 1809,[15] was rebuilt c. 1960;[16] Goose Green Farm was rebuilt of stone with a symmetrical south front c. 1800; and Grove Farm, at the north end on the west side, was standing in 1809 and rebuilt in brick in the later 19th century. By 1809 there had also been encroachments on the common, 2 or 3 cottages at Goose Green, c. 3 on the west side of the road at the north end, and c. 7 on the wide verge east of the road.[17] Those at Goose Green had been demolished by 1885.[18] The oldest of the others to survive is apparently Barn Gates, built near the north end of the settlement in the later 18th century and extended east in the 19th. After inclosure in 1809 Startley Farm was built on the west side of the road and White Lodge, with a symmetrical west front, on the east side, both in the earlier 19th century; a nonconformist chapel was built later; and in the later 19th century and the 20th houses and bungalows were built on both sides. Cottages north of Heath Road in 1773[19] were rebuilt in the 19th century.

MANORS AND OTHER ESTATES. There were seven separate Domesday estates in Great Somerford. The equal size of Edwin's and Alnod's, and of Alwin's, Alwi's, and Saieva's, may

[97] P. Hobbs, *Somerford Magna*, 102; *W.A.M.* xlix. 101.
[98] *Kelly's Dir. Wilts.* (1875); below, nonconf.
[99] Below, manors.
[1] O.S. Map 6″, Wilts. XIII (1888 edn.).
[2] Below, manors.
[3] W.R.O. 137/125/52; O.S. Map 6″, Wilts. XIII (1888 edn.).
[4] *Andrews and Dury, Map* (W.R.S. viii), pl. 14.
[5] W.R.O., EA/98.
[6] Date on ho., with initials S/TS.
[7] W.R.O., A 1/326/3.
[8] P.R.O., FS 3/408, no. 184.
[9] Ibid. HO 107/1181/32; Hobbs, *Somerford Magna*, 163.
[10] Exeter Coll., Oxf., Mun., K, box 3, no. 6.
[11] Hobbs, *Somerford Magna*, 165.
[12] Ibid. 149, 153, 155–9, 170, 174–7.
[13] Above, Malmesbury hund.
[14] *Andrews and Dury, Map* (W.R.S. viii), pl. 13.
[15] W.R.O., EA/98.
[16] Hobbs, *Somerford Magna*, 183.
[17] W.R.O., EA/98.
[18] O.S. Map 6″, Wilts. XIII (1888 edn.).
[19] *Andrews and Dury, Map* (W.R.S. viii), pl. 13.

imply the division of earlier large estates. In 1066 Edwin held 3 hides and 24 a. that became the manor of *SOMERFORD MAUTRAVERS*. Humphrey Lisle held the estate, with a house in Malmesbury, in 1086[20] and it passed to his daughter Adelize, wife of Reynold or Robert de Dunstanville. From their son Reynold (d. 1156) the overlordship passed with the barony of Castle Combe in the direct male line to Walter de Dunstanville[21] (d. 1270). It passed to Walter's daughter Parnel whose husband John de la Mare held it until his death in 1313. From John it passed to Bartholomew de Badlesmere, Lord Badlesmere (d. 1322), who bought the reversion from Parnel's son William de Montfort in 1309.[22] On the death of Badlesmere's son Giles in 1338, it was allotted to Giles's sister Elizabeth (d. 1356), the wife of William de Bohun, earl of Northampton.[23] The overlordship was afterwards held by Elizabeth's nephew Robert Tybotot, Lord Tybotot (d. *s.p.m.* 1372), whose heirs were overlords in 1380,[24] but no later mention of it has been found.

In 1086 Robert held the estate of Humphrey Lisle.[25] It was afterwards held by Roger son of Geoffrey. Roger's coheirs were his daughters Ela, wife of Richard of Herriard, and Alice (d. in or before 1180), wife of John Mautravers (d. 1200). In 1183–4 Alice's son Walter Mautravers (d. before 1201) was assigned the estate. He forfeited it after taking part in Prince John's rebellion of 1193,[26] and in 1194 it was apparently assigned to his uncle Richard of Herriard in right of Ela.[27] The estate was afterwards restored to Walter's brother John Mautravers (d. 1220). John forfeited it after joining the rebellion of 1215, but afterwards recovered it. The manor passed in the direct male line to John's son John (fl. 1242–3),[28] John (d. 1296 or 1297),[29] John (d. 1341), who was granted free warren in his demesne lands,[30] and John, Lord Mautravers (d. 1364). The manor passed to Lord Mautravers's relict Agnes (d. 1375)[31] and granddaughter Eleanor Mautravers, *suo jure* Baroness Mautravers (d. 1405), who married first John d'Arundel, Lord Arundel (d. 1379), and secondly Reynold Cobham, Lord Cobham (d. 1403).[32]

Eleanor was succeeded by her grandson John d'Arundel,[33] Lord Mautravers (d. 1421), whose relict Eleanor (d. 1455) married secondly Sir Richard Poynings (d. *c.* 1430) and thirdly Walter Hungerford, Lord Hungerford (d. 1449).[34] From that Eleanor the manor passed to her son William FitzAlan or Mautravers, earl of Arundel (d.

1487),[35] and descended from father to son with the Arundel title to Thomas FitzAlan (d. 1524), William FitzAlan (d. 1544),[36] and Henry FitzAlan (d. 1580).

In 1561 Henry, earl of Arundel, sold Somerford Mautravers manor to John Yew[37] (d. 1588). Yew was succeeded by his son John (d. by 1623),[38] and from the younger John the manor passed to his granddaughter Anne Long, who, with her father Gifford Long, sold it in 1623 to Robert Jason[39] (d. 1634). The manor descended in the direct male line to Sir Robert Jason, Bt. (d. 1675), and Sir Robert Jason, Bt. (d. 1687). The younger Sir Robert was foreclosed by the mortgagee, Sir Richard Hawkins (d. 1687),[40] whose trustees sold the manor in portions.

In 1699 John Smith (d. 1724) bought the manor house and demesne lands called Somerford farm. He was succeeded by his son John (d. 1765), who *c.* 1750 bought other parts of Somerford Mautravers manor. The younger John's daughter Elizabeth Smith (d. 1798) devised the estate to her kinsman William Jones (d. 1833), who took the name Smith in place of Jones in 1798, and to William's sister Mary (d. 1875), wife of Lazarus Birtill.[41] The estate was greatly reduced, apparently by sales in the later 19th or early 20th century, and 103 a. were sold in 1903 by the representatives of Mary Birtill's daughter-in-law Janetta Birtill,[42] who in 1910 owned only the Mount and 7 a.[43] The Mount was owned in 1927 by the Revd. W. J. Birtill,[44] from 1945 to 1955 by members of the Palmer family,[45] and from 1955 by Maj. P. W. G. Phillips,[46] the owner in 1988.

The Mount was built in the later 16th century as an **L**-shaped timber-framed house with a north–south hall range, entered through a two-storeyed east porch, and a south wing extending to the east. In the early 18th century a staircase was built in the angle between the hall and the wing, and a partition wall with heavily moulded panelling was made on the first floor. In the early 19th century the south elevation of the wing was made into a symmetrical entrance front with a central pediment, and all the walls were roughcast. In the later 20th century some 18th-century fittings, including panelling in the hall and a carved stone fireplace in the south wing, were introduced.

In 1726 Richard Knapp and others sold 10 a., formerly part of Somerford Mautravers manor, to Nathaniel Houlton.[47] The land became part of Houlton's Seagry estate, was sold in 1785 to Sir

---

[20] *V.C.H. Wilts.* ii, pp. 142, 144, 161.
[21] Ibid. pp. 110–11; G. Poulett Scrope, *Castle Combe* (priv. print. 1852), 19; I. J. Sanders, *Eng. Baronies*, 28.
[22] *Cal. Inq. p.m.* i, p. 232; *Bk. of Fees*, ii. 713; *Rot. Hund.* (Rec. Com.), ii (1), 272; Poulett Scrope, *Castle Combe*, 19, 54; for the Badlesmere fam., *Complete Peerage*, i. 371–3.
[23] *Cal. Inq. p.m.* viii, pp. 127, 137, 143; *Complete Peerage*, ix. 667.
[24] *Cal. Inq. p.m.* xv, pp. 77–8, 80; *Complete Peerage*, xii (2), 95–8.　　[25] *V.C.H. Wilts.* ii, p. 144.
[26] *Cur. Reg. R.* ix. 132; x. 17–18; for the Mautravers fam., *Complete Peerage*, viii. 557–86.
[27] *Pipe R.* 1194 (P.R.S. n.s. v), 201.
[28] *Bk. of Fees*, ii. 713.
[29] *Rot. Hund.* (Rec. Com.), ii (1), 272.
[30] *Feet of F.* 1272–1327 (W.R.S. i), p. 125; *Cal. Chart. R.* 1300–26, 391.
[31] *Feet of F.* 1327–77 (W.R.S. xxix), p. 109.
[32] *Cal. Inq. p.m.* xv, pp. 77–8, 80; xviii, pp. 250–1; *Cal. Close*, 1377–81, 315–16; 1402–5, 193.

[33] *Cal. Inq. p.m.* xviii, pp. 381–2.
[34] For the Arundel and FitzAlan fam., *Complete Peerage*, i. 247–53; *Cal. Close*, 1419–22, 190.
[35] *Cal. Close*, 1454–61, 90.
[36] P.R.O., REQ 2/75/46.
[37] Ibid. CP 25(2)/239/3 Eliz. I Hil. no. 125.
[38] Ibid. PROB 11/142, f. 483v.; *W.A.M.* ii. 280; xxxi. 288.
[39] *W.A.M.* xxxi. 288; P.R.O., CP 25(2)/372/21 Jas. I Mich.
[40] *W.N. & Q.* ii. 546–7; vii. 244, 361, 365, 398; *W.A.M.* xxxi. 294; P.R.O., C 142/555, no. 96; ibid. PROB 11/389, ff. 44v.–45v.
[41] P.R.O., PROB 11/1304, ff. 182–186v.; W.R.O. 2051/2; *W.N. & Q.* i. 407–10; iii. 68–9; *W.A.M.* xxxi. 295–6; *Changes of Name, 1760–1901*, comp. W. P. W. Phillimore and E. A. Fry, 293; mon. in church.
[42] W.A.S. Libr., sale cat. vii, no. 20.
[43] W.R.O., Inland Revenue, val. reg. 14.
[44] Ibid. G 7/515/3.　　[45] Ibid. G 7/516/1.
[46] Hobbs, *Somerford Magna*, 11.
[47] *W.A.M.* xliii. 300–1.

James Tylney-Long, Bt., and descended as part of the Draycot Cerne estate.[48] In 1865 the owner, Henry Wellesley, Earl Cowley, bought a 60-a. farm at Startley from Mary Birtill,[49] and in 1870 c. 18 a. at Startley from the Revd. Stephen Demainbray.[50] In 1920 Christian, Earl Cowley, offered c. 88 a. around Startley, including Startley farm, 32 a., for sale.[51] Startley farm was owned in 1988 by Mr. Robert Dickinson.[52]

In 1066 Alnod held 3 hides and 24 a. that became the manor of *SOMERFORD BOWLES* or *SOMERFORD EWYAS*. Alfred of Marlborough held the estate in 1086[53] and the overlordship passed like that of Teffont Evias manor with the honor of Ewyas to Robert Tregoze (d. 1265), who held it in 1242–3,[54] and to his son John Tregoze (d. 1300). John's grandson, John la Warre[55] (d. 1347), from 1307 Lord la Warre, was allotted 1 knight's fee in Great Somerford in 1306. The overlordship descended with the title to Roger, Lord la Warre (d. 1370), and John, Lord la Warre (d. 1398), and was last mentioned in 1370.[56] The manor was still considered part of the honor of Ewyas c. 1500.[57]

Siward held the estate of Alfred in 1086,[58] and Jordan Waters (*de aqua*) in 1275.[59] Between 1293 and 1300 it passed from Jordan and his wife Maud to John of Seagry.[60] John or a namesake held the manor in 1306,[61] and in 1321 John of Seagry and his wife Joan settled it on themselves and on John's son Simon.[62] The manor descended, presumably like a manor in Seagry,[63] to Emme Drew, who held it in 1384 and 1412, and Thomas Drew, who held it in 1451.[64] Like that manor it passed to John Mompesson (d. 1500), John Mompesson (d. 1511),[65] Edmund Mompesson (d. 1553),[66] and Anne Wayte. On Anne's death before 1571 it passed to her daughter Eleanor (d. 1592), wife of Richard Browning (d. 1573). Eleanor was succeeded by her son Richard Browning[67] (d. 1612), and Richard by his son Anthony (d. 1663).[68] Anthony's son Edmund in 1670 sold a farm of c. 217 a. to William Grinfield and in 1693 sold other portions of the manor to William Alexander, Michael Wickes, and Thomas Evans.[69]

The residue of Somerford Bowles manor, including the manorial rights and apparently the land called *MANOR* farm, was owned in 1751 by

Richard Serle[70] and afterwards passed to his nephew Richard Goodenough who sold the farm, apparently c. 1772 to John Timbrell. In 1774 Timbrell sold it to William Randall (d. 1809), from whom it passed to his relict Mary, and then to his son William Randall and grandson William Randall.[71] In 1847 the third William Randall offered the farm, 80 a., for sale:[72] it may have been part of the estate of William Beak (d. 1873) and W. E. Beak 1858–88.[73] In 1910 and 1927 Manor farm, 120 a., belonged to the representatives of Benjamin Porter,[74] and 1945–56 to the executors of C. Porter.[75] It was afterwards sold in portions. Manor Farm is a timber-framed house built in the early 17th century. It was encased in stone and the north end was rebuilt in the 18th century; in the early 19th century it was extended southwards and eastwards and given a double-gabled south entrance front.

The farm bought by William Grinfield in 1670 passed to his son Edward (d. 1759). Edward's son Steddy Grinfield sold it in 1775 to John Pyke[76] (will dated 1778), who devised Bridge, later *BROOK*, farm to his son John.[77] The younger John was succeeded by his brothers William (d. 1794) and Thomas (d. 1815). Thomas devised the farm for his children, including Thomas (d. s.p. 1839), John (d. s.p. 1842), and Henry (d. s.p. 1888). Henry Pyke devised it in undivided shares to Joseph, Isaac, and William Hanks and Ann Belcher, the children of his sister Elizabeth Hanks.[78] In 1896 Brook farm, 243 a., was sold to Sir Henry Meux, Bt. (d. 1900). Meux's relict Valerie offered the farm, 143 a., for sale in 1906.[79] It was owned in 1910 and 1939 by Frederick Cole,[80] in 1945–6 by W. G. Greenwood,[81] 1947–85 by Peter Sturgis, in 1988 by Mr. T. R. Sturgis.[82] Brook Farm has a main north–south range with north and south wings to the east, all of stone rubble. The oldest part of the house is the south wing which survives from a 16th-century building: its roof has re-used smoke-blackened rafters. The main range and the north wing are 17th-century. The west elevation was encased in ashlar to make a symmetrical entrance front for Thomas and Winifred Pyke in 1803,[83] and, also in the 19th century, the space between the wings was built over.

BLANCHARDS, the portion of Somerford

[48] Above, Draycot Cerne, manor; Seagry, manors.
[49] W.R.O. 969/25, abstr. of title.
[50] Ibid. 969/24, abstr. of title, 1870.
[51] Ibid. 1043/6, pp. 107, 149, 151, 166.
[52] Inf. from Miss P. Hobbs, Old School Ho.
[53] V.C.H. Wilts. ii, p. 142.
[54] Ibid. xiii. 187–8; Bk. of Fees, ii. 712.
[55] Rot. Hund. (Rec. Com.), ii (1), 272; Cal. Inq. p.m. iii, pp. 454–5.
[56] Cal. Close, 1302–7, 362; Cal. Inq. p.m. xiii, pp. 41, 44; for the la Warre fam., Complete Peerage, iv. 141–9.
[57] Cal. Inq. p.m. Hen. VII, ii, pp. 317–18.
[58] V.C.H. Wilts. ii, p. 142.
[59] Rot. Hund. (Rec. Com.), ii (1), 272.
[60] Feet of F. 1272–1327 (W.R.S. i), p. 38; Cal. Inq. p.m. iii, pp. 454–5.
[61] Cal. Close, 1302–7, 362.
[62] Feet of F. 1272–1327 (W.R.S. i), p. 107.
[63] Above, Seagry, manors.
[64] Feet of F. 1377–1509 (W.R.S. xli), pp. 14, 129; Feud. Aids, vi. 538.
[65] Cal. Inq. p.m. Hen. VII, ii, pp. 317–18.
[66] P.R.O., C 142/26, no. 117.
[67] Ibid. C 3/9/21; C 142/234, no. 25; C 142/236, no. 30;

ibid. CP 25(2)/239/4 Eliz. I East. no. 151; V.C.H. Wilts. xi. 173.
[68] V.C.H. Wilts. xi. 173; P.R.O., C 142/332, no. 169.
[69] W.N. & Q. iii. 26–7; W.A.M. xxxi. 292; W.R.O. 542/12, deed, Browning to Grinfield, 1670.
[70] Hobbs, Somerford Magna, 25.
[71] W.R.O., EA/98; ibid. 542/22, abstr. of title, 1834, geneal. notes for Randall fam.
[72] Ibid. 374/128/65.
[73] W.A.M. xxxi. 299; below.
[74] W.R.O., Inland Revenue, val. reg. 14; ibid. G 7/515/3.
[75] Ibid. G 7/516/1–2.
[76] Ibid. 542/12, deeds, 1670, 1775; abstr. of title, 1785.
[77] Ibid. 542/12, copy will of John Pyke.
[78] Ibid. 106/1, p. 64; 542/23, copy wills of Wm. Pyke, 1794, Thomas Pyke, 1815, Hen. Pyke, 1888; W.A.M. xxxi. 298, 319–20.
[79] W.R.O. 106/1, pp. 39, 64, 66.
[80] Ibid. Inland Revenue, val. reg. 14; Kelly's Dir. Wilts. (1939).
[81] W.R.O., G 7/516/1.
[82] Ibid. G 7/516/2–3; inf. from Mr. T. Sturgis, Brook Farm.
[83] W.R.O. 542/23, copy will of Thomas Pyke, 1815. The date 1803 and initials P/TW occur on rainwater heads.

Bowles manor bought in 1693 by William Alexander passed with his other land in the parish at his death in 1724 to his granddaughter Elizabeth Alexander (d. 1790), wife of John Smith (d. 1765). It was added to Smith's part of Somerford Mautravers manor.[84]

In 1695 Michael Wickes conveyed his part of Somerford Bowles manor, MAYO'S farm, c. 34 a., for charitable purposes in Malmesbury, including St. John's almshouse and the free school.[85] The land was sold in 1920.[86]

GROVE farm, Startley, the part of Somerford Bowles manor bought in 1693 by Thomas Evans, was sold in 1720 by his relict Ann Evans to Edward Yate, who charged it with £15 yearly for a dissenting minister in Malmesbury. Yate devised the farm to Abraham Sperring, who sold it to Thomas Hobbes in 1735. Hobbes devised it to his nephew Giles Bennett, who sold it in 1758 to John Pyke[87] (will dated 1778). Pyke devised Grove farm to his son William (d. 1794)[88] and it descended like Brook farm. It was held c. 1900 by Joseph Hanks,[89] whose representatives sold the 92-a. farm in 1910 to Wiltshire county council,[90] the owner in 1988.[91]

In 1066 Scirold held an estate of 3½ yardlands in Great Somerford. Edward of Salisbury held it in 1086, when a house in Malmesbury was held with it.[92] The overlordship of the manor of SOMERFORD descended in the direct male line to Walter of Salisbury (d. 1147), Patrick, earl of Salisbury (d. 1168), and William, earl of Salisbury (d. 1196), and afterwards passed to William's daughter Ela (d. 1261), wife of William Longespée, earl of Salisbury (d. 1226). Although the overlordship was last mentioned in 1242–3,[93] the manor was still considered part of the honor of Trowbridge 1653–64.[94]

Teodric held the estate of Edward in 1086.[95] It was held of the countess of Salisbury in 1242–3 by Geoffrey de Sifrewast,[96] possibly a kinsman of the Herriard family.[97]

The manor was held by Kington St. Michael priory in 1242–3, of Geoffrey de Sifrewast, and at the Dissolution.[98] In 1538 the Crown granted it to Sir Richard Long[99] (d. 1546),[1] who in 1544 conveyed it to his brother Robert (d. 1564). Robert was succeeded by his brother William,[2] who sold the manor to John Yew in 1570.[3] Yew sold it in 1577 to Sir John Thynne[4] (d. 1580), and it descended in the direct male line to Sir John Thynne[5] (d. 1604), Sir Thomas Thynne[6] (d. 1639), and

Sir James Thynne[7] (d. s.p. 1670). Sir James was succeeded in turn by his nephews Thomas Thynne (d. 1682) and Thomas Thynne, Viscount Weymouth (d. 1714). From Lord Weymouth the manor passed to his grandnephew Thomas, Viscount Weymouth (d. 1751), and in the direct male line to Thomas, Viscount Weymouth (cr. marquess of Bath 1789, d. 1796), and Thomas, marquess of Bath (d. 1837), who in 1810 sold the estate, three houses and 123 a., to John Parsloe (d. 1849).[8]

In 1853 Parsloe's trustees offered for sale the manor and other land owned by Parsloe in the parish, a total of 223 a.[9] William Beak (d. 1873)[10] was the owner in 1856.[11] His son W. E. Beak sold the estate, including Manor House and its 18-a. park, in portions in 1888.[12]

The Manor House was built of stone rubble in the mid 17th century. A long service range was built on the east side in the later 18th century. In the early 19th century, apparently for John Parsloe,[13] a tall block containing an entrance hall and staircase was built on the south side of the 17th-century block: it was extended eastwards in the later 19th. The 17th-century block was heightened and refronted c. 1900 to match the early 19th-century extension, and in the early 20th century a long north–south service range was built from the south side of the 18th-century range. Fittings of the 18th century were introduced into the house in the mid 20th century. The late 19th-century part of the house was demolished and the inside of the house rearranged and divided into two c. 1977. Stables were built north of the house in the earlier 19th century. To create the park south of the house in the later 19th century West Street was diverted to run between the house and stables,[14] a lodge was built on the Sutton Benger road c. 1900, and an avenue was planted across the park between it and the house.

In 1086 Alwin the priest, Alwi, and Saieva each held 2½ yardlands, and Edward held ½ hide.[15] Those estates were afterwards acquired by Edward of Salisbury and assigned to his daughter Maud, wife of Humphrey de Bohun.[16] The manor of GREAT SOMERFORD passed like Wilsford manor in Swanborough hundred to Maud's son Humphrey de Bohun (fl. 1131 × 1146), grandson Humphrey de Bohun (d. 1181), and great-grandson Henry de Bohun (cr. earl of Hereford 1200, d. 1220).[17] It afterwards descended with the earldom[18] and

[84] Hobbs, Somerford Magna, 24–5; above; below.
[85] Endowed Char. Wilts. (N. Div.), 672–4, 684; above, Malmesbury, educ., charities.
[86] Wilts. Cuttings, xiv. 257.
[87] W.A.M. xxxi. 297–8.
[88] W.R.O. 542/12, copy will of John Pyke; 542/23, copy will of Wm. Pyke.
[89] W.A.M. xxxi. 298.
[90] W.R.O., Inland Revenue, val. reg. 14.
[91] Inf. from Director of Property Services, Co. Hall, Trowbridge.
[92] V.C.H. Wilts. ii, p. 137.
[93] Complete Peerage, i. 373–82; Bk. of Fees, ii. 722.
[94] Longleat Mun., Thynne papers, box 43, f. 14; box 47, f. 13.
[95] V.C.H. Wilts. ii, p. 137.
[96] Bk. of Fees, ii. 722.
[97] V.C.H. Hants. iii. 367–8.
[98] Bk. of Fees, ii. 722; Valor Eccl. (Rec. Com.), ii. 113.
[99] L. & P. Hen. VIII, xiii (1), p. 488.
[1] Hist. Parl., Commons, 1509–58, ii. 545–6.

[2] Wilts. Pedigrees (Harl. Soc. cv/cvi), 117–18; Longleat Mun. 1975B; P.R.O., C 142/140, no. 200.
[3] Longleat Mun. 1976.   [4] Ibid. 8893.
[5] P.R.O., C 142/195, no. 118.
[6] Ibid. C 142/290, no. 110.
[7] Ibid. C 142/765, no. 47; Hist. Parl., Commons, 1558–1603, iii. 508.
[8] Burke, Peerage (1959), 168–9; W.A.M. xxxi. 294; W.R.O. 777/9.
[9] W.A.M. xxxi. 298–9; W.R.O. 137/125/52.
[10] Hobbs, Somerford Magna, 54.
[11] W.R.O., A 1/345/369.
[12] W.A.M. xxxi. 299.
[13] A tablet inscribed P/JA 1803 was found and built into the E. wall c. 1977.
[14] W.R.O. 137/125/52; O.S. Map 6", Wilts. XIII (1888 edn.); inf. from Mrs. Alison Davies, Manor Ho.
[15] V.C.H. Wilts. ii, p. 161.
[16] Ibid. p. 109; Complete Peerage, xi. 374.
[17] For the Bohun fam., Complete Peerage, vi. 457–77.
[18] Bk. of Fees, ii. 722; Rot. Hund. (Rec. Com.), ii (1), 272.

Humphrey de Bohun (d. 1373) was overlord of ½ and 1/10 knight's fee in Great Somerford. His daughter Mary,[19] wife of Henry of Lancaster, earl of Derby (Henry IV), was assigned ½ knight's fee in 1384.[20] No later mention of the overlordship has been found.

In 1242–3 Reynold of Somerford, probably Reynold son of William, held 1 knight's fee in Great Somerford of Humphrey, earl of Hereford.[21] Richard of Somerford's heirs held ½ knight's fee in 1275.[22] Great Somerford manor was held in 1373 by Thomas Drew,[23] in 1401–2 by Emme Drew,[24] and in 1428 by Thomas Drew.[25] It passed like a manor in Seagry to Isabel Drew, wife of John Mompesson (d. 1500). It was held for life by Agnes Trye (d. 1499), relict of John's and Isabel's son Drew Mompesson, and after her death like Somerford Bowles manor by her son John Mompesson (d. 1511).[26] The manor was afterwards held in moieties by Christopher Mompesson and Thomas Mompesson, brothers of John Mompesson (d. 1511). Christopher's moiety apparently passed to Thomas,[27] who held the entire manor at his death in 1560. The manor passed to his son Thomas[28] (d. 1582) and grandson Thomas Mompesson (d. 1612).[29]

In 1610 Thomas Mompesson sold land including *WEST STREET* farm to Nicholas Barrett (d. 1610), who devised it to his father Hugh in trust for his brother-in-law William Bayliffe. In 1617 Hugh Barrett and Bayliffe sold the farm to Hugh's son Richard, who in 1621 sold it to Edward, son of Nicholas Barrett. Edward sold it in 1627 to John Wells. The farm was afterwards owned by Henry Grayle, who in 1654 charged it with £10 yearly for apprenticing poor children of Malmesbury. In 1687 Grayle's grandson and heir Thomas Davys sold the farm to William Alexander[30] (d. 1724), and it descended to William's granddaughter Elizabeth Alexander (d. 1790), wife of John Smith (d. 1765).[31] West Street farm descended in the Smith and Birtill families to the representatives of Mary Anne, relict of Henry Birtill, who sold the 154-a. farm c. 1910 to Rowland Woolford[32] (d. 1935).[33] The farm was owned in 1965–6 by C. T. Ll. Palmer (d. 1978),[34] and in 1988 by Mrs. C. T. Ll. Palmer.[35]

West Street Farm was built of stone rubble as a long east–west range in the 17th century. In the 18th century a new block was built at the north-east corner. In the 18th century or early 19th the west end was heightened and the west end of the south front was encased in ashlar and decorated with bands of 12th-century chevron ornament, some

medieval roundels, and a shield of arms, possibly of the Mompesson family. Further alterations were made and a north wing was built at the west end in the later 19th century. The house was extensively restored c. 1988.

In 1610 Thomas Mompesson owned a small estate called *CULVERHOUSE* place[36] which was owned by Robert Jason in 1634[37] and, with an additional 20 a., by Sir Robert Jason in 1673. It descended with Somerford Mautravers manor to Sir Richard Hawkins's trustees,[38] who sold it to John Pyke c. 1699. From Pyke it descended to his son Henry (will dated 1764), who devised it to his son John (will proved 1778). That John Pyke bought *MILLS* farm, 20 a., formerly part of Somerford Mautravers manor, from Mary Leet in 1767.[39] Culverhouse place and Mills farm, together called Home farm c. 1815, descended in the Pyke family with Brook farm,[40] were held c. 1900 and in 1910 by Ann Belcher,[41] and, as Mills farm, 60 a., by Dee Bros. in 1927.[42]

Mills Farm was built of stone in the 17th century as a north–south range of one storey and attics. It was heightened to two storeys and attics in the later 18th century and a short wing was built at the centre of the east elevation. The wing was extended north in the early 19th century, perhaps for the school kept in the house,[43] and again c. 1985. The interior of the house was being altered and restored in 1989.

Between 1190 and 1290 Bradenstoke priory acquired by gift and purchase a total of c. 17 a.[44] The land passed to the Crown at the Dissolution.[45]

In 1920 Charles and Ernest Porter bought the glebe, Downfield farm.[46] The owner was C. E. Porter in 1945–6,[47] A. Ll. Palmer 1955–67,[48] and Julian Sturgis in 1988.[49] Broadfield farm was formed from several small portions of land in the 1960s by E. F. Porter, the owner in 1988.[50]

ECONOMIC HISTORY. Great Somerford was unusual for Wiltshire because it had seven estates in 1086. The estates had 4 hides in demesne on which were 2 ploughteams and 2 *servi*, and there were 3 *villani*, 12 bordars, 32 coscets, and 2 cottars, with a total of 5 ploughteams. Two of the estates, Humphrey Lisle's and Siward's, were assessed equally and each had 2 hides in demesne with 1 team: on the remaining 1 hide and 24 a. of each Humphrey had 7 bordars and 16 coscets with 2 teams, and Siward had 3 *villani*, 2 bordars, and 8 coscets with 2 teams. Humphrey's estate included pasture 3 furlongs by 1 furlong, Siward's included

---

[19] *Cal. Inq. p.m.* xiii, pp. 130, 139.
[20] *Cal. Close,* 1381–5, 512–15.
[21] *Bk. of Fees,* ii. 711, 722.
[22] *Rot. Hund.* (Rec. Com.), ii (1), 272.
[23] *Cal. Inq. p.m.* xiii, p. 139.
[24] *Feud. Aids,* vi. 632.
[25] Ibid. v. 236.
[26] *Wilts. Pedigrees* (Harl. Soc. cv/cvi), 132; *Cal. Inq. p.m. Hen. VII,* ii, p. 197; above, Seagry, manors.
[27] P.R.O., C 3/129/49.
[28] Ibid. C 142/131, no. 198.
[29] *V.C.H. Wilts.* xiii. 218.
[30] *W.N. & Q.* iii. 29–30, 32–4; *Endowed Char. Wilts.* (N. Div.), 678, 689; above, Malmesbury, charities.
[31] *W.N. & Q.* iii. 63–5, 68–9; *W.A.M.* xxxi. 320; above.
[32] W.R.O., Inland Revenue, val. reg. 14; mon. in church.
[33] Mon. in churchyd.
[34] Hobbs, *Somerford Magna,* 119, 170; W.R.O., G 7/516/3.

[35] Inf. from Miss Hobbs.
[36] *W.N. & Q.* iii. 29–30.
[37] P.R.O., C 142/555, no. 96.
[38] W.R.O. 542/14, deed, 1673.
[39] Ibid. 542/23, copy will of Hen. Pyke; *W.A.M.* xxxi. 296–7.
[40] Above; W.R.O. 542/23, copy will of Thomas Pyke, 1815.
[41] *W.A.M.* xxxi. 297; W.R.O., Inland Revenue, val. reg. 14.
[42] W.R.O., G 7/515/3.
[43] Below, educ.
[44] *Bradenstoke Cart.* (W.R.S. xxxv), pp. 71–3.
[45] P.R.O., SC 6/Hen. VIII/3985, rot. 54d.
[46] Ch. Com. file 86979; below, church.
[47] W.R.O., G 7/516/1.
[48] Ibid. G 7/516/2–3.
[49] Inf. from Mr. T. Sturgis, Brook Farm.
[50] Inf. from Mr. E. F. Porter.

woodland 2 furlongs by 1 furlong. Edward's estate of ½ hide could support ½ ploughteam but, because he had no tenant, may have been uncultivated. The seven estates had a total of 33 a. of meadow and, apart from Humphrey's, a total of 19 a. of pasture.[51]

Apart from small pastures in the village it is likely that in the Middle Ages all Great Somerford's land was in open fields and common meadows and pastures. The arable was in the centre of the parish, east, west, and south of the village. East, West, and South fields were so called in the later 13th century when the road to Sutton Benger may have divided East and West.[52] By the mid 16th century East field had been divided into Broad and Down fields.[53] By 1809 c. 700 a., nearly half, of the parish had been inclosed: west and south-west of the village arable had apparently been inclosed into fields averaging c. 7 a., north-west of the village many of the inclosures, south of the Rodbourne stream and averaging 2–3 a., were much smaller and were presumably of meadow land.[54] The main period of inclosure seems likely to have been the earlier 17th century[55] and the farmsteads in West Street and Heath Farm, Grove Farm, and Goose Green Farm at Startley may have been built then on newly inclosed land.[56] North of the Rodbourne stream and beside the Avon east and south-east of the village meadow land remained in common, and there were common pastures west of Startley called Startley marsh, c. 120 a., and east of Great Somerford village. All the remaining open field and common meadows and pastures were inclosed in 1809 by Act.[57]

Somerford Mautravers and Great Somerford manors are known to have consisted of demesne and copyhold. In 1622 Great Somerford manor included demesne of 94 a. and copyholds of 21 a. and 16 a., all presumably with extensive rights to feed animals in common: the copyholds had become leaseholds by 1748.[58] At inclosure in 1809 the rector was allotted land to replace his tithes. South of Dauntsey Road the rector thereafter had c. 215 a., most of which were in the farm called Downfield for which new buildings were erected c. 1824. He was also allotted 99 a. of Startley marsh which became Marsh farm. Other allotments included 269 a. to William Smith for Somerford Mautravers manor and 207 a. to Thomas Pyke, but most were of fewer than 100 a. each: they seem to have been added to existing farms rather than used for new ones, and most of the parish continued to be worked from farmsteads in Great Somerford village.[59]

In 1867 only a third of the parish was ploughed:

grain, chiefly wheat, was grown on two thirds of the arable, and root and fodder crops on the remainder. Of the two thirds of the parish under pasture, clover and grasses in rotation were grown on only a small acreage. There were 329 cows, 533 sheep, and 346 pigs on farms based in the parish. From 1876 to 1956 most of the parish was grassland. In that time an average of c. 270 a. was arable, and dairy farming increased at the expense of both sheep farming and pig keeping. After 1966 more land was ploughed. In 1985 c. 700 a. were arable, and wheat and barley were the chief crops. There were only 210 cows.[60]

Apart from Downfield, 186 a., West Street, 154 a., Brook, 143 a., and Manor, 120 a., the farms in the parish were of less than 100 a. in 1910, and some land was worked from outside the parish. All the farms based at Startley were small.[61] In 1927 Wiltshire county council owned 142 a. in four small farms based there, and a co-operative farming society, begun in Great Somerford c. 1911, owned 70 a. there. Goose Green farm, first named c. 1907, was then worked with Downfield farm, a total of 286 a.[62] In 1988 farms based at Startley were Goose Green, 60 a., Grove, 142 a., Heath, 65 a., and Startley, 32 a., and in and around Great Somerford village Broadfield, 140 a., Downfield, 215 a., Brook, 300 a., and West Street, 500 a. Mixed farming was practised on all except Startley, an arable farm, Goose Green, a pasture farm, and Grove, a dairy farm.[63] Broadfield farm, created in the 1960s, included a chicken farm, a market garden, and a commercial fishery, and in 1988 a 5-a. lake for trout fishing.[64] Also in the 1960s a chicken battery farm was established at Startley to supply the Sutton Benger factory of Buxted Chicken Ltd.[65] The only woodland in the parish was the extension of Seagry wood in the south-west corner: that woodland, 34 a., was presumably planted soon after the land became part of the Draycot Cerne estate in 1865.[66]

John Yew (d. 1588), who bought Somerford Mautravers manor in 1561 and lived at Great Somerford, and his son John were Bradford clothiers.[67] In 1831 most men living in Great Somerford were farm labourers, and some of the 21 described as tradesmen may have worked elsewhere.[68] Members of the Parsloe family were brewers at the Old Maltings by 1848 and until 1865 or later.[69] A building firm begun by George Martin and specializing in making ornamental pinewood brickmoulds for use at Rodbourne brickworks was based at Startley from the late 19th century: in 1988 it was a general building firm.[70] Bowprine Ltd., a firm of building contractors, was based at the Manor House in 1988.

[51] V.C.H. Wilts. ii, pp. 137, 142, 144, 161.
[52] Bradenstoke Cart. (W.R.S. xxxv), p. 72.
[53] P.R.O., STAC 3/9/135; W.R.O., D 1/24/184/1.
[54] W.R.O., EA/98.
[55] Ibid. D 1/24/184/1–3; Longleat Mun. 10652, p. 58.
[56] Above, introduction.
[57] Longleat Mun. 8892; 10652, pp. 52–3; W.R.O., EA/98; ibid. 490/1131.
[58] Longleat Mun. 8885, letter from Thomas Townsend, 1748; 8892; 10652, pp. 50–3, 56, 58.
[59] W.R.O., EA/98.
[60] P.R.O., MAF 68/151, sheet 3; MAF 68/493, sheet 5; MAF 68/1063, sheet 4; MAF 68/1633, sheet 6; MAF 68/2203, sheet 14; MAF 68/2773, sheet 10; MAF 68/3319, sheet 10; MAF 68/3814, no. 133; MAF 68/4182, no. 133; MAF 68/4552,

no. 133; MAF 68/5004, no. 133; MAF 68/5505, no. 133; MAF 68/5980, no. 133.
[61] W.R.O., Inland Revenue, val. reg. 14.
[62] Ibid. G 7/515/3; Hobbs, Somerford Magna, 102; Kelly's Dir. Wilts. (1907).
[63] Inf. from Miss Hobbs; Mr. Sturgis.
[64] Hobbs, Somerford Magna, 106, 163.
[65] Inf. from Personnel Manager, Buxted Chicken Ltd., Sutton Benger.
[66] W.R.O. 1043/6, pp. 107, 111–12, 120; above, manors.
[67] Above, manors; V.C.H. Wilts. vii. 43; Taxation Lists (W.R.S. x), 49.
[68] Census, 1831.
[69] Kelly's Dir. Wilts. (1848 and later edns.).
[70] Hobbs, Somerford Magna, 99–101.

In 1086 there was a mill on Alfred of Marlborough's estate. Each of five other estates then included a share in a mill but in what mill or mills is obscure.[71] No mill site in the parish is known.

LOCAL GOVERNMENT.

Records of courts, usually called views of frankpledge with courts of the manor, and possibly held twice a year, survive for 1513 and the period 1570–1652 for Kington priory's and the Thynnes' Somerford manor. Business included the election of a tithingman, the repair of tenements, the impounding of straying animals, and the overstocking of the common pastures. In 1652 the court required a copyholder, as a condition of admission, to plant fruit trees and oaks, ashes, or elms yearly until his holding was restocked, and to kennel for the lord a hound or a spaniel. Copyholders from Chipping, Little, or Old Sodbury (Glos.) and from Sevington in Leigh Delamere owed suit at the court in the earlier 17th century. Courts were held until 1748 or later.[72]

The amount spent on poor relief by Great Somerford was large for a parish of its size. In 1802–3 £302 was spent on continuous outdoor relief for a third of the inhabitants and on occasional relief for another 21.[73] In the years 1812–15 an average of £397 was spent on continuous relief for an average of 43 adults and on occasional relief for 18,[74] and later the amount spent varied between £259 in 1816 and £455 in 1830.[75] Other attempts to help the poor included the provision of allotment gardens and a poorhouse,[76] and subsidies to local farmers who employed paupers in 1822. The vestry assisted paupers to emigrate to Canada in 1831[77] and to North America in 1849.[78] The parish was included in Malmesbury poor-law union in 1835.[79] It became part of North Wiltshire district in 1974.[80]

CHURCH.

A church stood in Great Somerford in the late 12th century.[81] The benefice was a rectory, and in 1967 was united with the benefices of Little Somerford and Seagry. The benefice of Corston with Rodbourne was added to the united benefice in 1986.[82]

Between 1194 and 1198 Richard of Herriard, apparently lord of Somerford Mautravers manor, granted the advowson to Kington St. Michael priory.[83] The advowson was disputed in 1323–4

by the prioress and John Mautravers (d. 1341), and in 1334 it was adjudged that it belonged to Mautravers.[84] The lords of Somerford Mautravers manor thereafter presented rectors except in 1405 and 1421 when the king presented during minority[85] and in 1637 when the king presented because Sir Robert Jason was in the Fleet prison. Jason's right to present was unsuccessfully challenged by Edmund Browning c. 1676.[86] In 1699 the trustees of Sir Richard Hawkins sold the advowson to the rector, Edmund Wayte. In 1702 Wayte sold it to William Lake, whom the mortgagee presented as rector in 1702. Lake sold the advowson in 1704 to Robert Reeks, whose son Isaac was presented that year by the mortgagee. Later in 1704 Robert Reeks sold it to Richard Hutchins, who in 1708 gave it to Exeter College, Oxford, to provide a living for a fellow.[87] In 1967 the college was assigned the second and fourth of four turns of presentation, and in 1986 joint presentation at the first, third, and fifth of five turns.[88]

In 1291 the church was valued at £6 13s. 4d.[89] The rector took all the tithes and in 1341 had $\frac{1}{2}$ yardland and 2 a. of meadow.[90] The rectory was worth £13 5s. 8d. in 1535,[91] £100 in 1650.[92] The glebe was c. 55 a. in the 17th century.[93] At inclosure in 1809 the rector was allotted 302 a. to replace the tithes, and 22 a. to replace the open arable and pasture rights of the glebe. In the late 19th century he owned 322 a. in the parish.[94] The average income of £347 in the years 1829–31 made the benefice one of the richer in Malmesbury deanery.[95] All the land except 6 a. was sold in 1920.[96]

The rector had a house in 1341.[97] A new house, of stone with two storeys and a cellar, was built in the early 17th century, and in 1671 had newly built attics.[98] It was enlarged in stone to the southwest in the early 19th century and a service wing and yard were built on the west in 1863–4.[99] A new rectory house was built in 1974 and the old one was sold.[1]

In 1494 the church contained lights in honour of St. Catherine, St. Margaret, and St. Nicholas.[2] What was presumably a fourth light was endowed with a cottage and 2¼ a., later called St. Mary's lands. In 1575 St. Mary's lands were bought from the Crown through agents for the parish. The income, 6s. 8d. yearly in 1721 and 1828, was used for church repairs. After 1828 only part of the income was so used.[3]

John Cholsey, rector from 1384 to c. 1400, was

[71] V.C.H. Wilts. ii, pp. 58, 137, 142, 144, 161.
[72] W.A.M. xxxi. 323; Longleat Mun. 8885, 8887–8, 10,005; ibid. Thynne papers, box 54, bk. 4, ff. 133–4; box 55, bk. 5, ff. 70, 192; bk. 6, f. 16v.; bk. 7, f. 32; box 56, bk. 9, f. 15v.; bk. 12, ff. 34–5.
[73] Poor Law Abstract, 1804, 566–7; V.C.H. Wilts. iv. 357.
[74] Poor Law Abstract, 1818, 498–9.
[75] Poor Rate Returns, 1816–21, 189; 1822–4, 228; 1825–9, 219; 1830–4, 213.
[76] Below, charities.   [77] Hobbs, Somerford Magna, 40–1.
[78] W.A.M. xlvii. 151.
[79] Poor Law Com. 2nd Rep. App. D, 559.
[80] O.S. Map 1/100,000, admin. areas, Wilts. (1974 edn.).
[81] Dugdale, Mon. iv. 399.
[82] Inf. from Ch. Com.
[83] Dugdale, Mon. iv. 399; above, manors.
[84] Reg. Martival (Cant. & York Soc.), i. 292–3, 307; W.A.M. xlvii. 330–4.
[85] Phillipps, Wilts. Inst. (index in W.A.M. xxviii. 230); Cal. Pat. 1416–22, 401.

[86] Phillipps, Wilts. Inst. ii. 18, 34; W.N. & Q. vii. 294, 364.
[87] W.A.M. xxxi. 310; Exeter Coll., Oxf., Mun., M.V.6, A, Great Somerford deeds; M.V.6, C, list of inst.
[88] Inf. from Ch. Com.
[89] Tax. Eccl. (Rec. Com.), 189.
[90] Inq. Non. (Rec. Com.), 165.
[91] Valor Eccl. (Rec. Com.), ii. 140.
[92] W.A.M. xli. 6.
[93] W.R.O., D 1/24/184/1–3.
[94] Ibid. EA/98; Glebe Lands Return, H.C. 307, p. 56 (1887), lxiv, where the acreage is wrongly given as 222 a.
[95] Rep. Com. Eccl. Revenues, 846–7.
[96] Ch. Com. files, NB 5/86c/1; 86979.
[97] Inq. Non. (Rec. Com.), 165.
[98] W.R.O., D 1/24/184/2.
[99] Bristol R.O., EP/A/25/1.
[1] Inf. from Estates Bursar, Exeter Coll., Oxf.
[2] W.A.M. xxxi. 322.
[3] Cal. Pat. 1572–5, p. 409; Endowed Char. Wilts. (N. Div.), 897; Char. Com. file.

also a canon of Wells.[4] In 1413 a parishioner, John Fleming, was absolved from a sentence of excommunication imposed for his support of heretics.[5] Thomas Arnold, rector 1537–54, was deprived for his protestant views.[6] Several later rectors were pluralists and, from the 17th century to the 19th, curates either assisted them or served the cure.[7] William Lake, rector 1702–4, was also vicar of Chippenham, rector of Hardenhuish, and a canon of Salisbury.[8] Thomas Seale, rector 1728–71, was also rector of St. Clement's, Jersey, 1734–46.[9] From 1728 to 1951 the rectors were either fellows or graduates of Exeter College.[10] In 1783 William Tonkin, rector 1771–98 and a physician, held two services on Sundays, occasional weekday services, and administered the sacrament to c. 30 communicants on Christmas day, Easter day, Whit Sunday, and the Sunday after Michaelmas.[11] Stephen Demainbray, rector 1799–1854, was a chaplain to George III, rector of Long Wittenham (Berks.) from 1794, and astronomer at the royal observatory, Kew, 1782–1840;[12] he was an early proponent of village allotments. At Great Somerford he was usually assisted by curates.[13] In 1832 the curate lived in the rectory house and held two services on Sundays.[14] Congregations averaging 216 attended the three services on Census Sunday in 1851.[15] F. H. Manley, rector 1887–1945 and a canon of Bristol, wrote and published articles on the history of Great Somerford and other Wiltshire parishes.[16] The rectory was held in plurality with that of Little Somerford 1952–67,[17] and from 1967 the incumbent of the united benefice lived at Great Somerford.[18]

The church of *ST. PETER AND ST. PAUL*, so called in 1494[19] and 1763[20] but St. Peter's in 1421,[21] is of ashlar and rubble and consists of a chancel with north vestry, a nave with north aisle and south porch, and a west tower. The late 12th-century church was completely rebuilt between the later 14th and earlier 16th century,[22] although the nave retains what may be a 12th-century plan. The aisle, four-bayed arcade, and chancel arch were built in the later 14th century or earlier 15th. In the later 15th century the tower was built and the chancel rebuilt, and in the earlier 16th the south nave wall was rebuilt and given new windows, the porch was built, a turret with a square bottom stage and a semi-octagonal upper stage was built

to enclose a rood stair at the nave's outer south-east corner, and a stair turret of similar design was built in the south angle between the nave and tower. A north gallery was erected in 1826.[23] The church was restored in 1865 under the direction of J. H. Hakewill,[24] and the porch c. 1903 under that of Harold Brakspear.[25] The chancel ceiling was painted in 1901 to F. C. Eden's designs.[26] The royal arms of 1814 hang in the church.[27]

In 1553 the royal commissioners took 2 oz. of plate and left a chalice of 7 oz. In 1988 the parish had a chalice hallmarked for 1743 and a paten hallmarked for 1735.[28] In 1553 there were four bells, of which one, cast at Bristol in the 15th century, survives. The others were replaced by bells cast in 1634 by T. and W. Wiseman, 1663 by Roger Purdue, and 1731 by Abraham Rudhall. The bell of 1663 was recast in 1897 by Llewellins & James of Bristol. A treble, cast by Mears & Stainbank using a bell from Holy Trinity church, Bristol, was added in 1977 and became the second when another treble, cast by Taylor of Loughborough from a bell formerly in St. Barnabas's church, Bristol, was added to the peal in 1984.[29] The registers survive from 1707.[30]

NONCONFORMITY. Quakers, including members of the Sealy family, lived in Great Somerford 1656–1783,[31] and there were eight nonconformists in the parish in 1676.[32] Independents certified houses at Startley in 1797 and 1817 and at Great Somerford in 1827 and 1834.[33] A congregation of c. 30 Independents attended a chapel in Great Somerford in 1851,[34] but later record of it has not been found. A New Apostolic church was opened in 1953 but had been closed by 1971.[35]

A house in Great Somerford certified in 1829[36] was probably for Primitive Methodists. In 1882 Primitive Methodists bought for a chapel the village reading room,[37] and Methodists held services in it in 1988.

Primitive Methodists certified a building at Startley in 1843,[38] and in 1850–1 an average congregation of 90 attended services held on Sunday afternoons.[39] A chapel was built in 1854 and enlarged in 1860.[40] In the later 19th century half the families in Startley were nonconformists,[41] presumably Primitive Methodists. The chapel was

---

[4] Phillipps, *Wilts. Inst.* i. 69; *V.C.H. Wilts.* iii. 285.
[5] *Reg. Hallum* (Cant. & York Soc.), p. 123.
[6] Phillipps, *Wilts. Inst.* i. 206, 216.
[7] *W.A.M.* xxxi. 327; *Subscription Bk. 1620–40* (W.R.S. xxxii), pp. 65, 68; W.R.O., bishop's transcripts, bdles. 1–3; Bristol R.O., EP/V/4/128.
[8] *Alum. Oxon. 1500–1714*, iii. 870.   [9] Ibid. iv. 1329.
[10] Ibid. *1715–1886*, i. 24, 361; iii. 908; iv. 1426; *Crockford* (1955–6); Exeter Coll. Mun., D 6, Great Somerford coresp. file.
[11] *Alum. Oxon. 1715–1886*, iv. 1426; *Vis. Queries, 1783* (W.R.S. xxvii), pp. 195–6.
[12] *Alum. Oxon. 1715–1886*, i. 361; *D.N.B.*
[13] *Rep. Com. Eccl. Revenues*, 846–7; Bristol R.O., EP/V/4/128.
[14] Ch. Com. file, NB 5/86c/1.
[15] P.R.O., HO 129/252/1/11/11.
[16] *Alum. Oxon. 1715–1886*, iii. 908; Hobbs, *Somerford Magna*, 91.
[17] Exeter Coll. Mun., D 6, Great Somerford coresp. file.
[18] *Lond. Gaz.* 17 Nov. 1967, pp. 12581–2.
[19] *W.A.M.* xxxi. 322.   [20] J. Ecton, *Thesaurus* (1763), 403.
[21] *Cal. Pat. 1416–22*, 401.

[22] Cf. J. Buckler, watercolour in W.A.S. Libr., vol. vi. 18 (1809).   [23] W.R.O. 2076/1, p. 13.
[24] Pevsner, *Wilts.* (2nd edn.), 260.
[25] *W.A.M.* xxxiii. 335.   [26] Hobbs, *Somerford Magna*, 19.
[27] *W.A.M.* xlviii. 115.
[28] Nightingale, *Wilts. Plate*, 206; inf. from Miss Hobbs.
[29] Walters, *Wilts. Bells*, 200–1; *Ch. Guide*.
[30] W.R.O. 2051/2–5. Bishop's transcripts for several earlier periods are ibid. Marriages 1707–1812 are printed in *Wilts. Par. Reg. (Mar.)*, ed. W. P. W. Phillimore and J. Sadler, vi. 25–33; extracts are in *W.N. & Q.* vi. 409–12, 444–7.
[31] *W.N. & Q.* ii. 293; iii. 123; iv. 116–17; v. 403–5; vii. 8; *Vis. Queries, 1783* (W.R.S. xxvii), p. 195; W.R.O., D 1/54/1/1, no. 45; D 1/54/6/1, no. 1.
[32] *Compton Census*, ed. Whiteman, 129.
[33] *Meeting Ho. Certs.* (W.R.S. xl), pp. 47–8, 82, 114, 136.
[34] P.R.O., HO 129/252/2/11/14.
[35] G.R.O. Worship Reg. no. 63930; cancellations, no. 41779.   [36] *Meeting Ho. Certs.* (W.R.S. xl), pp. 121, 124.
[37] Hobbs, *Somerford Magna*, 60.
[38] *Meeting Ho. Certs.* (W.R.S. xl), p. 158.
[39] P.R.O., HO 129/252/2/11/13.   [40] Dates on bldg.
[41] Hobbs, *Somerford Magna*, 57, 59.

closed in 1985.[42]

EDUCATION. In 1808 a few children attended a school in the parish.[43] There were two schools attended by a total of c. 20 children in 1818. The rector then considered that widespread child employment and the scattered nature of settlement made it unlikely that a free day school would be well attended.[44] A cottage built in Hollow Street on St. Mary's land c. 1828 was used as a school.[45] A new schoolroom was built on the west in 1853 and extended in 1874:[46] 40–50 children were taught there in 1859,[47] and in 1871 on return day 49 children attended.[48] Between 1906 and 1938 attendance was highest, at 65, in 1911–14, lowest, at 39, in 1937–8.[49] The school was closed, and the Walter Powell school opened in Dauntsey Road, in 1982. The new school was attended by children from Great and Little Somerford,[50] and in 1988 there were 77 children on roll.[51]

A boarding school for c. 26 girls was opened in the parish in 1819.[52] It was kept in Mills Farm from 1841 or earlier to 1899 or later, by Ann Williams in 1855, by Jane Williams 1859–85, by the Misses Brown in 1890, and by Mrs. L. Cockey 1895–9.[53]

CHARITIES FOR THE POOR. In 1828 the cottage and 2½ a. called St. Mary's lands[54] were declared to be for general charitable purposes in the parish. That declaration was reiterated by a Scheme of 1983. A schoolhouse replaced the cottage c. 1828. Most of the land was sold c. 1954 and c. 1964. In 1985 investments produced £2,419, of which £1,000 was given to the school, £600 to parish youth organizations and clubs, £400 to the church, and £200 to the Methodist chapel.[55]

At inclosure in 1809, possibly at the instigation of the rector Stephen Demainbray, c. 2 a. at Seagry Heath and c. 6 a. south of Dauntsey Road, called the free gardens, were given as allotments for paupers. A poorhouse was built on part of the Dauntsey Road allotments after 1809. In 1835 it was converted to two cottages, the rent of which was paid to the overseers of the poor until 1867 and to Great Somerford school until 1894. From 1896 the cottages and allotments were administered by the parochial church council. There were 49 allotment holders in 1905.[56] The cottages were let for c. £40 1954–5[57] and sold in 1978. By a Scheme of 1981 the income was used for general charitable purposes and in 1986–7, from income of £3,238, payments of c. £300, c. £180, and £100 were made for, respectively, the upkeep of the free gardens, the upkeep of the churchyard, and old people's Christmas parcels.[58]

From 1967 inhabitants of Great Somerford were entitled to be admitted to an almshouse in Dauntsey.[59]

LITTLE SOMERFORD

LITTLE SOMERFORD,[60] in a bend of the Bristol Avon 4.5 km. south-east of Malmesbury,[61] was called Somerford Mauduit in the Middle Ages. The suffix was the surname of the lords of the manor.[62] The prefix Little, to distinguish the parish from Great Somerford, replaced the suffix from the 16th century.[63] In the early 1630s, after Braydon forest was inclosed, the men of Little Somerford were allotted Somerford common, 204 a. of the purlieus of the forest:[64] that land, c. 6 km. north-east of the village, became part of the parish. It was transferred to Brinkworth parish in 1884. Under an Act of 1882 a detached 5 a. to the north-west were transferred to Lea and Cleverton, and small areas were transferred to Lit-

tle Somerford from Great Somerford and from Lea and Cleverton. Thereafter Little Somerford contained 490 ha. (1,210 a.).[65]

About half the boundary of Little Somerford is marked by the Avon and its feeder Brinkworth brook and is presumably early. To the north-west the Avon divides Little Somerford from Malmesbury and to the south from Great Somerford. Between those two stretches the Avon divided Little Somerford from Rodbourne in Malmesbury in the late 11th century,[66] but land on the west bank was allotted to Little Somerford at an inclosure in 1281.[67] North of Great Somerford village the boundary follows not the present course of the Avon but possibly an old course.

[42] Inf. from Miss Hobbs.
[43] Lamb. Palace Libr., MS. 1732.
[44] Educ. of Poor Digest, 1037.
[45] Educ. Enq. Abstract, 1047; Hobbs, Somerford Magna, 82; above, church.
[46] P.R.O., ED 7/130, no. 136.
[47] Acct. of Wilts. Schs. 42.
[48] Returns relating to Elem. Educ. 420.
[49] Bd. of Educ., List 21, 1913 (H.M.S.O.), 550; 1914, 550; 1938, 423.
[50] Hobbs, Somerford Magna, 89–90.
[51] Inf. from Miss Hobbs.
[52] Educ. Enq. Abstract, 1047.
[53] Hobbs, Somerford Magna, 16, 43; Kelly's Dir. Wilts. (1848 and later edns.); P.R.O., HO 107/1181/32.
[54] Above, church.
[55] Endowed Char. Wilts. (N. Div.), 897–900; Char. Com. file.

[56] Endowed Char. Wilts. (N. Div.), 900–1; W.R.O., EA/98.
[57] W.R.O., Char. Com., Great Somerford.
[58] Hobbs, Somerford Magna, 163; Char. Com. file.
[59] Char. Com. file; above, Dauntsey, charities.
[60] This article was written in 1988.
[61] Maps used include O.S. Maps 1″, sheets 34 (1828 edn.), 157 (1968 edn.); 1/50,000, sheet 173 (1974 edn.); 1/25,000, ST 98 (1959 edn.); 6″, Wilts. XIII–XIV (1887–8 and later edns.).
[62] Cal. Pat. 1247–58, 283; P.R.O., CP 40/919, Carte rot. 1; below, manor.
[63] e.g. Valor Eccl. (Rec. Com.), ii. 119; P.R.O., CP 40/1305, Carte rott. 9–10.
[64] V.C.H. Wilts. iv. 406–7. For comment on the forest, above, Charlton, introduction, econ. hist.
[65] Census, 1891; P.R.O., IR 29/38/241; IR 30/38/241.
[66] Arch. Jnl. lxxvii. 88–90.   [67] Reg. Malm. ii. 219–20.

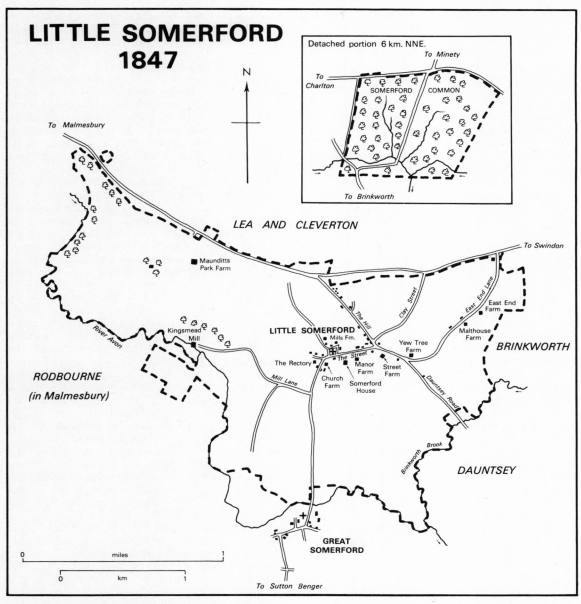

LITTLE SOMERFORD
1847

Detached portion 6 km. NNE.

To Minety

To Charlton

SOMERFORD   COMMON

To Brinkworth

LEA AND CLEVERTON

To Swindon

To Malmesbury

Maunditts
Park Farm

East End Lane
East End
Farm

The Hill
Clay Street

LITTLE SOMERFORD

Malthouse
Farm

Mills Fm.

Yew Tree
Farm

BRINKWORTH

Kingsmead
Mill

River Avon

The Rectory

The Street

Manor
Farm

Street
Farm

RODBOURNE
(in Malmesbury)

Mill Lane

Church
Farm

Somerford
House

Dauntsey Road

Brinkworth Brook

DAUNTSEY

miles

km

GREAT
SOMERFORD

To Sutton Benger

The parish slopes from *c*. 100 m. on its north boundary to *c*. 60 m. on its south. Apart from a small outcrop of Cornbrash in the west, Kellaways Clay, Oxford Clay, and Kellaways Sand outcrop over the whole parish, including Somerford common. Glacial deposits lie along the eastern part of the northern boundary, gravel and alluvium have been deposited by a small stream south of the village flowing eastwards to Brinkworth brook, and extensive deposits of alluvium flank the Avon and Brinkworth brook.[68] The parish seems always to have had more pasture than arable and is rich in meadow land.

The main Swindon–Malmesbury road along the northern boundary, the road leading south from it as the Hill and the Street through Great Somerford towards Chippenham, and the road from Little Somerford village to Dauntsey were turn-

piked in 1809 and disturnpiked in 1876.[69] A stone causeway for pedestrians was built on the west side of the road near Great Somerford village *c*. 1809. A lane with branches each side of the church ran in 1847 from the Street north to the Swindon–Malmesbury road:[70] it was a rough track in 1988. East End Lane may have been the main route north from Little Somerford village until the Hill was turnpiked, but afterwards declined in importance and, in the mid 20th century, the north end of it was closed.[71] In 1773 or earlier Mill Lane, leading west from the Great Somerford road, branched into lanes leading south and north-west:[72] when the north-west branch was severed by the railway line *c*. 1903, a new road was made north of the line.

The Malmesbury railway was built north-west and south-east across the parish close to the Avon

[68] Geol. Surv. Maps 1″, solid and drift, sheets 251 (1970 edn.), 252 (1974 edn.).
[69] *V.C.H. Wilts*. iv. 257, 263, 271; B.L. Maps, O.S.D. 169.

[70] P.R.O., IR 30/38/241.
[71] O.S. Maps 1″, sheet 157 (1958 edn.); 1/25,000, 31/98 (1949 edn.). [72] *Andrews and Dury, Map* (W.R.S. viii), pl. 14.

in 1877, with a station called Somerford west of the road near Great Somerford village. A goods depot was opened at the station in 1879, and in 1880 the line was vested in the G.W.R. In 1903 the G.W.R. line from Wootton Bassett to south Wales was constructed on an east–west course south of the village. It was carried by bridges over the Great Somerford road and the old line, and by a viaduct over the low ground near the Avon. Little Somerford station was opened south of the village. Somerford station was renamed Great Somerford in 1903 and in 1922 became an unstaffed halt. In 1933 a short stretch of new line was built to link the north-west part of the Malmesbury line and the main line near Kingsmead Mill, and the south-east part of the Malmesbury line and Great Somerford halt were closed. The line from Little Somerford to Malmesbury was closed to passengers in 1951. It and Little Somerford station were closed entirely in 1963.[73]

Part of a late Bronze-Age artifact and a hoard of Romano-British coins have been found in the parish.[74] Little Somerford had 77 poll-tax payers in 1377, a higher than average number for Malmesbury hundred.[75] In the 16th and early 17th century, when no lord of the manor lived there, its assessment for taxation was low.[76] The population rose from 255 in 1801 to 376 in 1831. A decrease to 337 by 1851 was attributed to inhabitants moving elsewhere for lack of housing in Little Somerford. Numbers had risen to 379 by 1881, declined to 232 by 1961, and risen to 351 by 1971 after new houses were built. The population was 347 in 1981.[77]

Little Somerford village consists of settlement along the several roads and lanes which converge in the centre of the parish, where the earliest settlement may have been along the east–west part of the Street. In 1773 there was settlement around the junction of the Street, the Hill, Clay Street,[78] so called c. 1513,[79] and Dauntsey Road, so called c. 1841,[80] and in East End Lane, so called in 1773. The junction of Dauntsey Road and East End Lane was called Collingbourne Green in 1773 and 1820.[81] Most of the larger buildings in the village are of stone. In 1988 few houses were earlier than the 20th century.

On the north side of the Street the church was standing in the 13th century, and the glebe house stood south-west of it in the 17th century or earlier. North-west of the church a small farmhouse was built of stone rubble in the 17th century. In the early 18th century it was incorporated as the east wing of a new house built of red brick with stone dressings: the house was called the Old Rectory after the rector lived there 1847–66.[82] East of the church Mills Farm was built in the early 17th cen-

tury. In the mid 19th century the west end was rebuilt to incorporate a mill.[83] On the south side of the Street, beyond wide verges, are three large farmhouses. The westernmost, Church Farm, was built in the late 16th or early 17th century and retains some carved and decorated beams. It was much altered in the 18th century. Somerford House was built for Richard and Margaret Estcourt in 1609.[84] It comprised an east–west range, on the south side of which at each end was a short wing. The west service wing was rebuilt in the 19th century. West of the house a large cattle yard and cattle sheds were built in the later 19th century. Manor Farm was built as a long east–west range in the 17th century and was altered internally in the 18th century and in the 19th when the ground floor was replanned. The village became a conservation area in 1975.[85] A station house was built of stone c. 1877 at Somerford station. In 1892 a cemetery was opened on the west side of the Great Somerford road,[86] and south of it eight council houses were built in 1931.[87]

A church house stood on the west side of the Hill until c. 1850, and a school later occupied the site. On the east side of the Hill a turnpike house was built c. 1809.[88] The King's Head north of the school had been opened by 1865 and was closed after c. 1956.[89] The Three Crowns, opened before 1895,[90] was north of the King's Head and was called the Little Somerford Arms in 1988. Houses on the east side of the Hill were pulled down between 1828 and 1847[91] and others were built further north on both sides of the road. On the south side of the Swindon–Malmesbury road, extending the line of settlement from the Hill, Hill House is a large house built between 1885 and 1898[92] and given a new Georgian west front in 1927.[93] West of it another large house, Coach House Farm, was adapted from stables built between 1869 and 1882.[94]

On the south side of Dauntsey Road, Street Farm was built of stone rubble with a roof of stone slates in the 17th and 18th centuries. Yew Tree Farm was built c. 1800 on the north side of the road at its junction with East End Lane; it is of red brick with a stone-slated mansard roof, and its south front has a doorway with fluted pilasters and an open pediment. Also in Dauntsey Road a pair of brick cottages was built beside the railway line c. 1903. A private estate of 29 houses, Vale Leaze, was built on the north side of Dauntsey Road, and more houses were built on the south side, in the 1960s.

Settlement in East End Lane in 1773 was around a small common.[95] Of the buildings on the east side in 1988, Malthouse Farm was built c. 1800 and north of it East End Farm was built of red

[73] V.C.H. Wilts. iv. 288–9; C. R. Clinker, Clinker's Reg. Closed Passenger Sta. 1830–1980, pp. 56, 76, 92, 163.
[74] V.C.H. Wilts. i (1), 83.   [75] Ibid. iv. 310.
[76] Taxation Lists (W.R.S. x), 29; P.R.O., E 179/197/153; E 179/198/261; E 179/199/356; E 179/199/399; E 179/259/20.
[77] V.C.H. Wilts. iv. 321, 357; Census, 1961; 1971; 1981.
[78] Andrews and Dury, Map (W.R.S. viii), pl. 14.
[79] P.R.O., SC 2/208/28, f. 34 and v.
[80] Ibid. HO 107/1181/33.
[81] Andrews and Dury, Map (W.R.S. viii), pl. 14; C. Greenwood, Map of Wilts. (1820).
[82] P.R.O., IR 29/38/241; IR 30/38/241; below, church.
[83] Below, econ. hist.

[84] W.R.O. 442/2, p. 306; the initials RE/ME and the date 1609 occur in the ho.
[85] Inf. from Co. Planning Officer, Co. Hall, Trowbridge.
[86] Below, local govt.   [87] Date on hos.
[88] W.N. & Q. vii. 272–5; P.R.O., IR 29/38/241; IR 30/38/241.
[89] Harrod's Dir. Wilts. (1865); W.R.O., G 7/516/2.
[90] Kelly's Dir. Wilts. (1895).
[91] O.S. Map 1", sheet 34 (1828 edn.); P.R.O., IR 30/38/241.
[92] Kelly's Dir. Wilts. (1898); O.S. Map 6", Wilts. XIII (1888 edn.).
[93] Date on ho.   [94] W.R.O. 212A/38/34/10.
[95] Andrews and Dury, Map (W.R.S. viii), pl. 14.

brick in the 18th century. On the west side the Cottage, a brick and thatch house of *c.* 1762, was replaced by a stone house *c.* 1980.[96] A farmstead which stood in 1773[97] and 1847[98] at the junction of East End Lane and the Swindon–Malmesbury road was demolished before 1885.[99]

Maunditts Park Farm, built in the 1950s on the site of a farmstead which stood in 1773, stands on high ground in the west.[1] South of it Kingsmead Mill stands beside the Avon. East of the mill Kingsmead House was built on the north side of Mill Lane in the early 20th century,[2] and Kingsmead Cottage was built north of it.

MANOR AND OTHER ESTATES. Between 934 and 939 King Athelstan granted to Malmesbury abbey 5 *mansae* at Somerford.[3] In 1066 Alward held the estate of the abbey by lease. A burgage tenement in Malmesbury was attached to it in 1086 and was still part of it in 1609.[4] The abbey's overlordship was last mentioned in 1369.[5]

In 1086 Gunfrid Mauduit held the manor of *LITTLE SOMERFORD* or *SOMERFORD MAUDUIT* of the abbey.[6] The manor may have passed with Nippred manor in Tisbury to Gunfrid's son Walkelin (fl. 1120 × 1130),[7] and *c.* 1141 Malmesbury abbey acknowledged that Walkelin's son Ancelin held it for ⅓ knight's fee.[8] Ancelin Mauduit, presumably another, held the manor in 1211–12.[9] It passed to Robert Mauduit (fl. 1212) and was held by his relict Beatrice Mauduit (fl. 1250) in 1242–3.[10] Sir John Mauduit (d. 1302), possibly the grandson of Robert (fl. 1212), was granted free warren in his Little Somerford demesne lands in 1254, and was succeeded by his nephew Sir John Mauduit[11] (d. 1347), who was granted free warren there in 1345. That Sir John was succeeded by his relict Agnes[12] (d. 1369), who married secondly Thomas de Bradeston, Lord Bradeston (d. 1360). Agnes's heir was her and Sir John Mauduit's grandson, Sir William Moleyns[13] (d. 1381), from whom the manor passed in the direct male line to Sir Richard (d. 1384) and Sir William[14] (d. 1425). William was succeeded by his relict Margery (d. 1439)[15] and granddaughter Eleanor Moleyns (d. 1476), who married Sir Robert Hungerford, Lord Hungerford and

Moleyns (attainted 1461, d. 1464), and secondly Sir Oliver Manningham (d. 1499).[16]

In 1460 the manor was conveyed to feoffees as security for money borrowed to pay Robert's ransom when he was a prisoner in Aquitaine,[17] but Eleanor and Sir Oliver held it in 1472,[18] and Sir Oliver apparently held it for life after Eleanor's death.[19] It reverted to Eleanor's granddaughter Mary Hungerford, *suo jure* Baroness Botreaux, Hungerford, and Moleyns (d. *c.* 1533), who married first Edward Hastings, Lord Hastings (d. 1506), and secondly Sir Richard Sacheverell (d. 1534). Mary's heir was her son George Hastings, Lord Hastings (cr. earl of Huntingdon 1529, d. 1544), from whom the manor passed to his son Francis, earl of Huntingdon (d. 1560). It was apparently held by Francis's relict Catherine (d. 1576),[20] and in 1572 she and their son Henry, earl of Huntingdon, sold it to Sir Christopher Hatton,[21] who sold it before 1581 to Sir Edward Hungerford (d. 1607). The manor passed like Corston manor in Malmesbury to Cecily, countess of Rutland, to Sir Anthony Hungerford, and to Sir Edward Hungerford,[22] who in 1682 sold it to Sir Stephen Fox.[23]

In 1689 Fox sold Little Somerford manor in two main parts. The manorial rights and most of the copyhold land were bought by John Hill, who in 1690 sold them to William White.[24] White was succeeded by his son William (d. 1722). Most of his estate descended to the younger William's daughter Susanna[25] (d. 1796 or 1797),[26] who married William Earle (d. 1774) of Eastcourt in Crudwell, and to her son Giles Earle.[27] In 1807 Earle sold a farm of 114 a. to Charles Wightwick (d. 1861), rector of Brinkworth from 1841, and one of 109 a. to Jonas Ady.[28] Ady sold his farm in 1818 to Henry Hulbert,[29] who in 1836 sold it to Wightwick.[30] Wightwick, who bought more land in 1817, in 1847 owned Church farm, East End farm, Yew Tree farm, and other land, a total of 241 a.[31] His estate passed to his nephew Henry Wightwick (d. 1884), rector of Codford St. Peter, part having first been held by his relict Mary Wightwick, who included his relict Sarah (d. 1907) and son H. K. Wightwick (d. 1907).[32] H. K. Wightwick's sisters, Lucy, Alice, Blanche, Louisa, and Maude

[96] Inf. from Mr. and Mrs. R. W. Gawthrop, East End Farm. A date tablet inscribed P/PA 1762 has been reset.
[97] *Andrews and Dury, Map* (W.R.S. viii), pl. 14.
[98] P.R.O., IR 30/38/241.
[99] O.S. Map 6", Wilts. XIII (1888 edn.).
[1] *Andrews and Dury, Map* (W.R.S. viii), pl. 14; inf. from Mrs. B. A. Marsh, Maunditts Park Farm.
[2] O.S. Map 6", Wilts. XIII. NE. (1900 edn.); W.R.O. 1343/2.   [3] Finberg, *Early Wessex Chart.* pp. 83–4.
[4] *V.C.H. Wilts.* ii. p. 125; W.R.O. 442/2, p. 315.
[5] *Wilts. Inq. p.m.* 1327–77 (Index Libr.), 353–4.
[6] *V.C.H. Wilts.* ii. p. 125.
[7] Ibid. xiii. 212.
[8] *Reg. Malm.* ii. 395.
[9] *Red Bk. Exch.* (Rolls Ser.), ii. 605.
[10] *Complete Peerage*, viii. 551; *Bk. of Fees*, ii. 733.
[11] *Complete Peerage*, viii. 551–2; *Wilts. Inq. p.m.* 1242–1326 (Index Libr.), 298–301; *Cal. Pat.* 1247–58, 283.
[12] *Wilts. Inq. p.m.* 1327–77 (Index Libr.), 175–6; *Cal. Chart. R.* 1341–1417, 43.
[13] *Wilts. Inq. p.m.* 1327–77 (Index Libr.), 262–3, 353–4; *Complete Peerage*, viii. 552–3.
[14] *Complete Peerage*, ix. 39–41; *Feet of F. 1377–1509* (W.R.S. xli), p. 66; *Feud. Aids*, vi. 530.
[15] *Complete Peerage*, ix. 41; *Cal. Close*, 1422–9, 242–3.

[16] *Complete Peerage*, vi. 618–21; *Cal. Close*, 1454–61, 451.
[17] *Feet of F. 1377–1509* (W.R.S. xli), p. 140; *Cal. Close*, 1454–61, 451.
[18] *Feet of F. 1377–1509* (W.R.S. xli), p. 152.
[19] P.R.O., CP 40/919, Carte rot. 1.
[20] *Complete Peerage*, vi. 618–24, 654–7; Phillipps, *Wilts. Inst.* i. 222; W.R.O. 442/2, p. 309.
[21] P.R.O., CP 40/1305, Carte rott. 9–10.
[22] Phillipps, *Wilts. Inst.* i. 230; W.R.O. 442/2, p. 306; above, Corston, manor.
[23] W.R.O. 177/39, deed, Hungerford to Fox, 1682.
[24] Ibid. 177/39, deeds, Fox to Hill, 1689, Hill to White, 1690.
[25] P.R.O., C 78/1746, no. 3.
[26] Ibid. PROB 11/1292, ff. 214–20.
[27] *Musgrave's Obit.* ii (Harl. Soc. xlv), 240; W.R.O., A 1/345/371; ibid. EA/34; ibid. 212A/38/94/1C.
[28] W.R.O., A 1/345/371; ibid. 212A/38/22/3; 374/128/66.
[29] Ibid. A 1/345/371; ibid. 212A/38/22/4, deed, 1818.
[30] Ibid. 212A/38/58/3A–B.
[31] *W.A.M.* xxxi. 313–14; P.R.O., IR 29/38/241; IR 30/38/241; below.
[32] *Alum. Oxon. 1715–1886*, iv. 1550; Princ. Regy. Fam. Div., wills of Chas. Wightwick, 1861, Mary Wightwick, 1863, Hen. Wightwick, 1884; W.R.O. 212A/38/18/9; 1438/8A.

Wightwick, c. 1918 sold 248 a. in Little Somerford, including Church, East End, and Yew Tree farms.[33] Church farm, 125 a., bought by Theodore Simmons, was owned in 1988 by Mr. P. T. Simmons, and East End farm, 63 a., bought by R. W. Gawthrop, was owned by another Mr. R. W. Gawthrop.[34] In 1808 Giles Earle sold to Henry Wightwick, rector of Little Somerford, the manorial rights and c. 63 a. mostly in the south-west.[35] Wightwick (d. 1846) devised the land to his daughter Susan, wife of his successor as rector, Arthur Evans (d. 1893).[36] It passed to Susan's and Arthur's son the Revd. Arthur Evans, and to the younger Arthur's daughter Catherine, wife of F. H. Manley, rector of Great Somerford.[37] Catherine's estate was apparently broken up in 1918.[38]

The rest of the younger William White's estate was sold in 1727 to Edmund Estcourt[39] (d. 1758),[40] and passed to his relict Anna Maria (will proved 1783).[41] The Estcourts' estate passed to their grandson William Edwards,[42] who in 1787 sold most of it to Abraham Young (d. 1787).[43] Young's son Abraham (d. 1794) inherited and devised it for his daughters Margaret (d. 1845), wife of the Revd. Henry Wightwick (d. 1846), Elizabeth (d. 1824), wife of John Ormond, and Mary (d. 1863), wife of the Revd. Charles Wightwick (d. 1861), as joint tenants.[44] By 1847 c. 66 a. and the house later called the Old Rectory had accrued to John Ormond, and the remainder of the land was in Charles Wightwick's Little Somerford estate.[45] Ormond's portion later reverted to the Wightwick estate and was sold with it in 1918.[46]

By will proved 1738 Thomas Browne devised a farm at Little Somerford to his daughter Arabella, who married William Calley (d. 1768). It passed to her son Thomas Calley (d. 1791), and grandson Thomas Calley,[47] who in 1804 sold the 78-a. farm to John Collingbourne.[48] In 1817 Collingbourne sold it to the Revd. Charles Wightwick,[49] and it became part of Wightwick's Little Somerford estate.

The demesne land of Little Somerford manor, *MAUNDITTS PARK* farm, was bought from Sir Stephen Fox by Thomas Powell (d. 1692), and passed to his son Thomas[50] (fl. 1736),[51] who devised it to his daughter Rachel, wife of John Sheppard. The estate was apparently afterwards owned by Rachel's nephew John Hayter, who settled it on his brother William Hayter. It passed

c. 1806 to William's son Francis, who in 1792 took his mother's surname, Egerton, in place of Hayter. Egerton sold it c. 1813 to W. P. Bendry,[52] who by will proved 1817 devised it to Samuel Brooke[53] (d. 1837). The farm descended to Brooke's son S. B. Brooke (d. 1869), and to S. B. Brooke's nephew, the Revd. Charles Kemble.[54] Kemble (d. 1874) devised it to his wife Charlotte, who assigned the 328-a. farm in 1882 to their son Stephen Kemble[55] (d. 1904). Kemble's relict Frances owned the farm in 1915.[56] Cornelius Wall was owner 1920–39,[57] W. H. Wilson 1945–6, and P. R. Marsh 1955–66.[58] Mr. B. A. Marsh owned the farm in 1988.[59]

Bradenstoke priory held land in Little Somerford worth 2s. a year in 1291.[60] The priory held a house and 3 a. in 1416[61] and at the Dissolution.[62]

ECONOMIC HISTORY. On the 5-hide estate at Little Somerford there were 3 *servi* and 2 ploughteams on the demesne hides in 1086. Elsewhere on the estate 7 *villani*, 5 bordars, and 12 coscets had 4 ploughteams. There were 40 a. of meadow.[63]

In 1303 the demesne included 140 a. of arable, 12 a. of meadow, and pasture worth 8s. yearly.[64] It had been leased in portions by 1449–50. Land, which later evidence suggests was in the north-west part of the parish, was inclosed to form a demesne park. The park was enlarged in 1426–7, was surrounded by a pale, and in 1449–50 was leased to a parker who in that year sent rabbits from it to the Hungerford family's estate at Rowden in Chippenham.[65] In 1609 the park was still leased and was stocked with 120 deer. It was disparked c. 1640, some of the land was ploughed,[66] and most was apparently later part of Maunditts Park farm.

There were 11 leaseholders in 1303. Two held farms of 2 yardlands each and five held ½ yardland each: all seven ploughed for a day in summer for the lord. There were 14 bondmen who each held ½ yardland, worked for the lord for three days a week throughout the year, and paid only 2½d. rent each year. Another 6 bondmen each held ¼ yardland and worked one day a week from 29 September to 1 August, two days a week during harvest. There were also 7 cottars.[67]

In 1609 of the six lessees, apart from the parker, one held the demesne farmhouse, three closes of

[33] W.A.S. Libr., sale cat. xii, no. 4; ibid. Manley MSS., box 53, file 16A.

[34] W.A.S. Libr., sale cat. xii, no. 4; inf. from Mrs. P. T. Simmons, Church Farm; Mr. R. W. Gawthrop, East End Farm.

[35] W.R.O. 212A/38/22/3; P.R.O., IR 29/38/241; IR 30/38/241.

[36] W.A.M. xxxi. 313–14; P.R.O., PROB 11/2055, f. 164v.

[37] W.A.M. xliii. 174; above, Gt. Somerford, church.

[38] W.R.O. 212A/38/43/11.

[39] Para. based on ibid. 212A/38/94/1E.

[40] *Musgrave's Obit.* ii (Harl. Soc. xlv), 280.

[41] P.R.O., PROB 11/1109, ff. 96v.–97v.

[42] W.R.O. 212A/38/94/2.

[43] Ibid. 1607/11; P.R.O., PROB 11/1156, ff. 334v.–335.

[44] P.R.O., PROB 11/1258, ff. 373–4; W.R.O. 1607/11; 2095/3; mon. in church; mon. in Brinkworth church; W.A.S. Libr., Manley MSS., box 53, file 16A.

[45] P.R.O., IR 29/38/241; IR 30/38/241; above.

[46] W.A.S. Libr., sale cat. xii, no. 4.

[47] V.C.H. Wilts. ix. 10; W.R.O. 1178/221–5.

[48] W.R.O., A 1/345/371; ibid. 212A/38/54/1A–B.

[49] Ibid. 212A/38/54/7A–B.

[50] *W.N. & Q.* vii. 126, 130–1; P.R.O., E 126/17, ff. 50v.–51.

[51] *Q. Sess. 1736* (W.R.S. xi), p. 143.

[52] W. P. W. Phillimore, *Changes of Name, 1760–1901*, 105; W.A.S. Libr., Manley MSS., box 53, file 16A; W.R.O., A 1/345/371.

[53] P.R.O., PROB 11/1588, ff. 14–17.

[54] *Kelly's Dir. Wilts.* (1867); W.R.O., A 1/345/371; ibid. 663/8; above, Charlton, manors.   [55] W.R.O. 856/3.

[56] *Kelly's Dir. Wilts.* (1915); Princ. Regy. Fam. Div., will of Steph. Kemble, 1904.

[57] *Kelly's Dir. Wilts.* (1920, 1939).

[58] W.R.O., G 7/516/1–3.

[59] Inf. from Mrs. B. A. Marsh, Maunditts Park Farm.

[60] *V.C.H. Wilts.* iii. 281.

[61] *Bradenstoke Cart.* (W.R.S. xxxv), pp. 173–4.

[62] *Cal. Pat.* 1558–60, 465.   [63] *V.C.H. Wilts.* ii, p. 125.

[64] *Wilts. Inq. p.m.* 1242–1326 (Index Libr.), 298–301.

[65] P.R.O., SC 6/1058/6.   [66] W.R.O. 442/2, p. 316.

[67] *Wilts. Inq. p.m.* 1242–1326 (Index Libr.), 298–301.

pasture, and 1¾ yardland apparently part of the demesne. One held a farm of c. 70 a., entirely pasture. Besides rights in the common meadows it included inclosed pastures of which the largest was England's, c. 20 a. west of the Avon and allotted to Little Somerford in 1281. The remaining four lessees, including the miller, held only small farms, of which one included land formerly in the park. Of 14 copyholders one held 55 a., five held 1 yardland each, and eight each held ½ yardland or less. In addition there were 7 cottagers.[68]

Idovers field was presumably on the sand southeast of the village towards the hamlet in Dauntsey called Idover, and Eggs field may have been south of the village on the sand. They may have been inclosed in the 16th century: no open field was mentioned after 1512.[69] Meadows beside the Avon were used in common with Rodbourne until 1281.[70] Thereafter they were used in common by the men of Little Somerford, and the lord of Charlton manor was entitled to c. 7 a., or 14 lots, in Little Kingsmead meadow c. 1600 and later.[71] Common rights were extinguished in 1808 when c. 109 a. of meadow land, possibly mainly southeast of Kingsmead Mill, were inclosed. Until then there was also common pasture beside the Swindon–Malmesbury road on open land called Little Somerford down in 1773, on the wide verges of the Street and other lanes near the village, and between East End Lane and Clay Street on land called Savage Green. Those pastures were also inclosed and allotted in 1808,[72] but a few acres in East End Lane were still common in 1847.[73]

Until the early 1630s the men of Little Somerford were accustomed to feed their animals in the open woodland and pastures of Braydon forest and its purlieus. They were excluded from the forest when it was inclosed in 1630 but, after dispute with the lords of manors nearer the forest, were allotted 204 a. of the purlieus, Somerford common, c. 1633.[74] The land was apparently used as a common pasture until 1792 when it was inclosed and allotted in portions.[75]

Maunditts Park, 288 a., was the largest farm based in the parish in 1847. The others were Manor, 77 a., Street, 79 a., that worked from Somerford House, 89 a., Church, 90 a., with which another 64 a. may have been worked, East End, 67 a., Malthouse, 23 a., Yew Tree, 10 a., and the glebe, 32 a. All were predominantly pasture: Maunditts Park farm included 58 a. of arable west of its farmhouse, the 154 a. apparently worked from Church Farm included 41 a. of arable, Street farm included 10 a. of arable, and the glebe 12 a.[76]

The arable acreage remained small, 189 a. in 1876, only 13 a. in 1936. It increased during or after the Second World War and there were c. 160 a. of arable in 1985. Crops for feeding stock were grown on c. 20 a., wheat and barley on c. 140 a. In the later 19th century and the 20th the area sown with clover or as temporary grassland varied, from 2 a. c. 1870 to 113 a. in 1976. An average of 390 cows was kept 1867–1976, an average of 190 sheep 1867–1946, and an average of 207 pigs 1867–1966. In 1985 there were 233 cows and 519 other cattle.[77] Farming in 1988 was still predominantly pastoral and three farms, Maunditts Park, Church, and East End, were based in the parish. Maunditts Park, which had c. 215 a. in the parish, and East End, c. 100 a., were dairy farms, and on Church farm, c. 210 a., corn was grown and cattle for beef were reared. The rest of the parish was still mostly grassland.[78]

There were 8 a. of woodland in 1086[79] and 10 a. in 1303.[80] After it was inclosed in 1792, 191 a. of Somerford common were planted with trees. All the woodland in the main part of the parish in 1847, 2 a. of plantations and a 4-a. coppice, were in Maunditts Park farm.[81] There were only a few acres of woodland in 1988.

A glover lived in the parish in 1582.[82] In 1831 most men in Little Somerford were agricultural labourers.[83] A mason or masons worked in the parish in 1841 and later; malting was carried on 1847–67 at Malthouse Farm by members of the Gantlett family, and in 1847 and later by Charles Hall at what became Mills Farm.[84] The auctioneering and cattle-dealing business of the Teagle family was based 1875–1927 at the farm worked from Somerford House. Two coal merchants were based at Little Somerford station from 1903, and from 1935 or earlier the Wiltshire Agricultural Co-operative Society Ltd. had a depot there.[85]

There was a mill at Little Somerford in 1086.[86] From 1303 or earlier a mill,[87] presumably on the Avon where Kingsmead Mill later stood, was part of the manor. Kingsmead Mill, so called in 1585,[88] descended with Maunditts Park farm from 1689 to 1910 or later.[89] Milling ceased in 1955, and in 1988 Kingsmead Mill was owned by Mr. David Puttnam, the film producer, and his wife. The mill was rebuilt in the 17th century or early 18th. In the late 18th century a mill house was built on the north side and a wing on the west. About 1828[90] the whole building was heightened and a brick range was built along the north part of its east front. The west front was altered in the 20th

[68] Reg. Malm. ii. 219–20; W.R.O. 442/2, pp. 306–16.
[69] P.R.O., SC 2/208/28.
[70] Reg. Malm. ii. 219–20.
[71] W.R.O. 88/2/34; 88/9/1J, deed, Palmer to Peddington or Tuck, 1647.
[72] Andrews and Dury, Map (W.R.S. viii), pl. 14; Little Somerford Inclosure Act, 48 Geo. III, c. 75 (Priv. Act).
[73] P.R.O., IR 29/38/241; IR 30/38/241.
[74] W.R.O. 88/9/11; 88/10/52.
[75] Ibid. EA/34.
[76] P.R.O., IR 29/38/241; IR 30/38/241.
[77] Ibid. MAF 68/151, sheet 3; MAF 68/493, sheet 5; MAF 68/1063, sheet 4; MAF 68/1633, sheet 6; MAF 68/2203, sheet 14; MAF 68/2773, sheet 10; MAF 68/3319, sheet 10; MAF 68/3814, no. 134; MAF 68/4182, no. 134; MAF 68/4552, no. 134; MAF 68/5004, no. 134; MAF 68/5505, no. 134; MAF 68/5980, no. 134.

[78] Inf. from Mrs. B. A. Marsh, Maunditts Park Farm; Mrs. R. W. Gawthrop, East End Farm; Mrs. P. T. Simmons, Church Farm.
[79] V.C.H. Wilts. ii, p. 125.
[80] Wilts. Inq. p.m. 1242–1326 (Index Libr.), 299.
[81] P.R.O., IR 29/38/241; IR 30/38/241.
[82] Sess. Mins. (W.R.S. iv), 77.   [83] Census, 1831.
[84] Kelly's Dir. Wilts. (1848 and later edns.); Harrod's Dir. Wilts. (1865); P.R.O., HO 107/1181/33; ibid. IR 29/38/241; IR 30/38/241.
[85] Kelly's Dir. Wilts. (1875 and later edns.).
[86] V.C.H. Wilts. ii, p. 125.
[87] Wilts. Inq. p.m. 1242–1326 (Index Libr.), 299.
[88] Extents for Debts (W.R.S. xxviii), pp. 93–4.
[89] Above, manor; W.R.O., Inland Revenue, val. reg. 14.
[90] Date in ho.; inf. from Mr. David Puttnam, Kingsmead Mill.

century. In the 1980s the inside of the house was extensively altered and refitted, a walled courtyard was built to the east, and landscaped gardens, incorporating the mill pond, were made to the south.

LOCAL GOVERNMENT. Views of frankpledge and manorial courts were held twice yearly c. 1450.[91] Records survive for 1510–14 and show the business of both to have been recorded together and to have included the election of a tithingman, the payment of cert money, the amercements of millers for overcharging, and presentments of flooded roads, waterlogged ditches, houses in need of repair, straying animals, and the deaths of customary tenants. Copyhold business was dealt with, and the use of the open fields after harvest was regulated.[92]

In 1689 William White conveyed a house to accommodate paupers.[93] It was presumably the church house so used in 1834.[94] The amount spent on the poor rose from £89 in 1775–6 to £203 in 1802–3 when, of a population of c. 255, 28 adults were relieved continuously and another 28 occasionally.[95] In 1813–15 c. £245 a year was spent on continuous relief and occasional relief for, respectively, averages of 24 and 14 adults.[96] The average of c. £270 yearly 1816–21 was low for Malmesbury hundred. Expenditure afterwards fluctuated greatly, £181 being spent in 1823, £376 in 1824, and £108 in 1825. Expenditure in 1833–5, £215 on average, was still low for the hundred. Little Somerford was included in Malmesbury poor-law union in 1835.[97] A burial board was formed in 1892 to administer the cemetery opened in that year.[98] The parish became part of North Wiltshire district in 1974.[99]

CHURCH. The church which stood in Little Somerford in 1251 may originally have been served from Malmesbury abbey. It became a parish church, possibly c. 1251, when the demesne tithes of Little Somerford manor were confirmed to the rector by the abbot in return for 2 lb. of wax yearly.[1] The rectory was united in 1967 with the rectory of Great Somerford and the vicarage of Seagry.[2] The benefice of Corston with Rodbourne was added in 1986.[3]

The advowson was held by Sir John Mauduit in 1312:[4] it descended with Little Somerford

manor until 1689 and the lords presented. From Sir Stephen Fox (d. 1716), the advowson descended in the direct male line to Stephen Fox (from 1758 Fox-Strangways, cr. Lord Ilchester 1741, earl of Ilchester 1755, d. 1776), Henry, earl of Ilchester (d. 1802), and Henry, earl of Ilchester (d. 1858).[5] The last Henry sold it in 1838 to the rector, Henry Wightwick (d. 1846). It descended to his son, the Revd. Henry Wightwick[6] (d. 1884), after whose death it was sold.[7] Mrs. Sarah Brown was the owner in 1892,[8] and in 1893 presented R. G. Brown (d. 1911), who afterwards acquired the advowson and devised it to the bishop of Bristol.[9] In 1967 the bishop became entitled to the first of four turns of presentation to the united benefice,[10] and in 1986 to the second and fourth of five turns.[11]

The benefice was valued at £10 in 1291[12] and at £8 19s. 4d. in 1535.[13] It had an average yearly income of £241 in the years 1829–31 when it was one of the poorer livings in Malmesbury deanery.[14] From 1251 the rector was entitled to all the tithes. A modus of £2 in place of tithes from the former demesne was confirmed in 1699.[15] In 1847 the tithes were valued at £262 and commuted.[16] The glebe c. 1341 comprised 1 carucate and 6 a. of meadow.[17] It was c. 30 a. in 1608 and later.[18] Between 1911 and 1922 all but 6 a. was sold.[19]

The rector had a house in 1341.[20] The rectory house was rebuilt in stone in the 17th or 18th century and c. 1783 contained a hall, wainscotted parlour, kitchen, and five bedrooms.[21] The rector considered it unsuitable for occupation c. 1830 and it was let.[22] Anne Evans (d. 1866), mother of Arthur Evans, rector 1847–93, occupied it from 1847. In 1866 a south wing with principal rooms and an east entrance front were built in stone, and Evans afterwards occupied the house himself.[23] It was sold c. 1948.[24]

In 1312 the rector, Thomas of Astley, was licensed to study for a year.[25] Sir William Moleyns, possibly he who died in 1381, gave a house and orchard in Little Somerford to endow a light in the church.[26] In 1421 Thomas Felix, rector 1409–35, was granted a corrody in Malmesbury abbey in return for attending when required to the abbey's business.[27] In 1553 no quarter sermon was preached and the parish lacked the *Paraphrases* of Erasmus,[28] and in 1585 the rector did not catechize, did not wear a surplice and a square cap, and was reported to have conducted a clandestine wedding.[29] William Palmer and his son

[91] P.R.O., SC 6/1058/6.
[92] Ibid. SC 2/208/28; SC 2/209/57.
[93] W.R.O. 212A/38/22/2.
[94] *Endowed Char. Wilts.* (N. Div.), 903.
[95] *Poor Law Abstract, 1804*, 566–7; *V.C.H. Wilts.* iv. 357.
[96] *Poor Law Abstract, 1818*, 498–9.
[97] *Poor Rate Returns, 1816–21*, 189; *1822–4*, 228; *1825–9*, 219; *Poor Law Com. 2nd Rep.* App. D, 559.
[98] Ch. Com. file 23135.
[99] O.S. Map 1/100,000, admin. areas, Wilts. (1974 edn.).
[1] *Reg. Malm.* ii. 218–19; *Tax. Eccl.* (Rec. Com.), 189.
[2] *Lond. Gaz.* 17 Nov. 1967, pp. 12581–2.
[3] Inf. from Ch. Com.
[4] *Reg. Ghent* (Cant. & York Soc.), ii. 775.
[5] Phillipps, *Wilts. Inst.* (index in *W.A.M.* xxviii. 230); *Complete Peerage*, vii. 46–7; above, manor.
[6] W.R.O. 700/133A/6, deeds, 1838, 1841.
[7] Princ. Regy. Fam. Div., will of Hen. Wightwick, 1884.
[8] Ch. Com. file 23135.
[9] Ibid. file 73057; *Crockford* (1896); *W.A.M.* xxviii. 180.

[10] *Lond. Gaz.* 17 Nov. 1967, pp. 12581–2.
[11] Inf. from Ch. Com.
[12] *Tax. Eccl.* (Rec. Com.), 189.
[13] *Valor Eccl.* (Rec. Com.), ii. 135.
[14] *Rep. Com. Eccl. Revenues*, 846–7.
[15] *W.N. & Q.* viii. 125–31.
[16] P.R.O., IR 29/38/241; IR 30/38/241.
[17] *Inq. Non.* (Rec. Com.), 165.
[18] *Glebe Lands Return*, H.C. 307, p. 56 (1887), lxiv; W.R.O., D 1/24/186/1–4; P.R.O., IR 29/38/241; IR 30/38/241.
[19] Ch. Com. files, NB 5/86c/1; 73057.
[20] *Inq. Non.* (Rec. Com.), 165.
[21] W.R.O., D 1/24/186/4.
[22] *Rep. Com. Eccl. Revenues*, 846–7; Ch. Com. file, NB 5/86c/1.   [23] *W.A.M.* xliii. 174; Bristol R.O., EP/A/25/1.
[24] Ch. Com. file, NB 5/86c/2.
[25] *Reg. Ghent* (Cant. & York Soc.), ii. 906.
[26] P.R.O., E 310/26/153, f. 7; ibid. SC 6/1058/6.
[27] Phillipps, *Wilts. Inst.* i. 97, 126; *Cal. Pat.* 1422–9, 263.
[28] W.R.O., D 1/43/1, f. 133v.   [29] Ibid. D 1/43/6, f. 32.

John were successive rectors 1618–89.[30] Nicholas Fenn, rector 1709–30, was from 1723 vicar of Staverton (Glos.), and Samuel Hill, rector 1730–53, was vicar of Eisey 1731–3, rector of Kilmington (then Som.) from 1733, and a canon of Wells (Som.) 1741–51.[31] Curates either served the cure or assisted the rector in 1639 and the earlier 18th century.[32] In 1783 the rector was assistant curate at Swindon, and the curate, who also served Sutton Benger, held a morning service each Sunday at Little Somerford. The sacrament was administered at Christmas, Easter, Whitsun, and Michaelmas to c. 6 communicants.[33] Henry Wightwick, rector 1794–1846, was lord of the manor from 1808 and patron of the living from 1838.[34] He was also curate of Brinkworth, where he lived, and held only one service each Sunday at Little Somerford in 1832.[35] In 1850–1 an average congregation of 30 attended Sunday morning services and one of 40 the afternoon services.[36] Wightwick's son-in-law and successor Arthur Evans was rector of Bremilham from 1840.[37] The rectory was held in plurality with that of Great Somerford 1952–67.[38]

The church of *ST. JOHN THE BAPTIST*, so called in 1786,[39] is built of stone rubble with ashlar dressings and has a structurally undivided chancel and nave with a south porch and west tower.[40] The nave may survive from the church which stood in 1251. The chancel was built, and a south window was inserted in the nave, in the later 13th century. The porch and west tower were built in the 15th or early 16th century. The chancel is divided from the nave by a screen made up from several pieces of wood carved in the 14th and 15th centuries. Above the screen is part of a boarded tympanum on which are painted the commandments flanked by censing angels. In the 17th century a royal coat of arms dated 1602[41] and a pulpit and reading desk dated 1626 were placed in the church, cartouches containing texts were painted on the nave walls, and the nave was fitted with box pews and a west gallery. The pews were later replaced by benches. About 1860 the chancel was restored and the east window was replaced by one in early 14th-century style. A window was inserted in the south chancel wall in 1905. The west gallery was removed c. 1900 and seating and a reredos

for the chancel were made from its wood.[42]

The church had much plate until 1553, when royal commissioners took 15 oz. of it and left a chalice weighing 3½ oz. In 1988 the parish held a chalice and paten cover hallmarked for 1714 and a chalice and paten bought in 1926.[43] There were three bells in 1553 and 1988: the second was recast in 1725 by John Tosier, and the treble and tenor by James Burrough in 1752 and 1753 respectively.[44] Registrations of baptisms, burials, and marriages survive from 1708.[45]

NONCONFORMITY. John Stockham of Little Somerford was a Quaker in 1662,[46] and he, his wife, and another woman were Quakers in 1674.[47] There were five nonconformists in Little Somerford in 1676.[48] In 1783 some parishioners were described as 'methodists',[49] Independents certified a room in 1799, and Calvinistic Methodists certified two houses in 1827.[50]

EDUCATION. A school in Little Somerford was attended in 1818 by 20 children,[51] in 1833 by 25,[52] and in 1846–7 by only 10.[53] A new schoolroom was built c. 1854, and in 1859 30–40 children were taught.[54] A new National school was built in 1872.[55] Average attendance was 60 in the period 1906–14 but after 1918 it gradually declined and in 1937–8 was 30.[56] There were 55 children on roll when the school closed in 1982.[57]

CHARITIES FOR THE POOR. The church house given in 1689 by William White was leased after 1835 for £5 yearly, with which blankets and sheets were bought for distribution to paupers on 21 December.[58] A blanket each for 14 people was bought in 1932, and blankets were still being given in 1945.[59] The cottage which replaced the church house c. 1850 was no longer owned in 1988. The charity's income was allowed to accumulate in the 1980s and grants to parishioners were made occasionally.[60] From 1967 inhabitants of Little Somerford were entitled to be admitted to an almshouse in Dauntsey.[61]

[30] Phillipps, *Wilts. Inst.* ii. 9, 42; *W.N. & Q.* viii. 128.
[31] *Alum. Oxon. 1500–1714*, ii. 491, 713.
[32] *Subscription Bk. 1620–40* (W.R.S. xxxii), p. 79; W.R.O., bishop's transcripts, bdle. 2.
[33] *Vis. Queries, 1783* (W.R.S. xxvii), p. 197.
[34] *Alum. Oxon. 1715–1886*, iv. 1550.
[35] Ch. Com. file, NB 5/86c/1; above, Brinkworth, church.
[36] P.R.O., HO 129/252/1/12/20.
[37] *Alum. Oxon. 1715–1886*, ii. 431; above, manor.
[38] *Lond. Gaz.* 17 Jan. 1967, p. 586; Ch. Com. file, NB 5/86c/2.
[39] J. Bacon, *Thesaurus* (1786), 886.
[40] Cf. J. Buckler, watercolour in W.A.S. Libr., vol. vi. 18 (1809).
[41] *W.A.M.* xlviii. 115.
[42] *Ch. Guide*.
[43] Nightingale, *Wilts. Plate*, 206–7; inf. from the rector, Great Somerford.
[44] Walters, *Wilts. Bells*, 201; inf. from the rector.
[45] W.R.O. 1149/1; 2095/1–3. Bishop's transcripts for several

earlier periods are ibid. Marriages are printed in *Wilts. Par. Reg. (Mar.)*, ed. W. P. W. Phillimore and J. Sadler, vi. 35–40.
[46] *W.N. & Q.* iv. 23; W.R.O., D 1/54/1/1, no. 46; Stockham was wrongly described as a recusant in *Misc.* v (Cath. Rec. Soc. vi), 323.
[47] W.R.O., D 1/54/6/1, no. 24.
[48] *Compton Census*, ed. Whiteman, 129.
[49] *Vis. Queries, 1783* (W.R.S. xxvii), p. 197.
[50] *Meeting Ho. Certs.* (W.R.S. xl), pp. 54, 113, 115.
[51] *Educ. of Poor Digest*, 1037.
[52] *Educ. Enq. Abstract*, 1047.
[53] Nat. Soc. *Inquiry, 1846–7*, Wilts. 10–11.
[54] *Acct. of Wilts. Schs.* 42.
[55] P.R.O., ED 7/130, no. 172; date on sch.
[56] *Bd. of Educ., List 21, 1908–38* (H.M.S.O.).
[57] W.R.O., F 8/600, Little Somerford sch. papers.
[58] *Endowed Char. Wilts.* (N. Div.), 904.
[59] W.R.O., Char. Com., Little Somerford.
[60] *W.N. & Q.* vii. 273; inf. from the rector.
[61] Char. Com. file; above, Dauntsey, charities.

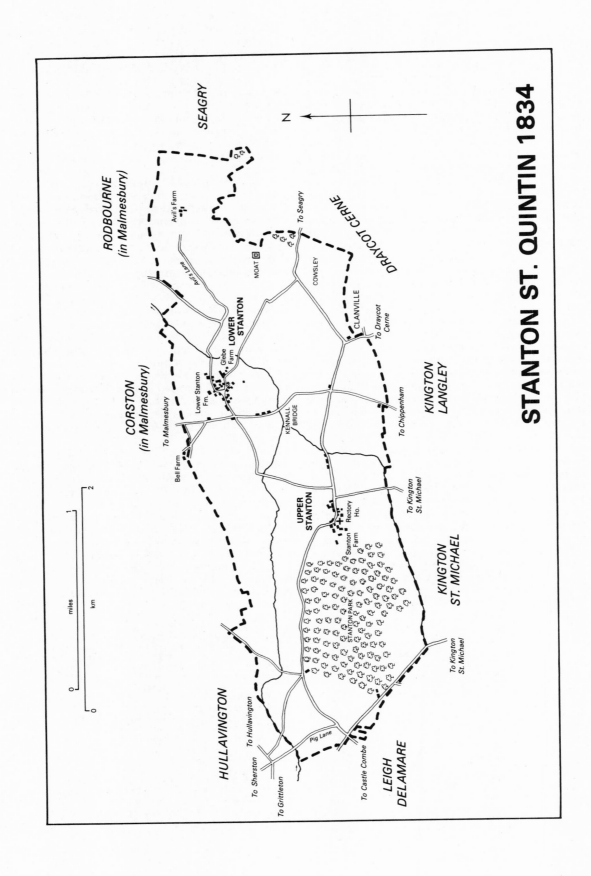

STANTON ST. QUINTIN 1834

STANTON ST. QUINTIN

STANTON St. Quintin church is 7 km. NNW. of Chippenham, 8 km. SSW. of Malmesbury.[62] The parish is 5 km. from east to west, c. 1.75 km. from north to south, and measures 731 ha. (1,807 a.). From the earlier 13th century, and possibly from the later 11th century or earlier, it has contained two markedly different villages, in 1223 called Stanton and Nether Stanton.[63] Stanton, the site of the church, manor house, and rectory house, was later called Upper Stanton, and Nether Stanton, the site of the tenantry farmsteads and a nonconformist chapel, was called Lower Stanton.[64] In 1989 they were called, respectively, Stanton St. Quintin and Lower Stanton St. Quintin. The suffix St. Quintin, in use by 1283–4,[65] and the alternative suffix FitzHugh, in use in the early 16th century,[66] were the surnames of lords of the manor.

The parish boundary is marked in several places by short stretches of road, the southern part followed a stream in the west, and the northern part follows another stream at its west end: especially in the east, however, no prominent feature marks it otherwise, and the southern stream was obscured when the London and south Wales motorway was built along the southern boundary. The long northern and southern boundaries are both apparently ancient. The boundaries of several of Stanton St. Quintin's neighbours, Corston and Rodbourne, both in Malmesbury, an estate called Langley, and Grittleton, were described in early charters.[67] To the north Stanton's boundary continues a line which divides pairs of parishes further east; to the south a charter mentions the southern stream and the place later called Clanville.[68] To the west the boundary was apparently defined by an agreement of 1236.[69] In the early Middle Ages Knabwell was apparently a farmstead or hamlet between Stanton St. Quintin and Seagry.[70] It was probably deserted in the later Middle Ages, and some of its land, including Nabals farm, was almost certainly added to Draycot Cerne parish.[71] In the 16th century, however, Knabwell was sometimes said to have been in Stanton St. Quintin parish,[72] and it is therefore likely that some of its land, perhaps pasture little used in the 15th century, was also added to Stanton St. Quintin, thus extending the parish eastwards or south-eastwards. A field of 10 a., projecting eastwards from the north-east corner of the parish, was considered

part of the parish in 1783, but it belonged to the owner of an estate in Seagry[73] and was in Seagry parish in 1840.[74] A minor adjustment of Stanton St. Quintin's boundary with Draycot Cerne was made in 1882.[75]

The parish contains roughly equal amounts of Cornbrash, clay of the Forest Marble, and Kellaways Clay, and is nearly flat. It is highest at 118 m. in the west, lowest at 77 m. north-east of Lower Stanton, and the two boundary streams cross the west part and meet south of Lower Stanton. The Cornbrash outcrops extensively in the centre and along the northern boundary west of the Malmesbury–Chippenham road: both villages stand on it, the open arable fields were on it, and the flat open land along the northern boundary was used for an airfield. The clay of the Forest Marble outcrops in the west, where the land has been used for both arable and pasture and some has long been woodland: the streams have cut through the Cornbrash to expose more of it, and in several places beside them limestone has been quarried from the 17th century or earlier. In the north-east and south-east the Kellaways Clay was used for common pastures. Kellaways Sand outcrops in the north-east corner.[76]

The Malmesbury–Chippenham road, called Kingway from c. 1100, turnpiked in 1756, and disturnpiked in 1874,[77] crosses the middle of the parish from north to south; a Draycot Cerne to Grittleton road, also turnpiked in 1756, disturnpiked in 1875,[78] crosses the parish from east to west. A road diverging from the Malmesbury–Chippenham road, passing east of Hullavington village, crossing the Draycot Cerne to Grittleton road in the west part of Stanton St. Quintin parish, and leading towards Castle Combe,[79] went out of use after a road further north, through Hullavington village, was turnpiked in 1820.[80] Pig Lane, an old road across the same part of the parish leading from Sherston towards Leigh Delamere, remains a road in Stanton St. Quintin parish but part of it further north has never been made up.[81] The lanes linking Upper Stanton to Lower Stanton and Kington St. Michael in 1989 followed the same courses as in 1719, as did Avil's Lane, so called in 1719,[82] but the lane from Lower Stanton to Seagry was straightened between 1834 and 1885.[83] The straight road running north-east from Clanville was presumably made in the mid 17th

---

[62] This article was written in 1989. Maps used include O.S. Maps 1", sheet 157 (1968 edn.); 1/50,000, sheet 173 (1974 edn.); 1/25,000, ST 87–8, ST 97–8 (1958–60 edns.); 6", Wilts. XIII, XX (1888–9 and later edns.).

[63] Cur. Reg. R. xi, p. 265; V.C.H. Wilts. ii, p. 155; below, manor, econ. hist., church.

[64] V.C.H. Wilts. iv. 310; W.R.O. 490/1529, ff. 48–52v.

[65] P.R.O., E 159/57, rot. 9d.

[66] Cal. Pat. 1494–1509, 536; L. & P. Hen. VIII, i (1), p. 819. [67] Arch. Jnl. lxxvi. 251–5; lxxvii. 44–5, 88–90.

[68] W.A.M. lxxvii. 67–70.

[69] P.R.O., CP 25(1)/250/10, no. 55.

[70] Cal. Inq. p.m. iii, p. 30.

[71] Knabwell manor or Nabals farm is traced above, Draycot Cerne, manor.

[72] Valor Eccl. (Rec. Com.), ii. 121.

[73] W.R.O., EA/24; ibid. 212A/27/48, survey, 1783; 490/1072; above, Seagry, manors.

[74] W.R.O., Seagry tithe award.   [75] Census, 1891.

[76] Geol. Surv. Map 1", solid and drift, sheet 265 (1965 edn.); below, econ. hist.; for the 17th-cent. quarrying, W.R.O. 212A/27/48, ct. bk. 1681–99, ct. 9 Sept. 1686.

[77] Above, Hullavington, introduction.

[78] V.C.H. Wilts. iv. 269; L.J. xxviii. 518.

[79] Andrews and Dury, Map (W.R.S. viii), pl. 13.

[80] W.R.O., A 1/370/24; above, Hullavington, introduction.

[81] Above, Hullavington, introduction.

[82] W.R.O. 212A/27/48, ct. bk. 1712–48, ct. 18 Oct. 1719; 490/1071.

[83] Ibid. 1781/29; O.S. Map 6", Wilts. XIII (1888 edn.).

century when common pasture was inclosed.[84] The London and south Wales motorway was opened in 1971,[85] and most of the roundabout at its junction with the Malmesbury–Chippenham road is in the parish. A new section of the Malmesbury–Chippenham road south of Lower Stanton, avoiding a bend at Kennall bridge, so called in 1773,[86] was opened in 1989.

In the west part of the parish is the site of a Roman villa.[87] Neither Upper Stanton nor Lower Stanton was populous until the 20th century: the total of 49 poll-tax payers in 1377 was low for a parish,[88] 16th-century taxation assessments were low,[89] and in the later 17th century John Aubrey said that the parish had only 23 houses.[90] The population was 193 in 1801. By 1821 it had risen to 285 and in 1851 reached a 19th-century peak of 346. A fall from 338 to 291 between 1861 and 1871 was attributed to emigration. With slight fluctuations the population had fallen to 236 by 1921, and it was 259 in 1931.[91] After R.A.F. Hullavington was opened the population rose sharply: in 1951 it was 1,184 of whom 1,016 were male. Fewer lived on the airfield later, and more houses were built in both villages in the parish. In 1971 there were 748 inhabitants, of whom 428 were male, and in 1981 933, of whom 585 were male.[92]

Upper Stanton is on the Draycot Cerne to Grittleton road, on the south side of which the church, standing in the 12th century, had a large manor house to the west and a large rectory house to the east.[93] In 1263 assizes were held in the village,[94] which in 1377 had 31 poll-tax payers.[95] In 1719 and 1783 only the manor house, the rectory house, and another house, all with farm buildings, and a few cottages and the church stood at Upper Stanton:[96] of the buildings of 1719 only the church survives. In 1834 the manor house, rectory house, and 13 cottages and houses were there:[97] of those only the rectory house and a house bearing a date stone of 1795 survive. A farmhouse replaced the manor house c. 1856.[98] About 1838 a pair of cottages, one of which was for use as a Sunday school, was built in 17th-century style on the north side of the road,[99] and later a schoolroom was built to adjoin it. East of it a pair of cottages was built in the later 19th century, a trio of three-storeyed cottages in 1873, and a pair of cottages in 1877.[1] West of the trio another pair of cottages was built in the early 20th century,[2] north-west of the school a trio of thatched cottages was built in 1925, and further north-west a house was built in vernacular style in 1930.[3] The village expanded after the

Second World War. A short distance north of it 43 houses were built in Valetta Gardens in 1950–1 for R.A.F. Hullavington,[4] and houses were built between Valetta Gardens and the village in the 1980s. South of the Draycot Cerne to Grittleton road 12 bungalows were built in Court Gardens and Kington Lane in the 1970s, and there was infilling in the village in the 1980s.

Lower Stanton had only 18 poll-tax payers in 1377,[5] but in the earlier 17th century was apparently more populous than Upper Stanton,[6] and in 1841 was twice as populous.[7] In 1719 and 1783 c. 7 farmsteads and c. 10 cottages stood there.[8] Glebe Farm, apparently 17th-century, is the oldest house in the village. A new double-pile stone farmhouse was built in the north part of the village c. 1830.[9] Other houses standing in 1834[10] and 1989 include on the north side of the street one apparently of the early 18th century, in the south-east two also apparently 18th-century, on the south side of the street a small farmhouse possibly of the early 19th century, and in Avil's Lane possibly a cottage bearing a datestone of the 1830s. A few cottages, including a pair of 1877 at the junction of the street and the Malmesbury–Chippenham road,[11] were built in the 19th century, but in 1989 most houses in the village were 20th-century. North of the village 5 houses were built in Blenheim Gardens for R.A.F. Hullavington in 1935–6 and a further 10 in 1950–1.[12] At the west end of the village 20 council houses were built in Newbourne Gardens in 1954,[13] and later there was infilling. At the east end extensive, mainly 19th-century, farm buildings were disused in 1989. A reading room on the south side of the street was open before 1920, reopened in 1953,[14] and later demolished.

At the east end of the parish a square moat encloses ½ a. If it is the site of a farmstead it, rather than Nabals Farm in Draycot Cerne, may be the site of Knabwell. The moat adjoins a field called the Hermitage in 1624 and later,[15] and the fine hermitage seen by John Aubrey inside a moat at Stanton St. Quintin in the later 17th century[16] was presumably a building or ruin within it. No evidence, however, of a building on the site has emerged from aerial photography or partial excavation.[17] Avil's farm in the north-east corner of the parish, so called c. 1700,[18] may be land formerly Knabwell's. The farmhouse is a later 17th-century house altered in the early 19th century and extended in the later 20th. An 18th-century barn stands among extensive 20th-century farm buildings.

84 Below, econ. hist.
85 *Rep. Co. Surveyor, 1971–2* (Wilts. co. council), 3.
86 *Andrews and Dury, Map* (W.R.S. viii), pl. 13.
87 *V.C.H. Wilts.* i (1), 107.
88 Ibid. iv. 310.
89 *Taxation Lists* (W.R.S. x), 29, 53.
90 Aubrey, *Nat. Hist. Wilts.* ed. Britton, 69.
91 *V.C.H. Wilts.* iv. 324, 358.
92 *Census*, 1961; 1971; 1981.
93 Below, manor, church.
94 *V.C.H. Wilts.* v. 20.
95 Ibid. iv. 310.
96 W.R.O. 490/1070–2.
97 Ibid. 1781/29.
98 Below, manor.
99 W.R.O. 490/500, deed, Radnor to Cotes, 1838.
1 Ibid. 1621/29; 1781/29; O.S. Map 6″, Wilts. XIII (1888 edn.).

2 O.S. Map 6″, Wilts. XIII. SW. (1900, 1925 edns.).
3 W.R.O. 1781/29.
4 Inf. from Defence Land Agent, Durrington.
5 *V.C.H. Wilts.* iv. 310.
6 W.R.O. 490/1529, ff. 48–52v.
7 P.R.O., HO 107/1181.
8 W.R.O. 212A/27/48, survey, 1783; 490/1070–2.
9 Ibid. 1781/29; O.S. Map 1″, sheet 28 (1834 edn.).
10 W.R.O. 1781/29.
11 Ibid. 1621/29.
12 Inf. from Defence Land Agent, Durrington.
13 W.R.O., G 3/132/43.
14 Ibid. 1781/15; Char. Com. file.
15 W.R.O. 490/1071; 490/1529, f. 50v.
16 Aubrey, *Topog. Coll.* ed. Jackson, 288.
17 J. Badeni, *Wilts. Forefathers*, 143–4; Wilts. co. council, air photos., 1981.
18 W.R.O. 490/698, acct. 1717.

Apart from Avil's Farm, the only buildings outside the two villages in 1719 were three north of the Draycot Cerne to Grittleton road and west of the Malmesbury–Chippenham road.[19] In 1773 there were two or three houses beside the Malmesbury–Chippenham road and buildings at Clanville;[20] beside the road one of the houses, apparently 18th-century, survives. By 1834 there had been more settlement. The buildings of 1719 had been removed, but most of the cottages and houses built between 1773 and 1834 survive: they include a cottage at the west end of Stanton wood, a possibly late 18th-century pair of cottages and another cottage on the waste beside the Draycot Cerne to Grittleton road east of Upper Stanton, a turnpike cottage at the junction of that road and the Malmesbury–Chippenham road, and two of three pairs of cottages on the waste beside the main road near Lower Stanton. At the north-west corner of Stanton wood a barn was built,[21] and a pair of cottages was built there in 1902.[22] In the 20th century a few small farmsteads and other houses, including a new rectory house, were built outside the villages, and in 1938 a village hall was built between the villages near the rectory house. Beside the Malmesbury–Chippenham road a garage has been open since 1925, and a police station was built near R.A.F. Hullavington in 1941.[23]

West of the Malmesbury–Chippenham road 168 a. were acquired for Hullavington airfield in 1935, and a further 45 a. were added later.[24] Most of the airfield buildings are in Stanton St. Quintin; the runways are mainly in St. Paul Malmesbury Without parish. The main buildings, of stone and including a three-storeyed officers' mess in neo-Georgian style and Greystones, a large house in similar style, were erected in 1936. R.A.F. Hullavington was opened in 1937. It was used mainly to train pilots and store aircraft. In the Second World War it was occasionally attacked, and in 1940 camouflaged. New buildings were erected in 1942 and 1956. The storing of aircraft ceased in 1959: flying and navigation training continued until 1965, since when the airfield has had various uses.[25]

MANOR AND OTHER ESTATES. Beorhtric held Stanton St. Quintin in 1066:[26] then and until 1719 or later the estate included 6 a. in Christian Malford.[27] Because the overlordship of Stanton St. Quintin manor was later part of the honor of Gloucester it is likely that Beorhtric was the son of Alfgar, that at Beorhtric's death soon after 1066 William I gave the estate to Queen Maud (d. 1083),

and that William II gave it to Robert FitzHamon. Robert's daughter Mabel married Robert, earl of Gloucester (d. 1147), whose heir was his son William, earl of Gloucester (d. 1183). About 1210 the overlordship of Stanton St. Quintin was part of the honor of Gloucester, then the inheritance of William's daughter Isabel, the divorced wife of King John and later wife of Geoffrey de Mandeville, earl of Gloucester.[28] The overlordship and, from the mid 13th century, the view of frankpledge held for Stanton St. Quintin[29] descended with the earldom of Gloucester until the death of Hugh de Audley, earl of Gloucester, in 1347.[30] The overlordship and view descended to Hugh's daughter Margaret, wife of Robert de Stafford, Lord Stafford[31] (cr. earl of Stafford 1351, d. 1372), and with the earldom to her son Hugh (d. 1386) and grandsons Thomas (d. 1392), William (d. 1395), and Edmund (d. 1403).[32] They descended to Edmund's son Humphrey, earl of Stafford, from 1444 duke of Buckingham (d. 1460), presumably to Henry, duke of Buckingham (d. 1483), and to Edward, duke of Buckingham (d. 1521), on whose attainder they passed to the Crown. The overlordship was not mentioned after 1428.[33] In 1585 the view was granted to Anthony Collins and James Maylard, possibly agents of Sir James Croft,[34] but the right to hold it was apparently not exercised and its later descent has not been traced.

In 1086 Osbern Giffard held the estate which was later *STANTON ST. QUINTIN* manor,[35] but by *c.* 1090 Richard de St. Quintin, a knight of Robert FitzHamon, may have been enfeoffed with it.[36] A successor of Richard was Herbert de St. Quintin (d. by 1154). Herbert had a son Richard (fl. 1166) and that Richard a son Herbert (d. by 1223), who held Stanton manor *c.* 1210.[37] That Herbert was succeeded in turn by his sons Herbert, John, who held the manor in 1236 and 1242–3,[38] and Anselm, whose successive heirs were his sons William and Hugh. The manor passed to William de St. Quintin (d. by 1268),[39] a fourth son of Herbert (fl. 1210), who may have been the William who held it in 1263.[40] It descended to his son Herbert (d. 1302), who in 1286 was granted free warren in his demesne lands of Stanton St. Quintin, to Herbert's grandson Herbert de St. Quintin[41] (d. 1338 or 1339), and to the younger Herbert's son Herbert (d. 1347). That last Herbert's heirs were his daughters Elizabeth (d. *s.p.*), wife of Sir John Marmion, and Lora, wife of Sir Robert Grey. The manor was held by his relict Margery, wife of Sir Roger Husee, until her death in 1361.[42] In the 1380s the manor belonged to Sir John de St. Quintin:[43] his relationship to Herbert

[19] Ibid. 490/1071.
[20] *Andrews and Dury, Map* (W.R.S. viii), pl. 13.
[21] W.R.O. 1781/29.   [22] Ibid. G 3/760/167.
[23] Ibid. 1621/29.
[24] Ibid.; inf. from Defence Land Agent, Durrington.
[25] C. Ashworth, *Action Stations*, v. 104–6.
[26] *V.C.H. Wilts.* ii, p. 155.
[27] Ibid. p. 124; W.R.O. 490/1070.
[28] *Complete Peerage*, v. 682–91; R. B. Patterson, *Earldom of Glouc. Chart.* 38; *Red Bk. Exch.* (Rolls Ser.), ii. 485.
[29] Below, local govt.
[30] e.g. *Bk. of Fees*, ii. 718; *Rot. Hund.* (Rec. Com.), ii (1), 272; *Cal. Close*, 1302–7, 38, 59; 1313–18, 415; 1346–9, 226–7; *Complete Peerage*, v. 694–719.
[31] *Cal. Inq. p.m.* xi, p. 69.

[32] Ibid. xvii, p. 93; xviii, p. 269; for the Staffords, *Complete Peerage*, xii (1), 174–81.
[33] *Feud. Aids*, v. 235, 264; P.R.O., C 142/80, no. 4; for the dukes of Buckingham, *Complete Peerage*, ii. 388–91.
[34] P.R.O., C 66/1254, no. 4.
[35] *V.C.H. Wilts.* ii, p. 155.
[36] For the St. Quintins, *Complete Peerage*, xi. 368.
[37] *Red Bk. Exch.* (Rolls Ser.), ii. 485.
[38] *Bk. of Fees*, ii. 718; P.R.O., CP 25(1)/250/10, no. 55.
[39] P.R.O., JUST 1/998A, f. 17.
[40] *Cal. Close*, 1261–4, 287.
[41] *Cal. Inq. p.m.* iv, p. 95; *Cal. Chart. R.* 1257–1300, 328.
[42] *Cal. Inq. p.m.* ix, p. 25; xi, p. 69.
[43] *Proc. before Justices*, ed. B. H. Putnam (Ames Foundation), 384; Phillipps, *Wilts. Inst.* i. 65, 67, 69, 71.

de St. Quintin (d. 1347) is obscure, but it is likely that he was Sir John Marmion.[44] Although in 1401–2 John de St. Quintin was said to hold the manor,[45] by 1397 it had apparently passed to the Greys' daughter Elizabeth and her husband Henry FitzHugh, Lord FitzHugh:[46] Henry held it in 1412.[47]

From Henry, Lord FitzHugh (d. 1425), and Elizabeth (d. 1427) Stanton St. Quintin manor descended in the direct male line with the Fitz-Hugh title to William (d. 1452), Henry (d. 1472), Richard (d. 1487), and George (d. s.p. 1513): Henry's relict Lady Alice FitzHugh may have held it until her death after 1503 and apparently before 1507. On George's death the manor passed to Richard's sister Alice Fiennes, and on her death, in 1516 or earlier,[48] to her son Thomas Fiennes, Lord Dacre (d. 1533). It descended to Lord Dacre's grandson and heir Thomas Fiennes, Lord Dacre (d. 1541), and to that Thomas's brother Gregory, Lord Dacre (d. 1594).[49] In 1572 Lord Dacre sold it to John Lennard[50] (d. 1591) who c. 1590 settled it on his son Sampson, the husband of Lord Dacre's sister Margaret, from 1594 suo jure Baroness Dacre, and on Sampson's and Margaret's son Henry.[51] In 1603 the Lennards sold it to Edward Read, who in 1619 settled it on himself and his daughter Elizabeth and her husband William Huntley.[52]

Read, then of Corsham, and the Huntleys sold Stanton St. Quintin manor to Edward, later Sir Edward, Hungerford (d. 1648) of Corsham and his wife Margaret in 1624.[53] Margaret (d. 1673) devised the manor to Sir Edward's grandnephew Edward Hungerford (d. s.p. 1681) from whom it passed to Sir Edward's brother Sir Giles (d. 1685). It was held by Sir Giles's relict Margaret until her death in 1711 when it passed to Robert Sutton, Baron Lexinton, the husband of her daughter Margaret (d. 1703), with remainder to Robert's and Margaret's daughter Bridget, wife of John Manners, marquess of Granby, from 1711 duke of Rutland. By Act of 1717 it was conveyed to trustees for sale.[54]

In 1718 the trustees sold the manor to Sir Edward des Bouverie, Bt.[55] (d. 1736) whose heir was his brother Sir Jacob, from 1747 Viscount Folkestone (d. 1761). It passed to Jacob's son William, Viscount Folkestone (cr. earl of Radnor 1765, d. 1776), and from father to son with the Radnor title to Jacob (d. 1828), William (d. 1869),

Jacob (d. 1889), William (d. 1900), and Jacob (d. 1930).[56] In 1909 Lord Radnor sold most of the manor to Meredith Meredith-Brown (d. 1920), whose wife was the daughter of a rector of Stanton St. Quintin and related to Lord Radnor by marriage,[57] and c. 1920 it was broken up.

The manor house, in which the arms of Marmion were depicted,[58] was a large building with two main east–west ranges. In it were windows of the 13th, 14th, and 15th centuries, and attached to its south-east corner was an embattled two-storeyed tower with first-floor oriel windows on two sides.[59] The tower was taken down in the early 19th century,[60] the remainder of the house in 1856.[61] A large stone farmhouse was built on its site, presumably in 1856–7. North of the house are a circular 18th-century dovecot and, among modern farm buildings, an early 19th-century barn.

In 1920 Manor farm, c. 335 a., was bought by B. H. A. Hankey (d. 1948), and it belonged to his relict Maud Hankey (d. 1972).[62] In 1971 the farm, 288 a., was sold by order of the Court of Protection[63] to R. A. Deeley: in 1983 Deeley sold it to his son-in-law and daughter, Mr. and Mrs. L. W. H. Plummer, the owners in 1989.[64] The farmhouse was sold separately in 1972[65] and in 1989 was a hotel. Wood Barn farm, 128 a., was bought in 1920 by Frank Hughes.[66] It was sold in 1947 by George Hughes to Wilfred Bishop (d. 1968), whose two sons, as Bishop Bros., added 70 a. in Hullavington in 1969 and owned the farm, 200 a., in 1989.[67] Lower Stanton farm, including c. 110 a. in the parish but mostly in Corston, was bought in 1919 or 1920 by S. H. Jones (d. 1947) and passed to his relict Amelia Jones (d. 1974). The land in Stanton St. Quintin descended to the Joneses' son R. D. Jones (d. 1986) whose son Mr. A. Jones owned it in 1989.[68] In 1920 F. J. Huntley bought 168 a. in the north-west part of the parish as part of Bell farm based in Corston. It was bought from Huntley by the state for Hullavington airfield in 1935.[69] Smaller farms, Cook's, Leaze, and Greenhill, descended separately after c. 1920,[70] and in 1989 Leaze belonged to Mr. L. W. H. Plummer.[71] Stanton wood, 145 a., was devised by Meredith-Brown to Lady Diana Somerset, and in 1989 was owned by the Beaufort hunt.[72]

Apart from the glebe and 24 a. owned by the lord of Draycot Cerne manor, Stanton St. Quintin

[44] Marmion arms were in the manor ho.: below.
[45] Feud. Aids, vi. 629.
[46] Phillipps, Wilts. Inst. i. 84; Complete Peerage, v, pedigree at pp. 432–3.
[47] Feud. Aids, vi. 538.
[48] Phillipps, Wilts. Inst. i. 167, 171, 184; Complete Peerage, v, pedigree at pp. 432–3; P.R.O., C 139/151, no. 43.
[49] Complete Peerage, iv. 9–11; P.R.O., SC 6/Hen. VIII/6129.
[50] W.R.O. 490/485, deed, Dacre to Lennard, 1572; P.R.O., C 2/Eliz. I/D 2/18.
[51] Complete Peerage, iv. 11–12; P.R.O., C 142/229, no. 143.
[52] W.R.O. 490/485, deeds, Lennard to Read, 1603, Read to Huntley, 1619.
[53] Ibid. 490/485, deed, Read to Hungerford, 1624; J. E. Jackson, Guide to Farleigh-Hungerford, 19.
[54] Complete Peerage, vii. 628–9; L.J. xx. 508; Mon. Inscr. in Salisbury Cath. 26 (copy in W.A.S. Libr.); Jackson, op. cit. 19; W.R.O. 490/73, abstr. of title, 1718.
[55] W.R.O. 490/73, conveyance, Rutland to Bouverie, 1718.

[56] Complete Peerage, v. 542; x. 717–21.
[57] W.A.M. xli. 305; Burke, Land. Gent. (1937), 491; Burke, Peerage (1949), 1651; W.R.O. 1621/29.
[58] Aubrey, Topog. Coll. ed. Jackson, 288.
[59] J. Buckler, watercolour in W.A.S. Libr., vol. x. 12; W.R.O. 490/1072; see below, plate facing p. 220.
[60] Soc. Antiq. MS. 817, x, ff. 103–4; W.R.O. 1781/29.
[61] Aubrey, Topog. Coll. ed. Jackson, 287.
[62] W.R.O. 1621/29; mon. in churchyd.; local inf.
[63] Wilts. Cuttings, xxvii. 60.
[64] Inf. from Mrs. J. Plummer, the Old Rectory.
[65] Wilts. Cuttings, xxvii. 112.   [66] W.R.O. 1621/29.
[67] Inf. from Bishop Bros., Wood Barn Farm.
[68] W.R.O. 1621/29; ibid. G 3/132/43; local inf.
[69] W.R.O. 1621/29; inf. from Defence Land Agent, Durrington.
[70] W.R.O. 1621/29; ibid. G 3/505/2/1.
[71] Inf. from Mrs. Plummer.
[72] W.R.O. 1621/29; inf. from Forestry Com., Postern Hill, Marlborough.

manor included nearly the whole parish in 1624.[73] Much was added to the glebe at inclosure in 1783 when 10 a. at the east end of the parish were part of the Seagry House estate.[74] After an exchange with the owner of the Draycot estate in 1791[75] Jacob, earl of Radnor, owned all but the glebe and 5 a., part of the Draycot estate.[76] In 1902 Jacob, earl of Radnor, sold Avil's farm, 236 a., to Henry Wellesley, Earl Cowley,[77] owner of the Draycot estate, who in 1904 bought 64 a. of glebe at Clanville.[78] In 1920 all the Draycot estate's land in Stanton St. Quintin was offered for sale.[79] Avil's farm was bought by John Smith, who sold it to A. Nuttall in the 1950s. In 1965 Nuttall sold it to N. C. Petrie, whose partner Mr. R. P. Voelcker owned it in 1989.[80] Glebe farm, c. 230 a., was bought in 1919 by Edward West (d. 1942), who was succeeded by a son and a daughter.[81] In the 1960s the farm, c. 205 a., was bought from J. West by Mr. W. E. Hayward, the owner in 1989.[82]

Margaret, Lady Hungerford (d. 1673), gave £60 a year from Stanton St. Quintin manor to a school and almshouse at Corsham.[83] From 1920 the £60 was a charge on Lower Stanton farm.[84]

ECONOMIC HISTORY. In 1086 Osbern Giffard had at Stanton St. Quintin 9 demesne hides with 7 *servi* and only 2 ploughteams; 9 *villani* and 3 coscets had 6 teams; and there were 6 a. of meadow, pasture said to be 1 league square, and woodland 1 league by 3 furlongs.[85] Those figures are compatible with later evidence of a large area of uncultivated demesne to the west and a separate village of small tenant farms with a large common pasture to the east. By 1236 land in the west had been imparked,[86] and most of Stanton park, 240 a. immediately west of the manor house,[87] may never have been agricultural land. The remainder of the parish was used for sheep-and-corn husbandry in common.

There were three open fields in the 14th century, and the demesne arable was in them. About 1303 the demesne was said to include 150 a. of arable and 15 a. of meadow: a free tenant, possibly the rector, held 4 yardlands, 11 customary tenants each held 2 yardlands, 9 customary tenants each held 1 yardland, and there were 6 cottars. It is likely that the customary farmsteads were then, as they were later, at Lower Stanton. In 1361 the demesne was said to include 320 a. of arable, 30 a. of meadow, and rights to feed 200 sheep: there were then 9 free tenants, 18 yardlanders, 3½-yard-landers, and 2 cottars.[88] It is likely that the

demesne was leased from c. 1400.[89] In the 16th and 17th centuries members of the Power family were lessees,[90] and in the later 17th century Aubrey said that they had been lessees for three centuries.[91]

In the early 17th century much of the demesne was probably several, but it still included rights to pasture in common. About 1615 the lessees of the demesne were among 14 who, with the rector, agreed to limit the use of Cowsley, a common pasture of 119 a. in the south-east corner of the parish, to feeding for a total of 91 cattle in summer, 240 sheep in winter, and nothing in spring and autumn. In 1624, however, nearly all the demesne, c. 550 a., was several, and an agreement by the parishioners to exchange lands in 1619 may have been part of a long process of separating the demesne, later called Stanton or Manor farm, from the other land in the parish. Such a process implied inclosure of both arable and pasture, and field names suggest that a West field in the north-west corner of the parish and a cattle pasture in the north-east corner were inclosed, mainly as part of the demesne.[92] Also before 1624 open field called Lent field and Puxey, adjoining that pasture to the west, was inclosed, divided among the other farms, and apparently converted to pasture.[93] In 1624 the demesne, including c. 300 a. of grassland and c. 240 a. of arable of which only 9 a. were in the open fields, was worked from two farmsteads at Upper Stanton: it also included 4 a. in a common meadow in Christian Malford. Between 5 and 10 farms were based in Lower Stanton, where c. 8 farmhouses stood: the glebe included a farmstead there in 1678 but may not have in 1624. Those farms, none of which was apparently much more than 100 a., had arable in West field, c. 290 a., and East field, c. 145 a., common pasture in Cowsley and Anfield, 86 a., and c. 250 a. of closes, most of which were pasture.[94] In the 17th century two sheep for each acre held could usually be fed on the open fields.[95]

Anfield was apparently inclosed soon after 1624[96] and Cowsley and a small part of the open field were inclosed between 1633 and 1678.[97] In 1719 the south-west corner of the parish was woodland, the other three corners were mainly pasture, and the centre was mainly arable. The 336 a. of open field were in Lower field, around and south-east of Lower Stanton, and Upper field, extending along the northern parish boundary west of Lower Stanton. The demesne grassland in the north-east was then a separate farm, Avil's, and possibly had been from when the farmhouse was built in the later 17th century. Stanton farm, 421 a. in c. 40

[73] W.R.O. 490/1529, ff. 48–52v.; for Draycot, above, Draycot Cerne, manor.
[74] W.R.O., EA/24; ibid. 212A/27/48, survey, 1783; 490/1072; above, Seagry, manors.
[75] W.R.O. 490/488, exchange, Radnor and Tylney-Long, 1791.
[76] Ibid. 1781/29.
[77] Ibid. 969/31.
[78] Ibid. 969/32.
[79] Ibid. 1043/6.
[80] Inf. from Mr. R. P. Voelcker, Avil's Farm.
[81] W.R.O. 1621/29; ibid. Inland Revenue, val. reg. 13; below, church.
[82] Inf. from Mr. W. E. Hayward, Manor Farm, Seagry.
[83] *Endowed Char. Wilts.* (N. Div.), 308, 310.
[84] W.R.O., G 3/132/43.
[85] *V.C.H. Wilts.* ii, p. 155.
[86] P.R.O., CP 25(1)/250/10, no. 55.

[87] W.R.O. 490/1072.
[88] *Wilts. Inq. p.m.* 1242–1326 (Index Libr.), 296–7; 1327–77 (Index Libr.), 286.
[89] Above, manor.
[90] P.R.O., SC 6/Hen. VIII/6129; W.R.O. 490/1529, ff. 48–9.
[91] Aubrey, *Topog. Coll.* ed. Jackson, 13.
[92] P.R.O., C 2/Jas. I/S 39/57; W.R.O. 490/1071; 490/1073, copy letter, Read to bp. of Salisbury, 1619; 490/1529, ff. 48–9, 51v.
[93] W.R.O. 490/488, lease, Long to Earle, 1631; 490/1071; 490/1529, ff. 49v.–51.
[94] Ibid. 490/1529, ff. 48v.–52v.; ibid. D 1/24/190/1.
[95] Ibid. 212A/27/48, ct. bk. 1681–99, ct. 17 Apr. 1684; 490/1541, ct. 11 Apr. 9 Chas. I.
[96] Ibid. 490/1529, f. 51v.
[97] Ibid. 490/1541, ct. 11 Apr. 9 Chas. I; ibid. D 1/24/190/1.

closes, included 76 a. of meadow, 176 a. of pasture, and 149 a. of arable; a farm of 94 a., later called Malthouse farm, was also based at Upper Stanton. Of the five main farms based at Lower Stanton the largest was 210 a., the smallest 62 a.[98] Apart from a copyhold of 6 yardlands most land was held by lease for lives.[99]

Apart from the woodland the parish was equally divided between arable and grassland in 1783 when by Act the arable was inclosed, the rector was allotted land to replace tithes, and many exchanges of land were made. Stanton, Malthouse, and Avil's farms were little affected, but Glebe farm was greatly increased and the other five or six farms based at Lower Stanton, of which the largest was 96 a., were reduced to a total of c. 400 a.[1] The number of farms in the parish was reduced to four between 1783 and 1834: Stanton farm, c. 584 a., was based at Upper Stanton, Lower Stanton farm, 325 a., and Glebe farm, c. 300 a., were based at Lower Stanton, and Avil's farm was c. 205 a. Apart from Avil's, which was mainly grassland, the farms were mixed.[2]

In the later 19th century and earlier 20th land was increasingly laid to grass: there were 621 a. of arable in 1887, 444 a. in 1927. In the early 20th century sheep farming declined and dairy farming and the number of farms increased.[3] About 1920 the buildings at Clanville became those of a farm of 34 a. in several parishes,[4] Cook's, based at Lower Stanton, and Leaze, Wood Barn, and Greenhill, all with buildings near Upper Stanton, became new farms,[5] and Lower Stanton farm, 422 a. in 1910 when it included 146 a. in Corston,[6] lost 168 a. west of the Malmesbury–Chippenham road to Bell farm, based in Corston. That 168 a., formerly Upper field, was pasture in 1936 when it was taken for the airfield.[7] Less than 200 a. in the parish was arable in 1937.[8] Manor farm was increased by c. 100 a., formerly woodland, between 1834 and 1885:[9] it was 613 a. in 1910,[10] later lost land to the smaller farms and the airfield, and from 1937 was c. 300 a.[11] Between 1939 and 1943 417 a. of grassland in the parish were ploughed.[12] Apart from the airfield the parish had more arable than grassland in 1989, most of the grassland being in the east. Manor, 288 a., was an arable and dairy farm, with which Leaze farm, c. 90 a., was worked;[13] Wood Barn farm, 200 a., was mainly arable;[14] Avil's, 294 a. including 56 a. in the new Seagry parish, was a corn and sheep farm on which there were also poultry houses for egg production;[15] and two or three smaller farms were based in the parish. By 1989 most of the many farm buildings in Lower Stanton had gone out of use: Lower Stanton farm was mainly arable, and Glebe, c. 205 a., was an arable and stock farm worked mainly from Seagry.[16]

In 1834 five fields in the parish, 14 a., were used as 65 garden allotments.[17] They were replaced by 50 a. given for allotments by C. G. Cotes, rector 1826–67, who was a keen farmer and also gave his parishioners seeds and implements: 25 a. west of Clanville were worked as allotments until the Second World War.[18]

Stanton park was said by Aubrey to have a wall high enough to prevent the escape of deer.[19] It was woodland in the early 17th century[20] and presumably long before. Apart from c. 100 a. at the east end grubbed up between 1834 and 1885 it remains so, and in the later 20th century was held on lease by the Forestry Commission. In 1989 oak, ash, Norway spruce, and Douglas fir were growing on its 145 a.[21] The parish has long contained little other woodland.

In 1361 the lord of Stanton St. Quintin manor owned a windmill which is likely to have been in the parish,[22] but the site is unknown. Apart from those deployed at R.A.F. Hullavington, no trade unconnected with agriculture has become prominent in the parish.

LOCAL GOVERNMENT. About 1258 Richard de Clare, earl of Gloucester, withdrew the men of Stanton St. Quintin from the Startley hundred tourn, and apparently required them to attend a tourn held for the honor of Gloucester. Under the authority of Richard's relict Maud, countess of Gloucester, and of his son Gilbert, earl of Gloucester, William de St. Quintin (d. by 1268) and his son Herbert continued to withdraw their men from the Startley tourn, by 1268 gallows had been erected at Stanton St. Quintin, and c. 1275 the assize of bread and of ale was being separately enforced. About 1268 the abbot of Malmesbury, who held Startley hundred at fee farm, demanded that the gallows should be removed and that Herbert's men should attend the hundred, and c. 1276 the sheriff apparently made an unsuccessful attempt to include Stanton St. Quintin in his tourn. The overlord continued to hold a view of frankpledge for Stanton St. Quintin, but the 16s. paid by the men of Stanton at Startley hundred before they were withdrawn, half to the king and half to the abbot of Malmesbury, was from c. 1276 again paid,[23] and Stanton St. Quintin was again attending the tourn for Malmesbury hundred in

---

[98] W.R.O. 490/1070–1; for Avil's Farm, above, introduction.
[99] W.R.O. 490/698, rent roll, 1718.
[1] Ibid. 212A/27/48, survey, 1783; 490/1072; ibid. EA/24.
[2] Ibid. 1781/29.
[3] P.R.O., MAF 68/1120, sheet 9; MAF 68/1690, sheet 11; MAF 68/2260, sheet 14; MAF 68/2830, sheet 4; MAF 68/3373, sheet 4.
[4] W.R.O. 1043/6.
[5] Ibid. Inland Revenue, val. reg. 13; ibid. G 3/505/2/1.
[6] W.R.O., Inland Revenue, val. regs. 9, 13.
[7] Inf. from Defence Land Agent, Durrington; [1st] Land Util. Surv. Map, sheet 111.
[8] P.R.O., MAF 68/3850, no. 45.
[9] W.R.O. 1781/29; O.S. Map 6″, Wilts. XIII (1888 edn.).
[10] W.R.O., Inland Revenue, val. reg. 13.
[11] Inf. from Defence Land Agent, Durrington; Wilts. Cuttings, xxvii. 60.

[12] W.R.O. 1621/29.
[13] Inf. from Mrs. J. Plummer, the Old Rectory.
[14] Inf. from Bishop Bros., Wood Barn Farm.
[15] Inf. from Mr. R. P. Voelcker, Avil's Farm.
[16] Inf. from Mr. W. E. Hayward, Manor Farm, Seagry; local inf.
[17] W.R.O. 1781/29.
[18] Ibid. 1621/9; Soc. Antiq. MS. 817, x, f. 101v.; O.S. Map 6″, Wilts. XIII. SW. (1925 edn.); inf. from Mr. J. P. M. Mann, the Old Post Office.
[19] Aubrey, Topog. Coll. ed. Jackson, 288.
[20] W.R.O. 490/1529, f. 48 and v.
[21] Inf. from Forestry Com., Postern Hill, Marlborough.
[22] Wilts. Inq. p.m. 1327–77 (Index Libr.), 286.
[23] Rot. Hund. (Rec. Com.), ii (1), 272; Cal. Inq. Misc. i, pp. 370–1; P.R.O., JUST 1/998A, rott. 17, 30; JUST 1/1004, rot. 82.

1439.[24] The only records to survive of the overlord's views are for 1460–1 when the king held them after the death of Humphrey, duke of Buckingham. Two views were held in 1460: at each the tithingman paid cert, and in one presented that animals had strayed and a tapster had sold ale from an unsealed measure.[25] Cert from a yearly view was still accounted for in the early 16th century[26] but there is no evidence that a court was convened. The gallows was replaced by a gibbet, on which a murderer was hung in 1764, standing on open arable land west of Lower Stanton.[27]

The lord of Stanton St. Quintin manor occasionally held courts in the earlier 16th century.[28] Eight courts baron were held between 1628 and 1640, and in the periods 1681–1700 and 1712–48 a court was held in most years. They were presumably not more frequent because most tenants were lessees. In addition to the copyhold business, orders were made to promote good common husbandry, in the late 17th century sheep tellers were sometimes appointed, and in the earlier 18th century orders were made to clear watercourses and ditches and to repair a bridge and the stocks.[29]

Expenditure on the poor was £51 in 1775–6. It increased from c. £75 a year in the early 1780s to £365 in 1802–3 when 24 adults and 68 children in a population of c. 200 were relieved continuously.[30] Between 1809 and 1836 the two overseers gave most relief as doles, but also paid rent and for shoes, clothing, fuel, and midwifery: in 1811 c. 27 adults were relieved, 23 in 1827, 14 in 1835.[31] Between 1820 and 1835, when the parish joined Chippenham poor-law union, expenditure averaging c. £212 was a little low for a parish with c. 300 inhabitants.[32] From 1769 the overseers were lessees of a cottage[33] and in 1834 held a pair of cottages in Lower Stanton.[34] The accounts of the two surveyors of highways survive from 1769 to 1836.[35] In 1974 the parish became part of North Wiltshire district.[36]

CHURCH. Stanton St. Quintin church was standing in the 12th century.[37] In 1312 the bishop collated a vicar to serve the church with the rector.[38] There is no evidence of a vicar before 1312 when a vicarage was ordained;[39] no record of the terms of the ordination survives. In 1341 the rector had a carucate of glebe and all tithes from the whole parish,[40] but how they were divided between him and the vicar is obscure. On a petition from the rector, who claimed that the church's income had declined and was then too small for two incumbents, the vicarage was consolidated with the rectory in 1434.[41] In 1967 the rectory was joined to the united benefice of Grittleton with Leigh Delamere, and in 1976 the vicarages of Hullavington and Norton were added.[42]

The right to present rectors descended with the lordship of Stanton St. Quintin manor. After 1312 rectors presented the vicars. In the 16th century and earlier 17th, although they had the advowson, the lords of the manor did not present the rectors. In 1507 the king presented because George, Lord FitzHugh, was a minor; by grants of a turn Sir Henry Long presented in 1555 and John Danvers (possibly Sir John Danvers, d. 1594) and Robert Franklin presented in 1574; the king presented by lapse in 1609; presumably by grant of a turn James Charnbury and his son James presented in 1639. From 1677 to 1911 the lords again presented.[43] In 1913 Jacob, earl of Radnor, conveyed the advowson to Meredith Meredith-Brown, and in 1921 Meredith-Brown's trustees transferred it to the bishop of Bristol who shared the patronage of the united benefice after 1967.[44]

Valuations at £8 in 1291,[45] £10 6s. in 1535,[46] £100 in 1650,[47] and £312 c. 1830[48] show the rectory to have been of slightly above average wealth and well endowed for a small parish. At inclosure in 1783 nearly all the tithes were exchanged for 256 a.: the rest were commuted for a rent charge of 8s. 9d.[49] The glebe measured 118 a. in 1624,[50] 135 a. in 1678,[51] and c. 150 a. in the early 18th century.[52] From 1783 the rector had a farmstead at Lower Stanton, acquired by exchange in 1783, and 409 a.: further exchanges, agreed in 1783, reduced the glebe to 358 a. after 1804.[53] The rector sold 64 a. in 1904.[54] In 1910 the rest included a farm of 232 a. and 50 a. of allotments.[55] The farm was sold in 1919,[56] and in 1989 the diocesan board of finance owned 25 a.[57]

In the early 16th century the glebe house was called the Vicarage.[58] It was a substantial stone house in which were coats of arms carved in stone.[59] It was replaced by a new double-pile house, of two storeys and attics with a south entrance front, built by the rector instituted in 1780. An east wing was built soon after 1826, and in 1868 the south front was rebuilt and the west,

[24] W.A.M. xiii. 117.
[25] Complete Peerage, ii. 388–9; P.R.O., SC 2/209/58.
[26] B.L. Add. Ch. 26874.
[27] Aubrey, Topog. Coll. ed. Jackson, 288; Andrews and Dury, Map (W.R.S. viii), pl. 13.
[28] P.R.O., SC 6/Hen. VIII/6129–31.
[29] W.R.O. 212A/27/48, ct. bks. 1681–99, 1712–48; 490/1541; above, econ. hist.
[30] Poor Law Abstract, 1804, 566–7; V.C.H. Wilts. iv. 358.
[31] W.R.O. 1621/16; 1781/21.
[32] Poor Rate Returns, 1816–21, 189; 1822–4, 228; 1825–9, 219; 1830–4, 213; Poor Law Com. 2nd Rep. App. D, 558, App. E, 406–7; V.C.H. Wilts. iv. 358.
[33] W.R.O. 1621/26.
[34] Ibid. 1781/29.
[35] Ibid. 1621/27.
[36] O.S. Map 1/100,000, admin. areas, Wilts. (1974 edn.).
[37] Below.
[38] Reg. Ghent (Cant. & York Soc.), ii. 775.
[39] W.R.O., D 1/2/9, f. (2nd foliation) 41v.
[40] Inq. Non. (Rec. Com.), 165.

[41] W.R.O., D 1/2/9, f. (2nd foliation) 41v.
[42] Ch. Com. file, NB 5/143B.
[43] Phillipps, Wilts. Inst. (index in W.A.M. xxviii. 230); W.R.O. 1621/29.
[44] Ch. Com. file 67515/1; ibid. NB 5/143B.
[45] Tax. Eccl. (Rec. Com.), 189.
[46] Valor Eccl. (Rec. Com.), ii. 135.
[47] W.A.M. xli. 8.
[48] Rep. Com. Eccl. Revenues, 848–9.
[49] W.R.O., EA/24.
[50] Ibid. 490/1529, f. 52.
[51] Ibid. D 1/24/190/1.
[52] Ibid. D 1/24/190/2; ibid. 490/1070.
[53] Ibid. EA/24; ibid. 212A/27/48, survey, 1783.
[54] Ibid. 969/32.
[55] Ibid. Inland Revenue, val. reg. 13.
[56] Ibid. 1621/29; Ch. Com. file 67515/1.
[57] Inf. from Deputy Dioc. Sec., Dioc. Bd. of Finance, Church Ho., 23 Gt. Geo. Street, Bristol.
[58] P.R.O., C 1/708, no. 13.
[59] Aubrey, Topog. Coll. ed. Jackson, 289–90.

with a new porch, was made the entrance front. The house was altered in 1871–2 to designs by Ewan Christian: the south front was again rebuilt, with two gables to replace three attic dormers, a north service wing was built, and the porch was moved to the north front. Panelling from the pulpit and reading desk of Purton church and a stone fireplace from Surrendell manor house in Hullavington were re-used in it. The house was sold in 1924, enlarged in 1926 when a west wing was built,[60] and later converted to five dwellings.[61] A new stone rectory house in vernacular style was built in 1928 beside the road between Upper Stanton and Lower Stanton.[62] That house was sold in 1975 and replaced by a new house built in Stanton St. Quintin village c. 1978.[63]

In 1300 the rector, Matthew of Ham, was licensed to visit Rome.[64] Only William of Stanton, vicar 1331–42, rector from 1342,[65] held both benefices. In 1410 the rector, Nicholas Sterre, was found not guilty of being absent from the church and of adultery, and accused of frequenting taverns.[66] His was one of five short incumbencies, ended by exchanges of benefice, between 1397 and 1414.[67] Thomas Bromhall, rector 1440–79,[68] was a canon of Wells (Som.) and held other livings:[69] Stanton St. Quintin was apparently served by a curate.[70] From the 16th century to the 20th, however, most rectors seem to have lived in the parish and to have served the church themselves, usually without the assistance of a curate.[71] William Charnbury, rector from 1639,[72] was sequestrated in 1646, and between then and 1660 there were four ministers: Charnbury was restored in 1660[73] and remained rector until 1677.[74] Francis Powell, rector 1732–59, was in 1735 ordered to live in the parish.[75] In 1783 the rector, Samuel Smith, was also rector of Hardenhuish. He lived at Stanton St. Quintin where he held a service every Sunday and celebrated communion thrice a year: there were only some eight communicants.[76] In 1851–2 the congregation averaged only c. 60.[77] F. J. Buckley of New Hall, Bodenham, a grandson and neighbour of his patron William, earl of Radnor (d. 1869), promised in 1867, when he was presented, that he would resign the rectory if Jacob, earl of Radnor (d. 1889), wished to present his son Bertrand Pleydell-Bouverie.[78] Pleydell-Bouverie, who had an assistant curate 1872–4, was rector 1870–80, and Buckley, a canon of Bristol from 1887, again from 1880 to 1905.[79] On most

Sundays in the 1930s three services were held, and in the 1940s often a fourth.[80] In 1719 or earlier the church held 2 a. in the open fields,[81] replaced by an allotment of 2 a. in 1783.[82] The land was let as allotments from which the income, £3 1s. in 1905, £2.50 in 1972, was used for church repairs.[83]

The church of *ST. GILES*, so called in 1763,[84] is of limestone rubble and ashlar and consists of a chancel, a central tower with north vestry, and a nave with south aisle and porch. The lower stages of the tower and most of the nave are 12th-century. The aisle was added c. 1200 and the small vestry was probably built about then as a chapel. The porch doorway, with 12th-century arch and capitals, may have been reset. In the 13th century the chancel may have been rebuilt, and in the 15th century a new west window and two north windows were inserted in the nave.[85] The chancel is said to have been shortened by 6 ft. in the late 18th century or early 19th,[86] and in 1827–8 the nave was lengthened and its west gallery replaced by a new one. In 1851 the aisle and porch were rebuilt, battlements were added to the tower, and the west window of the nave and pews installed in 1739 were replaced. The gallery was removed, presumably then. In 1888–9 the chancel was rebuilt to designs of C. E. Ponting.[87] On the outside west wall of the nave is a 12th-century carving. The pulpit was carved in stone by Bertrand Pleydell-Bouverie c. 1876 and placed in the church in 1893.[88]

In 1553 a chalice of 10 oz. was left and the king's commissioners took 2½ oz. of plate. The silver of a chalice of 1577 was used in making a new one given in 1738 when two offertory plates, a paten, and a flagon were also given: that plate was held by the parish in 1989. An almsdish and a wafer box were given in 1951.[89] There were two bells in 1553:[90] they were possibly the two cracked bells which in 1876 were replaced by a new bell cast by Mears & Stainbank.[91] The registers begin in 1679 and are complete.[92]

NONCONFORMITY. Quakers lived at Stanton St. Quintin in the later 17th century,[93] and eight nonconformists were there in 1676.[94] A Quaker burial ground, possibly in use as early as 1658,[95] was at Lower Stanton: none is known to have been buried there after 1800,[96] and the burial ground

---

[60] W.R.O. 1621/29; Soc. Antiq. MS. 817, x, f. 102.
[61] W.A.S. Libr., sale cat. xxxviii, no. 23.
[62] W.R.O. 1621/29.
[63] Inf. from Mrs. J. Plummer, the Old Rectory.
[64] *Reg. Ghent* (Cant. & York Soc.), ii. 843.
[65] Phillipps, *Wilts. Inst.* i. 27, 38.
[66] *Reg. Hallum* (Cant. & York Soc.), pp. 216–17.
[67] Phillipps, *Wilts. Inst.* i. 84, 87, 91, 94, 98, 104.
[68] Ibid. 131, 167.
[69] *Cal. Papal Reg.* x. 54.
[70] M. M. Condon, 'Wilts. sheriff's notebook', *Medieval Legal Rec.* ed. R. F. Hunnisett and J. B. Post, 415.
[71] e.g. W.R.O., bishop's transcripts, bdles. 1–3.
[72] Phillipps, *Wilts. Inst.* ii. 20.
[73] *Walker Revised*, ed. Matthews, 371.
[74] W.R.O., bishop's transcripts, bdle. 1.
[75] Phillipps, *Wilts. Inst.* ii. 64, 78; Soc. Antiq. MS. 817, x, f. 105.
[76] *Vis. Queries, 1783* (W.R.S. xxvii), p. 201.
[77] P.R.O., HO 129/253/4/4/16.
[78] Burke, *Land. Gent.* (1898), 193–4; W.R.O. 490/1073,

letter, Buckley to Folkestone, 1867; 1621/29.
[79] *W.A.M.* xxxvii. 180; W.R.O. 1621/29.
[80] W.R.O. 1621/6.   [81] Ibid. 490/1070.
[82] Ibid. EA/24.
[83] *Endowed Char. Wilts.* (N. Div.), 910–11; Char. Com. file.
[84] J. Ecton, *Thesaurus* (1763), 403.
[85] Buckler, watercolour in W.A.S. Libr., vol. vi. 15.
[86] W.R.O. 1621/29.
[87] Ibid.; 1621/11; Aubrey, *Topog. Coll.* ed. Jackson, 289; Wilts. Cuttings, x. 227.
[88] W.R.O. 1621/12; 1621/29.
[89] Nightingale, *Wilts. Plate*, 207; inf. from Mr. J. P. M. Mann, the Old Post Office.
[90] *W.A.M.* xii. 368.
[91] W.R.O. 1621/29.
[92] Ibid. 1621/1–4; bishop's transcripts for several earlier periods are ibid.
[93] *W.N. & Q.* ii. 292, 342, 345; iv. 24, 116; v. 365, 403.
[94] *Compton Census*, ed. Whiteman, 129.
[95] *V.C.H. Wilts.* iii. 117.   [96] *W.N. & Q.* vii. 9.

STANTON ST. QUINTIN
The manor house in 1808

FOXLEY
Foxley House *c.* 1800

A parliamentary election, as lampooned in 1792

The borough court meeting at St. John's almshouse in 1924

MALMESBURY

was a garden in 1989. A meeting house for Independents was certified in 1833. A meeting house certified in 1843[97] was presumably for the Primitive Methodists who formed a congregation of 95 at an evening service in a private house on Census Sunday in 1851.[98] A chapel at Lower Stanton south of the Seagry road was built for Primitive Methodists in 1873:[99] it was replaced in 1905 by a new stone chapel north of the road.[1] Services were held in the chapel in 1989.

EDUCATION. Only six or seven children attended a dame school in 1818: an earlier attempt to hold a school for children of the poor failed.[2] In 1833 a school, possibly held in the rectory house, was attended by 25–30.[3] A building erected for a Sunday school c. 1838 may also have been used for the day school which in 1846–7 incorporated a teacher's house and was attended by 41.[4] A new school was built c. 1848.[5] Only 32 attended on Census day in 1871.[6] The average attendance was 35 in 1902,[7] 60 in 1908–9, 42 in 1918–19, and 26 in 1937–8.[8] Extensions to the building were erected in 1954.[9] In 1988 there were 75 on roll.[10]

CHARITY FOR THE POOR. From, presumably, 1673 to, apparently, the early 20th century qualified paupers of Stanton St. Quintin were to be preferred at vacancies in the Hungerford almshouse at Corsham,[11] but how many from Stanton St. Quintin became almspeople is obscure. No other charity for the poor of Stanton St. Quintin is known.

SUTTON BENGER

SUTTON BENGER[12] church is 6 km. north-east of Chippenham[13] and, as its name indicates, the village is south of Malmesbury abbey which is likely to have owned it long before the Conquest. The parish is one of three in Wiltshire called Sutton: the suffix Benger, mistakenly derived from Berengar, the Domesday tenant of Sutton Mandeville, has been used from the later 14th century; in the late 15th century the parish was sometimes called Sutton Leonard, apparently in confusion with Sutton Veny where the church was called St. Leonard's.[14] Until 1884, when a detached part of Draycot Cerne parish, c. 90 a. beside the Bristol Avon, was added to it, Sutton Benger parish measured 1,198 a. (485 ha.), the area with which this article deals. In 1934 the whole of Seagry and Draycot Cerne parishes were added, increasing Sutton Benger parish to 3,385 a. (1,370 ha.). The lands of the new parish north of the London and south Wales motorway became the new Seagry parish in 1971, when Sutton Benger parish was left with 776 ha.[15]

The boundaries of Sutton were described in the late 11th or early 12th century. The northern and southern then, as later, followed tributaries of the Avon, and the eastern followed the Avon itself. Those boundaries suggest that the men of Draycot Cerne made good a claim to the c. 90 a. beside the Avon between c. 1100 and 1257.[16] The western boundary, which for part of its course was almost straight, followed no natural feature.

River deposits cover about a third of the old Sutton Benger parish which, except its northernmost part, is almost flat. Oxford Clay, Kellaways Clay, and Kellaways Sand outcrop in the north and west and the highest land reaches c. 90 m. In the south-east, valley gravel forms a wide terrace and extensive deposits of alluvium border the Avon. The lowest land, c. 50 m., is in the south-east corner. Alluvium has also been deposited beside Chissell brook, the southern boundary stream, and the other feeders of the Avon to the north.[17] Open fields were on the gravel and on sandy soils north-west of the village, the clay to the north supports woodland, and the alluvium gave the parish much meadow land.[18]

The main roads run east–west. The Swindon–Chippenham road was turnpiked through the village in 1756 and disturnpiked in 1875.[19] Its bridge over the Avon, linking Sutton Benger and Christian Malford, was built in the 18th century, possibly c. 1756: it has cutwaters separated by three segmental arches. It was widened in the 20th century. West of the bridge a stone causeway for pedestrians runs for c. 300 m. along the north side of the road. Further north the London and south Wales motorway was opened in 1971.[20] The northern tip of the parish is crossed by a road,

[97] Meeting Ho. Certs. (W.R.S. xl), pp. 134, 156.
[98] P.R.O., HO 129/253/4/4/5.
[99] W.R.O. 1621/29; O.S. Map 6", Wilts. XIII (1888 edn.).
[1] Date on bldg.   [2] Educ. of Poor Digest, 1037.
[3] Educ. Enq. Abstract, 1048; W.R.O. 1621/29.
[4] Nat. Soc. Inquiry, 1846–7, Wilts. 10–11; W.R.O. 490/500, deed, Radnor to Cotes, 1838.
[5] P.R.O., ED 7/130, no. 140.
[6] Returns relating to Elem. Educ. 420–1.
[7] W.R.O., F 8/220/1.
[8] Bd. of Educ., List 21, 1910 (H.M.S.O.), 510; 1919, 363; 1938, 425.
[9] Wilts. Tracts, 196, no. 19.
[10] Inf. from Chief Educ. Officer, Co. Hall, Trowbridge.
[11] Endowed Char. Wilts. (N. Div.), 308, 310; Char. Com.

file; above, manor.
[12] This article was written in 1987.
[13] The following maps have been used: O.S. Maps 1", sheet 34 (1828 edn.); 1/50,000, sheet 173 (1974 edn.); 1/25,000, ST 97–8 (1959 edn.); 6", Wilts. XIII, XX (1888–9 and later edns.); 1/10,000, ST 97 NE., NW., 98 SW. (1983 edn.).
[14] V.C.H. Wilts. ii, pp. 88, 152; viii. 71; P.N. Wilts. (E.P.N.S.), 74; Phillipps, Wilts. Inst. i. 175, 178.
[15] Census, 1881; 1891; 1931; 1971.
[16] Arch. Jnl. lxxvii. 53–4; below, econ. hist.
[17] Geol. Surv. Maps 1", solid and drift, sheet 265 (1965 edn.); 1/50,000, drift, sheet 266 (1974 edn.).
[18] Below, econ. hist.
[19] V.C.H. Wilts. iv. 257, 269; L.J. xxviii. 518.
[20] Rep. Co. Surveyor, 1971–2 (Wilts. co. council), 3.

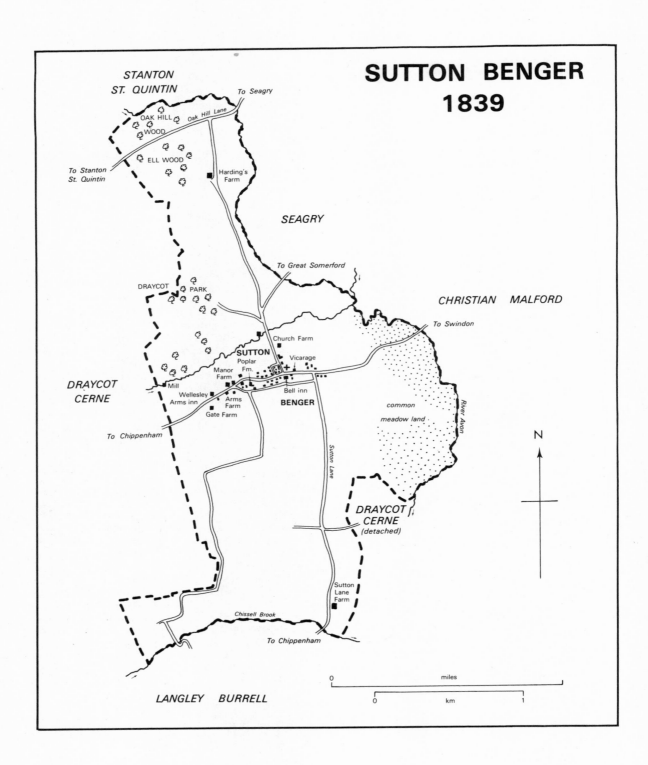

called Oak Hill Lane in 1736, between Seagry and Stanton St. Quintin.[21] Several north–south roads served Sutton Benger village. That leading north to Great Somerford was turnpiked in 1809 and disturnpiked in 1876.[22] Sutton Lane, so called in 1885, led south to Langley Burrell and was on its present course in 1773. Two others fell out of use between 1839 and 1885: one survives as a footpath west of and parallel to Sutton Lane; the other, part of which survives as a farm drive, linked the Great Somerford road and Oak Hill Lane.[23]

A palaeolithic artifact was found south-east of the church,[24] and there may have been a small farmstead between the site of the village and the Avon in the Iron Age and Romano-British period.[25] Sutton was not highly assessed for taxation in 1334, but in 1377 had one of the highest number of taxpayers, 125, in Malmesbury hundred.[26] In the 16th century and earlier 17th assessments were of moderate size for the hundred.[27] The population rose from 420 to 458 between 1801 and 1821 and declined to 336 in 1931. There was a temporary increase to 526 in 1841 because labourers building the G.W.R. line from London to Bristol lodged in the village.[28] After c. 1950 private and council housing estates were built in the village and the population increased. In 1981 the majority of the 854 inhabitants of Sutton Benger parish lived in the village.[29]

The village grew along the Swindon–Chippenham road, called High Street in Sutton Benger. The church was built on the north side, at what may then have been the east end of the village, in the 12th century, and a glebe house was built east of it.[30] In the later 13th century a demesne farmstead was built of stone,[31] presumably at the village's west end. Manor Farm, the demesne farmhouse, has a three-bayed north–south range. The north end was open to the roof and retains a smoke-blackened truss: the south end was of two storeys, and against its east side was a small two-storeyed wing. On the first floor, the east wing contained a small chapel and the 13th-century doorway by which it was entered from the main range survives. The east wall of the chapel retains parts of a blocked traceried window. The main range was altered in the later 17th century and the angle between it and the east wing was built over in the 19th.

Although Sutton Benger was a small parish the village was populous and contained several substantial farmhouses. Its prosperity presumably depended on the fertility of its land and its position on a main road, and an inn was mentioned in 1540.[32] Most of the older buildings are of stone, and the 19th-century estate cottages are of good quality. A malthouse and eight houses in the village were burned down in 1801. Six of the houses were immediately rebuilt.[33] On the north side of High Street at the east end are several cottages, timber-framed with thatched roofs, possibly of the later 16th century or earlier 17th. West of Manor Farm, the Tylney-Long or Wellesley Arms inn was built in the late 18th century: it was an inn in 1808,[34] and the Septennial Friendly Society met there c. 1845.[35] Ross Cottage, a two-storeyed stone house with a lobby entrance opposite the chimney, stands west of the Wellesley Arms. It was built in 1782, probably for Edward Russ.[36] Also on the north side of High Street are two pairs of early 19th-century cottages and, east of Manor Farm, four pairs of estate cottages, one built in 1868, the others in 1889.[37] On the south side are three large farmsteads. Gate Farm is of two storeys with attics. Its main north–south range was built in the earlier 17th century but may incorporate walls of a single-storeyed medieval building. A new staircase was built in the early 18th century, and in the 19th most of the windows were renewed. A wing which extends westwards from the north side of the main range was altered inside in the mid 20th century. The inside of the entire house was being altered and refitted in 1988. Arms Farm was possibly built in the later 18th century. It has a two-storeyed main north–south range with a symmetrical west entrance front. A narrow single-storeyed service wing along the east side was heightened to match the main range. Poplar Farm, incorporating a long east–west range, was apparently built in the 18th century. Also on the south side of High Street, opposite the church, the Bell inn, so called in 1797,[38] was built in the 17th and extended in the 19th and 20th centuries. It ceased to be an inn between 1839 and 1848.[39] In 1958 it was reopened as the Bell House hotel and restaurant.[40]

From the mid 20th century the village expanded south of High Street, a road parallel to which was named Chestnut Road. Ten council houses were built c. 1950 on the site of buildings of Poplar Farm,[41] a new school was built,[42] and small estates of private houses were built from the 1970s. North of High Street a factory was built[43] and a small estate of private houses replaced buildings of Manor Farm. In all parts of the village farm buildings have been converted for residence.

There was settlement along the Great Somerford road, called Seagry Road, in 1773 as far north as the feeder of the Avon which flows east across the parish:[44] a thatched cottage, possibly of the 18th century, survives there. A farmhouse north

[21] Q. Sess. 1736 (W.R.S. xi), p. 32.
[22] V.C.H. Wilts. iv. 271.
[23] Andrews and Dury, Map (W.R.S. viii), pls. 13–14; P.R.O., IR 30/38/254; O.S. Maps 6", Wilts. XIII, XX (1888–9 edns.).
[24] V.C.H. Wilts. i (1), 110; W.A.M. l. 290.
[25] W.A.M. lxxvi. 12.
[26] V.C.H. Wilts. iv. 298, 310.
[27] Taxation Lists (W.R.S. x), 30, 52–3; P.R.O., E 179/197/153; E 179/199/356; E 179/199/399.
[28] V.C.H. Wilts. iv. 320, 358.
[29] Census, 1981; below.
[30] Below, church.
[31] Reg. Malm. ii. 367; V.C.H. Wilts. iii. 230.
[32] P.R.O., SC 6/Hen. VIII/3986, rot. 2d.

[33] W.R.O. 542/10.
[34] Ibid. 1001/5; 2062/13, pp. 88–9.
[35] P.R.O., FS 4/Wilts./55, no. 214.
[36] W.R.O., A 1/345/385; date and initials on ho.
[37] Dates on hos.
[38] W.R.O. 542/10.
[39] Ibid. 969/26, deed, Wellesley to Edwards, 1848; P.R.O., IR 29/38/254; IR 30/38/254.
[40] Wilts. News, 6 Apr. 1962.
[41] O.S. Map 1/25,000, 31/97 (1949 edn.); W.R.O., G 3/516/1 (2).
[42] Below, educ.
[43] Ibid. econ. hist.
[44] Andrews and Dury, Map (W.R.S. viii), pl. 13.

of the stream was built in 1730 and extended in the 19th century,[45] west of the farmhouse a mill stood on the stream near the boundary with Draycot Cerne,[46] Church Farm, on the east side of Seagry Road, was built in the later 17th century, and Hazelwood Farm on the west side was built in the 18th. South of Church Farm large buildings for dealing in food were erected in the earlier 19th century; from c. 1920 they incorporated the Vintage public house, and in 1987 flats.[47] Opposite the Vintage, on the west side of the road, a school was built in the late 19th century.[48]

Cottages stood in a small group on the waste in Sutton Lane in 1773:[49] two survived in 1987. On the east side of the lane at the north end College Green, an estate of 14 bungalows for old people, was built c. 1960.[50] At the south end New House or Sutton Lane Farm, on a double-pile plan, was built shortly before 1773.[51]

North of Sutton Benger village Harding's, New, or Heath Farm, built between 1773 and 1808,[52] is a small house on a double-pile plan with a short east wing added in the 19th century. A large barn, possibly contemporary with the house, stands west of it.

MANOR. Sutton, mentioned in Malmesbury abbey's copy of a charter from King Ethelwulf in 854,[53] is likely to have been owned by the abbey long before the Conquest. The abbey later claimed that Edward the Confessor confirmed Sutton to it.[54] Sutton may have been part of the abbey's large estate called Brokenborough in 1086[55] but was later a separate estate[56] and belonged to the abbey until the Dissolution.[57]

In 1575 the Crown sold the manor of *SUTTON BENGER* to John Dudley and John Ayscough.[58] Sir Robert Long (d. 1581) owned it in 1576, and from then to 1920 it descended with Draycot Cerne manor. It passed to Sir Robert's son Sir Walter Long[59] (d. 1610), to Sir Walter's son Sir Walter[60] (d. 1637), and to that Sir Walter's son Sir James Long, Bt.[61] From Sir James (d. 1692) it passed to his grandsons Sir Robert Long, Bt. (d. 1692), Sir Giles Long, Bt. (d. 1697), and Sir James Long, Bt. (d. 1729).[62] The manor descended to Sir Robert Long, Bt. (d. 1767),[63] Sir James Long,[64] from 1784 Tylney-Long, Bt. (d. 1794), and Sir James Tylney-Long, Bt. (d. 1805).[65] It passed to the last Sir James's sister Catherine (d. 1825), wife

of William Pole-Tylney-Long-Wellesley, earl of Mornington. She was succeeded by her son William, earl of Mornington (d. 1863), who devised it to his cousin Henry Wellesley, Earl Cowley (d. 1884), and the manor passed to William, Earl Cowley (d. 1895), Henry, Earl Cowley (d. 1919), and Christian, Earl Cowley.[66] The manor was broken up in 1920 and from then to the 1980s was in about eight separately owned farms.[67]

The great tithes of Sutton Benger apparently belonged to Malmesbury abbey until 1265. Thereafter the *RECTORY* estate, a house, 1 yardland, and all the tithes arising from the parish, belonged to the dean and chapter of Salisbury. Probably in 1342 the land and in 1474 the small tithes were assigned to the vicarage.[68] The great tithes still belonged to the dean and chapter in 1839 when they were valued at £185 and commuted.[69]

ECONOMIC HISTORY. In 1086 and 1210 Sutton is likely to have been assessed as part of Malmesbury abbey's estate called Brokenborough.[70] In the Middle Ages there was open field land at Sutton[71] and sheep-and-corn husbandry prevailed.[72] A new demesne farmstead was built between 1260 and 1296.[73] Five customary tenants, including a miller, each held 1 yardland in 1283–4 and 36 others held smaller amounts of land.[74] There was a common meadow, in which the tenants' shares were apportioned by lot,[75] beside the Avon south of the main road.[76] From 1257 Sutton tenants were entitled, from 25 August to 2 February, to pasture rights in the detached part of Draycot Cerne south of the common meadow, and in return each Sutton team, at three days notice, ploughed ½ a. in the fields of Draycot Cerne.[77] Some customary tenants of Sutton Benger were obliged to mow in the demesne meadows of Brokenborough.[78]

In 1514 the open fields were South, Middle, and North, and in the later 16th century Barrow was a fourth open field. Between 1508 and 1539 an abbot of Malmesbury allowed Sir Henry Long to enclose land in the north-west part of Sutton Benger in Draycot park.[79] The demesne farm and most of the copyholds contained inclosed pasture in the 16th century,[80] and in 1656 the number of animals pastured on each lot in the common meadow was reduced by agreement from six to four.[81] The demesne farm, c. 230 a., was held by

[45] Date on ho., with initials S/DH.
[46] Below, econ. hist.
[47] Ibid.; inf. from Mrs. W. Mills, 36 High Street.
[48] Below, educ.
[49] *Andrews and Dury, Map* (W.R.S. viii), pl. 14.
[50] O.S. Map 1/25,000, ST 97 (1959 edn.); W.R.O., G 3/516/2 (2).
[51] *Andrews and Dury, Map* (W.R.S. viii), pl. 14.
[52] Ibid. pl. 13; W.R.O. 1001/5; 2062/13, pp. 60–1; O.S. Map 6″, Wilts. XIII (1888 edn.).
[53] *Reg. Malm.* i. 297–9; Finberg, *Early Wessex Chart.* pp. 200–1; *V.C.H. Wilts.* ii, p. 89.
[54] Finberg, *Early Wessex Chart.* p. 106; *V.C.H. Wilts.* ii, pp. 88–9.
[55] Above, Brokenborough, manor.
[56] *Bk. of Fees*, ii. 743.
[57] *Valor Eccl.* (Rec. Com.), ii. 119.
[58] *Cal. Pat.* 1572–5, p. 450.
[59] Ibid. 1575–8, p. 139; *Hist. Parl., Commons, 1509–58*, ii. 546; P.R.O., C 142/197, no. 95; above, Draycot Cerne, manor.
[60] P.R.O., C 142/334, no. 65.

[61] *Wilts. Inq. p.m.* 1625–49 (Index Libr.), 237–41.
[62] P.R.O., CP 43/479, rot. 30.
[63] Ibid. CP 43/605, rot. 297.
[64] Ibid. CP 43/769, rot. 366.
[65] W.R.O., A 1/345/385.
[66] Ibid. 1712/27; ibid. Inland Revenue, val. reg. 17; P.R.O., IR 29/38/254.
[67] W.R.O. 1043/6, pp. 46–51, 98; local inf.
[68] Below, church.   [69] P.R.O., IR 29/38/254.
[70] Above, Brokenborough, manor, econ. hist.
[71] B.L. Add. MS. 15667, ff. 76–77v.
[72] *Inq. Non.* (Rec. Com.), 167.
[73] *Reg. Malm.* ii. 367; *V.C.H. Wilts.* iii. 230.
[74] *Reg. Malm.* i. 170–2.
[75] P.R.O., SC 6/Hen. VIII/3986, rot. 102d.
[76] W.R.O. 1001/5.
[77] B.L. Add. MS. 15667, f. 76 and v.
[78] Longleat Mun. 10462.
[79] Ibid.; P.R.O., E 310/26/156, f. 59B.
[80] Longleat Mun. 10462.
[81] W.R.O. 473/304, agreement, 1656.

lease in the earlier 16th century. In 1540–1 there were 25 customary tenants holding 31 yardlands. The two largest holdings were of 4 and 3 yardlands, 5 were of 2 yardlands, 3 of 1½ yardland, 8 of 1 yardland, and 3 of ½ yardland.[82] In 1622 the holdings were roughly of the same size and number, and there were 32 holding cottages or small plots of land.[83] Of the 45 customary tenants in 1647, only 21 lived in Sutton Benger.[84]

Although a 12-a. inclosure was made in South field c. 1667,[85] common arable husbandry persisted until the open fields were inclosed by agreement in 1729.[86] The fields lay south-east and north-west of the village.[87] By 1731 the demesne had been divided into Manor farm, 80 a. in 1739, and two other farms, each c. 50 a. in 1731. There were 13 copyholds, each of between 20 a. and 50 a., and many smaller holdings in 1731.[88] Two new farms were created with buildings outside the village, New House later Sutton Lane farm in the south shortly before 1773, and New later Harding's farm in the north between 1773 and 1808.[89] In 1808 the largest farms were Poplar, 119 a., Manor, 116 a., Gate, 108 a., Arms, 84 a., Church, 47 a., Harding's, 87 a., and Sutton Lane, 58 a. The first four had farmsteads in High Street. In 1808 there were 10 other farms, each of 50 a. or less. Between 1808 and 1839 the extensive common meadows beside the Avon were inclosed and apportioned among the larger farms. In 1839 there were 405 a. of arable and 610 a. of grassland in the parish. During the 19th century most of the smaller farms were added to larger ones. In 1839 and 1872 Gate farm and Arms farm were worked together, and in 1839 Church and Harding's made up a 210-a. farm. Harding's was worked with Manor as a 267-a. farm in 1872, and Church farm was c. 122 a. in 1851 and 1872.[90] Between 1839 and 1863 the lord of the manor had in hand 97 a., of which some was in Draycot park,[91] and in 1872 c. 80 a. of Manor and Harding's farms and 6 a. of Church farm were added to the park.[92]

In the later 19th century the parish was a quarter arable and three quarters grassland. Most land was under grass in the earlier 20th century, and in 1936 only 98 a. were arable. Grain was grown on three quarters of the arable and fodder crops on the remainder. Between 1876 and 1936 grasses were grown in rotation on less than 100 a., and half the permanent grassland was mown. Sheep farming, with flocks averaging 400 in the parish, continued until c. 1880, but thereafter few sheep were kept. Average herds of c. 120 pigs were kept 1867–1936. Most farms had a dairy: c. 160 cows were kept in the parish in the later 19th century, c. 300 in the earlier 20th.[93]

Manor and Poplar farms were merged c. 1929,[94] and in 1987 the land, c. 242 a., was entirely arable.[95] Of the farms with farmsteads south of the Swindon–Chippenham road, Sutton Lane, including c. 140 a. in Sutton Benger, was a mixed farm in 1987,[96] Gate, c. 151 a., was a pasture farm on which cattle were reared for beef,[97] and Arms, c. 37 a., was a dairy farm.[98] Hazelwood farm, formed in the period 1923–7,[99] and enlarged c. 1978 when Church farm was broken up, was a dairy and pig farm in 1987.[1] Harding's farm, c. 90 a., supported a herd of Jersey cows in 1987,[2] and the c. 250 a. of North Draycot Park farm, formed c. 1971 and worked from buildings on land formerly in Draycot Cerne parish, were pasture on which sheep were kept and cattle were raised for beef.[3] Lake farm, also based in what was Draycot Cerne parish, in 1987 included c. 90 a. north of Sutton Benger village.[4]

There were 50–60 a. of woods, including Ell wood, c. 30 a., and Oak Hill wood, c. 20 a., in the north-west corner of the parish in the earlier 19th century.[5] Those two woods remained in 1987.

There was a fuller in the parish in 1611,[6] and clothworkers, among whom were Zephaniah Fry (d. 1724) and his son Zephaniah (d. 1716), in the later 17th century and the 18th.[7] Although most men in Sutton Benger in 1831 were agricultural labourers, 33 were tradesmen or artisans, more than usual in a small rural parish, and 5, including a surgeon, were professional men.[8] From 1779 or earlier Thomas Riley (d. 1801) and his wife Mary (d. 1809) were bakers and maltsters,[9] and in 1839 there was a malthouse east of Manor Farm on the north side of High Street. Between 1839 and c. 1911 members of the Hull family were in business in Seagry Road as grocers, spirit merchants, cheese factors, and bacon curers.[10] In 1920 Alfred Britton & Co., bakers, occupied the Hulls' premises, which were bought in 1920 by Wadworth & Co. and afterwards incorporated a public house.[11]

In 1822 three gravel pits lay north of the church,[12] c. 1948 Sheppard & Brown Ltd. extracted gravel from land between the church and

[82] P.R.O., SC 6/Hen. VIII/3986, rott. 102–3.
[83] Ibid. C 112/53/1, ct. of survey.
[84] Ibid. C 112/53/1, ct. roll.
[85] Ibid. C 112/53/1, deed, Long to Chaworth, 1667.
[86] W.R.O., D 1/24/197/4.
[87] P.R.O., IR 29/38/254; IR 30/38/254.
[88] W.R.O. 970/1, survey, 1731; 1081/118, assignment, Gotley to Atkins, 1739.
[89] Ibid. 1001/5; 2062/13, pp. 60–1, 94–7; *Andrews and Dury, Map* (W.R.S. viii), pl. 13; above, introduction.
[90] W.R.O. 1001/5; 2062/13, pp. 60–82, 84–9, 94–9, 104–13; 2062/14, ff. 5–6; 2062/15; P.R.O., IR 29/38/254; IR 30/38/254.
[91] P.R.O., IR 29/38/254; IR 30/38/254; W.R.O. 1712/27.
[92] W.R.O. 2062/15.
[93] P.R.O., IR 18/11163; ibid. MAF 68/151, sheet 2; MAF 68/493, sheet 5; MAF 68/1063, sheet 4; MAF 68/1633, sheet 5; MAF 68/2203, sheet 13; MAF 68/2773, sheet 4; MAF 68/3319, sheet 4; MAF 68/3814, no. 46.
[94] *Kelly's Dir. Wilts.* (1931); Ch. Com. file, N 5729.
[95] Inf. from Mrs. M. G. Baker, Hatt Farm, Old Jockey, Box.

[96] Inf. from Mr. D. O. Cooper, Sutton Lane Farm.
[97] Inf. from Mr. O. F. Titcomb, Gate Farm.
[98] Inf. from Mr. G. H. Carter, Arms Farm.
[99] *Kelly's Dir. Wilts.* (1923 and later edns.).
[1] Inf. from Mrs. W. Mills, 36 High Street; Mr. D. E. Isaac, Church Farm.
[2] Inf. from Lt.-Col. D. G. Williams, Harding's Farm.
[3] Inf. from Mr. F. B. Collins, N. Draycot Park Farm.
[4] Inf. from Mr. R. Greenhill, Lake Farm.
[5] W.R.O. 1001/5; 2062/13, p. 58; P.R.O., IR 29/38/254; IR 30/38/254.
[6] P.R.O., STAC 8/302/11.
[7] *W.N. & Q.* ii. 294, 519; vi. 226; *Wilts. Apprentices* (W.R.S. xvii), p. 140; W.R.O. 542/10.
[8] *Census*, 1831; W.R.O. 1093/20.
[9] *W.N. & Q.* vii. 9; W.R.O. 970/2.
[10] *Kelly's Dir. Wilts.* (1848 and later edns.); P.R.O., IR 29/38/254; IR 30/38/254.
[11] W.R.O. 1043/6, p. 61; ibid. G 3/516/1 (2); G 3/516/2 (2).
[12] Ibid. D 24/18, certificate, 1822.

the Avon,[13] and 1956–64 the Pyramid Sand & Gravel Co. worked pits in Sutton Benger.[14] A factory in which broiler hens were prepared for cooking was opened on the north side of High Street in 1958 by Western Poultry Packers. In 1987 the factory, owned by Buxted Chicken Ltd., prepared weekly c. 400,000 chickens reared in local broiler houses, including some beside Sutton Lane. Of the 535 employees at the factory only six lived in the parish.[15]

A mill stood in Sutton Benger c. 1283,[16] but not in the later 16th century.[17] The medieval mill may have been on the site of that which stood in 1773[18] and 1839 near the boundary with Draycot Cerne at the east end of the lake of Draycot House.[19] It was demolished before 1885.[20]

LOCAL GOVERNMENT. The abbot of Malmesbury held view of frankpledge in Sutton Benger.[21] Leet jurisdiction passed with the manor to Sir Robert Long (d. 1581).[22] Records of courts, called views of frankpledge and courts of the manor or courts baron, are extant for 1561–2, 1647–52, 1756, and 1765–1872. Leet and manorial business are undifferentiated in them. In the 16th and 17th centuries leet business included the payment of cert money, the appointment of a tithingman, and orders to repair hedges and ditches and to clean watercourses. Throughout the period manorial business included transfers of copyholds, the appointment of a hayward, and the repair of the pound. In 1801 the court ordered the rebuilding of the houses which were burnt down. The courts were held twice yearly until 1771 and thereafter once yearly in autumn and at other times when copyhold business required it.[23] Early 19th-century courts, at which little business was done, were marked, like those held for Draycot Cerne manor, by a dinner, probably at Sutton Benger, given by the lord for the tenants.[24]

At vestries held from 1745 or earlier parish officers were appointed and poor and highway rates were set. From the mid 18th century expenditure on the poor rose steadily[25] and in the early 19th sharply. It was claimed in 1801 that increased expenditure impoverished householders who were required to pay higher rates and discouraged the poor from helping themselves.[26] In 1802–3 £267 was spent on relieving 57 people continuously and 20 occasionally. The parish apparently had a small workhouse 1808–34: it had six inmates in 1812–13

when the parish also provided continuous relief for 29 and occasional relief for seven. The amount spent each year and the numbers relieved decreased 1813–15. Of the average of 37 relieved in 1814–15, 12 received occasional relief.[27] The annual sums 1816–34 represented average expenditure on the poor in Malmesbury hundred.[28] Sutton Benger was included in Chippenham poor-law union in 1835.[29] It became part of North Wiltshire district in 1974.[30]

CHURCH. A church which stood in Sutton Benger in the 12th century belonged to Malmesbury abbey and at least part of its revenues was assigned to the sacrist. In 1118 it was among Malmesbury properties taken by Roger, bishop of Salisbury. Henry I confirmed the church to the dean and chapter of Salisbury but in 1139 King Stephen may have restored it to the abbey.[31] It was disputed between the abbey, which called it a chapel and possibly considered it dependent on the abbey, and the dean and chapter, who called it a church and possibly appointed a rector, in the later 12th century and the 13th.[32] In a compromise the abbey apparently took the great tithes, appointed a rector from among the members of Salisbury chapter, and paid a pension of £13 6s. 8d. to the archdeacon of Wiltshire. It is not clear whether the abbey or the rector arranged for the church to be served.[33] The treasurer of the cathedral, Robert de Cardeville (d. 1264), was rector,[34] as, after him, was the chancellor, Ralph of Heigham. In 1265 Ralph resigned, Malmesbury abbey transferred the great tithes to the dean and chapter, the pension was extinguished, and a vicarage in the gift of the bishop of Salisbury was ordained.[35] Vicars served the church until in 1904 the benefice again became a rectory. In 1966 the benefices of Sutton Benger, Christian Malford, and Tytherton Kellaways were united.[36]

The bishop of Salisbury collated vicars from 1265 until 1696, except in 1416 when, possibly by grant of a turn, John Rober presented.[37] In 1719 the bishop transferred the advowson to the dean and chapter of Salisbury,[38] who became entitled to the first and fourth of five turns of presentation to the united benefice in 1966.[39]

From 1265 to 1474 or earlier the dean and chapter leased all the tithes of the parish to the vicar for £20 a year, possibly thereby augmenting the vicarage.[40] In 1535 the vicarage was worth £6,[41]

13 W.R.O., G 3/760/1376.
14 Ibid. G 3/516/1 (2); G 3/516/2 (2).
15 Inf. from Personnel Manager, Buxted Chicken Ltd.
16 Reg. Malm. i. 170–2.   17 Longleat Mun. 10462.
18 Andrews and Dury, Map (W.R.S. viii), pl. 13.
19 P.R.O., IR 29/38/254; IR 30/38/254.
20 O.S. Map 6", Wilts. XX (1889 edn.).
21 P.R.O., SC 6/Hen. VIII/3986, rot. 103.
22 Ibid. CP 25(2)/240/20 Eliz. I Hil.
23 Ibid. C 112/53/1, ct. rolls; ibid. SC 2/209/16, rott. 3–4d.; B.L. Eg. Ch. 8840; W.R.O. 542/10; 2062/30; above, introduction.
24 P.R.O., C 108/112/1, acct. bk. 1827–34.
25 W.R.O. 1712/18; 1712/28.
26 P.R.O., HO 67/23/120.
27 Poor Law Abstract, 1804, 566–7; 1818; 498–9; P.R.O., C 108/112/1, acct. bk. 1827–34; W.R.O. 1001/5; 2062/13, p. 100.
28 Poor Rate Returns, 1816–21, 189; 1822–4, 288; 1825–9, 219; 1830–4, 213.

29 Poor Law Com. 2nd Rep. App. D, 558.
30 O.S. Map 1/100,000, admin. areas, Wilts. (1974 edn.).
31 V.C.H. Wilts. iii. 216; Reg. Malm. ii. 232–4.
32 Reg. Malm. i. 348–52, 355–66; Reg. St. Osmund (Rolls Ser.), i. 204–6.
33 Reg. Malm. i. 411–12; ii. 232–4; W.R.O., D 24/18, Sutton Benger vicarage papers.
34 Sar. Chart. and Doc. (Rolls Ser.), 342–6, corrected by Ann. Winton. (Rolls Ser.), p. 102.
35 W. H. Jones, Fasti Eccl. Sar. 336; D. & C. Sar. Mun., press II, box 3, deed, abbot of Malmesbury to bishop of Salisbury, 1265; W.R.O., D 24/18, Sutton Benger vicarage papers.
36 Ch. Com. file 26699/1; inf. from Ch. Com.
37 Phillipps, Wilts. Inst. (index in W.A.M. xxviii. 231); Reg. Hallum (Cant. & York Soc.), p. 74; W.R.O., D 24/18, Sutton Benger vicarage papers.
38 W.R.O. 1712/17.   39 Inf. from Ch. Com.
40 W.R.O., D 1/24/197/3–4; D 24/18, Sutton Benger vicarage papers.
41 Valor Eccl. (Rec. Com.), ii. 135.

in 1651 £30.[42] The vicar was assigned £9 rent from the great tithes ,c. 1654.[43] In 1718 the dean and chapter of Salisbury gave £100, Edward Colston £100, and Queen Anne's Bounty £200 to augment the vicarage,[44] and from 1719 the dean and chapter again leased the great tithes to the vicar.[45] Its net yearly income of £285 c. 1830 made the vicarage one of the richer livings in Malmesbury deanery.[46]

constructed thatched hovel, was rebuilt.[57] New principal rooms to the west and a conservatory to the south were added c. 1841[58] in Gothic style. The house was sold c. 1969.[59]

A rent of 1s. 8d. from land in Seagry was given for a light in the church, and rents of 1s. from Sutton Benger and of 10d. from Langley Burrell were given for the rood light;[60] 1 a. was given for

ALL SAINTS' CHURCH

The rent charge for which the great tithes had been commuted was assigned to the vicar in 1904.[47]

In 1474 or earlier the dean and chapter of Salisbury assigned the small tithes to the vicarage.[48] In 1839 they were valued at £118 and commuted.[49]

The dean and chapter assigned the land of the rectory estate, 1 yardland, to the vicar, probably in 1342.[50] The vicar held the land, 18 a. in 1839,[51] until 1922 when 15 a. were sold.[52] Windmill Hill farm, 12 a. in Brinkworth, was bought for the vicar in 1728[53] and was sold in 1919.[54]

A vicarage house was mentioned from the later 16th century.[55] It needed repairs in 1683.[56] About 1783 the vicar's house, described as an ill-

church repairs, presumably also before the Reformation.[61] The 1 a. was leased for £2 yearly in 1837 and 1929,[62] and was held for the church in 1987.[63]

A curate apparently served the church in 1545,[64] and in 1553 no quarterly sermon was preached and the parish lacked Erasmus's *Paraphrases*.[65] In 1662 the vicar lacked a surplice and several parishioners refused contributions towards the purchase of new books and ornaments.[66] William Noble, vicar 1637–40,[67] was a composer of epitaphs.[68] Several later vicars were pluralists: they included John Stumpe, vicar from 1689 to c. 1696 and rector of Foxley,[69] and William Atkinson, vicar 1744–65 and rector of Fisherton Anger 1754–8 and

[42] *W.A.M.* xli. 13. [43] Ibid. xix. 210.
[44] C. Hodgson, *Queen Anne's Bounty* (1864), pp. cxxxii, cccxxxvi.
[45] W.R.O. 1712/17.
[46] *Rep. Com. Eccl. Revenues*, 848–9.
[47] Ch. Com. file 26699/1.
[48] W.R.O., D 1/24/197/3–4; D 24/18, Sutton Benger vicarage papers.
[49] P.R.O., IR 29/38/254.
[50] *Inq. Non.* (Rec. Com.), 167; *Hemingby's Reg.* (W.R.S. xviii), p. 112.
[51] P.R.O., IR 29/38/254; IR 30/38/254.
[52] Ch. Com., copy deeds, cccxcviii, no. 40151.
[53] Ibid. deed, Stratton to Thompson, 1728.
[54] W.R.O. 1712/21.
[55] Ibid. D 1/24/197/1; D 1/24/197/4; D 24/18, Sutton Benger vicarage papers.

[56] Ibid. D 1/54/10/1, no. 3.
[57] Ibid. D 1/24/197/4.
[58] Inf. from Mr. and Mrs. J. C. Timms, the Old Rectory.
[59] Ch. Com. file, NB 5/55.
[60] P.R.O., E 301/58, no. 129.
[61] Ibid. STAC 8/302/11; Aubrey, *Topog. Coll.* ed. Jackson, 292.
[62] W.R.O. 1712/21.
[63] Inf. from the rector, Christian Malford.
[64] *Taxation Lists* (W.R.S. x), 30.
[65] W.R.O., D 1/43/1, f. 134v.
[66] Ibid. D 1/54/1/1, no. 41.
[67] *Subscription Bk. 1620–40* (W.R.S. xxxii), pp. 74, 86.
[68] J. Stratford, *Wilts. and its Worthies*, 30.
[69] Phillipps, *Wilts. Inst.* ii. 36, 44, 60; *Alum. Oxon. 1500–1714*, iv. 1440; P.R.O., E 134/4 Wm. & Mary East./15; above, Foxley, church.

vicar of Lacock by 1765.[70] Charles Davies, vicar 1774–1810, was a fellow of Pembroke College, Oxford, and c. 1783 lived in Sutton Benger only during the university vacations and at Whitsuntide. A curate served the church 1743–5. A curate in 1783 also served the church of Little Somerford, where he lived. A service was held at Sutton Benger on Sunday afternoons and on Christmas day and Good Friday. Davies attributed the small number, c. 12, who received the sacrament, administered at Christmas, Easter, Whitsun, and Michaelmas, to his parishioners' fear of committing themselves to lead better lives.[71] Christopher Lipscomb, vicar 1818–24, was a fellow of New College, Oxford, and from 1824 bishop of Jamaica. His successor, E. C. Ogle, vicar 1824–36, was a canon of Salisbury from 1828[72] but lived in Sutton Benger. In 1832 he held two Sunday services, at one of which he preached.[73] G. T. Marsh, vicar 1836–62, was also rector of Foxley.[74] On Census Sunday in 1851 a congregation of 150 attended the morning service and one of 220 the afternoon service.[75] Richard Dawson, vicar 1862–1903, was chaplain of Chippenham union workhouse from 1886. The benefice was held in plurality with the rectory of Tytherton Kellaways 1920–66.[76]

The church of *ALL SAINTS*, so called in 1763,[77] is built of stone rubble with ashlar dressings. It comprises a chancel, a nave with south aisle and porch, and a west tower.[78] Some masonry in the nave may survive from the 12th century.[79] The chancel, in which two late 13th-century windows survive, was otherwise rebuilt c. 1345.[80] The south aisle, also built c. 1345, was separated from the nave by a five-bayed arcade with round columns, and the western respond forms a bracket on which was carved a male head emerging from foliage. The east end of the aisle is a chapel, and its east window contains, in the lower part of the central light, a canopied niche, on the exterior of which the entire window was formerly depicted in miniature.[81] In the 15th century the porch was rebuilt in ashlar with, on the east and west, three pairs of two-light openings separated by buttresses. Also in the 15th century the nave was shortened and widened, and the tower, with an openwork spirelet, was built. In 1849[82] the piers and arches of the aisle were renewed in a style earlier than that of c. 1345, and many original features of both nave and chancel were altered, during a restoration of the church by J. H. Hakewill.[83] An altar hanging, depicting saints and prophets and made from the orphreys of a pair of tunicles embroidered in England in the late 15th century, is preserved in the church.[84]

In 1553 the king's commissioners left a chalice of 10 oz. and took 2 oz. of plate.[85] The parish held a plate and a chalice with cover in 1783.[86] They were replaced by a chalice, paten, almsdish, and flagon, all hallmarked for 1848,[87] which, except for the almsdish, the parish held in 1987.[88] There was a ring of four bells in 1553. Of the five bells in the tower in 1987 the treble was cast by Nathaniel Boulter in 1638, the second in Bristol c. 1350, the third by Richard Purdue in 1631, the fourth by Llewellins & James of Bristol in 1902, and the tenor by Abraham Rudhall in 1706.[89] Registrations of baptisms are complete from 1653, of marriages and burials from 1654.[90]

NONCONFORMITY. A Quaker group in Sutton Benger by 1667[91] included Nathaniel Colman in 1669.[92] He was one of the separatists who declined to attend meetings or to remove their hats during prayer unless they felt divinely inspired to do so.[93] There were 25 nonconformists in the parish in 1676.[94] Colman and his son Nathaniel were among 19 Quakers in Sutton Benger in 1683 and 13 in 1689.[95] Another Quaker, Zephaniah Fry (d. 1724), lived in the parish but attended the Kington Langley meeting.[96] The houses in Sutton Benger of Zephaniah's son John (d. 1775) and William Price were certified for meetings in 1727.[97] John's son Joseph (d. 1787), also a Quaker, founded the chocolate-making firm of J. Fry & Co. He maintained a connexion with Sutton Benger, where he dated the preface of his *Select Poems* published in 1774.[98] Seven Quakers lived in Sutton Benger in 1783.[99]

In 1783 people from Sutton Benger attended a Congregationalist meeting in Christian Malford.[1] The group may have met in Sutton Benger in 1831.[2] It was perhaps for them, or for Wesleyan Methodists, that houses in the parish were certified in 1837 and 1839.[3] The Wesleyans built a chapel in Sutton Benger in 1850 and in 1850–1 an average congregation of 90 attended evening services in it.[4] No later record of it has been found.

EDUCATION. There was a school for girls in Sutton Benger in 1783.[5] In 1808 a school was attended by 24 pupils, of whom 15 were paid for

[70] Phillipps, *Wilts. Inst.* ii. 71, 75, 78, 82.
[71] *Vis. Queries, 1783* (W.R.S. xxvii), pp. 197, 208–9; *V.C.H. Wilts.* iii. 51; P.R.O., IND 17013, f. 340; ibid. PROB 11/1521, f. 71 and v.; W.R.O., bishop's transcripts, bdle. 2.
[72] *Alum. Oxon. 1715–1886*, iii. 855, 1037.
[73] Ch. Com. file, NB 5/55.
[74] *Alum. Oxon. 1715–1886*, iii. 916.
[75] P.R.O., HO 129/253/4/6/7.
[76] *Crockford* (1896 and later edns.); Bristol R.O., EP/A/7/6.
[77] J. Ecton, *Thesaurus* (1763), 888.
[78] Cf. J. Buckler, watercolours in W.A.S. Libr., vol. vi. 31; viii. 75.
[79] *W.A.M.* xix. 144–5.
[80] *Hemingby's Reg.* (W.R.S. xviii), pp. 121–2.
[81] *W.A.M.* xlvii. 595.
[82] P.R.O., HO 129/253/4/6/7; dated plan in church.
[83] Pevsner, *Wilts.* (2nd edn.), 502.
[84] *Proc. Soc. Antiq.* [2nd ser.], xvii. 239–42.
[85] Nightingale, *Wilts. Plate*, 224.
[86] W.R.O., D 1/24/197/4.

[87] Nightingale, *Wilts. Plate*, 224.
[88] Inf. from the rector.
[89] Ibid.; Walters, *Wilts. Bells*, 209–11, 289.
[90] W.R.O. 1712/1–2; 1712/4; bishop's transcripts for 1605–9, 1620–3, 1632–3, 1635–6 are ibid.
[91] *Cal. S.P. Dom.* 1666–7, 466.
[92] G. L. Turner, *Orig. Rec.* ii. 1077.
[93] N. Penney, *Jnl. of Geo. Fox*, ii. 446; *W.N. & Q.* iv. 274–5.
[94] *Compton Census*, ed. Whiteman, 129.
[95] W.R.O., D 1/54/10/1, no. 3; D 1/54/12/1, Sutton Benger.
[96] *W.N. & Q.* ii. 181; vi. 226.
[97] Ibid. iv. 259; vi. 319; *Meeting Ho. Certs.* (W.R.S. xl), p. 22.
[98] *D.N.B.*
[99] *Vis. Queries, 1783* (W.R.S. xxvii), p. 208.
[1] Ibid.; *V.C.H. Wilts.* iii. 131.
[2] Lewis, *Topog. Dict. Eng.* (1831), iv. 250.
[3] *Meeting Ho. Certs.* (W.R.S. xl), pp. 144–5, 148.
[4] P.R.O., HO 129/253/4/6/8.
[5] *Vis. Queries, 1783* (W.R.S. xxvii), p. 209.

by Catherine, Lady Tylney-Long (d. 1823).[6] A school had *c.* 90 children in 1818.[7] There were four schools in 1833. One was for 12 children: the others, begun in 1823, 1828, and 1829, were attended by 20 girls, 25 boys, and 56 boys and girls respectively.[8] One of the four was the National school in which 52 children were taught in 1846–7. A total of 32 children were then taught in the other three.[9] Only the National school survived in 1858 and a single teacher had 40–50 pupils in it.[10] In 1876 a master taught 51 children in a

new building of that year west of Seagry Road.[11] Average attendance fluctuated from 64 in 1906–7 to 41 in 1937–8,[12] and was *c.* 60 in 1964.[13] In 1966 the pupils were transferred to new buildings in Chestnut Road and six teachers taught 89 children there in 1987.[14] Harding's Farm was a preparatory school for boys in the 1930s.[15]

CHARITY FOR THE POOR. None known.

WESTPORT

WESTPORT was a separate settlement linked to Malmesbury by a short stretch of road along a narrow ridge and, as its name implies, it lay outside the west gate of Malmesbury.[16] It had a church in the late Saxon period, and later both Brokenborough and Charlton churches were dependent on Westport church.[17] Nearly all the land around the town of Malmesbury belonged to Malmesbury abbey, possibly from soon after its foundation in the 7th century and, perhaps before the Conquest when St. Paul's church in Malmesbury may have been standing,[18] the abbey assigned some of the land to Westport church as a parish. Apart from Brokenborough and Charlton, the parish had an irregular shape almost like a figure 8 with the church and main settlement in the centre: it comprised land north, west, and south-west of the town and included the hamlets or farmsteads called Filands and Thornhill and possibly a hamlet called Walcot.[19] As a suburb of Malmesbury, part of the settlement called Westport was within the boundary of Malmesbury borough. The land owned by the borough, in the early 17th century called King's Heath, was added to Westport parish and extended the parish south-westwards: most of King's Heath, the south-west part, was later called Malmesbury common.[20] In 1840 the parish was 2,036 a. (824 ha.). For reasons suggested elsewhere much of the parish boundary was irregular and six small areas, mainly embraced by Malmesbury and Brokenborough parishes, were detached.[21] The Westport parish boundary followed a tributary of the Sherston branch of the Bristol Avon south of Malmesbury, both the Sherston Avon and the Tetbury branch of the Avon west of Malmesbury, and short stretches of road in several places. For a short distance the boundary

was the town wall of Malmesbury. For most of its length, however, the parish boundary was not marked by prominent features, and to the west that with Brokenborough through Hyam park was defined only in 1838.[22]

Parts of Malmesbury common, a total of 16 a. belonging to the lord of Foxley manor and the rector of Foxley, were claimed by both Westport and Foxley *c.* 1840[23] and were in Foxley in 1885. Between 1840 and 1884 *c.* 13 a. in various fields north and north-west of the town were transferred from Westport to Brokenborough. Between 1882 and 1884 one of the detached areas of Westport was transferred to Brokenborough and five were transferred to Malmesbury, small exchanges were made between Westport and Malmesbury, and a detached part of Bremilham parish, 8 a. near the town, was transferred to Westport.[24] Most of the settlement was assigned to Malmesbury urban sanitary district when it was created in 1872 and was included in Malmesbury municipal borough in 1886.[25] The remainder of the parish, 1,961 a. (794 ha.), was added to St. Paul Malmesbury Without parish in 1896. In 1894 the Westport part of the municipal borough became the civil parish of Westport St. Mary Within. It absorbed the civil parish of Brokenborough Within in 1897 and thereafter measured 91 a. (37 ha.).[26] In 1934 it was merged with the other civil parishes of the borough to form a new Malmesbury parish. Lands west and north of the town and formerly in Westport parish were added to Malmesbury in 1984.[27]

Kellaways Clay outcrops over most of the former parish, especially in the south-west where Malmesbury common is flat and mostly below 80 m. Higher land lies at 91 m. in the north-east, where two areas of Oxford Clay outcrop, and in

[6] G.E.C. *Baronetage*, iii. 259; Lambeth Palace Libr., MS. 1732.
[7] *Educ. of Poor Digest*, 1038.
[8] *Educ. Enq. Abstract*, 1048.
[9] Nat. Soc. *Inquiry, 1846–7*, Wilts. 10–11.
[10] *Acct. of Wilts. Schs.* 43.
[11] P.R.O., ED 7/131, no. 267.
[12] Bd. of Educ., *List 21, 1908–9* (H.M.S.O.), 506; *1938*, 425.
[13] Wilts. Cuttings, xxii. 241.
[14] Inf. from Chief Educ. Officer, Co. Hall, Trowbridge; the headmaster, Sutton Benger Sch.
[15] *Kelly's Dir. Wilts.* (1935).
[16] This article was written in 1989. Maps used include O.S. Maps 1/50,000, sheet 173 (1974 edn.); 1/25,000, ST 98 (1959

edn.); 6″, Wilts. VIII, XIII (1888–9 and later edns.).
[17] Below, church.
[18] Above, Malmesbury, introduction, manors.
[19] W.R.O., tithe award; above, Malmesbury, introduction.
[20] Below, manors; econ. hist.
[21] W.R.O., tithe award; above, Malmesbury, introduction.
[22] W.R.O. 88/10/14.
[23] Ibid. tithe award; Foxley tithe award.
[24] Ibid. tithe award; *Census*, 1891; O.S. Maps 6″, Wilts. VIII, XIII (1888–9 edns.).
[25] Above, Malmesbury, introduction.
[26] *Census*, 1891; 1901.
[27] Above, Malmesbury, introduction; inf. from Chief Assistant (Environment), Dept. of Planning and Highways, Co. Hall, Trowbridge.

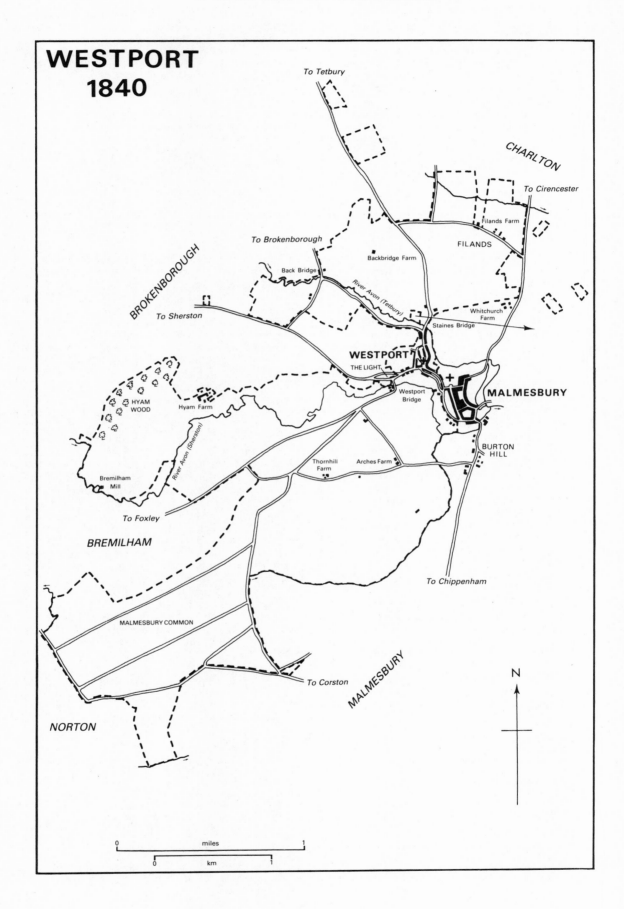

WESTPORT
1840

the west. Much of those areas of the parish was for long pasture. Both branches of the Avon and the south-east boundary stream have exposed terraces of Cornbrash and strips of clay of the Forest Marble: the Cornbrash favours tillage and limestone has been taken from quarries through the clay. Sand and gravel have been deposited in a small area near the northern boundary. The only steep slope in the parish is in the centre where the land rises from the rivers to the town wall. In the west Hyam wood, east of which was a park, was the only woodland.[28]

Two main roads from Malmesbury crossed Westport parish, that north to Tetbury (Glos.) and Gloucester and that west to Bristol via Sherston. Both were turnpiked in 1756.[29] Only a short stretch of the Sherston road, in the suburb of Westport, lay within the parish; it ran along part of the parish boundary further west, as did the Malmesbury–Cirencester road north-east of the town. The Tetbury road was disturnpiked in 1874, the Sherston road in 1876.[30] From the Sherston road a road ran north to Brokenborough, crossing the Tetbury Avon by Back bridge, apparently so called in 1478.[31] The settlements of Westport and Brokenborough were linked by a road which apparently forded the Tetbury Avon c. 500 m. north-west of the west gate:[32] by 1820 a new stretch of road had been made on the south bank and joined the road over Back bridge.[33] A road through Filands in use in 1773 carried much of the Chippenham–Tetbury traffic after an eastern bypass was built around Malmesbury in 1973.[34]

Before the Sherston road was turnpiked the main Malmesbury–Bristol road, part of an Oxford–Bristol road in the later 17th century, led through the south part of the parish towards Foxley: near Westport it crossed the Sherston Avon by a bridge, known in the Middle Ages as Turketyl and later as Westport bridge, and 400 m. south-west of the bridge a road diverged to Malmesbury common and Corston.[35] Both roads were in use in the late 20th century, when that to Corston was called Common Road. Lanes between Common Road and Burton Hill in Malmesbury, in use in the late 18th century, were not public roads in the late 20th. Others, across Malmesbury common, were replaced in 1832 by straight tracks, running north-east and south-west,[36] which were still in use in 1989.

The suburb of Westport was the main settlement in the parish. Filands and Thornhill, hamlets in the Middle Ages, had each dwindled to one or two farmsteads by the late 18th century.[37] In 1801 the population of the parish was 702. It had

risen to 1,023 by 1821 and continued to rise, with some fluctuations, until 1881, when it was 1,867. Although land and houses in Bremilham were added to Westport in the 1880s others were lost to Brokenborough, and by 1891, the last date for which a figure for the whole parish is available, the population had dropped to 1,669.[38]

Settlement had presumably extended from Malmesbury into the suburb of Westport by the late Saxon period.[39] Westport, so called in 1135,[40] is at the town's north-western corner and linked to it along the ridge by Abbey Row. Buildings on the west side of the town along lanes called Burnivale and King's Wall, between the town walls and the Sherston Avon, were also in Westport parish. In the 19th century the suburb comprised approximately a third of the borough's total area.[41] A guildhall stood in Westport c. 1200[42] and from the later 13th century until the 16th the parts of the borough in the two parishes were distinguished as Westport and Bynport.[43]

Most buildings of Westport were in King's Wall and Burnivale, in Abbey Row, in the Sherston and Tetbury roads leading respectively west and north from Abbey Row, and in the angle between the roads. In the late Saxon period the church was north of the Sherston road near what was until the 19th century the western edge of the settlement.[44] By the later 12th century the parish church had been built west of the Tetbury road, there later called Gloucester Road.[45] An open space south of the church, known from the 19th century as the Triangle, and another north-west of the church, called Horsefair from the 17th century, were presumably market places. A market for Malmesbury to be held in Westport was granted in 1252 and later markets and fairs were apparently held there.[46] From Horsefair a lane, called Milk Street in the late 18th century[47] and later West Street, ran south to the Sherston road, there called Bristol Street. Another, called St. Mary's Street, linked Horsefair to the Triangle. West Street and the Triangle were linked by Katifer Lane. In the late 17th century the buildings of Westport were probably clustered around those streets.[48] Early building in Burnivale and King's Wall included a chapel[49] and Postern Mill.[50]

Probably in 1643, when there were both royalist and parliamentary attacks on Malmesbury, Westport suffered considerable damage, including the destruction of the parish church. Later 17th-century buildings to survive include the Three Cups in the Triangle and several cottages in Horsefair and Gloucester Road. In King's Wall a large house was built c. 1700,[51] and no. 22 Horsefair

[28] Geol. Surv. map 1″, solid and drift, sheet 251 (1970 edn.); below, econ. hist.
[29] *Andrews and Dury, Map* (W.R.S. viii), pls. 13, 16; *L.J.* xxviii. 581.
[30] *V.C.H. Wilts.* iv. 269, 271; 36 & 37 Vic. c. 90.
[31] W.R.O. 88/1/16.
[32] *Andrews and Dury, Map* (W.R.S. viii), pl. 16.
[33] C. Greenwood, *Map of Wilts.* (1820).
[34] *Andrews and Dury, Map* (W.R.S. viii), pl. 16; above, Malmesbury, introduction.
[35] J. Ogilby, *Brit.* (1675), pl. 79; *Reg. Malm.* ii, p. xxxiii.
[36] *Andrews and Dury, Map* (W.R.S. viii), pls. 13, 16; W.R.O., EA/142.   [37] Below.
[38] *V.C.H. Wilts.* iv. 360; above, Brokenborough, introduction.

[39] Above.
[40] *Reg. Malm.* i. 342.
[41] Above, Malmesbury, introduction; Soc. Antiq. MS. 817, ix, f. 1.
[42] *Bradenstoke Cart.* (W.R.S. xxxv), p. 76.
[43] Above, Malmesbury, introduction.
[44] J. M. Moffatt, *Hist. Malm.* 101.
[45] Below, church.
[46] Above, Malmesbury, trade and ind. (mkts. and fairs).
[47] Moffatt, *Hist. Malm.* 101. Westport's streets are named on the map above, p. 130.
[48] Aubrey, *Topog. Coll.* ed. Jackson, pl. xxv.
[49] Below, church.
[50] Above, Malmesbury, trade and ind. (mills).
[51] Ibid. Malmesbury, introduction.

bears the date 1703. In the late 18th century lanes, later called Foundry Road and Harper's Lane, led respectively north from Horsefair to Gloucester Road and south-west from Bristol Street towards Westport bridge. By then settlement had spread north in Gloucester Road to Staines bridge and west in Bristol Street to the fork of the Foxley and Sherston roads.[52] In the late 18th century and the early 19th much of Westport was rebuilt.[53] A nonconformist chapel was built in Horsefair in 1788[54] and a double-fronted house of three storeys north of Abbey Row bears the date 1798, but most new building was of terraces of two-storeyed cottages with fronts of stone rubble.[55] A medieval range of building west of the church in St. Mary's Street, standing in 1809,[56] was apparently replaced soon afterwards. The increase in the population of Westport parish in the early 19th century[57] presumably resulted from new building in the suburb. There were c. 300 houses there in 1831;[58] most were apparently small, and in the 1840s it was reported that only one was occupied by a member of the professional classes.[59]

Another increase in population in the 1860s was ascribed to the sale of land and the building of new houses.[60] Some may have been built in Gastons Road, leading north from Bristol Street, where there were already a few houses in 1845,[61] and some in Burnham Road, which linked Gastons Road and Horsefair. Commercial and institutional building also took place in the later 19th century. A chapel was built in Bristol Street in 1856, a foundry was opened in Foundry Road c. 1870, and warehouses at the northern end of Gloucester Road and a hotel near Staines bridge may have been built in the 1870s.[62] Two large houses, Stainesbridge House and Verona House, were built near the bridge in 1871 and 1883 respectively,[63] and Euclid Villas, a pair of very tall Gothic houses south of Abbey Row, are of similar date. Cottages were replaced by new terraces in Bristol Street, where Avon Terrace bears the date 1888, and St. Mary's Street, where Mansfield Terrace bears the date 1899. In 1881 the population of the part of Westport which lay within Malmesbury urban sanitary district was 1,711; only 156 people lived elsewhere in the parish.[64]

In the mid 20th century most new building on the west side of Malmesbury was local authority housing in what had been Brokenborough parish. Within the former Westport parish a scattering of residential and industrial buildings grew up beside the Tetbury road, north of Staines bridge where it was called Tetbury Hill, and on the north side of Park Road west of Staines bridge. Two large estates of private houses were built, White Lion Park south-west of Park Road in the 1960s and Reed's Farm east of Tetbury Hill in the 1980s. A garage and light industrial and commercial buildings replaced earlier buildings north of Staines bridge in the 1970s and 1980s.

In 1620 four alehousekeepers were recorded in Westport.[65] One may have kept the Weaver's Arms, mentioned in 1666.[66] The Three Cups and the Castle, both in the Triangle, were open in 1822;[67] the Castle was closed after 1956,[68] the Three Cups was open in 1989. The Suffolk Arms, east of Tetbury Hill, was open in 1875 and 1989. The Bath Arms in Horsefair, the Railway hotel near Staines bridge, and the Plough beside the Sherston road, were opened between 1875 and 1885.[69] The Bath Arms was closed after 1956.[70] The Railway hotel, renamed the Flying Monk, was closed in the 1960s[71] and demolished c. 1980.[72] The Plough was closed in 1970.[73]

Thomas Hobbes (1588–1679), the philosopher, was born in a house near Westport church and received his schooling in Westport and Malmesbury. His father Thomas served Brokenborough church as curate in the early 17th century but lived at Westport: John Aubrey called him 'an ignorant Sir John' and wrongly described him as vicar of Westport.[74]

Filands was probably a hamlet in the late 13th century.[75] It had 17 poll-tax payers in 1377.[76] Orchard Farm, north of the road through the hamlet, is of 17th-century origin, and in 1773 the hamlet consisted of that and another farmstead east of it.[77] Filands Farm was built west of Orchard Farm in Malmesbury parish in the early 19th century, and between 1840 and 1885 a brickworks was built further west.[78] Two houses were built near the Cirencester road in the early 20th century, in the 1930s four pairs of houses were built between Filands Farm and the brickworks, and in the later 20th century the brickworks was replaced by a new farmstead called White Lodge Farm. In 1964 a school was built south-west of White Lodge Farm.[79]

Thornhill, also apparently a hamlet in the 13th century,[80] had 12 poll-tax payers in 1377,[81] and in the Middle Ages Malmesbury abbey had a grange called Thornhill.[82] The farmstead called Archars Farm in 1773[83] may mark the site of Thornhill. It was rebuilt c. 1800 and renamed

[52] Andrews and Dury, Map (W.R.S. viii), pl. 16.
[53] W.R.O. 212B/4362.
[54] Below, nonconf.
[55] See plate facing p. 236.
[56] J. Buckler, watercolour in W.A.S. Libr., vol. vi. 19; see below, plate facing p. 237.
[57] V.C.H. Wilts. iv. 360.
[58] Soc. Antiq. MS. 817, ix, f. 1v.
[59] Recollections of W. H. E. McKnight, ed. E. I. Thompson, 121.
[60] V.C.H. Wilts. iv. 324, 360.
[61] W.R.O. 815/27.
[62] Kelly's Dir. Wilts. (1875, 1885); above, Malmesbury, trade and ind.; below, nonconf.
[63] W.R.O. 149/101/2; date on bldg.
[64] V.C.H. Wilts. iv. 353, 360.
[65] Early-Stuart Tradesmen (W.R.S. xv), p. 30.
[66] W.A.M. xxvi. 403.

[67] W.R.O., A 1/326/3.
[68] Ibid. G 21/516/4.
[69] Kelly's Dir. Wilts. (1875, 1885).
[70] W.R.O., G 21/516/4.
[71] D. M. Fenton, Malm. Railway, 55.
[72] O.S. Map 1/2,500, ST 9287–9387 (1981 edn.).
[73] Wilts. Cuttings, xxiii. 300.
[74] D.N.B.; Aubrey, Topog. Coll. ed. Jackson, 263–4; A. Rogow, Thomas Hobbes, 23–7.
[75] Reg. Malm. i. 156–7.
[76] V.C.H. Wilts. iv. 309.
[77] Andrews and Dury, Map (W.R.S. viii), pl. 16.
[78] O.S. Map 6", Wilts. VIII (1889 edn.); W.R.O., tithe award.
[79] Above, Malmesbury, educ.
[80] Reg. Malm. i. 133–4.
[81] V.C.H. Wilts. iv. 310.
[82] P.R.O., E 134/2 Jas. I Mich./19.
[83] Andrews and Dury, Map (W.R.S. viii), pl. 16.

Thornhill Farm. By 1820 a new Arches Farm had been built east of it,[84] and cottages were built south-west of it beside Common Road in the late 19th century and the early 20th. Halcombe House, a substantial later 19th-century house, was built before 1885 north-east of Thornhill Farm near the junction of the Foxley road and Common Road,[85] and in the later 20th century houses and bungalows were built near the junction and along the north side of the Foxley road.

By 1538 a lodge had been built for the keeper of Hyam wood:[86] it was probably on the site of Hyam Park near the boundary between Westport and Brokenborough. Elsewhere in the parish, Bremilham Mill and a farmhouse called Back Bridge were standing in 1773[87] and survived in 1989. Between 1820 and 1840 a new Backbridge Farm was built north-east of, and cottages were built south of, Back bridge.[88] A 'smallpox house' stood west of Thornhill Farm apparently in Westport parish in 1773,[89] a fever (isolation) hospital near Back bridge was in use from the 1890s to 1933, and a cemetery for Westport and Malmesbury parishes was opened west of Tetbury Hill in 1884.[90]

MANORS AND OTHER ESTATES. The lands which became Westport parish, like those which became Malmesbury parish, are likely to have been held by Malmesbury abbey from or soon after its foundation in the 7th century.[91] They belonged to the abbey in the early Middle Ages, when they were recorded as part of a large estate called Brokenborough,[92] and the abbey kept them until the Dissolution.[93]

In 1547 the Crown granted lands south-west of Malmesbury as THORNHILL manor to Sir William Herbert[94] (cr. earl of Pembroke 1551).[95] By 1551 the estate had passed, presumably by sale, to William Stumpe (d. 1552), who settled it on his wife Catherine for life. Catherine later married William Basely and died in 1556. Thornhill passed to her son William Stumpe,[96] who sold it in 1576 to William Grymer.[97] In 1582 Grymer sold it to John Snell (d. 1587) and Snell's son Thomas,[98] who was later knighted. Sir Thomas (d. 1612) was succeeded by his son Sir Charles, who, probably c. 1617 and according to John Aubrey to raise money to provide a ship for Sir Walter Raleigh's last expedition, sold Thornhill to John Langton. In 1625 Langton settled the manor on his son John. By will dated 1660 the younger John's son John may have devised it with Easton Piercy manor in Kington St. Michael to his wife Elizabeth and sister Joan Lewis for 80 years. Either by inheritance or, with Easton Piercy, by release from Elizabeth and Joan, Thornhill passed to John's brother Sir Thomas Langton (d. c. 1672), who was succeeded in turn by his sons Thomas (d. c. 1696) and Robert.[99] In 1704 Robert sold the manor to Thomas Howard, earl of Berkshire (d. 1706).[1] It was conveyed by Joan Billers to William Robins and his wife Anne in 1758,[2] and by George Spackman to John Smith and his wife Elizabeth in 1767.[3] In 1788 the Smiths conveyed it to John Neate.[4] In 1827 it was apparently sold by Stephen Neate, and in 1839 Richard Blackford and Mary Garlick held Thornhill farm, 185 a. The farm was sold in 1869,[5] probably to C. W. Miles (d. 1892). It presumably passed with Miles's Burton Hill House estate in Malmesbury to C. N. Miles and A. C. Miles and was sold in 1919 by T. A. G. Miles. In 1921 Jesse Wootton sold the farm, 173 a.[6] R. S. Smith owned it in 1927 and 1931.[7] G. W. Sisum, the owner in 1939, sold the farm c. 1945. As a farm of 100 a. it was bought in 1962 by J. Neate and in 1969 by Mr. D. J. Grange, the owner in 1989.[8]

In the later 18th century there was a farm south-west of Malmesbury called ARCHARS.[9] At the Dissolution it is likely to have been granted by the Crown with Burton Hill manor in Malmesbury, which in 1577 was broken up by Adam Archard and Thomas Hall.[10] About 1800, when the farmstead was rebuilt and renamed Thornhill Farm,[11] it apparently belonged to the owner of Thornhill manor. In 1839 Arches farm, 100 a., belonged to Josiah Hanks.[12] With Thornhill farm it belonged to C. N. Miles in 1910, when it measured c. 150 a.,[13] and it was presumably sold like Thornhill farm in 1919. In 1927 Arches farm belonged to H. L. Storey[14] (d. 1933). Like Burton Hill House it was bought by the Shaftesbury Society, which sold it in 1948 to Percy Webb (d. 1985). Webb's sons Mr. Allen Webb and Mr. Roy Webb owned the farm, 180 a., in 1989.[15]

After the Dissolution Malmesbury abbey's land called HYAM, later Hyam park and Hyam farm, was part of Brokenborough manor. The manor was granted in 1552 to John Dudley, duke of Northumberland, who sold it in 1553 to Sir James Stumpe. It passed to Sir Henry Knyvett and in the Howard family with the earldoms of Suffolk and Berkshire.[16] In 1839 Hyam farm included c. 240 a. in Westport parish.[17] It was sold by an earl

[84] Greenwood, *Map of Wilts.*
[85] O.S. Map 6″, Wilts. VIII (1889 edn.).
[86] W.R.O. 88/1/24.
[87] *Andrews and Dury, Map* (W.R.S. viii), pl. 16.
[88] Greenwood, *Map of Wilts.*; W.R.O., tithe award.
[89] *Andrews and Dury, Map* (W.R.S. viii), pl. 16.
[90] O.S. Map 6″, Wilts. VIII (1889 and later edns.); above, Malmesbury, public services.
[91] Above, Malmesbury, manors.
[92] Ibid. Brokenborough, introduction, manor; *Arch. Jnl.* lxxvii. 42–8.   [93] *Valor Eccl.* (Rec. Com.), ii. 119.
[94] *Cal. Pat. 1547–8,* 193–4.
[95] *Complete Peerage,* x. 406–7.
[96] *W.N. & Q.* viii. 392–3, 481–4.
[97] *Cal. Pat. 1575–8,* p. 143.
[98] Glos. R.O., D 2697/17; P.R.O., C 142/221, no. 122.
[99] *W.A.M.* iv. 45 and pedigrees at pp. 45, 77.
[1] *Complete Peerage,* ii. 151; W.R.O. 212A/27/37, deed,

Langton to earl of Berks., 1704.
[2] P.R.O., CP 25(2)/1235/31 Geo. II Hil.
[3] Ibid. CP 25(2)/1445/8 Geo. III Mich.
[4] Ibid. CP 25(2)/1447/28 Geo. III East.
[5] W.R.O. 374/130/66; ibid. tithe award.
[6] Above, Malmesbury, manors; W.A.S. Libr., sale cat. xvii, no. 46.
[7] *Kelly's Dir. Wilts.* (1931); W.R.O., G 7/515/9.
[8] *Kelly's Dir. Wilts.* (1939); inf. from Mrs. J. D. Grange, Thornhill Farm.
[9] *Andrews and Dury, Map* (W.R.S. viii), pl. 16.
[10] Above, Malmesbury, manors.
[11] Ibid. introduction.   [12] W.R.O., tithe award.
[13] Ibid. Inland Revenue, val. reg. 9.
[14] Ibid. G 7/515/9.
[15] Above, Malmesbury, manors; inf. from Mr. A. Webb, Arches Farm.   [16] Above, Brokenborough, manor.
[17] W.R.O., tithe award.

of Suffolk after 1912,[18] and was bought in 1927 by T. L. Horn, who sold it in 1939 to his sister-in-law Ursula and her husband G. G. Cox Cox. In 1988 Mrs. Cox Cox owned Hyam farm which then included c. 150 a. of the former parish of Westport.[19] Hyam Park was built in the 17th century as a long north–south range with a main east front. In the 18th century a short west wing was added at the south end to make a new symmetrical south front, in 1922 a west wing was added at the north end, and in 1927 the south wing and south front were extended and other alterations were made to the house. Also in the 1920s a large cattle yard west of the house, bounded on the west by a stone barn probably of the 18th century, was made into gardens. Extensive 20th-century farm buildings are further west.

An estate called *FILANDS* was held in 1183–4 and in 1195 by Walter Mautravers (d. before 1201), presumably by knight service of Malmesbury abbey; it passed to his brother John (d. 1220),[20] and by 1248 may have reverted to the abbey.[21] In 1535 the abbey held lands in Westport formerly Mautravers's,[22] but after the Dissolution no separate estate was called Filands.

The land of Filands is likely to have been granted after the Dissolution as part of Whitchurch and Milbourne manor in Malmesbury, which included land in the north-east part of Westport parish. In 1782 William and Thomas Robins conveyed 42 a., formerly part of that manor, to John Jefferies, who devised them to Jane Coles. In 1820 she sold the land to Thomas Howard, Viscount Andover, later earl of Suffolk and of Berkshire,[23] and it was reunited with Whitchurch and Milbourne manor. Much of that manor descended with the Suffolk title and in 1989 belonged to Michael Howard, earl of Suffolk and of Berkshire,[24] but it is not clear whether the 42 a. were part of it. Another part of Whitchurch and Milbourne manor apparently passed with Whitchurch farm to Richard Kinneir, who in 1839 held 116 a. in Westport. That land passed with the farm to members of the Elwell family[25] who held 76 a. in Westport in 1927,[26] and to Mr. Edward Weaver, owner of Whychurch farm in 1989.[27]

In the Middle Ages the Crown held Malmesbury borough, including the part in Westport parish, and from 1215 to the Dissolution Malmesbury abbey held it in fee farm. The Westport part of the borough and the land adjoining it was from 1628 part of Malmesbury manor, sometimes called Malmesbury and Westport manor.[28] In 1839 the manor, then held by the Revd. George Rushout-Bowles, included c. 35 a. in Westport.[29] The lands passed to Elizabeth, Baroness Northwick (d.

1912), who in 1896 sold the reversion in lots.[30]

Malmesbury borough, which enjoyed certain privileges in or before the 11th century, may also have held lands; more land may have been granted by Malmesbury abbey after it became fee farmer of the borough in 1215,[31] and in the mid 13th century the guild merchant of Malmesbury received heath land south-west of the town from the abbey in an exchange.[32] The borough charter of 1381 ascribed a grant of 5 hides of heath near Norton, south-west of the town, to King Athelstan:[33] the charter clearly indicates that in 1381 the borough owned *KING'S HEATH*, but the claim that it had been given by Athelstan is implausible. In 1839 Malmesbury corporation owned Malmesbury common, 522 a., and c. 200 a. east and north-east of it.[34] In 1989 the burgesses and freemen of Malmesbury held a total of 718 a., of which c. 670 a. had been in Westport parish.[35]

In the 13th century Robert of Lea held 1 hide, apparently what later became *BACKBRIDGE* farm but then said to be in Thornhill.[36] The land probably passed with Lea manor in Lea and Cleverton parish until the later 16th century and with Boakley farm in Brokenborough until the early 19th.[37] In 1340 Sir John Mauduit and his wife Agnes conveyed 88 a. in Thornhill with Lea manor to their son-in-law John Moleyns.[38] The estate passed to Moleyns's son Sir William (d. 1381), who held it in 1370,[39] and probably thereafter in the Moleyns and Hungerford families and to members of the Hastings family, earls of Huntingdon. An earl of Huntingdon held an estate in Westport in the mid 16th century, part of which was sold in 1571 with Boakley farm by Henry Hastings, earl of Huntingdon, to Anthony Webb and in 1593 by Webb to William Bailey.[40] At his death in 1621 William held lands in Westport,[41] presumably the c. 130 a. held by his great-grandson Anthony Bailey (fl. 1655). As at Boakley farm, later owners were Giles Bailey, Daniel Bennett, Daniel's son Giles, and Giles Bailey Bennett. In 1822 Daniel's grandson Daniel Bennett sold Backbridge farm to Thomas Howard, earl of Suffolk and of Berkshire.[42] It passed with the earldoms to Henry, earl of Suffolk and of Berkshire, who owned the farm, 106 a., in 1912.[43] By 1927 it had been sold,[44] and it later had several different owners.

A small estate including Bremilham Mill passed with lands in Foxley from Thomas Bremilham to his son John, to John's son Richard (d. c. 1557), and to Richard's grandnephew Thomas Nicholas and great-grandnephew Robert Shipton. Thereafter it apparently passed with Player's farm in Foxley to Henry Vassall, Baron Holland,[45] who in 1839 held c. 70 a. and the mill in Westport

---

[18] W.R.O., G 7/500/1.
[19] Inf. from Mrs. U. Cox Cox, Hyam.
[20] *Cur. Reg. R.* x. 17; *Pipe R.* 1195 (P.R.S. n.s. vi), 46; above, Great Somerford, manors.
[21] *Reg. Malm.* i. 411–12.
[22] *Valor Eccl.* (Rec. Com.), ii. 121.
[23] *Complete Peerage*, xii (1), 479–80; W.R.O. 88/5/18.
[24] Above, Malmesbury, manors.
[25] Ibid.; W.R.O., tithe award.
[26] W.R.O., G 7/515/9.
[27] Above, Malmesbury, manors.
[28] Ibid.; P.R.O., PROB 11/1609, f. 232.
[29] W.R.O., tithe award.
[30] Ibid. 622/1; above, Malmesbury, manors.
[31] Above, Malmesbury, manors, local govt. (boro. govt.).

[32] *Reg. Malm.* ii. 150–60.
[33] *Cal. Pat.* 1381–5, 54; above, Malmesbury, local govt. (boro. govt.).   [34] W.R.O., tithe award.
[35] Inf. from the clerk to the burgesses and freemen, 1 Market Lane, Malmesbury.   [36] *Reg. Malm.* i. 247.
[37] Above, Brokenborough, manor; Lea and Cleverton, manors.
[38] *Feet of F.* 1327–77 (W.R.S. xxix), pp. 62–4.
[39] *Cal. Close*, 1369–74, 175.
[40] P.R.O., C 2/Eliz. I/E 4/68; above, Brokenborough, manor.   [41] P.R.O., C 142/415, no. 89.
[42] W.R.O. 88/5/24; above, Brokenborough, manor.
[43] W.R.O., G 7/500/1.   [44] Ibid. G 7/515/9.
[45] P.R.O., C 3/167/52; ibid. CP 25(2)/81/695, no. 21; above, Foxley, manor.

parish.[46] The estate passed with Foxley manor to Maj. A. R. Turnor whose son Mr. R. W. C. Turnor owned the mill and 54 a. in 1989.[47]

Humphrey Bridges (d. 1598) and his son Humphrey held jointly an estate in Westport and adjacent parishes.[48] At the younger Humphrey's death in 1609 it comprised c. 100 a. and rights of common pasture. He was succeeded by his brother Anthony[49] (d. 1617), whose heirs were his sisters Elizabeth, wife of Robert Bridges, Margaret, wife of John Breath, and Jane, wife of Richard Stevens, and his nephew Anthony Bridges.[50] The later history of the estate has not been traced.

The endowment of a chantry, founded in Westport church by 1478,[51] included c. 70 a. in Westport.[52] In 1564 the lands were conveyed by Henry Knyvett and his wife Elizabeth to Matthew King.[53] In 1569 they were successfully claimed by Thomas Estcourt,[54] who in 1571 sold them to John Stumpe[55] (d. 1600). Stumpe was succeeded by his son James, who at his death in 1602 held c. 140 a. in Westport and other parishes and was succeeded by his son William.[56] No later record of the Westport part of that estate has been found.

Rents from Westport were given to Bradenstoke priory by Henry le Bret in 1232 and by Andrew son of John of Malmesbury in the later 13th century, and in the mid 13th century the priory held other land there.[57] In 1535 the priory received rents totalling 13s. 4d. from Westport.[58]

Malmesbury abbey was licensed to appropriate Westport church between 1159 and 1181; the licence was apparently confirmed in 1191.[59] Thereafter the abbey owned the *RECTORY* estate until the Dissolution,[60] and afterwards most rectorial tithes probably passed with the estates from which they were derived. In the later 16th century rectorial tithes from Thornhill were apparently leased by the Crown with those from Corston.[61] The lessees claimed payment of tithes from the owners of Thornhill manor, apparently unsuccessfully.[62] Some tithes from Thornhill did, however, pass with those from Corston to R. H. Gaby.[63] In 1839 Gaby owned great tithes from 143 a. in Westport, the earl of Suffolk and of Berkshire those from 89 a., the vicar of Malmesbury those from 68 a., and the rector of Bremilham those from 10 a.: the tithes were all commuted in 1840. King's Heath was tithe free, and tithes from most other lands in the parish were merged.[64]

ECONOMIC HISTORY. Apart from King's Heath, which is treated separately below, nearly all the agricultural land of the parish was worked by Malmesbury abbey and its tenants in the Middle Ages. North of the town inhabitants of Filands may have shared lands with those of Whitchurch, as south of it those of Thornhill may have done with those of Burton Hill. To the west the abbey had woods and possibly parkland called Hyam in demesne.

In the late 13th century the abbey had 14 tenants at Filands and c. 12 at Thornhill; all were presumably customary tenants. Of those at Thornhill, one held 60 a., probably arable in open fields, four others had similar or greater holdings,[65] and all presumably had rights to common pasture. In the late 15th century the abbey had a grange at Thornhill and held demesne land there, apparently in hand. The land may have been mainly pasture on which the abbey kept sheep and cattle to supply its own larder.[66] In the 1530s the demesne, including arable in the open fields and c. 50 a. of several pasture and meadow, was leased, perhaps as a single holding.[67] In 1539–40 seven tenants shared 18 yardlands; another held 30 a. of arable and the grange. Works of cutting and gathering hay in meadows in Westport and Malmesbury parishes had been commuted,[68] probably much earlier. Woodland and a warren at Hyam were leased separately in 1538.[69] In 1340 Sir John Mauduit's 88 a. were shared by 5 tenants; the largest holding was of 60 a. of arable and 3 a. of meadow.[70] Of Westport chantry's c. 70 a., a single tenant held 63 a. in the open fields in 1548.[71]

In the mid 16th century c. 40 a. of Westport parish north of Malmesbury were part of Whitchurch marsh, a common pasture presumably used mainly by the men of Whitchurch. South of Malmesbury, Kemboro field, partly in Malmesbury parish, was worked by tenants of both Burton Hill and Thornhill manors. Thornhill manor also included Quarry field, south of the Sherston branch of the Avon, and Brokenborough field, perhaps north of the river. Its common pasture, part of Awls or Alice heath, was probably to the south beside the parish boundary. Between the mid 16th century and the 19th both arable and pasture were inclosed, apparently piecemeal, and the number of farms was reduced. The Thornhill part of Alice heath had been inclosed by the mid 16th century[72] and the latest reference to open-field cultivation in Westport dates from 1628.[73] Except for part of King's Heath, lands in the north half of the parish may have been the last to be inclosed. The Westport part of Whitchurch marsh was not mentioned when the Malmesbury part was inclosed in 1792 under an Act of 1790 and had almost certainly been inclosed earlier.[74] Common pasture or open field between the suburb of Westport and

[46] W.R.O., tithe award.
[47] Above, Foxley, manor; inf. from Maj. A. R. Turnor, Foxley Manor.
[48] P.R.O., C 142/281, no. 82.
[49] Ibid. C 142/310, no. 90.
[50] Ibid. C 142/371, no. 102.
[51] W.R.O. 88/1/16.
[52] P.R.O., E 301/58, no. 36.
[53] Cal. Pat. 1563–6, p. 135.
[54] P.R.O., C 3/58/7.
[55] Cal. Pat. 1575–8, p. 502.
[56] W.N. & Q. viii. 533–4.
[57] Bradenstoke Cart. (W.R.S. xxxv), pp. 76–8; Cal. Chart. R. 1226–57, 162.
[58] Valor Eccl. (Rec. Com.), ii. 123.
[59] Reg. Malm. i. 369–70, 374–5; below, church.
[60] L. & P. Hen. VIII, xix (1), p. 649.
[61] Cal. Pat. 1560–3, 330; above, Corston, manor.

[62] P.R.O., E 134/2 Jas. I Mich./19.
[63] Above, Corston, manor.
[64] W.R.O., tithe award.
[65] Reg. Malm. i. 130–3, 156–7; ii. 386–7.
[66] P.R.O., E 134/2 Jas. I Mich./19.
[67] Ibid. SC 6/Hen. VIII/3986, rot. 115; Valor Eccl. (Rec. Com.), ii. 120.
[68] P.R.O., SC 6/Hen. VIII/3986, rot. 115.
[69] W.R.O. 88/1/24.
[70] Feet of F. 1327–77 (W.R.S. xxix), pp. 62–4.
[71] P.R.O., E 301/58, no. 36.
[72] Ibid. SC 6/Hen. VIII/3986, rott. 113–14; W.R.O., tithe award; above, Malmesbury, agric.
[73] Wilts. Inq. p.m. 1625–49 (Index Libr.), 72–3.
[74] W.R.O., EA/34.

Brokenborough village is likely to have been inclosed long before 1822 when lands of Backbridge farm were called new inclosures.[75] The land of Hyam, which may have been a park in the Middle Ages, is known to have been one in the 16th century,[76] and in 1649 comprised 201 a. in Westport and Brokenborough parishes.[77] The park had been extended to c. 400 a., half in each parish, by c. 1785.[78]

In the early 19th century most of the parish was worked in small farms with a high proportion of pasture. In 1839 c. 750 a. were in farms of c. 70 a. or more. Hyam farm, 441 a. including 201 a. in Westport, was worked from the farmstead on the boundary of Brokenborough and Westport, and 116 a. in the north of the parish were worked from Whitchurch Farm in Malmesbury with lands in that parish. Thornhill farm was 160 a., Arches and Backbridge farms were each c. 100 a., and the farm attached to Bremilham Mill was 69 a. Of the remaining lands, c. 700 a. were in farms of 20–50 a. each and some were in smaller farms. Most of the farms of less than 50 a. had land near Malmesbury and were presumably worked as smallholdings from within the town or the suburb of Westport. Hyam wood was then 40 a.[79]

The pattern of farming in the parish had apparently changed little by the early 20th century. A market garden on 6 a. beside Tetbury Hill in 1910[80] had expanded to occupy 11 a. by 1927.[81] In the 1930s most of the agricultural land of the former parish was still pasture although some south of the town was arable.[82] In the 1980s sheep and beef cattle were reared on Hyam farm, Arches was an intensive dairy farm, and the lands of Thornhill farm were permanent pasture;[83] factories were built on part of Backbridge farm.

In the south-west part of the parish the names of Cooks heath, Portmans heath, Alice heath, and Great heath suggest that most of the land was pasture, but in the mid 13th century Cooks heath and other lands were cultivated. Except for part of Alice heath, which was used by the men of Thornhill, from the mid 13th century nearly all that land belonged to the borough of Malmesbury:[84] it was later called King's Heath, and from the 18th century the low lying and badly drained south-west part of it was called Malmesbury common.[85] There is no evidence that either pasture or arable was inclosed in the Middle Ages. In the late 14th century rights to feed animals on and to cultivate the land apparently belonged to members of the guild merchant of Malmesbury and to members of other privileged groups in the borough, but the details of how they used the land are obscure.[86] By c. 1570 lands near the town had been inclosed and allotted, c. 1570 Cooks heath was similarly dealt with,[87] and in 1607 there were

c. 100 a. in closes.[88] By 1610 more closes had been allotted[89] but most of the land was still subject to common grazing rights. In the early 19th century c. 210 a. were several and holdings varied from 1 a. to 15 a.[90] Closes were frequently broken in the late 16th century and the early 17th:[91] it is not clear how far the objection was to inclosure and how far the result of disputes about how the borough should be governed.[92]

Use of King's Heath was regulated by the borough court. Orders were made in 1620 for stinting on Hundred hill, and in the 1650s forbidding commoners to feed cattle not their own on the common pasture. In 1686 regulations for marking beasts and cutting gorse were issued and in 1691 it was agreed that winter grazing on the common pasture should be leased to the highest bidder. In 1669 a fine imposed on a capital burgess for ploughing his close was remitted because the change of use was to the general good. Under the terms of the borough charter of 1685 the alderman and 12 capital burgesses granted their closes on 21-year leases. The lessees improved the land by burnbaking and presumably brought them into cultivation and, when the leases were revoked under a charter restored in 1690, claimed compensation for the sums spent on improvement. In 1714 the borough court ruled that it was lawful for any close to be ploughed and sown providing it had been burned; there was to be a rotation of three crops, with clover sown in the fourth year.[93]

In 1760 and presumably earlier inhabitants of Foxley parish had the right to feed cattle on a small area of Malmesbury common near Foxley village.[94] In the early 19th century the common, described as a deplorable scene of waste and desolation, was overgrown with furze and gorse and so badly drained that it was impassable in bad weather.[95] Under an Act of 1821 c. 500 a. were inclosed and drained in 1832. All but 20 a. were allotted either to Malmesbury corporation, presumably to be added to the holdings of those who already had some inclosed land, or to the trustees of King's Heath, who were drawn from the corporation and regulated the commoners' lands. The allotments to the corporation and trustees were divided into 280 holdings of between 1 a. and 3 a. each. The remainder was allotted to neighbouring landowners who had grazing rights on the common, including 15 a. to Henry Vassall, Baron Holland, lord of Foxley manor.[96] Thereafter part of what was still known as Malmesbury common was cultivated. In 1886 only 30 a. were pasture; the main crops were wheat, grown on 82 a., and potatoes, grown on 126 a. Stubble was still grazed in common, and 150–200 pigs were usually kept on the allotments between 1886 and 1906. By 1930, however, much of the land had passed out of use. Few commoners took up their rights to cultivate land

[75] W.R.O. 88/5/24.
[76] Above, Brokenborough, econ. hist.
[77] Cal. Cttee. for Compounding, iii. 1969.
[78] W.R.O. 88/5/46/4.   [79] Ibid. tithe award.
[80] Ibid. Inland Revenue, val. reg. 9.
[81] Ibid. G 7/515/9.
[82] [1st] Land Util. Surv. Map, sheet 103.
[83] Inf. from Mr. A. Webb, Arches Farm; Mrs. U. Cox Cox, Hyam; Mrs. J. D. Grange, Thornhill Farm.
[84] Reg. Malm. ii. 150–4.
[85] B.L. Maps, M.T. 6e., 1 (2).
[86] Above, Malmesbury, local govt. (boro. govt.).
[87] P.R.O., E 134/9 Chas. I Mich./75.
[88] Ibid. STAC 8/130/3.   [89] Ibid. STAC 8/290/22.
[90] Rep. Com. Mun. Corp. [C. 2490–1], p. 73, H.C. (1880), xxxi.
[91] P.R.O., STAC 8/130/3; STAC 8/290/22.
[92] Above, Malmesbury, local govt. (boro. govt.).
[93] Hist. MSS. Com. 24, 12th Rep. VI, Ho. of Lords, pp. 432–3; Malmesbury boro. rec., ct. bk. 1600–1721.
[94] B.L. Maps, M.T. 6e., 1 (2).
[95] W.A.M. li. 151–2.   [96] W.R.O., EA/142.

MALMESBURY
The south part of High Street

WESTPORT
Early 19th-century cottages in West Street

WESTPORT: ST. MARY'S, DEMOLISHED *C.* 1840

LEA AND CLEVERTON: ST. GILES'S, MOSTLY DEMOLISHED 1879

CORSTON: ALL SAINTS', MOSTLY DEMOLISHED 1881

BREMILHAM: DEMOLISHED *C.* 1874

CHURCHES IN 1809

themselves and much of the common was managed by the trustees, who let part of it to neighbouring farmers. During the Second World War the common was again drained and part was again ploughed.[97] In 1989 both Malmesbury common and the older inclosures, *c.* 700 a. in all, were let to neighbouring farmers.[98]

MILLS. In the 13th century Robert of Lea held a mill in Westport.[99] Postern Mill on the river below King's Wall was on a site used for a mill from the 12th century or the 13th.[1]

Bremilham Mill was probably standing in the 1550s and may have been on the site of a much earlier mill.[2] In the later 19th century it was apparently the site of a considerable business, but milling ceased there between 1885 and 1899. In 1925 the wheel raised water for domestic use.[3] The mill and its outbuildings were demolished after 1945.[4] The mill house, a 17th-century stone building of one storey with attics, was standing in 1989, and the mill wheel was *in situ*. Another mill in the parish may have stood near Back bridge.[5]

TRADE AND INDUSTRY. Stone quarrying and iron working may have taken place on the site of Postern Mill in the late Saxon period and there may have been a tannery near the mill in the later Middle Ages.[6] A tanner lived in Westport in 1729[7] and others are recorded there later in the 18th century.[8] A tanyard near Back bridge in 1798[9] was probably that between Park Road and the Sherston road in use in 1823 and 1839.[10] From 1865 the yard was held by members of the Thompson family who until the 1880s had another at the Light, the detached part of Bremilham parish south of the Sherston road. Tanning ceased in Westport between 1895 and 1899.[11]

In the mid 18th century shafts were sunk on Malmesbury common in the hope of finding coal. Only lignite was found[12] but mining rights on the common were still leased in 1812.[13] In 1885 and 1912 there was a brickworks west of Filands; it had closed by 1919. On the western edge of the suburb several quarries were opened after 1885 but were mostly disused in 1924.[14] What was said to be a quarry on Malmesbury common in the 1920s[15] was perhaps a clay pit.

Some businesses associated with the town of Malmesbury were carried on from premises in Westport, and new factories west of Tetbury Hill and small industrial units in Park Road were built in the 1980s.[16]

LOCAL GOVERNMENT. The part of Westport in Malmesbury borough was subject to the borough courts, which also regulated King's Heath. Courts held for Malmesbury manor also had jurisdiction in the parish, chiefly over the suburb of Westport. In the earlier 18th century two constables for Westport were appointed at the borough sessions, and in the later 18th century two constables and two sidesmen were appointed at the manor court.[17]

Malmesbury abbey apparently held separate courts for Thornhill in the earlier 16th century.[18] No record of courts for Thornhill manor has been found.

In 1636 Malmesbury and Westport parishes disputed responsibility for relief of the poor living within the precinct of Malmesbury abbey. Westport was found to be responsible for those living in seven houses,[19] and a small part of the suburb was in Abbey parish which relieved its own poor in the later 18th century and the earlier 19th.[20] In 1648 Westport petitioned to set its own rates as other parishes did, giving as a reason the damage which had been suffered by the parish in military action and from the billeting of soldiers there. The petition may have been prompted by some alteration in the method of assessment following the garrisoning of Malmesbury in 1644; apparently before 1648 and certainly afterwards the parish set its own rates.[21]

In 1775–6 poor relief in Westport cost £125. Expenditure was £452 in 1802 when 53 adults and 90 children received permanent and 25 people occasional relief. The cost and numbers relieved were then approximately half those of Malmesbury parish. In 1813 permanent relief was given to 75 adults and occasional relief to 32; the total cost was £782. Expenditure was lower in the 1820s,[22] and between 1833 and 1835 the average annual cost was £408. In 1835 Westport became part of Malmesbury poor-law union.[23] In the late 18th century a building in Burnivale, which may have been St. Mary's chapel, was said to have long been used as a poorhouse.[24]

CHURCH. The church at Westport before the Conquest[25] may have been served by Malmesbury abbey. A new church had been built by the later 12th century, and between 1159 and 1181 the abbey was licensed to appropriate it. Until a vicarage was ordained in or before 1286 the abbey presumably served the cure.[26] From the later 13th

[97] *Country Life*, 22 Mar. 1941; Wilts. Cuttings, xi. 172; P.R.O., MAF 68/1063, sheet 2; MAF 68/2203, sheet 14.
[98] Inf. from the clerk to the burgesses and freemen, 1 Market Lane, Malmesbury.
[99] *Reg. Malm.* i. 247.
[1] Above, Malmesbury, trade and ind. (mills).
[2] P.R.O., CP 25(2)/81/695, no. 21; above, Brokenborough, econ. hist.
[3] Wilts. Cuttings, vi. 127; O.S. Maps 6", Wilts. VIII (1889 edn.), VIII. SW. (1900 edn.).
[4] Inf. from Lt.-Col. J. H. Pitman, Foxley Ho., Norton.
[5] Above, Brokenborough.
[6] *Medieval Arch.* xxi, p. 167; inf. from Mr. C. K. Currie, 15 Claudeen Close, Swaythling, Southampton.
[7] *Wilts. Apprentices* (W.R.S. xvii), p. 58.
[8] W.R.O. 212B/3992; 212B/4027.
[9] Ibid. 212B/4200.
[10] Ibid. 212B/4332; ibid. tithe award.

[11] *Harrod's Dir. Wilts.* (1865); *Kelly's Dir. Wilts.* (1875 and later edns.); above, Bremilham, econ. hist.
[12] *W.A.M.* ii. 159. [13] W.R.O. 315/27/6.
[14] O.S. Map 6", Wilts. VIII (1889 and later edns.); W.R.O., G 7/500/1. [15] Wilts. Cuttings, xi. 172.
[16] Above, Malmesbury, trade and ind.
[17] Malmesbury boro. rec., sessions order bk. 1712–41; W.R.O. 212B/3977; 1165/3.
[18] P.R.O., SC 6/Hen. VIII/3986, rot. 114v.
[19] Hist. MSS. Com. 55, *Var. Coll.* i, pp. 100–1.
[20] Above, Malmesbury, local govt. (par. govt.).
[21] Hist. MSS. Com. 55, *Var. Coll.* i, pp. 100–1, 116.
[22] *Poor Law Abstract, 1804*, 566–7; *1818*, 498–9; *Poor Rate Returns, 1816–21*, 189; *1822–4*, 228; *1825–9*, 219.
[23] *Poor Law Com. 2nd Rep.* App. D, 559.
[24] Moffatt, *Hist. Malm.* 95; below, church.
[25] Above, introduction.
[26] *Reg. Malm.* i. 369–70; ii. 322–3.

century or earlier Charlton church and from 1341 or earlier Brokenborough church were dependent chapels of Westport.[27] A united benefice with Malmesbury was formed between 1650 and 1658 but the two were separated after 1660.[28] In 1879 Brokenborough and Charlton were separated from Westport,[29] in 1946 the vicarage was reunited with that of Malmesbury and Westport church converted to a parish hall, and in 1984 Malmesbury with Westport and Brokenborough benefice was formed.[30]

Malmesbury abbey was patron of Westport vicarage. In 1528 Sir Anthony Hungerford presented a vicar by a grant of a turn. From the Dissolution until the late 19th century the Crown usually presented.[31] A presentation by the alderman and burgesses of Malmesbury in 1586 or 1587[32] was probably made by a grant from the Crown, and in 1670 the bishop of Salisbury may have collated a vicar.[33] In 1882 the advowson was transferred by exchange to Charlotte Kemble.[34] It passed with that of Malmesbury vicarage to the Church Trust Fund, patron of the united benefices formed in 1946 and 1984.[35]

Westport vicarage was valued in 1291 at £4 6s. 8d., well below the average for a living in Malmesbury deanery,[36] and at £18 8s. 8d., over twice the average, in 1535;[37] both valuations presumably included income from Brokenborough and Charlton. The vicar's annual income from the three parishes between 1829 and 1831 was c. £312, a little below the average for a Wiltshire living.[38] In 1535 a yearly pension of £1 was payable from the vicarage to Malmesbury abbey;[39] the pension apparently passed with the lordship of Malmesbury borough[40] and c. 1830 the vicar paid £2 yearly to the lord of Malmesbury manor.[41] In the early 19th century John, earl of Suffolk and of Berkshire, informally augmented the vicarage.[42]

Although in 1341 Malmesbury abbey was said to receive all tithes from Westport,[43] the vicar had apparently been entitled to some in 1286[44] and was so in 1535.[45] He was entitled to small tithes from Brokenborough, Charlton, and Westport, except where the land was tithe free. In Westport, King's Heath may have been tithe free early, and by the early 19th century vicarial tithes from other lands belonging to Malmesbury borough had been compounded.[46] In 1784–5 the vicar successfully disputed other compositions but accepted moduses for what was thought to have been demesne land of Malmesbury abbey including one of £4 for the

former Hyam park in Brokenborough and Westport.[47] In 1839 the vicar was entitled to small tithes from c. 800 a. in Westport. His tithes from Brokenborough, Charlton, and Westport were valued at £520 and commuted in 1840.[48]

The vicar had land and a house in Charlton, 46 a. in 1839,[49] but apparently neither in Westport or Brokenborough. In 1881–2 a house beside the Swindon road in Malmesbury parish was built for the vicar of Westport,[50] who was then and thereafter also vicar of Malmesbury. That house was sold in 1969.[51]

The small pre-Conquest church, of which the nave survives, stood north of Bristol Street. It was apparently known in the later Middle Ages as St. Helen's, and was presumably converted for other uses after the Dissolution.[52] A hermitage under the wall of Malmesbury borough in which Christine of Somerford was enclosed in 1250[53] may have been St. Mary's chapel in Burnivale, recorded in the later 13th century[54] and the 16th.[55] A building in Burnivale, ecclesiastical in style and known as the Hermitage, was demolished in the early 19th century.[56] A chantry of St. Mary in Westport church had been endowed by 1478, when it had land in Brokenborough.[57] At its dissolution its total income was £6 9s. 3d., of which £3 18s. was from Westport and Malmesbury. Its priest, a former monk, was described as honest, learned, and able to serve a cure.[58]

In 1303 keeping of the vicarage was committed to a chaplain because of the vicar's incapacity;[59] probably in 1413, men were excommunicated for wounding the vicar;[60] and in 1438 the vicar apparently lived at Charlton.[61] Presentments were made in 1553 of parishioners who had not attended church or paid their dues, in 1565 of a parishioner who had not taken communion for five years, and in 1585 of another for sorcery.[62] A woman of Westport was tried with others from Malmesbury for sorcery in the 1640s.[63] John Pearte, curate of Westport in 1565, was said to be neither a preacher nor a graduate.[64] John Aubrey reported that an early 17th-century vicar, William Stumpe, destroyed many manuscripts of Malmesbury abbey's library, using them to plug barrels.[65] Among charges brought against Matthew Whitley, vicar from 1650 or earlier until 1670, was his failure in eight years to perform any clerical duty in Westport except two baptisms. Like most of his successors until the late 19th century Whitley lived at Charlton.[66]

[27] Above, Brokenborough, church; Charlton, church.
[28] Ibid. Malmesbury, churches; Cal. S.P. Dom. 1658–9, 220.
[29] Lond. Gaz. 7 Mar. 1879, pp. 1957–60.
[30] Ch. Com. file, NB 5/116B.
[31] Phillipps, Wilts. Inst. (index in W.A.M. xxviii. 225).
[32] P.R.O., IND 17004, Wilts. p. 16.
[33] Ibid. IND 17007, p. 566; Phillipps, Wilts. Inst. ii. 31.
[34] Lond. Gaz. 7 Mar. 1882, pp. 536–7.
[35] Above, Malmesbury, churches.
[36] Tax. Eccl. (Rec. Com.), 189.
[37] Valor Eccl. (Rec. Com.), ii. 137.
[38] Rep. Com. Eccl. Revenues, 852–3.
[39] Valor Eccl. (Rec. Com.), ii. 137.
[40] Cal. Pat. 1563–6, pp. 463–4; above, Malmesbury, manors.
[41] Rep. Com. Eccl. Revenues, 852–3.
[42] Above, Charlton, church.
[43] Inq. Non. (Rec. Com.), 167.   [44] W.R.O. 88/5/46/4.
[45] Valor Eccl. (Rec. Com.), ii. 137; W.A.M. lxxvii. 104.
[46] W.R.O., tithe award.

[47] Ibid. 88/5/46/4.   [48] Ibid. tithe award.
[49] Above, Charlton, church.   [50] Ch. Com. file, NB 5/116B.
[51] Above, Malmesbury, churches.
[52] Cal. Pat. 1572–5, p. 478.   [53] Close R. 1247–51, 314.
[54] Reg. Malm. i. 121.
[55] L. & P. Hen. VIII, xxi (2), pp. 241–2.
[56] R. H. Luce, Hist. Malm. 38; Aubrey, Topog. Coll. ed. Jackson, 261; Buckler, watercolour in W.A.S. Libr., vol. vi. 35; see above, plate facing p. 173.
[57] W.R.O. 88/1/16.
[58] P.R.O., E 301/58, no. 36.
[59] Reg. Ghent (Cant. & York Soc.), ii. 624.
[60] Reg. Hallum (Cant. & York Soc.), pp. 119–20.
[61] Above, Charlton, church.
[62] W.R.O., D 1/43/1, ff. 24v., 133v.; D 1/43/5, f. 22v.; D 1/43/6, f. 31av.
[63] W.A.M. xxix. 159–60.
[64] W.R.O., D 1/43/5, f. 22v.
[65] Aubrey, Nat. Hist. Wilts. ed. Britton, 78–9.
[66] W.R.O., D 1/42/62; above, Charlton, church.

In 1783 morning service was held at Westport on alternate Sundays. There was no weekday service and *c.* 12 people received communion when it was celebrated at Easter, Whitsun, Michaelmas, and Christmas.[67] Services were still held on alternate Sundays in the early 19th century, when Westport was among six churches served by a single curate. In the late 1840s morning and evening services were held each Sunday; the morning congregation usually included fewer than 10 adults.[68] On Census Sunday in 1851, however, 100 people attended morning and 280 people evening service in Westport.[69] G. H. H. Hutchinson, vicar 1837–76, was largely responsible for rebuilding the church and founding a school at Westport.[70] His work was interrupted in 1861 when he was licensed to be absent because his wife had become a Roman Catholic.[71] The vicarage was held in plurality with that of Malmesbury from 1879 until the two were united.[72]

The church of *ST. MARY*, standing and so called in the later 12th century,[73] was described by Aubrey as a pretty church with very good windows; it probably had a chancel, a nave with two aisles, and a tower with a spire which may have been higher than that of St. Paul's in Malmesbury. It was destroyed during the Civil War, apparently by troops stationed in Malmesbury because it offered shelter to those attacking the town. A small church, with an undivided chancel and nave, was built after the war[74] and a north aisle was added later.[75] After it was rebuilt *c.* 1840,[76] in Tudor Gothic style of coursed rubble with ashlar dressings, it had an undivided chancel and nave with a south aisle of five bays and a western bellcot. A western gallery was later removed, and the arcade was blocked when the church was converted to a hall.

In 1553 plate weighing 9½ oz. was taken for the king and a chalice of 5 oz. was left in the church. A chalice of 1654 and mid 19th-century plate including two chalices, a paten, two almsdishes, and a flagon, all belonging to Westport church,[77] were used in Malmesbury abbey church after 1946.[78]

In 1553 three bells and a sanctus bell hung in the church. Five bells hanging there *c.* 1640 were either sold or melted down during the Civil War. A bell of 1739 hung in the church[79] until 1949, when it was melted down and the metal used for new bells for Malmesbury abbey church.[80]

Registers of baptisms and burials survive from 1678 and registers of marriages from 1685; those for some later years are missing.[81]

NONCONFORMITY. In 1676 there were 18 protestant nonconformists in Westport parish,[82] and until the late 18th century most nonconformists in Malmesbury apparently met in Westport. Presbyterian and Independent ministers in the town in the late 17th century probably preached in both Malmesbury and Westport.[83] William Conway, a Presbyterian expelled from Oxford university, was licensed in 1672 to preach in a barn in Westport and apparently continued to serve a congregation there until his death in 1694.[84] In 1689 two houses in Westport were certified for Presbyterian meetings,[85] and in 1715 the congregation numbered 160.[86] Although in 1783 the vicar of Westport reported that there was only one Presbyterian family in the parish,[87] a chapel was built in Horsefair in 1788. J. M. Moffatt, author of a *History of Malmesbury*, was minister from 1789 until 1804.[88] Probably from 1811 the church was Congregational. From 1812 until 1841 it was united with the Ebenezer chapel in Malmesbury.[89] In 1851 morning, afternoon, and evening services at the Westport chapel were attended by 178, 211, and 170 people respectively; congregations were usually larger, it was said.[90] A large new chapel, of stone, in Gothic style, and with a schoolroom, was built on a site adjoining that of the old chapel in 1867;[91] it remained open in 1989. Birth and baptism registers for the church survive from 1823.[92]

A house in Westport and another in Westport or Malmesbury were licensed for Baptist meetings in 1672.[93] By 1689 a pastor had been appointed,[94] and by 1695 a meeting house had been built in Abbey Row. It was a low stone building seating 60–70 and was replaced by a new Strict Baptist chapel, also of stone, built in 1802 and enlarged between 1814 and 1816. In the late 18th century baptisms took place in the Tetbury Avon north of the abbey church.[95] In 1851 services were usually held in the morning, afternoon, and evening on Sundays; on Census Sunday 208 people attended the morning service.[96] The chapel remained open in 1989. Birth and baptism registers survive from 1794.[97]

Methodists met in a barn said to be in St. Mary's Lane, possibly St. Mary's Street, in 1854. In 1856, when the church had 50 members, a Primitive

[67] *Vis. Queries, 1783* (W.R.S. xxvii), pp. 228–9.
[68] *Recollections of McKnight*, ed. Thompson, 68–9.
[69] P.R.O., HO 129/252/2/7/5.
[70] *Recollections of McKnight*, ed. Thompson, 69; *Alum. Cantab. 1752–1900*, iii. 503; W.R.O. 1795/6.
[71] P.R.O., PC 1/3966.
[72] *Clergy List* (1892); *Crockford* (1907 and later edns.).
[73] *Reg. Malm.* i. 369–70.
[74] Aubrey, *Topog. Coll.* ed. Jackson, 263.
[75] Buckler, watercolour in W.A.S. Libr., vol. vi. 19; see above, plate facing p. 237.
[76] W.R.O. 1795/6.
[77] Nightingale, *Wilts. Plate*, 203; *W.A.M.* xxxvii. 334.
[78] Inf. from the vicar, Malmesbury.
[79] Walters, *Wilts. Bells*, 230; Aubrey, *Topog. Coll.* ed. Jackson, 263.
[80] Inf. from the vicar, Malmesbury.
[81] W.R.O. 1589/47–54; bishop's transcripts for some earlier and missing years are ibid.

[82] *Compton Census*, ed. Whiteman, 129.
[83] Above, Malmesbury, prot. nonconf.
[84] *Calamy Revised*, ed. Matthews, 131.
[85] *Meeting Ho. Certs.* (W.R.S. xl), p. 2.
[86] Dr. Williams's Libr., Wilson MS. F i, p. 155.
[87] *Vis. Queries, 1783* (W.R.S. xxvii), p. 229.
[88] Moffatt, *Hist. Malm.* pp. xiii–xiv, 158.
[89] G. L. Jenkins, *Nonconf. in Malm.* (1895), 15, 22; above, Malmesbury, prot. nonconf.
[90] P.R.O., HO 129/252/2/7/6.
[91] *Lond. Gaz.* 15 Nov. 1867, p. 6063.
[92] P.R.O., RG 4/2595.
[93] *Meeting Ho. Certs.* (W.R.S. xl), pp. 174–5.
[94] Jenkins, *Nonconf. in Malm.* 18.
[95] R. W. Oliver, *Strict Bapt. Chapels Eng.* (Strict Bapt. Hist. Soc.), v. 27–9.
[96] P.R.O., HO 129/252/2/7/7.
[97] Ibid. RG 4/2238.

Methodist chapel of red brick with stone dressings was built in Bristol Street.[98] Another small chapel was built of stone in a mixed Gothic style in the Triangle in 1899[99] and remained open in 1989.

EDUCATION. In 1547 the priest serving the chantry in Westport church kept a school.[1] In the later 16th century Thomas Hobbes, the philosopher, was taught successively at a school in Westport church, by a clergyman of either Westport or Malmesbury, and, with two or three other boys, by Robert Latimer, then living in Westport and later rector of Leigh Delamere.[2] J. M. Moffatt, Presbyterian minister of Westport 1789–1804, also kept a school.[3]

There was no day school in the parish in 1846–7.[4] From 1851 the children of Westport have attended the same schools as children from Malmesbury, some of which were in Westport parish.[5]

Children were taught at a ragged school in Burnivale on Sundays and in the evenings from 1866 or earlier. From 1870 it was a day school; it had 53 pupils in that year and in 1873 a wooden schoolroom was built. In 1881–2 average attendance was 115. The school was closed in 1884.[6]

There was a private school in Westport in 1842;[7] another was attended by 57 boys and 49 girls in 1871.[8] In 1903 and 1927 Stainesbridge House was a girls' school.[9]

CHARITIES FOR THE POOR. Endowments, each yielding £1 a year, were provided for the poor of Westport by E. Waite (d. 1661) by will, and by Anne Rowles by deed in 1774. In 1904 the income from both was distributed to widows and others in need, each of whom received 6d. Residents of Westport were beneficiaries with those of parts of Malmesbury parish from Robert Cullerne's charity.[10]

[98] Jenkins, *Nonconf. in Malm.* 28–36.
[99] Wilts. Cuttings, xxvii. 311.
[1] P.R.O., E 301/58, no. 36.
[2] Aubrey, *Topog. Coll.* ed. Jackson, 263; *Alum. Oxon. 1500–1714*, iii. 884.
[3] *V.C.H. Wilts.* iii. 123 n.; above, nonconf.
[4] Nat. Soc. *Inquiry, 1846–7*, Wilts. 12–13.

[5] Above, Malmesbury, educ.
[6] W.R.O., F 8/600, Burnivale ragged sch.
[7] Pigot, *Nat. Com. Dir.* (1842), 20.
[8] *Returns relating to Elem. Educ.* 420–1.
[9] *Kelly's Dir. Wilts.* (1903, 1927).
[10] *Endowed Char. Wilts.* (N. Div.), 1017–19; above, Malmesbury, charities.

INDEX

NOTE. Page numbers in bold-face are those of the chapter on the parish, hundred, or tithing. A page number in italic refers to a map or illustration on that or the facing page. A page number followed by *n* is a reference only to the footnotes on that page.

Hibberd (*cont.*)
  Wm., 98
  fam., 98
Higgins:
  E. E., 91
  E. H., 91
  I. R., 91
Highman, A. R., 142
Hill:
  Francis, 142, 146
  Geo., 142
  John (fl. 1689), 207
  John (fl. 1840), 31
  Sam., rector of Little Somerford and of Kilmington, vicar of Eisey, canon of Wells, 211
  T. D., 141
Hill farm, *see* Oaksey: man.
Hinton:
  Ant., 84
  Thos., 84
Hislop:
  A. C., 97–8
  A. T., 97
  Dorothy, 97
Hitchings, J. T., 172
Hobbes:
  Thos., father of Thos. (d. 1679), curate of Brokenborough, 35, 232
  Thos. (d. 1679), philosopher, 35, 232, 240
  Thos. (fl. 1735), 199
  Wm., 146
hockey, 137
Hodges, Eliz., 35, 157, 160–1
Holford:
  Geo. (d. 1839), 10
  Sir Geo. (fl. 1915), 10
  Peter, 10
  R. S., 10, 12
  Rob. (d. 1753), 10
  Rob. (d. 1838), 10
Holland, Barons, 19; *and see* Fox
Hollinworth, John, curate of Charlton, vicar of Westport, 49
Hollis:
  Eliz., m. John Teagle, 190
  John, 190
  Rob. (fl. 1761), 190, 192
  Rob. (d. c. 1820, another), and his w. Eliz., 190
  Wm., 190
Holstein Friesian cattle, 60; *and see* Friesian cattle
Holtham:
  John, 180
  Ric., 180
Hooper:
  John, 111
  Wm., 111
  fam., 111
Hopkins, John, vicar of Hankerton, 103
Horn, T. L., 234
Horner:
  Susanna, *see* Strangways
  Thos., 85
horngeld, freedom from, 150
Hornidge, Thos., curate of Beverstone, vicar of Norton and of Coaley, 175
horses, 33, 145; *and see* steeplechases; stud farms
Horton:
  Edw., 109–10
  Thos. (d. 1530), and his w. Mary, 109
  Thos. (d. 1549), and his w. Margery, 109
  Wm., 110, 113
Hosed, Wal., 139
hospitals, *see* Burton Hill: hosp. of St. Mary Magdalene; Charlton; Gloucester: hosp. of St. Bart.; London: hosp. of the Savoy; Malmesbury: hosp., hosp. of St. Anthony, hosp. of St. John; Westport: 'smallpox ho.'
hotels, 31, 60, 180, 216, 223, 232; *and*

see Malmesbury: inns (Old Bell hotel)
Houlton:
  John, 189–90
  Jos., 189, 192
  Mary, w. of Nat., 189
  Nat., 189, 197
  fam., 190
hound, 202
housebreaking, 117
Howard:
  Cath., *see* Knyvett
  Chas., duke of Norfolk (d. 1815), 184
  Chas., earl of Berkshire (d. 1679), 41, 50
  Chas., earl of Suffolk and of Berkshire (d. 1876), 18, 41, 98
  Frances, m. —— Winchcombe, 23, 35, 49–50, 98, 103–4
  Hen., earl of Suffolk and of Berkshire (d. 1757), 41, 45
  Hen., earl of Suffolk and of Berkshire (d. 1779), 41–3, 155
  Hen., earl of Suffolk and of Berkshire (d. 1779, s. of Hen. d. 1779), 41
  Hen., earl of Suffolk and of Berkshire (d. 1898), 41
  Hen., earl of Suffolk and of Berkshire (d. 1917), 41, 234
  John, earl of Suffolk and of Berkshire, 33, 41, 43, 46, 49, 98, 100, 122, 142, 238
  Mary, dau. of Thos., earl of Berkshire (d. 1706), 50
  Mary, w. of Hen., earl of Suffolk and of Berkshire (d. 1898), 147
  Mic., earl of Suffolk and of Berkshire, 18, 41, 43, 91, 97, 101, 122, 142, 234
  Thos., earl of Berkshire (d. 1669), 18, 31, 41, 43, 45, 50, 89, 99
  Thos., earl of Berkshire (d. 1706), 41, 49–50, 98, 233
  Thos., earl of Suffolk (d. 1626), 6, 18, 41–3, 97, 148, 155
  Thos., earl of Suffolk and of Berkshire (d. 1783), 41
  Thos., Vct. Andover, earl of Suffolk and of Berkshire (d. 1851), 18, 30–1, 41, 46, 49–50, 91–2, 97, 99, 103, 122–3, 142, 234–5
  Victoria, 39
  fam., 2–3, 30, 39, 97, 233
Howe:
  Hen., Baron Chedworth, 6
  Joan, *see* Grobham
  John, 6
  Sir John, Bt. (d. by 1675), s. of John, 6
  John, Baron Chedworth (d. 1742), 6
  John, Baron Chedworth (d. 1762), 6
  John, Baron Chedworth (d. 1804), 6
  Sir Ric., Bt. (d. 1703), 6
  Sir Ric., Bt., (d. 1730), 6
Hugh, provost of Malmesbury, 139
Hughes:
  A., 158
  Frank, 216
  Geo., 216
  N. G., 55
  Ric., 192
Hulbert:
  Hen., 207
  Mic., 140
Hulberts Green, *see* Brinkworth
Hull, fam., 225
Hullavington:
  Hugh of, 109
  Ralph of, 109
  fam., 109
Hullavington, 5, 7, **104–18**, *106*, 160, 168, 175, 216
  adv., 116–17, 175
  agric., 112–14
  benefice, 116
  boundaries, 104–5, 127, 169

Bradfield, *q.v.*
  cemetery, 107
  chant., 117
  chap., 105, 116
  chaplains, 117
  char., 117–18
  ch., 88, 104–5, *109*, 112, 116–18
  ch. ho., 107, *108*
  common meadow, 113
  common pastures, 113
  cts., 115, 117
  curates, 88, 117; *and see* Jones, Thos.
  cust. tenants, 112–13
  dom. archit., 105, 107
    Court Ho., 105, 107
  farms, 109–10, 113–14, 164
  glebe, 112, 116
  inc., 1, 105, 113, 115–16
  inns, 107
  man., 105, 107–12, 115–16
    Rectory, 112, 116
  mills, 114
  Newtown, 107, 118
  Piccadilly, 107
  poor relief, 115–16
  pop., 105
  prehist. rem., 105
  priory, *see* Clatford: priory
  prot. nonconf., 107, 118
  R.A.F. sta., 104–5, 107, 110, 114, 129, 161, 163, 213–16, 218
  rly. sta., 108
  rectory, 112
  roads, 104–5
  schs., 118
  street, 104–5
  Surrendell, *q.v.*
  tithes, 112–13, 116
  tithing, 115
  trades, 114
  vestry, 116
  vicarage, 116, 174–5, 219
  vicarage ho., 107, 116
  vicars, 88, 113, 116–17; *and see* Adlam; Banks; Carter; Emly; Latimer, Wm.; Mandeville, John; Moore, John; Radcliffe; Stanley; Ward, Rob.
  village, 1–2, 104–5, 107
  woodland, 2, 110, 115
Hume-Campbell:
  Alex., Ld. Polwarth, 55
  Amabel, *see* Yorke
  and see Campbell
Humphrey, duke of Gloucester (d. 1447), 108
Humphrey (fl. 1086), 18
hundreds, *see* Chedglow; Chippenham; Damerham, North; Dunlow; Malmesbury hundred; Startley; Thorngrove
Hungerford:
  Sir Ant. (fl. 1528), 238
  Ant. (fl. early 17th cent.), 123
  Sir Ant. (d. 1657, ? another), 155, 162, 188, 192, 207
  Cecily, w. of Sir Edw. (d. 1607), m. 2 Francis Manners, earl of Rutland, 162, 188, 207
  Sir Edw. (d. 1607), 162, 188, 207
  Sir Edw. (d. 1648), 136, 216
  Edw. (d. 1681), 216
  Sir Edw. (d. 1711), 162, 188, 207
  Eleanor, w. of Sir Rob., Ld. Hungerford and Moleyns, *see* Moleyns
  Eleanor, w. of Wal., Ld. Hungerford, *see* Arundel
  Geo., and his w. Eliz., 166
  Sir Giles, 162, 188, 216
  Marg., m. Rob. Sutton, Baron Lexinton, 216
  Marg., w. of Sir Edw. (d. 1648), 216–17
  Marg., w. of Sir Giles, 162, 216
  Mary, Baroness Botreaux, Hungerford, and Moleyns, m. 1 Edw.